Birnbaum's 95 Germany

A BIRNBAUM TRAVEL GUIDE

Alexandra Mayes Birnbaum
EDITORIAL CONSULTANT

Lois Spritzer
Editorial Director

Laura L. Brengelman
Managing Editor

Mary Callahan
Senior Editor

David Appell
Patricia Canole
Gene Gold
Jill Kadetsky
Susan McClung
Associate Editors

A Division of HarperCollins*Publishers*

To Stephen, who merely made all this possible.

FIRST EDITION

ISSN 0749-2561 (Birnbaum Travel Guides)
ISSN 1068-7238 (Germany)
ISBN 0-06-278191-X (pbk.)

94 95 96 97 ❖/RRD 5 4 3 2 1

BIRNBAUM TRAVEL GUIDES

Bahamas, and Turks & Caicos
Berlin
Bermuda
Boston
Canada
Cancun, Cozumel & Isla Mujeres
Caribbean
Chicago
Country Inns and Back Roads
Disneyland
Eastern Europe
Europe
Europe for Business Travelers
France
Germany
Great Britain
Hawaii
Ireland
Italy
London
Los Angeles
Mexico
Miami & Ft. Lauderdale
Montreal & Quebec City
New Orleans
New York
Paris
Portugal
Rome
San Francisco
Santa Fe & Taos
South America
Spain
United States
USA for Business Travelers
Walt Disney World
Walt Disney World for Kids, By Kids
Washington, DC

Contributing Editors

Tom Bross
Roman Czajkowsky
Joan Gannij
Jerry Gerber
Michael Iachetta
Debra Jo Immergut
Roy Kammerer
Helmut Koenig
K. Michael Madden
Elsemarie Maletske
Caroline Sawyer
Theo Schlag
Susan C. Shipman
Kerry Stewart
Gillian Thomas
Donna Wilkinson
Candace Whitman

Maps

Mark Stein Studios

Contents

Getting Ready to Go

Practical information for planning your trip.

The Cities

Thorough, qualitative guides to each of the 12 cities most often visited by vacationers and businesspeople. Each section offers a comprehensive report on the city's most compelling attractions and amenities—highlighting our top choices in every category.

Diversions

A selective guide to a variety of unexpected pleasures, pinpointing the best places to pursue them.

Unexpected Pleasures and Treasures

Directions

The most spectacular routes and roads; most arresting natural wonders; and most magnificent palazzos, villas, and gardens—all organized into 10 specific driving tours.

Glossary

Foreword

Perhaps my purely Prussian heritage should have prepared me for my first and subsequent visits to Germany. But I remain amazed by my impressions: of Berlin today and before the Wall came down; of the Rhine's fairy-tale castles; of the rebuilt cities of Leipzig and Dresden; of the sybaritic pleasures of *Brenner's Park;* and of a tiny town in Bavaria named Birnbaum.

Just a simple recitation of the succession of events that have occurred in this formerly divided country provides the perfect punctuation for a history of life during the last two generations. From the rubble at the end of World War II to the economic miracle of the Berlin airlift to reunification a scant few years ago to today, Germany requires more than conventional coverage.

Germany is united geographically, but economically and emotionally, the reality is that the eastern and western regions remain worlds apart. After two world wars, crushing defeat, foreign occupation, division, and now unification, Germany is very much at the center of Europe. A country that has produced minds as disparate as Heine and Hitler and produced sounds as discordant as punk and *Parsifal* is fertile fodder for a guidebook.

That's why we've tried to create a guide to Germany that's specifically organized, written, and edited for today's demanding traveler, one for whom qualitative information is infinitely more desirable than mere quantities of unappraised data. We realize that it's impossible for any single travel writer to visit thousands of restaurants (and nearly as many hotels) in any given year and provide accurate appraisals of each. And even if it were physically possible for one human being to survive such an itinerary, it would of necessity have to be done at a dead sprint, and the perceptions derived therefrom would probably be less valid than those of any other intelligent individual visiting the same establishments. It is, therefore, both impractical and undesirable (especially in a large, annually revised and updated guidebook *series* such as we offer) to have only one person provide all the data on the entire world. Instead, we have chosen what we like to describe as the "thee and me" approach to restaurant and hotel evaluation, and, to a more limited degree, to the sites and sights we have included in the other sections of our text. What this really reflects is a personal sampling tempered by intelligent counsel from informed local sources.

This guidebook is directed to the "visitor," and such elements as restaurants have been specifically picked to provide the visitor with a representative, enlightening, and above all pleasant experience. Since so many extraneous considerations can affect the reception and service accorded a regular restaurant patron, our choices can in no way be construed as an exhaustive guide to resident dining. We think we've listed all the best places, in various price ranges, but they were chosen with a visitor's enjoyment in mind.

Other evidence of how we've tried to tailor our text to reflect modern travel habits is apparent in the section we call DIVERSIONS. Where once it was common for travelers to spend an urban visit seeing only the obvious sights, today's traveler is more likely to want to pursue a special interest or to venture off the beaten path. In response to this trend, we have collected a series of special experiences so that it is no longer necessary to wade through a pound or two of superfluous prose just to find exceptional pleasures and treasures.

Finally, I also should point out that every good travel guide is a living enterprise; that is, no part of this text is carved in stone. In our annual revisions, we refine, expand, and further hone all our material to serve your travel needs better. To this end, no contribution is of greater value to us than your personal reaction to what we have written, as well as information reflecting your own experiences while using the book. Please write to us at 10 E. 53rd St., New York, NY 10022.

We sincerely hope to hear from you.

Alexandra Mayes Birnbaum

ALEXANDRA MAYES BIRNBAUM, editorial consultant to the *Birnbaum Travel Guides*, worked with her late husband Stephen Birnbaum as co-editor of the series. She has been a world traveler since childhood and is known for her travel reports on radio on what's hot and what's not.

Germany

GERMANY
N
0 miles 60
0 kilometers 100
DENMARK
BALTIC SEA
NORTH SEA
POLAND
NETHERLANDS
Sylt
Rügen
Oderhaff
Oder
Elbe
Weser
Rhine
SCHLESWIG-HOLSTEIN
MECKLENBURG-WEST POMERANIA
BRANDENBURG
LOWER SAXONY
WESTPHALIA
LÜNEBURGER HEIDE
HARZ MOUNTAINS
Flensburg
Schleswig
Kiel
Husum
Rendsburg
Oldenburg
Neumünster
Travemünde
Itzehoe
Lübeck
Cuxhaven
Bremerhaven
Ratzeburg
Schwerin
Güstrow
Rostock
Stralsund
Greifswald
Neubrandenburg
Szczecin
Wilhelmshaven
Hamburg
Lüneburg
Neuruppin
Eberswalde
Berlin
Oranienburg
Oldenburg
Bremen
Celle
Brandenburg
Potsdam
Frankfurt
Lingen
Hannover
Wolfsburg
Magdeburg
Osnabrück
Minden
Lübbecke
Braunschweig
Cottbus
Wittenberg
Hildesheim
Wernigerode
Dessau
Bielefeld
Hameln
Elbingerode
Quedlinburg
Münster
Detmold
Hasselfelde
Halle
Göttingen
Nordhausen
Dresden
Görlitz
Essen
Bochum
Duisburg
Dortmund
Mülhausen
Naumburg
Leipzig

CZECH REPUBLIC
Prague
Chemnitz
Gera
Weimar
Eisenach
Düsseldorf
Cologne (Köln)
Aachen
Bonn
Siegen
THURINGIAN FOREST
Hof
Bayreuth
Bamberg
Frankfurt Am Main
Hanau
Offenbach
Seligenstadt
Aschaffenburg
Wiesbaden
RHEINGAU
Rüdesheim
Mainz
Koblenz
BELGIUM
RHEINLAND
Cochem
St. Goar
Beilstein
Zell
Traben-Trarbach
Bernkastel-Kues
Bingen
Trier
LUXEMBOURG
Luxembourg
Worms
Ludwigshafen
Mannheim
Heidelberg
Saarbrücken
Darmstadt
ODENWALD
Michelstadt
Miltenberg
Eberbach
Wertheim
Tauberbischofshain
Bad Mergentheim
Würzburg
Igersheim
Weikersheim
Creglingen
Rothenburg
Nuremberg
Regensburg
Passau
Dinkelsbühl
Nördlingen
ROMANTIC RD.
Heilbronn
Karlsruhe
Pforzheim
Stuttgart
Baden-Baden
Strasbourg
Tübingen
Freudenstadt
Ulm
Augsburg
BAVARIA
Munich (München)
Ammersee
Starnberger See
Chiemsee
Bad Reichenhall
Salzburg
Berchtesgaden
Reit Im Winkl
To Innsbruck
Bad Tölz
Tegernsee
Oberammergau
Füssen
BAVARIAN ALPS
Mittenwald
Garmisch-Partenkirchen
Zugspitze
AUSTRIA
Kempten
Ravensburg
Lindau
Friedrichshafen
Meersburg
Constance
Lake Constance (Bodensee)
Danube
Neckar
Tauber
Main
Lahn
Mosel
Rhine
BLACK FOREST
Triberg
Furtwangen
Freiburg
Titisee
Feldberg
Schaffhausen
Lörrach
Basel
SWITZERLAND
FRANCE
ROUTE NUMBERS
E = International European
A = National (primary)
Other = National (secondary)

How to Use This Guide

A great deal of care has gone into the organization of this guidebook, and we believe it represents a real breakthrough in the presentation of travel material. Our goal is to create a more modern generation of travel books, and to make this guide the most useful and practical travel tool available today.

Our text is divided into five basic sections in order to present information in the best way on every possible aspect of a vacation to Germany. Our aim is to highlight what's where and to provide basic information—how, when, where, how much, and what's best—to assist you in making the most intelligent choices possible.

Here is a brief summary of what you can expect to find in each section. We believe that you will find both your travel planning and en route enjoyment enhanced by having this book at your side.

GETTING READY TO GO

A mini-encyclopedia of practical travel facts with all the precise data necessary to create a successful trip to Germany. Here you will find how to get where you're going, currency information and exchange rates, plus selected resources—including pertinent publications, and companies and organizations specializing in discount and special-interest travel—providing a wealth of information and assistance useful both before and during your trip.

THE CITIES

Individual reports on the 12 cities in Germany most visited by travelers and businesspeople offer a short-stay guide, including an essay introducing the city as a historic entity and a contemporary place to visit. *At-a-Glance* contains a site-by-site survey of the most important, interesting, and unique sights to see and things to do. *Sources and Resources* is a concise listing of pertinent tourism information, such as the address of the local tourism office, which sightseeing tours to take, where to find the best nightspot, to play golf, to rent scuba equipment, to find the best beach, or to get a taxi. *Best in Town* lists our cost-and-quality choices of the best places to eat and sleep on a variety of budgets.

DIVERSIONS

This section is designed to help travelers find the best places in which to engage in a variety of exceptional experiences for the mind and body without having to wade through endless pages of unrelated text. In every case, our particular suggestions are intended to guide you to that special place where the quality of experience is likely to be highest.

DIRECTIONS

Here are ten itineraries that range all across the country, along the most beautiful routes and roads, past the most spectacular natural wonders, and through the most historic cities and countryside. DIRECTIONS is the only section of this book that is organized geographically, and its itineraries cover the touring highlights of Germany in short, independent journeys of three to five days' duration. Itineraries can be "connected" for longer sojourns or used individually for short, intensive explorations.

GLOSSARY

This compendium of helpful travel information includes a climate chart, a weights and measures table, and *Useful Words and Phrases,* a brief introduction to the German language that will help you to make a hotel or dinner reservation, order a meal, mail a letter, and even buy toothpaste in Germany. Though most large hotels, restaurants, and attractions in major German cities have English-speaking staff, at smaller establishments and in rural, out-of-the-way towns and villages, a little knowledge of German will go a long way.

To use this book to full advantage, take a few minutes to read the table of contents and random entries in each section to get a firsthand feel for how it all fits together. You will find that the sections of this book are building blocks designed to help you put together the best possible trip. Use them selectively as a tool, a source of ideas, a reference work for accurate facts, and a guidebook to the best buys, the most exciting sights, the most pleasant accommodations, the tastiest foods—*the best travel experience* you can possibly have.

Getting Ready to Go

Getting Ready to Go

When to Go

Germany has a temperate climate, although there is a good deal of variation between regions. In the northern lowlands, winters are chilly and damp and summers are mild. In central Germany's Harz Mountains and in the Bavarian Alps to the south, winters are cold and snowy and summers are cool. Overall, the country receives a fair amount of sunshine (except for the Alps, which often are shrouded in fog), but rain is not uncommon at any time of the year, especially in winter.

The period from mid-May to mid-September has long been—and remains—the peak travel period, traditionally the most popular vacation time. In addition, from December through March, the Alps, the Black Forest, the Harz Mountains, and other areas are popular destinations for skiing and other winter sports. For much of the country, however, the period from November to around Easter is the off season, and travel at this time—as well as during the so-called "shoulder" seasons (the months immediately before and after the peak months)—offers relatively fair weather and smaller crowds, and can be less expensive.

If you have a touch-tone phone, you can call *The Weather Channel Connection* (phone: 900-WEATHER) for current worldwide weather forecasts. This service, available from *The Weather Channel* (2600 Cumberland Pkwy., Atlanta, GA 30339; phone: 404-434-6800), costs 95¢ per minute; the charge will appear on your phone bill.

Traveling by Plane

SCHEDULED FLIGHTS

Leading airlines offering flights between the US and Germany include *Aer Lingus, Air France, Alitalia, American, Austrian Airlines, British Airways, Continental, Czechoslovak Airlines (CSA), Delta, Iberia, Icelandair, KLM Royal Dutch Airlines, Lufthansa, Northwest, SAS (Scandinavian Airlines System), Sabena, SwissAir, TAP Air Portugal, TWA, United,* and *USAir.*

FARES The great variety of airfares can be reduced to the following basic categories: first class, business class, coach (also called economy or tourist class), excursion or discount, and standby, as well as various promotional fares. For information on applicable fares and restrictions, contact the airlines listed above or ask your travel agent. Most airfares are offered for a limited time. Once you've found the lowest fare for which you can qualify, purchase your ticket as soon as possible.

RESERVATIONS Reconfirmation is strongly recommended for all international flights. It is essential that you confirm your round-trip reservations—*especially the return leg*—as well as any flights within Europe.

SEATING Airline seats usually are assigned on a first-come, first-served basis at check-in, although you may be able to reserve a seat when purchasing your ticket. Seating charts sometimes are available from airlines and also are included in the *Airline Seating Guide* (Carlson Publishing Co., 11132 Los Alamitos Blvd., Los Alamitos, CA 90720; phone: 310-493-4877).

SMOKING US law prohibits smoking on flights scheduled for six hours or less within the US and its territories on both domestic and international carriers. These restrictions do not apply to nonstop flights between the US and international destinations and, at press time, major carriers allowed smoking on all flights to Germany. A free wallet-size guide that describes the rights of nonsmokers under current regulations is available from *ASH* (*Action on Smoking and Health;* DOT Card, 2013 H St. NW, Washington, DC 20006; phone: 202-659-4310).

SPECIAL MEALS When making your reservation, you can request one of the airline's alternate menu choices for no additional charge. Though not always required, it's a good idea to reconfirm your request the day before departure.

BAGGAGE On major international carriers, passengers usually are allowed to carry on board one bag that will fit under a seat or in an overhead bin and to check two bags in the cargo hold. Specific regulations regarding dimensions and weight restrictions vary among airlines, but a checked bag usually cannot exceed 62 inches in combined dimensions (length, width, and depth), or weigh more than 70 pounds. There may be charges for additional, oversize, or overweight luggage, and for special equipment or sporting gear. Note that baggage allowances may be more limited for children (depending on the percentage of full adult fare paid) and on domestic routes abroad. Check that the tags the airline attaches are correctly coded for your destination.

CHARTER FLIGHTS

By booking a block of seats on a specially arranged flight, charter operators frequently can offer travelers bargain airfares. If you do fly on a charter, however, read the contract's fine print carefully. Federal regulations permit charter operators to cancel a flight or assess surcharges of as much as 10% of the airfare up to 10 days before departure. You usually must book in advance, and once booked, no changes are permitted, so buy trip cancellation insurance. Also, make your check out to the company's escrow account, which provides some protection for your investment in the event that the charter operator fails. For further information, consult the publication *Jax Fax* (397 Post Rd., Darien, CT 06820; phone: 203-655-8746; fax: 203-655-6257).

DISCOUNTS ON SCHEDULED FLIGHTS

COURIER TRAVEL In return for arranging to accompany some kind of freight, a traveler pays only a portion of the total airfare (and sometimes a small registration fee). One agency that matches up would-be couriers with courier companies is *Now Voyager* (74 Varick St., Suite 307, New York, NY 10013; phone: 212-431-1616; fax: 212-334-5243).

Courier Companies

Discount Travel International (169 W. 81st St., New York, NY 10024; phone: 212-362-3636; fax: 212-362-3236; and 801 Alton Rd., Suite 1, Miami Beach, FL 33139; phone: 305-538-1616; fax: 305-673-9376).

F.B. On Board Courier Club (10225 Ryan Ave., Suite 103, Dorval, Quebec H9P 1A2, Canada; phone: 514-633-0740; fax: 514-633-0735).

Halbart Express (147-05 176th St., Jamaica, NY 11434; phone: 718-656-8279; fax: 718-244-0559).

Midnite Express (925 W. Hyde Park Blvd., Inglewood, CA 90302; phone: 310-672-1100; fax: 310-671-0107).

Way to Go Travel (6679 Sunset Blvd., Hollywood, CA 90028; phone: 213-466-1126; fax: 213-466-8994).

Publications

Insiders Guide to Air Courier Bargains, by Kelly Monaghan (The Intrepid Traveler, PO Box 438, New York, NY 10034; phone: 212-569-1081 for information; 800-356-9315 for orders; fax: 212-942-6687).

Travel Unlimited (PO Box 1058, Allston, MA 02134-1058; no phone).

CONSOLIDATORS AND BUCKET SHOPS These companies buy blocks of tickets from airlines and sell them at a discount to travel agents or directly to consumers. Since many bucket shops operate on a thin margin, be sure to check a company's record with the *Better Business Bureau*—before parting with any money.

Council Charter (205 E. 42nd St., New York, NY 10017; phone: 800-800-8222 or 212-661-0311; fax: 212-972-0194).

International Adventures (60 E. 42nd St., Room 763, New York, NY 10165; phone: 212-599-0577; fax: 212-599-3288).

Travac Tours and Charters (989 Ave. of the Americas, New York, NY 10018; phone: 800-872-8800 or 212-563-3303; fax: 212-563-3631).

Unitravel (1177 N. Warson Rd., St. Louis, MO 63132; phone: 800-325-2222 or 314-569-0900; fax: 314-569-2503).

LAST-MINUTE TRAVEL CLUBS Members of such clubs receive information on imminent trips and other bargain travel opportunities. There usually is an annual fee, although a few clubs offer free membership. Despite the names of some of the clubs listed below, you don't have to wait until literally the last minute to make travel plans.

Discount Travel International (114 Forrest Ave., Suite 203, Narberth, PA 19072; phone: 215-668-7184; fax: 215-668-9182).

FLY ASAP (PO Box 9808, Scottsdale, AZ 85252-3808; phone: 800-FLY-ASAP or 602-956-1987; fax: 602-956-6414).

Last Minute Travel (1249 Boylston St., Boston, MA 02215; phone: 800-LAST-MIN or 617-267-9800; fax: 617-424-1943).

Moment's Notice (425 Madison Ave., New York, NY 10017; phone: 212-486-0500/1/2/3; fax: 212-486-0783).

Spur of the Moment Cruises (411 N. Harbor Blvd., Suite 302, San Pedro, CA 90731; phone: 800-4-CRUISES or 310-521-1070 in California; 800-343-1991 elsewhere in the US; 24-hour hotline: 310-521-1060; fax: 310-521-1061).

Traveler's Advantage (3033 S. Parker Rd., Suite 900, Aurora, CO 80014; phone: 800-548-1116 or 800-835-8747; fax: 303-368-3985).

Vacations to Go (1502 Augusta Dr., Suite 415, Houston, TX 77057; phone: 713-974-2121 in Texas; 800-338-4962 elsewhere in the US; fax: 713-974-0445).

Worldwide Discount Travel Club (1674 Meridian Ave., Miami Beach, FL 33139; phone: 305-534-2082; fax: 305-534-2070).

GENERIC AIR TRAVEL These organizations operate much like an ordinary airline standby service, except that they offer seats on not one but several scheduled and charter airlines. One pioneer of generic flights is *Airhitch* (2790 Broadway, Suite 100, New York, NY 10025; phone: 212-864-2000).

BARTERED TRAVEL SOURCES Barter—the exchange of commodities or services in lieu of cash payment—is a common practice among travel suppliers. Companies that have obtained travel services through barter may sell these services at substantial discounts to travel clubs, who pass along the savings to members. One organization offering bartered travel opportunities is *Travel World Leisure Club* (225 W. 34th St., Suite 909, New York, NY 10122; phone: 800-444-TWLC or 212-239-4855; fax: 212-564-5158).

CONSUMER PROTECTION

Passengers whose complaints have not been satisfactorily addressed by the airline can contact the *US Department of Transportation* (*DOT;* Consumer Affairs Division, 400 Seventh St. SW, Room 10405, Washington, DC 20590; phone: 202-366-2220). Also see *Fly Rights* (Publication #050-000-00513-5; *US Government Printing Office,* PO Box 371954, Pittsburgh, PA 15250-7954; phone: 202-783-3238; fax: 202-512-2250). If you have safety-related questions or concerns, write to the *Federal Aviation Administration* (*FAA;* 800 Independence Ave. SW, Washington, DC 20591) or call the *FAA Consumer Hotline* (phone: 800-322-7873). If you have a complaint against a travel service in Germany, contact the local tourist authorities.

Traveling by Ship

Your cruise fare usually includes all meals, recreational activities, and entertainment. Shore excursions are available at extra cost, and can be booked in advance or once you're on board. An important factor in the price of a cruise is the location (and sometimes the size) of your cabin. Charts issued by the *Cruise Lines International Association* (*CLIA;* 500 Fifth Ave., Suite 1407, New York, NY 10110; phone: 212-921-0066; fax: 212-921-0549) provide information on ship layouts and facilities and are available at some *CLIA*-affiliated travel agencies.

The *US Public Health Service (PHS)* inspects all passenger vessels calling at US ports; for the most recent summary or a particular inspection report, write to Chief, Vessel Sanitation Program, *National Center for Environmental Health* (1015 N. America Way, Room 107, Miami, FL 33132; phone: 305-536-4307). Most cruise ships have a doctor on board, plus medical facilities.

For further information on cruises and cruise lines, consult *Ocean and Cruise News* (PO Box 92, Stamford, CT 06904; phone/fax: 203-329-2787). And for a free list of travel agencies specializing in cruises, contact the *National Association of Cruise Only Agencies* (*NACOA;* 3191 Coral Way, Suite 630, Miami, FL 33145; phone: 305-446-7732; fax: 305-446-9732).

A potentially less expensive alternative to cruise ships is travel by freighter—cargo ships that also transport a limited number of passengers. For information, consult the *Freighter Travel Club of America* (3524 Harts Lake Rd., Roy, WA 98580; no phone), *Freighter World Cruises* (180 S. Lake Ave., Suite 335, Pasadena, CA 91101; phone: 818-449-3106; fax: 818-449-9573), *Pearl's Travel Tips* (9903 Oaks La., Seminole, FL 34642; phone: 813-393-2919; fax: 813-392-2580), and *TravLtips Cruise and Freighter Travel Association* (PO Box 188, 163-07 Depot Rd., Flushing, NY 11358; phone: 800-872-8584 or 718-939-2400; fax: 718-939-2047).

And finally, a number of companies—both in the US and abroad—also offer cruises along the Continent's inland waterways. In Germany, Elbe and Rhine river cruises are popular.

International Cruise Lines

Chandris Celebrity *and* ***Chandris Fantasy Cruises*** (5200 Blue Lagoon Dr., Miami, FL 33126; phone: 800-437-3111 or 305-262-6677; fax: 305-262-2677).

Cunard (555 Fifth Ave., New York, NY 10017; phone: 800-5-CUNARD or 800-221-4770; fax: 718-786-0038).

Epirotiki Lines (901 South America Way, Miami, FL 33132; phone: 800-221-2470 or 305-358-1910; fax: 305-358-4807).

Holland America Line (300 Elliot Ave. W., Seattle, WA 98119; phone: 800-426-0327; fax: 800-628-4855).

Princess Cruises (10100 Santa Monica Blvd., Los Angeles, CA 90067; phone: 800-421-0522; fax: 310-284-2844).

Renaissance Cruises (1800 Eller Dr., Suite 300, Ft. Lauderdale, FL 33316; phone: 800-525-2450; fax: 800-243-2987 or 305-463-8125).

Royal Caribbean Cruise Lines (1050 Caribbean Way, Miami, FL 33132; phone: 800-432-6559 in Florida; 800-327-6700 elsewhere in the US; fax: 800-722-5329).

Royal Cruise Line (1 Maritime Plaza, Suite 1400, San Francisco, CA 94111; phone: 800-792-2992 in California; 800-227-4534 elsewhere in the US; fax: 415-956-1656).

Royal Viking Line (95 Merrick Way, Coral Gables, FL 33134; phone: 800-422-8000; fax: 305-448-1398).

Seabourn Cruise Line (55 Francisco St., Suite 710, San Francisco, CA 94133; phone: 800-929-9595 or 415-391-7444; fax: 415-391-8518).

Swan Hellenic Cruises (c/o *Esplanade Tours,* 581 Boylston St., Boston, MA 02116; phone: 800-426-5492 or 617-266-7465; fax: 617-262-9829).

Freighter Companies

Deutsche Seereederei Rostock (c/o *Freighter World Cruises*; address above).

Egon-Oldendorff (c/o *Freighter World Cruises;* address above).

Grimaldi (c/o *Freighter World Cruises;* address above).

Mediterranean Shipping (c/o *Sea the Difference,* 420 Fifth Ave., Suite 804, New York, NY 10018; phone: 800-666-9333 or 212-354-4409; fax: 212-764-8592.

Inland Waterway Cruise Companies

AHI International (701 Lee St., Des Plaines, IL 60016; phone: 800-323-7373 or 312-694-9330; fax: 708-699-7108).

Elegant Cruises and Tours (31 Central Dr., Port Washington, NY 11050; phone: 800-683-6767 or 516-767-9302; fax: 516-767-9303).

Esplanade Tours (581 Boylston St., Boston, MA 02116; phone: 617-266-7465 in Boston; 800-426-5492 elsewhere in the US; fax: 617-262-9829).

Etoile de Champagne (89 Broad St., Boston, MA 02110; phone: 800-280-1492 or 617-426-1776; fax: 617-426-4689).

EuroCruises (303 W. 13th St., New York, NY 10014-1207; phone: 800-688-EURO or 212-691-2099; fax: 212-366-4747).

Europe Cruise Line (225 N. Michigan Ave., Suite 224, Chicago, IL 60601; phone: 800-880-0071 or 312-540-5500; fax: 312-540-5503).

European Cruises (241 E. Commercial Blvd., Ft. Lauderdale, FL 33334; phone: 800-327-8223 or 305-491-0333; fax: 305-772-9340).

Frontiers International (100 Logan Rd., Wexford, PA 15090; 800-245-1950 or 412-935-1577; fax: 412-935-5388).

INTRAV (7711 Bonhomme Ave., St. Louis, MO 63105-1961; phone: 800-456-8100; fax: 314-727-0908).

KD River Cruises of Europe (2500 Westchester Ave., Purchase, NY 10577; phone: 800-346-6525 or 914-696-3600; fax: 914-696-0833; 323 Geary St., San Francisco, CA 94102; phone: 800-858-8587 or 415-392-8817; fax: 415-392-8868).

Le Boat (215 Union St., Hackensack, NJ 07601; phone: 800-922-0291 or 201-342-1838; 800-992-0291 in Canada; fax 201-342-7498).

Skipper Travel Services (1500 41st Ave., Suite 8B, Capitola, CA 95010; phone: 408-462-5333; fax: 408-462-5178).

Traveling by Train

Deutsche Bahn (German Rail), the government-owned and -operated national railroad company, runs a network of some 32,000 trains. These include *EuroCity (EC)* trains, which provide international service; *InterCity (IC)* trains (featuring the high-speed *InterCityExpress*), which connect major German cities; and *InterRegio* trains, which provide service to smaller towns and villages throughout Germany. There also are car-carrying trains called *Autoreisezüge.*

All trains have first and second class cars, and many also have a dining car. Sleeping compartments also are available on some trains. Reservations are needed for some *EC* and *IC* trains, as well as for sleepers. Luggage often can be placed just inside the doors; otherwise, you can use the overhead racks. For an additional fee, you also can send some of your luggage ahead as rcgistered baggage. At most stations, porters are in short supply (and must be arranged for in advance), but self-service luggage carts are provided.

Various discount excursion tickets and rail passes are available, including the Eurailpass (which covers train travel throughout much of the Continent), the Europass (a more limited version of the Eurailpass), and the German Railpass (for travel only within Germany). The German Railpass *must* be purchased before you arrive in Germany. It is strongly recommended that you purchase your Eurailpass or Europass before leaving the US; these passes are more expensive abroad and can be purchased only in major train stations.

You can purchase the German Railpass from travel agents or from *German Rail*'s US representative, *DER Tours* (11933 Wilshire Blvd., Los Angeles, CA 90025; phone: 800-937-1234; fax: 310-479-3465; and 9501 W. Devon Ave., Rosemont, IL 60018-4832; phone: 800-782-2424 or 708-692-6300; fax: 800-282-7474). The Eurailpass and Europass can be purchased through travel agents or from *Rail Europe* (phone: 800-438-7245 or 914-682-2999; fax: 914-682-2821). A US agency specializing in rail travel is

Accent on Travel (112 N. Fifth St., Klamath Falls, OR 97601; phone: 503-885-7330).

FURTHER INFORMATION

Useful information about European rail travel, including rail passes, is provided in *Europe on Track,* issued by *Rail Europe* (phone above). Information on the German Railpass also can be obtained from *DER Tours* (address above). The *Thomas Cook European Timetable,* a compendium of European rail services, is available in bookstores and from the *Forsyth Travel Library* (9154 W. 57th St., PO Box 2975, Shawnee Mission, KS 66201-1375; phone: 800-367-7984 or 913-384-3440; fax: 913-384-3553). Other useful resources include the *Eurail Guide,* by Kathryn Turpin and Marvin Saltzman (Eurail Guide Annual, 27540 Pacific Coast Hwy., Malibu, CA 90265; no phone) and *Europe by Eurail,* by George and LaVerne Ferguson (Globe Pequot Press, 6 Business Park Rd., PO Box 833, Old Saybrook, CT 06475; phone: 203-395-0440; fax: 203-395-0312).

Once in Germany, city-to-city timetables are available at information desks in the main train stations. The *Städteverbindungen* (available only in German) provides scheduling and other information and can be ordered in the US from the Rosemont, Illinois office of *DER Tours* (address above).

Traveling by Car

Driving is the most flexible way to explore Germany. To drive in Germany, a US citizen must have a valid US driver's license. In addition, an International Driver's Permit (IDP) is recommended (although it is not required). The IDP—essentially a translation of your license into nine languages—can be obtained from US branches of the *American Automobile Association* (*AAA;* for locations, check the yellow pages or contact the central office: 1000 AAA Dr., Heathrow, FL 32746-5080; phone: 407-444-7000; fax: 407-444-7380).

Proof of liability insurance also is necessary and is a standard part of any car rental contract. To be sure of having the appropriate coverage, let the rental staff know in advance about the national borders you plan to cross. If buying a car and using it abroad, you must carry a Green Card *(Grüne Versicherungskarte),* which can be obtained from your insurance agent or through the *AAA.*

As in the US, driving in Germany is on the right side of the road and passing is on the left. Pictorial direction signs are standardized under the International Roadsign System and their meanings are indicated by their shapes: Triangular signs indicate danger; circular signs give instructions; and rectangular signs provide information. Distances are measured in kilometers (km) rather than miles (1 mile equals approximately 1.6 kilometers; 1 kilometer equals approximately .62 mile), and speed limits are in kilometers per hour (kph). In most towns, the speed limit is 50 kph (about 31 mph). On highways, the speed limit usually is 100 kph (62 mph), with the exception of the autobahn, which has no speed limit—although the recommended maximum speed is 130 kph (81 mph). There are no toll roads in Germany.

In Germany, seat belts are compulsory for both front and back seat passengers, and children under 12 must ride in the back seat. In many municipalities, honking is discouraged during the day and forbidden at night; flash your headlights instead. For more information, consult *Euroad: The Complete Guide to Motoring in Europe* (VLE Ltd., PO Box 444, Ft. Lee, NJ 07024; phone: 201-585-5080; fax: 201-585-5110).

MAPS

The *German National Tourist Office* distributes free countrywide and city maps. Comprehensive and up-to-date maps of Germany are published by *Michelin Travel Publications* (PO Box 3305, Spartanburg, SC 29304-3305; phone: 803-599-0850 in South Carolina; 800-423-0485 elsewhere in the US; fax: 803-599-0852). *Freytag & Berndt* maps cover most major destinations throughout Europe (including Germany), and can be ordered from *Map Link* (25 E. Mason St., Suite 201, Santa Barbara, CA 93101; phone: 805-965-4402; fax: 800-MAP-SPOT or 805-962-0884). The *American Automobile Association* (*AAA;* address above) also provides some useful reference sources, including a country map of Germany and an overall planning map of Europe, as well as the *Travel Guide to Europe* and *Motoring in Europe.*

AUTOMOBILE CLUBS AND BREAKDOWNS

To protect yourself in case of breakdowns while driving in Germany, and for travel information and other benefits, consider joining a reputable automobile club. The largest of these is the *American Automobile Association (AAA).* Before joining this or any other automobile club, however, check whether it has reciprocity with German clubs such as *Allgemeiner Deutscher Automobil Club* (*ADAC;* 8 Am Westpark, Munich 81373; phone: 89-76760; fax: 89-76762-500) and *Automobilclub von Deutschland* (*AvD;* 16 Lyoner Str., Frankfurt 60528; phone: 69-66060; fax: 69-6606-303).

GASOLINE

Gasoline is sold in liters (approximately 3.8 liters = 1 US gallon). Leaded, unleaded, and diesel fuel are available.

RENTING A CAR

You can rent a car through a travel agent or international rental firm before leaving home, or from a local company once in Germany. Reserve in advance.

Most car rental companies require a credit card, although some will accept a substantial cash deposit. The minimum age to rent a car is set by the company; some also may impose special conditions on drivers above a certain age. Electing to pay for collision damage waiver (CDW) protection will add to the cost of renting a car, but releases you from financial liability for the vehicle. Additional costs include drop-off charges or one-way service fees.

International Car Rental Companies

Alamo (phone: 800-522-9696).
Auto Depot (phone: 49-30-781-1011).
Auto Europe (phone: 800-223-5555).
Avis (phone: 800-331-1084).
Budget (phone: 800-472-3325).
Dollar Rent A Car (known in Europe as *Eurodollar Rent A Car;* phone: 800-800-6000).
Europa Service (phone: 49-30-891-1070).
Europe by Car (phone: 212-581-3040 in New York State; 800-223-1516 elsewhere in the US).
European Car Reservations (phone: 800-535-3303).
Foremost Euro-Car (phone: 800-272-3299).
Hertz (phone: 800-654-3001).
Kemwel Group (phone: 800-678-0678).
Meier's World Travel (phone: 800-937-0700).
National (known in Europe as *Europcar;* phone: 800-CAR-EUROPE).

Package Tours

A package is a collection of travel services that can be purchased in a single transaction. Its principal advantages are convenience and economy—the cost usually is lower than that of the same services purchased separately. Tour programs generally can be divided into two categories: escorted or locally hosted (with a set itinerary), and independent (usually more flexible).

When considering a package tour, read the brochure *carefully* to determine exactly what is included and any conditions that may apply, and check the company's record with the *Better Business Bureau.* The *United States Tour Operators Association* (*USTOA;* 211 E. 51st St., Suite 12B, New York, NY 10022; phone: 212-750-7371; fax: 212-421-1285) also can be helpful in determining a package tour operator's reliability. As with charter flights, to safeguard your funds, always make your check out to the company's escrow account.

Many tour operators offer packages focused on special interests such as the arts, nature study, sports, and other recreations. *All Adventure Travel* (5589 Arapahoe St., Suite 208, Boulder, CO 80303; phone: 800-537-4025 or 303-440-7924; fax: 303-440-4160) represents such specialized packagers. Many also are listed in the *Specialty Travel Index* (305 San Anselmo Ave., Suite 313, San Anselmo, CA 94960; phone: 415-459-4900 in California; 800-442-4922 elsewhere in the US; fax: 415-459-4974).

Package Tour Operators

Abercrombie & Kent (1520 Kensington Rd., Oak Brook, IL 60521; phone: 708-954-2944 in Illinois; 800-323-7308 elsewhere in the US; fax: 708-954-3324).

Adventure Golf Holidays (815 North Rd., Westfield, MA 01085; phone: 800-628-9655 or 413-568-2855).

Adventure Tours (9818-B Liberty Rd., Randallstown, MD 21133; phone: 410-922-7000 in Baltimore; 800-638-9040 elsewhere in the US; fax: 410-521-6968 or 410-922-8680).

AESU (2 Hamill Rd., Suite 248, Baltimore, MD 21210; phone: 800-638-7640 or 410-323-4416; fax: 410-323-4498).

AHI International (701 Lee St., Des Plaines, IL 60016; phone: 800-323-7373 or 312-694-9330; fax: 708-699-7108).

American Airlines FlyAAway Vacations (offices throughout the US; phone: 800-321-2121).

American Express Vacations (offices throughout the US; phone: 800-YES-AMEX).

American Museum of Natural History Discovery Tours (Central Park W. at W. 79th St., New York, NY 10024; phone; 212-769-5700).

Archaeological Tours (271 Madison Ave., Suite 904, New York, NY 10016; phone: 212-986-3054; fax: 212-370-1561).

AutoVenture (425 Pike St., Suite 502, Seattle, WA 98101; phone: 800-426-7502 or 206-624-6033; fax: 206-340-8891).

Bacchants' Pilgrimages (475 Sansome St., Suite 840, San Francisco, CA 94111; phone: 800-952-0226 or 415-981-8518; fax: 415-291-9419).

Backroads (1516 Fifth St., Berkeley, CA 94710-1740; phone: 800-462-2848 or 510-527-1555; fax: 510-527-1444).

Blue Marble Travel (2 Rue Dussoubs, Paris 75002, France; phone: 33-1-42-36-02-34; fax: 33-1-42-21-14-77; in the US, contact *Odyssey Adventures,* 305 Commercial St., Suite 505, Portland, ME 04101; phone: 800-544-3216 or 207-773-0905).

Brendan Tours (15137 Califa St., Van Nuys, CA 91411; phone: 800-421-8446 or 818-785-9696; fax: 818-902-9876).

British Airways Holidays (75-20 Astoria Blvd., Jackson Heights, NY 11370; phone: 800-AIRWAYS).

Caravan Tours (401 N. Michigan Ave., Chicago, IL 60611; phone: 800-CARAVAN or 312-321-9800; fax: 312-321-9810).

Catholic Travel (10018 Cedar Lane, Kensington, MD 20895; phone: 301-530-8963; fax: 301-530-6614).

Certified Vacations (110 E. Broward Blvd., Ft. Lauderdale, FL 33302; phone: 800-233-7260 or 305-522-1440; fax: 305-468-4781).

Classic Adventures (PO Box 153, Hamlin, NY 14464-0153; phone: 800-777-8090 or 716-964-8488).

Collette Tours (162 Middle St., Pawtucket, RI 02860; phone: 800-752-2655 in New England; 800-832-4656 elsewhere in the US; fax: 401-727-4745).

Contiki Holidays (300 Plaza Alicante, Suite 900, Garden Grove, CA 92640; phone: 800-266-8454 or 714-740-0808; fax: 714-740-0818).

Continental Grand Destinations (offices throughout the US; phone: 800-634-5555).

Dailey-Thorp (330 W. 58th St., New York, NY 10019-1817; phone: 212-307-1555; fax: 212-974-1420).

Delta's Dream Vacations (PO Box 1525, Ft. Lauderdale, FL 33302; phone: 800-872-7786).

DER Tours (11933 Wilshire Blvd., Los Angeles, CA 90025; phone: 800-782-2424 or 310-479-4140; fax: 310-479-3465; and 9501 W. Devon Ave., Rosemont, IL 60018; phone: 708-692-6300; fax: 800-282-7474).

EuroConnection (2004 196th St. SW, Suite 4, Lynnwood, WA 98036; phone: 800-645-3876 or 206-670-1140; fax: 206-775-7561).

European Tours Limited (5725 77th St., Lubbock, TX 79424; phone: 800-722-3679 or 806-794-4991; fax: 806-794-8550).

Extra Value Travel (683 S. Collier Blvd., Marco Island, FL 33937; phone: 813-394-3384; fax: 813-394-4848).

FITS Equestrian (685 Lateen Rd., Solvang, CA 93463; phone: 800-666-3487 or 805-688-9494; fax: 805-688-2493).

Five Star Touring (60 E. 42nd St., New York, NY 10165; phone: 800-792-7827 or 212-818-9140).

Forum Travel International (91 Gregory La., Suite 21, Pleasant Hill, CA 94523; phone: 510-671-2900; fax: 510-671-2993 or 510-946-1500).

4th Dimension Tours (1150 NW 72nd Ave., Suite 333, Miami, FL 33126; phone: 800-343-0020 or 305-477-1525; fax: 305-477-0731).

Funway Holidays Funjet (PO Box 1460, Milwaukee, WI 53201-1460; phone: 800-558-3050 for reservations; 800-558-3060 for customer service).

Globus/Cosmos (5301 S. Federal Circle, Littleton, CO 80123; phone: 800-221-0090, 800-556-5454, or 303-797-2800; fax: 303-347-2080).

GOGO Tours (69 Spring St., Ramsey, NJ 07446-0507; phone: 201-934-3500).

Golfing Holidays (231 E. Millbrae Ave., Millbrae, CA 94030; phone: 800-652-7847 or 415-697-0230; fax: 415-697-8687).

Himalayan Travel (112 Prospect St., Stamford, CT 06901; phone: 800-225-2380 or 203-359-3711; fax: 203-359-3669).

In Quest of the Classics (PO Box 890745, Temecula, CA 92589-0745; phone: 800-227-1393 or 909-694-5866 in California; 800-221-5246 elsewhere in the US; fax: 909-694-5873).

Insight International Tours (745 Atlantic Ave., Suite 720, Boston, MA 02111; phone: 800-582-8380 or 617-482-2000; fax: 617-482-2425).

International Bicycle Tours (PO Box 754, Essex, CT 06426; phone: 203-767-7005; fax: 203-767-3090).

Jefferson Tours (1206 Currie Ave., Minneapolis, MN 55403; phone: 800-767-7433 or 612-338-4174; fax: 612-332-5532).

KLM/Northwest Vacations Europe (c/o *MLT,* 5130 Hwy. 101, Minnetonka, MN 55345; phone: 800-727-1111; fax: 800-655-7890).

Liberty Travel (for the nearest location, contact the central office: 69 Spring St., Ramsey, NJ 07446; phone: 201-934-3500; fax: 201-934-3888).

Marathon Tours (108 Main St., Charlestown, MA 02129; phone: 800-444-4097 or 617-242-7845; fax: 617-242-7686).

Matterhorn Travel Service (2450 Riva Rd., Annapolis, MD 21401; phone: 410-224-2230 in Maryland; 800-638-9150 elsewhere in the US; fax: 410-266-3868).

Maupintour (PO Box 807, Lawrence, KS 66044; phone: 800-255-4266 or 913-843-1211; fax: 913-843-8351).

Meier's International (6033 W. Century Blvd., Suite 1080, Los Angeles, CA 90045; phone: 800-937-0700).

Mercator Travel (122 E. 42nd St., New York, NY 10168; phone: 212-682-6979; fax: 212-682-7379).

New England Hiking Holidays (PO Box 1648, N. Conway, NH 03860; phone: 800-869-0949 or 603-356-9696).

New England Vacation Tours (PO Box 560, West Dover, VT 05356; phone: 800-742-7669 or 802-464-2076; fax: 802-464-2629).

Odyssey Adventures (305 Commercial St., Suite 505, Portland, ME 04101; phone: 800-544-3216 or 207-773-1156; fax: 207-773-0943).

Olson Travelworld (970 W. 190th St., Suite 425, Torrance, CA 90502; phone: 800-421-2255 or 310-354-2600; fax: 310-768-0050).

Petrabax Tours (97-45 Queens Blvd., Suite 600, Rego Park, NY 11374; phone: 800-367-6611 or 718-897-7272; fax: 718-275-3943).

Pleasure Break (3701 Algonquin Rd., Suite 900, Rolling Meadows, IL 60008; phone: 708-670-6300 in Illinois; 800-777-1885 elsewhere in the US; fax: 708-670-7689).

Prospect Music and Art Tours (454-458 Chiswick High Rd., London W45TT, England; phone: 44-181-995-2151 or 44-181-995-2163; fax: 44-181-742-1969).

Saga International Holidays (222 Berkeley St., Boston, MA 02116; phone: 800-343-0273 or 617-262-2262).

Smithsonian Study Tours and Seminars (1100 Jefferson Dr. SW, Room 3045, Washington, DC 20560; phone: 202-357-4700; fax: 202-786-2315).

Take-A-Guide (main office: 11 Uxbridge St., London W8 7TQ, England; phone: 44-181-960-0459; fax: 44-181-964-0990; US office: 954 Lexington Ave., New York, NY 10021; phone: 800-825-4946; fax: 800-635-7177).

Tauck Tours (PO Box 5027, Westport, CT 06881; phone: 800-468-2825 or 203-226-6911; fax: 203-221-6828).

Thomas Cook (headquarters: 45 Berkeley St., Piccadilly, London W1A 1EB, England; phone: 44-171-499-4000; fax: 44-171-408-4299; main US office: 100 Cambridge Park Dr., Cambridge, MA 02140; phone: 800-846-6272; fax: 617-349-1094).

Trafalgar Tours (11 E. 26th St., Suite 1300, New York, NY 10010-1402; phone: 800-854-0103 or 212-689-8977; fax: 212-725-7776).

TRAVCOA (PO Box 2630, Newport Beach, CA 92658; phone: 800-992-2004 or 714-476-2800 in California; 800-992-2003 elsewhere in the US; fax: 714-476-2538).

Travel Bound (599 Broadway, Penthouse, New York, NY 10012; phone: 212-334-1350 in New York State; 800-456-8656 elsewhere in the US; fax: 800-208-7080).

Travel Concepts (62 Commonwealth Ave., Suite 3, Boston, MA 02116; phone: 617-266-8450; fax: 617-267-2477).

Travent International (PO Box 800, Bristol, VT 05443-0800; phone: 800-325-3009 or 802-453-5710; fax: 802-453-4806).

TWA Getaway Vacations (Getaway Vacation Center, 10 E. Stow Rd., Marlton, NJ 08053; phone: 800-GETAWAY; fax: 609-985-4125).

United Airlines Vacations (PO Box 24580, Milwaukee, WI 53224-0580; phone: 800-328-6877).

Value Holidays (10224 N. Port Washington Rd., Mequon, WI 53092; phone: 800-558-6850 or 414-241-6373; fax: 414-241-6379).

Worldwide Rocky Mountain Cycle Tours (PO Box 1978, Canmore, Alberta T0L 0M0, Canada; phone: 800-661-2453 or 403-678-6770; fax: 403-678-4451).

X.O. Travel Consultants (38 W. 32nd St., Suite 1009, New York, NY 10001; phone: 212-947-5530 in New York State; 800-262-9682 elsewhere in the US; fax: 212-971-0924).

Insurance

The first person with whom you should discuss travel insurance is your own insurance broker. You may discover that the insurance you already carry protects you adequately while traveling and that you need little additional coverage. If you charge travel services, the credit card company also may provide some insurance coverage (and other safeguards).

Types of Travel Insurance

Automobile insurance: Provides collision, theft, property damage, and personal liability protection while driving.

Baggage and personal effects insurance: Protects your bags and their contents in case of damage or theft at any point during your travels.

Default and/or bankruptcy insurance: Provides coverage in the event of default and/or bankruptcy on the part of the tour operator, airline, or other travel supplier.

Flight insurance: Covers accidental injury or death while flying.

Personal accident and sickness insurance: Covers cases of illness, injury, or death in an accident while traveling.

Trip cancellation and interruption insurance: Guarantees a refund if you must cancel a trip; may reimburse you for additional travel costs incurred in catching up with a tour or traveling home early.

Combination policies: Include any or all of the above.

Disabled Travelers

Make travel arrangements well in advance. Specify to all services involved the nature of your disability to determine if there are accommodations and facilities that meet your needs. Accessibility guides for hotels, restaurants, and other facilities are available from the *German National Tourist Office* in the US. Local tourist offices in Germany also can provide this information.

Service Ring Berlin (1 Wilhelm-Hauff-Str., Berlin 12159, Germany; phone: 49-30-859-4010) provides accessibilty information, wheelchairs, and other equipment, and organizes wheelchair tours throughout Germany. Agencies that rent hand-controlled cars include *Auto Depot* (phone: 49-30-781-1011) and *Europcar* (the German affiliate of *National Car Rental;* phone: 49-30-817-5016). Regularly revised hotel and restaurant guides, such as the *Michelin Red Guide to Deutschland* (Michelin Travel Publications; PO Box 3305, Spartanburg, SC 29304-3305; phone: 803-599-0850 in South Carolina; 800-423-0485 elsewhere in the US; fax: 803-599-0852), use a symbol of access (person in a wheelchair) to point out accommodations suitable for wheelchair-bound guests.

Organizations

ACCENT on Living (PO Box 700, Bloomington, IL 61702; phone: 800-787-8444 or 309-378-2961; fax: 309-378-4420).

Access: The Foundation for Accessibility by the Disabled (PO Box 356, Malverne, NY 11565; phone/fax: 516-887-5798).

American Foundation for the Blind (15 W. 16th St., New York, NY 10011; phone: 800-232-5463 or 212-620-2147; fax: 212-727-7418).

Holiday Care Service (2 Old Bank Chambers, Station Rd., Horley, Surrey RH6 9HW, England; phone: 44-1293-774535; fax: 44-1293-784647).

Information Center for Individuals with Disabilities (Ft. Point Pl., 27-43 Wormwood St., Boston, MA 02210; phone: 800-462-5015 in Massachusetts; 617-727-5540 elsewhere in the US; TDD: 617-345-9743; fax: 617-345-5318).

Mobility International (main office: 228 Borough High St., London SE1 1JX, England; phone: 44-171-403-5688; fax: 44-171-378-1292); German office: *Mobility International Germany,* c/o *Bundesarbeitsgemeinschaft der Clubs Behinderter und Ihrer Freunde (BAG-C),* Eupenerstr. 5, 55131 Mainz, Germany; phone: 49-6131-225514; fax: 49-6131-238834; US office: *MIUSA;* PO Box 10767, Eugene, OR 97440; phone/TDD: 503-343-1284; fax: 503-343-6812).

Moss Rehabilitation Hospital Travel Information Service (telephone referrals only; phone: 215-456-9600; TDD: 215-456-9602).

National Rehabilitation Information Center (8455 Colesville Rd., Suite 935, Silver Spring, MD 20910; phone: 301-588-9284; fax: 301-587-1967).

Paralyzed Veterans of America (*PVA;* PVA/ATTS Program, 801 18th St. NW, Washington, DC 20006; phone: 202-872-1300 in Washington, DC; 800-424-8200 elsewhere in the US; fax: 202-785-4452).

Royal Association for Disability and Rehabilitation (*RADAR;* 12 City Forum, 250 City Rd., London EC1V 8AF, England; phone: 44-171-250-3222; fax: 44-171-250-0212).

Society for the Advancement of Travel for the Handicapped (*SATH;* 347 Fifth Ave., Suite 610, New York, NY 10016; phone: 212-447-7284; fax: 212-725-8253).

Travel Industry and Disabled Exchange (*TIDE;* 5435 Donna Ave., Tarzana, CA 91356; phone: 818-368-5648).

Tripscope (The Courtyard, Evelyn Rd., London W4 5JL, England; phone: 44-181-994-9294; fax: 44-181-994-3618).

Publications

Access Travel: A Guide to the Accessibility of Airport Terminals (Consumer Information Center, Dept. 578Z, Pueblo, CO 81009; phone: 719-948-3334).

Air Transportation of Handicapped Persons (Publication #AC-120-32; *US Department of Transportation,* Distribution Unit, Publications Section, M-443-2, 400 Seventh St. SW, Washington, DC 20590; phone: 202-366-0039).

The Diabetic Traveler (PO Box 8223 RW, Stamford, CT 06905; phone: 203-327-5832; fax: 203-975-1748).

Directory of Travel Agencies for the Disabled *and* ***Travel for the Disabled,*** both by Helen Hecker (Twin Peaks Press, PO Box 129, Vancouver, WA 98666; phone: 800-637-CALM or 206-694-2462; fax: 206-696-3210).

Guide to Traveling with Arthritis (Upjohn Company, PO Box 989, Dearborn, MI 48121; phone: 800-253-9860).

The Handicapped Driver's Mobility Guide (*American Automobile Association,* 1000 AAA Dr., Heathrow, FL 32746-5080; phone: 407-444-7000; fax: 407-444-7380).

Handicapped Travel Newsletter (PO Box 269, Athens, TX 75751; phone/fax: 903-677-1260).

Handi-Travel: A Resource Book for Disabled and Elderly Travellers, by Cinnie Noble (*Canadian Rehabilitation Council for the Disabled,* 45 Sheppard Ave. E., Suite 801, Toronto, Ontario M2N 5W9, Canada; phone/TDD: 416-250-7490; fax: 416-229-1371).

Holidays and Travel Abroad, edited by John Stanford (*Royal Association for Disability and Rehabilitation,* address above).

Incapacitated Passengers Air Travel Guide (*International Air Transport Association,* Publications Sales Department, 2000 Peel St., Montreal, Quebec H3A 2R4, Canada; phone: 514-844-6311; fax: 514-844-5286).

Ticket to Safe Travel (*American Diabetes Association,* 1660 Duke St., Alexandria, VA 22314; phone: 800-232-3472 or 703-549-1500; fax: 703-836-7439).

Travel for the Patient with Chronic Obstructive Pulmonary Disease (Dr. Harold Silver, 1601 18th St. NW, Washington, DC 20009; phone: 202-667-0134; fax: 202-667-0148).

Travel Tips for Hearing-Impaired People (*American Academy of Otolaryngology,* 1 Prince St., Alexandria, VA 22314; phone: 703-836-4444; fax: 703-683-5100).

Travel Tips for People with Arthritis (*Arthritis Foundation,* 1314 Spring St. NW, Atlanta, GA 30309; phone: 800-283-7800 or 404-872-7100; fax: 404-872-0457).

Traveling Like Everybody Else: A Practical Guide for Disabled Travelers, by Jacqueline Freedman and Susan Gersten (Modan Publishing, PO Box 1202, Bellmore, NY 11710; phone: 516-679-1380; fax 516-679-1448).

Package Tour Operators

Accessible Journeys (35 W. Sellers Ave., Ridley Park, PA 19078; phone: 800-846-4537 or 215-521-0339; fax: 215-521-6959).

Accessible Tours/Directions Unlimited (Attn.: Lois Bonnani, 720 N. Bedford Rd., Bedford Hills, NY 10507; phone: 800-533-5343 or 914-241-1700; fax: 914-241-0243).

Beehive Business and Leisure Travel (1130 W. Center St., N. Salt Lake, UT 84054; phone: 800-777-5727 or 801-292-4445; fax: 801-298-9460).

Classic Travel Service (8 W. 40th St., New York, NY 10018; phone: 212-869-2560 in New York State; 800-247-0909 elsewhere in the US; fax: 212-944-4493).

Dialysis at Sea Cruises (611 Barry Pl., Indian Rocks Beach, FL 34635; phone: 800-775-1333 or 813-596-4614; fax: 813-596-0203).

Evergreen Travel Service (4114 198th St. SW, Suite 13, Lynnwood, WA 98036-6742; phone: 800-435-2288 or 206-776-1184; fax: 206-775-0728).

Flying Wheels Travel (143 W. Bridge St., PO Box 382, Owatonna, MN 55060; phone: 800-535-6790 or 507-451-5005; fax: 507-451-1685).

Good Neighbor Travel Service (124 S. Main St., Viroqua, WI 54665; phone: 800-338-3245 or 608-637-2128; fax: 608-637-3030).

The Guided Tour (7900 Old York Rd., Suite 114B, Elkins Park, PA 19117-2339; phone: 800-783-5841 or 215-782-1370; fax: 215-635-2637).

Hinsdale Travel (201 E. Ogden Ave., Hinsdale, IL 60521; phone: 708-325-1335 or 708-469-7349; fax: 708-325-1342).

MedEscort International (*ABE International Airport,* PO Box 8766, Allentown, PA 18105-8766; phone: 800-255-7182 or 215-791-3111; fax: 215-791-9189).

Prestige World Travel (5710-X High Point Rd., Greensboro, NC 27407; phone: 800-476-7737 or 910-292-6690; fax: 910-632-9404).

Sprout (893 Amsterdam Ave., New York, NY 10025; phone: 212-222-9575; fax: 212-222-9768).

Weston Travel Agency (134 N. Cass Ave., Westmont, IL 60559; phone: 708-968-2513 in Illinois; 800-633-3725 elsewhere in the US; fax: 708-968-2539).

Single Travelers

The travel industry is not very fair to people who vacation by themselves—they often end up paying more than those traveling in pairs. There are services catering to single travelers, however, that match travel companions, offer travel arrangements with shared accommodations, and provide information and discounts. Useful publications include *Going Solo* (Doerfer Communications, PO Box 123, Apalachicola, FL 32329; phone/fax: 904-653-8848) and *Traveling on Your Own,* by Eleanor Berman (Random House, Order Dept., 400 Hahn Rd., Westminster, MD 21157; phone: 800-733-3000; fax: 800-659-2436).

Organizations and Companies

Club Europa (802 W. Oregon St., Urbana, IL 61801; phone: 800-331-1882 or 217-344-5863; fax: 217-344-4072).

Contiki Holidays (300 Plaza Alicante, Suite 900, Garden Grove, CA 92640; phone: 800-466-0610 or 714-740-0808; fax: 714-740-0818).

Gallivanting (515 E. 79th St., Suite 20F, New York, NY 10021; phone: 800-933-9699 or 212-988-0617; fax: 212-988-0144).

Globus/Cosmos (5301 S. Federal Circle, Littleton, CO 80123; phone: 800-221-0090, 800-556-5454, or 303-797-2800; fax: 303-347-2080).

Insight International Tours (745 Atlantic Ave., Boston, MA 02111; phone: 800-582-8380 or 617-482-2000; fax: 617-482-2425).

Jane's International and Sophisticated Women Travelers (2603 Bath Ave., Brooklyn, NY 11214; phone: 718-266-2045; fax: 718-266-4062).

Marion Smith Singles (611 Prescott Pl., N. Woodmere, NY 11581; phone: 516-791-4852, 516-791-4865, or 212-944-2112; fax: 516-791-4879)

Partners-in-Travel (11660 Chenault St., Suite 119, Los Angeles, CA 90049; phone: 310-476-4869).

Singles in Motion (545 W. 236th St., Riverdale, NY 10463; phone/fax: 718-884-4464).

Singleworld (401 Theodore Fremd Ave., Rye, NY 10580; phone: 800-223-6490 or 914-967-3334; fax: 914-967-7395).

Solo Flights (63 High Noon Rd., Weston, CT 06883; phone: 800-266-1566 or 203-226-9993).

Suddenly Singles Tours (161 Dreiser Loop, Bronx, NY 10475; phone: 718-379-8800 in New York City; 800-859-8396 elsewhere in the US; fax: 718-379-8858).

Travel Companion Exchange (PO Box 833, Amityville, NY 11701; phone: 516-454-0880; fax: 516-454-0170).

Travel Companions (Atrium Financial Center, 1515 N. Federal Hwy., Suite 300, Boca Raton, FL 33432; phone: 800-383-7211 or 407-393-6448; fax: 407-451-8560).

Travel in Two's (239 N. Broadway, Suite 3, N. Tarrytown, NY 10591; phone: 914-631-8301 in New York State; 800-692-5252 elsewhere in the US).

Umbrella Singles (PO Box 157, Woodbourne, NY 12788; phone: 800-537-2797 or 914-434-6871; fax: 914-434-3532).

Older Travelers

Special discounts and more free time are just two factors that have given older travelers a chance to see the world at affordable prices. Many travel suppliers offer senior discounts—sometimes only to members of certain senior citizens organizations (which provide benefits of their own). When considering a particular package, make sure the facilities—and the pace of the tour—match your needs and physical condition.

Publications

Going Abroad: 101 Tips for Mature Travelers (*Grand Circle Travel,* 347 Congress St., Boston, MA 02210; phone: 800-221-2610 or 617-350-7500; fax: 617-423-0445).

The Mature Traveler (PO Box 50820, Reno, NV 89513-0820; phone: 702-786-7419).

Take a Camel to Lunch and Other Adventures for Mature Travelers, by Nancy O'Connell (Bristol Publishing Enterprises, PO Box 1737, San Leandro, CA 94577; phone: 510-895-4461 in California; 800-346-4889 elsewhere in the US; fax: 510-895-4459).

Unbelievably Good Deals & Great Adventures That You Absolutely Can't Get Unless You're Over 50, by Joan Rattner Heilman (Contemporary Books, 1200 Stetson Ave., Chicago, IL 60601; phone: 312-782-9181; fax: 312-540-4687).

Organizations

American Association of Retired Persons (*AARP;* 601 E St. NW, Washington, DC 20049; phone: 202-434-2277).

Golden Companions (PO Box 754, Pullman, WA 99163-0754; phone: 208-858-2183).

Mature Outlook (Customer Service Center, 6001 N. Clark St., Chicago, IL 60660; phone: 800-336-6330).

National Council of Senior Citizens (1331 F St. NW, Washington, DC 20004; phone: 202-347-8800; fax: 202-624-9595).

Package Tour Operators

Elderhostel (75 Federal St., Boston, MA 02110-1941; phone: 617-426-7788; fax: 617-426-8351).

Evergreen Travel Service (4114 198th St. SW, Suite 13, Lynnwood, WA 98036-6742; phone: 800-435-2288 or 206-776-1184; fax: 206-775-0728).

Gadabout Tours (700 E. Tahquitz Canyon Way, Palm Springs, CA 92262; phone: 800-952-5068 or 619-325-5556; fax: 619-325-5127).

Grand Circle Travel (347 Congress St., Boston, MA 02210; phone: 800-221-2610 or 617-350-7500; fax: 617-423-0445).

Grandtravel (6900 Wisconsin Ave., Suite 706, Chevy Chase, MD 20815; phone: 800-247-7651 or 301-986-0790; fax: 301-913-0166).

Insight International Tours (745 Atlantic Ave., Suite 720, Boston, MA 02111; phone: 800-582-8380 or 617-482-2000; fax: 617-482-2425).

Interhostel (*University of New Hampshire,* Division of Continuing Education, 6 Garrison Ave., Durham, NH 03824; phone: 800-733-9753 or 603-862-1147; fax: 603-862-1113).

Mature Tours (c/o *Solo Flights,* 63 High Noon Rd., Weston, CT 06883; phone: 800-266-1566 or 203-226-9993).

OmniTours (104 Wilmot Rd., Deerfield, IL 60015; phone: 800-962-0060 or 708-374-0088; fax: 708-374-9515).

Saga International Holidays (222 Berkeley St., Boston, MA 02116; phone: 800-343-0273 or 617-262-2262; fax: 617-375-5950).

Money Matters

The basic unit of currency in Germany is the **deutsche mark** (abbreviated "DM"), which is divided into 100 **pfennig** ("Pf"). German currency is distributed in coin denominations of 5 DM, 2 DM, 1 DM, 50 Pf, 10 Pf, 5 Pf, 2 Pf, and 1 Pf, and in bills of 1,000 DM, 500 DM, 200 DM, 100 DM, 50 DM, 20 DM, 10 DM, and 5 DM. At the time of this writing, the exchange rate for German currency was 1.66 deutsche marks to $1 US.

Exchange rates are posted in international newspapers such as the *International Herald Tribune.* Foreign currency information and related services are provided by banks and companies such as *Thomas Cook Foreign Exchange* (for the nearest location, call 800-621-0666 or 312-236-0042; fax: 312-807-4895); *Harold Reuter and Company* (200 Park Ave., Suite 332E, New York, NY 10166; phone: 800-258-0456 or 212-661-0826; fax: 212-557-6622); and *Ruesch International* (for the nearest location, call 800-424-2923 or 202-408-1200; fax: 202-408-1211). In Germany, you will find the official rate of exchange posted in banks, airports, money exchange houses, hotels, and some shops. Since you will get more deutsche marks for your US dollar at banks and money exchanges, don't change more than $10 for foreign currency at other commercial establishments. Ask how much commission you're being charged and the exchange rate, and don't buy money on the black market (it may be counterfeit). Estimate your needs carefully; if you overbuy, you lose twice—buying and selling back.

CREDIT CARDS AND TRAVELER'S CHECKS

Most major credit cards enjoy wide domestic and international acceptance; however, not every hotel, restaurant, or shop in Germany accepts all (or in some cases any) credit cards. (Some cards may be issued under different names in Europe; for example, *MasterCard* may go under the name *Access* or *Eurocard,* and *Visa* sometimes is called *Carte Bleue.*) When making purchases with a credit card, note that the rate of exchange depends on when the charge is processed; most credit card companies charge a 1% fee for converting foreign currency charges. It's also wise to carry traveler's checks while on the road, since they are widely accepted and replaceable if stolen or lost. You can buy traveler's checks at banks and some are available by mail or phone. Keep a separate list of all traveler's checks (noting those that you have cashed) and the names and numbers of your credit cards. Both traveler's check and credit card companies have international numbers to call for information or in the event of loss or theft.

CASH MACHINES

Automated teller machines (ATMs) are increasingly common worldwide, and most banks participate in international ATM networks such as *CIRRUS* (phone: 800-4-CIRRUS) and *PLUS* (phone: 800-THE-PLUS). Cardholders can withdraw cash from any machine in the same network using either a "bank" card or, in some cases, a credit card. Additional information on ATMs and networks can be obtained from your bank or credit card company.

SENDING MONEY ABROAD

Should the need arise, you can have money sent to you throughout Germany via the services provided by *American Express MoneyGram* (phone: 800-926-9400 for information; 800-866-8800 for money transfers) or *Western Union Financial Services* (phone: 800-325-6000 or 800-325-4176). If you are down to your last cent and have no other way to obtain cash, the nearest *US Consulate* will let you call home to set these matters in motion.

Accommodations

For specific information on hotels, resorts, and other selected accommodations see *Best in Town* in THE CITIES, *Best en Route* in DIRECTIONS, and sections throughout DIVERSIONS. Information on accommodations is available from the *German National Tourist Office* in the US and from local tourist offices in Germany. Hotels throughout Germany are listed in the *Deutscher Hotelführer,* a directory compiled by the *Deutscher Hotel und Gaststättenverband* (*DEHOGA;* 46 Kronprinzenstr., Bonn 53173; phone: 49-228-820080; fax: 49-228-820-0846), Germany's national hotel and restaurant association. Though written mostly in German, the guide includes an introduction in four languages (including English) which explains the symbols used.

RELAIS & CHÂTEAUX

Native to France, the *Relais & Châteaux* association, which consists of two groups of members—*Relais Châteaux* (hotels and other accommodations) and *Relais Gourmands* (restaurants)—has grown to include establishments in numerous countries. (At press time, there were 32 members in Germany.) All maintain very high standards in order to retain their memberships, as they are reviewed annually. An illustrated catalogue of properties is available from *Relais & Châteaux* (11 E. 44th St., Suite 707, New York, NY 10017; phone: 212-856-0115; fax: 212-856-0193).

PENSIONS AND BED AND BREAKFAST ESTABLISHMENTS

Usually small and family-run, pensions are among the most inexpensive accommodations in Germany. Only basic services are provided, but rooms are clean and comfortable, and breakfast usually is included. In addition, bed and breakfast properties (B&Bs—sometimes called *Garni-Hotels* in Germany) are becoming more and more common. The *German National Tourist Office* in the US distributes a brochure, *Bed and Breakfast in Germany,* which lists representatives of B&B-style guesthouses and pensions throughout Germany. Rooms also are sometimes available in private residences; local tourist offices generally are the best sources of information on such offerings.

RENTAL OPTIONS

An attractive accommodations alternative for the visitor content to stay in one spot is a vacation rental. For a family or group, the per-person cost can be reasonable. To have your pick of the properties available throughout Germany, make inquiries at least six months in advance. The *Worldwide Home Rental Guide* (369 Montezuma, Suite 338, Santa Fe, NM 87501; phone: 505-984-7080; fax: 505-989-7381) lists rental properties and managing agencies.

Rental Property Agents

Agentur Wohnwitz (55 Holsteinische Str., Wilmersdorf, Berlin 10717, Germany; phone: 49-30-861-8222; fax: 49-30-861-8272).

Berlin City Apartments (203 Landsberger Allee, Berlin 13055, Germany; phone: 49-30-978080; fax: 49-30-97808-450).

Erste Mitwohnzentrale (53 Sybelstr., Charlottenburg, Berlin 10629, Germany; phone: 49-30-324-3031; fax: 49-30-324-9977).

Europa-Let (92 N. Main St., Ashland, OR 97520; phone: 800-462-4486 or 503-482-5806; fax: 503-482-0660).

Freiraum (47 Marienburgerstr., Berlin 10405, Germany; phone: 49-30-441-5889 or 49-30-441-5890; fax: 49-30-442-6386; and 14 Wienerstr., Berlin 10999; phone: 49-30-618-2008; fax: 49-30-618-2006).

Interhome (124 Little Falls Rd., Fairfield, NJ 07004; phone: 201-882-6864; fax: 201-808-1742).

Property Rentals International (1 Park W. Circle, Suite 108, Midlothian, VA 23113; phone: 800-220-3332 or 804-378-6054; fax: 804-379-2073).

Rent a Home International (7200 34th Ave. NW, Seattle, WA 98117; phone: 206-789-9377; fax: 206-789-9379).

Villas International (605 Market St., Suite 510, San Francisco, CA 94105; phone: 800-221-2260 or 415-281-0910; fax: 415-281-0919).

HOME EXCHANGES

For comfortable, reasonable living quarters with amenities that no hotel could possibly offer, consider trading homes with someone abroad. The following companies provide information on exchanges:

Home Base Holidays (7 Park Ave., London N13 5PG, England; phone/fax: 44-181-886-8752).

Intervac US/International Home Exchange (PO Box 590504, San Francisco, CA 94159; phone: 800-756-HOME or 415-435-3497; fax: 415-386-6853).

Loan-A-Home (2 Park La., Apt. 6E, Mt. Vernon, NY 10552-3443; phone: 914-664-7640).

Vacation Exchange Club (PO Box 650, Key West, FL 33041; phone: 800-638-3841 or 305-294-3720; fax: 305-294-1448).

Worldwide Home Exchange Club (main office: 50 Hans Crescent, London, England SW1X ONA; phone: 44-171-589-6055; US office: 806 Brantford Ave., Silver Spring, MD 20904; phone: 301-680-8950).

HOME STAYS

United States Servas (11 John St., Room 407, New York, NY 10038; phone: 212-267-0252; fax: 212-267-0292) maintains a list of hosts worldwide willing to accommodate visitors free of charge. The aim of this nonprofit cultural program is to promote international understanding and peace, and *Servas* emphasizes that member travelers should be interested mainly in their hosts, not in sightseeing, during their stays.

Time Zones

Germany falls into the Greenwich plus 1 time zone, which means that the time is 6 hours later than in East Coast US cities. Germany moves its clocks ahead an hour in the spring and back an hour in the fall, corresponding to daylight saving time, although the exact dates of the changes are different from those observed in the US. German timetables use a 24-hour clock to denote arrival and departure times, which means that hours (*"Uhr"* in German) are expressed sequentially from 1 AM—for example, 1:30 PM would be "13.30 *Uhr.*"

Business and Shopping Hours

In most German cities, businesses and shops generally are open weekdays from 9 AM to 6:30 PM; some stores may stay open until 8 or 8:30 PM on Thursday nights and until 6:30 PM on Fridays. Many establishments also are open on Saturdays from 9 AM to 2 or 2:30 PM; on the first Saturday of the month, some stay open until 6 or 6:30 PM (4 or 4:30 PM in the summer). In small towns and villages, hours tend to be shorter—typically, weekdays from 8 AM to 4 PM, and Saturdays from 8 AM until noon. In addition, some shops may close in the early afternoon—or not open at all—on Monday or another day of the week. Most stores throughout Germany are closed on Sundays.

Banks are open weekdays from 8:30 AM to 2 PM—except on Wednesdays, when they close at noon, and another day of the week (usually Thursday or Friday), when they close at around 6 PM. Some bank branches at major airports are open seven days a week, from 8 AM to 10 PM.

Holidays

Below is a list of the public holidays in Germany and the dates they will be observed this year. (Note that the dates of some holidays vary from year to year; others occur on the same days every year.)

New Year's Day (January 1)
Good Friday (April 14)
Easter Monday (April 17)
Labor Day (May 1)
Ascension Day (May 25)
Whit Monday (June 5)
Day of German Unity (October 3)
Day of Prayer and Repentance (November 22)
Christmas (December 25 and 26)

NOTE

***Epiphany* (January 6) is observed only in Baden-Württemberg and Bavaria. *Corpus Christi* (June 15) and *All Saints Day* (November 1) are observed in Baden-Württemberg, Bavaria, North Rhine-Westphalia, Rhineland-Palatinate, and Saarland. At press time, the elimination of *Ascension Day* and *Whit Monday* as public holidays in Germany was under consideration.**

Mail

Although letters to and from Germany have been known to arrive in as short a time as 5 days, allow at least 10 days for delivery in either direction. Note that the inclusion of postal codes in German addresses is essential; delivery of your letter or parcel may depend on it.

Most post offices in Germany are open weekdays from 8 AM to 6 PM; some branches also are open on Saturdays from 8 AM to noon. Post offices in international airports are open from 7 AM to midnight. Stamps *(Briefmarken)* also can be bought at some of the larger hotels.

Letters can be placed in the yellow mail boxes found on the street, but it is better to send them directly from the post office. If your correspondence is especially important, you may want to send it via an international courier service, such as *Federal Express* or *DHL Worldwide Express.*

You can have mail sent to you care of your hotel (marked "Guest Mail, Hold for Arrival") or to a post office ("c/o *Postlagernd,*" the German equivalent of "General Delivery"). *American Express* offices also will hold mail for customers ("c/o Client Letter Service"); information is provided in their pamphlet, *Travelers' Companion.* Note that *US Embassies* and *Consulates* abroad will hold mail for US citizens *only* in emergency situations.

Telephone

Direct dialing and other familiar services are available in Germany. Note that the number of digits in phone numbers varies throughout the country.

The procedures for making calls to, from, or within Germany are as follows:

To call a number in Germany from the US: Dial 011 (the international access code) + 49 (the country code for Germany) + the city code + the local number.

To call a number in the US from Germany: Dial 00 (the international access code) + 1 (the US country code) + the area code + the local number.

To make a call between German cities: Dial 0 + the city code + the local number.

To call a number within the same city code: Dial the local number.

Note that German telephone directories and other sources often include the 0 (used for dialing within Germany) as part of the area code. When dialing from the US, follow the procedure described above, *leaving off the 0.*

Although many public telephones in Germany still accept coins, pay phones that take special phone debit cards are increasingly common. Issued by *Telekom,* the German national telephone company, phone cards are sold at *Telekom* branch offices and post offices.

You can use a telephone company calling card number on any phone, and some pay phones take major credit cards (*American Express, MasterCard, Visa,* and so on). Also available are combined telephone calling/bank credit cards, such as the *AT&T Universal Card* (PO Box 44167, Jacksonville, FL 32231-4167; phone: 800-423-4343). Similarly, *Sprint* (8140 Ward Pkwy., Kansas City, MO 64114; phone: 800-THE-MOST or 800-800-USAA) offers the *VisaPhone* program, through which you can add phone card privileges to your existing *Visa* card. Companies offering long distance phone cards without additional credit card privileges include *AT&T* (phone: 800-CALL-ATT), *Executive Telecard International* (4260 E. Evans Ave., Suite 6, Denver, CO 80222; phone: 800-950-3800), *MCI* (323 Third St. SE, Cedar Rapids, IA 52401; phone: 800-444-4444; and 12790 Merit Dr., Dallas, TX 75251; phone: 800-444-3333), *Metromedia Communications* (1 International Center, 100 NE Loop 410, San Antonio, TX 78216; phone: 800-275-0200), and *Sprint* (address above).

Hotels routinely add surcharges to the cost of phone calls made from their rooms. Long-distance telephone services that may help you avoid this added expense are provided by a number of companies, including *AT&T* (International Information Service, 635 Grant St., Pittsburgh, PA 15219; phone: 800-874-4000), *MCI* (address above), *Metromedia Communications* (address above), and *Sprint* (address above). Note that even when you use such long-distance services, some hotels still may charge a fee for line usage.

AT&T's Language Line Service (phone: 800-752-6096) provides interpretive services for telephone communications in German and numerous other languages. Additional resources for travelers include the *AT&T 800 Travel Directory* (phone: 800-426-8686 for orders); the *Toll-Free Travel & Vacation Information Directory* (Pilot Books, 103 Cooper St., Babylon, NY 11702; phone: 516-422-2225; fax: 516-422-2227); and *The Phone Booklet* (Scott American Corporation, PO Box 88, W. Redding, CT 06896; no phone).

Important Phone Numbers

Emergency assistance: 110
International operator: 00118
German information and operator: 01188

Electricity

Like most European countries, Germany uses 220-volt, 50-cycle alternating current (AC). Travelers from the US will need electrical converters to operate the appliances they use at home, or dual-voltage appliances, which can be switched from one voltage standard to another. (Some large tourist hotels may offer 110-volt current or may have converters available.) You also will need a plug adapter set to deal with the different plug configurations found in Germany.

Staying Healthy

For up-to-date information on current health conditions abroad, call the Centers for Disease Control's *International Travelers' Hotline:* 404-332-4559.

Travelers to Germany face few serious health risks. Tap water generally is clean and potable, but if you are at all unsure, bottled water is readily available in stores. Milk is pasteurized and dairy products are safe to eat, as are fruit, vegetables, meat, poultry, and fish. Because of pollution in the North and Baltic seas, however, seafood should be eaten cooked, and make sure it is *fresh.*

Most German cities and towns of any size have a public hospital, and even the tiniest village has a medical clinic or private physician nearby. All hospitals are prepared for emergencies, and many also have walk-in clinics.

Should you need non-emergency medical attention, ask at your hotel for the house physician or for help in reaching a doctor. Referrals also are available from the *US Embassy* or a *US Consulate.* Outside of the larger cities, most clinics and private practices close on weekends, but a list of doctors on call is published in local newspapers under the heading *Notarzt.* **In an emergency: Go to the emergency room of the nearest hospital, dial the emergency number given in *Telephone,* above, or call an operator for assistance.**

German drugstores, called *Apotheken,* usually are identified by a stylized Gothic "A" in front. Every major city has at least one pharmacy that is open 24 hours. Night duty rotates, and pharmacies that are closed display the address of the evening's all-night drugstore in the window. Although most pharmacies in smaller cities and towns are closed on weekends, local newspapers often provide a listing of those that are open under the heading *Not-Apotheke.*

Additional Resources

InterContinental Medical (2720 Enterprise Pkwy., Suite 106, Richmond, VA 23294; phone: 804-527-1094; fax: 804-527-1941).

International Association for Medical Assistance to Travelers (*IAMAT;* 417 Center St., Lewiston, NY 14092; phone: 716-754-4883; 40 Regal Rd.,

Guelph, Ontario N1K 1B5, Canada; phone: 519-836-0102; fax: 519-836-3412).

International Health Care Service (440 E. 69th St., New York, NY 10021; phone: 212-746-1601).

International SOS Assistance (PO Box 11568, Philadelphia, PA 19116; phone: 800-523-8930 or 215-244-1500; fax: 215-244-2227).

Medic Alert Foundation (2323 Colorado Ave., Turlock, CA 95382; phone: 800-ID-ALERT or 209-668-3333; fax: 209-669-2495).

Travel Care International (*Eagle River Airport,* PO Box 846, Eagle River, WI 54521; phone: 800-5-AIR-MED or 715-479-8881; fax: 715-479-8178).

TravMed (PO Box 10623, Baltimore, MD 21285-0623; phone: 800-732-5309 or 410-296-5225; fax: 410-825-7523).

Consular Services

The American Services section of the *US Consulate* is a vital source of assistance and advice for US citizens abroad. If you are injured or become seriously ill, the consulate can direct you to sources of medical attention and notify your relatives. If you become involved in a dispute that could lead to legal action, the consulate can provide a list of English-speaking attorneys. In cases of natural disasters or civil unrest, consulates handle the evacuation of US citizens if necessary.

The *US State Department* operates an automated 24-hour *Citizens' Emergency Center* travel advisory hotline (phone: 202-647-5225). You also can reach a duty officer at this number from 8:15 AM to 10 PM, eastern standard time on weekdays, and from 9 AM to 3 PM on Saturdays. At all other times, call 202-647-4000. For faxed travel warning and other consular information, call 202-647-3000 using the handset on your fax machine; instructions will be provided. With a PC and a modem, you can access the consular affairs electronic bulletin board (phone: 202-647-9225).

Offices of the US Embassy and Consulates in Germany

Embassy

Bonn: *Main Embassy,* 29 Deichmanns Aue, Bonn 53170 (phone: 49-228-3391; fax: 49-228-339-2663).

Berlin: *US Embassy Office—Berlin,* Neustädtische Kirchstr., Berlin 10117 (phone: 49-30-238-5174; fax: 49-30-238-6290; *Consular Section,* 170 Clayallee, Berlin 14195 (phone: 49-30-819-7454; fax: 49-30-831-4926).

Consulates

Frankfurt: *Consulate General,* 21 Siesmayerstr., Frankfurt 60323 (phone: 69-753-50; fax: 69-753-52260).

Hamburg: *Consulate General,* 27 Alsterufer, Hamburg 20354 (phone: 40-411-71315; fax: 40-443-004).

Leipzig: *Consulate General,* 4 Wilhelm-Seyfferth-Str., Leipzig 04107 (phone: 37-41-211-7866; fax: 37-41-211-7855).

Munich: *Consulate General,* 5 Königinstr., Munich 80539 (phone: 89-2-8881; fax: 89-283047).

Entry Requirements and Customs Regulations

ENTERING GERMANY

A valid US passport is the only document a US citizen needs to enter Germany. As a general rule, a passport entitles the bearer to remain in Germany for up to 90 days as a tourist. A visa is required for study, residency, work, or stays of more than three months. Proof of means of independent financial support is pertinent to the acceptance of any long-term–stay application. US citizens should contact the nearest *German Consulate* or the *German Embassy* well in advance of their trip.

You are allowed to enter Germany with the following items duty-free: 200 cigarettes; 50 cigars (or 250 grams of pipe tobacco); two liters of wine, and either one liter of liquor with over 22% alcohol or two liters of liquor with less than 22% alcohol; and personal effects and sports equipment appropriate to a pleasure trip. Note that only those over 17 (the legal drinking age in Germany) are permitted to bring alcohol into the country. Gifts valued at up to 115 deutsche marks (about $69 US, at press time) can be brought into Germany duty-free.

DUTY-FREE SHOPS

Located in international airports, duty-free shops provide bargains on the purchase of goods imported to Germany from other countries. But beware: Not all foreign goods are automatically less expensive. You *can* get a good deal on some items, but know what they cost elsewhere. Also note that although these goods are free of the duty that *German Customs* normally would assess, they will be subject to US import duty upon your return to the US (see below).

VALUE ADDED TAX (VAT)

Called *Mehrwertsteuer* in Germany, this sales tax is applicable to most goods and services. Although everyone must pay the tax, foreigners often can obtain a partial refund.

Many stores participate in the *Europe Tax-Free Shopping (ETFS)* program, which enables visitors to obtain cash refunds at the airport upon departure. The procedure is as follows: Request a tax-free shopping voucher at the store when you make your purchase. At the airport, have this voucher stamped by *German Customs* officials, and then take it to the cash refund desk or agent (customs officials can direct you) for your refund.

If you purchase goods at a store that does not participate in the *ETFS* program, you still may be able to obtain a refund, although the procedure is somewhat more complicated and, unfortunately, subject to long delays. You must request special refund forms for this purpose when making your purchase. These must be stamped by *German Customs* officials at the airport upon departure, and then mailed back to the *store,* which processes the refund. The refund will arrive—eventually—in the form of a check (usually in deutsche marks) mailed to your home or, if the purchase was made with a credit card, as a credit to your account.

Note that stores are under no obligation to participate in either of the VAT refund programs, so ask if you will be able to get a refund *before* making any purchases. For additional information, contact the German office of *Europe Tax-Free Shopping* (Postfach 260162, Düsseldorf 40094; phone: 49-211-301040; fax: 49-211-3010411) or the German tourist authorities.

RETURNING TO THE US

You must declare to the *US Customs* official at the point of entry everything you have acquired in Germany. The standard duty-free allowance for US citizens is $400. If your trip is shorter than 48 continuous hours, or if you have been outside the US within 30 days of your current trip, the duty-free allowance is reduced to $25. Families traveling together may make a joint customs declaration. To avoid paying duty unnecessarily on expensive items (such as computer equipment) that you plan to take with you on your trip, register these items with *US Customs* before you depart.

A flat 10% duty is assessed on the next $1,000 worth of merchandise; additional items are taxed at a variety of rates (see *Tariff Schedules of the United States* in a library or any *US Customs Service* office). Some articles are duty-free only up to certain limits. The $400 allowance includes one carton of (200) cigarettes, 100 cigars (not Cuban), and one liter of liquor or wine (for those over 21); the $25 allowance includes 10 cigars, 50 cigarettes, and four ounces of perfume. With the exception of gifts valued at $50 or less sent directly to the recipient, *all* items shipped home are dutiable.

Antiques (at least 100 years old) and paintings or drawings done by hand are duty-free. You must obtain a permit from the local *Kulturamt* (Cultural Office) to take archaeological finds or other artifacts out of Germany.

FORBIDDEN IMPORTS

US regulations prohibit the import of some goods sold abroad, such as fresh fruits and vegetables, meat products (except certain canned goods), dairy products (except fully cured cheeses), and anything made from plants or animals on the endangered species list.

FOR FURTHER INFORMATION Consult one of the following publications, available from the *US Customs Service* (PO Box 7407, Washington, DC 20044): *Currency Reporting; GSP and the Traveler; Importing a Car; International Mail Imports; Know Before You Go; Pets, Wildlife, US Customs; Pocket Hints;* and *Travelers' Tips on Bringing Food, Plant, and Animal Products into the United States.* For tape-recorded information on customs-related topics, call 202-927-2095 from any touch-tone phone.

For Further Information

Branches of the *German National Tourist Office* in the US are the best sources of travel information. Offices generally are open on weekdays, during normal business hours. For information on entry requirements and customs regulations, contact the *German Embassy* or a *German Consulate.*

German National Tourist Office

California: 11766 Wilshire Blvd., Suite 750, Los Angeles, CA 90025 (phone: 310-575-9799; fax: 310-575-1565).

New York: 122 E. 42nd St., 52nd Floor, New York, NY 10168-0072 (phone: 212-661-7200; fax: 212-661-7174).

The German Embassy and Consulates in the US

Embassy

Washington, DC: 4645 Reservoir Rd. NW, Washington, DC 20007-1998 (phone: 202-298-4000 during business hours; 202-298-4355 at other times; fax: 202-298-4249).

Consulates

California: *Consulate General,* 6222 Wilshire Blvd., Suite 500, Los Angeles, CA 90048 (phone: 213-930-2703 or 213-930-2709; fax: 213-930-2805); *Consulate General,* 1960 Jackson St., San Francisco, CA 94109 (phone: 415-775-1061; fax: 415-775-0187).

Florida: *Consulate General,* 100 N. Biscayne Blvd., Suite 2210, Miami, FL 33132 (phone: 305-358-0290 or 305-358-0291; fax: 305-358-0307).

Georgia: *Consulate General,* Marquis Two Tower, 285 Peachtree Center Ave. NE, Suite 901, Atlanta, GA 30303-1221 (phone: 404-659-4760/1/2; fax: 404-659-1280).

Illinois: *Consulate General,* 676 N. Michigan Ave., Suite 3200, Chicago, IL 60611 (phone: 312-580-1199; fax: 312-580-0099).

Massachusetts: *Consulate General,* 3 Copley Pl., Boston, MA 02116 (phone: 617-536-4414; fax: 617-536-8573).

Michigan: *Consulate General,* Edison Plaza, 660 Plaza Dr., Suite 2100, Detroit, MI 48226-1271 (phone: 313-962-6526; fax: 313-962-7345).

New York: *Consulate General,* 460 Park Ave., New York, NY 10022-1906 (phone: 212-308-8700; fax: 212-308-3422).

Texas: *Consulate General,* 1330 Post Oak Blvd., Suite 1850, Houston, TX 77056 (phone: 713-627-7770; fax: 713-627-0506).

Washington State: *Consulate General,* One Union Square, 600 University St., Suite 2500, Seattle, WA 98101 (phone: 206-682-4312; fax: 206-682-3724).

The Cities

Baden-Baden

The echo of *Bad,* the German word for "bath," in the name Baden-Baden says almost everything you need to know about this spa city: If you are seeking hot-springs bathing in ultimate luxury, then stop and stay awhile; if not, then pass on by.

Its elegant spa facilities, which have been operating in some form or another since Roman times, made Baden-Baden a tony vacation spot long before the *Kurhaus* casino, run by Parisian entrepreneur Jacques Bénazet, became wildly popular in the 1830s. But that casino, one of the most formal and elegant in Europe, cemented Baden-Baden's international reputation as a playground for the rich and famous. During the 19th century, this was a prime getaway for kings, emperors, and other celebrated figures the world over, who came here to gamble in the casino at night and nurse their hangovers in a healing mud bath the next day. Today, Baden-Baden (pop. 50,000) remains one of the most exclusive resorts in all of Europe. You don't have to be a millionaire to live or visit here—but it helps.

In the 19th century, this small town at the edge of the Black Forest near the border of Alsace was visited by such historic German figures as Frederick Nietzsche, Richard Wagner, Johannes Brahms, Richard Strauss, and composer and pianist Clara Schumann (wife of the legendary composer Robert Schumann)—not to mention Kaiser Wilhelm I and Otto von Bismarck. Russian novelist Fyodor Dostoyevski made a beeline for the gambling tables here, and contemporary Ivan Turgenev maintained a lavish villa in the town. Former British prime minister Benjamin Disraeli also visited, as did Victor Hugo, Leo Tolstoy, Louis-Hector Berlioz, and Camille Saint-Saëns. (Mark Twain, another famous visitor during this period, was less enamored of the place. He once commented, "[Baden-Baden] is an inane town filled with sham and petty fraud and snobbery, but the baths are good.") In recent years, Baden-Baden's celebrated guests have included Elizabeth Taylor, Joan Collins, Plácido Domingo, and José Carreras. Heads of state are still seen here, too, often participating in one of the many international conferences held at the town's major resorts.

Baden-Baden's founding dates from the time of the earliest Roman invasions of Germany. The first legions arrived in AD 70, setting up their base camp at this strategic point near the Rhine, along a tributary now called the Oos River. Discovering the underground hot springs, they named their newly founded city Aquae and built a modest spa; by the time of Emperor Caracalla's reign (211–217), the growing popularity of the baths had elevated Aquae into a thriving metropolis and the country's first spa center. The emperor was the first member of royalty to "take the waters" here, claiming that the baths did wonders for his rheumatism.

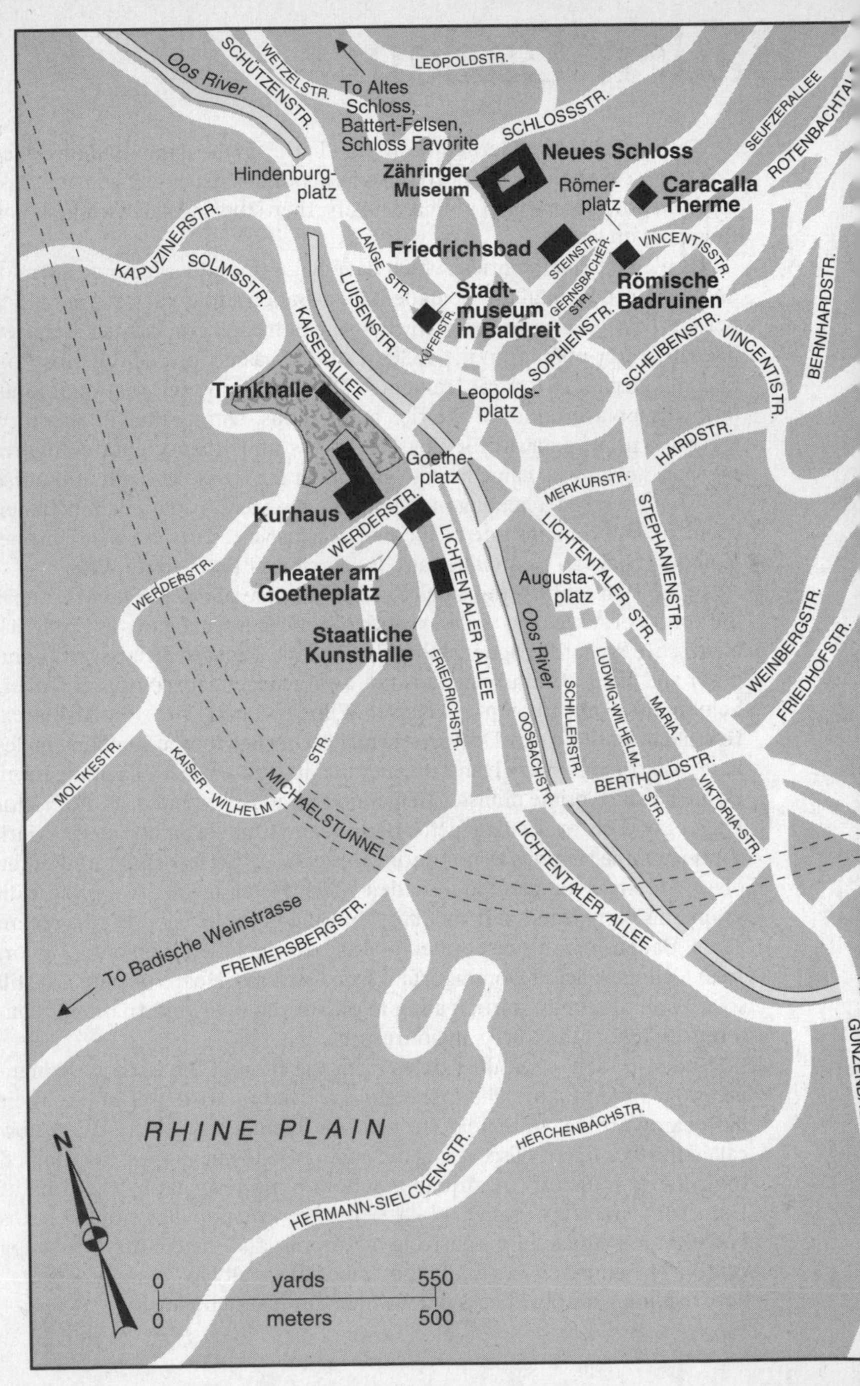

Oos River
SCHÜTZENSTR.
WETZELSTR.
To Altes Schloss, Battert-Felsen, Schloss Favorite
LEOPOLDSTR.
SCHLOSSSTR.
Neues Schloss
Zähringer Museum
Hindenburg-platz
Römer-platz
Caracalla Therme
SEUFZERALLEE
ROTENBACHTAL
Friedrichsbad
KAPUZINERSTR.
SOLMSSTR.
LANGE STR.
STEINSTR.
GERNSBACHER-STR.
VINCENTISSTR.
Römische Badruinen
LUISENSTR.
KAISERALLEE
Stadt-museum in Baldreit
KÜFERSTR.
SOPHIENSTR.
SCHEIBENSTR.
VINCENTISTR.
BERNHARDSTR.
Trinkhalle
Leopolds-platz
HARDSTR.
Goethe-platz
MERKURSTR.
Kurhaus
WERDERSTR.
STEPHANIENSTR.
LICHTENTALER STR.
Theater am Goetheplatz
Augusta-platz
Staatliche Kunsthalle
LICHTENTALER ALLEE
Oos River
FRIEDRICHSTR.
WEINBERGSTR.
FRIEDHOFSTR.
LUDWIG-WILHELM-STR.
SCHILLERSTR.
OOSBACHSTR.
MARIA-VIKTORIA-STR.
MOLTKESTR.
KAISER-WILHELM-STR.
MICHAELSTUNNEL
BERTHOLDSTR.
LICHTENTALER ALLEE
FREMERSBERGSTR.
To Badische Weinstrasse
GUNZENBACH
RHINE PLAIN
HERCHENBACHSTR.
HERMANN-SIELCKEN-STR.
N
0 yards 550
0 meters 500

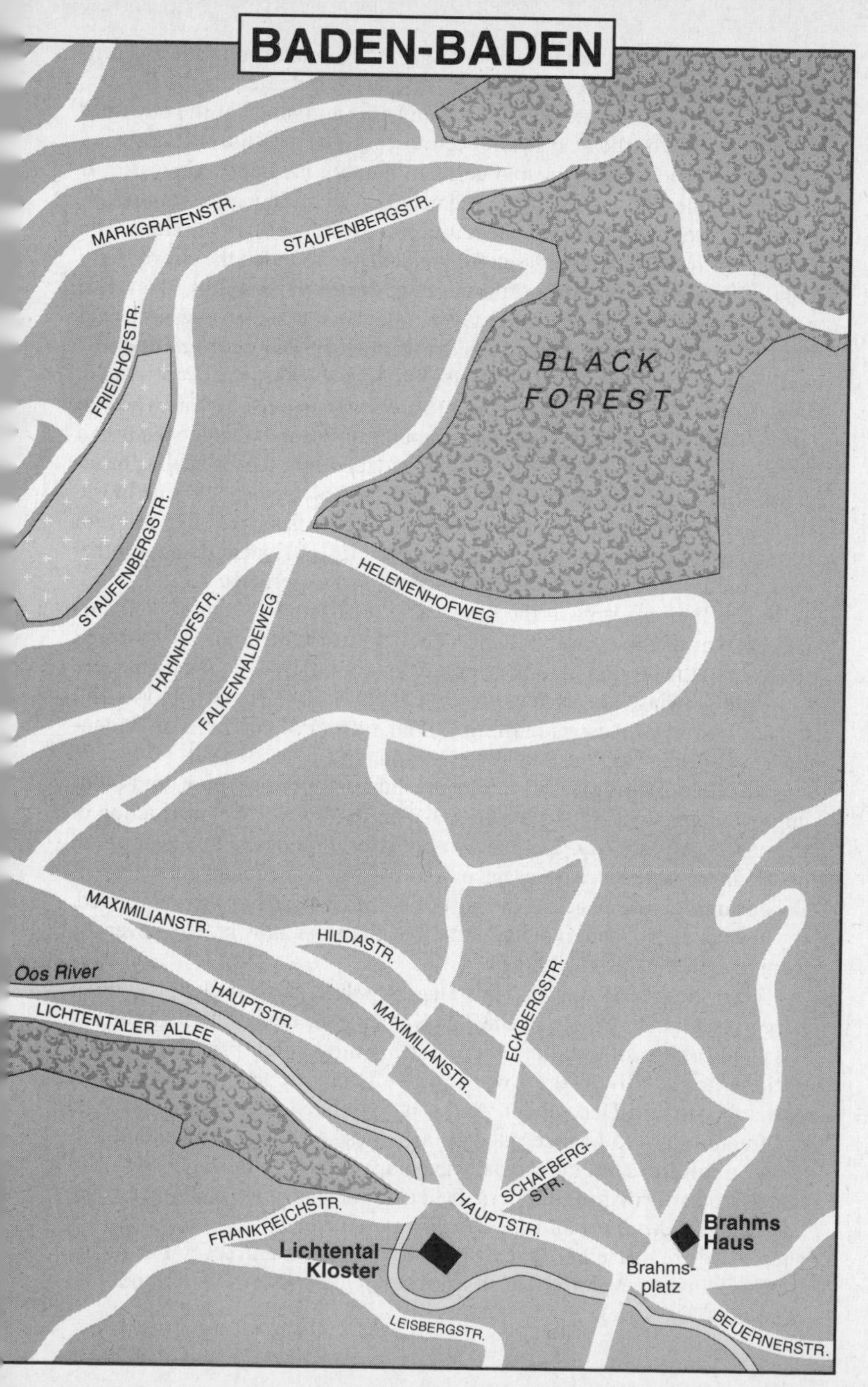
BADEN-BADEN
MARKGRAFENSTR.
STAUFENBERGSTR.
FRIEDHOFSTR.
BLACK
FOREST
STAUFENBERGSTR.
HAHNHOFSTR.
FALKENHALDEWEG
HELENENHOFWEG
MAXIMILIANSTR.
HILDASTR.
Oos River
HAUPTSTR.
LICHTENTALER ALLEE
MAXIMILIANSTR.
ECKBERGSTR.
SCHAFBERG-
STR.
FRANKREICHSTR.
HAUPTSTR.
Lichtental
Kloster
Brahms
Haus
Brahms-
platz
LEISBERGSTR.
BEUERNERSTR.

The Alemanni, a German tribe, drove the Romans out in the 3rd century; they stayed for about 300 years until being defeated by the Franks, under Clovis I. In the battle, the Roman baths and much of the city were destroyed, and for the next several centuries Aquae was little more than a small wine-producing town connected to the famous Baden vineyards. It wasn't until the 12th century that it reemerged as a city under the Zähringens, a German noble family who chose the site as their principal home. The family, which also had holdings in Switzerland and founded the city of Bern, built new palaces and public buildings and restored the baths. They also gave the town its present name. Over time, Baden-Baden reestablished itself as a spa retreat. During the mid-15th century, Emperor Friedrich III was among the crowds that flocked here to take *die Kur* (the cure). And in 1480, Hans Foltz, a local *Meistersinger* (a medieval singer/songwriter) helped spread the word throughout the noble houses of Europe when he published a book about Baden-Baden's hot springs and their miraculous healing properties. Philippus Paracelsus, a Swiss doctor and alchemist, and one of the first to advocate using minerals as medicinal remedies, arrived in the 16th century as a nobleman's personal physician; in 1601, local doctors introduced mud-pack treatments to enhance the spa experience.

Baden-Baden's fame at the time was short-lived. In August 1689, during the War of the Grand Alliance, French troops of Louis XIV burned the town to the ground; it took a century to rebuild. By 1796 the baths were again in full swing, with such royalty as Czar Nicholas, Queen Victoria, and Queen Louise of Austria making it their retreat of choice. For Baden-Baden, La Belle Epoque had arrived—and it hasn't ended yet.

Over the following decades, new steambaths, a pump room, and other improvements were added to the spa. The 1820s saw the construction of the now-legendary *Kurhaus* casino and, later, one of the loveliest opera houses in Europe. Since it was never a site of war-related industries, Baden-Baden largely escaped attack during both world wars. After the wars ended, the town picked up where it had left off, with the wealthy meeting over the gaming tables and in the baths.

Today, despite Baden-Baden's elegant, *sehr exklusiv* cachet, you don't have to be Donald Trump or the Aga Khan to stay here. Although the city has plenty of luxurious hotels, there also are moderately priced accommodations (especially in the low season—from July to mid-August and November to mid-December). And you don't need to confine yourself to spa treatments and Las Vegas–style activities: Although Baden-Baden is hardly a cultural center (especially in comparison with Berlin or Munich), many fine performances of opera, ballet, drama, musicals, and concerts are staged in the *Kurhaus* and the *Theater am Goetheplatz.* As for historical sites, there are the ruins of the original Roman baths and several 19th-century buildings to explore, as well as *Neues Schloss* (New Castle) and *Altes Schloss* (Old Castle).

Despite its fancy, high-tone facilities, Baden-Baden has maintained a certain Old World charm. In the older part of town, east of the Oos River, cobblestone streets lined with elegant shops run uphill to the town hall; this is also where you'll find the historic baths (including relics of the original Roman baths), the *Neues Schloss,* and Baden-Baden's churches, towers, and steeples, all silhouetted against a backdrop of wooded hills. Here most streets are tree-lined and traffic-free. The surrounding countryside, with the northern edge of the Black Forest to the east and the Rhine plain to the west, provides a pleasant, bucolic respite from the bustle of the city. The area's climate is one of the most pleasant to be found in Germany: Spring begins early and autumn tends to be long and sunny.

To the west of the Oos River, the *Kurhaus* complex—the main pavilion containing the casino—and neighboring *Trinkhalle* (Drinking Hall), the *Theater am Goetheplatz,* and the *Kunsthalle* (Art Gallery) dominate the vast green manicured garden setting of the spa grounds. South of that is the *Lichtentaler Allee,* a beautiful promenade that runs alongside the Oos. Once the favorite of such luminaries as Queen Victoria and Napoleon III, it is the ideal place to quietly reflect upon the long and celebrated history of this small city.

Baden-Baden At-a-Glance

SEEING THE CITY

Some of the best views of the city, the countryside, the Rhine plain, and even France can be seen from the *Bühlerhöhe* castle hotel (see *Checking In*) and the ruins of *Altes Schloss,* a former German nobleman's palace on Alter Schlossweg (see *Special Places*). Another good vantage point for panoramic views of the entire area is the Merkur, a 2,204-foot mountain at the east edge of the city limits; a funicular (which operates daily from 10 AM to 6 PM) is available to make the steep climb to the top. The fare is 5 DM ($3). There is a lookout tower, as well as a restaurant and barbecue facilities. To get there, take the No. 5 bus from Leopoldsplatz to the *Merkur* station. The spa district can be seen from the public gardens of *Neues Schloss* (see *Special Places*).

SPECIAL PLACES

Known almost exclusively as a spa resort and gambling center, as a study of the indulgences of Europe's leisure classes in the 19th century, Baden-Baden is second to none. The neoclassical *Kurhaus,* the main casino building, has been restored several times but still appears much as it did when it opened in the 1820s. Though not of great architectural interest, other public buildings have attractive façades in a variety of styles, ranging from the Romanesque of the *Trinkhalle* to the neo-Baroque of the *Theater am Goetheplatz.* Because the Michael Tunnel extends in a 1¼-mile (2-km) arc beneath the city, above ground Baden-Baden is one of the most traffic-free cities in Germany, which makes exploring it on foot particularly enjoyable; indeed, walking is de rigueur along the *Lichtentaler Allee* and on the pedestrians-only streets of the Altstadt (Old City). A self-guided walking tour of the city's highlights will take only a few hours. Pick up a detailed map (for a small fee) at the *Haus des Kurgastes* (Spa Visitors' Center; see *Tourist Information*).

KURHAUS In the heart of town, this opulent two-story gaming palace and social center was constructed between 1821 and 1824 according to plans by architect Friedrich Weinbrenner for what was then referred to as a *maison de conversation* (gathering place). Extensively renovated several times, this elegant white building, with intricately detailed red-and-white friezes on its façade and a porticoed entrance hall supported by eight Corinthian columns, consists of a center section and two wings.

With enormous crystal chandeliers suspended from the coffered ceiling, the great hall of the *Weinbrenner Salon*—directly inside the main entrance—was once the original casino. Today it is used as a venue for community events and concerts. The four salons in the right wing were created in the mid-1850s by Charles Séchan, a Parisian theatrical set designer who sought to emulate the lavish chambers of the royal palaces of France. The *Roter Salon* (Red Salon) is decorated in the style of Louis XIV, with chandeliers, mirrors, and a vast frescoed ceiling, and the *Weisser Salon* (White Salon)—also known as the *Wintergarten* (Winter Garden)—reflects the Louis XVI period, with fountains and statuary set into the niches along its gold leaf walls and twin roulette tables rimmed by an oval "border" of Chinese vases. The *Grüner Salon* (Green Salon) dates to the period of Louis XIII, with fine frescoed walls and a cupola that can be raised to accommodate an orchestra on special occasions. The *Pompadour Salon,* with a portrait of Madame de Pompadour, mistress of Louis XV, looks as though it came directly from Versailles.

The main building has more salons; in the left wing are two restaurants and two cafés, a large recital hall, and several conference rooms. The entire structure is crowned by rooftop gardens. Guided tours are given in the morning at half-hour intervals daily except *All Saints' Day* (November 1) and *Christmas Eve.* Admission charge. 1 Kaiserallee (phone: 275245).

TRINKHALLE (DRINKING HALL) While the casino is the domain of the champagne set and late-night revelers, the *Trinkhalle* is where health-conscious visitors gather by day to sip spring water. Also known as the *Pump Room* (a term used by the British), this monumental structure—a splendid example of Romanesque architecture—was built between 1839 and 1842; its 100-yard-long arcade is decorated with 14 romantic frescoes depicting legends of Baden-Baden and the Black Forest; and water nymphs grace the carvings over the entrance. Beyond the arcade is a row of 16 Corinthian columns. The liquid you'll see people drinking here is likely to be rather salty water laced with (putatively) health-enriching substances, including lithium and arsenic (yes, arsenic!) drawn from springs on the Florentinerberg mountain. In season (autumn), fresh grape juice is also offered for a small fee. Open daily. No admission charge. 3 Kaiserallee (phone: 275277).

THEATER AM GOETHEPLATZ Considered among Germany's most beautiful theaters, this neo-Baroque landmark was built between 1860 and 1862 according to a design similar to that of the *Paris Opéra.* Sculptures of the nine Muses adorn the tympanum high above the entrance; busts of Germany's venerated writers Johann Wolfgang von Goethe and Friedrich von Schiller are set within niches over the left and right windows. Today, the magnificent interior looks the same as it did on the theater's opening night in 1862, when the royalty of Europe attended the premiere of the Berlioz opera *Beatrice and Benedict* (based on Shakespeare's *Much Ado About Nothing*), created expressly for the occasion; since then, the theater has served as Baden-Baden's opera house. Also presented here are ballet performances, classic German drama, and popular musicals. Closed to the public except for group tours (by prior arrangement) and performances. Goethepl. (phone: 275268).

LICHTENTALER ALLEE This world-famous promenade runs along the bank of the Oos River from Goetheplatz to *Lichtental Kloster* (see below), a distance of about a mile and a half. The original avenue was laid out in 1655, starting from a point near where today's *Kurhaus* is located. This serene, tree-shaded, flower-lined pathway traverses the most fertile part of the Oos Valley, where medieval knights once jousted on an adjoining meadow and court minnesingers declared their always unrequited love for the wives of the town's margraves (noblemen). By 1850, an English-style garden—with some 300 different kinds of trees and shrubs imported from all over the world—replaced what once was an arbor of ancient oaks. Dominant today are magnolias, rhododendrons, azaleas, and gingko, chestnut, and trumpet trees. The cream of European society has strolled here; Edward VII, the dandy Prince of Wales, once rode to a costume party along this route dressed as a ghost in a sheet. And in 1861, in the shade of an oak tree, a student named Oskar Becker attempted to assassinate the King of Prussia, Wilhelm I. (The king escaped with only slight wounds, and survived to become Emperor of Germany in 1871—and to take retreats at Baden-Baden, which he did for a total of 40 years.) Quaint iron bridges span the river, linking the historic route with stately villas and grand hotels, and bridle paths branch off across the valley.

STAATLICHE KUNSTHALLE (STATE ART GALLERY) This gallery is part of a two-building complex south of the theater. The older structure was a residence of Queen Dorotea Vilhelmina Fredrika of Sweden from 1821 to 1826; since 1872 it has served as headquarters for the *International Club,* an organization that sponsors races at the *Iffezheim* racetrack. The art gallery, a two-story Art Nouveau structure built in 1909 in a peaceful garden setting, hosts international exhibits of contemporary art in a brightly lit, modern interior. Closed Mondays. Admission charge. 8a *Lichtentaler Allee* (phone: 23250).

LICHTENTAL KLOSTER (LICHTENTAL CLOISTER) At the end of the *Lichtentaler Allee,* in what was formerly the village of Lichtental but is now part of Baden-Baden, is the formidable complex of a Cistercian abbey. Founded in 1245, the abbey is now a girls' school; the nuns who teach here also produce religious arts and crafts, some of which are sold in the abbey shop. Tombs of the first families of local nobility are housed in the royal chapel, its spare, white walls adorned by early Gothic woodwork and statuary. There are gilt paintings of biblical scenes, and in the recessed altar is a portrait of the Holy Family. A small museum displays religious artifacts reflecting the abbey's history. Tours of the chapel and museum are given to groups of seven or more at 3 PM, Tuesdays through Sundays (except the first Sunday of the month, when the cloister is closed to visitors); reservations must be made in advance. Admission charge. 40 Hauptstr. (phone: 72332).

BRAHMS HAUS (BRAHMS HOUSE) Near the cloister is the only remaining former residence of noted composer Johannes Brahms. A member of the circle of musicians who often met at the nearby Hauptstrasse home of Clara Schumann, Brahms spent the summers from 1865 to 1874 here. The composer wrote a number of major works while in Lichtental, including his *Second Symphony,* also known as the "Lichtental Symphony." Brahms's former quarters are now a museum, with memorabilia related to his life and work. Open Mondays, Wednesdays, and Fridays from 3 to 5 PM; Sundays from 10 AM to 1 PM; and by appointment. Admission charge. 85 Maximilianstr. (phone: 71172).

RÖMISCHE BADRUINEN (ROMAN BATHS) About a 10-minute walk from the *Kurhaus* (northeast along Gernsbacher Strasse), located underneath Römerplatz on the grounds of the main spa of *Friedrichsbad,* are the remains of the original Roman baths, dating from AD 117. Uncovered in 1847, and extensively restored since, they sit behind glass walls, affording viewers a vivid picture of the ancient thermal baths used by the Roman legions almost 2,000 years ago. The therapeutic regime at the time was similar to the one practiced today, including taking steambaths, sweating and drying out in hot-air rooms, and swimming in icy waters. Open daily from *Good Friday* through October. Even when the ruins are closed, parts can be viewed through the windows of the underground parking garage in front of the *Friedrichsbad.* Admission charge. Römerpl. (phone: 275936).

FRIEDRICHSBAD When it was completed in 1877, this magnificent spa was considered Europe's most modern thermal bath. Completely renovated in 1981, it occupies an enormous Renaissance-style building with a green cupola and corner towers, its façade enhanced with statuary and balconies. The interior, inspired by classical Roman baths, is strikingly handsome, with white marble pools, graceful columns, and tile-inlaid archways beneath a Beaux Arts dome. For details on the various programs offered here, see *Sybaritic Spas.* Closed *Good Friday, All Saints' Day* (November 1), and *Christmas Eve.* 1 Römerpl. (phone: 275920).

CARACALLA THERME Next door to the *Friedrichsbad,* this ultramodern, five-story structure—completed in 1985 on the site of the former *Augustabad*—is built in the spare, box-like style of the Bauhaus school. See *Sybaritic Spas* for information on the wide variety of spa regimes available here. Closed *Good Friday, All Saints' Day* (November 1), and *Christmas Eve.* 11 Römerpl. (phone: 275940 or 275941).

NEUES SCHLOSS (NEW CASTLE) This structure, the former palatial homestead of the Zähringens, was originally built in 1437; it was severely damaged by fire in 1669 and rebuilt over the next 200 years. The castle is located a short distance from the baths, east of the city center along the hilltop rim of the Altstadt. The terraces afford expansive views of the *Trinkhalle, Kurhaus, Theater am Goetheplatz,* and the *Kunsthalle* along the Oos River. Although a hodgepodge of different building styles, with its Baroque main building completed in 1847, the castle retains its 15th-century tower and huge copper-embossed gargoyles on wrought-iron supports. There's also a large park for strolling beneath the lovely foliage of trees rarely seen in Germany: Judas, cypresses, and figs. You can visit the part of the castle devoted to the *Zähringer Museum,* which includes art and artifacts collected over the centuries. Salons and private chambers of former dukes and duchesses have been preserved with their original furnishings and elegant artifacts in porcelain, crystal, and silver. An outdoor café is open afternoons (weather permitting). The museum can be visited from May through September on a guided tour, given on weekdays at 3 PM, with leaflets in English provided. No admission charge. On the Schlossstr. (phone: 25593).

STADTMUSEUM IM BALDREIT (MUNICIPAL MUSEUM IN THE BALDREIT) Occupying the former *Baldreit Inn* in the Altstadt, the collection details the highlights of Baden-Baden's 2,000-year history. Included are relics from the Roman period, the Middle Ages, and the spa's 19th-century heyday, as well as exhibits about the springs, fountains, and other spa facilities used in medieval times, such as wooden tubs with unusual basket-weave designs. Also included are crude pieces from gambling games that date back to the Middle Ages. One room traces the history of the *Kurhaus* casino. Closed Mondays. Admission charge. 3 Küferstr. (phone: 932271).

ALTES SCHLOSS (OLD CASTLE) In a dramatic cliffside setting near the Battert-Felsen (Battert Rocks), a 1,874-foot mountain, the ruins of the former *Schloss Hohenbaden* (Hohenbaden Castle) surround a courtyard where a pillar is decorated with a St. Andrew's cross. Only ruins of the walls remain to mark the site of the former stronghold of the leading noble family of Baden-Baden, which stood on this site from the 12th century until the end of the 16th century. The castle was destroyed by fire around the year 1600, but restoration work in the early 1800s saved the wall fragments from further deterioration. There are magnificent views from here of the central city, the Rhine plain, and across the Rhine River to the Vosges Mountains in France. Lower areas of the Battert Rocks are traversed by marked footpaths; the upper reaches, with their steep pinnacles, serve as training grounds for mountain climbers who come here from all over Germany to hone their skills. Open daily. No admission charge. A café is also on the premises (closed Mondays). A trail map of the area, including the Battert Rocks, is available at the site. You can get here either by footpath from the *Neues Schloss* or by car via the Schlossberg Tunnel. 10 Alter Schlossweg (phone: 26948).

ENVIRONS

BADISCHE WEINSTRASSE (BADEN WINE ROAD) Along this road—heading south from the city limits and paralleling the Rhine—are several quaint-looking wine villages, their orchards and vineyards extending to the eastern edge of the Black Forest. Take the Fremersbergstrasse out of Baden-Baden; Wine Road signs (which depict bunches of grapes) point the way to Durbach, a distance of about 31 miles (50 km). Among the highlights along the way are the ruins of *Yburg,* a former knight's castle atop a hill overlooking vineyards and forests, the Rhine River, and France. In the village of Bühl, *Altwindeck,* another former hilltop fortress with fabulous views, has a restaurant with a terrace that is open in good weather. It serves both regional and continental fare (104 Kappelwindeckstr., Bühl; phone: 7223-40015; closed Mondays). Other fine restaurants in the area include *Zum Alde Gott* and *Schloss Neuweier* in Neuweier, and the *Bühlerhöhe* in Bühl (see *Eating Out* for all three).

SCHLOSS FAVORITE In the opposite direction from the Wine Road, 5 miles (8 km) north at Förch on the way to Rastatt, this Baroque summer palace (circa 1711) has an extensive porcelain collection in the kitchen. Also of interest are lavishly furnished state rooms and a hall of mirrors, which were refurbished as part of a 20-year restoration project that was completed in 1990. In summer, candlelight concerts are presented, with musicians in 18th-century costume playing period music. There's a café serving light meals, and the grounds, including a well-maintained English garden, are open daily. Guided tours (in English by prior arrangement only) are given Tuesdays through Sundays mid-March through mid-November. Open daily. Admission charge. Located just off the autobahn (No. 5) at Förch (phone: 7222-41207).

Sources and Resources

TOURIST INFORMATION

The *Haus des Kurgastes* (Spa Visitors' Center; 8 Augustapl.; phone: 275200 or 275201; fax: 275202) is open daily. Available (for a small fee) are maps and brochures. An information counter at the *Kurhaus* (see *Special Places*) may also be able to answer some of your questions. A complimentary *Kurkarte* (Spa Card) entitles the visitor to free admission to the *Promenadenkonzert* at the *Kurhaus* (see *Theater and Music*) and to discounts for theater performances and local attractions. Ask for the card at your hotel upon checking in.

LOCAL COVERAGE The *Haus des Kurgastes* (above) publishes a bimonthly program of events and attractions (in German only). There are no English-language newspapers published locally.

TELEPHONE The city code for Baden-Baden is 7221.

GETTING AROUND

AIRPORT An airport at Karlsruhe, 18 miles (30 km) from Baden-Baden, handles domestic flights; the nearest international airport is at Strasbourg, France, 45 miles (72 km) from the city. Car and taxi service between Baden-Baden and either airport can be arranged at the *Haus des Kurgastes* (see *Tourist Information*).

BUS Typical fares on city buses are about 2.50 DM ($1.50). For further information on city transit, call 2771. *Deutsche Bundesbahn* (German National Railways) buses (phone: 7222-35791) leave from the Augustaplatz on excursions along the Schwarzwaldhochstrasse (Black Forest High Road) to mountain spa resorts and the Mummelsee, a lovely, romantic lake about 3,400 feet above sea level.

CAR RENTAL Major firms include *Avis* (54 Maximilian Str.; phone: 71088); *Hertz* (101 Lange Str.; phone: 1201); and *Europcar* (29 Rheinstr.; phone: 64031). Before reserving a car, check at the information counter of the *Kurhaus* (see *Tourist Information*); discount specials are frequently available.

TAXI Taxi stands are located at the *Kurhaus* and at the *Hauptbahnhof* (see *Train*). Taxis on 24-hour radio call can be reached by calling 62112, 53888, or 62110. Your hotel also can get you a cab.

TOURS Several times a week in the summer, afternoon guided walking tours of the city (in German only) leave from the *Haus des Kurgastes* on Augustaplatz; guided hikes into the surrounding Black Forest also are available by arrangement. Tours are free with the *Kurkarte.* For schedule information, check with the *Haus des Kurgastes* (see *Tourist Information*).

TRAIN Located at the *Hauptbahnhof* (4 Ooser Bahnhofstr.; phone: 61445) in the Oos quarter at the northwestern rim of the city, *InterCityExpress* and *Trans-Europe Express,* service divisions of *Deutsche Bundesbahn* (German National Railways), offer connections to Stuttgart; Frankfurt; Basel, Switzerland; Strasbourg, France; and other major continental cities. To arrange "door-to-door" luggage service, which provides baggage pick-up and delivery at both ends of the journey, call 61495.

SPECIAL EVENTS

The major annual events are two horse races: the *Frühjahrs-Meeting* (Spring Meeting), a six-day event held at the end of May into early June, and the *Grosse Woche* (Grand International Race Week), one of the country's premier social and sporting events, which is held from late August through early September. Both take place at the *Iffezheim* racetrack in the community of the same name northwest of the city. *Frühjahrs-Meeting* is celebrated with a weekend festival of singing and dancing at the *Kurhaus*. Other events during the *Frühjahrs-Meeting* include variety shows and the *Grand-Prix-Ball,* with international entertainers and a fireworks display. The *Baden-Grand-Prix* horse race, one of the events during *Grosse Woche,* has a purse of close to $50,000 and attracts some of Europe's leading mounts. For information about either event, contact the *International Club* (8 *Lichtentaler Allee;* phone: 21210; fax: 211222). *Musikalischer Sommer* (Musical Summer), a program featuring regional musicians performing primarily classical music, is held the first three weeks in July. A weekend in mid-August is devoted to *Bade-Tage* (Bath Days), a street festival held in the spa district, the Altstadt, and the marketplace (near the *Friedrichsbad*). Right after *Christmas* comes the *Casino Treff–Rendezvous Baden-Baden* (Casino Meet–Rendezvous Baden-Baden), a program primarily of music and dancing at several venues throughout the city. *Silvester* (New Year's Eve) in the *Kurhaus* is celebrated with an elaborate variety show, dinner, and a gala ball.

SHOPPING

The main emphasis in Baden-Baden's shops is on designer fashions for men and women—at prices that are higher than in most other German cities. Budget-conscious shoppers head to Strasbourg, France (41 miles/61 km from the city), or Karlsruhe (26 miles/39 km). The pedestrian zones of Sophienstrasse, Gernsbacher Strasse, and part of Lange Strasse are lined with elegant boutiques. A rewarding shopping promenade (either for serious buying or just browsing) starts at the Kurgarten Kolonnaden in front of the casino. Walk east toward the Altstadt along Sophienstrasse, then cross Leopoldsplatz, continuing along Sophienstrasse. While strolling on Sophienstrasse to Gernsbacher Strasse on the eastern edge of the Altstadt, make short detours along Lange Strasse to the north, and Stephanienstrasse to the south. For standard shopping hours, see GETTING READY TO GO. The following are among the best shops in town:

Boulevard A centrally located gift shop filled with such charming bibelots as Schwarzwald cuckoo clocks, marionette puppets, and locally made souvenirs. 21 Lichtentaler Str. (phone: 24495).

ESCADA Boutique German-designed womenswear. 18 Sophienstr. (phone: 390448).

Herrenkommode A trendy store offering stylish men's clothing. 16 Sophienstr. (phone: 29292).

Homann Small and cozy, this antiques shop specializes in exquisite pieces of Meissen and KPM Berlin porcelain. 24 Gernsbacher Str. (phone: 22572).

Inka A top outlet for leather goods, including *Gold Pfeil.* 26 Sophienstr. (phone: 23955).

Münchener Moden Here is women's sportswear made of Loden wool. The rustic look of these fashions is very popular with trendy Europeans. 3 Gernsbacher Str. (phone: 31090).

Schulmeister One of the best places in town to buy the area's renowned wines and spirits, including the flavorful cherry and raspberry *eau de vie* (clear brandy) that bears the store's name. 9 Lange Str. (phone: 24170).

Schwarzwald Bienen-Honig-Haus An unusual specialty shop that offers products made from the labors of bees, including several varieties of honey, cosmetics containing pollen, and honey schnapps. 38 Lange Str. (phone: 31453).

SPORTS AND FITNESS

In keeping with its role as a recreational refuge from the stress and pollution of Germany's overcrowded cities, Baden-Baden offers a wide range of fitness and sports activities.

GOLF On the Fremersberg, just west of town, the *Baden-Baden Golf Club* (127 Fremersbergstr.; phone: 23579) has an 18-hole course that is open to the public; call ahead.

GYMNASTICS Gymnastics, fitness training, aerobics, and jazz dancing are offered by the *Arena Gymnastica* in the *Caracalla Therme* (11 Römerpl.; phone: 32226).

HORSEBACK RIDING The *Baden-Baden Riding Club* (phone: 52525) maintains an exercise area in nearby Balg, just north of the city near the *Altes Schloss.* It also offers guided riding excursions into the Black Forest. The *Baden-Baden Riding Center* (4A Gunzenbachstr.; phone: 31876), with an equestrian hall and training track near *Lichtental Kloster,* offers riding instruction and organizes daily rides through the countryside.

HORSE RACING Twice a year the *Iffezheim* racetrack at Iffezheim, 8 miles (13 km) northwest of Baden-Baden, hosts world class races—the *Spring Meeting* in late May and the *Grand International Race Week* in late August (see *Special Events*).

JOGGING Neither congested nor polluted, and with a large network of marked paths and multiple pedestrian-only zones, Baden-Baden is a runner's delight. One excellent run of about 6 miles (10 km) extends from the end of the *Lichtentaler Allee* west into the Oos Valley.

ROCK CLIMBING AND MOUNTAINEERING With craggy peaks and sheer towers of rock, the 1874-foot Battert Rocks (located near the *Altes Schloss*) provide terrain for everyone from the novice to the expert climber. To receive the

Battert Climbers' Guide (in English), contact the Baden-Baden branch of the *German Alpine Club* (7 Rathauspl., Baden-Baden-Haueneberstein 76531; phone: 17200).

SPAS The hot mineral springs are Baden-Baden's raison d'être; visiting here without taking the waters at least once is unthinkable. Formal "cures," or spa treatments under a doctor's care, generally run for four weeks, although three-week courses are available. Shorter arrangements (three, four, and eight days), starting and ending with a doctor's checkup, are also offered. Most spa packages include accommodations. Listed below are our favorite places for indulging yourself in style.

SYBARITIC SPAS

Caracalla Therme Next door to the *Friedrichsbad,* this ultramodern, five-story structure built on the site of the former *Augustabad* is like a spa supermarket, offering something for almost everyone: hot- and cold-water grottoes, bubbling pools, Jacuzzis, a sauna and solarium, and huge indoor and outdoor swimming pools. Also available here are various kinds of medicinal treatments and hydropathic services, including tub baths, exercise baths, massage and underwater massage, inhalation cures, mud-pack treatments, group therapy, and aerobics programs, as well as drinking fountains spouting different kinds of mineral water. There's also a cafeteria. Closed *Good Friday, All Saints' Day* (November 1), and *Christmas Eve.* 11 Römerpl. (phone: 275940 or 275941).

Friedrichsbad Here, the health-conscious can undergo several different regimes, including the "Roman-Irish Bath": The two-hour, relatively inexpensive treatment features steambaths at various temperatures, vigorous soap-and-brush massage, a high-pressure jet-stream bath, submersion in ice-cold water, and finally a nap in a vast room with your fellow bathers. (If you decide to undergo the procedure, don't schedule any heavy activity for the rest of the day, as you'll probably come out feeling like you've been put through a wringer.) Those with more time (and money) can try the "anti-stress cure," an intense, seven-day hydrotherapy treatment that combines the Roman-Irish Bath with medicinal baths, massage, walks in the countryside, deep-breathing exercises, a low-fat diet, and minimal intake of alcohol. Open daily. 1 Römerpl. (phone: 275920).

For information on other spas in Baden-Baden, contact the *Badeärztlicher Verein Baden-Baden* (Spa Doctors' Association), 115 Fremersbergstr. (phone: 32336).

SWIMMING In addition to the various pools in the *Caracalla Therme,* there is an indoor pool (closed during school vacations) and a heated outdoor pool (closed in winter) at *Bertholdbad* (24 Ludwig-Wilhelm Str.; phone: 932611).

TENNIS The *Tennis-Club Rot-Weiss* (5 *Lichtentaler Allee;* phone: 24141) operates 10 indoor tennis courts and has a bar and restaurant; closed Mondays. The *Rösinger Tennis Center* (17 Leopoldstr.; phone: 22131) has three indoor courts and two lighted outdoor grass courts; open daily.

WALKING AND HIKING Altogether, some 250 miles of marked and signposted woodland paths and trails fan out from Baden-Baden, some reaching deep into the Black Forest. Guided walks can be arranged through the *Haus des Kurgastes* (see *Tourist Information*). Another popular hiking destination is the Merkur (see *Seeing the City,* above), which has numerous marked trails snaking through a landscape of boulders and towering firs.

THEATER AND MUSIC

The *Baden-Baden Symphonie* (phone: 275245) presents regular concerts in the opulent *Weinbrenner Salon* of the *Kurhaus;* guest artists and orchestras perform here as well. Another musical event at the *Kurhaus* is the *Promenadenkonzert,* a performance presented by the *Baden-Baden Symphonie* several afternoons a week. In spring and summer, the one-hour concerts of light classical music and Viennese waltzes are given in the bandshell outside the *Kurhaus;* in cold weather, they are held inside. The neighboring *Theater am Goetheplatz* (phone: 275268) puts on opera, ballet, musicals, and plays. Consult the monthly program available at the *Kurhaus* for schedules.

NIGHTCLUBS AND NIGHTLIFE

As might be expected, much of Baden-Baden's after-dark activity is concentrated in and around the *Kurhaus* (see *Special Places*), which houses one of the world's most glamorous casinos. The gambling salons are open daily except for a number of holidays—including *Good Friday, All Saints' Day* (November 1), *Christmas Eve,* and *Christmas*—from 2 PM until 2 AM Sundays through Thursdays; until 3 AM Fridays and Saturdays. Games of chance include roulette, blackjack, baccarat, and poker.

You must be 21 years of age or older to enter the casino. Bring your passport with you. Jacket and tie are required for men, evening wear for women; jeans, shorts, and sports shoes are forbidden. You can purchase tickets for a single day, two days, a weekend, or a full week. The minimum bet is 5 DM (about $3); the maximum is 20,000 DM (about $12,000). Those unfamiliar with the games can attend free demonstrations and explanations of rules for roulette, baccarat, and blackjack on Fridays from 10:30 to 11:30 AM.

There are no slot machines at the *Kurhaus* casino, but there are some in a small casino in the former railroad station on Lange Strasse. It's open from 2 to 11 PM Sundays through Thursdays; until midnight Fridays and Saturdays. There's an admission charge.

For music and dancing, the *Kurhaus* houses the *Paddock Bar* (phone: 9070), a popular spot for young people, and *Equipage* (phone: 32375), featuring live music by Euro-rock and pop bands from all over Europe; also try *Club Taverne* (1 Kaiserallee; phone: 29666), the town's leading disco. Popular hotel piano bars include the *Jockey Bar* in the *Steigenberger Badischer Hof* and the *Oleander Bar* in *Brenner's Park* (see *Checking In* for both).

Best in Town

CHECKING IN

With Baden-Baden's reputation for luxury and high living, it's no surprise that rooms at most of its hotels cost a king's ransom (though many agree they're worth every pfennig). Yet the budget traveler also has a number of options. Prices drop somewhat in the off season (which for most hotels is July, the first three weeks in August, and early December through February). Some hotels offer economical package plans, and there also are some small, out-of-the-way but high-quality places that offer reasonably priced rooms year-round.

For a double room in a place listed as very expensive, expect to pay $300 or more (much more!) in high season; in a place in the expensive category, between $200 and $300; in a moderate place, $120 to $200; and in a place described as inexpensive, under $120. Unless otherwise indicated, all rooms have a private bath or shower, a TV set, and a telephone, and breakfast is included in the rate. All telephone numbers are in the 7221 city code unless otherwise indicated.

For an unforgettable experience in Baden-Baden, we begin with our favorites (both in the very expensive category), followed by our cost and quality choices, listed by price category.

ROOMS AT THE TOP

Brenner's Park One of Germany's (and the world's) most luxurious properties, this mansion hotel is very expensive—but worth it. Here monarchs and other heads of state mingle with celebrities and lions of industry. Each of its 100 rooms (many with balconies overlooking the Oos River and the tree-lined *Lichtentaler Allee*) is decorated with period antiques, in either rustic or elegant palatial style. Indoor and outdoor pools, a complete spa, an exclusive health clinic in a separate building, gracious service, public areas with river views, as well as music, dancing, miniature golf, riding, and two dining rooms—among the best in the area (see *Eating Out*)—complete the picture. 6 Schillerstr. (phone: 9000; 800-323-7500; fax: 38772).

Bühlerhöhe Nestled on a 6-square-mile mountaintop overlooking the Rhine, this mock Baroque castle 9 miles (14 km) south of Baden-Baden was built in 1912 as a soldiers' convalescent home; it became a hotel in 1920. After World War II, Konrad Adenauer, chancellor of West Germany, was a frequent visitor; more recent celebrity guests have included Shirley Bassey and José Carreras. In 1986, television-manufacturing magnate Max Grundig bought the property and lavishly renovated its interior; some highlights are the two-story rotunda, circular staircase, and ballrooms. Of the 90 rooms, with modern mahogany furnishings, 42 have Rhine views. The service here is first-rate. Amenities include a lounge and bar, two fine restaurants (see *Eating Out*), a huge indoor pool, a sauna, two tennis courts (one indoor and one outdoor), jogging and cross-country ski trails, a beauty spa, and a spa-clinic with medical staff. Inquire about special sports, spa, and meal plan packages. Non-guests can request tours. 1 Schwarzwaldhochstr., Bühl 77815 (phone: 7226-55100; fax: 7226-55777).

EXPENSIVE

Der Kleine Prinz Its name is German for *The Little Prince,* the children's book by Antoine de Saint-Exupéry. Occupying two townhouses in the heart of downtown, this retreat favored by Americans has 33 individually decorated rooms and suites. The "Prince" and "Princess" suites are furnished with fine antiques; one room is fashioned à la Biedermeier (comfortable, home-like furnishings first introduced in the early 19th century), another is an "Olde English" bedroom decorated with Laura Ashley–designed fabrics. There's even a "Manhattan" room, whose bed has a headboard that's a backlit cutout of the lower Manhattan skyline. There's an elegant restaurant and a cozy lobby bar. Guests start their day with a generous breakfast buffet. Rooms have mini-bars and cable TV. The hotel also offers packages that include all meals. 36 Lichtentaler Str. (phone: 3464; fax: 38264).

Steigenberger Badischer Hof This former cloister in a garden setting has been converted into an elegant spa hotel; there are thermal springs on the grounds. Several of the 140 rooms overlook the Oos River, and some have thermal waters piped directly into the bathtubs. Amenities include spa facilities (supervised by on-site doctors) with pool and sauna, plus a beauty clinic, a three-story-high lobby lounge, and a restaurant. 47 Lange Str. (phone: 9340; 800-223-5652; fax: 28729).

Steigenberger Europäischer Hof One of Baden-Baden's original grande dames, it has been extensively renovated to restore the neoclassical splendor of its heyday during the first half of the 19th century. Centrally located on the Oos River across from the *Kurhaus,* the property has 135 handsomely appointed rooms, a popular terrace café, a bar, and a restaurant. 2 Kaiserallee (phone: 9330; 800-223-5652; fax: 28831).

MODERATE

Atlantic With a central location, right on the *Lichtentaler Allee* and across from the theater, this low-key establishment offers a warm welcome that recalls the classic spa hotels of a bygone era. It has been owned and operated by the Kötter family for 74 years. There are 51 comfortably furnished rooms, lounges with fireplace, and a pleasant terrace café in a garden setting. 2a Sophienstr. (phone: 24111; fax: 26260).

Haus Reichert In a townhouse in the pedestrian zone, this place has been run since the late 19th century by several generations of the Schmidtz family. A number of the 24 high-ceilinged rooms have balconies overlooking downtown shops and restaurants. There's also a pool and sauna, but no restaurant. 4 Sophienstr. (phone: 24191; fax: 29534).

Plättig The exterior of this 100-year-old property is reminiscent of a ski lodge of its time (late 19th century), but its interior has been extensively renovated and modernized. There are 57 comfortable rooms, a pool, a sauna, tennis courts, and two first-rate restaurants. Located across from the castle hotel *Bühlerhöhe* (see above), it's under the same management. 2 Schwarzwaldhochstr., Bühl 77815 (phone: 7226-55300; fax: 7226-55444).

Der Quellenhof In the pedestrian zone of the Altstadt close to the baths, this link in the Best Western chain offers 51 rooms. A rustic atmosphere prevails in the lobby, the restaurant, and the *Alte Badische Weinstube* (wine room). There are special low-cost weekend packages including meals, and a program that includes visits to *Caracalla Therme* and the *Kurhaus.* 27-29 Sophienstr. (phone: 9380; 800-528-1234; fax: 28320).

Zum Hirsch The oldest hostelry in the area, this 300-year-old establishment's guest list reads like an international *Who's Who:* Balzac, Niccolò Paganini, and the Rothschilds were once regulars here and partook of the thermal spring waters that poured into bathtubs in their rooms. Today's guests may enjoy that same indulgence in all of the 59 rooms. The property underwent an extensive renovation to restore it to its original appearance. Its exterior resembles an English country home, draped in wisteria vines; the guestrooms boast such antique treasures as Second Empire walnut dressing tables, Louis Philippe chairs, and Baroque-framed crystal mirrors. The elegant decor extends to the public rooms, the bar, and the fine restaurant (for hotel guests only). Located in the heart of the Altstadt, the property is a member of the Steigenberger chain. 1 Hirschstr. (phone: 9390; 800-223-5652; fax: 38148).

INEXPENSIVE

Deutscher Kaiser Popular with Americans, this property is conveniently located on a quiet side street near the city center. Its 35 clean, spacious rooms are decorated with rustic furniture and feature mini-bars. The cozy *Bierstüble* downstairs serves light meals and snacks. 9 Merkurstr. (phone: 2700).

Am Friedrichsbad Directly across from the *Friedrichsbad,* this 14-room hostelry was built on the site of the *Roten Löwen,* once a popular hotel, which burned down in 1689. Though the accommodations are modest, the ground-floor restaurant, *Prager Stuben,* is one of the city's best (see *Eating Out*). 31 Gernsbacher Str. (phone: 271046).

Am Markt Small and intimate, this 27-room, family-run townhouse on the market square of the Altstadt is an excellent choice for the budget traveler. Dinner is served (guests only) in the dining room. (There is no breakfast or lunch.) 17-18 Marktpl. (phone: 22747).

Römerhof The 24 rooms tend to be somewhat spartan, but this hotel is ideally located in the Altstadt near the baths; the breakfast room (no restaurant) has a rustic charm, with a huge, old-fashioned tile stove as its centerpiece. 25 Sophienstr. (phone: 23415).

EATING OUT

Part of the ultimate spa experience is good food, served in a dining room not far away—or better yet, by room service. Here, the dining experience is especially pleasurable, as the regional fare is among Germany's best. At resorts like Baden-Baden, you're likely to have more meals in your hotel than anywhere else. A typical nightly scenario might be a leisurely aperitif at the bar, followed by dinner in the restaurant at "your" table with "your" waiter or waitress; after the meal, you repair to the lounge for coffee. Social life is much like what occurs at sea on ocean liners, with diners forming tight, intimate relationships. Expect to pay $160 or more for a dinner for two, not including drinks or wine, at a restaurant listed as very expensive; $110 to $155 at expensive places; $75 to $105 at moderate restaurants; and under $75 at inexpensive spots. The service charge and taxes are always included; however, you should add a small additional tip to reward very good service. Unless otherwise indicated, all restaurants are open for lunch and dinner. All telephone numbers are in the 7221 city code unless otherwise indicated.

VERY EXPENSIVE

Zum Alde Gott Located in Neuweier on the Wine Road, 6 miles (10 km) south of town, this dining spot is set high among the vineyards in a handsomely renovated farmhouse. Its specialties, however, are down-to-earth: Try the seafood salad, roast duck with lentils and *Spätzle* (short, thick noodles), rabbit and goose liver, and for dessert, homemade chocolate cake. Closed Thursdays, Friday dinner, and most of January. Reservations necessary. Major credit cards accepted. 10 Weinstr. (phone: 7223-5513).

Brenner's Park This luxury hotel has two fine restaurants: the more formal, high-ceilinged, white-glove *Park,* and the intimate, rustic but chic *Schwarzwaldstube.* The *Park* features such international dishes as Parma ham, Dover sole, local trout, and beef Wellington; the *Schwarzwaldstube* offers regional fare such as *Forelle mit Mandeln* (trout with almonds) and *Maultaschen* (a large ravioli that may be stuffed with anything from meat to nuts). Both restaurants are open daily. Reservations necessary. Major credit cards accepted. 6 Schillerstr. (phone for both: 9000).

Bühlerhöhe With two of the area's finest restaurants located right here, some castle guests don't get to town too often. Meals are prepared in a single kitchen, but the two dining rooms (the *Schloss* and the *Imperial*) have separate chefs and distinctly different atmospheres. The *Schloss* has a relatively plain decor, but the view through large picture windows across the Rhine plain is glorious. Meals here feature simple preparations of salmon, poultry, veal, and lamb served with lightly cooked vegetables. The regal *Imperial,* on the other hand, lives up to its name. Candlelight reflects off the polished woodwork, and the tables are set with fine china and silver. The menu features such elegant continental specialties as dumplings with chanterelles in a cream sauce and baby Atlantic turbot with basil-flavored noodles. The *Schloss* is open daily; the *Imperial* is closed Wednesdays, Thursdays, and weekday lunches. Reservations necessary for both. Major credit cards accepted. 1 Schwarzwaldhochstr., Bühl 77815 (phone: 7226-55100).

Pospisil's Merkurius This is the place to sample baby lobster or leg of lamb; the menu changes seasonally, but no matter what is offered, the preparations are always inspired and innovative. Closed Mondays and Tuesday and Saturday lunch. Reservations advised. No credit cards accepted. 2 Klosterbergstr., in nearby Varnhalt (phone: 7223-5474).

EXPENSIVE

Schloss Neuweier Another popular eatery along the Wine Road, it offers traditional German home-style dishes such as boiled beef with a light horseradish sauce. The fresh-baked pastries, cherry pies in season, and fruit tarts are inspired. There's alfresco dining on a garden terrace in fine weather. Closed Tuesdays, *Christmas* week, and a week in early January. Reservations necessary. American Express accepted. 21 Mauerbergstr. (phone: 7223-57944).

Stahlbad In a villa surrounded by trees and facing the Oos River and *Lichtentaler Allee,* this 30-year-old local favorite is equally attractive on the inside: The elegant decor features tasteful prints on the walls and fresh flowers. The menu features pâté de foie gras, veal and lamb dishes, and a variety of seafood entrées, including lobster. The chocolate mousse is irresistible. Service is friendly and personal. The shady garden terrace is an ideal setting in warm weather. Closed Sundays and Mondays. Reservations necessary. Major credit cards accepted. 2 Augustapl. (phone: 24569).

MODERATE

Badner Stuben This small, family-run restaurant features such regional Swabian fare as *Maultaschen* (large ravioli), liver and *Spätzle* (short, thick noodles), rye noodles, and almond-studded potato croquettes. Closed Mondays and Sunday dinner. Reservations unnecessary. No credit cards accepted. 4 Rettigstr. (phone: 22039).

Nest Here you have a choice of traditional German food, Hungarian specialties, and vegetarian meals, well prepared and reasonably priced. Closed Tuesdays. Reservations advised. Major credit cards accepted. 1 Rettigstr. (phone: 23076).

La Provence Romantically located in a large, vaulted room that was formerly the chancery of the *Neues Schloss,* this popular dining spot offers classic southern French fare. Menu highlights are Provençal fish soup with rouille and gruyère cheese, baked scampi with aioli, and cassoulet with duck, goose, and lamb. Open daily. Reservations advised. Major credit cards accepted. 20 Schloss Str. (phone: 25550).

La Terrazza Tucked away in an inner courtyard of the Goldenes-Kreuz-Gang (Passage), a narrow walkway off Lichtentaler Strasse, this elegant place offers northern Italian dishes. Closed Mondays. Reservations necessary. Major credit cards accepted. 13 Lichtentaler Str. (phone: 32727).

INEXPENSIVE

Café König This popular pastry shop is an ideal spot for lunch or afternoon coffee and cake. Light meals—salads and sandwiches—are served, as well as pastries. Try for a table in the tree-shaded garden. Open daily. No reservations. No credit cards accepted. 12 Lichtentaler Str. (phone: 23573).

Eis-Crêpes A great place for a quick, informal, and inexpensive meal. This little café in the Altstadt's pedestrian zone serves more than 100 varieties of crêpes filled with meats, vegetables—and even ice cream. Pizzas and pasta dishes are also offered. Closed Mondays. No reservations. No credit cards accepted. 26 Gernsbacher Str. (phone: 23839).

Feinkost Fritz A deli with a few stand-up counters and a limited number of tables, it's a good place for a quick bite or a light lunch. Menu items include foie gras and smoked salmon, along with daily specials. Open for breakfast and lunch only; closed Sundays. No reservations. No credit cards accepted. 5 Kreuzstr. (phone: 29212).

Münchener Löwenbräu A cavernous place decorated in typical rustic *Biergarten* style in a townhouse near the baths. A wide, tree-shaded terrace overlooks a cobbled square. The food is also typical of a Bavarian beer garden—sausages, dumplings, roasts, and sauerkraut, washed down with large mugfuls of Munich's best-known beer. The service can be indifferent and hurried, but the atmosphere is nonetheless pleasant, especially on sunny days. Open daily until midnight. Reservations unnecessary. Major credit cards accepted. 9 Gernsbacher Str. (phone: 22311).

Prager Stuben The central European food served in this light and airy hotel dining room is one of the best bargains in town. Owner Prokop Pustina, who hails from the former Czechoslovakia, presents a variety of tasty dishes such as duckling served with bread dumplings, free-range chicken with wild mushrooms, baked trout, and goulash made with Pilsner beer. You also can enjoy a glass of Budweiser beer—*not* the American brand, but the famous Czech brew that gave the American beer its name. Open daily. Reservations advised. Major credit cards accepted. In the *Am Friedrichsbad Hotel,* 31 Gernsbacher Str. (phone: 271046).

Berlin

The years since its infamous Wall came tumbling down have been a period of dramatic change for Berlin. Since December 1989, when Berliners from both East and West could finally walk through the historic *Brandenburger Tor* (Brandenburg Gate) on their way from one sector of the long-divided city to the other, Berlin has embarked on what will undoubtedly be a long process of transformation, growth, and assimilation. The 30-mile-long Wall has been dismantled (except for a short stretch that serves as a reminder); Checkpoint Charlie has been "brought in from the cold"; and Germans in general—and Berliners in particular—enjoy free access to all of Berlin for the first time since the city was partitioned at the end of World War II. East and West Berliners, after living in vastly different historical and economic climates for almost a generation, have been getting reacquainted with each other over the last several years in their attempts to forge a new political and social identity. And the various institutions that have existed in duplicate since the Cold War—government departments, museums, and so forth—are slowly being combined. But the most significant transition is yet to come: By the turn of the century, Berlin will again become Germany's capital.

The world will be watching as this reestablished capital—once in the vanguard of Cold War tension and later reduced to the role of a "political wallflower"—leads Germany's transition into a united country. For it is in Berlin, where two different social and economic systems have contrasted so sharply, that the post-1989 changes are more noticeable than anywhere else in Germany.

As Berliners are discovering, unification exacts its own price, chiefly in the economic sector. The city is feeling the effects of the general recession that Germany has been struggling with for several years, and the energetic surge of investment interest that began with the fall of the Wall in 1989 seems to have dried up for the time being. Many prospective developers are biding their time until Berlin once again assumes its place as a world capital. And although the Kempinski group has announced long-range plans to rebuild the *Adlon* (the "Grand Hotel" of film and Broadway musical fame) on its original site, and a Four Seasons luxury property is set to open in the *Hofgarten am Gendarmenmarkt* complex in the Mitte district next year, there are no other major construction projects in the works. Eastern Berlin continues to deal with severe financial problems, and in many ways the city still is divided culturally and sociologically. But make no mistake: For the first time in a generation, Berlin has the opportunity to develop into the German metropolis of tomorrow. It is, after all, the center of a huge metropolitan area with a population of five million—the largest

BERLIN

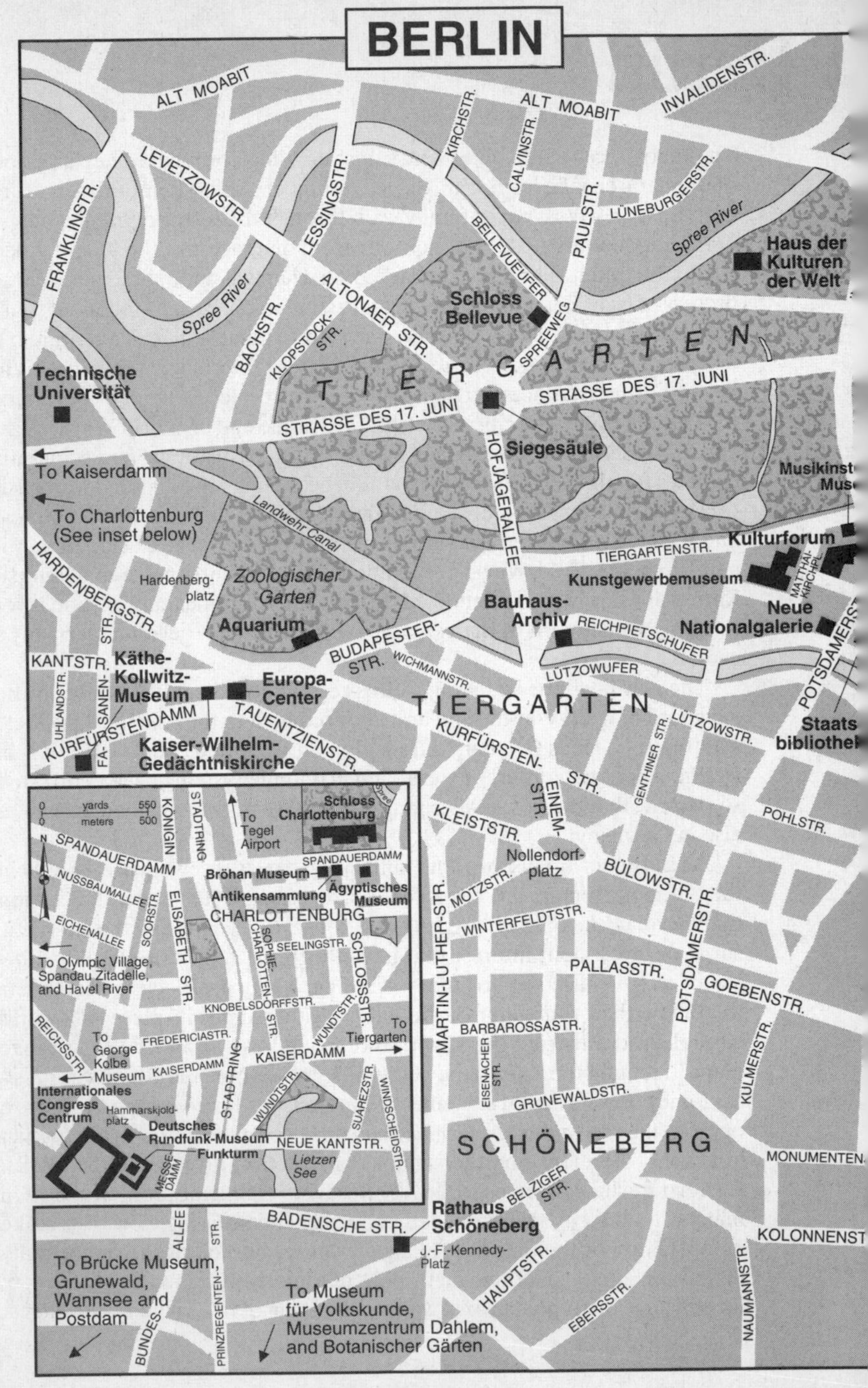

ALT MOABIT
INVALIDENSTR.
LEVETZOWSTR.
LESSINGSTR.
KIRCHSTR.
CALVINSTR.
PAULSTR.
LÜNEBURGERSTR.
Spree River
Haus der Kulturen der Welt
FRANKLINSTR.
BELLEVUEUFER
BACHSTR.
ALTONAER STR.
KLOPSTOCK-STR.
Schloss Bellevue
SPREEWEG
TIERGARTEN
Technische Universität
STRASSE DES 17. JUNI
Siegesäule
HOFJÄGERALLEE
To Kaiserdamm
To Charlottenburg (See inset below)
Landwehr Canal
Kulturforum
TIERGARTENSTR.
Kunstgewerbemuseum
MATTHÄI-KIRCHPL.
HARDENBERGSTR.
Hardenberg-platz
Zoologischer Garten
Aquarium
Bauhaus-Archiv
Neue Nationalgalerie
REICHPIETSCHUFER
LÜTZOWUFER
BUDAPESTER-STR.
WICHMANNSTR.
KANTSTR.
Käthe-Kollwitz-Museum
Europa-Center
UHLANDSTR.
SANEN-STR.
FA-
KURFÜRSTENDAMM
TAUENTZIENSTR.
Kaiser-Wilhelm-Gedächtniskirche
KURFÜRSTEN-STR.
GENTHINER STR.
LÜTZOWSTR.
POTSDAMERSTR.
Staats bibliothek
EINEM-STR.
KLEISTSTR.
Nollendorf-platz
POHLSTR.
BÜLOWSTR.
MOTZSTR.
MARTIN-LUTHER-STR.
WINTERFELDTSTR.
PALLASSTR.
GOEBENSTR.
POTSDAMERSTR.
BARBAROSSASTR.
EISENACHER STR.
GRUNEWALDSTR.
KULMERSTR.
SCHÖNEBERG
MONUMENTEN
BELZIGER STR.
Rathaus Schöneberg
BADENSCHE STR.
J.-F.-Kennedy-Platz
KOLONNENST
HAUPTSTR.
EBERSSTR.
NAUMANNSTR.
To Brücke Museum, Grunewald, Wannsee and Postdam
To Museum für Volkskunde, Museumzentrum Dahlem, and Botanischer Gärten
BUNDES-ALLEE
PRINZREGENTEN-STR.
0 yards 550
0 meters 500
KÖNIGIN
STADTRING
To Tegel Airport
Schloss Charlottenburg
SPANDAUERDAMM
Bröhan Museum
Antikensammlung
Ägyptisches Museum
NUSSBAUMALLEE
EICHENALLEE
SOORSTR.
ELISABETH STR.
CHARLOTTENBURG
SOPHIE-CHARLOTTEN STR.
SEELINGSTR.
SCHLOSSSTR.
To Olympic Village, Spandau Zitadelle, and Havel River
KNOBELSDORFFSTR.
REICHSSTR.
To George Kolbe Museum
FREDERICIASTR.
WUNDTSTR.
To Tiergarten
KAISERDAMM
Internationales Congress Centrum
Hammarskjold-platz
SUAREZSTR.
WINDSCHEIDSTR.
Deutsches Rundfunk-Museum
Funkturm
NEUE KANTSTR.
MESSE-DAMM
Lietzen See

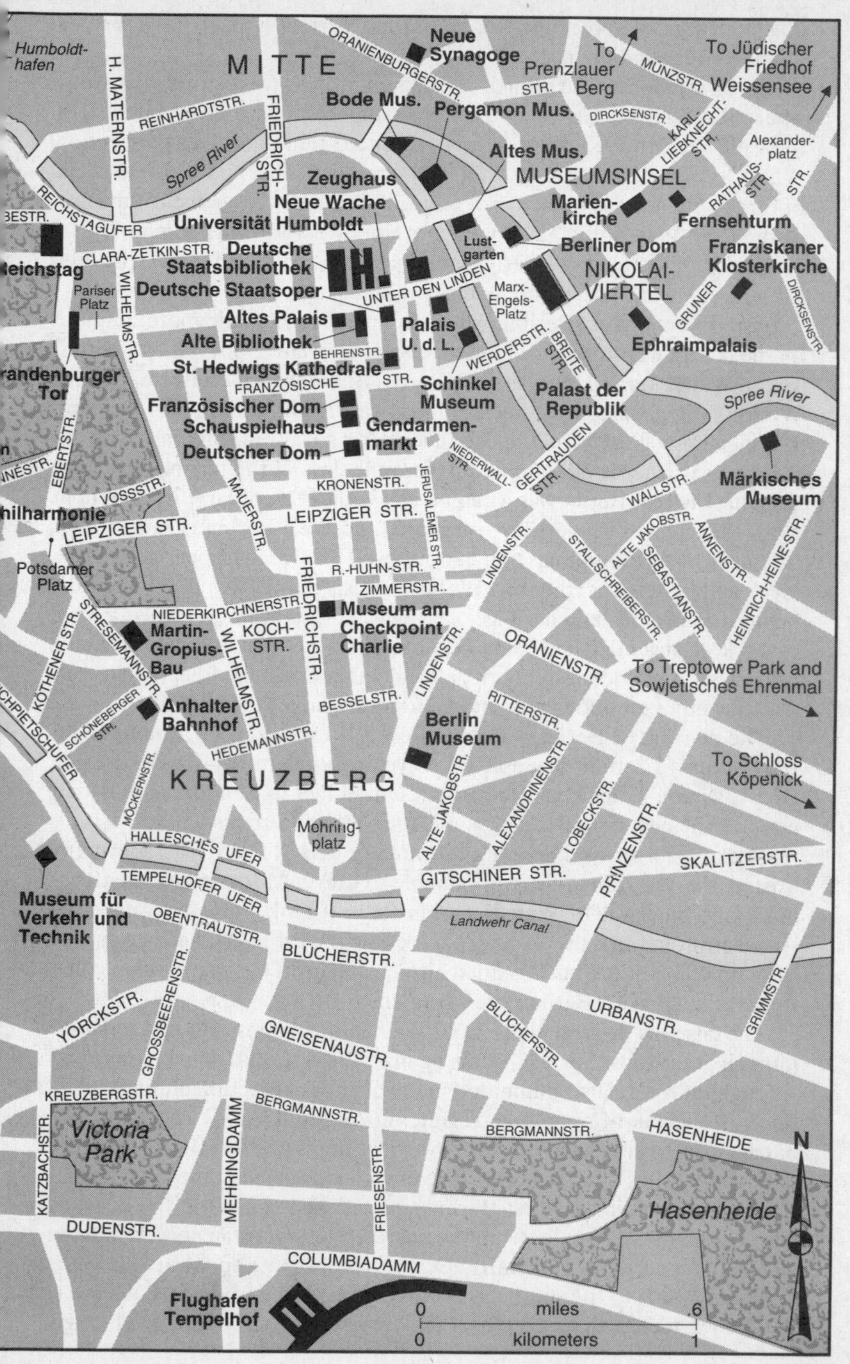
MITTE
Humboldt-hafen
Neue Synagoge
Bode Mus.
Pergamon Mus.
Altes Mus.
MUSEUMSINSEL
Zeughaus
Neue Wache
Universität Humboldt
Deutsche Staatsbibliothek
Deutsche Staatsoper
Altes Palais
Alte Bibliothek
St. Hedwigs Kathedrale
Französischer Dom
Schauspielhaus
Deutscher Dom
Gendarmenmarkt
Palais U. d. L.
Schinkel Museum
Lustgarten
Marx-Engels-Platz
Berliner Dom
Marienkirche
Fernsehturm
Franziskaner Klosterkirche
NIKOLAIVIERTEL
Ephraimpalais
Palast der Republik
Märkisches Museum
Alexanderplatz
To Prenzlauer Berg
To Jüdischer Friedhof Weissensee
Reichstag
Pariser Platz
Brandenburger Tor
Philharmonie
Potsdamer Platz
Martin-Gropius-Bau
Anhalter Bahnhof
Museum am Checkpoint Charlie
Berlin Museum
KREUZBERG
Mehringplatz
To Treptower Park and Sowjetisches Ehrenmal
To Schloss Köpenick
Museum für Verkehr und Technik
Landwehr Canal
Victoria Park
Hasenheide
Flughafen Tempelhof
Spree River
ORANIENBURGERSTR.
REINHARDTSTR.
H. MATERNSTR.
FRIEDRICHSTR.
REICHSTAGUFER
CLARA-ZETKIN-STR.
WILHELMSTR.
UNTER DEN LINDEN
BEHRENSTR.
FRANZÖSISCHE STR.
WERDERSTR.
BREITE STR.
GERTRAUDENSTR.
NIEDERWALLSTR.
KRONENSTR.
LEIPZIGER STR.
VOSSSTR.
EBERTSTR.
MAUERSTR.
JERUSALEMER STR.
R.-HUHN-STR.
ZIMMERSTR.
NIEDERKIRCHNERSTR.
KOCHSTR.
STRESEMANNSTR.
KÖTHENER STR.
SCHÖNEBERGER STR.
BESSELSTR.
HEDEMANNSTR.
LINDENSTR.
ORANIENSTR.
RITTERSTR.
ALTE JAKOBSTR.
ALEXANDRINENSTR.
LOBECKSTR.
PRINZENSTR.
STALLSCHREIBERSTR.
SEBASTIANSTR.
ANNENSTR.
HEINRICH-HEINE-STR.
WALLSTR.
MÜNZSTR.
DIRCKSENSTR.
KARL-LIEBKNECHT-STR.
RATHAUSSTR.
GRUNERSTR.
MÖCKERNSTR.
HALLESCHES UFER
TEMPELHOFER UFER
GITSCHINER STR.
SKALITZERSTR.
OBENTRAUTSTR.
BLÜCHERSTR.
YORCKSTR.
GROSSBEERENSTR.
GNEISENAUSTR.
URBANSTR.
GRIMMSTR.
KREUZBERGSTR.
BERGMANNSTR.
HASENHEIDE
KATZBACHSTR.
MEHRINGDAMM
FRIESENSTR.
DUDENSTR.
COLUMBIADAMM
N
0 miles .6
0 kilometers 1

economic region between the Ruhr basin and Moscow—and it has a decided talent for rebounding from adversity.

Berlin symbolizes the rebirth of freedom in a city (and an entire nation) where the Wall was for years the most tangibly monstrous monument of the Cold War. In 1963, when John F. Kennedy told thousands of cheering West Germans that he, too, was a Berliner, he made a political statement of rare depth and resonance. Not only did it sum up the then current state of the Cold War, but its unspoken promise of a worldwide community of sympathy for the plight of Berliners managed to touch and soothe the profound anxiety of the city and its residents.

For 45 years, West Berliners lived in an isolation made more desolate by the overpowering cultural and historic importance of their city before World War II. Long gone was the Imperial Berlin that ruled Germany until World War I; gone, too, was the devil-may-care Berlin of the 1920s and early 1930s, whose gaiety and decadence were so admirably captured by Christopher Isherwood; gone even were the days of the terrible power of the Third Reich. Berlin was a capital city without a country. And then, in 1961, the city was irreversibly truncated, and West Berliners saw the few treasured historic buildings that had survived the war disappear behind the blank and pitiless concrete face of the Wall. As the Wall went up, they lost family, friends, city, and heritage overnight. This radical surgery left a wave of shock, an anger that had hardly begun to dissipate when President Kennedy paid a visit. It also left a stubborn determination to remain free, which more than any other emotion from that dark period drives the city still.

The division of Berlin, a fact of life for West Berlin's 2.1 million and East Berlin's 1.2 million people for 45 years, began in 1944, when the US, Great Britain, France, and the Soviet Union met in London and divided not only the city, but all of Germany, into occupied zones.

Because no written Soviet guarantee of access from West Germany existed, the Western Allies were unable to prevent Moscow from launching a land blockade of West Berlin in 1948. It took a massive, year-long Allied airlift to force the Soviets to back down. West Berlin had been saved from slow starvation, but 70 Allied airmen and eight German workers died trying to keep West Berlin's lifeline open.

The city was divided along Cold War political lines into two separate municipal entities. Soviet threats against West Berlin, which continued throughout the 1950s, culminated in the overnight erection of the Wall by the East German Communist regime on August 13, 1961. The concrete barrier effectively sealed off the 185 square miles of West Berlin from the 156 square miles of East Berlin. The city's location made the Wall particularly problematic for West Berlin, since it existed right in the heart of East Germany—110 miles from the nearest West German border, and the same distance from the Baltic Sea to the north and what was once Czechoslovakia to the south. (Berlin is only 52 miles from the Polish border, which means that it is closer to Warsaw than to Munich.) The ugly nine-foot-high symbol of what ailed Europe's body politic kept the people of West Berlin separated from East Berlin. Nevertheless, thousands of Berliners on either side of the dividing line continued to maintain bonds of blood and friendship.

This effort was made easier in 1971 when the three Western Allies met with the Soviet Union and produced the Four Power Agreement on Berlin to reduce East-West tensions over the city. Afterward, access to West Berlin from West Germany was assured, and both halves of the city settled down to a relatively normal existence. Nevertheless, West Berlin continued to be the only city in Europe under military occupation. In the Western sectors, sovereignty was still exercised by the Americans, the British, and the French; and the 13,000 Allied troops here were a visible reminder for the West Berliners that Western guarantees enabled them to live and work in freedom.

From early October to early November of 1989, the entire world watched in rapt attention as East Berliners and citizens in other East German cities took to the streets almost daily to demand the basic democratic freedoms that had been denied them for decades. At virtually the same time, tens of thousands of other citizens of the German Democratic Republic (East Germany) were making their way to the West through gaps in the Iron Curtain that were increasingly widening in Budapest, Prague, and Warsaw. Using any means of conveyance possible, the East Germans let their leaders know that totalitarian domination over their lives was at an end.

When it became clear that Soviet troops would not be used to support the ruling Communist bloc in East Germany, the Socialist Unity party (the regime that had ruled East Germany since 1945) suddenly announced, on the evening of November 9, 1989, that the Berlin Wall would come down. And it did, just a little over a month later. In September 1990, a treaty ended the 45-year occupation of Berlin and other German territory, and gave Germany full sovereignty. All foreign troops are scheduled to leave the city by the beginning of this year.

One of the initial far-reaching changes for the reunited country was the reintroduction of all-German elections on December 2, 1990, which placed Chancellor Helmut Kohl and his Christian Democratic Party at the head of the new Germany. That same year, the West German deutsche mark (DM) replaced the East German mark as the country's currency. Despite such unifying steps, however, it will take many more years for the two sides to become fully integrated and for the scars of Germany's stormy postwar history to heal.

Architecturally, postwar eastern Berlin and ancient Imperial Berlin are curiously intermixed. On the site of the modern *Palast der Republik* (where the former East German Parliament met), the Hohenzollern family built a palace and ruled first as Electors of Brandenburg (from the early 15th century), then as Kings of Prussia, and finally as German emperors. They made their small capital an architectural jewel, lining the main street, Unter den Linden, with magnificent Baroque palaces and other noble edifices. (Although World War II destroyed or severely damaged every one of these historic monuments, the Communist regime restored many of them to their former splendor.)

Near the end of the 19th century, another architectural look flourished here in Berlin, as well as in the rest of the country. Known as *Jugendstil* (which literally translates to "Youth Style"), this Art Nouveau–like movement was popular from 1880 to 1915. Proponents of the style spurned the symmetry and symbolism of more classical architecture in favor of an innovative and richly ornamental design. Many structures built in this style can still be seen today in both halves of the city.

Although World War II and its aftermath gave the heart of the Altstadt (Old City) to East Berlin, the new, truncated West Berlin, rising from the ashes of the war, created its own urban essence. That it succeeded in this massive enterprise is an understatement. Since the war devastated West Berlin, construction of new buildings greatly changed the appearance of the city. A small part of the architecture of the past—the majestic *Schloss Charlottenburg* and *Schloss Bellevue,* for example—were somewhat damaged by the war, but largely salvageable. On the other hand, *Flughafen Berlin-Tegel* (Tegel Airport), as well as numerous hospitals, schools, factories, businesses, and housing projects, were all built in a kind of anonymous contemporary style—many of the buildings are high-rises—and at an accelerated rate. In 1987, the city's *International Building Exhibition,* a massive program that entailed the reconstruction and renovation of many war-struck districts in West Berlin, was completed. The glitz and glitter of the Kurfürstendamm, West Berlin's prestigious international thoroughfare (affectionately called the Ku'damm by locals), is only one of this program's legacies.

What makes today's Berlin an outstanding place in which to live and visit is its culture. Continuing its prewar role, the rejoined city remains a cultural center of the very first order. It has some 30 theaters and two theater companies, the *Schaubühne* and the *Berliner Ensemble,* said by critics to be two of the world's best German-speaking troupes. Also of international rank are the famed *Berliner Philharmonisches Orchester* (Berlin Philharmonic Orchestra) and numerous museums, such as the great *Museumszentrum Dahlem* (Dahlem Museum Center), the *Neue Nationalgalerie* (New National Gallery), and the *Bauhaus-Archiv,* as well as the magnificent museum complex on Berlin's famed *Museumsinsel* (Museum Island). A new museum focusing on the Berlin Wall and its history (still under construction at press time) will be located near the *Bernauerstrasse U-Bahn* station. There is a kind of creative ferment and a cult of quality in Berlin that has attracted writers, artists, composers, architects, and actors for centuries.

Berlin is not only a cultural but an educational center, and one of the finest in Europe. The *Freie Universität* (Free University), *Technische Universität* (Technical University), and *Universität Humboldt* (Humboldt University) enjoy excellent reputations. Despite the great many older citizens living in Berlin, this is a city of—and for—the young, a city of pop music, experimental movies and theaters, and student hangouts. Berlin also is Germany's largest industrial center, with many firms headquartered here. The city's large foreign population—more than 250,000 non-Germans live and work here—adds a special spice to the melting pot, although some residents think the continuing flood of Eastern Europeans is spoiling the stew. And a small, rabidly xenophobic nationalist minority regularly conducts protests and occasionally goes on rampages.

People who live in Berlin have a reputation for being somewhat brusque and impatient, and concierges and restaurant personnel are often less than courteous. But in general, Berliners are extremely proud of their city, and are happy to give directions or assist visitors in any way they can. It is hard to do justice to the remarkable variety of life here. In constant flux, Berlin is a place for people who thrive on exchanges of high energy. Writer Christopher Isherwood would no doubt feel at home in this new, highly sophisticated, and ever-changing Berlin. The indomitable spirit of the courageous, pugnacious, and worldly Berliners would certainly remind him of the city he wrote about more than half a century ago.

SAFETY NOTE

Compared to many American and European cities, Berlin is relatively safe; wandering around town, even at night, is not risky. Occasionally, muggings do occur in Charlottenburg and Mitte, so stick to the main streets in those neighborhoods. Also, watch your purse or wallet: Pickpockets are numerous and very skillful. "Skinheads" or neo-Nazis—young thugs who cruise around looking for trouble—are a problem here, though tourists are in little danger. Most of these criminals tend to stay on their own turf, usually the poorer suburbs. But it's a good idea to be alert while riding the *S-Bahn* late at night, particularly on weekends.

Berlin At-a-Glance

SEEING THE CITY

The tallest structure in Berlin is the slender spire of the *Fernsehturm* (Television Tower; between Alexanderplatz and the Lustgarten; phone: 24040), which climbs to a height of 1,209 feet. Built in 1969, it is Europe's second-tallest tower. A revolving sphere at 655 feet is decked out with studio and transmission facilities, as well as with a good restaurant/café (see *Eating Out*), from which there is a magnificent view of the city. The tower is open daily; there's an admission charge.

The *Funkturm,* Berlin's radio tower (Messedamm; phone: 303-82996), is a steel-latticed spire 453 feet above the town that resembles the Eiffel Tower. An elevator ascends the structure to a viewing platform that, weather permitting, offers a good view of Germany's largest city; there is also a restaurant on a lower floor. The *Funkturm* is open daily; admission charge.

SPECIAL PLACES

Berlin is easy to get around. Most of the downtown area was laid out in the late 19th century, and the streets form a sensible grid. You can see much of that part of the city by foot, if you familiarize yourself with the main thoroughfares. Running from east to west in the western part of the city are Kurfürstendamm (the closest thing to Main Street), Hardenbergstrasse, Kantstrasse, and Strasse des 17. Juni; the chief north-to-south connections are Potsdamer Strasse, Joachimstaler Strasse, and Wilmersdorfer Strasse. In Berlin's eastern section, the important down-town streets are Friedrichstrasse, which runs north to south, and Unter den Linden (which becomes Strasse des 17. Juni in "West" Berlin) and Karl-Marx-Allee, both running east to west. The city is divided into 23 districts, but most of the best-known tourist attractions are in Mitte, especially along Unter den Linden and around Potsdamer Platz. Berlin's historical center is on an island in the Spree (pronounced *Shpray*) River. To reach outlying areas of the city, use the *U-Bahn* (subway), buses, street-cars, or *S-Bahn* (aboveground trains). For more information, see *Getting Around.*

THE MITTE DISTRICT (AROUND UNTER DEN LINDEN)

UNTER DEN LINDEN Some 1,500 yards long and almost 70 yards wide, this avenue is in the very heart of what was East Berlin. Originally laid out to connect the royal palace with the hunting preserve, the *Tiergarten,* it got its name from the rows of linden trees that were planted on both sides (and in the center) of the wide boulevard. In the 18th and 19th centuries, a number of magnificent structures were built along the boulevard. Although many were bombed during World War II, the former East German government faithfully restored those that survived.

BRANDENBURGER TOR (BRANDENBURG GATE) There is very little of historical interest between the *Deutsche Staatsbibliothek* and this massive Berlin landmark at the western end of Unter den Linden. The *Brandenburger Tor,* formerly inaccessible to cars and pedestrians because of the Wall, now is open to everyone; the gate turned 200 years old in 1991. The *Quadriga,* a beaten copper replica of the goddess of victory in a chariot drawn by four horses, was restored to the top of the gate for the bicentennial ceremonies. The triumphal arch is brilliantly lit at night (also see *Quintessential Germany* in DIVERSIONS). Pariser Pl.

DEUTSCHE STAATSBIBLIOTHEK (GERMAN STATE LIBRARY) Built in the early 20th century, the library occupies the site of the former *Preussische Staatsbibliothek* (Prussian State Library); that institution's stock of books that remained in Berlin during the war has been stored here. The rest are at the *Staatsbibliothek* (see below). Open daily. 8 Unter den Linden (phone: 203-8435).

UNIVERSITÄT HUMBOLDT (HUMBOLDT UNIVERSITY) Erected in the mid-18th century, it became *Friedrich-Wilhelm Universität* (Friedrich Wilhelm University) in 1810. Since 1949, this, the largest university in what was East Germany, has been known by its present name. Famous teachers included Hegel, Max Planck, and Einstein; Marx and Engels were students here. 6 Unter den Linden (phone: 20930).

NEUE WACHE (NEW GUARDHOUSE) Built in 1818, from 1960 until the Wall came down in 1989, it served as an East German monument to the victims of fascism and militarism. The Kohl administration has transformed the monument into a memorial to *all* German war dead. An engraving on the neoclassical structure reads, "To the victims of war and the rule of violence." Inside there is a sculpture by Käthe Kollwitz. Open daily. No admission charge. 4 Unter den Linden (no phone).

ZEUGHAUS (ARSENAL) Built between 1695 and 1706, this lovely Baroque structure is the oldest on Unter den Linden. Set on the Spree River, it overlooks the historic *Museumsinsel* (Museum Island). Originally an arsenal (hence the name), the building now houses the *Deutsches Historisches Museum* (German Historical Museum), with temporary displays about the country's history. Closed Wednesdays. Admission charge. 2 Unter den Linden (phone: 215020).

ALTES PALAIS (OLD PALACE) Built in 1836, this structure was the residence of Emperor William I during the last 50 years of his life. It is now used by *Universität Humboldt.* 9 Unter den Linden.

ALTE BIBLIOTHEK (OLD LIBRARY) This late-18th-century building housed the *Preussische Staatsbibliothek* (Prussian State Library) until 1914. Now known as the *Alte Bibliothek,* it is part of *Universität Humboldt.* Set back from Unter den Linden, on Bebelplatz (formerly Opernplatz, made famous during the Nazi burning of books in 1933).

DEUTSCHE STAATSOPER (GERMAN STATE OPERA) The opera house was built in 1743 and burned down 100 years later. Rebuilt, it was twice destroyed by bombs during World War II. It seats nearly 1,500 people (for ticket information, see *Music*). The interior is closed to the public except during performances. 7 Unter den Linden (phone: 203540).

ST. HEDWIGS KATHEDRALE (ST. HEDWIG'S CATHEDRAL) This Roman Catholic cathedral dates from the late 18th century and was built according to plans laid out by Frederick the Great (who was, by all appearances, impressed by the Pantheon in Rome). Gutted in the war, it has been just as carefully restored as most other Unter den Linden landmarks. Bebelpl.

PALAIS UNTER DEN LINDEN (UNTER DEN LINDEN PALACE) Converted from a house into a Baroque palace in the 17th century, it was known as the *Kronprinzenpalais* (Crown Prince Palace) until 1945. Emperor Wilhelm II was born here in 1859, and during the Weimar Republic the handsome building was used as a museum of contemporary art. More recently—in August 1990—the Treaty of Unification between East and West Germany was signed here, and it is currently being considered as the official residence of Germany's federal president. The palace is reserved for state functions and is closed to the public; however, the adjacent and equally opulent *Opernpalais* (formerly the "Princesses' Palace," where the daughters of Queen Luise lived in the 19th century) houses two of the city's best restaurants, *Abend-Restaurant Königin Luise* and the *Operncafé* (see *Eating Out* for both). Unter den Linden (no phone).

MUSEUMSINSEL (MUSEUM ISLAND) On the north side of the Lustgarten, surrounded on three sides by the Spree River, is one of the world's largest and most magnificent museum complexes. The impressive buildings date to the 19th and early 20th centuries. The *Altes Museum* accommodates contemporary paintings and the *Kupferstichkabinett* (Cabinet of Engravings), which contains 135,000 prints by German and foreign masters (15th to 18th centuries), including Botticelli's illustrations of scenes from Dante's *Divine Comedy.* Also here is the *Pergamon Museum,* the site of three astounding architectural feats: the *Pergamon Altar,* named after the ancient Greek city in which it was discovered (south of the historic city of Troy in what is now Turkey) and including huge bas-reliefs of most of the major Greek gods; the *Market Gate,* from a Roman settlement at Miletus (also in what is now Turkey), which towers more than two stories high; and the Babylonian *Ishtar Gate* and processional way, the 2,600-year-old entrance to the legendary city of Babylon. These are among the most imposing sights on view at any museum anywhere. In this building, too, are the *Vorderasiatisches Museum* (Far Eastern Collection), the *Museum für Völkerkunde* (Museum of Ethnography), and the *Islamisches Museum* (Islamic Museum).

At the northernmost tip of this island of museums is the *Bode Museum,* which now houses the *Agyptisches Museum* (Egyptian Museum; there's another museum of the same name that houses the bust of Queen Nefertiti—see *Museums*), the *Gemäldegalerie* (Picture Gallery), the *Museum für Bildhauerkunst* (Sculpture Collection), the *Münzekabinett* (Cabinet of Coins), and the *Museum für Vor- und Frühgeschichte* (Museum of Pre- and Proto-History). Among the treasures here are such masterpieces of German sculpture as the 12th-century *Naumburg Crucifix* and the *Winged Altarpiece* from *Minden Cathedral* (15th century). Closed Mondays and Tuesdays, except for the *Pergamon Museum,* which is open daily. Admission charge to each museum. 1-3 Bodestr. (phone: 203550).

STAATSRATSGEBÄUDE (STATE COUNCIL BUILDING) Not in use at press time (though it may reopen this year), this modern structure is still worth seeing from the outside; it's where the former East German government, the State Council, used to meet in the days of Communist boss Erich Honecker's rule. The centerpiece is one of the portals from the former royal palace. South side of the Lustgarten.

BERLINER DOM (BERLIN CATHEDRAL) This monumental (243 feet high and 116 feet in diameter), domed church was built around the turn of the century by the Hohenzollern family, whose palace stood across the street. After an 18-year, multimillion-dollar restoration, the lavish main sanctuary reopened in 1993; the crypt, containing the Hohenzollern mausoleum, also may be visited. Lustgarten.

MARIENKIRCHE (ST. MARY'S CHURCH) Just past the *Museumsinsel,* in the shadows of the *Fernsehturm* (Television Tower), is Berlin's second-oldest church. First erected in 1240, it is a pleasant combination of Gothic and neoclassical styles. Karl-Liebknecht-Str.

OTHER MITTE LANDMARKS

GENDARMENMARKT (GENDARMES' MARKET) The square, which takes its name from the 18th-century gendarmes who quartered their horses here, was a lively marketplace until the onset of World War II. Now a lovely plaza with elegant cast-iron street lamps, geometric stone pavement, and a statue of playwright Friedrich Schiller, it is framed by two historic churches and a concert hall. The *Französischer Dom* (French Cathedral), on the northern side of the plaza, was built in the early 18th century by Berlin's Huguenot community, which left France following Henry IV's Edict of Nantes. You can climb to the tower's balustrade for a view of the Mitte district. The church also houses the *Hugenottenmuseum* (Huguenot Museum), with exhibits tracing the history of the exiled community. The museum is closed Mondays and Fridays; admission charge (phone: 229-1760). Facing the *Französischer Dom* and dating from the same period, the towers of the *Deutscher Dom* (German Cathedral) dominate the quarter. Severely damaged during World War II, its façade was restored in 1985, but its interior is still undergoing repair and remains closed to the public; it is scheduled to reopen next year. Between the two cathedrals stands the *Schauspielhaus.* Designed in 1818 by the renowned neoclassical architect Karl Friedrich Schinkel, this 1,650-seat concert hall, with its sparkling crystal and gold interior, offers classical music concerts (see *Music*).

EPHRAIMPALAIS (EPHRAIM PALACE) More a mansion than a palace, this elaborate home in the neighborhood known as the Nikolaiviertel (see below) was built in the 1760s as a gift from Friedrich II to his court jeweler and banker, Heine Ephraim. Demolished in 1935, the rococo masterpiece was reconstructed in the 1980s and is used today for changing exhibits of local art and history. Museum hours vary, depending upon the exhibition, so call ahead for information. Admission charge. 16 Poststr. (phone: 238-0900).

NIKOLAIVIERTEL (NIKOLAI QUARTER) A charming 16th-century neighborhood, destroyed by bombs in World War II and later rebuilt, it's perfect for a leisurely stroll through narrow streets, replete with gas lanterns and several period taverns. Note the *Nikolaikirche* (St. Nicholas's Church; Nikolaikirchpl.);

the oldest building in Berlin, it was founded around 1200 and renovated in 1812. Its twin steeples overlook the cobbles, nooks, and crannies of this charming quarter. Between the Spree and the *Rathaus* (City Hall).

FRANZISKANER KLOSTERKIRCHE (FRANCISCAN CLOISTER CHURCH) Founded in 1249, its walls are among only a few remnants of medieval Berlin. The structure was heavily bombed in 1945; the ruins remain a grim reminder of the war. Klosterstr.

NEUE SYNAGOGE (NEW SYNAGOGUE) Opened in 1866 as Berlin's main Jewish sanctuary (it once had 3,500 seats), this golden-domed, Moorish-style structure was plundered and set on fire during the anti-Jewish raids on *Kristallnacht* (November 9, 1938). It was further damaged by bombs during a 1943 air attack and torn down in 1958 (although the anterooms, a smaller sanctuary, and the façade survived). Still a major tourist site, the black marble plaques on its façade hauntingly recall the tragic events. High above the street, a blue-and-gold cupola topped with a golden Star of David sits flanked by two towers; below, colorful brickwork and arched portals and windows are still impressive. Restoration work on the interior is scheduled for completion next year. The building will then reopen as the *Centrum Judaicum* (Jewish Cultural Center). 30 Oranienburger Str. (phone: 280-1253).

DOROTHEENSTÄDTISCHER FRIEDHOF (DOROTHEENSTADT CEMETERY) Not far from the *Friedrichstrasse* train station, this tranquil oasis is the final resting place of many notables of German culture, including Bertolt Brecht and his wife, the actress Helene Weigel. Other illustrious names on the tombstones include Georg Wilhelm Friedrich Hegel, Heinrich Mann, and Johannes Becher. 126 Chausseestr.

BRECHT-WEIGEL-GEDENKSTÄTTE (BRECHT-WEIGEL MEMORIAL) Bertolt Brecht and Helene Weigel's former apartment is located next to the *Dorotheenstädtischer Friedhof* (see above). Boasting its original furnishings, it's now a memorial and a study center devoted to Brecht's works. Closed Sundays and Mondays. Admission charge. 125 Chausseestr. (phone: 282-9916).

AROUND POTSDAMER PLATZ

POTSDAMER PLATZ (POTSDAM SQUARE) Ever since the demise of the Wall, Berlin has become a building contractor's dream, especially in this section of the city. Before World War II, it was the city's "Times Square," and Europe's busiest intersection. During the postwar years, Potsdamer Platz was a Cold War desert bisected by the Wall and chiefly frequented by East German border guards and a host of rabbits. During the next decade, this gigantic construction site will become Berlin's largest commercial and residential district. Offices, apartment buildings, hotels, a conference center, and a theater will be in place when it is completed.

MARTIN-GROPIUS-BAU (MARTIN GROPIUS BUILDING) This huge, red brick neoclassical building houses rotating history and contemporary art exhibits; the *Berlinische Gallerie* (Berlin Gallery), which features works by local artists; and a collection of religious items, photographs, and documents tracing the history of Berlin's Jewish community. Closed Mondays. Admission charge. 110 Stresemannstr. (phone: 254860).

PRINZ ALBRECHT GELÄNDE (TOPOGRAPHY OF TERRORS) On this site stood the headquarters of Nazi terror mechanisms: the Gestapo and the SS. It now houses a moving and informative documentary exhibition devoted to the victims of the Third Reich. A small contemporary structure displays photos and documents, and contains the excavated Gestapo cellars where hundreds of people were interrogated and tortured. Walking into the cells is a deeply chilling experience. Outside, signs point out the few remaining building remnants and the former locations of other structures; the whole complex was torn down after the war. A 200-yard stretch of the Wall still stands here as a reminder of days past. Closed Mondays. No admission charge. 110 Stresemannstr. (phone: 254-86703).

ANHALTER BAHNHOF (ANHALTER TRAIN STATION) All that remains of what was once Berlin's busiest long-distance train station is a single broken portal, a haunting reminder of a lively neighborhood where hotels, cafés, restaurants, and bars were always packed. An unusual sight, and worth a look. Askanischer Pl.

MUSEUM AM CHECKPOINT CHARLIE The collection here chronicles the history of the Wall and of Berlin during the Cold War years, with a special emphasis on the creative ways East Germans tried to flee their country. The museum is next to the former site of Checkpoint Charlie, the most famous border crossing between eastern and western Berlin. A guard tower and a section of the Wall still stand here, but this may change when an American business center goes up at the site in a few years. Open daily. Admission charge. 43-44 Friedrichstr. (phone: 251-1031).

PHILHARMONIE The home of the world-renowned *Berliner Philharmonisches Orchester* (Berlin Philharmonic Orchestra) is just a few blocks south of the *Reichstag* (Parliament Building), at the southern fringe of the *Tiergarten.* The building's asymmetrical architecture has been controversial ever since it was completed in 1963. Smaller ensembles perform in the adjoining *Kammermusiksaal* (Chamber Music Hall; see *Music*). Free guided tours of the building (in German only) are given once every morning. Kemperpl. (phone: 254880).

MUSIKINSTRUMENTEN MUSEUM (MUSEUM OF MUSICAL INSTRUMENTS) This museum holds an intriguing collection of European instruments that date from the 16th century. Music lovers will particularly enjoy such rarities as

Frederick the Great's flute and Edvard Grieg's piano. Closed Mondays. Admission charge. 1 Tiergartenstr. (phone: 254810).

KUNSTGEWERBEMUSEUM (MUSEUM OF DECORATIVE ARTS) Next door to the *Philharmonie,* in the city's developing cultural center, is this imposing museum that houses a unique collection of German crafts from the past 900 years, including pottery, glassware, and furniture. Closed Mondays. Admission charge. 6 Tiergartenstr. (phone: 266-2911).

NEUE NATIONALGALERIE (NEW NATIONAL GALLERY) Designed by Ludwig Mies van der Rohe in 1968, this striking, glass-walled building houses the city's collections of late 19th- and 20th-century art. If you plan a visit to Potsdam, pay special attention to the works of Adolph von Menzel, whose paintings of *Sanssouci* and its inhabitants were done during the palace's prime. The Monets will delight, but the more recent works—Jasper Johns, Francis Bacon, and Paul Klee—are strongest. Spend some time in the quiet sculpture garden during the summer months. Closed Mondays. Admission charge for special exhibitions. 50 Potsdamer Str. (phone: 266-2662 or 266-2663).

STAATSBIBLIOTHEK (STATE LIBRARY) Directly opposite the *Neue Nationalgalerie* is the starkly modern *Staatsbibliothek,* Berlin's successor to the *Preussische Staatsbibliothek* (Prussian State Library). Its collection of more than three million volumes makes it one of the world's largest libraries. Exhibitions and lectures also are presented. Closed Sundays. No admission charge to exhibitions. 33 Potsdamer Str. (phone: 2661).

GEDENKSTÄTTE DEUTSCHER WIDERSTAND (GERMAN RESISTANCE MEMORIAL) Plaques and impressive statuary are grouped in the courtyard of this building—which housed the German Armed Forces Supreme Command during World War II—to honor the German officers who were shot here for the ill-fated uprising against Hitler on July 20, 1944. There also is a historical document center. Open daily. No admission charge. Near the *Neue Nationalgalerie,* at 14 Stauffenbergstr. (phone: 265-42202).

THE TIERGARTEN

TIERGARTEN This beautiful public park—far more extensive than the *Zoologischer Garten* (Zoological Garden; see below), which is at its western fringe—originally was the royal hunting preserve. It now is one of the world's largest and most beautifully landscaped urban parks and is dotted with charming lakes and ponds. The *Tiergarten* extends from the zoo to within several hundred yards of the *Brandenburger Tor,* a total length of about 2 miles (3 km).

REICHSTAG (PARLIAMENT BUILDING) At the eastern edge of the *Tiergarten,* just north of the *Brandenburger Tor,* is Germany's once and future Parliament building, built in the late 19th century in Italian High Renaissance style. Gutted by fire by Hitler's supporters in 1933, it was rebuilt and currently is used for political conclaves. A permanent display is devoted to recent

German history, and there is also the excellent *Im Reichstag* restaurant (see *Eating Out*). It will take several years to renovate the building to accommodate the Bundestag—the seat of Germany's government. By the end of this decade, the entire area around the *Reichstag* is scheduled to be occupied by new government buildings. Closed Mondays. No admission charge. Pl. der Republik (phone: 39770).

SIEGESSÄULE (VICTORY COLUMN) Completed in 1873 to commemorate the Prussian campaigns against Denmark, Austria, and France, this 223-foot-high monument stands at the center of the *Tiergarten.* At the top are an observation platform and a gold statue of Victory. The platform is closed November through March. Admission charge.

HAUS DER KULTUREN DER WELT (HOUSE OF WORLD CULTURES) A gift from the American people in 1957, the ultramodern structure stands in the *Tiergarten,* on the banks of the Spree. Always controversial because of its bold design, it offers exhibitions, concerts, and theater devoted to the world's ethnic groups. In addition, it has a charming riverside restaurant and café-bar. Nearby is a 140-foot-tall carillon, whose 68 bells resound daily at noon and 6 PM. Open daily; restaurant and café-bar closed Mondays. No admission charge. 10 John Foster Dulles Allee (phone: 397870).

ZOOLOGISCHER GARTEN (ZOOLOGICAL GARDEN) On the southeastern edge of the *Tiergarten,* one block north of the *Gedächtniskirche* (see below), is one of Berlin's two zoos (*Tierpark* is the other; see below). Germany's first, the zoological gardens were laid out in 1841 and still have more species than any other zoo in the world. Open daily. Admission charge. 8 Hardenbergpl. (phone: 254010).

AQUARIUM Next door to the *Zoologischer Garten,* it has the most comprehensive collection of marine animals in the world. In the *Tropical Hall,* you can watch large numbers of alligators and crocodiles in their own environments; your vantage point is a bridge a mere 10 feet or so above the bloodthirsty creatures. Open daily. Admission charge. 32 Budapester Str. (phone: 254010).

THE CHARLOTTENBURG DISTRICT (WEST OF THE TIERGARTEN)

KAISER WILHELM GEDÄCHTNISKIRCHE (KAISER WILHELM MEMORIAL CHURCH) Designed by Franz Schwechten, this huge neo-Romanesque church was built toward the end of the 19th century to honor Kaiser Wilhelm I. The structure was almost completely destroyed by Allied bombing during World War II, and the ruins remained untouched for many years as Berliners debated what to do with them. A poll in 1957 showed that most people wanted the remains preserved—but moved to a more remote location, away from the center of the newly created West Berlin. However, a decision was finally made to leave them where they were. The hexagonal bell tower and the octagonal chapel were added in the 1960s; some locals facetiously refer to them as "the compact and lipstick case." The old west tower, 207 feet tall, was preserved in its ruined state. Partially new, partially old, partially preserved, and partially destroyed, to Berliners the church has become a symbol of the city. Breitscheidpl.

GEDENKSTÄTTE PLÖTZENSEE (PLÖTZENSEE MEMORIAL) About 2 miles (3 km) northwest of the *Gedenkstätte Deutscher Widerstand,* tucked behind the *Gefängnis Plötzensee* (Plötzensee Prison), is a memorial to the people who died in the Holocaust. Here stand two small brick buildings where "undesirables," such as Jews, Gypsies, and homosexuals, as well as many members of the resistance movement against the Nazis, were executed. In front of the buildings are a small garden, a wall bearing a tribute to the victims, and a stone urn containing soil from all the Nazi concentration camps. Open daily. No admission charge. Hüttigpfad (phone: 344-3226).

SCHLOSS CHARLOTTENBURG (CHARLOTTENBURG PALACE) Begun in 1695 and completed 10 years later, this sprawling Baroque castle on the outskirts of Berlin was to Prussia what Versailles was to France: the sometime residence of the royal family. It was also a great stone monument to the aspirations of the Hohenzollern regime, and a bronze statue of the Great Elector Frederick William (1620–88), the iron-fisted tyrant who forged the Prussian juggernaut, sternly welcomes visitors to the *Ehrenhof* (Court of Honor). The cavernous bedrooms and endless hallways in this castle built for Queen Sophie-Charlotte are gracefully feminine, albeit not exactly cozy. Adjacent to the palace is the *Galerie der Romantik* (Gallery of Romantics) in the Knobelsdorff Wing, devoted to 19th-century art from the neoclassical, Romantic, and Biedermeier periods. Displayed here are the works of artists who tried to capture the complex German soul—brooding, idealistic, dramatic. Good examples are Caspar David Friedrich's paintings (particularly *Morgen im Riesengebirge*), which often depict the Germans' mystical stance toward nature. On a lighter note are the paintings of Antoine Watteau, whose *Embarcation for Cythera* is a work of whimsical beauty. The *Galerie der Romantik* is closed Mondays. The palace also houses the *Museum für Vor- und Frühgeschichte* (Museum of Pre- and Proto-History; closed Fridays). The beautifully laid-out park behind the palace is one of the nicest areas in the city. The castle is open daily. Separate admission charges to the castle and museums. Luisenpl. (phone: 320911).

INTERNATIONALES KONGRESSCENTRUM UND MESSEGELÄNDE (INTERNATIONAL CONGRESS CENTER AND FAIRGROUNDS) The modern *ICC,* as it is called, is about 1½ miles (2 km) southwest of *Schloss Charlottenburg.* Across the street from this looming convention center and concert hall, and connected to it by a covered pedestrian walkway, are the rambling fairgrounds, the site of year-round fairs and exhibitions, which include *Internationale Grüne Woche* (International Green Week; see *Special Events*) and the

German radio and TV exhibition. On the fairgrounds is the *Funkturm* (Radio Tower; see *Seeing the City*). Masurenallee and Messedamm (phone: 30380).

OLYMPIASTADION (OLYMPIC STADIUM) Another 2 miles (3 km) to the west of the *ICC,* this huge sports arena casts its shadow over the low-lying houses of a pleasant residential area. It was built for the *1936 Olympic Games,* and if you look hard, you can still make out the "royal" box from which Hitler and his cohorts took in the spectacle. Open daily unless a sports event is being held here. Admission charge. Olympischer Pl. (phone: 304-0676).

ELSEWHERE IN THE CITY

TIERPARK Also in the city's suburbs, this zoo was opened in 1955 on the grounds of *Schloss Friedrichsfelde* (Friedrichsfelde Palace; also see *Museums*). As much as possible, the animals are shown in herds or family groups in spacious enclosures that blend with the landscape. Open daily. Admission charge. 125 Am Tierpark (phone: 515310).

SOWJETISCHES EHRENMAL (SOVIET WAR MEMORIAL) In the suburbs of eastern Berlin, within the confines of verdant *Treptower Park* and not far from the left bank of the Spree, is this huge, impressive monument. Dedicated in 1949, it honors more than 5,000 Soviet soldiers who fell in the battle for Berlin in 1945. Much of the material used came from the ruins of Hitler's *Reich Chancellery.* Open daily. Entrance from Puschkinallee and Am Treptower Park.

JÜDISCHER FRIEDHOF WEISSENSEE (JEWISH CEMETERY) In the Weissensee district, this is said to be the largest Jewish cemetery in Europe. Restored by the former East German government, it contains thousands of graves, most marked by large, ornate tombstones in late 19th- and early 20th-century style. Male visitors must wear hats. Closed Saturdays. 45 Herbert-Baum-Str.

EAST SIDE GALLERY Shortly after the two Berlins were united, artists from over 20 nations were invited by city officials to paint sections of the longest extant piece of the Berlin Wall. Their creations are wildly different, but the central theme is the fall of the Wall. This "canvas" runs for more than a half mile along the Spree River in Friedrichshain. Mühlenstr., near the *Hauptbahnhof* (Main Train Station).

MUSEUM FÜR VERKEHR UND TECHNIK (MUSEUM OF TRANSPORT AND TECHNOLOGY) Across the Landwehrkanal (Landwehr Canal) and a bit east is this showplace, which houses a very interesting collection devoted to the historic development of the railroad, the automobile, the bicycle, and the airplane. Closed Mondays. Admission charge. 9 Trebbiner Str. (phone: 254840).

RATHAUS SCHÖNEBERG (SCHÖNEBERG CITY HALL) This building, Berlin's city hall, also functions as the seat of government for the borough of Schöneberg. In 1991, the mayor moved his offices here, and other government officials followed. The city council has since moved to larger quarters in eastern

Berlin. There is a good panoramic view from the top of the spireless tower, which contains a replica of the American Liberty Bell, presented to the city by General Lucius Clay in 1950. On June 26, 1963, President John F. Kennedy made his *"Ich bin ein Berliner"* speech from the balcony here to a gathering of over 450,000 citizens. The tower is open Wednesdays and Sundays from April through September. No admission charge. John-F.-Kennedy-Pl. (phone: 7831).

SPANDAU ZITADELLE (SPANDAU CITADEL) Even farther west, on the Havel River, is this historic citadel. The oldest edifice on the grounds, the *Juliusturm* (Julius Tower) dates from the 14th century. The citadel, which has served as a fortification, a prison, and the royal treasury, now is a local history museum. Nazi war criminals were not housed here, but at the prison on Wilhelmstrasse, in the middle of the Spandau district; the prison was torn down in 1987, after the suicide of its sole remaining occupant, Rudolf Hess. Closed Mondays. Admission charge. Am Juliusturm (phone: 33911).

MUSEUMSZENTRUM DAHLEM (DAHLEM MUSEUM CENTER) To the south, in the fashionable and lovely section of Dahlem, is one of Berlin's largest museum complexes. (The others are at *Schloss Charlottenburg,* near the *Tiergarten,* and on the *Museumsinsel.*) Its extensive buildings accommodate several institutions, and you can spend at least a full day going through them: The *Gemäldegalerie* (Painting Gallery) houses masterpieces of European painting before 1800, with the Italian Renaissance and Dutch and Flemish collections the standouts. Highlights include Cranach's *Fountain of Youth* and Botticelli's *Madonna and Child with Six Angels.* Also at *Museumszentrum Dahlem* is the *Museum für Völkerkunde* (Ethnology Museum), which displays cultural artifacts from around the world—such as sailing boats, a men's clubhouse from the South Pacific, and a range of other exotica. The museum's accessible exhibits make it a great choice for families with young children. There is also a small sculpture department, with Byzantine and European sculpture from the 3rd to the 18th centuries, as well as the *Museum für Islamische Kunst* (Museum of Islamic Art), *Museum für Indische Kunst* (Museum of Indian Art), and *Museum für Ostasiatische Kunst* (Museum of Far Eastern Art), as well as a collection of prints and engravings. Closed Mondays. No admission charge on Sundays and holidays. 8 Lansstr. (phone: 83011).

BOTANISCHER GARTEN (BOTANICAL GARDENS) About half a mile east of *Museumszentrum Dahlem* are the largest botanical gardens in Germany, and one of the world's most significant collections of flora. Of special interest in the 104-acre gardens are the geographical gardens, where plants from various parts of the world flourish in carefully maintained native environments. There is a fascinating botanic display at the museum, next to the entrance to the gardens. The gardens are open daily; the museum is closed Mondays. Separate admission charges to museum and gardens. 6 Königin-Luise-Str. (phone: 830060).

GEDENKSTÄTTE HAUS DER WANNSEE-KONFERENZ (WANNSEE HOLOCAUST MEMORIAL CENTER) In 1942, this peaceful lakeside mansion 5 miles (8 km) west of Berlin was the site of a grisly summit. Here members of the Nazi Party, including Adolf Eichmann, convened to discuss the "final solution to the Jewish question." More than 50 years later, the building serves as a Holocaust memorial and educational center, with a permanent exhibition that documents the history of Germany's acts of genocide. Closed Mondays. No admission charge. 56-58 Am Grossen Wannsee (phone: 805-0010).

EXTRA SPECIAL

Largely unknown to most tourists, who rarely leave the downtown area, the outlying districts of Berlin are mostly forests, including the Grunewald and the Tegel and Spandau Wälder, and waterways, such as the Havel and Spree Rivers, the Tegeler See, and the Wannsee. To see the Havel and the forests, board one of the 70 ships that make daily trips on the river. Between *Easter* and the end of September, boats leave eight times a day from numerous points, including Wannsee Hafen (Wannsee Harbor) in the Zehlendorf district. The main cruise company in Berlin is *Stern und Kreisschiffahrt* (60 Sachtlebenstr.; phone: 810-0040).

Along the way, get off at any number of points and explore to your heart's content, then reboard a subsequent boat. Stopping-off points include the *Grunewaldturm* (Grunewald Tower), formerly known as *Kaiser-Wilhelm Turm* (Kaiser Wilhelm Tower), dating from the 19th century and affording a good view of Berlin from the top; Lindwerder Insel (Lindwerder Island), with restaurants offering snacks of beer, coffee, and cake; Pfaueninsel (Peacock Island), a beautiful example of an 18th-century formal garden with small pavilions, ponds, and a château dating from 1796 that is open to the public; and Potsdam, the former Prussian royal residence, just outside the city (for information, call the *Potsdam Tourist Office* at 331-21100). For more information about Potsdam, see *The Harz Mountains* in DIRECTIONS. All stops on this trip are well provisioned with restaurants and beer gardens. (The only catch is that since these boats are mostly for Germans and rarely cater to foreign visitors, English usually is not spoken by the guides.)

The sights passed on the Havel also may be visited by land (via subway, streetcar, *S-Bahn,* or bus). Bear in mind that many of the sights are closed on Mondays and Tuesdays.

A similar tour is offered on the Spree River, whose tributaries flow through the city for a total of 20 miles before joining the Havel. The white excursion ships run by *Stern und Kreisschiffahrt* (see above) ply the Spree and its tributaries every day from March through early October; you can get on and off as often as you wish. Along the way you might want to stop

off at these sights: the *Müggelturm,* a 98-foot-high tower near Berlin's largest lake, Müggelsee; the *Mecklenburger Dorf,* in Köpenick, a replica of a 19th-century northern German village, offering typical snacks and beverages at very reasonable prices; and the *Rathaus,* a neo-Gothic brick structure built in 1904. Boats depart eight times a day from the piers on the Spree at the *Treptower Park S-Bahn* station. (Again, this trip is mostly for Germans, so English is rarely spoken on board.)

Sources and Resources

TOURIST INFORMATION

The *Verkehrsamt* (Tourist Office) is in the large complex of shops and restaurants at *Europa-Center* (entrance on Budapesterstr.; phone: 21234; fax: 212-32520). It also maintains branches at *Flughafen Berlin-Tegel* (Tegel Airport; phone: 410-3145), as well as at the foot of the *Fernsehturm* (phone: 242-4675) and at the *Bahnhof Zoologischer Garten* train station (phone: 279-5209). The tourist offices will supply you with all sorts of free information in English about Berlin, including a general tourist map and numerous brochures. All branches are open daily.

Another source of information is *Dial Berlin,* a private tourism reservation service that has a telephone hotline in the US (phone: 800-237-5469).

LOCAL COVERAGE There is no newspaper in English, but a monthly calendar of events called *Berlin Programm* is available at the tourist office and at newsstands; some of the information is in English. *Tip* and *Zitty,* two German-language biweekly city magazines, list local events along with information on places of interest in Berlin. Both are available at most newsstands. One of the best-detailed and most up-to-date local maps of Berlin is the *Berlin Stadtatlas,* available at many bookstores and larger newsstands for about 16 DM ($10).

Even if you don't read German, you'll find *Marcellino's Restaurant Report* (Verlag Marcellus Hudvilla; about 16 DM/$10) helpful. Available at most local bookstores, this guide reviews 250 dining establishments, cafés, bars, and nightclubs, and rates each establishment numerically (on a scale of 0–25) on *Essen* (food), *Trinken* (drinks), *Bedienung* (service), and *Ambiente* (ambience).

Kiepert (4-5 Hardenbergstr.; phone: 311-0090) has an entire section devoted to travel tomes and maps; there are some books in English. *Wohlthat's* (44 Budapester Str., across from the *Europa-Center;* phone: 262-3636) has a smaller selection of English-language travel books; it is open until 11 PM. We also immodestly suggest that before you leave home, you pick up a copy of *Birnbaum's Berlin 95* (HarperCollins; $12).

TELEPHONE The city code for Berlin is 30.

GETTING AROUND

AIRPORT *Flughafen Berlin-Tegel* (Tegel Airport), a 20- to 30-minute ride from downtown, handles most domestic and international flights. The No. 109 bus provides service from the airport to downtown and leaves from just outside Gate 8 every 15 minutes between 5:30 AM and midnight. *Flughafen Berlin-Schönefeld* (Schönefeld Airport), just outside the city and about a 45-minute drive to downtown, handles some international traffic. *S-Bahn* lines 9 and 10 run directly to *Schönefeld;* you can also take the No. 171 bus from Rudow (the last stop on *U-Bahn* line 7) to the *Schönefeld* air terminal. *Flughafen Tempelhof* (Tempelhof Airport), in the city center, caters to a limited number of domestic carriers; it's 15 minutes by taxi from downtown. The No. 119 bus also runs to *Tempelhof,* as does the *U-Bahn* line 6 to the *Platz der Luftbrücke Station.*

CAR RENTAL The major American firms are represented, as well as several European companies. Information can be obtained at any hotel.

SUBWAY AND BUS Berlin has one of the world's most efficient public transportation systems. The subway, or *U-Bahn,* with its snappy little yellow cars, has been a fact of life here since 1902, and its eight lines serve almost every part of the city. The *U-Bahn* is fast, clean, convenient, and one of the least expensive in Germany. Its eastern and western sections have been reunited, so trains now run from the *Olympiastadion* in the west to Pankow, northeast of the city. The "El," or *S-Bahn,* carried its first passengers in 1882, and is still in service today. Both lines travel to points in eastern Berlin. A ticket for 3 DM (about $1.80) is valid for a trip from one end of the city to the other, and you can transfer as often as you wish within the *U-Bahn* system, the elevated *S-Bahn,* and to any of the many bus and streetcar lines that ply Berlin's streets. A *carnet,* valid for four rides, is available for 12 DM ($7.20). The *Berlin Transport Authority* also sells a ticket valid for 24 hours unlimited travel on all *U-Bahn, S-Bahn,* and bus lines throughout Berlin (11 DM/$6.60) and a six-day, unlimited-travel ticket (30 DM/about $18).

TAXI Berlin's cream-colored cabs are spacious and often luxurious (many are Mercedes-Benzes). Taxis can be hailed in the streets, and there are cabstands all over town and at the major hotels; fares are posted near the stands. To call a cab, which can be ordered around the clock and up to 24 hours in advance, call 69022, 210202, or 261026. Many dispatch operators understand English.

TOURS Several bus companies—among them *BVB* (phone: 885-9880), *BBS* (phone: 213-4077), and *Severin und Kühn* (phone: 883-1015)—offer two- and four-hour motorcoach tours of Berlin's major sights; most coaches are equipped with headphones, allowing visitors to hear the commentary in their own language. Reservations are unnecessary; you'll see the ticket booths (most have a sign saying "Tours") all along the Ku'damm (Kurfürstendamm), at

Breitscheidplatz, and on Unter den Linden. Tours leave approximately every half hour from 10 AM to 6 PM daily.

Though guided walking tours are plentiful, almost all of them are conducted in German. If you understand enough to get by, pick up a copy of *Tip* (see *Local Coverage*) for a daily schedule. *Stadtreisen Berlin* (4 Turmstr.; phone: 394-8354; fax: 394-7910) offers custom-designed, English-language tours for small groups.

TRAIN The city's main stations are *Bahnhof Zoologischer Garten* (also known as *Zoo Station;* Hardenbergpl.; phone: 19419) in western Berlin, and *Hauptbahnhof* (Holzmarkt; phone: 19419) in eastern Berlin. Though Germany still has two train companies—the East German *Deutsche Reichsbahn (DR)* and the West German *Deutsche Bundesbahn (DB)*—tickets to eastern destinations such as Dresden and Leipzig can be purchased at the *DB* offices. (The difference between the two systems is mostly in the age of the cars—the *DR*'s can be ancient.)

SPECIAL EVENTS

Berlin's calendar is filled with a variety of annual festivals and celebrations. For additional information and exact dates, check with the tourist office at *Europa-Center* (see *Tourist Information*). *Internationale Grüne Woche* (International Green Week), a 14-day agricultural and food festival, takes place at the convention hall in Charlottenburg in January. The annual two-week *Berlinale* (International Film Festival Berlin) is held in February. The *Theatertreffen Berlin,* a gathering of performers and directors from throughout the nation, takes place in May. The *Internationale Polo Turniers* (International Polo Tournaments) are held on the Maifeld at the *Olympiastadion* (see *Special Places*) in August. In September, *Berliner Festwochen,* a month-long festival of the arts, features concerts and plays (in German only) performed by the world's leading musicians and actors; most of the big-name performers appear at the *Philharmonie* (see *Special Places*). Also in September, runners thread their way through the streets of western Berlin in the 26-km (16-mile) *Berlin Marathon.* (Shorter races are also held on *New Year's Eve* and *New Year's Day.*) The *Berlin Oktoberfest* (in October, natch) brings food, drink, and a carnival atmosphere to the fairgrounds near the *Funkturm.* For two weeks in October, international soloists gather at bars and nightclubs across the city for *Jazz Fest Berlin.* November also marks Berlin's annual six-day *Sechstagerennen,* a cycling contest that attracts international competitors. And during the *Christmas* season, the city hosts several *Christkindlesmarkts* at various locations; the most famous one is held around the *Kaiser Wilhelm Gedächtniskirche* on Breitscheidplatz.

MUSEUMS

In addition to those described in *Special Places,* other museums worth seeing include the following:

AGYPTISCHES MUSEUM (EGYPTIAN MUSEUM) Directly opposite *Schloss Charlottenburg* is this unusual collection whose priceless treasures include the world-renowned bust of Queen Nefertiti and the magnificent *Kalabsha Gate,* which dates from 2000 BC and was found in a temple in Kalabsha, Egypt. Closed Mondays. Admission charge. 70 Schlossstr. (phone: 320911).

ANTIKENSAMMLUNG (ANTIQUITIES MUSEUM) Masterpieces of Greek, Roman, and Etruscan art, including sculpture, jewelry, and portraits, are displayed in a palatial building across from the *Schloss Charlottenburg* complex. Closed Fridays. Admission charge. 1 Schlossstr. (phone: 32011).

BAUHAUS-ARCHIV Housed in a striking white building, this collection of manuscripts, tools, and blueprints documents the work of the famed Bauhaus School of architecture and applied and graphic arts. Founded by Walter Gropius in 1919, the group counted Paul Klee, Marcel Breuer, Wassily Kandinsky, and Mies van der Rohe among its masters and students; the school was forced into exile by the National Socialist government in the 1930s. Closed Tuesdays. Admission charge. 14 Klingelhöferstr. (phone: 254-0020).

BRÖHANMUSEUM Adjacent to the *Antikensammlung* (see above), this lovely, small facility features a collection of 20th-century art—especially *Jugendstil* paintings, sculptures, graphic arts, and furniture. Closed Mondays. Admission charge. 1A Schlossstr. (phone: 321-4029).

BRÜCKEMUSEUM This contemporary building in the Grunewald serves as a gallery and archive for the works of Die Brücke (The Bridge)—an influential group of early 20th-century German Expressionist artists. Displays include paintings, watercolors, drawings, and sculptures by Karl Schmidt-Rottluff and Ernst Ludwig Kirchner, among others. Closed Tuesdays. Admission charge. 9 Bussardsteig (phone: 831-2029).

DEUTSCHES RUNDFUNK-MUSEUM (GERMAN RADIO MUSEUM) Located at the base of Charlottenburg's radio tower, the exhibits offer a complete overview of German broadcasting history, from primitive radios to modern television sets. Closed Tuesdays. Admission charge. 1 Hammarskjöldpl. (phone: 302-8186).

FRISEURMUSEUM (HAIRDRESSING MUSEUM) A unique collection documenting over 500 years of the barber's art. Displays include a magnificent *Jugendstil* workstation from a hair salon that served members of the Prussian royal court, medieval surgical equipment, and elaborate powdered wigs. Closed Fridays. Admission charge. 8 Husemannstr. (phone: 449-5380).

GEORG KOLBE MUSEUM The former home and studio of one of Berlin's best-known sculptors houses a display of his works, along with those of his local contemporaries. Closed Sundays and Mondays. Admission charge. 25 Sensburger Allee, in Charlottenburg (phone: 304-2144).

GRÜNDERZEITMUSEUM MAHLSDORF (MAHLSDORF FOUNDING ERA MUSEUM) During the 1870s, when Germany was united by Iron Chancellor Otto von Bismarck, the nation underwent a rapid period of industrialization, and the appearance of the German household changed enormously—factory-made furniture and such luxury items as gramophones came into widespread use. Furnishings, housewares, and other domestic treasures from this era are displayed in an old villa in the suburbs; there's also a pub in the basement that dates to the decadent 1920s. Open Sundays for guided tours (in English on request) beginning at 11 AM and noon, or by appointment. No admission charge. 333 Hultschiner Damm (phone: 527-8329).

KÄTHE KOLLWITZ MUSEUM The works of this eponymous local artist, including sculptures, drawings, prints, and posters, are housed in a charming villa just off the Ku'damm (Kurfürstendamm). Kollwitz's subjects included the city's downtrodden population; the collection is renowned for its emotional impact. Closed Tuesdays. Admission charge. 24 Fasanenstr. (phone: 882-5210).

KUNSTGEWERBEMUSEUM IM SCHLOSS KÖPENICK (APPLIED ARTS MUSEUM AT THE KÖPENICK PALACE) Built by Prince Friedrich in the late 17th century on the site of a medieval Slav castle, this historic palace on the Spree River houses a museum of European arts and crafts. The collection, which spans 900 years, include gold and silver work, glass, porcelain, and furniture. Closed Mondays and Tuesdays. No admission charge Sundays. About 12 miles (20 km) outside the city center at Schlossinsel Köpenick (Köpenick Palace Island; phone: 657-1504).

MÄRKISCHES MUSEUM One of the best of its kind in Europe, it surveys Berlin's history. Closed Mondays and Tuesdays. Admission charge. 5 Am Köllnischen Park (phone: 270-0514).

MUSEUM BERLINER ARBEITERLEBEN (BERLIN LABOR MUSEUM) Created by the former East German government, the exhibits chronicle the lifestyle of the city's proletariat at the turn of the century; there's also a replica of an apartment of the period. Closed Sundays and Mondays. Admission charge. 12 Husemannstr. (phone: 448-5675).

MUSEUM FÜR VOLKSKUNDE (FOLKLORE MUSEUM) A collection of tools, household goods, clothing, and furniture from the 16th century to the present. Closed Mondays. No admission charge Sundays. 6-8 Im Winkel (phone: 839-01287).

OTTO-NAGEL-HAUS This branch of the *Neue Nationalgalerie* (see *Special Places*) exhibits typical works of proletarian art from 1918 to 1945. Closed Fridays and Saturdays. No admission charge Sundays. 16-18 Märkisches Ufer. (phone: 279-1402).

SCHINKEL-MUSEUM The great local architect Karl Friedrich Schinkel changed the face of Berlin in the early 19th century. His life and works are depicted in this collection housed in one of Schinkel's churches—the neo-Gothic

Friedrichswerdersche Kirche. Closed Mondays and Tuesdays. Werderstr., near Unter den Linden (phone: 208-1323).

SCHLOSS BRITZ (BRITZ PALACE) Originally part of an 18th-century country estate, this luxurious mansion displays the beautiful furniture and decorations of the Wilhelmine era (mid- to late 19th century). There also are rotating historical exhibits and exquisitely landscaped grounds. Closed Mondays and Tuesdays. Admission charge. 73 Alt-Britz (phone: 606-6051).

SCHLOSS FRIEDRICHSFELDE (FRIEDRICHSFELDE PALACE) This pink-and-white Baroque palace was built in 1695 by the Prussian royalty for members of their court. Sixteen of its rooms, which have been painstakingly restored, house displays on the art and culture of the 18th and 19th centuries. Open only for guided tours (in English on request) at 11 AM and 1 and 3 PM; closed Mondays. Admission charge. 125 Am Tierpark (phone: 510-0111).

SCHWULES MUSEUM (GAY MUSEUM) Located in the heart of Kreuzberg, this museum features rotating exhibits on gay history, art, and culture. Closed Mondays and Tuesdays. Admission charge. 61 Mehringdamm (phone: 693-1172).

NOTE

The history of Berlin's Jewish community is not only a chronicle of persecution and tragedy, but of achievement and vitality as well. The Berlin of the 1920s—the golden age of the theater, cabaret, and film industry—would have been impossible without the contributions of Jewish performers, directors, and writers. Several of the city's greatest doctors, architects, and merchants were part of one of the world's most productive Jewish communities. Many of their graves can be seen in the cemeteries in Prenzlauer Berg and Weissensee.

When the Nazis came to power in 1933, Berlin's thriving Jewish community was doomed. On January 20, 1942, the infamous "final solution" was resolved at the *Wannsee Villa* in Berlin's Zehlendorf district; it's now a Holocaust memorial center (see *Special Places*). Two of Brandenburg's concentration camps are also dedicated to the victims of the Nazis' attempt at genocide. The *Sachsenhausen* camp (Str. der Nationen, Oranienburg; phone: 3301-803715), where many Jews, political prisoners, homosexuals, Poles, and Russians were sentenced to forced labor, can be reached by taking the *S-Bahn* No. 1 line to the last stop in Oranienburg. From there, it's a short bus or cab ride to the camp. The camp is closed Mondays; no admission charge. The other camp, *Ravensbruck,* is located in Furstenburg (phone: 33093-2025). To get there, take an *S-Bahn* train from *Lichtenberg Station* to *Furstenburg-Havel Station* (about an hour's ride) and take a taxi from there. *Ravensbruck* is also closed Mondays; no admission charge.

Today, Berlin's Jewish community is thriving, due in part to a large influx of Jews from the former Soviet republics. To find out about services in the city's five active synagogues, contact the *Jüdisches Gemeindehaus* (Jewish Community Center; 79-80 Fasanenstr.; phone: 884-2030). For a tour of the community, contact the *Stadtreisen Berlin* (4 Turmstr.; phone: 394-8354; fax: 394-7910). This company offers many special-interest excursions, with German commentary; custom-designed group tours in English are also available.

Artifacts from the collection of the *Jüdisches Museum* (Jewish Museum) are temporarily being displayed in the *Martin-Gropius-Bau* (see *Special Places*), while a new home for the museum is being constructed next to the *Berlin Museum,* which is also currently closed; both facilities are scheduled to reopen in 1998.

SHOPPING

Berlin has an abundance of interesting shops. There is hardly anything you cannot buy here, and some of the items offered for sale are truly unique. The best shopping is in the western part of the city. If you just want to browse before making up your mind, go through *Europa-Center,* at the foot of Kurfürstendamm in the middle of the downtown area. This city within a city has scores of small shops and boutiques offering a variety of typical German specialties. German cameras, including those by Leica, Rollei, and Zeiss, are available here, but it is necessary to do very careful comparison shopping; the same brands often are less expensive in the US. Optical goods such as binoculars, telescopes, and microscopes also are German specialties, and there are good buys in china and porcelain; great names in the latter are Meissen, Rosenthal, and KPM (Staatliche Porzellan Manufaktur Berlin, the state porcelain factory). Toys, cutlery, and clocks are good buys, too. For standard shopping hours, see GETTING READY TO GO. Although you might want to do some exploring on your own, here is a small sample of recommended stores:

Antik und Flohmarkt Friedrichstrasse (Friedrichstrasse Antiques and Flea Market) As its name implies, it offers a little bit of everything you never even knew you wanted. Closed Tuesdays. Under the tracks of *Friedrichstrasse Station* (phone: 215-02129).

Ararat Over 32,000 different postcard designs. 99a Bergmannstr. and other locations (phone: 693-5080).

Arno Offers pricey lamps and chandeliers cleverly shaped into spiders, and assorted other whimsical creations. 12 Savignypl., under the *S-Bahn* (phone: 312-9010).

Bannat For the globetrotter, everything from Gore-Tex jackets to compasses and maps. 65 Lietzenburger Str. (phone: 882-7601).

Berliner Zinnfiguren Wonderful miniature toy soldiers and other collectible pewter figurines. 88 Knesebeckstr. (phone: 310802).

Boris Schoenherr Handmade musical instruments. 17 Sophienstr. (phone: 281-7064).

Bücherbogen am Savignyplatz Berlin's best source for art and architecture books. Savignypl., under the *S-Bahn* (phone: 312-1932).

Design Pur Sleek accessories for the home and office. 17 Dahlmannstr. (phone: 324-0756).

Durchbruch Designer Christina Ueckermann features quality casual womenswear. 54 Schlüterstr. (phone: 881-5568).

FNAC A household name in France, this unusual emporium carries books, records, cassettes, and CDs in both German and English. 20-24 Meinekestr. (phone: 884720).

Freimuth Traditional, well-made hats for men and women. 33 Kurfürstendamm (phone: 881-6865).

Horn's The latest in women's fashions. 213 Kurfürstendamm (phone: 881-4055).

J. A. Henckels Cutlery and top-of-the-line kitchen utensils. 33 Kurfürstendamm (phone: 881-3315).

Jazzcock LPs, cassettes, and CDs—a paradise for jazz fans. 17 Fürbringer Str. (phone: 693-6133).

Jil Sander Boutique Chic womenswear. 48 Kurfürstendamm (phone: 883-3730).

KaDeWe Germany's largest, grandest, and best-stocked department store (the name is short for *Kaufhaus des Westens*), it's simply got everything, including an enormous food shop with a score of lunch counters on the sixth floor. 21-24 Tauentzienstr. (phone: 21210).

Kaufhaus Schrill Fun fashions and outrageous tics and jewelry. 46 Bleibtreustr. (phone: 882-4048).

Kiepert Berlin's most comprehensive bookstore has an excellent selection of English books—everything from murder mysteries to romance novels. 4-5 Hardenbergstr. (phone: 311-0090).

Kostümhaus This eastern Berlin shop features clothes by young German designers. 22 Veteranenstr. (phone: 281-5224).

Kramberg Expensive designer clothing for men and women. 56 Kurfürstendamm (phone: 323-6058).

Kunsthandwerk Stroh Handmade *Christmas* tree ornaments, dolls, and other unique creations—all made from straw. 9 Sophienstr. (phone: 281-2888).

Leysieffer Fine cakes, preserves, and chocolates. Marzipan and flavored truffles are specialties. There's also a café serving these delicacies on the second floor. 218 Kurfürstendamm (phone: 882-7820).

Marga Schoeller English and American books. 33 Knesebeckstr. (phone: 881-1112).

Musikalienhandlung Hans Riedel The city's best sheet music selection, plus records. 38 Uhlandstr. (phone: 882-7395).

Porzellan-Manufaktur Meissen Porcelain from the famous Meissen factory. Two locations: 39b Unter den Linden (phone: 229-2691) and 30 Mohrenstr. (phone: 238-24150).

Rogacki Berlin's oldest smoked-fish shop. 145 Wilmersdorferstr. (phone: 341-4091).

Rosenthal Studio-Haus Porcelain from modern to classic designs from one of Germany's top manufacturers. 226 Kurfürstendamm (phone: 881-7051).

Rutz Fine bedding and lingerie. 7b Tauentzienstr. (phone: 262-4055).

Schuhtick The city's best outlet for trendy shoes. Alexanderpl. (phone: 242-4012) and 11 Savignypl. (phone: 312-4955).

Staatliche Porzellan Manufaktur Berlin (KPM) Known until 1918 as *Königliche Porzellan Manufaktur* (Royal Porcelain Manufacturers), this company's beautiful china has been made in Berlin for centuries. 26a Kurfürstendamm (phone: 390090).

Triebel An outlet for traditional clothes from Bavaria and Austria, as well as hunting and riding outfits. 12 Schönwalder Str., Spandau (phone 335-5001).

Virgin Megastore True to its name, this shop carries an enormous selection of records, cassettes, and CDs. 14 Kurfürstendamm (phone: 880-0810).

Vom Winde Verweht (Gone with the Wind) An Anglo-American kite emporium featuring fascinating European kites at low prices. 43 and 81 Eisenacher Str. (phone: 784-7769 or 788-1992).

SPORTS AND FITNESS

BICYCLING You can rent a bike by the hour for a jaunt through the expansive Grunewald Forest from *F. Damrau* (Schmetterlingspl.; phone: 811-5829; call before 9 AM). Also try *Fahrradbüro* (146 Hauptstr.; phone: 783-5562) and *Räderwerk* (14 Körtestr.; phone: 691-8590); both companies require a 24-hour-minimum rental.

FITNESS CENTER *Fitness-Studio* (182-183 Kurfürstendamm; phone: 882-6301 or 881-3371) is open to visitors for a fee.

GOLF The *Golf und Landclub* (Stölpchenweg, Berlin-Wannsee; phone: 805-5075) has a nine-hole golf course.

HORSE RACING Berlin's renowned *Trabrennbahn Mariendorf* (222-298 Mariendorfer Damm; phone: 74010) has harness racing year-round on Wednesdays and Sundays. Harness racing at *Trabrennbahn Karlshorst* (129 Treskowallee; phone: 509-0891) is on Saturdays and Tuesdays year-round. Thoroughbreds race on weekends from April through October at the historic *Hoppegarten* (1 Goetheallee, Dahlwitz-Hoppegarten; phone: 559-6102).

ICE HOCKEY From November through April, you can see professional games at the *Eissporthalle* (Jafféstr.; phone: 30380). Berlin's resident teams are the *Preussen* (Prussians) and the *Eisbären* (Polar Bears).

ICE SKATING In the winter, there are various public indoor rinks in the city, including the *Sportforum Berlin* (Konrad-Wolf-Str.; phone: 97810) and the *Eisstadion Wilmersdorf* (9 Fritz-Wildung-Str.; phone: 823-4060).

JOGGING The best place is the *Tiergarten,* where there are trails. Farther out, runners prefer Grunewald Forest or the long, winding trails of the *Volkspark Wilmersdorf.*

SOCCER A very special sport here, as West Germany won the *1990 World Cup* in its final season before reunification. *Hertha* and *Blau-Weiss,* Berlin's professional soccer teams, play on autumn Saturdays at the *Olympiastadion* (Olympischer Pl.; phone: 304-0676).

SWIMMING Aquatic sports can be enjoyed at a number of indoor and outdoor pools; each of Berlin's 23 boroughs has at least one public facility. In addition, there is a sandy beach at Wannsee and another at Müggelsee.

TENNIS Courts can be reserved by the hour at *Tennis and Squash City* (53 Brandenburgische Str.; phone: 879097). In addition, the city has a number of indoor and outdoor public courts. For locations and hours of admission, consult the tourist office.

THEATER

Theater in Berlin, still Germany's theatrical metropolis, is mostly an all-German affair. But some places are worth visiting despite a possible language barrier.

CENTER STAGE

Berliner Ensemble For 30 years, seeing *The Threepenny Opera* performed by the *Berliner Ensemble* was one of the best reasons to visit East Berlin. Here, Bertolt Brecht's radicalism is a proud heritage to be preserved. But if the theater's cutting edge was dulled a bit by posthumous veneration of its founding father, it is now being resharpened. In the last few seasons, the *Ensemble,* which has its permanent home at the *Theater am Schiffbauerdamm,* has been wooing talent from the German-speaking world's most lustrous institutions. 1 Bertolt-Brecht-Pl. (phone: 282-3160).

Deutsches Theater (German Theater) Founded in 1883, this repertory company was long locked in the GDR and is now trying to claim its rightful throne in a unified Germany's theater world. The *Deutsches Theater*'s longtime director was Gustav Gründgens, the actor who steered his career through the shoals of Nazi cultural policy and was the inspiration for the character played by Klaus-Maria Brandauer in Istvan Szabo's film *Mephisto.* Other German theatrical legends who trod these boards were Otto Brahm, Max Reinhardt, and the late Marlene Dietrich (in 1922, she made her stage debut here). 13a Schumannstr. (phone: 284-41225).

Schaubühne am Lehninerplatz This once subversive theater has shed its angry bent, but its bold productions are still the rage. It was founded along idealistic lines in 1962 by the visionary director Peter Stein, who shared decision making with the acting team. These days, the political points have been made, Stein has left, and the troupe has become more affable (even a bit timid). 153 Kurfürstendamm (phone: 890020; box office: 890023).

For an example of classical repertoire, go to the intimate *Kammerspiele* (same address as the *Deutsches Theater,* see above; phone: 287-1226), which was founded in 1906 by Max Reinhardt. Another small stage, the *Maxim Gorki Theater* (2 Am Festungsgraben; phone: 208-2783), offers both classical and contemporary dramas. Eastern Berlin's *Volksbühne* (Rosa-Luxemburg-Pl.; phone: 282-8978) features innovative productions of new and classic plays. Other prominent theaters are the *Renaissance* (6 Hardenbergstr.; phone: 312-4202); *Theater am Kurfürstendamm* (206 Kurfürstendamm; phone: 882-3789); *Komödie* (206 Kurfürstendamm; phone: 882-7893); and *Tribühne* (18-20 Otto-Suhr-Allee; phone: 341-2600). One of Europe's most successful children's theaters is *Grips* (22 Altonaer Str.; phone: 391-4004).

Berlin also boasts a variety of fringe theaters, whose productions range from the sublime to the ridiculous. An important venue for the avant-garde scene is the *Hebbel Theater* in Kreuzberg, a district on the outskirts of the city (29 Stresemannstr.; phone: 251-0144). Other well-respected alternative theaters are the *Vaganten-Bühne* (12a Kantstr.; phone: 312-4529); *Schmalen Handtuch* (91 Frankfurter Allee; phone: 588-4659); *Theater unterm Dach* (101 Dimitroffstr.; phone: 420-0610); *Fliegendes Theater* (54 Hasenheide; phone: 692-2100); and *Theater am Halleschen Ufer* (32 Hallesches Ufer; phone: 251-0941). The *Zan Pollo* in Schöneberg (45 Rheinstr.; phone: 852-2002) mounts rarely staged classics. Two of eastern Berlin's wildest experimental theaters are the *Tacheles* cultural center (53-56 Oranienburgerstr.; phone: 282-6185), housed in a turn-of-the-century former shopping arcade, and the *Kesselhaus* in the *Kulturbrauerei* complex (36-39 Schönhauser Allee, entrance on Knaackstr.; phone: 440-9243). Several *Kneipen* (pubs) host theatrical performances, including *Rost Bühne* (29 Knesebeckstr.; phone: 881-1699). There's also the *Freunde der Italienischen Oper* (40 Fidicinstr.; phone: 691-1211), a tiny theater/cabaret in Kreuzberg that often has performances in English.

Tickets for all performances can be purchased at box offices (you can almost always call ahead for reservations); you can buy tickets for the mainstream theaters at just about any ticket booth around town, including *Wildbad Kiosk* (1 Rankestr.; phone: 881-4507); *Theaterkasse Zanke* (16 Kurfürstendamm; phone: 882-6563); and the *Theaterkasse* in the *Radisson Plaza* hotel (see *Checking In*).

The best venues for ballet are the *Deutsche Oper* and the *Komische Oper* (see *Music,* below). Berlin's lively contemporary dance scene centers around the *Hebbel* (see above) and the *Tanzfabrik* (68 Möckernstr.; phone: 786-5861).

Should you feel a bit homesick, take in the latest Hollywood movie in English at the *Odeon* (116 Hauptstr.; phone: 781-5667). Other cinemas show movies in English on occasion; check the *Tip* or *Zitty* listings for showings labeled "OmU" (original version with German subtitles) or "OF" (original version). Beware: All other movie theaters show English-language films dubbed in German.

MUSIC

Berlin is one of the world's musical centers, with performances of everything from classical to pop and rock.

HIGH NOTES

Berliner Philharmonisches Orchester This is quite simply the world's best orchestra. The baton has passed from the late Herbert von Karajan to a baby-boom Italian, Claudio Abbado, but the *Berliner Philharmonisches Orchester* has lost none of its musical splendor. The ensemble is at its greatest playing the colossal works of such titans as Richard Strauss, Anton Bruckner, and Johannes Brahms. Whatever the program, the *Philharmonie* concert hall is filled with a sound that is no less than divine. Kemperpl. (phone: 254880; no telephone ticket orders accepted).

Berlin's Operatic Trio The 40-year rivalry between East and West has left Berlin with two of everything—except in opera, where there are three companies. The oldest, the *Deutsche Staatsoper* (7 Unter den Linden; phone: 200-4762)—which until a few years ago was East Germany's state opera—celebrated its 250th anniversary in 1992. Now restored to its imperial luster, the 18th-century scale of the opera house makes it far more intimate than larger, modern spaces that singers have to strain to fill. Here, you can feel a diva's anguish up close, and a tenor's heroic high C will part your hair.

Unlike most of the rest of Germany, which was painstakingly reconstructed to look exactly like its prewar self, the gutted, turn-of-the-century opera house in the western suburb of Charlottenburg was rebuilt into the modern *Deutsche Oper* (35 Bismarckstr.; phone: 34381), which opened in 1961. In addition to performances by such luminaries as Lucia Aliberti, Alfredo Kraus, René Kollo, and Karan Armstrong, the *Deutsche Oper*'s productions are intermingled with evenings of ballet. The *Komische Oper* (55-57 Behrenstr.; phone: 229-2555) is the custodian of the repertoire's lyric froth, but it does not stick slavishly to jolly presentations. Recent productions have ranged from an acerbically updated version of Wagner's politically charged *Rienzi* to traditional versions of operas by Rimsky-Korsakov and Rossini.

In addition, chamber music can be heard at the *Kammermusiksaal* (phone: 254880) in the *Philharmonie.* The *Schauspielhaus* (Gendarmenmarkt; phone: 209-02129), built in 1820, also hosts other world-famous orchestras. The *Rundfunk-Sinfonieorchester Berlin* (Berlin Radio Symphony Orchestra) gives most of its concerts at *Sender Freies Berlin,* the radio station (8-14 Masurenallee; phone: 302-7242). Concerts and recitals of classical music can be heard at the *Hochschule der Künste* (College of Arts; 1 Fasanenstr.; phone: 318-52374). Operettas and musicals are launched at *Theater des Westens* (12 Kantstr.; phone: 319-03193). Pop concerts, many by visiting international stars, are performed at the *ICC* (see *Special Places*), the *Metropol* (see *Nightclubs and Nightlife,* below), and the *Deutschlandhalle* (Messedamm; phone: 303-84387). For the latest in jazz and rock music, attend one of the concerts that are frequently given at *Tempodrom* (In den Zelten; phone: 394-4045) and at *Huxley's Neue Welt* (108-114 Hasenheide; phone: 786-6048). In the summer, the *Waldbühne* (Passenheimer Str.; phone: 305-5079), an open-air amphitheater, is a pleasant place to hear a concert, either rock or classical.

NIGHTCLUBS AND NIGHTLIFE

Berlin's nightlife—immortalized in story, song, the cartoons of George Grosz, and films like *Cabaret*—is legendary. London's *Time Out* magazine once hailed Berlin as "Europe's most decadent city," and the description still fits. Even if decadence is not your style, Berlin's after-dark scene offers something for every taste, from the tame to the outlandish.

For some nostalgic cheek-to-cheek dancing, try *Clärchen's Ballhaus* (24-25 Auguststr.; phone: 282-9295) and *Ballhaus Berlin* (102 Chausseestr.; phone: 282-7575); the latter even has telephones on the tables so you can call that attractive person in the corner and ask for a dance. *Annabelle's* (64 Fasanenstr.; phone: 883-5220) in Charlottenburg is a chic club favored by the champagne set; you must ring the bell and get the doorman's approval before entering. *First* (26 Joachimstaler Str.; phone: 882-2686) is a popular club for those over 30; so are the *Bristol Bar* at the *Bristol Kempinski* hotel (27 Kurfürstendamm; phone: 884-34756) and *Salsa* (13 Wielandstr.; phone: 324-1642), which features Latin American music.

Those eager to sample Berlin's radical nightlife scene have a variety of choices. The demise of East Berlin resulted in the birth of discos in way-out settings: ruins, bunkers, abandoned underground restrooms, and so on. Many in what used to be West Berlin occupy factory space. *Neunzig Grad* (Ninety Degrees; 37 Dennewitzstr.; phone: 262-8984) offers a mixture of musical styles and decor. *Planet* (52 Köpenicker Str.; no phone) is housed in an old chalk factory on the Spree. *Tresor* (Leipziger Str. and Otto-Grotewohl-Str.; no phone) has an underground disco in the former treasury of an old bank.

Also popular with the young crowd, but housed in more conventional settings, are the huge *Metropol* (5 Nollendorfpl.; phone: 216-4122); *Orpheo* (2 Marburger Str.; phone: 211-6445); and *Abraxas* (134 Kantstr.; phone: 312-9493).

Local bands and those from abroad perform at *Knaack* (224 Greifswalder Str.; phone: 426-2351) and *Franz* in the *Kulturbrauerei* complex (36-39 Schönhauser Allee, entrance on Knaackstr.; phone: 448-5567), where the sounds range from Russian punk to an eclectic music mix called "African-Latin Jazz Rock." Try *Go In* (17 Bleibtreustr.; phone: 881-7218) or *Café Zapata* in the *Tacheles* cultural center (see *Theater,* above) for folk music.

Berliners love jazz, and the city boasts myriad first-rate jazz clubs. *Quasimodo* (12a Kantstr.; phone: 312-8086) attracts big names to its classic smoky cellar. *A-Trane* (1 Bleibtreustr., near Savignyplatz; phone: 313-2550) is the city's classiest hot spot. *Flöz* (37 Nassauische Str.; phone: 861-1000), *Lohmeyer's* (24 Eosanderstr.; phone: 342-9660), and *Badenscher Hof* (29 Badensche Str.; phone: 861-0080) offer intimate settings that attract laid-back jazz lovers. In Mitte, the *Podewil* cultural center (68-70 Klosterstr.; phone: 24030) and *Sophienclub* (6 Sophienstr.; phone: 282-4552) often have jazz on the musical menu. *Yorckschlösschen* (77 Yorckstr.; phone: 215-8070) offers live jazz on Sundays performed in its shady outdoor beer garden (weather permitting).

And don't forget Berlin's famous—or should we say infamous—cabarets. Both *Stachelschweine* (*Europa-Center;* phone: 261-4795) and *Wühlmäuse* (Lietzenburger Str., corner of Nürnberger Str.; phone: 213-7047) put on interesting performances, devoted chiefly to literary and political satire. At *Kartoon* (24 Französischestr.; phone: 229-9305), the waiters, who perform as well as serve, specialize in skits that satirize German politics. As its name implies, *Chamäleon Varieté* (40-41 Rosenthaler Str.; phone: 282-7118) offers an ever-changing bill. Also good choices for an evening out are *BKA* (34 Mehringdamm; phone: 251-0112), housed in a Kreuzberg factory loft; *Bar Jeder Vernunft* (24 Schaperstr., phone: 883-1582), in an ornate circus tent in Charlottenburg; and *Die Distel* (101 Friedrichstr.; phone: 200-4704), once the state-sponsored cabaret of East Germany. The *Wintergarten* (96 Potsdamer Str.; phone: 262-7070) and *Friedrichstadtpalast* (107 Friedrichstr.; phone: 284-66474) feature flashy variety shows with scantily clad chorus girls.

Nightclubs featuring transvestite shows have long been a German specialty. If you like this sort of thing (if you think you don't, you may be pleasantly surprised) visit *La Vie en Rose* (in the *Europa-Center;* phone: 323-6006) or *Chez Nous* (14 Marburger Str.; phone: 213-1810). If gambling is one of your sins, visit the city's one and only licensed casino, on the ground floor at the Budapester Strasse side of *Europa-Center,* for roulette, baccarat, and blackjack. The casino is open daily from 3 PM to 3 AM (phone: 250-0890). Minimum age is 21; you must present your passport at the door. Jacket and tie are required.

Berlin is known for its multitude of *Kneipen* (pubs) and *Biergärten* (beer gardens), which dispense well-drawn glasses of beer, homemade schnapps, good eats, and lots of *Gemütlichkeit* (congeniality). Some of them are in town, while others are *Ausflugslokale* (on the city's fringes) and ideal for an outing—day or night. All are great fun. Unless otherwise noted, the *Kneipen* and *Biergärten* are open daily and require reservations. Those worthy of mention include *Die Kleine Weltlaterne* (22 Nestorstr.; phone: 892-6585), which caters to an arty crowd; *Lutter und Wegener* (see *Eating Out*), a wine cellar of note; *Zwiebelfisch* (7-8 Savignypl.; phone: 317363), a haunt for journalists and students; and *Zur letzten Instanz* (14 Waisenstr.; phone: 212-5528).

Best in Town

CHECKING IN

In Berlin, visitors can choose from among one of the best assortments of hotels in all of Germany. Nearly all the hotels in the city's eastern section have been privatized (many are now run by US and other Western hotel chains), adding to the number of good-quality accommodations available. Since there always seems to be something happening in this scintillating city, it is always advisable to make advance reservations—either directly with the hotel of your choice or through the city's efficient tourist office; *Dial Berlin* can also help here (see *Tourist Information*).

Our selection includes some of the luxury hotels, as well as establishments that can be classified as moderate and inexpensive. Many of the latter are attractive little houses, noted for their charm. A word of caution: Hotel accommodations in Germany are expensive, and Berlin is no exception. Should you prefer more modest, although somewhat less comfortable, rooms, check with the tourist office. The hotels listed below have a bath or a shower in every room, and in almost every case the rooms have telephones; breakfast is included in the rates, unless otherwise noted. Most of Berlin's major hotels have complete facilities for the business traveler. Those hotels described as having "business services" usually offer such conveniences as an English-speaking concierge, meeting rooms, photocopiers, computers, translation services, and express checkout, among others. Call the hotel for additional information. For a double room in those hotels we have classed as expensive, expect to pay $200 or more; in places in the moderate category, from $100 to $200; and in inexpensive hotels, under $100. All telephone numbers are in the 30 city code unless otherwise indicated.

For an unforgettable Berlin experience, we begin with our favorites (all in the expensive category), followed by our cost and quality choices, listed by price category.

ROOMS AT THE TOP

Bristol Kempinski Like so much in Berlin, the "Kempi" is a fine old name wrapped in a new package. At the corner of patrician Fasanenstrasse and the Ku'damm—Germany's best and brightest boulevard—this 358-room establishment is right in the middle of the city's golden mile. It also boasts a renowned restaurant, the *Kempinski Grill* (see *Eating Out*); and a table at the *Kempinski-Eck* café feels like sitting on the 50-yard line of all of Europe. Other amenities include 24-hour room service, foreign currency exchange, and business services. Breakfast is not included. 27 Kurfürstendamm (phone: 884340; 800-426-3135; fax: 883-6075).

Maritim Grand Hotel Berlin In the center of the historic downtown area in what was East Berlin, it offers the height of luxury and comfort. The 350 well-appointed rooms, spacious lobby, and six cafés and restaurants (especially good is *Silhouette;* see *Eating Out*) all seem so "Western" that it's hard to imagine that you're in the middle of what used to be a workers' state. Other amenities include 24-hour room service, foreign currency exchange, and business services. 158-164 Friedrichstr. (phone: 23270; 800-843-3311; fax: 232-7362).

EXPENSIVE

Am Zoo When Thomas Wolfe came to Berlin in the early 1930s, he stayed at this 145-room hotel, one of the traditional downtown establishments. Amenities include a restaurant, 24-hour room service, foreign currency exchange, and business services. 25 Kurfürstendamm (phone: 884370; fax: 884-37714).

Berlin Hilton Beautifully designed, this property in the eastern part of the city overlooks the *Deutscher Dom* and *Französischer Dom,* along with the 19th-century Gendarmenmarkt and the *Schauspielhaus* concert hall (see *Special Places*). The 505 rooms and suites are all luxuriously appointed. Several restaurants, taverns, and bars, as well as a pool, sauna, and fitness center are among the extensive facilities. Other amenities include 24-hour room service, foreign currency exchange, and business services. 30 Mohrenstr. (phone: 23820; 800-HILTONS; fax: 238-24269).

Curator With an ideal location—between Savignyplatz and the Ku'damm—this quiet, chic place is perfect for tourists or business travelers. Amenities such as king-size beds and telephones in the bathrooms make the 100 rooms especially comfortable; the English-speaking concierge is very helpful. There's an elegant bar and a restaurant off the lobby. Business services are available. 41-43 Grolmanstr. (phone: 884260; fax: 884-26500).

Forum In the eastern downtown area, its 994 rooms make it one of the largest in town. There is a fine restaurant (the *Panorama;* see *Eating Out*), plus a sauna and a garage. Although guestrooms are fairly small, the convenient location in front of Alexanderplatz is this establishment's main draw; closed to automobile traffic, the square is ringed by restaurants, stores, the *Fernsehturm,* and other public buildings. Other amenities include 24-hour room service, foreign currency exchange, and business services. Alexanderpl. (phone: 23890; fax: 212-6437).

Grand Hotel Esplanade With 400 rooms, plus 17 suites, this fine hostelry is idyllically set on the Landwehr Canal—but it's downtown Berlin, not Amsterdam, that's just around the corner. The rooms, service, and other amenities are well above standard, and the popular *Harlekin* restaurant (see *Eating Out*) is on the premises. Other amenities include 24-hour room service, foreign currency exchange, and business services. Breakfast is not included. 15 Lützowufer (phone: 261011; 800-223-5652; fax: 262-9121).

Inter-Continental In the heart of western Berlin—with wall-size windows to keep the weather out and the luxury in—this modern 600-room establishment is somewhat removed from the city's hustle and bustle. Request a room overlooking the green, expansive *Tiergarten;* you'll feel as if you're miles from the tumult of the Kurfürstendamm—but in fact you're only a short walk away. Acres of pale marble cover the lobby, and there's a fine selection of restaurants, including a rooftop dining room with live entertainment, as well as a popular ballroom. Located next to the *Zoologischer Garten,* its other amenities include 24-hour room service, foreign currency exchange, and business services. Breakfast is not included. 2 Budapester Str. (phone: 26020; 800-327-0200; fax: 260-80760).

Metropol This handsome 340-room high-rise was built in the mid-1970s by a Swedish firm. Extras are a fine dining room (see *Eating Out*), a sauna, and a garage. In former East Berlin, the hotel has always appealed to those used to Western European luxury. Other amenities include 24-hour room service, foreign currency exchange, and business services. 150-153 Friedrichstr. (phone: 23875; fax: 2387-4209).

Mondial In the heart of Ku'damm, it has 75 large, elegantly decorated rooms, plus a pool and a first-rate restaurant. Other amenities include foreign currency exchange and business services. 47 Kurfürstendamm (phone: 884110; fax: 884-11150).

Palace Just behind the *Kaiser Wilhelm Gedächtniskirche* and within the orb of the *Europa-Center,* this imposing downtown hostelry has a large number of apartments and 160 well-appointed rooms, as well as a restaurant, pool, and sauna. Other amenities include 24-hour room service, foreign currency exchange, and business services. Breakfast is not included. 42 Budapester Str. (phone: 25020; fax: 262-6577).

Penta With 425 rooms, this is one of Berlin's largest and most modern properties. On the premises are a restaurant, a bar, a beer cellar, a pool, a sauna, a solarium, and an underground garage. Other amenities include 24-hour room service, foreign currency exchange, and business services. Breakfast is not included. Centrally located at 65 Nürnberger Str. (phone: 210070; 800-225-3456; fax: 213-2009).

President In a sleek, modern building, this 132-room hostelry boasts a prime location—across the street from the *Urania,* the city's famed lecture hall, and within easy walking distance of Wittenbergplatz and *KaDeWe,* the great department store. Its topnotch restaurant, *Die Saison* (see *Eating Out*), attracts business and theater people. Children under 14 stay free in their parents' room. Other amenities include foreign currency exchange and business services. 16-18 An der Urania (phone: 219030; fax: 214-1200).

Radisson Plaza Formerly the *Palast,* this 600-room hotel in the city's eastern section provides first class service, luxurious accommodations, and a good view of the city. Its restaurants serve a variety of ethnic fare, from Asian to French. Other amenities include 24-hour room service, foreign currency exchange, and business services. 5 Karl-Liebknecht-Str. (phone: 23828; 800-333-3333; fax: 2382-7590).

Savoy In a prewar building, this 128-room establishment radiates Old World charm with its plush lobby and elegant bar. The rooms on the sixth floor are especially posh, with TV sets that double as computers, and fresh flowers daily. Other amenities include a restaurant, 24-hour room service, foreign currency exchange, and business services. 9-10 Fasanenstr. (phone: 311030; 800-63-SAVOY; fax: 311-03333).

Schweizerhof This 441-room establishment is opposite the *Inter-Continental* and is managed by that same chain. The motif is Swiss, as the name implies, and the service is excellent. There is a restaurant. Breakfast is not included. 21-31 Budapester Str. (phone: 26960; 800-327-0200; fax: 269-6900).

Seehof Only 2½ miles (4 km) down the road from the downtown area, on the lovely Lietzensee, this 80-room hotel overlooks a small park. Amenities include a restaurant, 24-hour room service, foreign currency exchange, and business services. Breakfast is not included. 11 Lietzenseeufer (phone: 320020; fax: 320-02251).

Steigenberger This modern, comfortable establishment with 400 rooms—plus several restaurants and bars, a pool, a sauna, and a shopping arcade—is a link in one of Germany's largest hotel chains. The location is prime. Other amenities include 24-hour room service, foreign currency exchange, and business services. Breakfast is not included. Downtown, facing lovely Los Angeles Platz. 1 Los Angeles Pl. (phone: 21080; 800-223-5652; fax: 210-8117).

MODERATE

Am Studio A modern place, it offers a magnificent view of the city from each of its 78 rooms. There's no restaurant, but breakfast is included. There's also an English-speaking concierge. 80 Kaiserdamm (phone: 302081; fax: 301-9578).

Art Hotel Sorat An unusual 75-room establishment that is a cross between a hotel and an art gallery. Modern paintings and sculpture by German artist Wolf Vostell enliven the building's façade and its unusually tasteful interior. Its equally attractive dining room, *Anteo,* serves fine continental fare (see *Eating Out*). Other amenities include 24-hour room service, foreign currency exchange, and business services. 28-29 Joachimstaler Str. (phone: 884470; fax: 884-47700).

Askanischer Hof A favorite with journalists and actors, this 17-room property—a country inn in the heart of Berlin—has a charming, antique-filled decor. The lobby and breakfast room, on the second floor of the prewar building, are cozy and welcoming. There's no restaurant. 53 Kurfürstendamm (phone: 881-8033; fax: 881-7206).

Berlin With 470 rooms (those in the older—circa 1960—section are especially spacious), this is one of the city's largest properties. An old-fashioned pub, the *Berlin Eck,* offers hearty snacks, while the *Globe* restaurant (see *Eating Out*) is considered one of the city's best hotel dining rooms. 17 Lützowpl. (phone: 26050; 800-843-6664; fax: 260-52716).

Berlin Excelsior Just off Kurfürstendamm in the center of town, this pleasant property offers 325 rooms with refrigerators; public rooms include a breakfast room, restaurant, bar, and banquet room. Other amenities include 24-hour room service, foreign currency exchange, and business services. 14 Hardenbergstr. (phone: 31550; fax: 315-1053).

Börse Right in the middle of downtown Berlin, this 44-room hotel offers little peace and quiet, as it's surrounded by shops, cafés, restaurants, theaters, and movie houses. But it's fine if you like a lively location. There's no restaurant, but breakfast is included. Other amenities include 24-hour room service, foreign currency exchange, and business services. 34 Kurfürstendamm (phone: 881-3021; fax: 883-2034).

Castor Located on a quiet side street in the middle of Berlin's antiques district, just four blocks from the *KaDeWe* department store, is this unpretentious, no-frills hostelry. Each of the 78 small rooms is prettily decorated with French fabrics, and the corner rooms have porthole windows. A good restaurant serving fine regional fare is a plus. Other amenities include an English-speaking concierge and foreign currency exchange. 8 Fuggerstr. (phone: 213030; fax: 213-03160).

Domus Set on a charming side street in the city center, this pleasant establishment offers 70 comfortable rooms. There's no restaurant, but a generous buffet breakfast is included. 49 Uhlandstr. (phone: 882041; fax: 882-0410).

Forsthaus Paulsborn Housed in a former hunting lodge on the Grunewaldsee (Grunewald Lake), this 10-room gem offers a quiet and romantic atmosphere in a lovely setting. The vaulted-ceiling bar and restaurant feature lake views and fine German cooking. Am Grunewaldsee (phone: 813-8010; fax: 814-1156).

Frühling am Zoo Located on the busiest corner in town, this place can be noisy, but its prices are reasonable. The 66 guestrooms have high ceilings and comfortable beds. There's no elevator, however, and no restaurant. 17 Kurfürstendamm (phone: 881-8083; fax: 881-6483).

Luisenhof This comfortable, elegant hostelry is housed in a beautiful 19th-century building that was formerly used as a Communist Party training center. It has 28 rooms, a bar, and a restaurant. 92 Köpenicker Str. (phone: 279-1109).

Novotel With 187 rooms, and right next to *Flughafen Berlin-Tegel* (Tegel Airport), it provides efficiency without any sacrifice of comfort. There's a restaurant, sauna, solarium, and pool on the premises. Other amenities include an English-speaking concierge and foreign currency exchange. 202 Kurt-Schumacher-Damm (phone: 41060; 800-221-4542; fax: 410-6700).

Plaza Just around the corner from the Kurfürstendamm is this 131-room alternative to more expensive accommodations. Amenities include a restaurant, an English-speaking concierge, and foreign currency exchange. 63 Knesebeckstr. (phone: 884130; fax: 884-13754).

Residenz A favorite of German TV stars who sometimes stay for months, this 90-room property boasts *Jugendstil* interiors, an excellent French restaurant, and a wonderful location—just off the Ku'damm. Ask about their special packages. 9 Meineckestr. (phone: 884430; fax: 882-4726).

Riehmer's Hofgarten This offbeat 25-room hostelry, which looks out onto the courtyard of a large turn-of-the-century apartment complex, is located in

Kreuzberg, a neighborhood popular with artists. Guests enjoy comfort without frills. There is a restaurant on the ground floor (not connected to the hotel). 83 Yorckstr. (phone: 781011; fax: 786-6059).

Viktoria Hotelschiff For those who envision sailing over the bounding main but can't stand the sight of a wave, this floating hostelry on the River Spree is the perfect choice. Once a private yacht, this now-moored boat offers 38 cozy, comfortable rooms decorated with—what else?—a nautical theme. The on-board dining room serves good seafood dishes. Other amenities include 24-hour room service, foreign currency exchange, and business services. Pier 3 at *Treptower Park* (phone: 272-7117 or 272-7873; fax: 272-7435).

INEXPENSIVE

Christliches Hospiz Near *Friedrichstrasse Station* and the Scheunenviertel, this clean, well-run place has no frills, but its 70 rooms are comfortable and reasonably priced. The concierge speaks little English. The restaurant is open to the public on weekdays; to guests only on weekends. 82 Auguststr. (phone: 284970; fax: 284-97109).

Econtel Midway between *Flughafen Berlin-Tegel* (Tegel Airport) and downtown and near the *Deutsche Oper* and *Schloss Charlottenburg,* it puts its accent on simple comfort rather than luxury, but doesn't sacrifice modern facilities. Other amenities include an English-speaking concierge and foreign currency exchange. There's no restaurant, but breakfast is included in the rate. 24-26 Sömmeringstr. (phone: 346810; fax: 344-7034).

PENSIONS

The European tradition of the family-run pension is alive and well here. For travelers on a budget, a pension can be the perfect antidote to Berlin's sky-high hotel rates—a double room and breakfast costs from about $50 to $80 a night at a pension, depending on location and amenities. Even the least expensive establishments are usually spotlessly clean; Germans wouldn't have it any other way.

Here are some standout pensions (none has a restaurant, but breakfast is included at each):

Alpina Sixteen comfortable rooms (some with private baths) in a suburban setting near the Grunewald. 3 Trabener Str. (phone: 891-6090).

An der Weide Located in a quiet eastern Berlin neighborhood, this modern 14-room pension (a few with private baths) is run by a friendly family. 20 Alt-Mahlsdorf (phone: 527-7975).

Charlottenburg With 14 rooms (some with private baths), it's a wonderful bargain with a prime location near Savignyplatz. 32-33 Grolmanstr. (phone: 881-5254).

Charlottenburger Hof Clean, well-managed, and convenient, it offers 45 rooms, some with private baths. 14 Stuttgarter Pl. (phone: 324-4819).

Kettler This seven-room place is situated on one of the loveliest streets in the city; some of the units have private baths. 19 Bleibtreustr. (phone: 883-4949).

Kleistspark An exceptionally well maintained pension with 20 rooms (some with baths) in the pleasant Schöneberg district. 1 Belziger Str. (phone: 781-1189).

Seeblick Located near the lovely Lietzensee (Lietzen Lake), this 10-room place is within easy commuting distance of downtown Berlin. Some of the rooms have private baths. 14 Neue Kantstr. (phone: 321-3072).

EATING OUT

At its best, German food is hearty and tasty; at its worst, it's as heavy as lead. Main courses usually consist of roasted or stewed meat with boiled potatoes or dumplings (called *Knödel,* which are very heavy) and sauerkraut, cabbage, or other vegetables, such as string beans. Wiener schnitzel and sauerbraten are well-known specialties.

Like other continentals, Germans like rolls for breakfast, occasionally the sweet, cruller-like pastries called *Krapfen* and *Berliner Pfannkuchen*. At mid-morning, they often have a snack of sausages and bread for *Brotzeit* (literally, "breadtime").

Sausages are the specialty in Germany at any time of day or night; they are made from pork, veal, and game. The frankfurter, which originated in Vienna, is longer, slimmer, and better than the American variety. *Weisswurst* is a boiled white sausage made mostly of veal; bratwurst is a grilled pork sausage; a *Regensburger* is a spicy pork sausage.

Interesting appetizers include herring, which is very popular and comes in many varieties, and *Lachs* (smoked salmon). Soups are popular and very substantial: *Leberknödelsuppe* (liver dumpling soup), *Erbsensuppe* (pea soup), and *Kohlsuppe* (cabbage soup) are just a few. *Schwarzbrot,* or dark bread, is very tasty, especially Westphalian pumpernickel.

Although Berlin restaurants serving traditional German fare offer many of these dishes, they are more commonly served throughout other regions of the country. For a typical Berlin treat, stop in at a *Konditorei,* a little shop that offers excellent cakes and pastries with coffee or tea. Special desserts are *Schwarzwälder Kirschtorte,* a Black Forest cherry cake with whipped cream; *Kugelhupf,* a marvelous coffee cake; or *Käsekuchen,* a cheesecake. Another Berlin specialty is *Eisbein* (pigs' knuckles).

The past several years have seen a dramatic increase in the number of ethnic restaurants in the city, adding variety to Berlin's dining scene. Italian and Chinese establishments seem to be on every corner—but not all of them are good. More reliable bets are the Indian, Turkish, and Greek restaurants, with loads of bright vegetables and tasty grilled meat. Other treats include Afghan, Thai, and Japanese fare.

Germans are justifiably famous for their beer and wine. *Helles* (light) and *Dunkles* (dark) beers from southern Germany come in many sizes and varieties. Most beers come from Munich, but you might want to try *Berliner Weisses* in the summer, a whitish beer made from wheat and often served *mit Schuss* (with raspberry juice). *Bierkeller* (beer restaurants) serve food as well as beer.

Germany produces a lot of wine, some of it very good. You may be disappointed in *Liebfraumilch,* which is not a place-name (it means "Milk of Our Lady") and thus is not reliable. Best bets are the Moselles—light, pleasant, and often cheap—like *Wehlener Sonnenuhr, Piesporter,* or *Zeltinger.* Rhine wines, of course, are famous—some of the best are *Niersteiner, Oppenheimer,* and *Schloss Johannisberger.* Baden wines are equally renowned, especially *Weissherbst,* a rosé.

For a dinner for two, expect to pay $100 or more at restaurants in the expensive category; between $40 and $100 at places in the moderate range; and less than $40 at places classed as inexpensive. Unless otherwise noted, the restaurants listed below are open for lunch and dinner. Prices do not include drinks and wine. Taxes and tips are included in the bill, but leave a few extra deutsche marks (DM) for good service. All telephone numbers are in the 30 city code unless otherwise indicated.

For an unforgettable dining experience, we begin with our culinary favorites, followed by our cost and quality choices, listed by price category.

DELIGHTFUL DINING

Abend-Restaurant Königin Luise Set in the handsome *Opernpalais* restaurant complex, formerly the "Princesses' Palace," where Queen Luise's three daughters lived in the early 19th century, this is one of Berlin's most elegant dining rooms. The palace's exterior was recently restored to its former splendor; the decor is 19th-century Imperial, with antique furnishings, china, and silver. The menu of nouvelle German fare is equally elaborate: Breast of guinea hen with walnut sauce and broccoli timbales, and filet of goat with rosemary sauce and vegetable lasagne are just a few of the selections. The dining experience is pricey, but well worth it. In the same building and under the same management is the *Operncafé,* with less expensive coffee and cakes (see below). Open daily for dinner only. Reservations necessary. Major credit cards accepted. 5 Unter den Linden (phone: 200-2269).

Bamberger Reiter Although this rustic restaurant in the center of the city opened in 1984, the tasteful renovations and dark wood paneling give it a patina of antiquity. Austrian owners Franz and Doris Ranburger have created a sumptuous menu (honored with a Michelin star) which features perch in rosemary butter with spinach and pumpkin noodles, Breton lobsters, Italian truffles, and the more traditional pot roast and dumplings; the sommelier will have just the wine to go with all of it. Open for dinner only; closed Sundays and Mondays. Reservations necessary. No credit cards accepted. 7 Regensburger Str. (phone: 218-4282; fax: 214-2348).

Frühsammers Twenty minutes from downtown Berlin, this country cottage has none of the French ambitions of its tonier competition. Peter Frühsammer prides himself in dishing out the very best in local products—he works with farmers and fishers, urging them to grow the finest vegetables and herbs, raise free-range livestock, fish the region's lakes, and gather wild mushrooms and berries. These ingredients are then melded into subtle delights such as *Milchlammleber mit Ofenschalotten* (an appetizer of milk-fed lamb's liver with roasted shallots) and *Lendchen vom Neuland-Schwein in Sherryrahm mit Rösti* (roast pork loin in a sherried cream sauce, served with fried potatoes). Open for dinner only; closed Sundays. Reservations necessary. Major credit cards accepted. 101 Matterhornstr. (phone: 803-2720 or 803-8023; fax: 803-3736).

Rockendorf's This turn-of-the-century villa in a northern suburb of Berlin is not a place to grab a bite between sights—a meal here is a production. Since there is no à la carte option, you should allow as much time for the parade of courses as you would for a tour of a museum. There is something almost religious in the veneration with which each meal is borne out of the gleaming kitchen, where Siegfried Rockendorf, one of Germany's high priests of gastronomy, watches over his potions. His efforts have been rewarded by one Michelin star. The fixed- (and high-) price menu changes daily, so call ahead if you're picky. Possible choices include North Sea crab parfait with chervil and oysters, breast of pheasant in an herb and champagne sauce, crayfish tails on a bed of artichoke leaves, and saddle of venison. A dazzling array of cheeses, and spiced coffee mousse in cinnamon sauce with a rum and fruit parfait, make for happy endings. And, should you still be in the mood for a nibble, a handful of petit fours will see you back to your hotel. A suitably epic wine list is also on hand. Closed Sundays and Mondays. Reservations necessary. Major credit cards accepted. 1 Düsterhauptstr. (phone: 402-3099).

EXPENSIVE

Alt-Luxemburg The nouvelle cuisine at this cozy bistro near the city center (which has earned a Michelin star) has made this a favorite among locals and visitors alike. Try the seafood specialties—especially halibut topped with fresh greens and salmon with kumquat sauce. Closed Sundays, Mondays, and three weeks in July. Reservations advised. Major credit cards accepted. 31 Windscheidstr. (phone: 323-8730).

Chalet Corniche This beautiful former country mansion on the western fringe of the city in the Grunewald section is a special place indeed. Not only does the impressive architecture give you the feeling of bonhomie (the house was built around a big old tree), but the view through the tall windows onto wide lawns and a beautiful lake is as soul-satisfying as the food. We recommend the veal steaks and the seafood specialties. Open daily. Reservations advised. Major credit cards accepted. 5b Königsallee (phone: 892-8597).

Conti Fischstuben As its name implies, this elegant, small dining room in the *Ambassador* hotel is for seafood lovers. Open for dinner only; closed Sundays and Mondays. Reservations advised Major credit cards accepted. 42 Bayreuther Str. (phone: 219-02362).

Daitokai Close to the Kurfürstendamm, this Japanese dining place offers good food and friendly service. Guests can sit on the floor Japanese-style. Closed Mondays. No reservations. Major credit cards accepted. *Europa-Center,* Budapester Str. (phone: 261-8099).

Ermeler Haus Away from the hustle and bustle of downtown, this lovely rococo building in the eastern part of the city is one of only a few historic buildings still standing here (except for those on Unter den Linden). Housed on the building's second floor, the restaurant offers good continental dishes in intimate surroundings. The *Raabe-Diele* beer cellar and the first-floor café also are popular. Open daily for dinner only. Reservations advised. Major credit cards accepted. 10-12 Märkisches Ufer (phone: 279-4028).

Globe One of the best hotel dining rooms in town, with continental dishes served in elegant surroundings. You can dine either in the main dining room or in the smaller grillroom. Grillroom closed Sundays. Reservations advised. Major credit cards accepted. In the *Berlin Hotel,* 17 Lützowpl. (phone: 26050).

Grand Slam In a quiet suburb, about 7 miles (11 km) from downtown Berlin, it offers first-rate fare that has earned a Michelin star—we recommend the cream of spinach soup with a side dish of black truffle slices, or any one of several succulent lamb creations. This is one of the few restaurants in the Berlin area that requires men to wear jackets and ties. Closed Sundays and Mondays. Reservations necessary. Major credit cards accepted. 47-55 Gottfried-von-Cramm-Weg (phone: 825-3810).

Harlekin This stylish dining room in the *Grand Hotel Esplanade* features refined "New German" fare—try the lentils with saddle of rabbit or the lamb filet. The wine list boasts some unusual selections. Closed Sundays.

Reservations advised. Major credit cards accepted. 15 Lützowufer (phone: 261011).

Kardell Specialties are leg of lamb, game, steaks, and fish. Owner Heinz Kardell runs the place with obsessive attention to detail—and it shows. Open daily; closed Saturday lunch. Reservations necessary. Major credit cards accepted. 24 Gervinusstr. (phone: 324-1066).

Kempinski Grill The candlelit glow, creamy decor, and piano music are all serenely old-fashioned in Berlin's number one hotel dining room. The menu features lobster (a Berlin obsession) in salads, soups, and sauces. Grilled fish and steaks also are recommended. Round off the evening with a stop at the hotel's soothing *Bristol Bar* (see *Nightclubs and Nightlife* above). Closed Sundays. Reservations necessary. Major credit cards accepted. 27 Kurfürstendamm (phone: 884-34792).

Landhaus am Poloplatz Overlooking a polo field in the exclusive northern suburb of Frohnau, this place serves classic German cooking. Closed Mondays and for three weeks during the summer (usually in July). Reservations necessary. Major credit cards accepted. 9 Am Polopl. (phone: 401-9035).

Lutter und Wegener One of the oldest dining spots in Berlin, this elegant place moved to its present location in Charlottenburg after its original 19th-century building in the Mitte district was bombed during World War II. It offers well-prepared nouvelle cuisine, fine wine, and soft jazz in a relaxed setting. Try the stuffed roast lamb with rosemary served with zucchini and dumplings. Open daily for dinner only. Reservations advised. Major credit cards accepted. 55 Schlüterstr. (phone: 881-3440).

Marjellchen A cozy establishment specializing in East Prussian cuisine. The goose and the *Königsberger Klopse* (meatballs in a caper sauce) are especially good. Open daily for dinner only. Reservations advised. Major credit cards accepted. 9 Mommsenstr. (phone: 883-2676).

Metropol This elegant hotel dining room features rustic decor, *Gemütlichkeit* (a warm, welcoming atmosphere), and fine continental fare. Open daily. Reservations advised. Major credit cards accepted. 150-153 Friedrichstr. (phone: 22040 or 203070).

Ming's Garden If you crave Peking duck, this lushly decorated dining room is the place. But though it serves the city's finest Chinese cooking, don't expect the quality or variety available in most US cities. Open daily. Reservations advised. Major credit cards accepted. 16 Tauentzienstr., entrance on Marburger Str. (phone: 211-8728).

Panorama A fitting name for a restaurant on the 37th floor of the *Forum* hotel. The fare, which includes seafood dishes, pork, and steaks, almost equals the marvelous view. Try the daily specialties. Open daily. Reservations necessary. Major credit cards accepted. Alexanderpl. (phone: 238-94347).

Paris-Bar A traditional bistro that is a magnet for intellectuals and artists drawn by its equally traditional French cuisine. Closed Sundays. Reservations advised. Major credit cards accepted. 152 Kantstr. (phone: 313-8052).

Paris-Moskau Not far from the *Reichstag* in a somewhat undistinguished neighborhood, this nevertheless distinguished restaurant offers excellent continental dishes in three dining rooms in a charming two-story house. Open daily for dinner only. Reservations advised. Major credit cards accepted. 141 Alt-Moabit (phone: 394-2081).

Restauration 1900 Located in Prenzlauer Berg, this renowned eastern Berlin eatery was named for the famous Bertolucci film. The city's cultural elite come here to dine and look. The food is continental-Mediterranean. Try the bouillabaisse. Open for dinner only; closed Sundays and Mondays. Reservations necessary. Major credit cards accepted. 1 Husemannstr. (phone: 449-4052).

Die Saison In a plant-filled space lined with colorful paintings, an ever-changing menu of seasonal specialties makes this hotel dining room a favorite among locals and visitors alike. Our favorites are the asparagus soup and calf's liver with brandy. Open daily. Reservations advised. Major credit cards accepted. In the *President Hotel,* 16-18 An der Urania (phone: 219030).

Silhouette This dining room (with one Michelin star) is the pride of the *Maritim Grand* hotel. The food and decor are Thuringian, with such specialties as roast goose and grilled sausages with bacon-laden potato salad. Native red wines are featured. Open daily. Reservations necessary. Major credit cards accepted. 158-164 Friedrichstr. (phone: 209-2400).

MODERATE

Alter Fritz One of Berlin's oldest restaurants, this former coach stop on the road north of the city serves up hearty German food and beer in a charming country atmosphere. Open daily. Reservations advised. Major credit cards accepted. 12 Karolinenstr. (phone: 433-5010).

Anselmo A must for devotees of Italian fare, this intimate spot has an imaginative and well-run kitchen, rustic decor, and a pleasant atmosphere. Closed Mondays. Reservations advised. Major credit cards accepted. 17 Damaschkestr. (phone: 323-3094).

Anteo Contemporary and avant-garde art adorn the walls of this hotel dining establishment. A continental menu offers simple, flavorful fare such as Greek hors d'oeuvres, tortellini with Gorgonzola sauce, and beef steaks with roasted potatoes. There's terrace dining in fine weather. Open daily. Reservations advised. Major credit cards accepted. In the *Art Hotel Sorat,* 29 Joachimstaler Str. (phone: 883-4407).

Aphrodite This dining place in the Prenzlauer Berg district offers continental dishes and wines at reasonable prices. Try the lamb filet with a glass of chardonnay. Open for dinner only; closed Sundays and Mondays. Reservations advised. Major credit cards accepted. 61 Schönhauser Allee (phone: 448-1707).

Ax-Bax The beautiful people often hang out in this nicely designed bar that has no identifying sign on the door. In addition to the drinks and glitter, it also has good pub-style food, including bratwurst and steaks. Open for dinner only; closed Mondays. Reservations advised. Major credit cards accepted. 34 Leibnitzstr. (phone: 313-8594).

Blockhaus Nikolskoe The perfect restaurant for fans of German history and good continental food, this place, high above the wide Havel River, was built in log cabin fashion in 1819 by Prussian King Friedrich Wilhelm III for his daughter Charlotte and her husband, Grand Duke Nicholas (later Russian Czar Nicholas I). It looks like a Russian dacha. The location is remote, so ask directions when you make reservations. Closed Thursdays and in the winter after 7 PM. Reservations advised. Major credit cards accepted. On Nikolskoer Weg in Wannsee (phone: 805-2914).

Bovril This tony bistro is the best place in town for fine French-German food at a reasonable price. The menu changes daily; try the salad appetizers and the fresh fish dishes. Closed Sundays. Reservations advised. Major credit cards accepted. 184 Kurfürstendamm (phone: 881-8461).

Chamisso Situated on one of the city's few remaining perfectly preserved 19th-century squares, this charming Italian eatery specializes in fine pasta. Open daily for dinner only. Reservations advised. Major credit cards accepted. 25 Willibald-Alexis-Str. (phone: 691-5642).

Don Quijote Appropriately named, this eatery features first-rate Spanish fare in a friendly, festive atmosphere. Ask for the daily fish special—waiters present an assortment and let you choose. Other favorites include a *tapas* plate (a variety of Spanish appetizers) and garlic shrimp. Be sure to sample the sangria. Open daily for dinner only. Reservations advised. Major credit cards accepted. 41 Bleibtreustr. (phone: 881-3208).

Exil This out-of-the-way place is well worth the trip. On a canal in Kreuzberg, it features well-prepared Viennese dishes, including Wiener schnitzel and strudel. You can dine on the bower-like terrace, weather permitting. The service also is charmingly Viennese, and the ambience is sophisticated but relatively informal. Open for dinner only; closed Mondays. Reservations advised. No credit cards accepted. 44A Paul-Lincke-Ufer (phone: 612-7037).

Fernsehturm Europe's second-tallest tower (see *Seeing the City*) has a revolving café/restaurant that, in addition to offering decent international fare, affords diners a breathtaking panoramic view of Berlin. Good choices are the salads, pork cutlets, and sausages. Open daily. Reservations unnecessary. Major credit cards accepted. Alexanderpl. (phone: 212-3333 or 210-4232).

Florian A finely tuned crew maintains this admirable dining spot. The menu emphasizes French, Austrian, and Bohemian fare, and the wines and the service are as good as the food. The neighborhood is currently "in," so the place is frequented by artists, film people, and the so-called New Wave set. Open for dinner only; closed *Christmas Eve* through *New Year's Eve.* Reservations advised. No credit cards accepted. 52 Grolmanstr. (phone: 313-9184).

Fofi's A Greek-style bistro that has become a magnet for the "in" crowd; the attractions here are the Greek food and the clientele. Open for dinner only; closed *Christmas Eve.* Reservations advised. Major credit cards accepted. 70 Fasanenstr.—look for the *"estiatorio"* sign (phone: 881-8785).

Foyer Tucked in a rear courtyard just off the Ku'damm, this unpretentious dining spot is somewhat hard to find, but if you crave Turkish food, it's worth the effort. Open for dinner only; closed Sundays. Reservations advised. Major credit cards accepted. 28 Uhlandstr. (phone: 881-4268).

Hard Rock Café Berlin's member of the ubiquitous Hard Rock dynasty, which extends from London to Singapore. Die-hard rock fans can eat to the beat, munching on hefty hamburgers and salty French fries while their favorite tunes fill the air. Rock 'n' roll memorabilia on the walls include the microphone first used by the *Beatles* in concert, Jimi Hendrix's vest, a poster of the *Who* signed by John Entwhistle and Keith Moon, and a tour jacket signed by Madonna. Open daily. Reservations unnecessary. Major credit cards accepted. 21 Meinekestr. (phone: 881-2995).

Good Friends This Chinese eatery boasts tasty barbecued pork and chicken, as well as efficient service and a convenient location. Open daily. Reservations advised. Major credit cards accepted. 210 Kurfürstendamm (phone: 881-5756).

Im Reichstag One wing of this late 19th-century building, the former (and future) seat of the German Parliament (see *Special Places*), has been set aside as a restaurant. Solid German food is served in a historic setting. Closed Mondays. Reservations advised. No credit cards accepted. Pl. der Republik (phone: 397-73172).

Istanbul The food at Berlin's oldest Turkish restaurant is excellent, but the real attraction is the atmosphere. The rooms are ornate and colorful, and on weekends belly dancers work the crowd into a delighted frenzy. Open daily. Reservations advised. Major credit cards accepted. 77 Knesebeckstr. (phone: 883-2777).

Katschkol In the city's only Afghan eatery, diners can sit on the floor or at regular tables; dishes are wonderfully spiced and served with cool yogurt sauces. Service can be erratic, but the food is worth the wait. Open daily for dinner only. Reservations advised. Major credit cards accepted. 84 Pestalozzistr. (phone: 312-3472).

Lanna A friendly staff serves topnotch Thai food in this dimly lit, wood-paneled dining room. Try the octopus with basil and garlic, green curry chicken, or spicy Thai noodles. Open for dinner only; closed Sundays. Reservations advised (a few days in advance for Fridays and Saturdays). Major credit cards accepted. 4 Pfalzburger Str. (phone: 883-2373).

Lucky Strike Located just a few steps from the *Pergamon Museum,* this trendy eatery is Berlin's first foray into New Orleans–style cooking. Menu items include jambalaya, barbecued ribs, and seafood gumbo. An adjacent lounge features live jazz and blues by various artists. This spot is hopping well into the wee hours of the morning. Open daily; closed weekday lunch. Reservations advised. Major credit cards accepted. Georgestr., under the *S-Bahn* tracks (phone: 308-48822).

Müggelsee-Perle The fish, fowl, and game dishes are best; also try the Berlin pea soup. On the shore of the Grosser Müggelsee, the restaurant is accessible by excursion ship (see *Extra Special*) as well as by bus and car. Closed November through April. Reservations unnecessary. Major credit cards accepted. Am Grossen Müggelsee (phone: 65882).

Mundart In Kreuzberg, a former working class district that has gone arty, it features French cuisine, though Jacques, the imaginative chef, is no disciple of nouvelle. The decor, service, and excellent wines are also highly commendable. Open for dinner only; closed Mondays, Tuesdays, and July. Reservations advised. No credit cards accepted. 33-34 Muskauer Str. (phone: 612-2061).

November On the south bank of the Landwehrkanal, oppposite the *Neue Nationalgalerie,* this intimate, bistro-like place is a favorite of writers, artists, and others belonging to the cultural scene. The bohemian ambience is in charming contrast to the upmarket tone of the fare offered by an extremely obliging staff. Try the leg of lamb or game dishes. Open daily for dinner only. Reservations advised. Major credit cards accepted. 65 Schöneberger Ufer (phone: 261-3882).

Offenbach Stuben Intimate and cozy, this is one of the few eateries in the city's eastern section that always has been privately run. The German and continental fare are fine, as are the beverages. Closed Sundays and Mondays. Reservations necessary. Major credit cards accepted. 8 Stubbenkammerstr. (phone: 448-4106).

Osteria No. 1 Always crowded, this Italian eatery offers fine pasta, seafood, and meat dishes in a bright and cheerful dining room. The ravioli is excellent. Open daily. Reservations advised. Major credit cards accepted. 71 Kreuzbergstr. (phone: 786-9162).

Schipkapass A rustically decorated Czech eatery, featuring those two mainstays of every good Bohemian kitchen: Prague ham and pilsner beer. You can feast on the large portions. Open daily for dinner only. Reservations advised. No credit cards accepted. 185 Hohenzollerndamm (phone: 871941).

Shell Café For elegantly presented fare served all hours of the day, this centrally located eatery is a real find. Set in a former gas station (and named for the oil company), it features brunch with American-style bacon and eggs. Open daily. No reservations, but the place gets very crowded after 4 PM, so expect a wait. Major credit cards accepted. 22 Knesebeckstr. (phone: 312-8310).

Storch Alsatian specialities offered here include *Flammenkuchen,* a crispy flat pastry topped with cheese, ham, and onions; as a dessert, it's covered with cheese and apples, then drizzled with Calvados and flambéed. The big wooden tables make this a good choice for large groups. Open daily for dinner only. Reservations advised. No credit cards accepted. 54 Wartburgstr. (phone: 784-2059)

Terzo Mundo A favorite of actors and journalists, its menu features hearty Greek fare; there's often an entertainer who sings Greek folk songs. Open daily for dinner only. Reservations advised. Major credit cards accepted. 28 Grolmanstr. (phone: 881-5261).

Tres Kilos Berlin's only good Tex-Mex restaurant, it's a great spot for hot summer evenings; the open-air terrace overlooks the lively Marheinekeplatz, and the margaritas are first-rate. The dining rooms are filled to overflowing almost every night. Open daily for dinner only. Reservations advised. Major credit cards accepted. 3 Marheinekepl. (phone: 693-6044).

Tuk-Tuk Indonesian food served in a tropical setting. Friendly service and a large selection of vegetarian dishes make this place a Schöneberg favorite. Open daily for dinner only. Reservations advised. Major credit cards accepted. 2 Grossgörschenstr. (phone: 781-1588).

Weinstube am Savignyplatz Grilled steaks and fresh fish, complemented by a carefully chosen list of French wines, are served in a warm, candlelit dining room. Near the *Theater des Westens,* it's a fine choice for a pre- or post-theater dinner. Open for dinner only; closed Mondays. Reservations advised. Major credit cards accepted. Corner of Savignypl. and Kantstr. (phone: 313-8697).

Wirtshaus Schildhorn Steaks cooked on the grill are a specialty at this upscale beer garden and outdoor restaurant. With its lovely location—on a tiny peninsula by the Havel River—it is very popular in summer. Open daily. Reservations advised on summer weekends. Major credit cards accepted. 4A Am Schildhorn (phone: 305-3111).

Yukiguni A delicate pale-wood interior provides the perfect setting for the chef's artful versions of Japanese specialties. There's also an excellent sushi bar.

Closed Sunday lunch and Tuesdays. Reservations advised. Major credit cards accepted. 30 Kantstr. (phone: 312-1978).

INEXPENSIVE

El Bodegón This lively Spanish *finca,* featuring a wide range of Iberian dishes, is much frequented by students, musicians, and artists. The atmosphere is genuinely Iberian, including guitar music, chiefly flamenco. Open daily for dinner only. Reservations unnecessary. Major credit cards accepted. 61 Schlüterstr. (phone: 312-4497).

Brasserie You will find a true French bistro here. The decor, food, and wine are typical of the Gallic provinces. There also is a small enclosed terrace. Open daily. Reservations unnecessary. Major credit cards accepted. 3 Wittenbergpl. (phone: 218-5786).

Café Möhring This traditional German *Konditorei* has two locations in the city. Here you can enjoy rich cakes, light Danish pastry, and other wonders from their own bakery to go along with your coffee or tea. Light hot meals also are available. Open daily. Reservations unnecessary. No credit cards accepted. 213 Kurfürstendamm (phone: 881-2075) and 55 Charlottenstr. (phone: 209-02240).

Café Oren Located near the *Neue Synagoge,* this popular vegetarian eatery features innovatively prepared Eastern European and Israeli dishes. The soups, especially the yogurt and the borscht, are outstanding. A great place to stop while touring the Scheunenviertel, but be prepared to wait in a long line. Open daily. Reservations necessary on weekends. Major credit cards accepted. 28 Oranienburger Str. (phone: 282-8228).

Häagen-Dazs A refreshing taste from home, its name notwithstanding. The same good ice cream (you won't have any trouble translating from the German *Eiskrem*); ask for one *Kugel* (scoop) or two *Kugeln.* Open daily. Major credit cards accepted. 224 Kurfürstendamm (phone: 882-1207).

Hardtke Two traditional restaurants with traditionally hearty German food such as fresh *Leberwurst* and *Blutwurst.* All meat dishes come from its own butcher shops. The atmosphere is rustic and friendly. A very good value. Open daily. Reservations advised. Major credit cards accepted. 27 and 27B Meinekestr. (phone: 881-9827).

Hollandstüb'l Dutch fare, with the accent on dishes from the East Indies (*nasi goreng, rijsttafel,* and so on). The decor is a holdover from the 1920s, when this was one of Berlin's more popular restaurants. Open daily. No reservations. Major credit cards accepted. 11 Martin-Luther-Str. (phone: 218-8593).

India Haus A bit out of the way, this place is worth the detour for its better-than-average Indian food. The butter chicken and curried lamb are scrumptious. Open daily; closed weekday lunch. Reservations unnecessary. Major credit cards accepted. 38 Feurigstr., at the corner of Dominicusstr. (phone: 781-2546).

Jimmy's Diner Right out of *American Graffiti,* this spot in the heart of town is a larger-than-life replica of the good old American diner, complete with canned music piped in everywhere, even in the WC. The menu is what you'd expect: luscious cheeseburgers, coleslaw (the only place in town that serves it), pasta, salads, sandwiches, and steaks. For dessert, have a slice of apple pie and a cup of coffee. Open daily. No reservations, and it's crowded in the evening. Major credit cards accepted. 41 Pariser Str. (phone: 882-3141).

Kellerrestaurant im Brecht-Haus The decor may be downscale, but this dining spot in the eastern part of town is a great place to grab a bite. Classic Austrian fare and a jovial atmosphere are in abundance here, not to mention a bit of history—German playwright Bertolt Brecht spent the last 10 years of his life in the upstairs rooms. Try the Wiener schnitzel with fried potatoes. Dinner only; closed Sundays. Reservations advised. Major credit cards accepted. 125 Chausseestr. (phone: 282-3843).

Litfass Not far from the Kurfürstendamm and the famous *Schaubühne* theater is this unpretentious Portuguese place. Among the specialties are shark steaks and potted chicken in garlic sauce. Open daily for dinner only. No reservations. No credit cards accepted. 49 Sybelstr. (phone: 323-2215).

Luisen-bräu Locals flock here for the hearty, traditional German fare, including homemade sausages, cabbage soup, and house-brewed beer (the waiters will keep refilling your small mug until you put a coaster on top of it—that's the signal for "enough already"). In the summer, guests may dine alfresco on big picnic tables. There's no extra charge for the fine view of *Schloss Charlottenburg,* directly across the street. Open daily. Reservations unnecessary. No credit cards accepted. 1 Luisenpl. (phone: 341-0232).

Nordsee Fish is the only dish served in this conveniently located place in the city center. Seafood also reigns supreme (but at slightly higher prices) at *Rendezvous für Feinschmecker,* a fancy grill located a floor below street level in the same building and under the same ownership. Open daily. Reservations unnecessary. Major credit cards accepted. Spandauer Str., at the corner of Karl-Liebknecht-Str. (phone: 212-3296).

BERLIN BREAKFAST

The first meal of the day is an event in Berlin, especially on weekends. The typical Berlin café breakfast consists of a large plate overflowing with slices of Gouda and Camembert cheese, slices of ham, chunks of fruit, jam and butter, and little bowls of yogurt or a fluffy cream called *Quark.* You may also be served a soft-boiled egg and a basket of fresh bread and rolls. Another specialty is the *Bauernfrühstück* (farmer's breakfast), a hearty omelette made with potatoes, onions, and ham or bacon.

It's a real delight to linger over Sunday breakfast as the Berliners do—eating a bit, reading a bit, then eating some more, as the morning stretches into afternoon. Many places serve until 2 PM, so the meal makes for an ideal brunch or lunch as well. If you do decide to forgo your hotel breakfast one morning, here are a few suggestions. All open at 10 AM unless otherwise noted. None accept credit cards.

Café Einstein This grand homage to the Viennese coffeehouse is set in a palatial villa with an outdoor terrace in back. A favorite of the established arts community, it's more expensive than most cafés, but it's worth every pfennig. Try the eggs Florentine for breakfast. 58 Kurfürstenstr. (phone: 261-5096).

Café Tiago Inexpensive and popular with students. 9 Knesebeckstr. (phone: 312-9042).

Café Tomasa One of the best breakfast spots in town; serves until 4 PM. 60 Motzstr. (phone: 213-2345).

Operncafé An extensive breakfast buffet is served from 8:30 AM to 2 PM in a beautiful Old World setting. 5 Unter den Linden (phone: 200-2269).

Cologne

The most dramatic vantage point for a first-time view of Cologne is from the deck of a Rhine steamer sailing in to its riverside dock, near the city center. It is a view of lacy spires etched against the sky, incongruously delicate accents to the massive *Kölner Dom* (Cologne Cathedral), which dominates the city.

As the ship nears the shore, images come into sharper focus—the tree-lined riverside with its neat row of narrow three- and four-story slate-roofed houses, their façades painted white, vivid blue, yellow, or deep purple, with bright trim around windows and doors. Though it's lovely, Cologners confess that their Altstadt (Old City)—faithfully reconstructed into a pretty-as-a-picture-postcard version of the Cologne of long ago—is by no means symbolic of the vibrant, working class metropolis beyond.

It is the *Kölner Dom,* however, that commands your attention as the cruise liner docks. Cologne's image is indelibly tied to its great twin-spired, Gothic cathedral, the largest in Germany: Solemn and majestic, it is as well known as Chartres and Notre Dame de Paris. A masterpiece of ecclesiastical architecture, *Kölner Dom* first attracts and then enchants the first-time visitor; it was—and still is—the heart and soul of the city.

But Cologne is not only about its cathedral. It is probably best known for *eau de Cologne,* the scented toilet water first introduced here around 1705; based on an Italian formula, it was originally used for medicinal purposes only, in the treatment of various afflictions (gout, apoplexy, and ailments both real and imaginary), and, according to some healers, to counteract effects of the plague. Originally dubbed *L'eau admirable,* the best-known brand comes with a blue-and-gold label and the trademark 4711 (taken from the street number on the Glockengasse where the Mühlens family set up the first shop to market the product back in 1794). An indication of 4711's importance to Cologne's economy is the fact that the site of the original store (where 4711 products are still sold today) is a main stop on city sightseeing tours.

Cologne is also one of Europe's contemporary art centers, a status that dates from the end of World War I, when Hans Arp and Max Ernst introduced the avant-garde Dadaism movement here. In the early 1980s, a style that became known as neo-Expressionism created a sensation in Cologne; its art galleries exhibited such artists as Anselm Kiefer (whose works were later featured at New York City's *Museum of Modern Art*), George Baselitz, and Gerhard Richter, and postmodernists Sigmar Polke, Martin Kippenberger, and Rosemary Trockel. However, the major catalyst of Cologne's dominance in the modern art world was the 1986 opening of a new building for the *Wallraf-Richartz/Ludwig Museum,* with a large, significant collection of 20th-century art as well as exhibits dating from the 1300s.

Although some have accused the Cologne art market of sacrificing creativity to commercialism (Cologne has more galleries per square foot than any other city in Europe; see *Galleries*), the fact remains that many of the Continent's best contemporary artworks can be found here.

Cologne's beginnings can be traced back more than 2,000 years, when in 38 BC the invading Romans set themselves up along this stretch of the Rhine river. Its name comes from the Latin *colonia,* or "colony," the original name of the garrison. By the middle of the 1st century the settlement was accorded the rights of a Roman city under the name Colonia Claudia Ara Agrippinensis, incorporating the names of both the then-ruling emperor, Claudius, and his empress Agrippina, a Cologner, into the official title. The name would in time be shortened simply to Colonia, and, in German, to Köln.

For the next four centuries Cologne prospered in its role as the northeastern cornerstone of the Roman Empire. Traces of the urbanization of that period can be found in the Cologne of today: Large sections of original city walls remain, as well as parts of a 50-mile-long aqueduct that brought spring water to the city from the Eifel Hills. There are also remnants of underground sewage and drainage systems that are amazingly modern in concept. Cologne was linked to the empire's extensive road network; today the old Roman "high road," the main thoroughfare of Roman Cologne, lives on as the Hohe Strasse, the city's main pedestrian shopping mall.

Early in the Middle Ages the Romans were driven out by the Franks, who established a bishopric here. In the early 9th century under Charlemagne, the bishopric became an archbishopric; the Archbishops of Cologne evolved into Prince Electors of the Holy Roman Empire, ruling over all of the Rhineland. During the Middle Ages Cologne grew to be the largest city—as well as one of the richest and most powerful—in what is now Germany. Some 40,000 people lived within its four-mile semicircular city wall; the largest fortification of its time, it had 12 city gates. Gaining the status of a Hanseatic city on a par with the Baltic and North Sea ports of Hamburg and Lübeck, Cologne became the continent's major inland trading post, controlling traffic on the Rhine and selling its goods to points as distant as England, Sicily, and Scandinavia. Cologne held its first trade fair in 1360.

As a free imperial city in the Holy Roman Empire, Cologne minted its own coins and established its own army. The city's armorers, goldsmiths, and cloth makers became famous. Printing and publishing flourished. Martin Luther's Reformation passed Cologne by, however, and the city stayed a bastion of Catholicism within a predominantly Protestant part of Germany.

In 1794 French troops occupied Cologne and ruled for 20 years, only to be replaced by Prussian soldiers in 1815. In the 19th century, the Industrial Revolution propelled the city to the forefront of Germany's manufacturing centers: Private railway companies and Rhine ports established it as a major transportation hub. Late in the century, the city's area expanded to

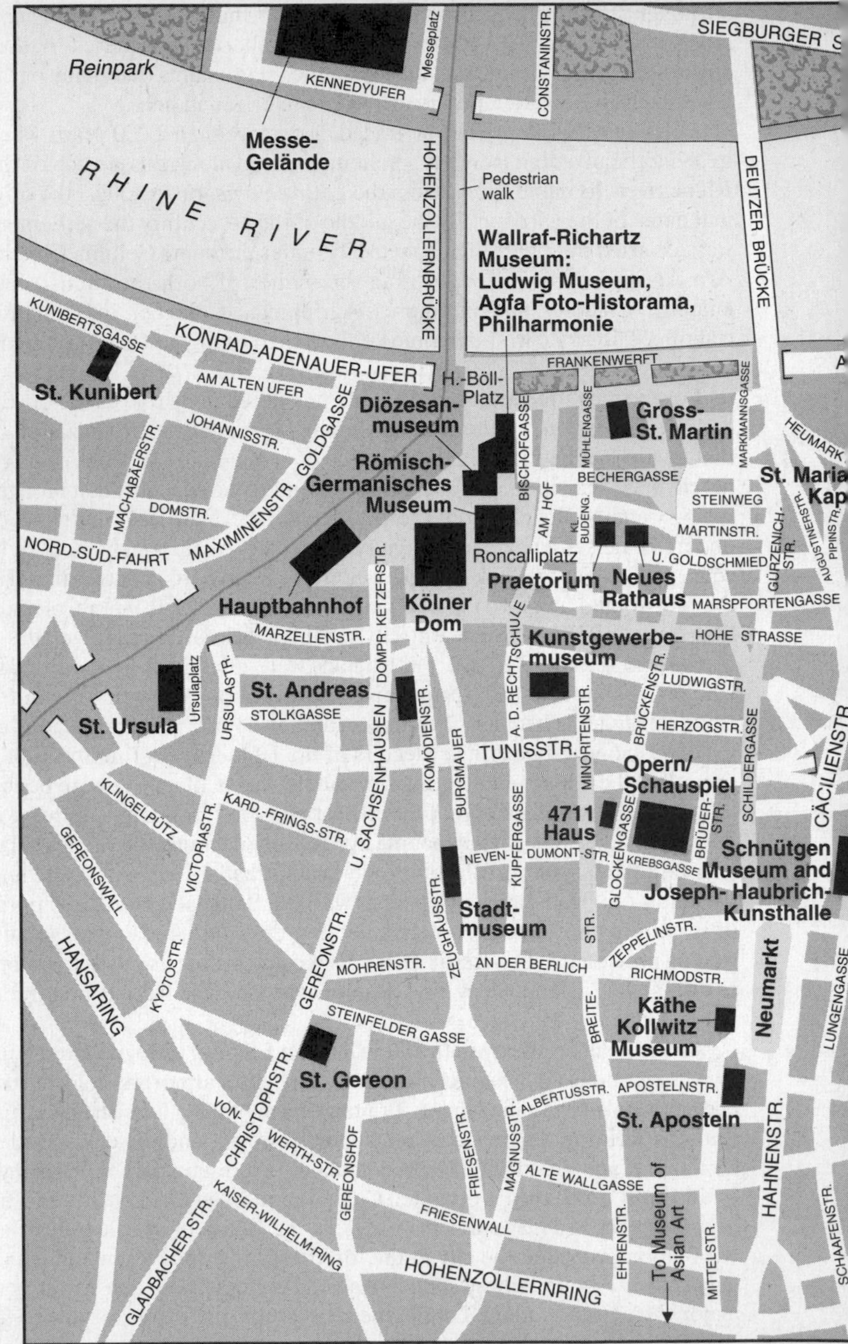

Reinpark
KENNEDYUFER
Messeplatz
CONSTANINSTR.
SIEGBURGER S
Messe-
Gelände
RHINE RIVER
HOHENZOLLERNBRÜCKE
Pedestrian
walk
DEUTZER BRÜCKE
Wallraf-Richartz
Museum:
Ludwig Museum,
Agfa Foto-Historama,
Philharmonie
KUNIBERTSGASSE
KONRAD-ADENAUER-UFER
FRANKENWERFT
St. Kunibert
AM ALTEN UFER
H.-Böll-
Platz
Diözesan-
museum
Gross-
St. Martin
JOHANNISSTR.
MACHABÄERSTR.
GOLDGASSE
MAXIMINENSTR.
Römisch-
Germanisches
Museum
BISCHOFGASSE
MÜHLENGASSE
MARKMANNSGASSE
HEUMARKT
St. Maria
Kap
BECHERGASSE
STEINWEG
DOMSTR.
AM HOF
KL. BUDENG.
MARTINSTR.
GÜRZENICH-STR.
AUGUSTINERSTR.
PIPINSTR.
NORD-SÜD-FAHRT
Roncalliplatz
U. GOLDSCHMIED
Praetorium
Neues
Rathaus
MARSPFORTENGASSE
Hauptbahnhof
Kölner
Dom
DOMPR.
KETZERSTR.
MARZELLENSTR.
A. D. RECHTSCHULE
Kunstgewerbe-
museum
HOHE STRASSE
Ursulaplatz
URSULASTR.
St. Andreas
LUDWIGSTR.
BRÜCKENSTR.
St. Ursula
STOLKGASSE
HERZOGSTR.
U. SACHSENHAUSEN
KOMÖDIENSTR.
BURGMAUER
TUNISSTR.
MINORITENSTR.
Opern/
Schauspiel
SCHILDERGASSE
CÄCILIENSTR.
KLINGELPÜTZ
KARD.-FRINGS-STR.
VICTORIASTR.
KUPFERGASSE
4711
Haus
GLOCKENGASSE
BRÜDER-STR.
GEREONSWALL
NEVEN-
DUMONT-STR.
KREBSGASSE
Schnütgen
Museum and
Joseph- Haubrich-
Kunsthalle
ZEUGHAUSSTR.
Stadt-
museum
STR.
ZEPPELINSTR.
GEREONSTR.
Neumarkt
HANSARING
KYOTOSTR.
MOHRENSTR.
AN DER BERLICH
RICHMODSTR.
LUNGENGASSE
STEINFELDER GASSE
BREITE-
Käthe
Kollwitz
Museum
St. Gereon
CHRISTOPHSTR.
ALBERTUSSTR.
APOSTELNSTR.
HAHNENSTR.
St. Aposteln
VON-
WERTH-STR.
FRIESENSTR.
MAGNUSSTR.
ALTE WALLGASSE
GEREONSHOF
KAISER-WILHELM-RING
FRIESENWALL
EHRENSTR.
To Museum of
Asian Art
MITTELSTR.
SCHAAFENSTR.
GLADBACHER STR.
HOHENZOLLERNRING

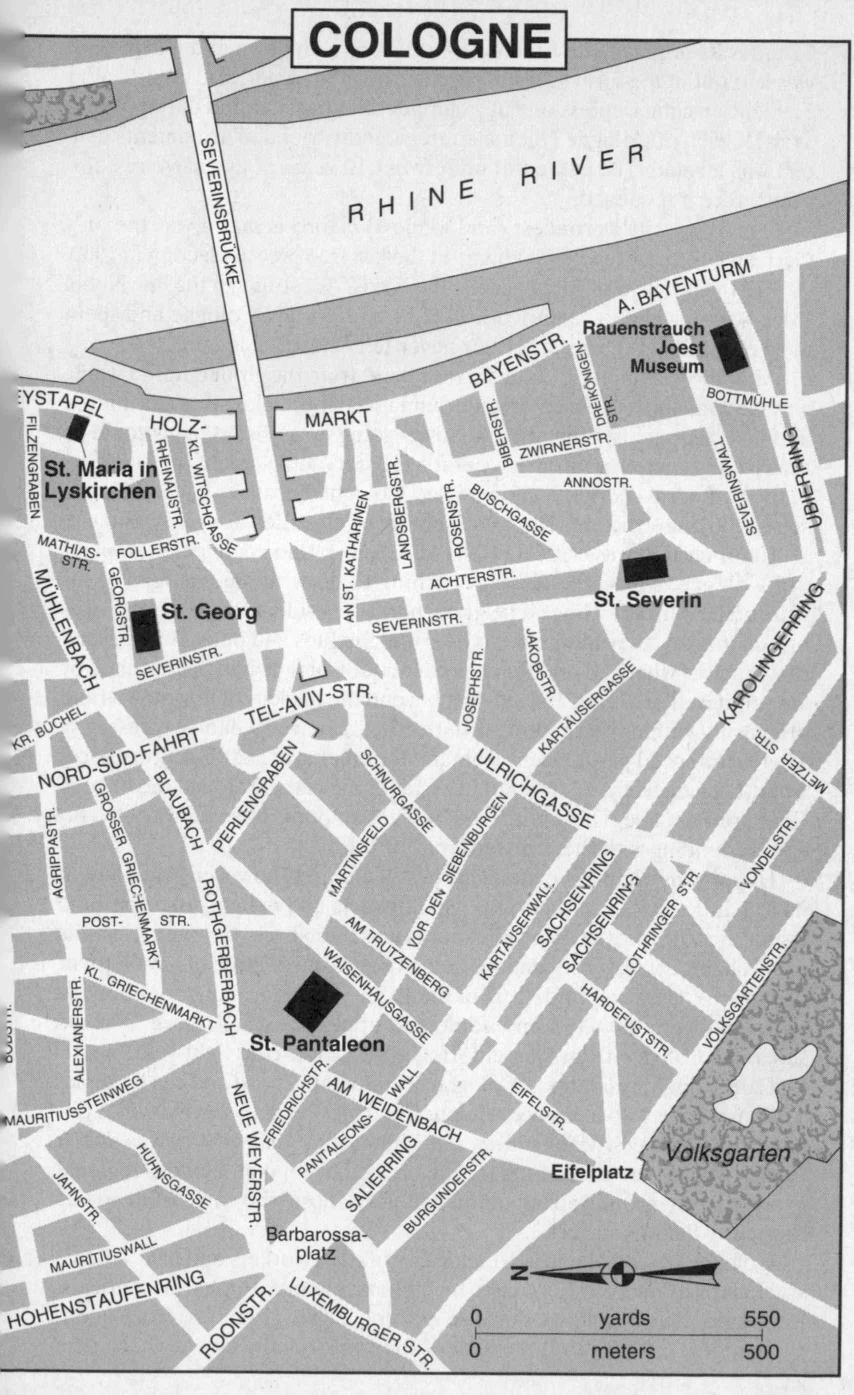
COLOGNE
RHINE RIVER
SEVERINSBRÜCKE
A. BAYENTURM
BAYENSTR.
Rauenstrauch Joest Museum
BOTTMÜHLE
DREIKÖNIGEN-STR.
ZWIRNERSTR.
BIBERSTR.
ANNOSTR.
UBIERRING
SEVERINSWALL
EYSTAPEL
HOLZ-
MARKT
FILZENGRABEN
St. Maria in Lyskirchen
RHEINAUSTR.
KL. WITSCHGASSE
BUSCHGASSE
ROSENSTR.
LANDSBERGSTR.
AN ST. KATHARINEN
MATHIAS-STR.
FOLLERSTR.
GEORGSTR.
MÜHLENBACH
St. Georg
ACHTERSTR.
St. Severin
SEVERINSTR.
KAROLINGERRING
JOSEPHSTR.
JAKOBSTR.
KARTÄUSERGASSE
TEL-AVIV-STR.
KR. BÜCHEL
NORD-SÜD-FAHRT
BLAUBACH
PERLENGRABEN
SCHNURGASSE
ULRICHGASSE
METZER STR.
AGRIPPASTR.
GROSSER GRIECHENMARKT
ROTHGERBERBACH
MARTINSFELD
VOR DEN SIEBENBURGEN
KARTÄUSERWALL
SACHSENRING
LOTHRINGER STR.
VONDELSTR.
POST-
STR.
AM TRUTZENBERG
WAISENHAUSGASSE
KL. GRIECHENMARKT
ALEXIANERSTR.
St. Pantaleon
HARDEFUSTSTR.
VOLKSGARTENSTR.
MAURITIUSSTEINWEG
NEUE WEYERSTR.
FRIEDRICHSTR.
AM WEIDENBACH
PANTALEONS-WALL
EIFELSTR.
Volksgarten
HUHNSGASSE
JAHNSTR.
SALIERRING
BURGUNDERSTR.
Eifelplatz
Barbarossa-platz
MAURITIUSWALL
HOHENSTAUFENRING
ROONSTR.
LUXEMBURGER STR.
N
0 yards 550
0 meters 500

11 times its original size. Medieval walls were torn down and a new town was laid out in the form of a semicircle around an inner core. World War I and the ensuing Depression put a damper on expansion, and during World War II, 95% of Cologne (then a strategic industrial and armaments center) was leveled. The cathedral underwent 10 years of extensive restoration before it reopened.

One of the city's proudest (and loudest) claims is that it was the only German city to actively resist Hitler. In the last free prewar election in 1932, 70% of the population voted against the Nazis. According to the late Nobel Prize–winning author Heinrich Böll (who was born in Cologne and spent most of his life in the city), "Hitler never felt comfortable here."

After the war, most of Cologne was rebuilt from the ground up—a whole new city was superimposed on the foundation of the old, all of it achieved as if in a race against time, with buildings going up as fast as plans could be drawn and concrete poured. Except for the storybook look of the buildings in the cathedral district, contemporary Cologne became a place of uninspired-looking structures that could hardly be classified as eye-pleasing.

Heinrich Böll was critical of just about everything connected to postwar Cologne, a place he felt had nothing to do with the Cologne of his youth. The Altstadt—once a neighborhood of residences and shops—was turned into an entertainment quarter of nightclubs and pubs. Böll insisted that much of what had once been great about Cologne had been ruined by the proliferation of cars. Indeed, just beyond the nucleus of downtown (and practically within the shadow of the cathedral) are six-lane expressways where cars speed past ancient Roman monuments at a 20th-century pace; a parking garage has been fitted in beneath the cathedral; and the bucolic Rhine promenade is now bordered by what amounts to a raceway of vehicles resounding with the incessant roar of traffic.

Happily, much of Cologne's charm still endures, however. And though its romantic-looking cathedral is what attracts and delights the first-time visitor, it is the spirit of its people that brings them back. Cologne residents are probably the least ostentatious and most relaxed of those of any German metropolis. Here one finds little of the stiffness and formality traditionally associated with the German middle and upper classes. A mere 25 miles separates Cologne from Düsseldorf, yet the cities seem light-years apart. Not surprisingly, residents of Cologne are straightforward and can be somewhat truculent, with a cocky confidence in their ability to survive under difficult circumstances. Many still speak a lilting Rhine dialect known as *Kölsch* (which is also the name of the locally brewed beer) that includes regional expressions remaining all but unintelligible to those who come from no farther away than Frankfurt.

Cologne has long been a dynamic city of hard workers and heavy industry. Factories turn out Ford cars, machinery, chemicals, pharmaceuticals, perfumes, and chocolates. Because it is only 28 km (17 miles) from Bonn, the national capital (until the turn of the century), the city has become a base for journalists and government officials; many foreign embassies, including Romania's, are located here as well. A large number of broadcasting companies are headquartered in Cologne, including WDR, the main German radio and television station; and RTL, Luxembourg's national radio and television station. And, like Hartford in the US, Cologne is the hub of the insurance industry in Germany; most of the country's top firms have offices here. Over the years, tens of thousands of foreign "guest workers" have swelled the city's labor force (the current population is 992,000). Cologne fairly bustles with activity: Seagoing vessels are loaded and unloaded at the city's huge inland ports; 10 major motorways feed into the ring road encircling the city; eight bridges span the Rhine; and 1,000 trains a day cross the Hohenzollernbrücke (Hohenzollern Bridge) near the cathedral. A major trade-fair city, Cologne hosts several hundred such events each year.

A magnet for business people and a haven for art aficionados, Cologne affords the visitor a little bit of everything. It has a reputation for being a good-time city, particularly during *Carnival;* the scent of its famous 4711 fills the air; *Kölner Dom* is a sightseer's delight; and with an even dozen magnificently restored Romanesque churches, numerous outstanding museums, and many impressive Roman ruins, Cologne is a delight for all the senses.

Cologne At-a-Glance

SEEING THE CITY

The best place for panoramic views of the cathedral and its surroundings is from the *Messeplatz* (trade fairgrounds) on the other side of the Rhine. You can walk there (about 10 minutes) across the Hohenzollernbrücke, the bridge near the cathedral, or take the ferry that offers shuttle service across the river from alongside the bridge. Expansive vistas also can be enjoyed from above, on the cable car that crosses the Rhine (departing from the *Flora U-Bahn* station). And for those who don't mind the climb, a view of the city on both sides of the Rhine, the river itself, and the surrounding countryside can be enjoyed from the top of the south tower of *Kölner Dom* (see *Special Places*)—a 509-step climb up a winding staircase (whew!).

SPECIAL PLACES

Though the cathedral is the core of Cologne, other sites, particularly the city's museums and Romanesque churches, also are worthy of note.

KÖLNER DOM (COLOGNE CATHEDRAL) This flamboyant cathedral, the heart and soul of the city, seems somehow both meticulously planned and spontaneously conjured up by a great sorcerer. The Romans chose this spot for a temple 2,000 years ago; an early Christian church was built and extended here in the 6th century; and a Carolingian cathedral, built by the Franks, replaced the original church in the 9th century. In 1248, Holy Roman Emperor Frederick II ordered work to begin on a splendid cathedral that would house relics of the Magi (which remain on display inside the golden shrine behind the altar). The construction continued in fits and starts over the centuries, but it was not until 1880—when the city was under Prussian rule—that the cathedral was finally completed.

Despite the delay, the structure was built in much the way that Frederick envisioned it. Every detail—arches, pillars, pointed gables, and sculptures—was fashioned after the original plans of Frederick's master builder. Its western façade is studded with statuary and intricate stone filigree. The cathedral reflects the Gothic tradition of making buildings ever taller and thinner, blurring the boundaries between sandstone and air, between heaven and earth. Slender flying buttresses shoulder the weight of the angular vaulting and allow the walls to be almost paper-thin, making the cathedral look like a fragile spider web laced with droplets of stone. When the finishing touches had been put on the 515-foot south tower in 1880, the cathedral—then the tallest structure in the world—was hailed as an architectural masterpiece.

The interior is no less splendid. Graced by a splendid vaulted nave, a massive Gothic choir, a high altar, and towering stained glass windows, it contains oak choir stalls carved around 1310 and the great 10th-century carved oak crucifix of Archbishop Gero (the oldest wooden crucifix north of the Alps). The huge altar triptych, *Adoration of the Three Wise Men,* is by Stefan Lochner, master of the 15th-century Cologne School. Be sure to visit the *Domschatz* (Cathedral Treasury), whose entrance is in the north transept. Here are some liturgical objects, including reliquaries, codices, gold-threaded vestments, finely carved ivory, and beautiful illuminated manuscripts; also here is the silver shrine of Archbishop Engelbert, who was murdered in 1225. Open daily. Admission charge to the treasury and the tower. Dompl. (phone: 244546).

RÖMISCH-GERMANISCHES MUSEUM (ROMAN-GERMANIC MUSEUM) Housing the finest repository of remains from the far-flung Roman Empire in Germany, this ultramodern, white stone building was opened in 1974 primarily to showcase the Dionysus Mosaic, a mosaic floor from the dining area of a Roman merchant's 3rd-century villa. (In 1941, workmen digging an air-raid shelter alongside the cathedral happened upon the mosaic.) Further digs in the area unearthed such treasures as a triumphal chariot, frescoes, and statuary, as well as household items, including glassware, ceramics, coins, and jewelry. All are handsomely displayed throughout the three-story building, but the highlight is the vast floor (showcased on the museum's lower level), which features millions of tiny stones and pieces of glass depicting Dionysus, the god of wine, surrounded by representations of mythical figures, along with animals, fish, fowl, and fruit. Examine it up close and then from the second-floor gallery to best appreciate its harmony of colors, variety of geometric designs, and exquisite detail. The other major attraction is the enormous pillared tomb of the legionnaire Lucius Poblicius (from about AD 40); the three-story tomb was discovered in 1960 by two Cologne men digging in their backyard. Closed Mondays. Admission charge. 4 Roncallipl. (phone: 221-4590).

DIÖZESANMUSEUM (DIOCESAN MUSEUM) Operated by the Cologne archdiocese, this museum of medieval sacred art—housed in a well-lit, modern building alongside the *Römisch-Germanisches Museum*—displays jewelry from the tombs of Frankish princes, discovered during excavations beneath the cathedral. Among the masterpieces here is the exquisite *Madonna and Child* by Stefan Lochner. Closed Thursdays. Admission charge. 2 Roncallipl. (phone: 257-7672).

WALLRAF-RICHARTZ/LUDWIG MUSEUM In a modern building housing several diverse art collections—from Gothic to contemporary—this museum includes exhibits from Cologne's first museum of art, founded in 1824. On display here are canvases of the Cologne School; major examples of the Gothic period, including works by such German masters as Cranach the Elder and Albrecht Dürer; paintings by Stefan Lochner (note his luminous *Madonna in the Rose Garden*); Dutch panel paintings; and the works of the Flemish masters (such as Rubens and Franz Hals), Italy's Old Masters (Tiepolo, Canaletto), and the giants of the French period (Renoir, Monet, and Cézanne). The *Ludwig Collection,* a gift of chocolate magnate Peter Ludwig, is devoted entirely to 20th-century art, including important works by Picasso, Braque, Gris, and German Expressionist painters such as Max Beckman and Ernst-Ludwig Kirchner. Another collection, the *Agfa Foto-Historama,* boasts just about everything related to photography, including cameras and various types of photo equipment—lenses, projectors, viewers—and photographs from all periods. There also are temporary exhibits by such photographers as Henri Cartier-Bresson, Bill Brandt, and Marc Riboud. *Note:* Consult the schematic diagrams of the building in the front foyer to best chart your course through the museum. Closed Mondays. Admission charge. 1 Bischofsgartenstr. (phone: 221-2379).

ROMAN COLOGNE Few places in Europe hold so many excellent artifacts from the era of their erstwhile conquerors. To see one of the city's most notable Roman sites (not on the regular bus-tour routes), walk south from Domplatz (Cathedral Square) along the onetime main north-south Roman road (now Hohe Strasse, the city's main pedestrians-only shopping street). After two short blocks, turn left on Grosse Budengasse to Kleine Budengasse, a cobblestone alleyway running off to the left along the rear of the *Neues Rathaus* (New Town Hall; built in 1953). A full city block below street level, at the bottom of a long flight of steps, are a palace and the *Praetorium* (the Roman city government headquarters) with large sections of foundations and partial standing walls, along with an entrance to the city sewage system. Glass cases along the sides display Roman artifacts, including household objects and small stone sculptures. Closed Mondays. Admission charge. No street number; entrance is directly across from the well-signed *Oldtimer Bar* on Kleine Budengasse (phone: 221-2394).

On the other side of the Domplatz, along the Komödienstrasse, walk west away from the Rhine to see ruins of the original Roman walls, which roughly follow the modern roadway. Continue under the overpass a few short blocks to the corner of Zeughausstrasse (near the *SAS Royal* hotel) to Cologne's most remarkable structure from Roman times: a beautifully restored, complete Roman tower from AD 50 (not open to the public).

ROMANESQUE CHURCHES Cologne is known as the "Rome of the North" and the "Holy City" because of its lordly Rhineland Romanesque churches, most built between 1150 and 1250. Romanesque style predates the towering spires of Gothic architecture and is typified by such design features as blind arcades, round, squat towers, and roofs shaped like bishop's miters. All of the following 12 churches were severely damaged (or destroyed) during World War II, but over a 40-year period they have been painstakingly restored. Roman Catholic services are held in most of these churches; check with the tourist office for schedules.

St. Andreas Easily recognizable by its octagonal-shape lantern tower, this parish church and Dominican monastery, built in 1225 and still in use today, has a choir that dates from the late Gothic period. Its nave and west side boast a fine collection of late Romanesque architectural sculpture. West of the cathedral off Komödienstr.

St. Aposteln Located at Neumarkt (New Marketplace) in the heart of central Cologne on what had been the medieval route to Aachen, this massive triple-towered 11th-century structure rates as a masterpiece of Rhineland Romanesque architecture and is considered the most beautiful of Cologne's churches.

St. Cäcilien This unpretentious, flat-roofed mid-12th-century building with a Romanesque pillared basilica has been desanctified and converted into the *Schnütgen Museum.* Its collection includes Romanesque and Gothic sacred sculpture—miniatures in ivory, gold, and bronze—along with stained glass, liturgical objects, and a medieval wooden crucifix. Closed Mondays. Admission charge. 29 Cäcilienstr. (phone: 221-2310).

St. Georg A former seminary, its interior boasts a crucifix from the early 14th century. In the *Waidmarkt,* on Georgstr.

St. Gereon Part of this vast structure dates from the late Roman classical period (4th century). Twin towers and a high dome with ribbed vaults and flying buttresses were added in the 12th century. Inside are frescoes and a Renaissance altarpiece designed in Gothic style. Go down into the crypt to view the 11th-century mosaic floor. Off the Christophstrasse, due west of the *Kölner Dom.*

St. Kunibert Overlooking the Rhine, north of the cathedral quarter, this 13th-century church boasts some of Germany's most beautiful stained glass windows in its choir and transept.

St. Maria im Kapitol Built on the foundation walls of the Roman Capitol, this huge 11th-century church has a cloverleaf choir modeled on the one in the Church of the Nativity in Bethlehem. Note the remarkable wooden doors, with 26 reliefs illustrating the life of Christ, and the 12th-century stone sculpture of the Virgin Mary.

St. Maria in Lyskirchen On the Rhine south of the Deutzer Brücke (Deutzer Bridge), the vaults of this small church contain a series of renowned 13th-century paintings of scenes from the Old and New Testaments.

Gross St. Martin Near the Rhine in the Altstadt just south of the cathedral, this fortress-like church with its imposing square tower rimmed with four smaller towers has been a commanding presence on the city skyline for generations, second only in impact to the *Kölner Dom.*

St. Pantaleon The city's oldest Romanesque church (started in the 10th century) features a late Gothic roodscreen (a screen that separates the chancel from the nave). An elegantly arched treasury contains two Romanesque shrines. Located in a southwest district of central Cologne near a popular park, the *Volksgarten.*

St. Severin Excavations beneath the church reveal remains of four preceding buildings that occupied this spot (the first known incarnation was a 4th-century Roman graveyard). The excavations can be visited on guided tours (in German only) Mondays and Fridays at 4:30 PM. Admission charge. Severinstr. (phone: 316870).

St. Ursula This Romanesque church was built in 1135 on the site of a Roman graveyard, resting place of virgin martyrs. Later, relics of the saints were collected and put on display in the great Baroque-style *Golden Chamber,* which is open to visitors Mondays and Thursdays from 11 AM to noon; Wednesdays and Fridays from 3 to 4 PM; and Saturdays from 4 to 5 PM. Admission charge. Located north of *St. Andreas* on Ursulapl.

Sources and Resources

TOURIST INFORMATION

The *Cologne Tourist Office* (19 Unter Fettenhennen; phone: 221-3345; fax: 221-3320), offering English-language brochures, booklets, and maps for a small fee, is open daily.

LOCAL COVERAGE *Köln Monatsvorschau,* a monthly German-language publication available at the tourist office, lists special events plus opening hours of churches and museums and starting times for guided tours of the city.

TELEPHONE The city code for Cologne is 221.

GETTING AROUND

The cathedral quarter (including *Kölner Dom*), the major museums, the Altstadt, and the Rhine promenade can easily be covered on foot. (Most streets follow the straight grid pattern originally plotted by the Romans.) Walking is the best way to reach many of the city's notable Romanesque churches, too, although visits to *St. Severin, St. Pantaleon, St. Cäcilien, St. Gereon,* and *St. Aposteln* are a subway ride away.

AIRPORT *Flughafen Köln-Bonn* (Cologne-Bonn Airport; phone: 2203-404001 for flight information), 12 miles (17 km) southeast of the city at Wahn, is connected to Cologne by city bus No. 170, which leaves every 20 minutes from the *Hauptbahnhof* (main railway station) near the cathedral.

BOAT During the warm-weather months, steamer cruises on both the Rhine and the Mosel leave from the docks directly in front of the Altstadt between the Hohenzollern and Deutzer Bridges. Rhine cruises are organized by *Köln-Düsseldorfer Deutsche Rheinschiffahrt* (15 Frankenwerft; phone: 20880). Mosel trips are run by *Köln Tourist-Personenschiffahrt* (Konrad-Adenauer-Ufer; phone: 121600). Sightseeing excursions and evening cruises on the Rhine also are offered by *Dampfschiffahrt Colonia* (18 Lintgasse; phone: 257-4225). Longer Rhine cruises—including weekend trips between Cologne and Frankfurt and Cologne and Strasbourg, France—can be booked in advance through *KD River Cruises of Europe* (170 Hamilton Ave., Suite 317, White Plains, NY 10601; phone: 914-948-3600).

CABLE CAR From *Easter* through October a cable car runs daily between the *Flora U-Bahn* station and the *Rheinpark* (across the Rhine from the cathedral), offering scenic views of the cathedral quarter and the sprawling Rhineland city beyond. Take *U-Bahn* 5, 16, or 18 from *Hauptbahnhof* to the *Flora* station.

CAR RENTAL *Avis* (29 Clemensstr.; phone: 234333), *Hertz* (19-21 Bismarckstr.; phone: 515084), *EuropCar-InterRent* (2 Christophstr.; phone: 132071), and *Sixt Budget* (38 Weisshausstr.; phone: 414026) have offices in the city, as well as counters at the airport.

SUBWAY AND TRAM Cologne is served by an extensive network of *U-Bahn* and *S-Bahn* routes, going underground through the city center, aboveground beyond. A zone-based pricing system—the greater the distance the higher the price—is used, but there are various discount schemes, such as one-day (5 DM/$3) and three-day (7 DM/$4.20) passes. There's a traveler's information center at 25 Neumarkt (phone: 547-4646; 547-3333 for 24-hour information).

TAXI Cab stands can be found at the airport, the railway station, and major hotels. For 24-hour service, call 2882 or 212231.

TOURS From April to October, *ETRAV* (7-11 Steinweg; phone: 258-0791) offers guided bus tours of the city several times daily; they depart from the cathedral quarter next to the tourist office (see *Tourist Information*).

TRAIN The *Hauptbahnhof* (main train station; phone: 19419) is directly north of the cathedral, with trains connecting to all parts of Germany and the rest of Europe.

SPECIAL EVENTS

The most important annual event in Cologne is *Carnival,* considered to be Germany's most colorful celebration—even wilder than Munich's better-known *Oktoberfest.* The buildup to the *Drei Tolle Tage* (Three Mad Days) prior to *Lent* actually begins on *New Year's Eve,* when a fancy dress ball is held (the first of more than 300 that take place between the beginning of the year and *Lent*). On the last Thursday before *Lent,* taverns stay open around the clock, and the spirit of *Carnival* reigns in the streets, public squares, and beer halls. The highlight is the Monday before *Lent*—known as *Rosenmontag* (Rose Monday)—when a parade of gaily decorated floats, 60 marching bands, and a sea of costumed revelers, all led by the three main *Carnival* figures—Prince, Peasant, and Maiden—pass in review before crowds that number in the hundreds of thousands.

Other annual events include the *International Kölner Sechs Tage Radrennen* (International Cologne Six-Day Bicycle Race) in January and summer music concerts (folk, pop, jazz, and rock) on weekends at the *Rheinpark* (across the Rhine from the cathedral). The city also hosts numerous trade fairs, including *Photokina,* one of the photography industry's best-known fairs (in September), and *Art Cologne,* an international art trade fair (in November) that draws dealers from around the world.

MUSEUMS

In addition to those listed in *Special Places,* several other museums in Cologne are worth a visit. All have admission charges.

IMHOFF-STOLLWERCK MUSEUM The city's newest and most unusual museum, devoted to the history and production of chocolate, is the brainchild of Hans Imhoff, head of the Stollwerck Chocolate Company. The cultivation of the cocoa plant and the processing of its "fruit" into chocolate (both past and present methods) are described in various displays; the roles of this mouth-watering sweet throughout history are also explored. There's also a machine that dispenses chocolate in various forms, as well as the mother of all temptations: a fountain that spouts warm melted chocolate. Open daily. Set in the former *Customs House,* at Rheinau Harbor (phone: 931-8880).

JOSEF HAUBRICH KUNSTHALLE (JOSEF HAUBRICH ART GALLERY) This spacious gallery offers temporary exhibits with such international themes as "Romans on the Rhine" and "State and Temple Treasures." In the same building, the *Köln Kunstverein* (Cologne Art Association) mounts contemporary art exhibits, including painting, sculpture, and photography. *Josef Haubrich Kunsthalle* is open daily; the *Köln Kunstverein* is closed Mondays. Josef Haubrich Hof (phone: 221-2335).

KÄTHE KOLLWITZ MUSEUM A collection of over 200 sculptures, sketches, and prints by this renowned artist. Closed Mondays. 18-24 Neumarkt (phone: 227-2899).

KUNSTGEWERBEMUSEUM (MUSEUM OF APPLIED ART) Located in the building that formerly housed the *Wallraf-Richartz/Ludwig Museum,* the collection (mostly by local artists) consists of some 30,000 items, including clothing, jewelry, household objects, furnishings, ceramics, and artwork from the past 200 years. Closed Mondays. An der Rechtschule (phone: 221-2995).

OSTASIEN KUNSTMUSEUM (MUSEUM OF EAST ASIAN ART) Assembled from private donations are the arts of China, Japan, and Korea, including Buddhist paintings and sculpture, Chinese stone objects dating from as far back as the 6th century, and Japanese wood sculpture, scrolls, ceramics, lacquerwork, and silk screens. Closed Mondays. 100 Universitätsstr. (phone: 405038).

RAUTENSTRAUCH JOEST MUSEUM This museum of ethnology displays art and artifacts of cultures from around the world, including those of pre-Columbian America, Africa, North American Indians, and the Far East. Closed Mondays. 45 Ubierring (phone: 311065).

STADTMUSEUM (MUNICIPAL MUSEUM) Housed in a building erected around 1600 as the city arsenal, this museum was established to serve as "the city's memory." Its two floors display artifacts, documents, and household objects depicting local industries, art, science, and customs of leisure. Closed Mondays. 1-3 Zeughausstr. (phone: 221-2352).

GALLERIES

In general, this Rhine city is not known for its shopping; in fact, even locals head for nearby Düsseldorf (25 miles/40 km away) when they're in the mood to browse. Cologne has branches of the major national department stores, *Kaufhof* (Hohe Str.; phone: 2251) and *Karstadt* (103 Breite Str.; phone: 20391), but aside from picking up a souvenir flask of 4711 Eau de Cologne, you won't find much else to interest you—that is, unless you're an art lover. In recent years Cologne has emerged as the contemporary art capital of Europe; chockablock with galleries, it is a treasure trove for true collectors—even though prices are on the high side. The most prestigious of these galleries tend to specialize in contemporary German art and sculpture, much of it produced by émigrés from the former East Germany. The monthly *Vorschau* (see *Tourist Information*) lists more than 30 private galleries mounting exhibitions. For standard shopping hours, see GETTING READY TO GO.

Our favorite haunts include *Amerika-Haus* (13-15 Apostelnkloster; phone: 311-6500); *Artothek* (50 Am Hof; phone: 221-2332); *Galerie im Atelier Theater* (78 Roonstr.; phone: 463-9111); *Galerie Baukunst* (7 Theodor Heuss Ring; phone: 771-3335); *Galerie Boisseree* (7-11 Drususgasse; phone: 603-9191); *Galerie Carla Stützer* (21 Kamekestr.; phone: 518214); *Galerie Inge Baecker* (13 Zeughausstr.; phone: 257-0401); *Galerie Janine Mautsch* (15-17 Ehrenstr.; phone: 256902); *Galerie Johannes Schilling* (2-4 Breite Str.; phone: 257-8538); *Galerie Karsten Greve* (3 Wallrafpl.; phone: 257-1012); *Galerie Kunsthandwerk* (12 Heumarkt; phone: 311-4050); *Galerie Michael Werner* (24-28 Gertrudenstr.; phone: 925-4620); *Galerie Rolf Ricke* (10 Volksgartenstr.; phone: 315717); *Galerie der Spiegel* (328 Bonner Str.; phone: 385799); *Galerie Ucher* (39 Grosser Griechenmarkt; phone: 215956); *Kunsthandlung Goyert* (18 Hahnenstr.; phone: 389-6454); *Kunsthaus Lempertz* (3 Neumarkt; phone: 396-2414); *Kölner Maler Kreis* (33 Meiningstr.; phone: 903603); *Naive Kunst Galerie Marianne Kühn* (5 Roteichenweg; phone: 221-3989); and *Olaf Clasen Gallerie* (17-21 St. Apern Str.; phone: 252104).

SPORTS AND FITNESS

Though not as much of a sportmen's haven as Munich or Berlin, Cologne has plenty of facilities for athletic pursuits.

FITNESS CENTERS Fully equipped centers include *Freizeit und Fitness Center* (51 Trierer Str.; phone: 216253); *Sport Center Fit Cologne* (30-32 Neusser Str.; phone: 779392); *Sportstudio Brinkmeier* (76 Aachener Str.; phone: 527513); and *Sport Studio Nord* (26 Neusser Str.; phone: 720070). There's also a sauna, a solarium, and massage facilities at the *Eis- und Schwimmstadion* (30 Lentstr.; phone: 726026).

ICE SKATING The *Eis- und Schwimmstadion* (see *Fitness Centers*) has an ice rink and skates for rent.

JOGGING Both the Rhine Promenade and the *Rheinpark* (across the Rhine from the cathedral) are ideal venues for walking, jogging, and running. Other greenbelts are somewhat farther afield, such as the *Stadtwald,* on the western edge of the city, which has plenty of jogging and walking trails.

SWIMMING The *Müngersdorfer Stadion* (Aachener Str.; phone: 693-5430) offers a variety of facilities, including a heated outdoor pool; it's closed October through April. Take *U-Bahn* No. 1 toward Junkersdorf and get off at the next-to-last stop, marked *Stadion.* There's also a heated pool with a water slide at the *Eis- und Schwimmstadion* (see *Fitness Centers*).

TENNIS Two of the more centrally located facilities are *Tennis INN* (325 Aachener Str.; phone: 407964) and *Tennishalle Bell* (57 Wilhelm Mauser Str.; phone: 583800). There are also tennis courts in the *Müngersdorfer Stadium* (see *Swimming*).

THEATER

In a modern building on Offenbachplatz, the *Kölner Schauspiele* (Cologne Theater Company; phone: 221-8400) performs original works and hosts visiting drama groups, including those offering English-language productions. Other small theaters are *Theater der Keller* (6 Kleingedankstr.; phone: 318059); *Theater am Dom* (2 Glockengasse; phone: 258-0153); *Bühne 48* (48 Aachener Str.; phone: 318059); *Kabarett* (24 Gertrudestr.; phone: 242101); *Kleine Komödie* (Turiner Str.; phone: 122552); *Atelier Theater* (78 Roonstr.; phone: 242485); and *Comedia Colonia* (7-9 Löwengasse; phone: 247670). For general information about theater performances in Cologne and information about scheduled English-language productions, call these box offices: *Theaterkasse am Neumarkt* (phone: 214232) and *Theaterkasse in Kaufhof* (phone: 216692 or 217692).

MUSIC

The *Oper der Stadt Köln* (Cologne State Opera), one of Germany's finest companies, offers a richly rounded repertoire. It occupies the same building as the *Kölner Schauspiele* (see *Theater,* above). The renowned *Köln Gürzenich* orchestra and many visiting ensembles perform in the *Philharmonie,* a huge underground concert hall in the *Wallraf-Richartz/Ludwig Museum* complex (1 Bischofsgartenstr.; phone: 204080). *Köln Ticket* (phone: 2801), the *Philharmonie* ticket and information office, is located on Roncalliplatz between the cathedral and the *Römisch-Germanisches Museum.*

NIGHTCLUBS AND NIGHTLIFE

Cologne has a fairly active night scene, much of it concentrated in the Altstadt, with jazz cellars, discos, strip joints, revues, gambling clubs, pick-up bars, and seemingly countless *Kneipen,* the intimate beer bars spread from one end of the city to the other.

But if it's local color you're after, check out the old-fashioned beer taverns. Cologners are as loyal to these as Londoners are to their favorite pubs. There are still some 30 small breweries in Cologne and each one runs its own tavern, featuring *Kölsch,* a light and tasty local brew that is fairly low in alcohol but high on locals' list of favorites. Taverns are virtually devoid of decoration: One sits at long, plain, scrubbed wooden tables; no-nonsense waiters known as *Köbes* tend to be brash and familiar, and to speak in *Kölsch,* a Cologne dialect unintelligible to Berliners and New Yorkers alike. Favorites among the taverns are *Sion* and *Früh am Dom,* not only for good beer and plenty of traditional atmosphere, but also for first-rate regional fare at reasonable prices (see *Eating Out* for details on both).

Jazz, particularly the old-time, two-beat rhythm of Dixieland, is popular here: The best-known club is *Papa Joe's Jazzlokal em Streckstrump* (37 Buttermarkt; phone: 217950), with a different band playing every night. On Sundays from 11 AM to mid-afternoon it offers *Jazzfrühschoppen,* a brunch accompanied by a jazz band. Under the same management is *Papa Joe's Biersalon Klimperkasten* (50-52 Alter Markt; phone: 216759) in Altstadt. Here, in a room decorated in memorabilia of the Gay '90s, a piano player belts out barrelhouse, boogie-woogie, and show tunes. Sunday midday jazz sessions are featured at *Küppers Biergarten* (157 Alteburger Str.; phone: 373242) and the *Biergarten* of the *Hyatt Regency* hotel (see *Checking In*). *Atelier am Dom* (in the *Dom* hotel; see *Checking In*) features "After Shopping" jazz on Saturday afternoons. In summer, *Tanzbrunnen Rheinterrassen* (1 Rheinparkweg; phone: 887381) holds a "Moonlight Party" dance every Saturday night that lasts until the wee hours of Sunday morning.

Nightclubs with shows and striptease include *Chez Nous* (13 Grosse Budengasse; phone: 217029); *Coconut Grove* (5 Salzgasse; phone: 217604); and *Moulin Rouge "Tingel Tangel"* (68 Maastrichter Str.; phone: 262601). On Friday and Saturday nights the old waiting room of the *Hauptbahnhof* is converted into a popular disco, *Alter Wartesaal* (phone: 133061). Other popular discos include *Bierdorf* (Neue Langgasse; phone: 248989); *Das Ding* (30-34 Hohenstaufenring; phone: 246348); and *Disko 42* (22 Hohenstaufenring; phone: 247971).

Best in Town

CHECKING IN

As is typical in popular German trade-fair cities, Cologne's hotel rates tend to be high. However, also typical of hotels catering to the business traveler, special weekend discount packages are available. Package deals also are available during July and August. For a double room (including breakfast, unless otherwise indicated) in hotels we have listed as expensive, expect to pay between $270 and $400 per night; in places we describe as moderate, $160 to $270; and in places in the inexpensive category, less than $160. Most of Cologne's major hotels have complete facilities for the business traveler. Those hotels listed below as having "business services" usually offer such conveniences as English-speaking concierge, meeting rooms, photocopiers, computers, translation services, and express checkout, among others. Call the hotel for additional information. All telephone numbers are in the 221 city code unless otherwise indicated.

For an unforgettable experience in Cologne, we begin with our favorite, followed by our cost and quality choices of accommodations, listed by price category.

A ROOM AT THE TOP

Dom A temple of extravagance, this outstanding 126-room property is brazenly close to the cathedral that is Cologne's spiritual center. All guests—who in the past have included well-heeled celebrities and well-oiled sheikhs—are indulged by a staff of consummate professionals. Choose a room on the Domplatz (Cathedral Square), so you can study the Gothic spires over breakfast in bed in the morning and listen to the pedestrian bustle percolate into the hotel's patrician repose in the evening. Also on the premises is the charming winter garden restaurant *Atelier am Dom* and a congenial bar. Business services are available. 2 Domkloster (phone: 20240; fax: 202-4444).

EXPENSIVE

Excelsior Ernst On the opposite side of the cathedral from the *Dom* hotel, this 160-room grande dame has a skylit atrium in the lobby, and there's a stunning circular marble staircase. Most of the rooms in the recently renovated wing are bright and spacious, with large marble baths; those in front look out on the twin spires. Note that some rooms in the older section can be fairly plain and somewhat cramped. *Die Hansestube,* the hotel's elegant restaurant, offers a changing continental menu. Business services are available. Dompl. (phone: 2701; fax: 135150).

Hotel im Wasserturm Once the largest water tower in Europe, this property was transformed into a luxurious 12-story jewel box of a hotel. The 90 rooms are wedge shape (as would be expected from a circular structure), but the ultramodern decor (African hardwoods with the coarse earthiness of burnt brick) is extremely attractive, and the location—in the heart of the Altstadt—can't be beat. With a staff of 130, service is second to none, and the *Restaurant im Wasserturm* on the top floor serves international specialties. Reduced-rate weekend packages are offered year-round. Breakfast is not included. Business services are available. 2 Kaygasse (phone: 20080; fax: 200-8888).

Hyatt Regency Few places are as popular as this property on the far side of the Rhine. Many visitors come for a stroll through its three-story glass atrium—with a 15-foot waterfall and lush greenery—which affords spectacular views of the Cologne skyline, or for a bite in the *Glashaus* restaurant. The 300 spacious rooms have functional furnishings, but the big attractions are the facilities: a fitness club, a gym, an indoor pool, a whirlpool, a sauna, a Roman steambath, a solarium, and a massage room. There are discount weekend packages. Breakfast is not included. Business services are available. 2a Kennedy-Ufer (phone: 828-1234; 800-233-1234; fax: 828-1370).

SAS Royal Located just outside the cathedral quarter, this 290-room establishment offers a high level of service and spacious, comfortable rooms. Amenities include a pool, a solarium, a massage room, a restaurant, and a popular bar. Summer and weekend packages are offered. Breakfast is not included. Business services are available. 14 Helenenstr. (phone: 2280; 800-327-0200; fax: 228-1301).

MODERATE

Dorint Good value is the hallmark of this off-the-beaten-path property. On the edge of the city center, its exterior is plain and its lobby and public areas are without grandeur, although there's a cheerful winter garden lobby. The 103 rooms are big and bright with pleasant furnishings, and there is a restaurant. There are special weekend packages. Breakfast is not included. Business services are available. 44-48 Friesenstr. (phone: 16140; fax: 161-4100).

Eden Centrally located, this 33-room, family-run hostelry is pleasantly furnished; some rooms feature cathedral views. There's no restaurant, but business services are available. 18 Am Hof (phone: 258-0491; fax: 258-0495).

Haus Lyskirchen This downtown place with a touch of country-inn charm (a gabled façade, a wood-paneled restaurant) has 95 sleek, functional rooms. Facilities include a pool and sauna. Business services are available. 26-32 Filzengraben (phone: 20970; fax: 209-7718).

Königshof There are 85 comfortable rooms (some with cathedral views) in this centrally located property. Its fairly plain exterior belies its dazzling public areas, including a chic bar. There's no restaurant. Business services are available. 14-16 Richartzstr. (phone: 234883; fax: 238642).

REMA-Europa Ideally located (ask for a room with a cathedral view), this elegant 100-room hostelry (formerly *Europa am Dom*) is Bauhaus-style on the outside, Biedermeier (a common style of furnishings popular in post-Napoleonic Germany) on the inside. There's also a first-rate restaurant, *Ambiance am Dom* (see *Eating Out*). Business services are available. 38-46 Am Hof (phone: 20580; fax: 211021).

Senatshotel A neat, small spot within a stone's throw of the cathedral, it offers 60 tastefully furnished rooms, personalized service, and a good restaurant. Business services are available. 9-17 Unter Goldschmied (phone: 20620; fax: 247863).

Viktoria North of the cathedral quarter near the Rhine, this 47-room place is in a neoclassical, turn-of-the-century building. Accommodations are modern; many rooms offer a Rhine view. There's no restaurant. Business services are available. 23 Worringer Str. (phone: 720476; fax: 727067).

INEXPENSIVE

Altstadt Located in the Altstadt, this 28-room hotel is long on charm (all rooms are individually decorated). There's no restaurant. 7 Salzgasse (phone: 234187; fax: 234189).

Arcade At the edge of the Altstadt in a modern building with a no-frills lobby, its 203 rooms are bright, clean, and functional. There is a restaurant that serves regional dishes. 4 Neue Weyerstr. (phone: 20960; fax: 209-6199).

Krone Another uninspired box-like structure, but its Altstadt location (near the *Praetorium*—see *Special Places*) and its 40 attractively decorated rooms make it a worthy choice. There's no restaurant. Business services are available. 15 Kleine Budengasse (phone: 210253; fax: 253532).

EATING OUT

In this predominantly middle class and working class city, steakhouses, particularly those of the Churrasco chain, are popular, as are brewery restaurants, which serve down-home regional fare along with the local beer (*Kölsch*) in sparsely decorated, cavernous settings. There is another side to the Cologne dining scene, however: the Cologne devoted to businesspeople here for the trade fairs, or art collectors making the rounds of the city's galleries. The nouvelle cuisine featured in the more elegant places compares well with that found in any European city of its size. Expect to pay $100 or more for a meal for two at restaurants in the very expensive category; $70 to $100 at places in the expensive range; $40 to $70 at moderate restaurants; and less than $40 at places we list as inexpensive. Prices do not include drinks, wine, or beer. Taxes and service charge are always included in the bill, but you should leave a small additional amount to reward good service. Unless otherwise noted, the restaurants listed below are open daily for lunch and dinner. All telephone numbers are in the 221 city code unless otherwise indicated.

For an unforgettable dining experience, we begin with our culinary favorite, followed by our cost and quality choices, listed by price category.

DELIGHTFUL DINING

Goldener Pflug It's a retreat of tasteful discretion, from the half-lit glow and sprays of ferns to the barely heard piano. This grande dame of the gastronomic world, nestled in a suburb across the Rhine, offers the area's most sophisticated fare, with such sumptuous entrées as *Frische Gänseleber pochiert mit Linsencreme* (goose-liver pâté with creamed lentils) and the *Marinierter Lachs auf weissem Tomatengelee* (marinated salmon glazed in a tomato aspic). Closed Sundays. Reservations necessary. American Express accepted. 421 Olpener Str., Merheim (phone: 895509 or 896124).

VERY EXPENSIVE

Chez Alex In a Belle Epoque–style setting worthy of a museum—all plush and silk brocade, with antiques, deep leather chairs, and walls hung with tapestries and dark paintings—this is one of Germany's most luxurious dining establishments. Located in the Altstadt, close to the cathedral, its menu features nouvelle cuisine such as rack of lamb with artichoke confit, turbot with lobster sauce, and for dessert, *tarte tatin* with white coffee ice cream. It has the finest (and most expensive) wine list in the city. Service is impeccable. Prix fixe lunch menus are an exceptional value. Closed Sundays and holidays; dinner only on Saturdays. Reservations necessary. Major credit cards accepted. 1-3 Mühlengasse (phone: 258-1069).

Rino Casati Although this is a favorite place for Italian food in Cologne, it takes an eclectic approach to cooking, borrowing most notably from the French. Typical starters include salmon, carpaccio, and seafood salad, with main courses of duck or tournedos with goose liver. The decor is tasteful and elegant, with pale pastel walls and fine napery and silver; the large tables spaced well apart give a sense of intimacy and romance. Open for dinner only; closed Sundays. Reservations necessary. Major credit cards accepted. 3 Ebertpl. (phone: 721108).

EXPENSIVE

Ambiance am Dom This hotel dining room offers fine German dishes such as salmon with lemon ginger sauce and veal roast ringed by seasonal vegetables. The prix fixe luncheon menu is an excellent value. Closed Sundays, holidays, and Saturday lunch. Reservations advised. Major credit cards accepted. In the *REMA-Europa Hotel,* 38 Am Hof (phone: 258-2092).

Die Bastei The chief lure of this old-time favorite is its location: North of the city center, overlooking the Rhine, it affords stunning river views. In fact, there isn't a more pleasant place to enjoy a leisurely dinner in the fading light of a summer evening. Try the Rhine version of sauerbraten, here called *Soorbrode*—beef marinaded in a spicy sauce and served with apple sauce and dumplings. Closed Saturday lunch. Reservations advised. Major credit cards accepted. 80 Konrad-Adenauer-Ufer (phone: 122825).

Ratskeller Forget the concept of rustic German *Ratskellers.* This one is anything but: a glamorous setting of dark stonework, Renaissance archways, a fireplace, and an inner courtyard for alfresco dining in summer. The menu features German dishes, including smoked trout and rack of salt marsh lamb from the district of Schleswig-Holstein. Open daily. Reservations advised. Major credit cards accepted. 1 Rathauspl. (entrance on Alter Markt; phone: 218301).

MODERATE

Chalet Suisse A glamourized version of a Swiss mountain inn, with knotty pine woodwork, kitschy touches, and lots of greenery, this is a pleasant place at which to enjoy such Swiss specialties as fondue and raclette and veal dishes, plus fresh greens at the salad buffet. Open daily. Reservations unnecessary. MasterCard and Visa accepted. 26 Am Hof (phone: 233891).

El Gaucho An Argentine steakhouse with waiters dressed as rancheros (in sombreros and ponchos) in a simulated Pampas hacienda, it may appear overdone, but the charcoal-grilled steaks (imported from Argentina) are always cooked to perfection. Portions are huge. Closed Mondays. Reservations unnecessary. Major credit cards accepted. 4A Barbarossapl. (phone: 246797).

Pan e Vin A smaller and more modest branch of the *Rino Casati* (above), its focus is also on Italian cooking, including such memorable dishes as black ink pasta with lobster sauce and risotto with lobster, shrimp, and squid. There are excellent Italian wines by the glass. This place is extremely popular on Sundays. Open for dinner only; closed Mondays. Reservations necessary. American Express accepted. 75 Heumarkt (phone: 248410).

Weinhaus im Walfisch In a magnificently restored, step-gabled townhouse (ca. 1626) located in the Altstadt close to the Rhine, this is a longtime favorite of Cologne residents, who enjoy the menu's traditional German fare. Highlights include *Hämchen* (cured pigs' knuckles), which are cooked in vegetable broth and served with sauerkraut and potato purée; and oxtail soup seasoned with spices and sherry. It's famed for its excellent wines, but serves no other alcohol. (A bit of historical trivia: This building was the only one in the Altstadt to emerge from World War II completely undamaged.) Closed Sundays, holidays, and Saturday lunch. Reservations unnecessary. Major credit cards accepted. 13 Salzgasse (phone: 257-7879).

INEXPENSIVE

Café Reichard In a glass-enclosed pavilion in an impressive neo-Gothic building directly in front of the cathedral, this eatery is the city's favorite place for afternoon coffee and cake. The menu also offers a luncheon buffet along with sandwiches and light meals, such as herring plates and smoked salmon samplers. Open daily. Reservations unnecessary. No credit cards accepted. 11 Unter Fettenhennen (phone: 233892).

Churrasco The restaurants of the Churrasco chain, with branches in some two dozen German cities, are invariably crowded, and for good reason. At the three outlets here, at most hours of the day and into the night, you can enjoy thick, juicy, charcoal-grilled Argentine steaks, along with a baked potato with chive-laced sour cream, big portions of salad, garlic bread, and good German beer or wine by the glass, at hard-to-beat prices. There are also weekday lunch specials. Open daily. Reservations unnecessary. Major credit cards accepted. 12-14 Steinweg (phone: 217767); 1-9 Dompropst-Ketzer Str. (phone: 134798); and 11 Mittelstr. (phone: 257-0162).

Früh am Dom Right near the cathedral, this *Kölsch* brewery tavern has frescoed vaulted ceilings, paneled walls, and long wooden tables where previously unacquainted diners sit next to one another in the *Tischnachbar* (table neighbor) tradition. Sample the traditional Cologne specialty, *Hämchen* (cured pigs' knuckles). Also on the menu are hearty soups, sauerbraten with dumplings, sausage and cold-cut platters, and smooth *Kölsch* beer.

Open daily. Reservations unnecessary. Major credit cards accepted. 12-14 Am Hof (phone: 212621).

Haus Töller Another longtime local favorite, this one is a short *U-Bahn* ride from the *Hauptbahnhof* to *Barbarossaplatz,* and worth the trip for the atmosphere alone. Pigs' knuckles, spicy salads, dark country bread, schnapps, and beer are served in a Baroque setting. Open daily. Reservations unnecessary. Major credit cards accepted. 96 Weyerstr. (phone: 214086).

Sion Another legendary *Kölsch* brewery tavern—this one in business since 1811—it's set in the heart of the Altstadt near the cathedral. The walls are decorated with old-time brewery equipment. There's seating for 500 in the numerous wood-paneled rooms, and terrace seating is available in warm weather. Portions are enormous, so order one course at a time. Open daily. Reservations unnecessary. MasterCard and Visa accepted. 5-7 Unter Taschenmacher (phone: 214203).

Dresden

A high point of any trip through Germany, the city of Dresden is alive with cultural tradition and political history. Among Germany's largest urban centers, with a population of over half a million, its art collections rank among the most valuable in the world. Yet to visitors from around the world (particularly Great Britain and the US), its name, like that of Hiroshima, is synonymous with the horrors of modern warfare. Tens of thousands of people died in the Anglo-American bombing raids on February 13 and 14, 1945, and some 80% of the town center, with its narrow old streets and passageways, was leveled in a devastating firestorm.

The *Hofkirche* (Catholic Court Church), the *Semperoper* (Semper Opera House), and the galleries along the *Brühlsche Terrasse* (Brühl Terrace) on the Elbe River were rebuilt to restore to Dresden the silhouette made famous by court painter Bernardo Bellotto (1720–80)—nicknamed "Canaletto," after his famous uncle, the Venetian painter Canaletto (1697–1768). Bellotto's cityscapes earned Dresden its nickname, "Florence on the Elbe." Inland from the waterfront, much of the city center was rebuilt in characterless concrete and glass. However, work is in progress to restore Old Dresden to its former Baroque and rococo splendor.

Today the Elbe flows past princely villas, the nearby vineyards of Sächsische Elbland (Saxon Wine Country), and the sandstone cliffs and bizarre rock formations in *Sächsische Schweiz Nationalpark* (Saxon Switzerland National Park). Vintage paddle-wheel steamboats of the *Weisse Flotte* (White Fleet), in business since 1837, tie up at the Terrassenufer embankment, and take passengers upriver and downriver on day trips. Unlike the flatland locales farther northwest in Saxony, Dresden lies in a deep valley rimmed by foothills.

Founded in 1206, Dresden was an undistinguished trading city until 1475, when the dukes and electors of the Wettin dynasty's Albertine branch made it their official residence. When Martin Luther delivered a sermon here in 1518, the city was transformed into a bastion of his Protestant Reformation. And in the late 17th century, the spendthrift Saxon princes chose Dresden for their court. Legend has it that one of them, Friedrich Augustus I (aptly dubbed Augustus the Strong), sired 352 children and regularly drank lion's milk. His chief architect, Matthäus Daniel Pöppelmann, teamed up with Bavarian sculptor Balthasar Permoser in designing and building palaces, ornate bridges, and formal gardens in the Baroque style of Rome, Vienna, and Versailles. Among their works is the now restored *Zwinger* museum complex. During this time, the goldsmiths' guild crafted a fortune in metal objects, such as exquisite jewelry, fine carvings, and inlaid cabinetry for Augustus. Today the treasures are housed in the *Grünes Gewölbe* (Green Vault) chamber of the *Albertinum* (see *Special Places*).

After Napoleon made Dresden capital of the kingdom of Saxony in 1806, the electors reigned as full-fledged monarchs; one of the most celebrated of them all, King Albert, had the *Albertinum* built to house his treasures and those collected by his forebears. The Albertines ruled until the Weimar Republic was established in 1918.

Art and music have always played an important part in Dresden's history. It was in the mid-18th century that Bellotto was appointed court painter, and during that time a fortune was spent acquiring art for palace galleries. The *Sächische Kunstakademie* (Saxon Academy of Arts), now known as the *Hochschule für bildende Kunst* (Academy of Fine Art), was founded in 1764, and not long afterward philosopher Johann Gottfried von Herder (1744–1803) referred to Dresden as the German Florence. Just prior to World War I, painters and sculptors started the Expressionist *Brücke* (Bridge) movement in Dresden, later attacked as "degenerate art" by the Nazis. As for music, Carl Maria von Weber began his directorship of the court orchestra in 1817 and was followed by Richard Wagner 31 years later. Not one but two world class symphony orchestras, the *Saxon Staatskapelle* and the *Dresden Philharmonic,* were established in Dresden. In the 19th century, Wagner's *Rienzi, The Flying Dutchman,* and *Tannhäuser* premiered in Dresden's prestigious *Semperoper,* designed by Gottfried and Manfred Semper.

The renowned Altstadt (Old City) skyline above the Elbe River embankment has come to symbolize a process of painstaking revival following the wartime bombing. It's readily apparent that the city is still recovering. Landmark buildings are slowly being reconstructed. Others—interspersed with the banal structures of the former Communist regime—are actually faithfully detailed replicas of the Baroque and Renaissance originals. Bellotto's cityscapes have been consulted by Dresden restorers who seek to re-create this golden age.

Although sizable portions of the city center have never been rebuilt (witness the wide-open, windy spaces), some districts retain vestiges of their prewar elegance. One is Blasewitz, east of the city center, leading toward the 19th-century *Blaues Wunder* (Blue Wonder) steel suspension bridge. Across the Elbe, the hillside Weisser Hirsch and Bühlau neighborhoods border the southern reaches of the 20-square-mile *Dresdner Heide,* a municipal nature reserve. Its cobweb pattern of paths and roadways was laid out during Augustus the Strong's freewheeling reign. Nearly two-thirds of the city's total area consists of woods and parks.

Unlike Berlin and Leipzig, its more sophisticated counterparts, Dresden, which is located close to the Czech and Polish frontiers, was relatively untouched by Western influences during the Cold War. International trade fairs, Western cultural exchanges, even West German broadcast signals were not regularly received here. But after having been isolated for so long, this former cultural capital is once again taking its place in the world of the arts, with numerous world class music festivals (see *Music*) and notable

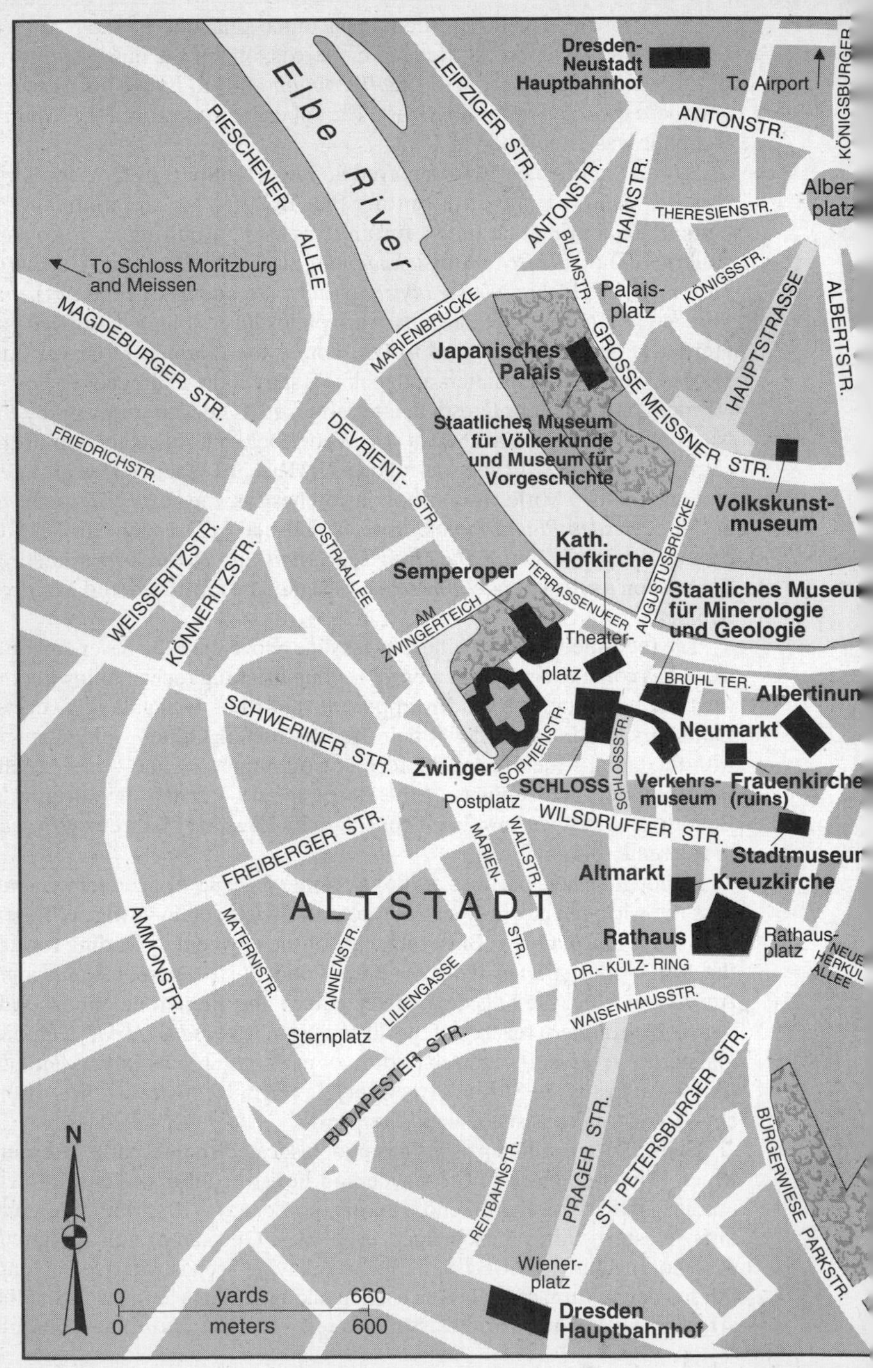

Elbe River
Dresden-Neustadt Hauptbahnhof
To Airport
ANTONSTR.
KÖNIGSBURGER
Albert platz
LEIPZIGER STR.
PIESCHENER ALLEE
ANTONSTR.
HAINSTR.
THERESIENSTR.
BLUMSTR.
Palais-platz
KÖNIGSSTR.
HAUPTSTRASSE
ALBERTSTR.
To Schloss Moritzburg and Meissen
MAGDEBURGER STR.
MARIENBRÜCKE
Japanisches Palais
GROSSE MEISSNER STR.
Staatliches Museum für Völkerkunde und Museum für Vorgeschichte
FRIEDRICHSTR.
DEVRIENT-STR.
Volkskunst-museum
AUGUSTUSBRÜCKE
Kath. Hofkirche
Semperoper
TERRASSENUFER
Staatliches Museum für Minerologie und Geologie
WEISSERITZSTR.
KÖNNERITZSTR.
OSTRAALLEE
AM ZWINGERTEICH
Theater-platz
BRÜHL TER.
Albertinum
SCHWERINER STR.
SOPHIENSTR.
SCHLOSSSTR.
Neumarkt
Zwinger
SCHLOSS
Verkehrs-museum
Frauenkirche (ruins)
Postplatz
WILSDRUFFER STR.
FREIBERGER STR.
MARIEN-STR.
WALLSTR.
Stadtmuseum
Altmarkt
Kreuzkirche
ALTSTADT
AMMONSTR.
MATERNISTR.
ANNENSTR.
Rathaus
Rathaus-platz
NEUE HERKUL ALLEE
DR.- KÜLZ- RING
LILIENGASSE
WAISENHAUSSTR.
Sternplatz
BUDAPESTER STR.
ST. PETERSBURGER STR.
PRAGER STR.
REITBAHNSTR.
BÜRGERWIESE PARKSTR.
N
0 yards 660
0 meters 600
Wiener-platz
Dresden Hauptbahnhof

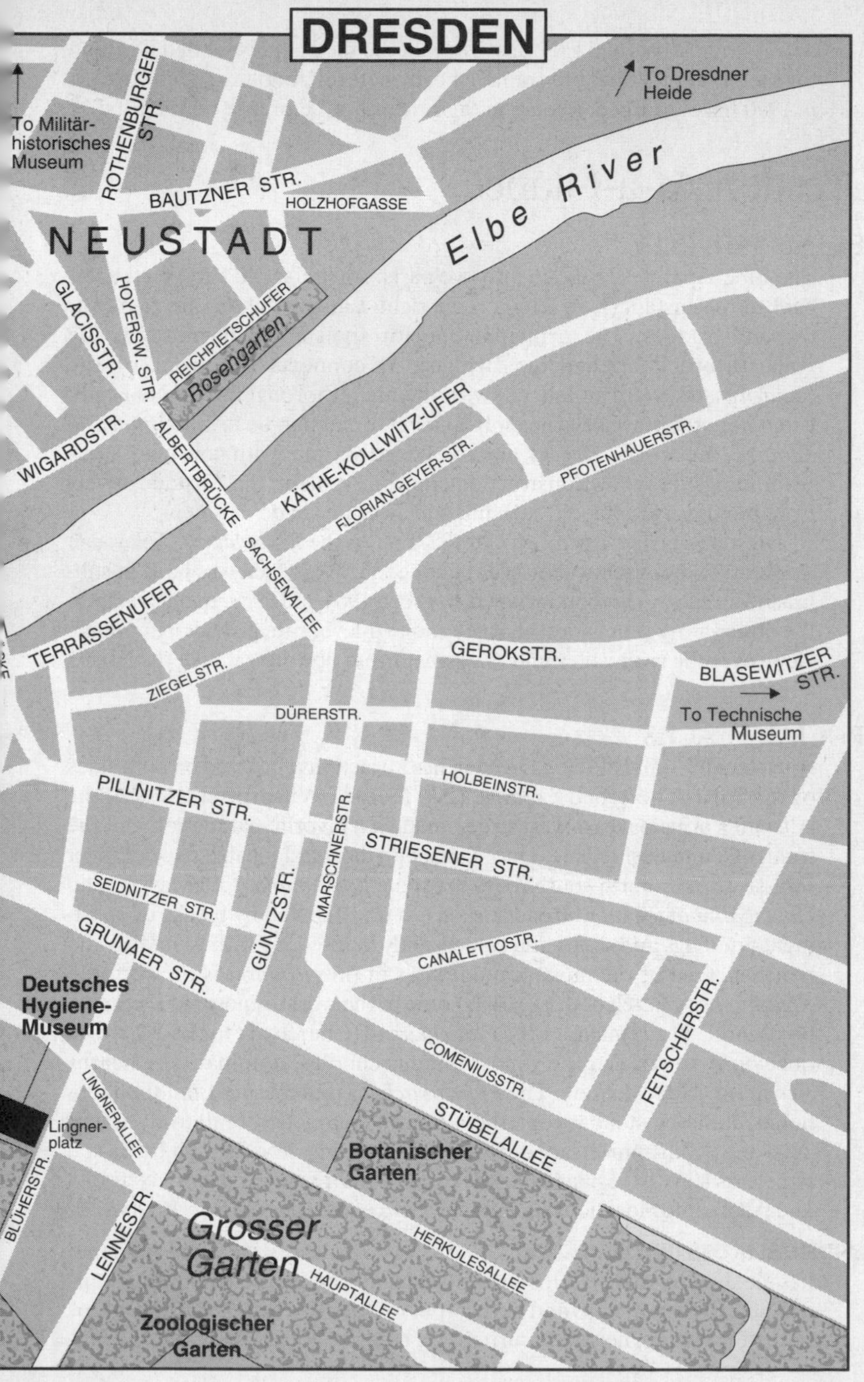
DRESDEN
To Dresdner Heide
To Militär-historisches Museum
ROTHENBURGER STR.
BAUTZNER STR.
HOLZHOFGASSE
Elbe River
NEUSTADT
GLACISSTR.
HOYERSW. STR.
REICHPIETSCHUFER
Rosengarten
WIGARDSTR.
ALBERTBRÜCKE
KÄTHE-KOLLWITZ-UFER
FLORIAN-GEYER-STR.
PFOTENHAUERSTR.
SACHSENALLEE
TERRASSENUFER
GEROKSTR.
BLASEWITZER STR.
To Technische Museum
ZIEGELSTR.
DÜRERSTR.
HOLBEINSTR.
PILLNITZER STR.
STRIESENER STR.
MARSCHNERSTR.
SEIDNITZER STR.
GÜNTZSTR.
GRUNAER STR.
CANALETTOSTR.
FETSCHERSTR.
Deutsches Hygiene-Museum
COMENIUSSTR.
LINGNERALLEE
Lingner-platz
STÜBELALLEE
Botanischer Garten
BLÜHERSTR.
LENNÉSTR.
Grosser Garten
HERKULESALLEE
HAUPTALLEE
Zoologischer Garten

avant-garde artists and galleries. Many of the thousands who fled Dresden for the West on "freedom trains" shortly before Germany's reunification in 1990 have returned, joining in the renewal of "Florence on the Elbe."

Dresden At-a-Glance

SEEING THE CITY

The Elbe separates Dresden into two parts: Altstadt (Old City) on the left bank and Neustadt (New City) on the right. Linking the two are four central-city bridges. The principal one for sightseeing purposes is the Augustusbrücke (Augustus Bridge). It connects the front of the *Residenzschloss* (Royal Palace) with the main thoroughfare in Neustadt. From here the view is of the embankment, excursion boats, the *Brühlsche Terrasse* (see *Special Places*), and the fabled skyline (with now-ubiquitous scaffolding and yellow construction cranes). At night, the Altstadt's riverfront buildings are floodlit in white and an eerie shade of green.

Dresden's tallest structure by far (827 feet) is the *Fernsehturm* (Television Tower; 37 Oberwachtwitzer Weg; phone: 36759), which was built in suburban Wachwitz, east of downtown, between 1964 and 1969. In fair weather, the observatory (admission charge) and two-level café provide panoramic views over the river valley and cityscape. From downtown, take the No. 93 streetcar.

SPECIAL PLACES

A thoroughly walkable city, Dresden has attractions clustered on both sides of the Elbe. The broad expanse (200 feet) of Wilsdruffer Strasse, the Altstadt's principal east-west street, made it a favorite parade route of the former Communist regime. Once Dresden's most fashionable street, Prager Strasse, the key north-south route between the *Altmarkt* (Old Market) and *Hauptbahnhof* (main railroad station), is now flanked by blocks of apartment buildings and shops and is pleasantly landscaped with fountains and benches. One of the most popular sites in the *Altmarkt* is the restored *Kreuzkirche* (Church of the Cross), home of the world-renowned *Kreuzchor* boys' choir. The remains of the *Frauenkirche* (Church of Our Lady), which once bore one of Europe's most famous cupolas, dominate the nearby *Neumarkt* (New Market). The *Frauenkirche* is undergoing a multimillion-dollar, stone-by-stone reconstruction, with completion tentatively set for 2006, the 800th anniversary of Dresden's founding. Mass-transit buses and streetcars leave at regular intervals from transfer stations in both Neustadt and Altstadt for locations outside the city center (see *Getting Around*).

RESIDENZSCHLOSS (ROYAL PALACE) The Albertine dynasty's imposing residence has the dubious distinction of being Germany's biggest remaining war ruin, a jumble of broken walls and burned-out towers. The neo-Renaissance look of the four wings, however, currently is being restored. Recently, the high

Georgianisches Tor (Georgian Gate) facing the Elbe was rebuilt and a copper turret and spire again were placed atop the *Hausmannsturm* (main tower). The restoration project is expected to cost $320 million and to take 11 more years; work is scheduled to be completed by Dresden's 800th anniversary in 2006. Tours (in German) combine the history of the palace's past glory with details about the construction project. Closed Thursdays. Admission charge. Entrance on Sophienstrasse (phone: 495-3110).

HOFKIRCHE (CATHOLIC COURT CHURCH) Completed in 1751, gutted by fire in the 19th century, and heavily damaged by Allied bombing in 1945, this restored late-Baroque edifice with an onion-dome tower, Saxony's largest church, was born of political necessity. Augustus the Strong was the first of the post-Reformation Saxon kings to convert to Catholicism (in order to obtain the Polish throne) and was succeeded by his son Friedrich Augustus II (1733–63), a Catholic born in a Lutheran town. Working under architect Gaetano Chiaveri, Italian artisans labored stealthily so as not to unduly inflame the Protestant burghers. The soaring white interior features *The Ascension of Christ* by court painter Anton Raphael Mengs above the high altar; sculptor Balthasar Permoser fashioned the snow-white cherubs in the rococo pulpit. Guardian angels adorn the 3,000-pipe organ built by the master instrument maker himself, Gottfried Silbermann. The abstract Meissen porcelain *Pietà*—sculpted in 1975 by Friedrich Press for the *Gedächtniskapelle* (Memorial Chapel)—commemorates the victims of World War II bombing. Also here in four crypts are 49 former members of the ruling Wettin lineage, along with a black egg-shaped urn containing the heart of Augustus the Strong. In 1980, the church became the Dresden-Meissen diocese's *Katholische Hofkirche* (Catholic Cathedral).

Each Wednesday, half-hour Silbermann organ recitals begin at 11:45 AM, and on Saturdays from April though October organ vespers are presented at 4 PM. Guided tours (in German only) are conducted Mondays through Thursdays at 11 AM and 2 PM; Fridays and Saturdays at 1 and 2 PM; and Sundays at 11:45 AM. Admission charge for tours. Schlosspl. (phone: 495-5135).

BRÜHLSCHE TERRASSE (BRÜHL TERRACE) It was reputedly Napoleon who first described this promenade as the "Balcony of Europe." The terrace, overlooking the Elbe from atop the walls of the 16th-century town fortifications, was laid out in 1739–48 for the pleasure of Prime Minister Heinrich von Brühl of Saxony. Lampposts, trees, and fountains recapture some of the old-time elegance. Among several statues, one is of architect Gottfried Semper; also here is Pierre Courdray's 18th-century Dolphin Fountain and, providing futuristic contrast, a stainless-steel tribute to Romanticist landscape painter Caspar David Friedrich. Buildings lining the promenade are in various stages of war damage and repair. The fully restored 19th-century exception is a cream-colored palace, *Sekundogenitur* (Second Generation), intended for the second-born Wettin prince, and now a part of the *Dresden Hilton* (see *Checking In*). In one of the vaults beneath the terrace, an alchemist under the employ of Augustus the Strong, Johann Friedrich Böttger, labored in vain to turn base metals into gold. Instead, in 1708, he manufactured the first porcelain objects in Europe. Tours (in German only) of the rampart's casements are held weekdays at 2, 3:30, and 5 PM, and Saturdays on the hour from 9 AM to 3 PM. Admission charge. Access at Georg-Treu-Platz (phone: 237-1008).

SEMPEROPER (SEMPER OPERA HOUSE) Completed in 1841, the richly ornamented building facing Theaterplatz is a second reincarnation of Semper's masterpiece. After a destructive fire in 1869, his son Manfred redesigned this home of the *Sächsische Staatsoper,* Saxony's state opera company, shifting the style from Italian to German Renaissance and adding a bronze panther quadriga high above the front portico. Several major operas debuted here, including Richard Strauss's *Elektra, Salome,* and *Der Rosenkavalier.* Gutted again during the World War II bombing raids of February 1945, Dresden's grand opera house reopened 40 years later to the day. The production that evening was *Der Freischütz* by Carl Maria von Weber, operatic music director from 1816 to 1826. The acoustically praised interior is decorated in gilded white and velvety crimson, and the florid curtain, reproduced from the original by Ferdinand Keller, displays an image of the Goddess of Imagination sitting on a throne. Guided tours are offered at 11 AM and 1 PM Thursdays; make reservations at the ticket office in the *Schinkelwache,* a neoclassical building across Theaterplatz (phone: 48420). For English-language tours, book at least four weeks in advance. On the Theaterplatz.

FÜRSTENZUG (PRINCES' PROCESSION) Narrow Augustusstrasse would be a nondescript street behind the *Brühlsche Terrasse* were it not for its artistic showpiece, a 1908 tribute to the Wettin dynasty's 800th anniversary. A 330-foot-long mosaic made of 24,000 Meissen porcelain tiles depicts a mounted procession of 37 margraves, dukes, electors, and kings from the 11th to the 19th centuries. The rulers are shown accompanied by a retinue of musicians, standard-bearers, page boys, influential representatives of Saxon arts and sciences, and finally, as if rushing to catch up, Wilhelm Walther, the muralist himself. All but 200 of the kiln-baked tiles withstood the intense heat of the firestorm in 1945, and the entire regal extravaganza underwent cleanup and full restoration between 1979 and 1980.

FRAUENKIRCHE (CHURCH OF OUR LADY) The most emblematic image of the Dresden bombing is a postwar photograph of a statue of Martin Luther standing before two jagged fragments of walls. These pieces were all that was left of the city's prized landmark, the *Frauenkirche,* which now is being meticulously restored in preparation for the city's 800th anniversary. Built between 1726 and 1743, the church was originally paid for by local Lutherans in angry response to the commissioning of the Catholic *Hofkirche* nearby. It became Germany's largest Protestant church and Dresden's centerpiece, with a 312-foot bell-shaped cupola designed by George Bähr early in the 18th century. A comprehensive restoration had been finished a mere two years before the bombs fell. The church survived the triple attack itself, but heat stress caused the combustion of its Luftwaffe film archives and the next morning the sandstone dome collapsed. The current phase of reconstruction—which involves sorting the stones and fitting them into their original places using a computerized replication of the church—is enormous and attracts crowds of onlookers.

ALBERTINUM Named for Saxony's King Albert, the glass-domed building has been a museum since it opened in the late 19th century; currently it houses four of Dresden's most important collections. Supreme among them is the *Grünes Gewölbe* (Green Vault), a trove of precious objects—jewelry, carvings, china, crystal glassware, alabaster goblets, swords, mirrors, and inlaid cabinetry—crafted by goldsmiths and jewelers from the 15th to the 18th centuries and amassed by successive generations of ruling Albertines. The collection includes Augustus the Strong's golden coffee service and a tableau depicting an Indian mogul's birthday party, consisting of 137 enameled figurines and 3,000 diamonds, emeralds, rubies, and pearls. Before the war these treasures were housed in the *Residenzschloss;* palace restorers say that by 2001, five rooms of objects will be returned there. More than 200,000 coins, medals, bank notes, stamps, and seals are in the *Münzkabinett* (Numismatic Collection). The *Skulpturensammlung* (Sculpture Collection), begun by Augustus the Strong in 1717, features Egyptian, Etruscan, Greek, and Roman antiquities. The largest section of the building contains the *Gemäldgalerie Neue Meister* (Gallery of the New Masters), devoted to 19th- and 20th-century artworks, including paintings by French Impressionists and two sculptures by Rodin. The main focus is on works by such German artists as Adrian Ludwig Richter, Caspar David Friedrich, Max Liebermann, Max Slevogt, and the antiwar, antifascist artists Otto Dix and Hans Grundig. Closed Thursdays. Admission charge. Georg-Treu-Pl. (phone: 495-3056).

ZWINGER A ceremonial showplace built between 1710 and 1722 at the height of Augustus's reign, it was lovingly restored in the postwar years. In magnificent Baroque style, with graceful sculptures and courtyard fountains, the *Zwinger* houses one of the world's most stunning art collections, the *Gemäldegalerie Alte Meister* (Gallery of the Old Masters), as well as several other museums (see below). Architect Matthäus Pöppelmann designed the formal quadrangle surrounded by a curving, linked ensemble of six pavilions, and sculptor Balthasar Permoser fashioned the porcelain nymphs, fauns, satyrs, maidens, and fat cherubs. Flourishes include 40 Meissen porcelain bells on the *Glockenspielpavillon*'s pediment, and the façade of the *Wallpavillon,* upon which Hercules bears the globe on his shoulders. The north side was later enclosed by a seventh, larger pavilion, designed by Gottfried Semper to house Dresden's fabled art collection. All but destroyed in the war, the complex was rebuilt in the city center by 1964, then fell victim to imperfect workmanship and acid rain, which marred the soft sandstone ornamentation. The most recent reconstruction was completed in late 1992. The main entrance is on Sophienstrasse.

Gemäldegalerie Alte Meister (Gallery of the Old Masters) This masterpiece gallery contains more than 650 canvases from such pre-19th-century greats as Raphael, Rubens, Rembrandt, Titian, Tintoretto, Botticelli, Correggio, Dürer, Cranach, Holbein, and Vermeer. Meticulously detailed perspectives of 18th-century Dresden by Bernardo Bellotto (nicknamed "Canaletto") hang at the top of the staircase and in a side gallery. Among the many famous paintings here are Raphael's *Sistine Madonna,* Vermeer's *Girl Reading a Letter by an Open Window,* Giorgione's *Sleeping Venus,* Ribera's *St. Agnes in Prison,* and Jean-Etienne Liotard's *The Chocolate Girl.* In a downstairs gallery is the Dresden altar triptych, *Seven Agonies of Mary;* side-by-side depictions of *Adam and Eve,* both by Albrecht Dürer; and another passionate triptych by Lucas Cranach the Elder. In addition, there is a large and impressive collection of china, coins, and hunting weapons. Closed Mondays. One admission charge allows entrance to both the *Gemäldgalerie Alte Meister* and the *Rüstkammer* (see below). In the north side of the *Zwinger* complex (phone: 484-0119).

Rüstkammer (Armory Chamber) More commonly known as the *Historisches Museum* (Historical Museum), this museum holds an impressive collection of battle gear, including suits of armor for horses, men, and children, as well as swords, lances, bows and arrows, pistols, battle axes, shields, powder horns, and other implements of war. Articles of ceremonial dress and the tournament trappings of the Saxon princes and electors are preserved in exquisite detail. There's also a full-length portrait of Augustus the Strong, completed in 1718 by Louis de Silvestri. Closed Mondays. In the north side of the *Zwinger* (phone: 484-0126).

Tierkundemuseum (Zoological Museum) A small but wide-ranging menagerie of stuffed creatures is housed here, including penguins, a North American bald eagle, a grizzly bear, a mountain goat, Ethiopian springboks and impalas, an African python, and birds and mammals of the nearby *Sächsische Schweiz Nationalpark* (Saxon Switzerland National Park; see below). Closed Mondays. Admission charge. In the southwest pavilion of the *Zwinger* (phone: 495-2503).

Porzellansammlung (Porcelain Collection) Housing one of the most significant collections of early porcelain objects in Europe, this museum has pieces crafted in 1710 by Augustus the Strong's alchemist, Johann Friedrich Böttger. The vintage red items exemplify the earliest phase of the Dresden craft, and were followed by white glazed pieces created by mid-18th-century porcelain designers Johann Joachim Kändler and Johann Gottlieb Kirchner. Many are monumentally huge—cats and dogs, lions and monkeys, spread-feathered peacocks—but there are also dozens of detailed, vividly colored figurines of harlequins, cavaliers, musicians, farmers, cooks, and turbaned Turks. Among the dinnerware sets is Augustus II's Japanese service from 1760. In addition to famous Dresden and Meissen porcelain and pewter, Oriental and French Sèvres objects are on display. Closed Thursdays. Admission charge. On two levels of the *Zwinger*'s southeastern pavilion (phone: 484-0127).

Mathematisch-Physikalischer Salon (Mathematical–Physical Sciences Salon) An extensive collection of early terrestrial and celestial globes, compasses, atlases, clocks, telescopes, scales, and scientific instruments is displayed. Closed Thursdays. Admission charge. In the southwestern pavilion of the *Zwinger* (phone: 495-1364).

STALLHOF (ROYAL STABLES) This open-air courtyard, located behind the palace and dating from the 16th-century reign of Duke Moritz, once hosted jousts and tournaments. Saxon coats of arms on the 22 Tuscan arches underscore the heraldic past. Today it's used for occasional outdoor exhibitions. The *Neumarkt* entrance, across from the *Frauenkirche* ruins, is always open.

KREUZKIRCHE (HOLY CROSS CHURCH) The single surviving prewar edifice in the *Altmarkt,* the church was built from 1764 to 1792. (Its façade has yielded to a checkerboard look because fresh stones have replaced old to keep the blackening body and 370-foot clock tower intact.) A church has stood in one form or another in this same location for the past 700 years. The present structure, predominantly Baroque on the exterior but with a surprisingly austere interior, is the fourth to bear the name *Kreuzkirche.* It's home to the famous *Kreuzchor* boys' choir, a fixture in Dresden since the 13th century. The 150-member choir sings at 6 PM Saturdays and regularly for 9:30 AM Sunday services. An interior display near the front doors documents the church's history, which includes extensive fire damage in 1897. Photos taken from the tower show the market square as a bombed-out wasteland in 1945, and continue in sequence, detailing the progress of reconstruction. In 1989, the *Kreuzkirche* became Dresden's main gathering place for peaceful protests against repressive German Democratic Republic government policies. *Altmarkt.*

RATHAUS (CITY HALL) As a statement of municipal authority, the tower that survived the Dresden bombing was made taller than those of the *Hofkirche* and *Kreuzkirche* when this sprawling, *Jugendstil* (Art Nouveau) building was constructed in 1910. The tower, crowned by a gilded Hercules, is two feet shorter than the restored *Hausmannsturm* (main tower) of the *Residenzschloss.* Like most German city halls, it has a large restaurant downstairs (see *Eating Out*). On Rathauspl., two blocks east of the *Altmarkt.*

GROSSER GARTEN Dresden's largest park covers an area southeast of the city center. Originally designed in the Baroque style for the private use of the electors in the 17th century, it was enlarged 200 years later on the model of English landscape gardens and opened to the public. At its center are a pond and sandstone statues. The park's three outdoor stages and a puppet theater draw crowds, and the Carolasee lake is a favorite place for boating and ice skating (the *Carolaschlösschen* buffet restaurant at lakeside is also popular). A long-standing feature, a narrow-gauge railroad run by schoolchildren since 1950, loops the park from April through September. In the southwestern corner of the park is the *Zoologischer Garten* (Zoological Garden; Tiergartenstr.; phone: 471-5445). Founded in 1861, this is one of the oldest zoos in Germany; it keeps about 2,500 animals of 500 different species. It's open daily; admission charge. To the north, the *Botanischer Garten* (Botanical Garden; Stübelallee; phone: 459-3185) includes outdoor and greenhouse arrangements of tropical flowers and plants. It's open daily; admission charge.

HAUPTSTRASSE Across the Elbe, Neustadt's main street is arguably the most attractive pedestrian zone in eastern Germany. Sooner or later, most visitors to Dresden find themselves strolling along this strip past rows of statues, linden trees, and two Baroque fountains adorned with nymphs. Also on this street are a few distinctive stores, including *Hohlfeldt KG, Bücherstube Gutenberg,* and *Kunst und Handwerk Etzol* (see *Shopping* for details on all), as well as several fine restaurants, including the ritzy *Meissner Weinkeller* and the grillroom and café of the *Kügelgen Haus* (see *Eating Out* for both). The focal point, at the southern end of the street, is the *Goldener Reiter* (Golden Rider), a gilded statue of Augustus the Strong mounted on a Lippizaner stallion. Hauptstrasse suffered considerable war damage and was renamed Strasse der Befreiung (Street of Liberation) under Communist rule. However, some of the Baroque burgher houses along the west side of the street have been carefully restored. Also on the west side stands the towering, 18th-century *Dreikönigskirche* (Epiphany Church), which was designed in the Baroque style by Matthäus Pöppelmann and George Bähr. Nearby (take streetcar No. 11 from the Hauptstrasse) is *Schloss Albrechtsburg* (130 Bautzner Str.; phone: 55655), a terraced Elbe palace built in mid-19th-century Berlin classical style for a Hohenzollern prince, Albrecht of Prussia. There is a wine restaurant in the downstairs vaults, and chamber music and symphony concerts are presented periodically in the *Kronensaal* (see *Music*). The palace is open daily; admission charge.

ENVIRONS

MEISSEN Less than an hour's drive (50 miles/80 km) west of Dresden, this romantic city on the Elbe escaped damage during World War II bombing. Chief among the attractions here is the workshop where alchemist Johann Böttger developed and perfected Dresden china. Pieces housed in the *Staatliche-Porzellan-Manufaktur* (Porcelain Workshop) and the *Schauhalle* (Showroom/Museum; 9 Talstr.; phone: 3521-458541) rival those of Dresden's

Porzellansammlung. Other sightseeing favorites: with its elaborately decorated twin spires, the hilltop Gothic cathedral, parts of which date to the mid-13th century; and the adjacent *Schloss Albrechtsburg* (not to be confused with the palace of the same name in Dresden), built between 1471 and 1525 with a complex of vaulted interiors. Located on Domplatz (phone: 3521-452920), it is closed Mondays; admission charge. The restored gabled buildings around the central market square were first built in the 15th century. Meissen—where the influential Wettin dynasty originated—became the residence of Saxony's powerful margraves in AD 968. The tourist office is at 3 An der Frauenkirche (phone: 3521-454470).

SCHLOSS PILLNITZ Another of Pöppelmann's 17th-century Baroque fantasy creations, this palace along the Elbe River is a popular riverside destination in the eastern suburbs. Built as the Saxon electorate's summer palace, it is replete with French and English pleasure gardens. Motorcoach tours of Dresden and the castle are available (see *Tours*). Open daily. Admission charge. Located in Pillnitz, about 9 miles (15 km) southeast of Dresden (phone: 351-39325).

CARL-MARIA-VON-WEBER GEDENKSTÄTTE (CARL MARIA VON WEBER MEMORIAL HOUSE) Located in the southeastern suburb of Hosterwitz (just beyond the city center), this museum houses music memorabilia, including a favorite piano of the composer and his notebooks. Closed Mondays. Admission charge. 44 Dresdner Str., Hosterwitz (phone: 39234)

RICHARD WAGNER MUSEUM Graupa, a suburb about 5 miles (8 km) east of Dresden, is where Richard Wagner, another of the city's celebrated court conductors, retreated to compose his opera *Lohengrin* in 1846. This town's Wagner museum houses memorabilia and original notebooks. Tours are given on the hour from 10 AM to 3 PM (weekends from 11 AM). Closed Fridays through Sundays. Admission charge. 6 Richard-Wagner-Str., Graupa (phone: 3501-48229).

FESTUNG KÖNIGSTEIN On a promontory above the Elbe, about a one-and-a-half-hour drive south of downtown Dresden, is this imposing medieval fortress, built about 1200. Never overthrown by force, the fortress was chosen during World War II to temporarily house the treasures of the *Grünes Gewölbe* (see *Albertinum*). Guided tours (available in English) are given several times daily; reservations necessary. Open daily. Admission charge. On Rte. 172 (phone: 35021-374 or 35021-375).

SÄCHSISCHE SCHWEIZ NATIONALPARK (SAXON SWITZERLAND NATIONAL PARK) Located near the German-Czech border, about 25 miles (40 km) southeast of central Dresden, this national park (one of only three in Germany) features reddish and gray sandstone rock formations, great hiking trails, and peaceful riverfront villages. Open daily. No admission charge. For information, contact the *Fremdenverkehrsverband Sächsische Schweiz* (Saxon

Switzerland Tourist Office; 9 Zehistaer Str., Pirna; phone: 3501-85455; fax: 3501-8456).

BAROCKSCHLOSS MORITZBURG (MORITZBURG BAROQUE CASTLE) Just outside the little town of Moritzburg, on an island in the middle of an artificial lake, this was once the electors' rambling hunting lodge. There's a pleasant restaurant. Closed Mondays. Admission charge. About 11 miles (18 km) north of Dresden (phone: 35207-439).

RADEBEUL This vineyard town along the Elbe Valley's Sächsische Weinstrasse (Saxon Wine Road) is the site of the *Karl May Museum* (5 Karl-May-Str.; phone: 762723), the former home of the writer whose cowboys-and-Indians adventure novels have inspired three generations of Germans to romanticize the early American West. The museum is closed Mondays; admission charge.

EXTRA SPECIAL

For stunning, high-level views of metropolitan Dresden and the Elbe, take a train from Körnerplatz in suburban Loschwitz (about 2 miles/3 km east of the palace), which follows a suspension railway (circa 1901) up to the Oberloschwitz hill station. In south-suburban Freital, the *Windbergbahn*—Germany's oldest mountain train, a narrow-gauge steam engine operating since 1857—makes a steep, winding, 40-minute ascent from a deep valley to the Oberglittersee Plateau. Freital is close to the Tharandtwald (Tharandt Forest), a leafy city-dwellers' sanctuary. Both railroads are owned by *Dresdner Verkehrsbetrieb* (Dresden Municipal Public Transportation Company; phone: 471-8727).

Sources and Resources

TOURIST INFORMATION

Tourist-Information (10 Prager Str.; phone: 495-5025; fax: 495-1276), the main information office in the Altstadt, is open daily. It's a good source for maps, hotel listings, schedules of events, transportation information, tour availability, guidebooks, and English-language brochures. It also has currency exchange tellers. The Neustadt branch (Neustädter Markt; phone/fax: 53539), in the pedestrian underpass connecting the Augustus Bridge with the Hauptstrasse, is open daily as well. Both offices also function as reservation bureaus for accommodations in hotels and private residences.

LOCAL COVERAGE There is no English-language newspaper in Dresden. Pocket-size *Dresden Life,* available at the tourist offices and most hotels, is a monthly German-language calendar of events that also includes a city map and selected hotel and restaurant listings. A similar German-language publication, *Dresden-Information,* covers monthly events more comprehensively, with the addition of a pictorial city map, public-transit network plan, and a handy listing of banks, fitness facilities, sports locations, museums, cinemas, and nightclubs. It's available at the tourist offices.

TELEPHONE The city code for Dresden is 351.

GETTING AROUND

AIRPORT *Flughafen Dresden-Klotzsche* (Dresden-Klotzsche Airport), located 5 miles (8 km) north of the city center, handles flights from and to 17 German cities, plus Budapest, Moscow, Paris, and Zurich. For flight information call 589-3080. *Airport City-Liner* van service (phone: 412-1423) offers frequent round-trip service. In-town pickup points include the *Dresden Hauptbahnhof* (Dresden Railroad Station; in the *Altmarkt*) and the *Dresden-Neustadt Hauptbahnhof* (Dresden-Neustadt Railroad Station; in Neustadt), as well as Pirnaischer Platz and Terrassenufer (at the *Dresden Hilton*) in Altstadt, and the Augustus Bridge (near the *Maritim Bellevue* hotel) in Neustadt.

BOAT The *Sächsische Dampfschiffahrt* cruise line (1-2 Terrassenufer; phone: 502-2611)—colloquially known as *Weisse Flotte (White Fleet)*—arranges trips on the Elbe. From the Altstadt embankment terminal, cruise boats travel downriver to Radebeul and Meissen (one-day trips are popular) and as far as Riesa, and upriver through the *Sächsische Schweiz Nationalpark* and into the Czech Republic as far as the little town of Decin. A popular stopover point is Pillnitz, site of the former Saxon court's summer palace, *Schloss Pillnitz* (see *Special Places*). Daily sailings leave at 8:30 AM to Meissen and 9:30 AM to Pillnitz. There are also disco cruises in the evening. In addition, the *Krippen,* a passenger steamer launched in 1882, sails from Meissen on a scenic 15-mile (24 km) round trip along the Elbe past the villages of Diesbar-Seusslitz and Radebeul. For information, contact Klaus Junghans (2A Siebeneichener Str.; phone: 3521-452-6000), who operates the boat.

BUS AND STREETCAR The city's efficient, wide-ranging *DBV* public transit system, in service since 1872, consists of 17 streetcar lines linked to 27 bus lines. Tickets can be purchased at automatic machines and sales booths located at main transfer points in Altstadt and Neustadt. Fares range from 1 to 2 DM (60¢ to $1.20), depending on the length of the ride; also, one-day ($3), one-week ($7.20), and one-month ($21.60) passes are available.

CAR RENTAL Rental counters for *Avis* (phone: 589-4600), *Hertz* (phone: 589-4580), *Sixt-Budget* (phone: 589-4570), *Europcar* (phone: 589-4591), *Autohansa* (phone: 589-4575), and *SLS* (phone: 589-4586) are at the airport. The major city hotels also have car rental services.

TAXI Stands are at the *Dresden Hauptbahnhof* in the *Altmarkt, Dresden-Neustadt Hauptbahnhof* in Neustadt, and Postplatz. Taxis also congregate in front of the *Dresden Hilton* in Neumarkt and on the Neustadt side of the Augustus Bridge near the *Maritim Bellevue* hotel. For a radio taxi, call 459-8112.

TOURS Daily motorcoach tours of the city and *Schloss Pillnitz,* with English-speaking guides, depart daily from the intersection of Prager Strasse and Dr.-Külz-Ring, and from the Altstadt side of the Augustus Bridge. For more information on this and other excursions, including trips to Meissen, *Sächsische Schweiz Nationalpark,* and *Barockschloss Moritzburg,* call *Strand Stadtrundfahrt Dresden* (phone: 494-0038) or the tourist offices (see *Tourist Information*).

TRAIN Dresden is an important Central European railroad junction, with both German and European connections at two stations: Altstadt *Hauptbahnhof* (phone: 471-0600 or 476-1502) and Neustadt *Hauptbahnhof* (phone: 51185). The *SV-Bahn* suburban railroad lines, with double-decker passenger cars, serve such locations as Meissen, Radebeul (on the Saxon Wine Road), Tharandt Forest, Dresdner Heide meadowlands, and towns in the *Sächsische Schweiz National Park.* Also, high-speed *InterCity Express* trains are scheduled to begin running between Berlin and Dresden this year.

SPECIAL EVENTS

Each year, concerts in the *Kreuzkirche, Semperoper,* and *Kulturpalast* commemorate the February 13–14 anniversary dates of the bombing of Dresden. The *Film Festival* takes place each spring (dates vary) at the *UFA-Palast* cinema. The *Kulturpalast* and several other concert halls and churches in the city play host to the annual *Internationales Dixieland-Festival,* the largest festival of its kind in Europe, during the second weekend in May; the *Dresdner Musikfestspiele* (Dresden Music Festival), with performances of classical music and operas, in the last week of May and the first week of June; and the *Sommerfest der Volksmusik* (Summer Festival of Folk Music) in July. Also in July is the *Dresdner Kunstfest* (Dresden Art Festival). *Filmnächte am Elbufer* (Outdoor Film Nights), with movies shown in front of the Saxon state finance ministry in Neustadt, attracts film buffs from early July to mid-August. In parks and squares around town, a *Country-Festival,* featuring US-style country music and German-language and English-language performers, with a "special guest" singing star from the United States, is held during the last weekend of August. The 10-day *Dresdner Tage der zeitgenössischen Musik* (Dresden Days of Contemporary Music); *Kabarett-Tage* (Cabaret Days), featuring satirical performances in German; and *Jazz Herbst* (Jazz Autumn) weekend are October highlights. Most festivals are held at the *Kulturpalast. Striezelmarkt* is Dresden's traditional *Christmas* fair, held from late November to December 22 on the *Altmarkt.*

MUSEUMS

In addition to those mentioned in *Special Places,* the following museums are worth a visit. Unless otherwise indicated, all are closed Mondays and charge admission.

DEUTSCHES HYGIENE-MUSEUM (GERMAN MUSEUM OF HYGIENE) The only one of its kind in the world, it opened as a museum in 1930, 19 years after serving as the main pavilion of the first *International Exhibition of Hygiene.* Included are life-size glass models of two women (one pregnant, one not), a man, a horse, and a cow. A good natural food restaurant, *Vitanova,* is on the premises. From downtown, take streetcar No. 10, 13, or 26. 1 Lingnerpl. (phone: 48460).

MILITÄRHISTORISCHES MUSEUM (MUSEUM OF MILITARY HISTORY) Six thousand artifacts cover six centuries of European wars and revolutions. From downtown, take streetcar No. 8 north. In Neustadt at 3 Olbrichtpl. (phone: 592-3250).

STAATLICHES MUSEUM FÜR MINEROLOGIE UND GEOLOGIE (MINEROLOGICAL AND GEOLOGICAL MUSEUM) The collection includes 50,000 minerals and 350,000 different fossils. On the *Brühlsche Terrasse* in the *Ständehaus,* Saxony's prewar administrative center. Closed Mondays and Tuesdays. 1 Augustusstr. (phone: 495-3002).

STAATLICHES MUSEUM FÜR VÖLKERKUNDE UND MUSEUM FÜR VORGESCHICHTE (ETHNOLOGY MUSEUM AND PREHISTORY MUSEUM) Exhibits of anthropological and archaeological interest in the 18th-century *Japanisches Palais* (Japanese Palace) along the riverbank in Neustadt. Closed Fridays. Palaispl. (phone: 52591).

STADTMUSEUM (CITY MUSEUM) Artifacts from old Dresden, such as vintage typewriters and memorabilia from the Communist era, in the beautifully restored 18th-century *Landhaus.* Closed Fridays. 2 Wilsdruffer Str. (phone: 495-2302).

TECHNISCHES MUSEUM (MUSEUM OF TECHNOLOGY) Located in a nearby suburb, this recently renovated museum focuses on technological feats of the last 200 years. There are displays on electronics, computers, photography, motion pictures, and gramophone players. Closed Sundays. From downtown, take streetcar No. 1 or No. 6 two stops past Schillerplatz. 5 Reinhold-Becker-Str., Blasewitz (phone: 35485).

VERKEHRSMUSEUM (TRANSPORT MUSEUM) Established in 1956 in the Renaissance *Johanneum,* which became the electors' art gallery in the 18th century, this place features everything from buggies to bicycles, from locomotives to luxury liners. Half-price admission on Fridays. Neumarkt (phone: 495-3002).

VOLKSKUNSTMUSEUM (FOLK ART MUSEUM) Located in the oldest building in the Neustadt, the *Jägerhof*—a royal hunting lodge built between 1568 and 1617—this museum was gutted during the firebombing and reopened in 1950. Note its three rounded staircase towers. The collection includes national costumes, toys, and rare Erzgebirge woodcarvings. From central Dresden, take the No. 11 streetcar. 1 Köpckestr. (phone: 570817).

SHOPPING

German reunification had a speedy impact on the variety and quality of merchandise offered in Dresden. Most stores are concentrated in the city center on Prager Strasse, along wide Wilsdruffer Strasse, at the *Altmarkt,* and on Neustadt's pedestrians-only Hauptstrasse. *Karstadt* (19 Prager Str.;

phone: 48470), a full-service department store, is housed in an ugly aluminum building. A newer, smaller annex stocks sportswear and sporting goods exclusively. For standard shopping hours, see GETTING READY TO GO. The following is a list of specialty stores worth browsing:

Antiquitäten The best of the few antiques shops in central Dresden. 17-19 Hauptstr. (phone: 570740).

Bücherstube Gutenberg A well-stocked, likable bookstore in Neustadt. 38 Hauptstr. (phone: 53257).

Hohlfeldt KG Stylish menswear and women's clothing occupy the first two floors of a Baroque building facing a courtyard. 9 Hauptstr. (phone: 55942).

Hutschenreuther AG High-quality Bavarian porcelain tableware bears the 1814 Hutschenreuther trademark. Also featured are modern patterns and designs. 6 Wilsdruffer Str. (phone: 495-2542).

IB Internationale Bücher A well-stocked Altstadt bookstore with English-language selections on the second level. 4 Kreuzstr. (phone: 495-4190).

Kunst und Handwerk Etzol A cute one-room place crammed with wood-carved toys, figurines, nutcracker soldiers, and typical *Christmastime* windmill pyramids and nativity cribs handmade in Saxony's Erzgebirge highland region. 19 Hauptstr. (phone: 53893).

Meissen Porcelain An exclusive outlet in the arcade of the *Dresden Hilton.* Neumarkt (phone: 484-1871).

Resi Hammerer A branch of Vienna's ultrastylish women's fashion boutique. 10 Wilsdruffer Str. (phone: 284-3574).

Rhythmus 2011 Recordings from English-language Dixieland to Dresden opera. 28 St. Petersburger Str. (phone: 495-1221).

Sächsische Werk-Kunst-Stube Folkloric Saxon textiles, pottery, and miscellany in traditional deep blue with white highlights. Striking, reasonably priced Pulsnitzer earthenware, too. 1 Wallstr. (phone: 495-1487).

Skyline Ladies' coats, jackets, sweaters, and accessories. 44 Hauptstr. (phone: 55314).

Vitzhum Upscale jewelry and watches. 21 *Altmarkt* (phone: 495-2564).

GALLERIES GALORE

Dresden has an emerging visual art scene, with dozens of galleries, ranging from the more traditional to the experimentally radical. Ask at the tourist office for a free *Kunst Angebot* directory, which lists nearly three dozen of these privately owned galleries. Those closest to the city center include *Galerie Lehman* (4 Institutsgasse; phone: 495-5245), *Galerie Kunst der Zeit* (7 Wilsdruffer Str.; phone: 495-2467), and, in Neustadt, *Galerie*

Königstrasse (11 Königstr.; phone: 578204), _Galerie Autogen_ (11 Pulsnitzer Str.; phone: 502-2147), and _Kunstausstellung Kühl_ (12 Zittauer Str.; phone: 55588).

SPORTS AND FITNESS

Extensive public greenery and forests, plus the wide Elbe meadows on both sides of the river, give Dresdeners the best of the country in the city.

BICYCLING Bikes can be rented by the hour or day at *Radsportshop* (Körnerpl.; phone: 377945) for rides along the Elbe. Within the city limits are 20 miles (32 km) of bike lanes, some of which extend along the Elbe and the *Grosser Garten.*

FITNESS CENTER *Bodyx* gym and aerobics studio (5 Gerichtsstr.; phone: 281-1902) is open daily except Sundays. *Freier's Sauna* (phone: 459-3312) is located in the same building.

FOOTBALL The Dresden *Monarchs* play American-style football against other German teams on Saturdays from September through December in the *Sportpark Ostragehege,* just northwest of the Altstadt. For information, contact the tourist office (see *Tourist Information*) or call 36680.

GOLF The area's sole public 18-hole golf course is in Possendorf, 3 miles (5 km) south of the city center (phone: 35206-3376).

HORSE RACING The season at *Pferderennbahn* racetrack (1 Oskar-Röder-Str.; phone: 237-1125 or 237-1103) starts in April and extends until mid-November.

ICE SKATING AND ROLLER-SKATING Both roller-skating (spring through fall) and ice skating (in winter) are available at the indoor *Eissporthalle* in the *Friedrichstadt* sports complex (1 Pieschener Allee; phone: 437211), a short distance east of Altstadt's city center. In addition, there's outdoor skating at the *Eislaufbahn* (phone: 432-7806), also at the *Friedrichstadt* complex. Skate rental is available.

JOGGING Elbe riverside trails, a series of wide walkways and pathways that extend for miles on the Neustadt side, are best for the serious runner; there's also a pleasant 2-mile (3-km) circuit around *Grosser Garten* in Altstadt.

SOCCER *FC Dynamo Dresden* plays against other first-division *Bundesliga* squads in the 38,000-seat *Rudolf Harbig Stadium* (entrance on Dr.-Georg-Sorg-Str.; phone: 495-6046) near the *Grosser Garten.*

SWIMMING Indoor pools are located at the *Schwimmhalle* (Steinstr.; phone: 459-3048); there are outdoor pools at *Georg-Arnold-Bad* (Dr.-Georg-Sorg-Str.; phone: 495-2097), next to the *Rudolf Harbig Stadium.*

TENNIS There are no public courts. But visitors can use the courts at the private *TC Grün-Weiss* club (Wiener Str.; phone: 477491).

THEATER

The Saxon state *Schauspielhaus* (3 Ostra-Allee; phone: 484-2429), scheduled to reopen at press time after an extensive renovation, stages works by Shakespeare, Schiller, Ibsen, Brecht/Weill, Fassbinder, Arthur Miller, and Neil Simon, as well as experimental offerings. Its repertory company performs at *Kleines Haus* in Neustadt (28 Glacisstr.; phone: 52631). The *Herkuleskeule* cabaret (1 Sternpl.; phone: 495-1446) does political satire, particularly on the strains of *Ossi-Wessi* (East-West) "togetherness." There are performances Tuesday through Friday nights, with two shows on Saturdays. *Dresdner Brettl* (17 Maternistr.; phone: 495-4123), another satirical-revue cabaret, also features drama, music, and literary readings. Tiny 50-seat *Theater 50* delves mainly into snappy comedy and pantomime (44 Clara-Zetkin-Str.; phone: 412-1375). *Kleine Szene* (107 Bautzner Str.; phone: 484-2323) offers contemporary plays on a small stage. *Projekttheater* (47 Louisenstr.; phone: 53041) puts on alternative versions of the classics, new-wave productions, and vintage international films. Plays for both grownups and children are staged at *Theater Junge Generation* (4 Meissner Landstr.; phone: 437267), and puppetry for children has been the attraction at Neustadt's *Puppentheater* (220 Leipziger Str.; phone: 51124) since 1952. Classical and modern ballet is performed in the *Semperoper* (see *Music*). Theater and cabaret tickets can be purchased at the respective box offices, most of which open an hour before curtain time. Or try the Altstadt and Neustadt tourist offices. Make advance bookings for *Schauspielhaus* performances at the *Schinkelwache* ticket office on the Theaterplatz (phone: 484-2393; fax: 484-2692). It's open Mondays through Wednesdays and Fridays from noon to 5 PM; Thursdays from noon to 6 PM; and Saturdays from 10 AM to 1 PM; closed Sundays.

MUSIC

Grand opera usually sells out in the glorious *Semperoper* (see *Special Places*), which is also the home of one of Europe's most critically acclaimed symphony orchestras, the *Staatskapelle.* The light opera of Johann Strauss and Franz Lehar is the primary repertoire of the *Staatsoperette* (131 Pirnauer Landstr.; phone: 223-8763), but Broadway-type musicals play here, too. Tickets for *Semperoper, Staatskapelle,* and *Staatsoperette* performances are available at the *Schinkelwache* ticket office on Theaterplatz. Concerts by the other big-time local symphony orchestra, the *Dresden Philharmonic,* are held in the *Kulturpalast* (2 Schlossstr.; phone: 486-6286). Its box office is open weekdays from 9 AM to 6 PM; weekends from 10 AM to 2 PM. *Hochschule für Musik* (Music Conservatory; 13 Wettiner Pl.; phone: 495-2103) and *Zentrum für zeitgenössische Musik* (Center for Contemporary Music; 17 Schevenstr.; phone: 378281) both schedule a wide variety of musical concerts, from rap to classical and pop music, plus works of innovative contemporary composers from all over the world, including Hungary, Russia, the US, and Argentina. Chamber concerts at 4 PM Sunday are a tradition at the *Kronensaal* of *Schloss Albrechtsburg* (see *Special Places*). Other musical highlights are Silbermann organ recitals in the *Hofkirche* and performances by the famed *Kreuzchor* in the *Kreuzkirche,* where the boys' choir is joined by the *Philharmonic* on special occasions (see *Special Places* for details about both). Organ recitals are regular events at 5:30 PM Mondays and Fridays in Neustadt's *Dreikönigskirche* (23 Hauptstr.; phone: 562-4103).

NIGHTCLUBS AND NIGHTLIFE

Jazz Club Tonne (3 Tzschirnerpl.; phone: 495-1354), in the cellar of a bombed-out building across from the *Albertinum,* attracts a young crowd for live jazz and disco music. Jazz is featured, too, at *Club Passage* (5 Leutewitzer Ring; phone: 491-2665), while *Podium* in Neustadt (11 Hauptstr.; phone: 53266) offers jazz, folk music, and Monday amateur nights. The *Herkuleskeule* cabaret (see *Theater*) has a piano bar with jazz music. *Amadeus* is a stylish restaurant (see *Eating Out*) with dance bands on weekend nights. Saturday is disco night at *Club Bärenzwinger* (phone: 492-3860), in echoing vaults beneath the *Brühlsche Terrasse* gardens. Another hot disco spot is *Maximilian's* (phone: 484-1755) in the *Dresden Hilton;* upstairs at the *Galeriecafé* in *Haus Altmarkt* (on the *Altmarkt;* phone: 495-1212); and *Hollywood 118* (Bautzner Str.; phone 502-2451), located in an Elbe-side villa that used to be Stasi secret police headquarters. *Weisse Flotte* disco cruises are popular; tickets can be purchased at a kiosk near the boat (2 Terrassenufer; phone: 502-2661). Congenial bars in Neustadt include *Gin Gin* (Am Albertpl.; phone: 53372) and *Der Löwe* (48 Hauptstr.; phone: 51138); on *Neumarkt* in Altstadt, try *Café zur Frauenkirche* (formerly *Blaues Ei;* phone: 484-1836). The city's only casino, with blackjack, roulette, and one-armed bandits, is in the *Maritim Bellevue* hotel (see *Checking In*). It's open daily from 7 PM until dawn. You must bc 18 to get in; bring your passport.

Best in Town

CHECKING IN

The two most important words on the subject of Dresden hotels? Book early. Forty years after the Dresden bombing the city did not have a bona fide luxury hotel. Now there are three, with several being planned for the near future, including four that were under construction at press time: the *Grand Hotel Taschenbergpalais,* a 200-room property across from the *Zwinger;* the 242-room *Dorint* hotel; the *Art'Hotel,* with 100 rooms; and the small *Classic,* with 20 rooms. Check with the tourist offices (see *Tourist Information*) for more information on the status of these hotels. However, at least for now, there's nowhere near enough quality hotel space to meet the growing demand fostered by first-rate festivals, concerts, and theatrical productions that draw four million visitors annually. Because events are spread out during the calendar year, room availability and rates remain basically stable year-round. The tourist offices in Altstadt and Neustadt keep up-to-date room-reservation records; write or call for information regarding budget-rate pensions, private residences, youth hostels, and hotels beyond the city limits. Many of Dresden's major hotels have complete facilities for the business traveler. Those hotels listed below as having "business services" usually offer such conveniences as English-speaking concierge, meeting rooms, photocopiers, computers, translation services, and express check-out, among others. Call the hotel for additional information. A double room (with private bath, TV set, and breakfast included, unless otherwise indicated) at those properties listed as very expensive is priced at $250 or more per night; at expensive places, $185 to $250; at places in the moderate category, $150 to $185; and at inexpensive hotels, less than $150. All telephone numbers are in the 351 city code unless otherwise indicated.

VERY EXPENSIVE

Dresden Hilton Deluxe in every respect, this modern-style chain member, formerly the *Dresdner Hof,* is Swedish-built with Swiss-designed interiors and furnishings in a black-and-white motif. All paintings, graphics, sculptures, and mobiles throughout the building are by Dresden artists. Adjoining is a congress center with full business services, including secretarial services, and computer and fax lines. There are 333 rooms, with 67 designated as non-smoking. Facing the *Neumarkt* and the *Frauenkirche* ruins, it has 13 restaurants, including the excellent *Ristorante Rossini* (see *Eating Out*), bistros, an espresso bar, a piano bar, a Viennese-style café, coffeehouses, bakeries, and snack bars. There's also an athletic club with a pool, saunas, and a bowling alley. A glass passageway attaches the main building to the historic *Sekundogenitur* (see *Special Places*) for access onto the *Brühlsche Terrasse.* 5 An der Frauenkirche (phone: 48410; 800-HILTONS; fax: 484-1700).

Maritim Bellevue A Baroque 17th-century burgher's mansion with a marble lobby and corridors, restored and skillfully blended into the low-rise cluster of newer wings, this member of the prestigious Maritim chain boasts 330 regally outfitted rooms and suites, business services, a shopping gallery, and the city's most complete fitness club—a gym, a pool, a solarium, bowling lanes, and a refreshment bar. Along with the *Semperoper,* it opened to rave reviews 40 years after the Dresden bombing raids. Business services are available. The fine restaurants include a wraparound outdoor terrace, the genteel *Palais* dining room, Polynesian *Buri-Buri,* a café in the Baroque courtyard annex, and the first-rate *Canaletto,* specializing in French cuisine (see *Eating Out*). 15 Grosse Meissner Str. (phone: 56620; 800-843-3311; fax: 55997).

Palais Hotel Gewandhaus This 50-room hostelry, in an 18th-century Baroque building first transformed during the Communist era into a mediocre hotel, is Dresden's newest topflight luxury property. Its creamy white exterior and four-story atrium make a most fashionable statement. All rooms have outside views, gold-plated bathroom fixtures, and individual whirlpools. Amenities include a fully equipped fitness center, an indoor pool, and business services. The best in-house restaurant is the *Weissen Sammlung*, and there's a 25-seat *Teezimmer* (tea room) and lounge areas under the glass atrium in the *Palmgarten*. Centrally located next to the *Rathaus*. 1 Ringstr. (phone: 495-6180; fax: 495-6120).

EXPENSIVE

Mercure Newa Although not up to the standards of the previous entries, this monolithic 14-story structure popular with Russian officials in the pre-*glasnost* era has been upgraded. All 310 rooms have shower-only bathrooms, telephones, mini-bars, and large windows with good skyline views, particularly on the upper floors. Amenities include a sauna, massage, and a beauty salon, plus business services. The *Newski* lobby bar is pleasant, and Russian specialties are served in the *St. Petersburg* restaurant. Close to the main railroad station. 34 St. Petersburg Str. (phone: 481-4109; fax: 495-5137).

Prinz Eugen Noted for its efficient, English-speaking reception staff, this modern place with a curved, central skylight has been open for a couple of years. There's no restaurant, but each of the 47 rooms has its own kitchenette with refrigerator, as well as bright, light-colored, modern furnishings, a telephone, and a washing machine and dryer. Business services are available. The location, close to the Elbe River, is in east-side Dresden's Laubegast suburb, an upscale, tree-shaded, quiet neighborhood. 4 Gustav-Hartmann-Str. (phone: 251-5998; fax: 251-5986).

Am Terrassenufer Savvy developers proved the truth of the real estate adage "location, location, location" when they transformed this 21-year-old, 12-story building of uninspiring Communist-era design into an upscale hotel overlooking the Elbe and the Altstadt skyline. All of the 196 spacious rooms are equipped with the usual amenities, including telephones; some are reserved for nonsmokers. Dining is in the skylit *Pavilion* restaurant. Business services are available. 12 Terrassenufer (phone: 495-9500; 800-223-5652; fax: 440-9600).

Windsor This turn-of-the-century building on a quiet residential side street off the main thoroughfare of Leipziger Strasse, 15 minutes by streetcar from the Augustus Bridge, is an intimate hideaway. Each of the 25 rooms features a mini-bar, a TV with built-in radio, a telephone, white and brass furnishings, a bathroom with a shower, a hair dryer, monogrammed robes, and sandals. Premium rooms have balconies and twin bathroom vanities. There's a good breakfast buffet, a lobby bar, and a Bavarian cellar tavern, but no restaurant. The personable, English-speaking owner, Dr. Fritz Walter Merker, is a yachtsman whose love of the sea is expressed in the nautical pictures that adorn the guestrooms and public areas. 13 Rossmässlerstr. (phone: 52941; fax: 52944).

MODERATE

Alpha Located in an impressively renovated building about 2 miles (3 km) west of the Augustus Bridge and Hauptstrasse in Neustadt, it features bathrooms with showers, direct-dial telephones, radios, and color TV sets with nine-channel hookups in all 80 rooms. German-style buffet breakfasts are offered in the *China-Restaurant,* which serves typical Chinese meals for lunch and dinner. Other features include a cellar wine bar, a sauna, a whirlpool, and a solarium. 21 Fritz-Reuter-Str. (phone: 502-2441; fax: 571390).

Ambiente A popular choice, this 20-room boutique of a place is located in the serene suburb of Niedersedlitz. Greco, the resident parrot, welcomes you (in German, *natürlich*) as you pass the etched-glass public-area doors. Interiors are of cherry wood; the furnishings, custom-made. Room amenities include TV-radios, telephones, and hair dryers. The buffet breakfasts are abundant. Nearby is Pöppelmann's *Schloss Pillnitz* (see *Special Places*). 23 Meusegaster Str. (phone: 221880; fax: 221-8836).

Bastei This semi-high-rise example of Socialist architecture (ca. 1969), a typically bland-looking building of glazed white tiles on the Prager Strasse pedestrian mall, has now been somewhat spruced up. Mini-bars and telephones are standard in the 306 rooms, and the restaurant serves tasty Saxon specialties for lunch and dinner. Bedrooms are spacious, and horizontal windows let in plenty of light (though the furnishings and carpeting are tired-looking and ordinary). As a hospitable gesture, a basket at the front desk is always filled with apples. Business services are available. Prager Str. (phone: 485-6385; fax: 495-4076).

Bülow Residenz A Baroque townhouse built in 1730, this property located a block west of Hauptstrasse has been completely renovated and transformed into a fine hotel. The 31 rooms are huge, attractively decorated with cherry-wood furnishings, and equipped with mini-bars, safes, telephones, and tiled bathrooms with hair dryers and either tubs or showers. Some of the rooms have a view of the street, but the others are quieter. Other amenities include *Das Caroussel,* a romantic restaurant; the cozy *Caroussel Bar,* which occupies a vaulted space downstairs that was used as a bomb shelter in 1945; and business services. This is a particularly good value for the money. 19 Rähnitzgasse (phone: 44033; fax: 440-3410).

Coventry Cottage Named after Dresden's sister city in England, this attractive hostelry is located in the suburb of Altreick, which is easily accessible by streetcar from the Altstadt *Hauptbahnhof.* The 51 rooms are well-appointed and feature modern amenities; some have balconies. There are also four suites with high, curved ceilings (they are set inside rooftop barrel vaults). The *Coventry Gardens* restaurant offers superb food (see *Eating Out*), and there's a lobby bar with a grand piano. 1 Hülstr., Altreick (phone: 281-6311; fax: 281-6310).

Florentina Anchored on the Altstadt side of the Elbe, this is one of several former excursion boats that have been converted into floating hotels in order to increase the city's supply of overnight accommodations. The 140 small cabins are equipped with showers, direct-dial telephones, radios, and satellite TV. The cabins have bunk-type beds and shelves rather than clothing drawers. There's a good restaurant, serving a breakfast buffet and à la carte meals; a cocktail lounge; and the top-deck, glass-canopied *Wintergarten,* a beer garden used for group functions. If possible, stay in a portside cabin, which offers views of Elbe boating traffic and the Saxon state chancellery on the Neustadt shore. Terrassenufer (phone: 459-0169; fax: 459-5036).

Königstein A clone of the *Bastei* (see above) next door, it has the same GDR developer, same utilitarian concept, same late-1960s vintage, same room rates, same restaurant quality, and a comparable basket of apples; it has also recently undergone renovation. Business services are available. Prager Str. (phone: 485-6362; fax: 495-4054).

Lilienstein The third hotel in a look-alike row of tile-surfaced triplets, alongside the *Bastei* and *Königstein* (see above). It's the same size, and offers the same features (including business services), restaurant quality, and rates. Prager Str. (phone: 485-6372; fax: 495-2506).

INEXPENSIVE

Cosel For a taste of Dresden in all its turn-of-the-century glory, try this charming mansion set in the Strehlen district, a charming neighborhood of zigzag streets a few blocks south of the *Grosser Garten.* Formerly known as *Gästehaus Strehlen,* its 19 small rooms have basic furnishings which include radios and telephones, and bathrooms with tubs and showers or showers only. What used to be the ballroom is now a small conference facility, and there's a good restaurant with a well-chosen wine list. Breakfast service begins at 6:30 AM. The friendly and attentive manager, Brigitte Melcher, adds a personal touch. Nearby is the Wasaplatz shopping and public-transport hub. 46 August-Bebel-Str. (phone: 471-9495; fax: 471-0171).

Elbresidenz This Terrassenufer "hotel ship" used to be the *Nederland* in the *KD German Rhine Line* fleet. It offers 66 double-bed and 20 triple-bed cabins on two decks; rooms are equipped with TV sets, radios, and telephones. Superb meals are served in *Salon Meissen* (see *Eating Out*) on the promenade deck, where there's also a cocktail lounge and a salon for private gatherings. Its fitness-related features include a sauna, exercycles, and a sundeck pool. Rates are appreciably lower for weekend stays. Terrassenufer (phone: 459-5003; fax: 459-5137).

Martha Hospiz Centrally located on a quiet side street two blocks west of the Hauptstrasse pedestrian zone in Neustadt, this hostelry is a little gem of polished woodwork and deep-pile carpeting. The 36 rooms are bright and comfortable with telephones, color TV sets, and bathrooms with either tubs and showers or showers only. (Ask for a room facing the street—

most of them do.) An elevator is an added nicety in the refurbished four-story structure built in 1899. The buffet breakfast is hearty. The hostelry is part of the *Christian Hotels Association,* a European-wide network of clean, well-run, economical properties. 11 Nieritzstr. (phone: 56760; fax: 53218).

Schloss Eckberg The next-door neighbor of *Schloss Albrechtsburg* (see *Special Places*) shares a Neustadt promontory above the Elbe. Built for a rich merchant in the mid-19th century, this neo-Gothic villa is now a hotel with a fitness center, a sauna, and business services. The 80 small rooms have TV sets, radios, telephones, and bathrooms with tubs and showers or showers only. *Remise,* a reasonably priced restaurant, overlooks the river; dance music for the younger set is featured Friday and Saturday evenings in the *Schlossbar.* 134 Bautzner Str. (phone: 52571; fax: 55379).

EATING OUT

Dresden's once-stodgy culinary tradition has taken a sharp turn for the better since reunification. For Germans the cuisine of choice remains sauerbraten, pork, wursts, and sauerkraut, but restaurants serving continental fare have made marked inroads. On most menus the category called *Sächsisch regionale Gerichte* (roughly translated as the specialties of Saxony) lists such mainstays as *Kartoffelsuppe* (potato soup) with sausages, bacon bits, and parsley, and *Quarkkeulchen,* a baked appetizer made from boiled potatoes, flour, sugar, and raisins, topped with cinnamon and served with a side dish of cream-topped applesauce. Saxon-style potato salad often includes vegetables, bits of sausage, fish, apples, or cucumbers. Two favorite meat dishes, *Schmorhaxe* (roast veal or beef) and *Dickbein* (pickled pork shank), are cooked in beer sauce with sauerkraut and dumplings. For dessert it's *Eierschecke,* a sugar-covered egg concoction speckled with raisins, *Pflaumenkuchen* (plum cake), and Saxon Pulsnitz *Pfefferkuchen* (gingerbread). At *Christmas* have a slice of Dresdner stollen, the rum-spiced fruit and almond cake that's been a staple here since 1474.

The city-brewed beer is Radeberger Pilsner. White wines from the nearby Elbtal vineyard region are commendable. Meissner rühlander, kerner, rosengrünchen, scheurebe, müller-thurgau, and weissburgunder vintages tend to be the best. Farther north are the Saale-Unstrut vineyards. For a dinner for two without drinks and wine, expect to pay $90 or more in establishments classified as very expensive, $75 to $90 in those in the expensive category, $35 to $75 in moderate places, and less than $35 in inexpensive spots. Taxes and tips are included, but you should leave a small additional amount for good service. Unless otherwise noted, restaurants are open for lunch and dinner. All telephone numbers are in the 351 city code unless otherwise indicated.

VERY EXPENSIVE

Canaletto The tastefully decorated, candelit dining room of the *Maritim Bellevue* hotel affords splendid views of its colorful gardens. Chef Helmut Ott offers a French-style menu in what ranks as the most elegant place in town. Meat, seafood, and game entrées (including breast of pheasant) are superb. Open for dinner only; closed Sundays. Reservations necessary. Major credit cards accepted. 15 Grosse Meissner Str. (phone: 56620).

Meissner Weinkeller Part of a bland Communist-era building block, this place, with one of the best wine cellars in Saxony, nonetheless offers a warm, welcoming interior. Cozy and old-fashioned, with dark woodwork, a "country Saxon" atmosphere, and superior service, it's favored by those looking for sophisticated, German-style cuisine. One of its most popular dishes is honey-glazed breast of duck in red wine sauce. The wine list is extensive, including the finest of Saxony's white Elbtal varietals. Closed Sundays. Reservations advised. Major credit cards accepted. 1B Hauptstr. (phone: 55814).

Ristorante Rossini Graciously attentive service is a hallmark of the *Hilton* hotel's top dining room. (The menu is operatically categorized: overture, first act, intermezzo, second and third acts, and grand finale.) A favorite entrée is the lamb cutlets sprinkled with rosemary herbs, with a side dish of fresh zucchini. Open daily. Reservations necessary. Major credit cards accepted. 5 An der Frauenkirche (phone: 484-1741).

EXPENSIVE

Amadeus An elegant restaurant in the *Haus Altmarkt* complex, this place features big-band music and dancing every evening, romantically in tune with the expertly prepared meals. Favorite dishes from the German/continental menu include salmon steak with crabmeat and sauerbraten with apple dumplings. Open daily for dinner only. Reservations necessary. Major credit cards accepted. 19-21 Wilsdruffer Str. (phone: 495-1212).

Laterne The view of the city lights of the Albertplatz, Neustadt's traffic hub, and Altstadt in the near distance make this wine restaurant a favorite nighttime destination. Each banquette seating arrangement faces bronze-tinted, floor-to-ceiling windows on the fifth and sixth floors of a postmodern building. Try the Dresden potato soup, beef roulade with red cabbage and apples, and Saxon egg pancakes with raisins, apples, and whipped cream. Open daily. Reservations advised. Major credit cards accepted. 1 Bautzer Str. (phone: 53094).

Opernrestaurant und Steakhaus These two places—in the same building and under the same management—are a surprisingly harmonious contemporary addition to the *Semperoper.* The *Opernrestaurant* dining room occupies the upper level, while the more casual *Steakhaus* downstairs boasts a large alfresco terrace. Among the most popular of the Saxon specialties served in both places are *Seusslitzer* duck soup (must be ordered in advance), and *Moritzburger* venison goulash with sauerkraut and *Klitscher* (potato fritters); the *Steakhaus* also offers steaks and chops. Open daily. Reservations advised. Major credit cards accepted. 2 Theaterpl. (phone: 484-2521, *Opernrestaurant;* 484-2506, *Steakhaus*).

MODERATE

Altmarktkeller Scurrying waitresses dish out hearty German food in this rustically authentic *Bierstube* in a cellar area of the *Haus Altmarkt* complex. The salad bar is a good value. Open daily. Reservations unnecessary. Major credit cards accepted. *Altmarkt* (phone: 495-1212).

China-Palast Although very large, with an elaborate pagoda entryway, this is a welcoming, family-owned place. Typical Chinese dishes, Thai delicacies, and Polynesian cocktails are featured. Open daily. Reservations unnecessary. Major credit cards accepted. 19 Wilsdruffer Str. (phone: 495-4061).

Coventry Gardens This dining room enjoyed a stellar reputation long before it became part of the *Coventry Cottage* hotel a few years ago. Now, under the direction of master chef Frank Berg, it is better than ever. The menu primarily features French-Alsatian dishes and fresh seafood; try the salmon roulade stuffed with spinach and served with red sea bass, snow peas, and tomato rice. In warm weather, diners can eat on an attractive terrace. Open daily. Reservations advised. Major credit cards accepted. 1 Hülstr. (phone: 281-6311).

Kügelgen Haus This Baroque burgher's mansion in Neustadt houses three separate facilities: a *Kaffeestübe* (coffee parlor) serving light fare, a meat-and-sauerkraut *Bierkeller* (beer cellar), and a formal grillroom. In the grillroom, try the regional Saxon lunch and dinner courses, such as Erzgebirgische-style chicken breast and mushrooms, or Lausitzer pork with prune sauce. Its walls are covered with engravings and woodcuts of musicians and writers from Dresden's prewar years. All three places are open daily; the *Kaffeestübe* serves lunch only. Reservations advised. Major credit cards accepted. 13 Hauptstr. (phone: 52791).

Im Kulturpalast Don't be put off by the garish color scheme and peacock curtains—chintzy holdovers from the GDR years. The staff is politely eager to please, the meat dishes—such as sauerbraten and pork ribs—are good, and the price is right. Located in the upstairs floor of the *Kulturpalast,* Dresden's performing arts center, it affords impressive views of the *Altmarkt* and the *Kreuzkirche.* Open daily for breakfast, lunch, and dinner. Reservations unnecessary. Major credit cards accepted. Entrance on Galeriestr. (phone: 486-6298).

Maredo The presence of a high-quality, Western-style steakhouse has caused quite a stir in post-reunification Dresden. The favorite fare offered here is prime Argentinian beef; there's also a well-stocked salad bar. Centrally located around the corner from the *Altmarkt.* Open daily. Reservations advised. Major credit cards accepted. 9 Dr.-Külz-Ring (phone: 495-6083).

Maygarten Linie 6 For a decidedly offbeat experience, board streetcar No. 4 or No. 10 (*not* No. 6) from downtown to the east side of town. The funky assemblage of antique trolley cars and transit esoterica here includes more than 400 conductors' hats. Wearing one while eating is part of the fun. The traditional German food, served in very generous portions, is good, and the basement "subway" bar is an inviting spot for a nightcap. Open daily. Reservations advised. No credit cards accepted. 24 Schaufussstr. (phone: 30268).

Piccolo Designed in a combination of Art Nouveau and Art Deco—a pastiche of gray, black, and white—this Neustadt spot with a sidewalk patio offers a regularly changing menu. Try the lamb cutlets in garlic butter or wild boar goulash with cranberries and brussels sprouts. A vegetarian alternative is tomato-purée zucchini. Open daily. Reservations necessary. Major credit cards accepted. 26 Königstr. (phone: 53168).

Ratskeller With seating for 400, this town hall restaurant is typically large, but a tasteful color scheme of cream and brown, with decor of hanging plants and potted palms, softens the atmosphere. The menu offers regional fare; there's also a popular bar. Open daily. Reservations unnecessary. Major credit cards accepted. 19 Dr.-Külz-Ring (phone: 488-2950).

Salon Meissen The dining room of the *Elbresidenz* hotel ship is far more elegant than most floating riverfront restaurants, which tend to be tacky and touristy. Here service is gracious, and the food—Dresden Dickbein pork and pasta dishes are specialties—is among the best in the city. Open daily. Reservations advised, except during winter. Major credit cards accepted. Terrassenufer (phone: 459-5003).

Szeged What was once a drowsy Hungarian restaurant has perked up since reunification. Wood, exposed brick, and pink napery blend attractively in the upstairs dining room, with its bank of wraparound windows opening onto views of downtown Dresden. Specialties include catfish soup, different variations on stuffed vegetables, and the Hungarian version of Wiener schnitzel. On street level is the bistro-café *Zum Tip,* among the Altstadt's most hospitable places for daytime coffee or after-hours drinks. Open daily. Reservations advised for dinner. Major credit cards accepted. 4-6 Wilsdruffer Str. (phone: 495-1371).

Zum Goldener Ring Woodsy kitsch and cheerful *Gemütlichkeit* (friendliness, good cheer) are attributes of this old-timer in an upstairs space overlooking the *Altmarkt.* The food is no-nonsense hearty, making it an affordable place for a beginner's sampling of Saxon specialties. Try potato soup followed by a full-course Dresden Dickbein pork dinner, washed down with Radeberger beer. Open daily. Reservations advised. Major credit cards accepted. 18 *Altmarkt* (phone: 495-2320)

INEXPENSIVE

Bella Donna This Italian pizzeria and ristorante with a minimalist black-and-white decor is tiny, but there's nothing small about the antipasto, or the pizza, pasta, and meat entrées offered here. Open daily. No reservations. Major credit cards accepted. 16-17 *Altmarkt* (phone: 495-1135).

Bistro Café This small, avant-garde eatery is a popular choice among locals, particularly in warm weather, when tables are set up on an outdoor terrace. The food here is simple: pastries and coffee for breakfast or a quick afternoon bite, and light lunch and supper fare (sandwiches, soups, etc.). Live music sometimes plays in the upper alcove in the evenings. Open daily. Reservations unnecessary. Major credit cards accepted. In the *Haus Altmarkt* complex, 19-21 Wilsdruffer Str. (phone: 495-1212).

Bistro Café am Schloss A pleasant spot (not to be confused with the *Bistro Café*, above), it features regional Saxon fare—sausages with eggs and potatoes—along with *Kaffeekuchen* (coffee cakes) for snack time. Thanks to full-length windows and an outdoor terrace, you can watch stonemasons rebuilding the *Residenzschloss* while you eat. Open daily for breakfast, lunch, and dinner. Reservations unnecessary. Major credit cards accepted. 7-9 Schlossstr. (phone: 495-1154).

Eis Café Venezia A well-known Neustadt destination for ice-cream lovers, the big draw is the selection of Italian gelato, with 16 flavors on the big board, plus 22 different sundae extravaganzas. Espresso and cappuccino are also available. This is the best of Dresden's regrettably few *Milchbars.* Open daily. No reservations. No credit cards accepted. 2a Hauptstr. (phone: 55458).

Kreutzkamm For a wistful bit of prewar Dresden try this *Konditorei* (cake shop), which dates back to 1825. Looking out on the *Kreuzkirche* and the *Altmarkt* arcades, it's the preferred place in town to sample local *Eierschecke* pastry with tea or coffee; light lunch fare is served, too. Open daily for breakfast and lunch. No reservations. No credit cards accepted. 18 *Altmarkt* (phone: 495-4172).

Mandarin Red lanterns hang from the ceiling in this, the best of central Dresden's small-size Chinese eateries. Located on a short side street off Wilsdruffer Strasse, it is one of the few non-hotel restaurants with English-language menus. Open daily. Reservations unnecessary. Major credit cards accepted. 5 Gewandhausstr. (phone: 496-3193).

Nordsee The popular western German seafood chain, which relies on cafeteria efficiency, is long on value, short on ambience. The quality of its fresh (caught daily) Atlantic seafood far exceeds typical buffet fare. Closed Sundays. No reservations. No credit cards accepted. 14 Hauptstr. (phone: 55605).

7 Schwaben Near the Neustadt riverbank, this barn-like structure (better known as *Narrenhäusel* among locals) is the place to find the best in Swabian fare, such as *Maultaschen* (a large ravioli stuffed with meat, fruit, or nuts), *Roggennudeln* (rye noodles), or light almond-studded potato croquettes. There's even Swabian beer, direct from Baden-Württemberg. Select a table by the south-side windows for views of the Altstadt with the Augustus Bridge in the foreground. Open daily. Reservations unnecessary. Major credit cards accepted. Am Augustusbrücke (phone: 55502).

Düsseldorf

At first glance the former fishing village at the confluence of the Rhine and the Düssel Rivers (*das Dorf an der Düssel*) doesn't compare to the Cinderella-castle style of Cologne, just 25 miles upriver. But look again. Almost 185 years ago, Napoleon dubbed Düsseldorf his "Little Paris," and it's easy to see why. North of city center a tree-shaded promenade extends along the banks of the Rhine and opens onto acres of green space in *Rhein Park* and the *Hofgarten.* Downtown, the world-famous Königsallee shopping district—spanned by delicate cast-iron pedestrian bridges and lined with well-tended flower beds, charming cafés, and expensive boutiques—flanks a narrow canal (originally a city moat) that is home to families of ducks and swans. At the city's northern edge, the *Tritonbrunnen* (Triton Fountain)—a stone sea god and huge sculptured fish—is a commanding presence. Though it may not be the Magic Kingdom or the Champs-Elysées, Düsseldorf has a charm all its own; it has made the transformation from fishing village to major city with grace and style.

What Düsseldorf lacks in Romanesque churches, Roman ruins (the Romans did not settle here), and cathedral spires, it makes up for in intellectual and physical variety. The city is the unrivaled fashion center of Germany, and it also offers a rich cultural history—Brahms, Schumann, Mendelssohn, and Goethe lived here, as did poet Heinrich Heine as a child—and an eclectic architectural mix. Here, it's not unusual to see a modern glass skyscraper looming behind a squat medieval tower.

This onetime village is now considered by Germans to be a great place to live—at least for the well-to-do. Residents here traditionally have had the highest per-capita income in the country (not surprisingly, everything costs more here). Two-thirds of the city's 578,000 citizens work at white-collar jobs. The work force produces a staggering 15% of Germany's foreign trade. Even during the first years of reunification, when economic slowdowns dogged heavy industries throughout the nearby Ruhr basin, Düsseldorf suffered to a lesser degree (with an unemployment rate of about 10%) than the Ruhr Valley itself.

Düsseldorf also is rich in artworks: In addition to the *Tritonbrunnen,* the city has several Henry Moore sculptures; an enormous green bronze of *Father Rhine and His Daughters,* created in 1898 by local artist Jansen Tushaus and situated in *Schwanenspiegel Park* on Haroldstrasse; the *Pallas Athena,* a huge gold statue of the Greek goddess of wisdom standing next to the *Tonhalle* (Music Hall); and contemporary and historic figures in stone, metal, and plastic guarding entrances to museums and galleries, perched on rooftops, and taking refuge among the greenery of parks and gardens. Even the cobblestone passageways in the Altstadt (Old City) are decorated with life-like bronze figures.

If you're lucky, some enterprising Düsseldorf youngsters with a flair for tradition will reenact a scene depicted at one of the most popular Altstadt landmarks: the *Radschlägerbrunnen* (Cartwheelers' Fountain). The cartwheeler tradition is said to have started in the 17th century at the wedding of the popular ruler Johann Wilhelm (locally known as Jan Wellem). During the ceremonial procession, a wheel of the wedding coach came off, and a young boy attached himself to the axle. Twisting himself into the shape of a human wheel, he "turned cartwheels" for the rest of the parade and was given a gold coin for his troubles. Today, boys known as *Radschläger* still take great pride (and earn pocket money) turning cartwheels near the fountain and along the sidewalks in front of the Königsallee cafés in summer.

Unlike Cologne and such other riverside cities as Frankfurt and Trier, Düsseldorf never enticed the Romans to stay. It wasn't until the 3rd century that the Dukes of Berg claimed the right banks of the Rhine and the Düssel for their home, and enclosed it within fortified walls studded with turrets and towers. In the late 17th century, the city came under the rule of the Neuburg-Palatinate electors, and Jan Wellem, one of the clan, presided over a talented court of architects, painters, poets, and musicians who built glorious castles, created colossal artworks, and turned the once-sleepy village into a vibrant city of the arts.

After the French Revolution, Düsseldorf was occupied by French troops and remained under French domination until 1815. Napoleon made it the capital of the Grand Duchy of Berg, and established his brother-in-law, Joachim Murat, as ruler. The French embarked on an extensive beautification program to turn Düsseldorf into not only the liveliest and most sophisticated city along the Rhine, but also the loveliest.

By the mid-19th century Düsseldorf had established its ties to the Industrial Revolution, developing ironworks and other heavy industries in the Ruhr Valley. Railway lines and Rhine steamers linked the city to the rest of Europe. During World War I, factories produced armaments, tanks, and armored vehicles. Between the two world wars, the French occupied Düsseldorf again, this time for four years.

Postwar Düsseldorf was rebuilt more or less from the ground up (as headquarters for the Ruhr basin's heavy industry, the city was a key target for bombing during World War II): Landmarks of old were restored to their original luster—even the riverside quarter of the Altstadt regained its romantic medieval look. The financiers and industrialists who constructed the postwar city exemplified the so-called German economic miracle, building fortunes in the steel, coal, and automotive industries. Today, manufacturers of machinery, steel tubing, and automobiles are the major employers. Top German companies Daimler-Benz, Henkel, Krupp, Salzgitter, and Thyssen have significant operations here. It is said that virtually all commercial transactions tied to the Ruhr's industrial output are conducted within an area of several blocks in downtown Düsseldorf.

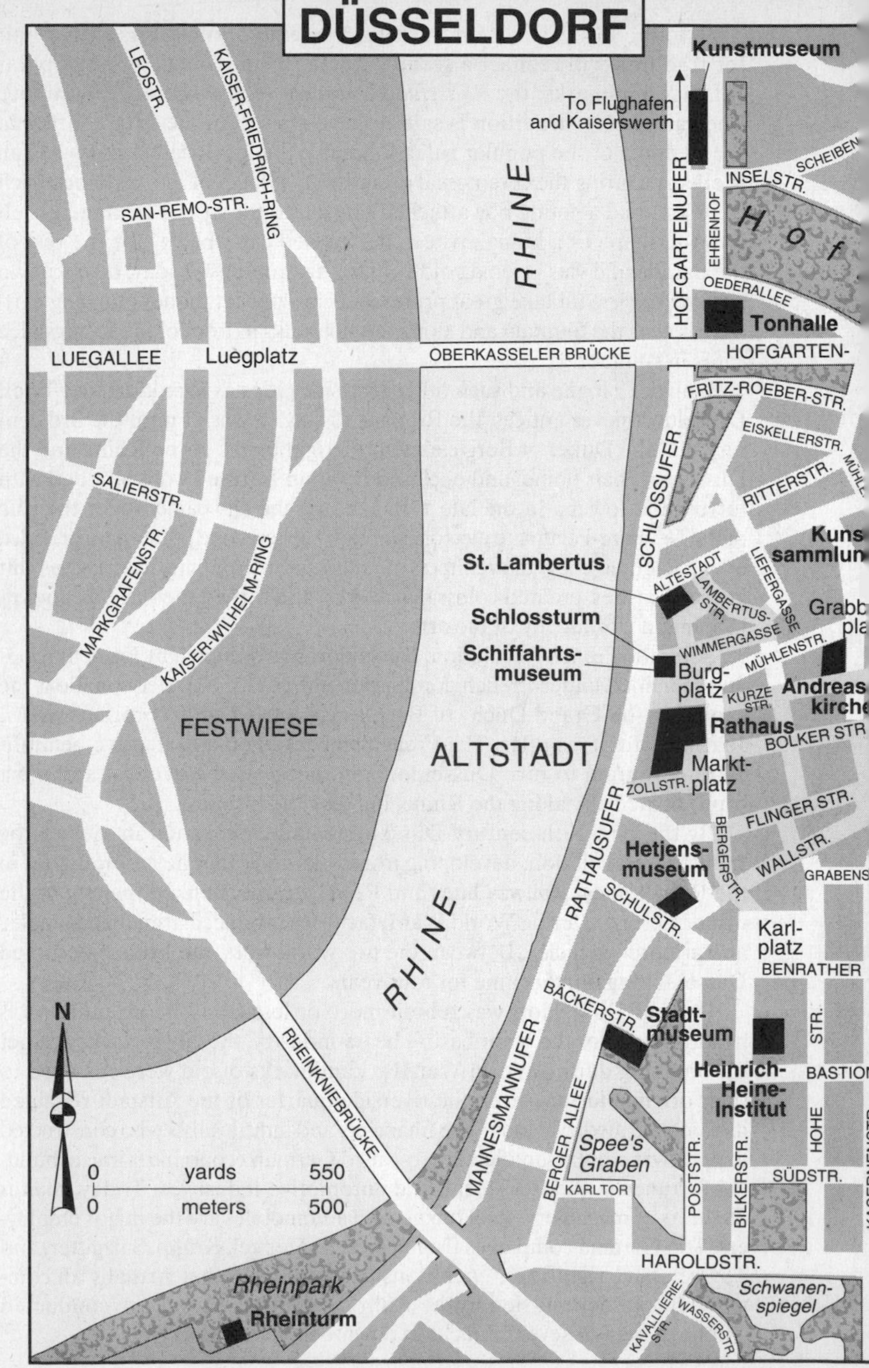

DÜSSELDORF
Kunstmuseum
To Flughafen and Kaiserswerth
LEOSTR.
KAISER-FRIEDRICH-RING
SAN-REMO-STR.
RHINE
HOFGARTENUFER
EHRENHOF
INSELSTR.
SCHEIBEN
Hof
OEDERALLEE
Tonhalle
LUEGALLEE
Luegplatz
OBERKASSELER BRÜCKE
HOFGARTEN-
FRITZ-ROEBER-STR.
EISKELLERSTR.
SALIERSTR.
SCHLOSSUFER
RITTERSTR.
MARKGRAFENSTR.
KAISER-WILHELM-RING
St. Lambertus
ALTESTADT
LAMBERTUS-STR.
LIEFERGASSE
Schlossturm
WIMMERGASSE
MÜHLENSTR.
Schiffahrts-museum
Burgplatz
KURZE STR.
Andreas kirche
Rathaus
BOLKER STR.
FESTWIESE
ALTSTADT
Markt-platz
ZOLLSTR.
RATHAUSUFER
FLINGER STR.
Hetjens-museum
BERGERSTR.
WALLSTR.
SCHULSTR.
RHINE
Karl-platz
BENRATHER
STR.
BÄCKERSTR.
Stadt-museum
N
RHEINKNIEBRÜCKE
MANNESMANNUFER
BERGER ALLEE
Heinrich-Heine-Institut
BASTION
HOHE
Spee's Graben
0 yards 550
0 meters 500
KARLTOR
POSTSTR.
BILKERSTR.
SÜDSTR.
HAROLDSTR.
Rheinpark
Rheinturm
KAVALLIERIE-STR.
WASSERSTR.
Schwanen-spiegel

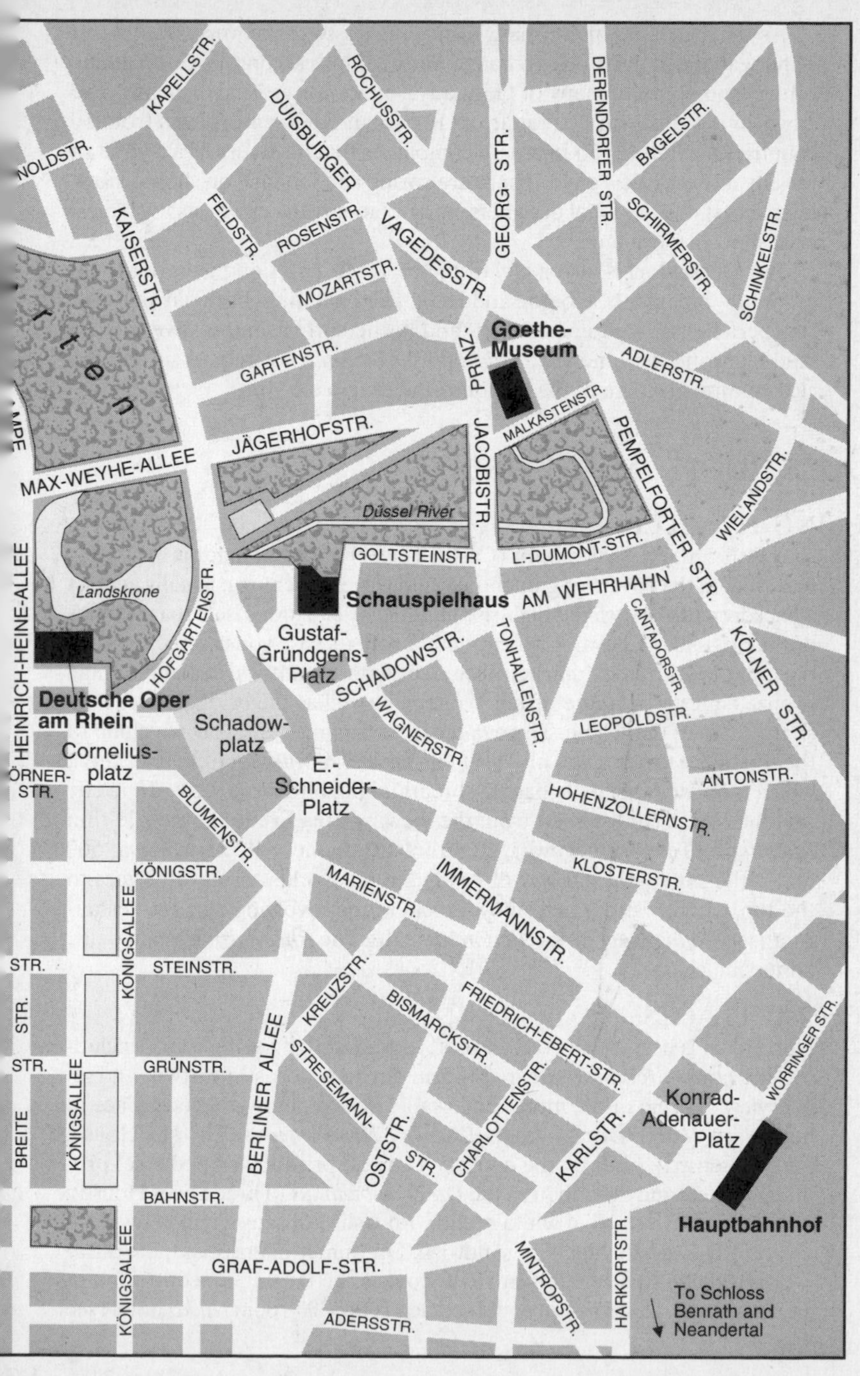

KAPELLSTR.
NOLDSTR.
KAISERSTR.
DUISBURGER
ROCHUSSTR.
FELDSTR.
ROSENSTR.
VAGEDESSTR.
GEORG- STR.
DERENDORFER STR.
BAGELSTR.
SCHIRMERSTR.
SCHINKELSTR.
MOZARTSTR.
GARTENSTR.
PRINZ-
Goethe-Museum
ADLERSTR.
rten
JÄGERHOFSTR.
JACOBISTR.
MALKASTENSTR.
PEMPELFORTER STR.
MAX-WEYHE-ALLEE
Düssel River
WIELANDSTR.
GOLTSTEINSTR.
L.-DUMONT-STR.
HEINRICH-HEINE-ALLEE
Landskrone
HOFGARTENSTR.
Schauspielhaus
AM WEHRHAHN
CANTADORSTR.
TONHALLENSTR.
KÖLNER STR.
Gustaf-Gründgens-Platz
SCHADOWSTR.
Deutsche Oper am Rhein
Schadowplatz
WAGNERSTR.
LEOPOLDSTR.
Corneliusplatz
E.-Schneider-Platz
ANTONSTR.
ÖRNER-STR.
BLUMENSTR.
HOHENZOLLERNSTR.
KÖNIGSTR.
MARIENSTR.
IMMERMANNSTR.
KLOSTERSTR.
KÖNIGSALLEE
STR.
STEINSTR.
KREUZSTR.
BISMARCKSTR.
FRIEDRICH-EBERT-STR.
WORRINGER STR.
STR.
STR.
GRÜNSTR.
STRESEMANN-STR.
CHARLOTTENSTR.
Konrad-Adenauer-Platz
BREITE
KÖNIGSALLEE
BERLINER ALLEE
OSTSTR.
KARLSTR.
BAHNSTR.
Hauptbahnhof
KÖNIGSALLEE
GRAF-ADOLF-STR.
MINTROPSTR.
HARKORTSTR.
ADERSSTR.
To Schloss Benrath and Neandertal

As the heartland of Germany's amazing postwar recovery, Düsseldorf is the seat of a major stock exchange, the country's second-largest banking center, and home to many of Germany's major advertising agencies. The city also is European headquarters for about 5,000 enterprises from 50 countries, including 450 Japanese companies that have turned a district of the city into a Little Tokyo. There are spring and fall fashion shows, drawing the best international designers, and in January the city hosts the largest boat show in Germany.

But Düsseldorf is also a city of the arts. Museums and galleries focus on two literary giants, Goethe and Heine, and paintings both old and new. Its opera house, theaters, cabaret, and particularly its impressive concert hall, featuring the renowned *Düsseldörfer Sinfonie,* all help to sustain the rich cultural heritage of the Neuburg-Palatinate electors.

Düsseldorf At-a-Glance

SEEING THE CITY

The 14th-century *Schlossturm* (Castle Tower) in the Altstadt is invariably featured on the covers of guidebooks and travel brochures, usually against a backdrop of glass-walled high-rise buildings. (The tower is all that remains of the original medieval fortifications.) From its base you can see the cobblestone Marktplatz (marketplace), set with chestnut trees and a huge bronze equestrian statue of Jan Wellem, as well as the bridges across the sharp curve of the Rhine. To get a more panoramic view, you can climb to the top of the tower if you also visit the *Schiffahrt Museum* (see *Museums*), which is located inside its base. A breathtaking bird's-eye view of the city and the Rhine can be seen from the viewing area inside the needle-thin *Rheinturm* (Television Tower; 20 Stromstr.; phone: 84858), which at 569 feet is the 11th highest tower of its kind in the world. An elevator goes to the top, where visitors can enjoy a meal at the revolving *Top 180* restaurant (see *Eating Out*) or the *Panorama* café. The *Rheinturm* is open daily; admission charge.

SPECIAL PLACES

Düsseldorf is best discovered on foot. A guided sightseeing tour—including the commercial harbor, parks and gardens, a castle or two, and an overview of some of the more remarkable skyscrapers—is a good place to begin (see *Tours*). Don't miss the 26-story *Thyssen-Haus* (Thyssen House; on Thyssenstr.); built by the country's largest privately owned steel producer in 1959 and described as the *Dreischeibenhaus* (Three Slices House), it resembles two slabs of white bread with a slice of sausage in between—a sort of Dalí-esque high-rise sandwich. On Immermannstrasse, the ultramodern *Japan Center,* built in 1979, houses the largest concentration of Japanese enterprises in Europe. Included is the 300-room *Nikko* hotel (see

Checking In), a number of Japanese restaurants, shops, a branch of the Bank of Tokyo, and an office of the *Japan Travel Bureau.*

KÖNIGSALLEE Many first-time visitors find they never stray far from this street, colloquially known as the Kö. With the most enlivening café life this side of Munich, the strip is a must-see. It's the Champs-Elysées, Rue du Faubourg St-Honoré, Via Veneto, and the Gran Vía in Madrid all rolled into one, with touches of Venice's Grand Canal thrown in for good measure.

The Kö is actually two spacious boulevards divided by a waterway (a former city moat). The east side is lined with elegant townhouses with Art Nouveau façades which have been converted into office buildings—mostly banks and other financial institutions. The west side is home to restaurants and cafés, including *Von Eiken* (No. 48; phone: 323166), which serves good Italian food, and the *Benrather Hof* (see *Eating Out*), as well as about 250 luxury shops, including those of the exclusive *Kö Galerie* (see *Shopping*). Both sides have Art Nouveau street lamps from a 1910 design and turn-of-the-century phone booths and kiosks.

Napoleon set the tone for the Kö during the French occupation when he issued his "beauty decree," which linked the street's design with that of the public parks. By 1865 the avenue had developed into an exclusive residential area; in 1902, the monumental neo-Baroque *Tritonbrunnen* (Triton Fountain) was built at the northern edge. Then the city's first department store (no longer extant) was established here; elegant cafés flourished; and Düsseldorf's first cinema came to the neighborhood.

Two wars and the Great Depression took their toll on the Kö, but today the strip—rebuilt and better than ever—has regained its place as a fashion and style center. Cafés and restaurants spill out onto the streets, with tables topped by colorful umbrellas and white "Paris chairs," reminiscent of those of Napoleon's time.

ALTSTADT (OLD CITY) A relief map of Düsseldorf from the 14th century shows a walled settlement along the eastern bank of the Rhine, the little Düssel River forming its southern boundary. The original settlement expanded within successive rings of fortifications, and by 1801 it occupied much of the city center. Today the Altstadt embraces the area between the Rhine and Heinrich-Heine-Allee.

Described as the longest bar in Europe, with some 260 eating and drinking establishments crowded into an area measuring no more than half a square mile, the Altstadt has none of the cachet of the Kö. Instead, it caters to less pretentious (and sometimes rowdy) types, offering down-home regional fare and strong beer in a pedestrians-only area of narrow alleys rimmed with pubs, restaurants, music bars, and nightclubs.

For a taste of Düsseldorf's famous dark Altbier (Old Beer), this is the place. Try *Zum Schiffchen,* a first-rate tavern restaurant, or *Zum Uerige,* one of the city's four remaining small breweries (see *Eating Out* for both). Prior to World War I there were about 75 small "house" breweries in

Düsseldorf, each turning out its own version of Altbier, the only beer produced in town. (Altbier is aged longer than most beer and is brewed according to a process established prior to the 15th century.) Beer is served straight from the wooden barrel in which it is lagered, and waiters, who answer to the name of *Köbes* (a variation of Jacob in the local dialect), draw up to 30 servings at a time into narrow glasses. *Note:* In Altstadt taverns, the *Köbes* will keep serving you until you tell them to stop. As soon as you finish one glass of beer, they will automatically bring you another.

HOFGARTEN (COURT GARDENS) Dating from 1769, these gardens fan out from the northern end of the Kö. With lakes and waterways along the southern edge, this is a delightful setting for strolling on a network of paths near centuries-old trees and past fountains and statuary. Expanded under Napoleon's rule, the *Hofgarten* was a favorite of the emperor. Looking down from atop its only hill (dubbed Napoleonsberg), the little emperor declared that Düsseldorf was his "Little Paris." The Henry Moore sculpture *Reclining Nude* now stands on that site. Also here are the *Ratinger Tor,* a classically designed gate at the west entrance that was built from 1811 to 1815, and the *Schloss Jägerhof,* an 18th-century hunting lodge in late Baroque style that now houses the *Goethe Museum* (see *Museums*).

ENVIRONS

KAISERSWERTH Located 6 miles (10 km) north of city center—accessible by trams U-78 and U-79—this district was founded in AD 700 on the banks of the Rhine. The site of a Benedictine cloister, it later served as the residence of emperors and kings. Holy Roman Emperor Frederick Barbarossa settled here in 1174. Ancient structures remain, such as the medieval *St. Suitbertuskirche* (Church of St. Suitbertus) and partial ruins of the *Kaiserpfalz,* the onetime imperial palace. Now a popular tourist destination, it's busiest during the summer months as a destination for Düsseldorfers seeking to escape the fast-paced downtown core. Here they bask in the charm of the authentic Altstadt, with its tree-shaded Marktplatz bordered by exquisite period-piece houses with brick façades. In one of these historic houses is *Im Schiffchen,* one of the Düsseldorf area's finest restaurants (see *Eating Out*).

SCHLOSS BENRATH This combination palace and hunting lodge, built for Elector Karl Theodor between 1755 and 1773, is located 6 miles (10 km) south of the city (take *S-Bahn* No. 6 or tram 701 or 703). Ranked among the finest of Germany's late Baroque buildings, and one of the most beautiful palaces of its time in Europe, the structure's elegant interiors feature intricate parquet floors and detailed stuccowork ceilings. The most notable resident was Joachim Murat, Napoleon's brother-in-law, who ruled here from 1806 to 1808. Closed Mondays. Admission charge. 104 Benrather Schlossallee (phone: 899-7271).

NEANDER VALLEY The Neander Valley, 10 miles (15 km) southeast of the city (reached either by car or via *S-Bahn* No. 8 to Erkrath, then bus 743), is named after Joachim Neander (1650–80), a very popular poet who lived in Düsseldorf. The term "Neanderthal Man" is derived from the fact that bones discovered here in 1856 were the first physical evidence of this stage of prehistoric human development. The *Neandertal Museum* (Thekhauser Vall; phone: 210-431149), in the small town of Erkrath, contains those bones, as well as a life-size replica of what scientists believe a Neanderthal man would have looked like and other exhibits pertaining to these cave people. The museum is closed Mondays; admission charge. Another attraction in the Altstadt is the *Neanderkirche* (Neander Church; Bölkerstr.), which was also named after the poet. Built in 1710, it was the area's first Protestant church.

Sources and Resources

TOURIST INFORMATION

The *Düsseldorf Tourist Association* has two offices that offer general information, including brochures and maps: at 24 Heinrich-Heine-Allee (phone: 899-2346), which is closed weekends; and at 65 Immermannhof, on Konrad-Adenauer-Platz in front of the *Hauptbahnhof* (Main Railway Station; phone: 172020; fax: 161071), which is closed Sundays. The tourist office also has a kiosk (Konrad-Adenauer-Pl; no phone) where hotel reservations can be arranged; it's open daily.

LOCAL COVERAGE The official *Monatsprogram,* on sale at tourist offices and hotels, lists just about everything going on in the city; it comes out on a monthly basis. Also published monthly is *Düsseldorf Führer,* a booklet available free at hotels, which lists special attractions, plus restaurants, bars, and nightclubs. Both are German-language publications. An annual magazine called *Highlights* is published in both English and German and is available at the tourist offices.

TELEPHONE The city code for Düsseldorf is 211.

GETTING AROUND

Central Düsseldorf (the Altstadt, the Rhine promenade, and the Kö) can easily be covered on foot. For anything beyond that, use public transportation. As in most major German metropolitan areas, a car is of little use except for excursions into the countryside. Most hotels have arrangements for leaving cars in underground garages (albeit at high rates). Street parking at meters is even more expensive.

AIRPORT The *Flughafen Düsseldorf-Lohausen* (Düsseldorf-Lohausen Airport), which is second only to Frankfurt in terms of the number of scheduled flights, is located at Lohausen, 5 miles (8 km) from the city center. Take *S-Bahn* No. 7, which takes 13 minutes from the airport to the city center, or mass-transit bus lines; each costs about 3 DM ($1.80). For international and domestic flight information, call 4211.

BOAT Düsseldorf serves as an overnight port for *KD Rhine River Cruises* sailing between Basel and Rotterdam. *KD* also runs shorter Rhine and Mosel cruises that originate in Düsseldorf; for information, call 375020. The terminal is at the Theodor Heuss Bridge (Rheinterrasse; phone: 326072). *Weisse Flotte* (phone: 326124) also operates excursions between the *Rheinturm* and Kaisersworth. Short trips—including shuttle service to the harbor, Ruhr district, and Kaiserswerth—are offered between March and October by the *Rheinische Bahn Gesellschaft* (Rhine Transportation Authority; 5 Graf Adolf Pl.; phone: 58201 or 58228).

BUS, TRAM, SUBWAY, AND SUBURBAN TRAINS As in most German cities, Düsseldorf's public transportation system works like a dream. In and around the city, the best way to go is by streetcar. The cost of a trip depends on the distance covered, but a discount pass that allows four rides in the span of 24 hours is available for between 4.80 and 8 DM (about $2.80 to $4.80). Tickets and passes can be purchased from the driver or from machines at bus stops and subway stations; they must be stamped at the start of your journey. Route maps are available at tourist offices. For more information contact the *Rheinische Bahn Gesellschaft* (see *Boat* above).

CAR RENTAL Among the major rental firms are *Avis* (32 Berliner Allee; phone: 329050) and *Hertz* (65 Immermannstr.; phone: 357025; and at the airport; phone: 420024). A car and English-speaking driver can be hired at *Ronald Buch Holtz* (18 Stressemannstr.; phone: 327373).

TAXI Cab stands are located at the railway terminal, at major hotels, and at various other places throughout the city. For 24-hour service call 33333.

TOURS Two-hour guided sightseeing tours (in English and German) organized by the *Düsseldorf Tourist Association* (see above) depart twice daily April through October at 11:15 AM and 2:45 PM; the rest of the year, the trips can be arranged for groups of seven or more. In August and September, the 2:45 PM tour is extended to include a half-hour scenic Rhine boat ride. Tours leave from the *Parcel Post Office* next to the railway station.

TRAIN Domestic and international connections can be made at the *Hauptbahnhof* (main train station; Konrad-Adenauer-Pl.; phone: 19419), a veritable city within a city, with a wide range of shops and eating places.

SPECIAL EVENTS

Düsseldorf is a big trade-fair city, with the *Internationales Boot* (International Boat Show) in January, and spring and fall fashion shows that attract some of the world's foremost designers. One of the biggest events of the year, however, is *Karneval,* which is celebrated during the six weeks preceding *Lent.* In July there's the *Rheinfest* (Rhine Festival,) a gigantic folkloric music and dance extravaganza, and weekend musical concerts in a variety of venues. September marks the *Königsallee Festival,* an open-air street carnival.

MUSEUMS

Though by no means on a par with Munich or Berlin, Düsseldorf has an impressive number of museums for a city of its size. All are closed Mondays and charge admission.

GOETHE MUSEUM What Beethoven was to German music, Johann Wolfgang von Goethe (1749–1832) was to German literature. (Goethe visited Düsseldorf regularly and stayed for extended periods in 1774 and 1792.) Housed in the *Schloss Jägerhof* in the *Hofgarten,* this museum contains a vast collection of Goethe's letters, drawings, original manuscripts, first editions, and other memorabilia. 2 Jacobistr. (phone: 899-6262).

HEINRICH-HEINE-INSTITUT Devoted to the life, work, and times of Düsseldorf's most famous literary son, the museum displays original manuscripts, first editions, letters, portraits, and household memorabilia. 12-14 Bilker Str. (phone: 899-5571).

HETJENS MUSEUM (GERMAN CERAMIC MUSEUM) In the elegant Baroque *Palais Nesselrode* is an extensive private collection of ceramics from all over the world, some dating back as far as 8,000 years. 4 Schulstr. (phone: 899-4210).

KUNSTMUSEUM (FINE ARTS MUSEUM) One of Germany's leading collections of European art from the Middle Ages to the present is housed in this dramatic Bauhaus structure at the northern edge of the *Hofgarten* near the Rhine. Paintings range from Old Masters to German Expressionists. 5 Ehrenhof (phone: 899-2460).

KUNSTSAMMLUNG NORDRHEIN-WESTFALEN (ART COLLECTION OF NORTH RHINE-WESTPHALIA) A strikingly modern, dark stone structure resembling a concert grand piano, the city's cultural showpiece houses 93 paintings and drawings by Klee, along with major works by Beuys, Bonnard, Braque, Chagall, Ernst, Kandinsky, Léger, Matisse, Picasso, and Pollock. 5 Grabbepl. (phone: 83810).

SCHIFFAHRT MUSEUM (NAVIGATION MUSEUM) Located in the historic *Schlossturm,* this museum boasts displays chronicling 2,000 years of shipping on the Rhine. Included are more than 100 ship models, along with navigation-related documents and graphics. 30 Burgpl. (phone: 899-4195).

STADTMUSEUM (CITY MUSEUM) In a restored 18th-century palace, it traces the city's development—from a tiny fishing village on the right bank of the Rhine to one of the world's most modern business, fashion, and arts centers. 2 Bergerallee (phone: 899-6170).

SHOPPING

Style and fashion are taken very seriously in Düsseldorf. Clothes shopping revolves around the Kö, particularly its two most famous shopping plazas: the *Kö Galerie,* with 100 designer shops and boutiques, several restaurants and bars, and even a fitness center with a sauna and a swimming pool; and the open-air *Kö Center,* also with about 100 shops. These malls are ideal venues for those who can afford the luxury items offered here—although window-shoppers can have a good time, too. More affordable merchandise is offered at two department stores on Schadowstrasse: *Kaufhof* (phone: 16031) and *Karstadt* (phone: 36860). (About 1 billion DM is spent in the shops on Schadowstrasse every year—more than any other street in Germany.) Antiques mavens can have a good time browsing through the many fine shops on Hohestrasse and Bastionstrasse in the Altstadt, including *Arts Decoratifs, Heintzen & Adams,* and *Päpke & Janowitz* (see below for details on all three). During the *Christmas* season, there are two *Weihnachtsmarkts* (Christmas Fairs), where a colorful variety of handmade decorations, crafts, and food is sold at several little stalls. One is held at Jan-Wellem-Platz near Schadowstrasse; the other takes place at various sites throughout the Altstadt. For standard shopping hours, see GETTING READY TO GO. The following is just a sampling of the city's best shops:

Anena Stylish shoes for women. *Kö Center* (phone: 325935).

Arts Decoratifs Furniture and household accessories, primarily in Art Deco style. 28 Hohestr. (phone: 324553).

Balluf A huge gift shop offering such traditional German souvenirs as candles, dried flowers, and handicrafts. 15 Schadowstr. (phone: 136300).

Bogner Sportswear for men and women, especially skiwear. 6-8 Königsallee (phone: 134222).

Carsch Haus The city's most exclusive department store, with designer clothes and stylish furniture and housewares. In the basement are several delicatessens and small restaurants (see *Eating Out*). 1 Heinrich-Heine-Pl. (phone: 83970).

Chanel High-quality cosmetics, perfume, and other beauty products from the famous designer label. *Kö Center* (phone: 325992).

Etienne Aigner One of Germany's leading designers of leather goods, including wallets, luggage, and handbags. *Kö Galerie* (phone: 323-0955).

Façonnable A two-floor branch of the French firm specializing in casual clothes for men. *Kö Karree,* 58 Königsallee (phone: 327566).

Frankonia Jagd Casual wear for men and women, including hunting and riding outfits. *Kö Galerie* (phone: 132163).

Georg Jensen Here you can get anything you could possibly want, as long as it's silver. *Kö Galerie* (phone: 324281).

Giorgio Armani The world-famous designer's chic fashions and accessories for men and women. 72 Königsallee (phone: 324422).

Guido Boehler Local designer Boehler's fashions for women, as well as the creations of fellow Germans Ursula Conzen, Daniela Bechtoff, and Reimer Clausen. *Kesting Galerie,* 36 Königsallee (phone: 326225).

Heintzen & Adams Antique pine chairs, tables, and desks, as well as traditional Rhineland furniture. 12 Hohestr. (phone: 327552).

Jil Sander One of Germany's leading designers of women's clothing. *Kö Center* (phone: 328444).

Lothar Heubel Home furnishings imported from China, India, and Africa, including rugs, chests, furniture, and statuary. The shop also carries jewelry. 27 Bastionstr. (phone: 134103).

Louis Feraud Women's fashions by the noted French designer. *Kö Galerie* (phone: 132909).

Louis Vuitton Elegant leather goods, including luggage and accessories. *Kö Center* (phone: 323230).

MCM The initials stand for *Michael Cromer München,* a leading German designer of fine luggage, handbags, and other leather items. 68 Königsallee (phone: 322350).

Päpke & Janowitz An antiques shop offering fine European 18th- and 19th-century furniture and artwork. 27 Hohestr. (phone: 131680).

Ritterskamp This boutique in a passage just off Königsallee features men's and women's fashions by designers from Italy, England, the US, and Japan, including Donna Karan, Calvin Klein, Roberto Gigli, and Yohji Yamamoto. 7 Trinkausstr. (phone: 329994).

Sarah Lingerie Frilly undergarments of silk, satin, and lace. *Kö Center* (phone: 323525).

Walter Steiger Schuhe High-fashion shoes for men and women. *Kö Galerie* (phone: 134104).

Wempe Juwelier This family-run enterprise, begun in 1878, is now one of Europe's leading jewelers, with Swiss watches and gold, silver, and precious gems. 14 Königsallee (phone: 327287).

SPORTS AND FITNESS

The parks and gardens (including the *Hofgarten*) in and around the city and the Rhine promenade offer myriad opportunities for outdoor sports.

BICYCLING Rentals are available from *Fahrrad Egert* (143 Ackerstr.; phone: 662134) and *Burda & Egert* (112 Kölnerlandstr.; phone: 763599).

FITNESS CENTERS Saunas, massages, and fitness equipment are available at most major hotels. *Kö-Thermen,* the fitness center on the top floor of the *Kö-*

Galerie (Königsallee; phone: 323220), offers a sauna and squash courts; there's even a jogging track on the roof.

GOLF About 6 miles (10 km) east of the city center, the *Hubbelrath Golf Club* (in Mettmann; phone: 2104-72178) has a couple of 18-hole courses; you must bring a letter from your golf club at home to play here. Another possibility is the *Auf der Lausward* nine-hole public golf course (Auf der Lausward, near the Rhine harbor; phone: 396617).

ICE HOCKEY *DEG* (Deutsches Eishockey Gemeinschaft), the local team, plays Federal League opponents at the *Eisstadion* (27 Brehmstr.; phone: 627101).

ICE SKATING From July through April, you can skate at the *Eisstadion* (see *Hockey*), which offers equipment for rent.

SWIMMING There are three indoor pools open to the public: *Bad Stockum/Rheinstadion* (65 Beckbuschstr.; phone: 821-2575); *Stadtbad Derendorf* (13 Münsterstr.; phone: 821-2632); and *Wellenbad Stadtmitte* (15 Grünstr.; phone: 821-6413).

TENNIS The best facilities in town are *Tennis Center am Seestern* (22 Emmanuel-Leutze-Str.; phone: 592959) and *Tennis Center Düsseldorf* (5 Ullenbergstr.; phone: 152544).

THEATER

The city's major theater, the *Schauspielhaus* (Gustav-Gründgens-Pl.; phone: 369911), along the southern rim of the *Hofgarten,* is an arresting sight: a brilliant white, freestanding structure that looks as though it has been carved out of a giant mushroom. Even if you have no special interest in attending one of the German-language performances offered here, look in on the spectacular foyer. For children, there's the *Marionettentheater* (7 Bilkerstr.; phone: 328432) and *Puppentheater am Fürstenplatz* (38 Helmholtzstr.; phone: 372401).

MUSIC

For opera lovers, there's the elegant *Deutsche Oper am Rhein* (16A Heinrich-Heine-Allee; phone: 890-8211). The main concert venue is the *Tonhalle* (7 Hofgartenufer; phone: 89955); a converted music hall with exquisite acoustics, it is home to the city's first-rate *Düsseldörfer Sinfonie* and the setting for the *Niederrheinisches Musikfest,* held during the summer, which features some of Germany's finest classical musicians.

NIGHTCLUBS AND NIGHTLIFE

Düsseldorf nightlife has two very distinct personalities: the crowded discos and glittering bars of the Kö, and the loud, smoky, traditional beer halls of the Altstadt (the conviviality and atmosphere of these Altstadt bars are just as enjoyable during the day). For the former, try the city's popular disco, *Sam's West* (27 Königsallee; phone: 328171), or *Checkers,* in a high-tech setting in the *Kö Center* (Königsallee; phone: 134068). The best of the latter is *Zum Uerige* (see *Eating Out*), which is most appealing late on a weekend afternoon and busiest on Friday and Saturday evenings until after midnight.

Popular late-night piano bars (some with dancing) include *Bei Tino* (21 Königsallee; phone: 326463) and *Em Pöötzke* (6 Mertensgasse; phone: 326973).

Düsseldorf is also home to a lively jazz and rock scene; there are a number of music clubs, including *Miles Smiles* (6 Akademiestr.; phone: 329655), a very hip place for modern music; and *Dr. Jazz* (11 Flingerstr.; phone: 329463), owned by nationally prominent jazz singer Lous Dassen, who also performs here regularly.

Best in Town

CHECKING IN

As can be expected in a business city, hotel rates in Düsseldorf are on the high side. However, weekend visitors can reap a veritable harvest of package deals if they plan their stay during the off-season (that is, not during trade fairs) or arrange to arrive on a Friday evening. Be sure to ask about summer discount specials and weekend deals. Most of Düsseldorf's major hotels have complete facilities for the business traveler. Hotels listed as having "business services" usually offer such conveniences as an English-speaking concierge, meeting rooms, photocopiers, computers, translation services, and express checkout, among others. Call the hotel for additional information. For a double room (including private bath, TV set, and breakfast, unless otherwise indicated) at those hotels we have listed as expensive, expect to pay between $275 and $375 per night; $150 to $275 at places in the moderate category; between $100 and $150 at hotels in the inexpensive category. All telephone numbers are in the 211 city code unless otherwise indicated.

EXPENSIVE

Breidenbacher Hof The finest hotel in town, this legendary property, centrally located between the Kö and the Altstadt, is Düsseldorf's premier celebrity haunt. When they are in town, kings and queens, film stars, and symphony conductors stay here. In business since 1814, and rebuilt and restored at various times, each of the 132 rooms and suites is decorated with antiques and artworks. Dining places include the excellent *Breidenbacher Eck* (see *Eating Out*), a *Trader Vic's,* and a popular bar. Business services are available. 36 Heinrich-Heine-Allee (phone: 13030; 800-223-6800; fax: 130-3830).

Düsseldorf Hilton Situated just north of the city center, this link in the international chain offers 372 attractive guestrooms with a contemporary decor and amenities such as mini-bars. Other facilities at this modern property include a recreation and leisure club featuring a pool, a sauna, a solarium, and a fitness center; business services; a buffet dining room with a garden terrace; and a Thai restaurant. 20 Georg-Glock-Str. (phone: 43770; 800-HILTONS; fax: 437-7791).

Nikko Not far from the railway terminal, this ultramodern high-rise serves as the linchpin of the city's large Japanese community. Both the surroundings and the service are of world class caliber. The elegant decor in the vast lobby is also reflected in the 300 spacious guestrooms. Amenities include street-level shopping arcades and *Benkay,* a Japanese restaurant; the penthouse health club features a fitness center, a heated pool, saunas, massage, solariums, and great views across the city and the Rhine. Business services are available. 41 Immermannstr. (phone: 8340; 800-NIKKO-US; fax: 161216).

SAS Royal Scandinavian This link in the renowned chain boasts 309 rooms, an indoor pool, and a fitness center with a sauna, whirlpool, and massage. It also has one of the best restaurants in town, *Les Continents* (see *Eating Out*), and *Café de la Paix,* a popular bistro. Located about 2 miles (3 km) from the city center, it is a five-minute *U-Bahn* ride away. Business services are available. 5 Karl-Arnold-Pl. (phone: 45530; 800-221-2350; fax: 455-3110).

Steigenberger Park Built in 1902, this palatial structure overlooks the Kö, *Hofgarten,* and the opera house and is just steps away from the Altstadt. Many of the 160 comfortable rooms have balconies. Amenities include the popular *Etoile Bar* and the *Menuett,* a good restaurant with a terrace for outdoor dining. Business services are available. 1 Corneliuspl. (phone: 13810; 800-223-5652; fax: 131679).

MODERATE

Eden Conveniently located a short distance from the Kö, this hostelry has a spacious lobby, the cozy *Bierstube* restaurant on the main floor, 129 pleasantly furnished rooms, and business services. 29-31 Aderstr. (phone: 38970; fax: 389-7777).

Günnewig Savoy A fine 19th-century hotel in the city center, it has 130 rooms (the quietest are in the rear). Amenities include a fitness center, a pool, a sauna, a solarium, massage facilities, and business services. There's a stylish restaurant, and the renowned bakery and sweetshop *Bierhof Hofkonditorei,* court confectioners since 1856. 128 Oststr. (phone: 360336; fax: 356642).

Holiday Inn Favored among Americans, it has 177 good-size rooms, plus a restaurant, a pool, a sauna, a solarium, and business services. Friendly, accommodating service is another plus. 10 Graf-Adolf-Pl. (phone: 38480; 800-HOLIDAY; fax: 384-8390).

Queens This modern hotel is conveniently located a short walk from the *Hauptbahnhof.* Its 120 rooms are immaculate, comfortable, and well-appointed (amenities include a mini-bar that dispenses a limited number of complimentary drinks). There is also a restaurant, a whirlpool, a sauna, a steamroom, and shiatsu massage. Business services are available. 3 Ludwig-Erhard-Allee (phone: 777-1717; fax: 777-1888).

INEXPENSIVE

An der Oper Conveniently located directly across the street from the opera house and the *Hofgarten,* this modern place has an attractive lobby and 48 spartan but comfortable rooms. Only breakfast is served. 15 Heinrich-Heine-Allee (phone: 323062; fax: 328656).

Günnewig Uebachs A less expensive sibling of the *Günnewig Savoy* (above), this cozy property sits on a quiet street convenient to shopping and other attractions. It has 82 simply furnished rooms, a restaurant, a homey, friendly bar, and a very hospitable staff. Guests are allowed to use the facilities at the *Savoy,* which is a seven-minute walk away. 3-5 Leopoldstr. (phone: 360566; fax: 358064).

Herzog Clean and basic, this 20-room hotel has a convenient location within walking distance of the Königsallee. Breakfast is not included; there's no restaurant. 25 Herzogstr. (phone: 372047; fax: 379836).

Ibis Attached to the *Hauptbahnhof,* this 166-room member of the French-based chain offers no-frills accommodations at down-to-earth prices. Among its pluses are pleasantly furnished rooms, a friendly staff, generous breakfast buffets, and an animated bar scene. There's no restaurant. Business services are available. 14 Konrad-Adenauer-Pl. (phone: 16720; 800-873-0300; fax: 167-2101).

EATING OUT

When well-to-do Düsseldorfers make an occasion of dining out, it is usually to partake of foreign fare—French, Italian, or some of the best Japanese food this side of Toyko. At the other end of the scale, there are many places serving standard German fare and tasty regional Rhineland specialties. For a three-course lunch or dinner for two, expect to pay $200 or more at restaurants in the very expensive category; $130 to $200 at places in the expensive range; $85 to $130 at restaurants we call moderate; and less than $85 at places described as inexpensive. Prices do not include drinks and wine or beer, but taxes and service charges are always included. If you receive particularly good service, however, leave a small additional tip. Unless otherwise noted, all restaurants are open for lunch and dinner. All telephone numbers are in the 211 city code unless otherwise indicated.

For an unforgettable dining experience, we begin with our culinary favorite, followed by cost and quality choices, listed by price category.

DELIGHTFUL DINING

Im Schiffchen Not to be confused with *Zum Schiffchen* (see below), this has long been rated as the city's premier dining place. Loire Valley–born chef Jean-Claude Bourgueil is the founding father of this beacon of Gallic perfection, which, in the 16 years since its inception, has become a Düsseldorf institution (and has earned three Michelin stars). Located on the upper floor of a historic brick house near the Rhine in the suburb of Kaiserswerth, its charming nautical decor, first-rate fare, and impeccable service are about as upscale as you can get. The menu features such superbly prepared specialties as foie gras, Breton lobster, Bresse duck, and steamed turbot with wild mushrooms. At street level is the one-Michelin-star *Aal-schokker,* a rustic eatery which shares management and kitchen facilities and serves German regional cooking at somewhat lower prices than those upstairs. Make your reservations here first, and *then* call the airline; this is a meal worth planning a trip around. Open for dinner only; closed Sundays and holidays. Reservations necessary. Major credit cards accepted. 9 Kaiserswerther Markt (phone: for *Aal-schokker,* 403948; for *Im Schiffchen,* 401050).

VERY EXPENSIVE

Les Continents Probably the best hotel dining room in town, this elegant but cozy place in the *SAS Royal Scandinavian* boasts cordial service, fine wines, and such expertly prepared dishes as champagne mustard cream soup, gratinée catfish with creamed lentils, and lamb curry. Both the lunch and dinner menus are exceptional values. Closed Sundays and Saturday lunch. Reservations advised. Major credit cards accepted. 5 Karl-Arnold-Pl. (phone: 455-31136).

Edo Among Düsseldorf's dozen Japanese restaurants, this one gets the highest praise. Set amid the tall office blocks on the far side of the Rhine, this rustic wooden Japanese teahouse serves eight or more courses, with such dishes as sushi, tofu steak, and fish carpaccio. Another branch, on the second floor of the *Kö Galerie,* has a somewhat less ambitious menu and lower prices; both offer luncheon specials. The main restaurant is closed Sundays and Saturday lunch. Reservations necessary. 3 Am Seestern (phone: 591082). The *Kö Galerie* branch is open daily; closed Sunday lunch. Reservations advised. Major credit cards accepted. Königsallee (phone: 132838).

Victorian On the second floor of an office building near the Kö, this place is true to its name in decor—fin de siècle English dark woodwork and brass—but it's Teutonic in its specialties: Dishes prepared by the Düsseldorf-born chef are a lighter version of traditional German fare. Of special note are goose-liver terrine with apple salad, crabmeat on a bed of spinach, and a salad of oysters and new potatoes. The relatively inexpensive luncheon menu attracts a weekday office crowd. On a lower floor, its sibling, the *Victorian Lounge,* is a spacious bistro—done up with antique mirrors, leather, and oak—offering excellent light meals until midnight. Closed Sundays and holidays. Reservations necessary. Major credit cards accepted. 3a Königstr. (phone: 320222).

EXPENSIVE

Amalfi With Felliniesque ambience—white statuary and columns against bright red walls—this is the city's favorite Italian restaurant. A pasta sensation is *fettucine con salsa di noci* (fettucine with walnut sauce). Friendly service adds to its appeal. Closed Sundays. Reservations advised. Major credit cards accepted. 122 Ulmenstr. (phone: 433809).

Breidenbacher Eck One of three dining rooms in the *Breidenbacher Hof,* this is noted for its German fare. There also are continental dishes, but stick with the sauerbraten, lamb, and traditional-style noodles. Excellent wines are available by the glass. Service is topnotch. Open daily. Reservations advised. Major credit cards accepted. 36 Heinrich-Heine-Allee (phone: 130-3877).

Top 180 Located atop the *Rheinturm* (Television Tower), this restaurant has the most spectacular setting in Düsseldorf. The revolving dining room gives patrons a 360° view of the Rhine and the entire city. The views inside are equally attractive, with tasteful murals on the walls, simple but elegant furnishings, and a smart bar. The menu offers well-prepared and beautifully presented continental dishes; the cream of lobster soup with armagnac is especially good. Open daily. Reservations advised. Major credit cards accepted. 20 Stormstr. (phone: 84858).

MODERATE

Carl Maassen A family business that dates back 190 years. The Maassens own the two busiest fish restaurants in town, plus a thriving retail shop. One restaurant (split into two dining rooms) is in the Altstadt, linked to the retail store; the other, with a more formal atmosphere, is on the harbor. The vast shop and dining annex in the Altstadt is designed in Art Deco style, with white tile walls and floor and dark woodwork. In warm weather, tables are set up under umbrellas on the pedestrian cobblestone street out front. The harbor restaurant is decorated in a simple, elegant style, with leather upholstery and subdued lighting. In both locations, the menu changes frequently but always features the freshest seafood. Try the bouillabaisse, smoked salmon, herring, thick fish stew, crab soup, or lobster bisque. The downstairs dining room is open daily; the upstairs restaurant is closed Sundays. The harbor restaurant is closed Sundays and Saturday lunch. Reservations advised for the upstairs restaurant and the harbor restaurant; downstairs, reservations unnecessary. Major credit cards accepted. In the Altstadt, 37 Berger Str. (phone: 326057); and at the harbor, 4 Kaistr. (phone: 304547).

Im Goldenen Ring Established in 1873, this home-style eatery is located in the heart of Altstadt, next to the *Radschlägerbrunnen* and the *Schlossturm.* It's a favorite gathering place for residents, largely because of its menu of tasty, traditional German fare and the fun, friendly atmosphere. Try the delicious *Düsselsteak,* seasoned with a special mustard produced in the region. For dessert, mixed berries with fresh cream is another popular local specialty. Open daily. Reservations advised for dinner. Major credit cards accepted. 21-22 Burgpl. (phone: 133161).

N. T. Tables at the sidewalk café are especially coveted at this, the city's quintessential "in" spot. *N. T.* stands for *Nachrichten Treff*, which translates as "News Meeting Place." The decor is best described as "English gentlemen's club"—exposed brick columns, beamed ceiling, dark woodwork and brass, black leather booths and banquettes, tasseled lamps. There's a kiosk with newspapers and magazines from around the world, a telex running continuously with dispatches from the various wire services, big TV screens tuned to all-news channels, and electronic ticker tapes of late-breaking news. Not surprisingly, the bar and dining room attract more than their share of journalists. The menu features solid, well-prepared international fare (try the smoked salmon platter or the steak and fries); the place is famous for the selection of mixed drinks offered at its bar. There's beer and wine, too. Open daily. Reservations unnecessary. Major credit cards accepted. 27 Königsallee (phone: 132311).

Zum Schiffchen In a 17th-century house in the Altstadt, near the riverbank, this is the most atmospheric—and the most authentic—of the city's brewery taverns. It is Düsseldorf's oldest restaurant (dating from 1628)— Napoleon ate here in 1811. With a capacity of 420, the restaurant is divided into a series of smaller rooms with long wooden tables. Beer—including the local special dark Altbier—comes straight from the barrel. Try the grilled pork, smoked salmon, or cold ham and asparagus in season. Open daily. Reservations advised for dinner. Major credit cards accepted. 5 Hafenstr. (phone: 132-4021).

INEXPENSIVE

Benrather Hof A huge beer hall–type establishment in the center of the Kö, this dining place (seating up to 350) has been in operation since 1887. It's strictly home-style dining: long wooden tables that you share with others, no tablecloths, and paper napkins. The meat comes from the in-house butcher shop. The menu offers mainly traditional German dishes such as *Reibekuchen* (potato pancakes) and sausages made on the premises, along with a wide range of beers on tap and wines by the glass. The beer garden is a popular summertime venue. Open daily for breakfast, lunch, and dinner. Reservations unnecessary. No credit cards accepted. 1 Steinstr., corner of Königsallee (phone: 325218).

Mövenpick In the *Kö Galerie,* this rustic branch of the Swiss chain offers a wide range of tasty dishes, including grilled lamb and fish. Among the most popular attractions is a nightly all-you-can-eat, make-it-yourself pizza buffet. There's also a reasonably priced, unlimited salad bar, including soup, salad, rolls, and a glass of wine. Open daily for breakfast, lunch, and dinner. Reservations unnecessary. Major credit cards accepted. Königsallee (phone: 320681).

Zum Uerige Though people visit this renowned brewery set in a restored 19th-century building mainly for the dark beer that has been brewed on site for 125 years, it also features such down-home specialties as thick pea soup with chunks of bacon, sausage with sauerkraut, and potato salad with spicy mustard. You'll need to acquire a taste for two favorite Rhineland bar foods: *'Ne halve Hahn* (literally "Half a Hen"), a rye roll stuffed with a wedge of aged Dutch cheese and caraway seeds; and *Mett,* finely chopped raw pork served with onions and spices. A favorite throughout Germany, *Grieben Schmaltz* (rendered pork fat flecked with fine pieces of fried apple), is served in a little pot, or set up on the bar on a help-yourself basis: Spread it on rye bread and sprinkle it with salt. Open daily for breakfast, lunch, and dinner. Reservations unnecessary. No credit cards accepted. 1 Berger Str. (phone: 84455).

SHOP 'N' SUP

The *Carsch-Haus* department store devotes a full floor to deli and fine foods, including numerous counters and mini-restaurants serving snacks and light meals—pasta, pizza, grilled chicken, quiche, seafood, sandwiches, salads, and sausage platters—along with beer, champagne, and wines. Closed Sundays. Major credit cards accepted. 1 Heinrich-Heine-Pl. (phone: 83970).

Frankfurt

Trade and traffic have formed the destiny of Frankfurt am Main (Frankfurt on the Main) since its earliest existence as a community (in 1994, the city celebrated its 1,200th anniversary). Its location on the Main River at the heart of the European continent made it the crossroads of prehistoric trade routes linking northern Europe with the Mediterranean areas, and eastern with western Europe. The city grew, spreading out to meet the imperial forest of Dreieich in the south and the wooded Taunusberg (Taunus Mountains) which encircle the broad plain formed by the Main as it flows toward the Rhine. Frankfurt today is a bustling commercial center with a genuine international flair; it's also a city with many parks and museums. Look behind the imposing glass and steel of modern Frankfurt and you will find lovingly restored landmarks that highlight the city's long history.

The Celts were here first, but were forced west across the Rhine by migrating German tribes. Romans had settled along the Main by the 1st century, but they fled the Saxon tribes, who, in turn, were driven out by the Franks in 496. The little settlement on the Main became the site of the Franks' ford—where Saxons from south of the river could cross over to trade. The city's name, Frankfurt, literally translates to "Franks' Ford."

Ludwig the German, the first ruler of the German Empire and a grandson of Charlemagne, made Frankfurt his capital, and from 1356 to 1792 the Holy Roman emperors were elected here. The city was granted the right to mint money in the 16th century, and since that time the name Frankfurt has been synonymous with finance and trade. The Rothschild financial dynasty started here with Meyer Amschel Rothschild (1743–1812); his sons who succeeded him in business were known as "the five Frankfurters." Frankfurt also can claim Germany's greatest poet, Johann Wolfgang von Goethe, as its own. Goethe was born here in 1749.

Over the years, Frankfurt has earned a reputation as a center of liberal ideas and actions. The *Pauluskirche* (St. Paul's Church), where the country's first National Assembly met in 1848, has become a symbol of German liberalism, and in this century, pockets of opposition to the Nazis could be found here. Although a massive Allied air attack during World War II destroyed much of the city, Frankfurt was quick to rebuild after the war and never really stopped. The city has made a conscious attempt to relieve the coldness of modern skyscrapers with attractive pedestrian precincts for shopping and strolling or simply relaxing in an outdoor café. Frankfurt's parks, forest, and neighboring greenbelts are much used by city residents.

Frankfurters sometimes refer to their city as "Mainhattan" (Manhattan on the Main) and "Bankfurt" (over 400 national and international banks have offices here). Around 660,000 people live in Frankfurt proper, but the greater Frankfurt area, extending across the fertile Maintal (Main Valley) and up into the Taunus Mountains, has a population of more than a million. Frankfurt's citizens work in its financial center and in the advertising, communications, chemical, electronics, machine-tool, and printing industries. They are cosmopolitan and used to sampling the world's best goods as a result of the role Frankfurt plays as an international trade center. Like many Germans, some Frankfurters are anxious about the adverse effects German unification may have on their local economy (and pocketbooks), but for the present there seems to be no noticeable difference in their standard of living.

Frankfurt still is a city of superlatives: It has faster trains, more cars per capita, more banks, a larger airport, and more skyscrapers than almost any other German metropolis. The 52-story, 842-foot-high *Messeturm* (Fairgrounds Tower), a pencil-shaped structure designed by the Chicago-based, German-born architect Helmut Jahn, is Europe's tallest office building. In spite of their success in the business world, Frankfurters have maintained a casual approach to life that exists almost nowhere else in Germany. This is, after all, the city that shuts down the afternoon of the Tuesday following *Pfingstmontag* (Whitmonday) so that its citizens can walk in the woods.

Frankfurt At-a-Glance

SEEING THE CITY

Unfortunately, the 1,086-foot *Europaturm* television tower (Western Europe's tallest)—the best place to get an overall view of the city and surrounding area—is temporarily closed for renovation; its reopening date was uncertain at press time. However, a good aerial view of Frankfurt can be seen from the tower of the *Dom* (Cathedral; see *Special Places*). You also can get a sense of the region by riding the historic *Eisenbahn* steam train along the Main River, which runs one weekend per month. For information, call 436093.

SPECIAL PLACES

Central Frankfurt is on the right bank of a bend in the Main. Most of the commercial and historic areas are in a small area ringed by a series of green parks that follow the Altstadt (Old City) walls. Across the Main is a district called Sachsenhausen. Both these areas are ideal for exploring on foot.

DOWNTOWN

AN DER HAUPTWACHE This little square on the right side of the Main is considered the hub of Frankfurt. The centerpiece is the *Hauptwache,* a beautifully reconstructed Baroque building dating from 1730 that once served as a sentry house. You can get your bearings at the adjacent *Hauptwache Café* (phone: 281026), a lovely little eatery that serves coffee and cake and attracts locals and tourists alike; in spring and summer, tables are set up on the sidewalk outside. Just in front of the café is an escalator leading from the street to a huge underground shopping mall. Before leaving the square,

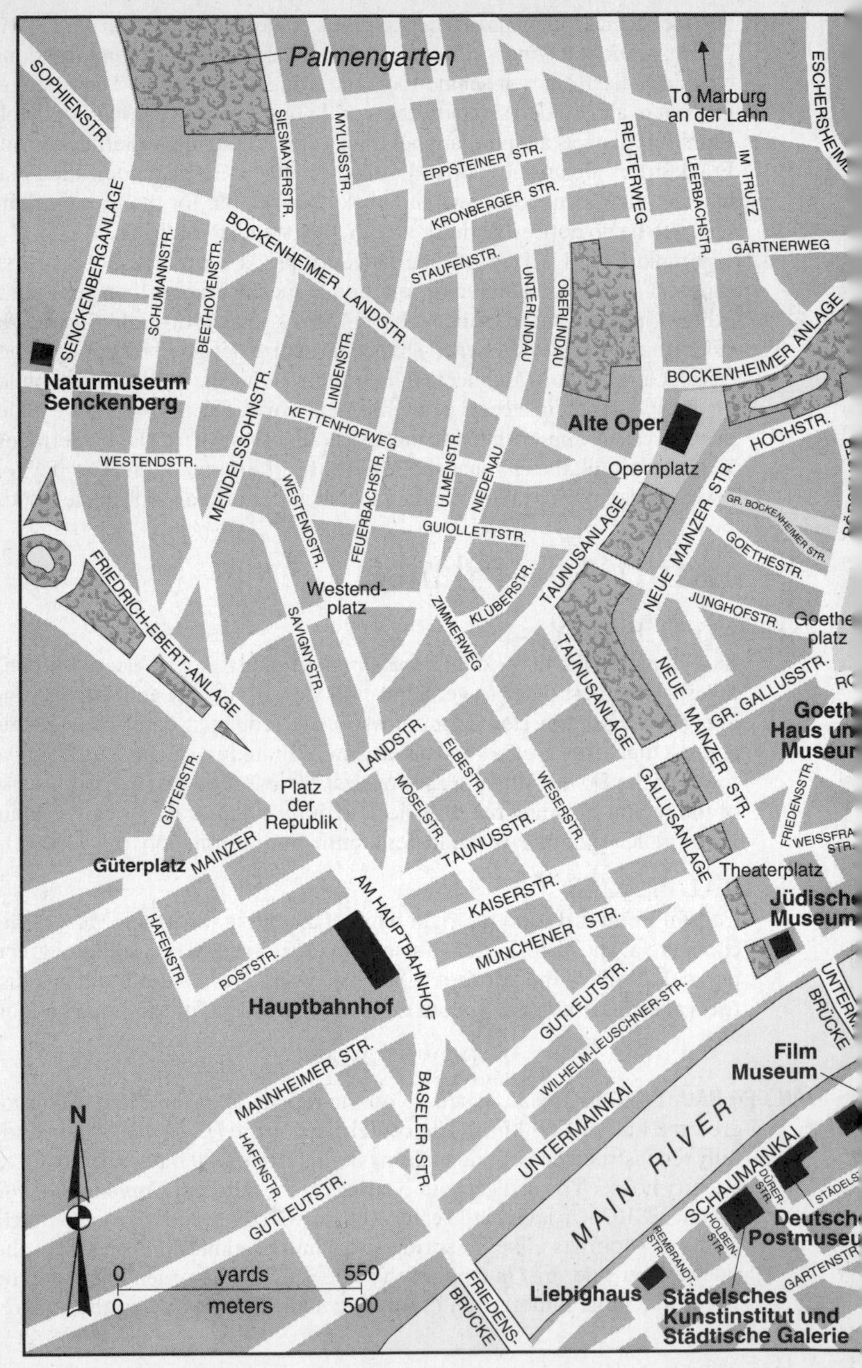
Palmengarten
To Marburg an der Lahn
SOPHIENSTR.
SIESMAYERSTR.
MYLIUSSTR.
EPPSTEINER STR.
KRONBERGER STR.
REUTERWEG
LEERBACHSTR.
IM TRUTZ
ESCHERSHEIM
GÄRTNERWEG
SENCKENBERGANLAGE
SCHUMANNSTR.
BEETHOVENSTR.
BOCKENHEIMER LANDSTR.
STAUFENSTR.
UNTERLINDAU
OBERLINDAU
BOCKENHEIMER ANLAGE
Naturmuseum Senckenberg
LINDENSTR.
MENDELSSOHNSTR.
KETTENHOFWEG
Alte Oper
Opernplatz
HOCHSTR.
WESTENDSTR.
FEUERBACHSTR.
ULMENSTR.
NIEDENAU
GR. BOCKENHEIMER STR.
GOETHESTR.
NEUE MAINZER STR.
TAUNUSANLAGE
GUIOLLETTSTR.
FRIEDRICH-EBERT-ANLAGE
Westend-platz
SAVIGNYSTR.
ZIMMERWEG
KLÜBERSTR.
JUNGHOFSTR.
Goethe platz
GR. GALLUSSTR.
Goeth Haus un Museur
LANDSTR.
ELBESTR.
GÜTERSTR.
Platz der Republik
MOSELSTR.
WESERSTR.
GALLUSANLAGE
FRIEDENSSTR.
WEISSFRA STR.
Güterplatz
MAINZER
TAUNUSSTR.
Theaterplatz
KAISERSTR.
Jüdische Museum
HAFENSTR.
AM HAUPTBAHNHOF
MÜNCHENER STR.
POSTSTR.
GUTLEUTSTR.
UNTERM. BRÜCKE
Hauptbahnhof
WILHELM-LEUSCHNER-STR.
MANNHEIMER STR.
Film Museum
BASELER STR.
UNTERMAINKAI
MAIN RIVER
N
SCHAUMAINKAI
DÜRER-STR.
STÄDELST
GUTLEUTSTR.
HOLBEIN-STR.
Deutsche Postmuseu
REMBRANDT-STR.
0 yards 550
0 meters 500
GARTENSTR
Liebighaus
FRIEDENS-BRÜCKE
Städelsches Kunstinstitut und Städtische Galerie

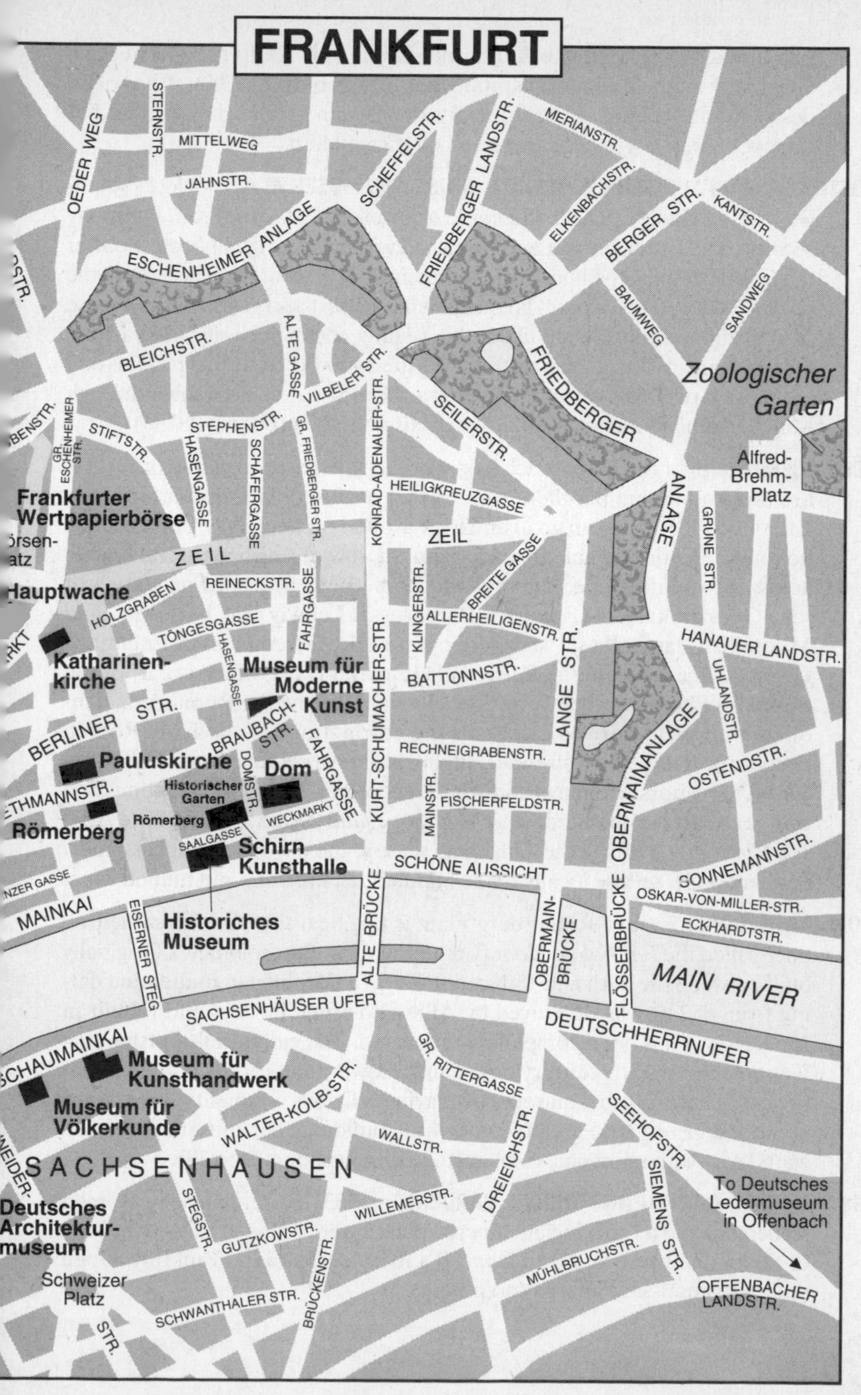

FRANKFURT
OEDER WEG
STERNSTR.
MITTELWEG
JAHNSTR.
SCHEFFELSTR.
FRIEDBERGER LANDSTR.
MERIANSTR.
ELKENBACHSTR.
BERGER STR.
KANTSTR.
ESCHENHEIMER ANLAGE
BAUMWEG
SANDWEG
BLEICHSTR.
ALTE GASSE
VILBELER STR.
FRIEDBERGER
Zoologischer Garten
Alfred-Brehm-Platz
GR. ESCHENHEIMER STR.
STIFTSTR.
STEPHENSTR.
HASENGASSE
SCHÄFERGASSE
GR. FRIEDBERGER STR.
KONRAD-ADENAUER-STR.
SEILERSTR.
HEILIGKREUZGASSE
ANLAGE
GRÜNE STR.
Frankfurter Wertpapierbörse
ZEIL
ZEIL
REINECKSTR.
FAHRGASSE
BREITE GASSE
KLINGERSTR.
Hauptwache
HOLZGRABEN
TÖNGESGASSE
ALLERHEILIGENSTR.
LANGE STR.
HANAUER LANDSTR.
UHLANDSTR.
Katharinenkirche
HASENGASSE
Museum für Moderne Kunst
BATTONNSTR.
BERLINER STR.
BRAUBACH-STR.
FAHRGASSE
KURT-SCHUMACHER-STR.
OBERMAINANLAGE
RECHNEIGRABENSTR.
OSTENDSTR.
Pauluskirche
DOMSTR.
Dom
Historischer Garten
MAINSTR.
FISCHERFELDSTR.
Römerberg
WECKMARKT
Römerberg
SAALGASSE
Schirn Kunsthalle
SCHÖNE AUSSICHT
SONNEMANNSTR.
MAINKAI
EISERNER STEG
ALTE BRÜCKE
OBERMAIN-BRÜCKE
FLÖSSERBRÜCKE
OSKAR-VON-MILLER-STR.
ECKHARDTSTR.
Historiches Museum
MAIN RIVER
SACHSENHÄUSER UFER
DEUTSCHHERRNUFER
SCHAUMAINKAI
Museum für Kunsthandwerk
Museum für Völkerkunde
GR. RITTERGASSE
WALTER-KOLB-STR.
SEEHOFSTR.
WALLSTR.
DREIEICHSTR.
SACHSENHAUSEN
Deutsches Architekturmuseum
STEGSTR.
WILLEMERSTR.
SIEMENS STR.
To Deutsches Ledermuseum in Offenbach
GUTZKOWSTR.
BRÜCKENSTR.
MÜHLBRUCHSTR.
Schweizer Platz
SCHWANTHALER STR.
OFFENBACHER LANDSTR.
STR.

you may want to visit the *Katharinenkirche* (St. Katharine's Church). Originally a convent and hospital when it was built in 1343, it has been destroyed and rebuilt several times; its main claim to fame, however, is that the poet Goethe was christened and confirmed here.

GOETHE HAUS UND MUSEUM (GOETHE'S HOUSE AND MUSEUM) A few blocks southwest of the Hauptwache is the home of Frankfurt's favorite son. Faithfully reconstructed after the war and furnished with many original possessions of the Goethe family, the house offers a fascinating peek at the place where the prolific poet and playwright did much of his work; it also gives visitors a sense of what 18th-century life was like in this wealthy, commercial city. In an adjoining museum are documents on Goethe's life and work as well as pictures and sculpture by well-known artists of his era. Closed weekends October through March. Admission charge. 23 Grosser Hirschgraben (phone: 282824).

RÖMERBERG South of the Hauptwache, on a broad square with a statue of Justice, are three adjoining burghers' houses that have served as Frankfurt's city hall since 1405. You can go in and look around on weekdays, but there are no tours. The three gabled façades and the row of seven medieval houses across the street are the symbol of the Römerberg; also here are statues of four German kaisers (Friedrich Barbarossa, Ludwig II, Charles IV, and Maximilian), as well as a sculpture of an eagle, the emblem of Frankfurt. History comes alive in the *Kaisersaal* (Imperial Hall), which is part of the complex of buildings that forms the city hall. During the Roman era, banquets were held here to celebrate the coronations of the Holy Roman Emperors; today, the *Kaisersaal* still hosts important functions. The hall is closed to visitors Mondays and when receptions are going on; admission charge. Nearby is the modern *Schirn Kunsthalle* (Schirn Hall of Fine Arts; see *Museums*). During the *Christmas* season, the city holds a special market here daily, selling locally made handicrafts, pretzels, and mulled wine.

DOM (CATHEDRAL) East of Römerberg Platz is this beautiful Gothic cathedral, once called the *Bartholomödom* (Cathedral of St. Bartholomew). Originally built between the 13th and 15th centuries on a Carolingian foundation dating from 852, it was destroyed by Allied bombing in 1944 and rebuilt in 1953. Now it has been completely renovated. The cathedral's outstanding features are its 15th-century dome and a tower that affords a fine view of the city. There is also a museum displaying religious vestments and exhibits about the history and architecture of the building. The museum is closed Mondays. Admission charge. Am Kaiserdom (phone: 289229).

HISTORISCHER GARTEN (HISTORICAL GARDEN) In 1953, the remains of a Roman settlement and a Carolingian imperial palace were found at this site in front of the main entrance to the *Dom.* It's the oldest site in Frankfurt. Open daily. No admission charge (no phone).

ALT-SACHSENHAUSEN A few steps from Römerberg, near where the ancient Franks forded the river, the Eiserner Steg footbridge leads across the river into another old section of the city. (*Sachsenhausen* means "Saxons' houses.") Here you can enjoy the jumble of half-timbered houses and rough cobbled streets with their inviting pubs and restaurants, as well as charming little squares and pretty fountains that are particularly lively meeting places at night and on weekends. There are also several museums along Schaumainkai near the river, including the *Deutsches Architekturmuseum* (Museum of German Architecture), *Deutsches Filmmuseum* (German Film Museum), and the *Museum für Völkerkunde* (Museum of Ethnology; see *Museums* for details on all three). A colorful flea market is held beside the river every Saturday, and there is a short but pleasant stretch of greenery where you can sit and gaze at the city skyline. Visit the local pubs for the special apple cider called *Stöffche* and the Frankfurt dishes *Rippchen* (pork ribs) or *Haxen* (pork foot and sauerkraut). For listings of pubs to visit in Alt-Sachsenhausen, see *Nightclubs and Nightlife.*

PALMENGARTEN (PALM GARDEN) One of Europe's most famous botanical gardens, these 55 acres of trees, meadows, ponds, gardens, and footpaths offer a welcome sanctuary from the bustling city. Over 12,000 varieties of plants grow in the park and thousands of orchids and cacti are displayed in its conservatories. A traditional Sunday afternoon entertainment in Frankfurt is a stroll through the flower gardens, perhaps pausing to listen to one of the concerts, followed by an elaborate ice-cream sundae on the flower-bedecked terrace of the *Palmengarten* restaurant (phone: 975-7510). Open daily. Admission charge. Entrance at Palmengartenstrasse (phone: 212-33939).

ZOOLOGISCHER GARTEN (ZOOLOGICAL GARDEN) This is one of Europe's oldest zoos, but nonetheless one of its most up-to-date. Founded in 1858, the zoo is noted for its beautifully landscaped open-air enclosures, its aviary, its collection of nocturnal animals, and its success in breeding rare species. Open daily. Admission charge. 16 Alfred-Brehm-Pl. (phone: 212-33735).

FRANKFURTER WERTPAPIERBÖRSE (FRANKFURT STOCK EXCHANGE) Frankfurt is one of the most important financial centers in the world. More than 400 German and overseas banks have headquarters or subsidiaries in the city. Although public access is extremely limited, no tour of the financial district would be complete without a visit to the spectators' gallery to watch the activity on the floor. Tours (available in English) are given weekdays at 10 and 11 AM and at noon, but reservations must be made at least a month in advance. No admission charge. Börsenpl. (phone: 299770).

STÄDELSCHES KUNSTINSTITUT UND STÄDTISCHE GALERIE (STÄDEL ART INSTITUTE AND MUNICIPAL GALLERY) Famous works of Flemish primitives and German masters of the 16th century are on display in the second-floor picture gallery. Closed Mondays. Admission charge. 63 Schaumainkai (phone: 605-0980).

ALTE OPER (OLD OPERA HOUSE) A victim of wartime bombing, this 100-year-old landmark was finally rebuilt in 1981. No opera is performed here, however; the ultramodern complex of rooms and halls now is used for concerts and conferences. The façade and the vestibule have been fully restored. The building is closed to the public except during performances. Opernpl. (phone: 13400).

ENVIRONS

WIESBADEN The famous hot springs of this lovely spa city 19 miles (30 km) west of Frankfurt have been attracting visitors since Roman times. The mineral-laced waters are used for both bathing and drinking. A casino has been an added attraction in more recent times (see *Nightclubs and Nightlife*). The leafy Kurhausplatz in the center of town and elegant villas dating from the 19th century, both of which were largely untouched during World War II, also contribute to Wiesbaden's charm. As a special treat, dine at the superb, one-Michelin-star *Die Ente vom Lehel* in the elegant *Nassauer Hof* hotel (3-4 Kaiser-Friedrich-Pl.; phone: 611-1330). The restaurant, which serves dinner only, is closed Sundays, Mondays, holidays, and July. Reservations necessary. Major credit cards accepted. (For more information about Wiesbaden, see *Taking the Waters: Spas* in DIVERSIONS.)

DEUTSCHES LEDERMUSEUM (GERMAN LEATHER MUSEUM) Exhibitions of the history of shoes and handbags are displayed in a wonderfully fragrant museum in Offenbach just 5 miles (8 km) southeast of Frankfurt. Open daily. Admission charge. 86 Frankfurterstr., Offenbach (phone: 813021).

FREILICHTMUSEUM HESSENPARK (HESSENPARK OPEN-AIR MUSEUM) Located in a northern suburb about 16 miles (25 km) from Frankfurt, this collection of typical dwellings and rustic buildings representing various regions of the state of Hesse includes houses, barns, stables, and even a church. The look is of a re-created 19th-century village. Tours are given in English, each focusing on a different craft, such as pottery or weaving. Open daily. Admission charge. Hessenpark, Neu Anspach, Taunus (phone: 6081-5880).

EXTRA SPECIAL

The charming old town of Marburg an der Lahn, remarkable for its university, its castle, and the first Gothic church ever built in Germany (between 1235 and 1285), is 59 miles (94 km) north of Frankfurt in the Hesse region. The church is dedicated to St. Elizabeth of Hungary, who lived and performed good works here. The university is a center for Protestant theology. On the market square in the old quarter of town, you can see several old half-timbered houses dating from the mid-16th century. As you wander the twisting alleys of the old quarter, you may meet country people in traditional costume, particularly if you visit on a market day (Wednesdays and Saturdays).

Sources and Resources

TOURIST INFORMATION

For information, maps, brochures, hotel and restaurant listings, plus special sightseeing tours and tickets to local events, visit the *Frankfurter Verkehrsamt* (Frankfurt Tourist Board). It has information bureaus on the north side of the *Hauptbahnhof* (Main Train Station), opposite track 23 (phone: 212-38849 or 212-38851), and at 27 Römerberg (phone: 212-38708 or 212-38709). Both tourist information bureaus are open daily.

LOCAL COVERAGE The tourist office issues *Journal,* a bimonthly publication in English that lists all special events, plus museum and restaurant information.

TELEPHONE The city code for Frankfurt is 69.

GETTING AROUND

Frankfurt has a clean, efficient, and quiet rapid-transit system of buses, streetcars, subways, and trains. The trip from the *Flughafen Frankfurt Main* (Frankfurt-Main Airport) to the city's main railway station takes only 12 minutes by train. The same kind of ticket is used for the entire system. Be advised that individual ride tickets are more expensive during morning and late afternoon–evening rush hours than they are during nonpeak hours (3 DM/$1.80 as opposed to 2.50 DM/$1.50). Buy tickets from automatic dispensers before boarding. There also are passes that allow unlimited travel for one day (6 DM/$3.60) or three days (17 DM/$10.20); they can be purchased at the tourist information bureaus (see *Tourist Information*). Maps and timetables arc conveniently posted throughout the system. For information on service, contact the public transportation system (*FVV;* 15-19 Mannheimer Str.; phone: 269402).

AIRPORT Frankfurt's *Flughafen Frankfurt Main* (Frankfurt-Main Airport) handles both domestic and international flights. It's about a 20-minute drive from the airport to downtown. Various lines of the *S-Bahn* inter-urban train system speed their way to downtown Frankfurt in just 12 minutes (look for signs to the *S-Bahn,* and take the S-14 or S-15 train).

BUSES AND STREETCARS *Stadtbus* (city buses) and *Strassenbahn* (streetcars) transport passengers inexpensively to all parts of the city and to many suburbs.

CAR RENTAL Among major international firms represented are *Avis* (170 Mainzer Landstr.; phone: 230101); *Europcar* (at the airport; phone: 690-5464); and *Hertz,* with two locations (106-108 Hanauer Landstr.; phone: 449090; and at the airport; phone: 690-5011). If driving a special German vehicle—Porsche, BMW, Mercedes—on the autobahn at top speed is one reason you're visiting Germany, get in touch with *Budget-Sixt* (52 Allerheiligenstr.; phone: 290066; or at the airport; phone: 697-0070), which offers luxury cars (despite its name).

SUBWAYS AND TRAINS The subway system, called the *U-Bahn,* and the fast trains to outlying areas, *S-Bahn,* get you where you want to go quickly and comfortably. The main stops are at Hauptwache and the *Hauptbahnhof* (Main Train Station).

TAXI There are stands near major hotels, stations, and at some intersections, and taxis (they are expensive) can easily be hailed on the streets. Most public telephone booths have a taxi call-number posted. For 24-hour service call 230001, 230033, or 545011.

TOURS The Frankfurt tourist board offers two-and-a-half-hour guided bus tours of the city which depart daily from in front of the office on Römerberg (see *Tourist Information*). *Gray Line Limousine and Coach Travel Service* (39 Wiesenhüttenpl.; phone: 230492) offers daily guided tours in English of Frankfurt and its neighboring cities. *Fahrgastschiff Wikinger II* (phone: 293960) offers Main River sightseeing cruises on steamers; the excursions leave from the dock at Eiserner Steg weekdays at 2, 3, and 4 PM (weather permitting); Sundays and holidays every half hour between 1 and 6 PM.

On weekends, you also can circle the city on the gaily painted streetcars of the *Ebbelwei Express* (phone: 213-22425). The tours are given every 30 minutes between 1:30 and 5:30 PM; commentary is available in English as well as German. You'll get music with your ride, and you can buy some of Frankfurt's famous *Apfelwein* (apple wine) to sip along the way. Hop aboard at any of the 18 *Ebbelwei Express* stops, including those in Willy-Brandt-Platz, at the *Hauptbahnhof* (Main Train Station), or at the intersection of Gartenstrasse and Schweizerstrasse in Sachsenhausen.

SPECIAL EVENTS

Frankfurt is at its busiest during the more than a dozen trade fairs that draw some 1.2 million visitors to the city each year. The biggest of these are the *Internationale Frankfurter Messe Premiere* (International Frankfurt Trade Fair) held in winter, and the *Frankfurter Buchmesse* (Frankfurt Book Fair) in October. Most of these events are held at the *Messegelände* (Fairgrounds), a huge exhibition center near the main railway station. The tradition of trade fairs in Frankfurt dates back 800 years. There also are numerous public fairs, such as the *Mainmesse* (Main Fair), held in August in the streets between the river and the *Pauluskirche;* and *Dippemess,* a big country fair that takes place in front of the *Eissporthalle* (see *Sports*) in April and September, with colorful stalls of crockery being the main attraction. One other very special local holiday deserves mention: *Wäldchestag.* On the Tuesday afternoon following *Pfingstmontag* (Whitmonday—the seventh Monday after *Easter*), most Frankfurters leave the city to walk in the neighboring woods, eat sausages and drink beer, and dance in the *Oberforsthaus* (Forest House).

MUSEUMS

In addition to those described in detail in *Special Places,* Frankfurt has several other interesting museums, the best of which are listed below. Unless otherwise noted, the museums listed are closed Mondays.

DEUTSCHES ARCHITEKTURMUSEUM (MUSEUM OF GERMAN ARCHITECTURE) The country's only museum specifically focusing on German architecture has exhibits on the country's building styles throughout history, as well as presentations on theoretical issues pertaining to architecture (ecology, responsibility to people, and more). The "house within a house," featuring several rooms of a house built within a self-contained exhibit, is especially interesting. No admission charge on Wednesdays. 43 Schaumainkai (phone: 212-38844).

DEUTSCHES FILMMUSEUM (GERMAN CINEMA MUSEUM) Offers permanent and changing displays about the history of films and filmmaking, both in Germany and all over the world. It also has a cinema that regularly shows movies (in German only), a bookstore, and a café. No admission charge on Wednesdays. 41 Schaumainkai (phone: 212-38830).

DEUTSCHES POSTMUSEUM (GERMAN POSTAL MUSEUM) Housed in two adjacent buildings are exhibits relating to the history of the communications industry in Germany, including the postal service and the development of telecommunications technology. There's also a large collection of postage stamps. No admission charge on Wednesdays. 53 Schaumainkai (phone: 60600).

HISTORISCHES MUSEUM (HISTORICAL MUSEUM) The life of Frankfurt and its people throughout the years is explored via models of the Altstadt, graphics, and coin collections, among other exhibits. There's also a children's museum, a library, and a café. No admission charge on Wednesdays. 19 Saalgasse, at the Römerberg (phone: 212-35599).

JÜDISCHES MUSEUM (JEWISH MUSEUM) Set in the magnificent palace of the Rothschilds, this museum details the social and cultural lives of Jews in Germany through permanent and temporary exhibitions, seminars, readings, and films. Admission charge. 14-15 Untermainkai (phone: 212-35000).

LIEBIEGHAUS (LIEBIEG HOUSE) Displays many types of sculpture, including those from ancient Greece, Egypt, and Rome. Periods covered include the Middle Ages and the Renaissance. No admission charge on Wednesdays. 71 Schaumainkai (phone: 212-38617).

MUSEUM JUDENGASSE (JEWS' LANE MUSEUM) Like the *Jüdisches Museum* (see above), this place has exhibits about Jewish life, but here they focus specifically on the history and culture of Frankfurt's Jewish quarter. Admission charge. 10 Kurt Schumacher Str. (phone: 297-7419).

MUSEUM FÜR KUNSTHANDWERK (MUSEUM OF APPLIED ARTS AND CRAFTS) Over 30,000 European books, prints, and handicrafts are housed in an elegant villa designed by American architect Richard Meier. The café here is a popular local meeting place. No admission charge on Wednesdays. 17 Schaumainkai (phone: 212-34037).

MUSEUM FÜR MODERNE KUNST (MUSEUM OF MODERN ART) One of Frankfurt's newer museums, it displays controversial works by international artists and examples of avant-garde architecture from the 1960s to the present. No admission charge on Wednesdays and Saturdays. 10 Domstr. (phone: 212-38819).

MUSEUM FÜR VÖLKERKUNDE (MUSEUM OF ETHNOLOGY) Changing exhibitions, with emphasis on the cultures of Third World countries. No admission charge on Wednesdays. 29 Schaumainkai (phone: 212-35391).

NATURMUSEUM SENCKENBERG (SENCKENBERG MUSEUM OF NATURAL HISTORY) Animals, plants, fossils, and geological items, including an impressive collection of dinosaurs and prehistoric whales, are displayed. Open daily. No admission charge on Wednesdays. 25 Senckenberganlage (phone: 75421).

SCHIRN KUNSTHALLE (SCHIRN HALL OF FINE ARTS) A museum that offers changing exhibits of modern painting and sculpture by internationally renowned artists. No admission charge on Wednesdays. Am Römerberg (phone: 299-8820).

SHOPPING

As befits Europe's major transportation hub, Frankfurt is filled with goods from all over the world. It is said that more money passes through the cash registers of the well-stocked department stores on the Zeil than on any other street in Europe. The best-known department stores are *Kaufhof* (116 Zeil; phone: 21910) and *Hertie* (90 Zeil; phone: 29861). There are several pedestrian shopping streets besides the Zeil, including Grosse Bockenheimerstrasse, with its chic boutiques and elegant apparel stores. Incidentally, this street is known locally as Fressgass (a rough English equivalent is "Gluttony Alley") because it is lined with so many restaurants, wine bars, and delicatessens, including one of the best delis in town, *Plöger* (No. 30; phone: 20941). Two other streets, Goethestrasse and Schillerstrasse, offer a tempting variety of designer clothing stores and fine boutiques. The best buys are the well-known German cutlery, expensive but superbly made leather clothing, and Frankfurt's distinctive blue and gray pottery. For standard shopping hours, see GETTING READY TO GO.

Cris Bittong Distinctive women's clothing from this local designer, including silk blouses and shirts with asymmetrical patterns. 19 Oppenheimer Landstr. (phone: 628464).

Fink Exklusiv Schuhe A local favorite, this shoe store is packed with high-quality footwear in conservative styles. 9 Goethestr. (phone: 289904).

Francofurtensien The perfect place to pick up a visual reminder of Frankfurt, this store is stocked with prints and paintings of local scenes, woodcuts, etchings, and even a map of the city in 1549. 11 Bethmannstr. (phone: 292324).

Freiraum Tin figures, glass jewelry, and decorative housewares, all locally designed and crafted. 15 Braubachstr. (phone: 296566).

Friedrich Brothers Christoph and Stephan Friedrich are among Germany's most famous jewelry designers; their pieces in gold, silver, and precious gems are beautiful, classic—and pricey. 17 Kaiserstr. (phone: 284353).

Hut Lange Hats, hats, and more hats, in a staggering variety of shapes and styles. 99 Fahrgasse (phone: 284687).

Der Laden Vivi Leonhardt creates and sells wonderful leather items in her workshop, from handbags to backpacks, including custom-made pieces. 16 Danneckerstr. (phone: 617180).

Lorey A veritable paradise of gift items, including Hummel, Meissen, and Rosenthal figurines. 16 Schillerstr. (phone: 299950).

Pfuller Kinderhaus Children's clothing in classic, yet modern, styles. 12 Goethestr. (phone: 284547).

Rosenthal am Kaiserplatz World-renowned porcelain. 38 Kaiserstr. (phone: 239822).

SPORTS AND FITNESS

One out of every six Frankfurt residents belongs to some type of sports club, and walking and jogging along the river or the marked paths in the city forest and in the nearby Taunus Mountains are almost universal activities. Physical fitness is even sponsored by the state government, which maintains a *Trimm Dich* ("keep yourself trim") trail, a 1½-mile (2.5-km) illustrated course of exercises and jogging in the Stadtwald (City Forest; see *Jogging*).

BICYCLING Numerous cycling events are scheduled during the summer (check with the tourist office for details), and there are paths in the city parks and the forest. Bicycles can be rented at *Fahrrad Burger* (73 Bergerstr.; phone: 432453) and *Theo Intra* (273 Westerbachstr.; phone: 342780), which also rents touring and mountain bikes and tandems.

FITNESS CENTER Many major hotels have fitness facilities on their premises (see *Checking In*). In addition, two well-equipped fitness centers are *Sport- und Fitnesszentrum Judokan* (109 Zeil; phone: 280565) and *Sportschule Petrescu* (55-57 Bleichstr.; phone: 295906).

FOOTBALL Frankfurt's team, *Galaxy,* faces fellow members of the World League of American Football at the *Waldstadion* (362 Mörfelder Landstr.; phone: 530-9935) between April and June.

GOLF The 18-hole course at *Frankfurter Golfclub* is just west of *Waldstadion* (41 Golfstr.; phone: 666-2318); to play here, you must be a member of a golf club at home.

HORSE RACING AND HORSEBACK RIDING Flat races and steeplechase races are held at *Frankfurt-South Racecourse* in suburban Niederrad (Schwarzwaldstr.; phone: 678-7018). Horses can be rented by the hour from *Frankfurter Reit- und Fahrclub* (85 Hahnstr.; phone: 666-7585) and *Reiterbund Frankfurt* (87 Hahnstr.; phone: 666-7485).

ICE SKATING You can skate or just watch other people at various rinks, including one at the *Waldstadion* (362 Mörfelder Landstr.; phone: 678040) and another at the spacious *Eissporthalle Frankfurt* (Am Bornheimer Hang; phone: 212-30825).

JOGGING There are paths through the Stadtwald, south of the Main River and 4 miles (6 km) from downtown; take streetcar No. 14; exit Oberschweinstiege.

SOCCER Frankfurt is a major soccer city. Its professional club, *Eintracht,* plays to large, enthusiastic crowds at the *Waldstadion* (see *Football*) almost every other weekend from September through January.

SWIMMING Several hotels have swimming pools, and there are numerous indoor and outdoor pools throughout the city. For indoor swimming, visit *Rebstockbad* (7 August-Euler-Str.; phone: 708078 or 708079) or *Brentanobad* (Rödelheimer Parkweg; phone: 212-39020).

TENNIS Exhibition matches arc played at *Waldstadion* (see *Football*) and the *Festhalle* at the *Messegelände* (Fairgrounds); contact the tourist office (see *Tourist Information*) for details. It is difficult for visitors to get court time at parks and clubs because of local demand, but three places usually have open times: *Tennisanlage Füssenich* (Sigmund-Freud-Str.; phone: 542318); *Tennisplätze Eissporthalle* (Am Bornheimer Hang; phone: 419141); and *Tennis & Squash Park Europa* (49 Ginnheimer Landstr.; phone: 532040).

THEATER

Frankfurt has more than 20 theaters. Most performances are in German, but there are some English-language theaters, including the *Theater in Bornheim* (*TIB;* 35 Bornheimer Landwehr; phone: 493-0503) and the *English Theater* (52 Kaiserstr.; phone: 242-31620). *The Städtisches Theater* (City Theater) is in the *Städtische Bühnen* complex on Theaterplatz (phone: 236061). The *Fritz Rémond-Theater* is at the *Zoologischer Garten* (16 Alfred-Brehm-Pl.; phone: 435166), and often produces current British and American hits in German. The *Theater am Turm (TAT)* offers drama (2 Eschersheimer Landstr.; phone: 154-5110); light comedy is the specialty at *Die Kömodie* (18 Neue Mainzer Str.; phone: 284580). *Ballet Frankfurt,* a local company under the direction of American choreographer William Forsythe, presents avant-garde, often provocative productions at the *Oper* (11 Untermainanlage; phone: 236061)—not to be confused with the *Alte Oper* on Opernplatz.

MUSIC

Whatever your taste in music, from opera or jazz to punk or pop, you'll hear it in Frankfurt. The *Städtische Oper* (City Opera) performs on the stage of the theater in the *Städtische Bühnen* arts complex (see *Theater*). There are frequent choral, symphony, and chamber music concerts at *Hessischer-Rundfunk* (8 Bertramstr.; phone: 1551), at the huge *Jahrhunderthalle* in suburban Hoechst (phone: 360-1240), and at the *Alte Oper* (see *Special Places*). Upcoming music events are posted on billboards around the city and in the daily newspaper.

NIGHTCLUBS AND NIGHTLIFE

All of Frankfurt's big hotels offer music and dancing, and discotheques are cropping up all over the city. One of the most popular discos is *Dorian Gray* (at the airport; phone: 690-2212), modeled after New York's late *Studio 54. Tiger-Palast* (16-20 Heiligkreuzgasse; phone: 289691) features an international circus-style show with magic acts, acrobats, and juggling; there's also a bar and a restaurant where locals gather. Other good clubs include *Chamäleon* (13 Kaiserhofstr.; phone: 289977); *Cooky's* (4 Am Salzhaus; phone: 287662); *Omen* (14 Junghofstr.; phone: 282233); and *Plastic* (14 Seilerstr.; phone: 285055).

Jazz lovers will love Frankfurt, which is purported to have more than 100 daily performances, ranging from traditional New Orleans to modern jazz. *Der Jazzkeller* (18A Kleine Bockenheimerstr.; phone: 288537) is the best-known club, but you should also stop in at *Jazzkneipe* (70 Berlinerstr.; phone: 287173); *Sinkkasten Arts Club* (9 Brönnerstr.; phone: 280385); *Jazzhaus* (12 Kleine Bockenheimerstr.; phone: 287194); *Jazz-Life Podium* (22 Kleine Rittergasse; phone: 626346); and *Lorbascher Tal* (49 Grosse Rittergasse; phone: 616459).

Pub-hopping in Sachsenhausen gets merrier and merrier as the night wears on. Look for the traditional green wreath hanging over the door to identify taverns that serve Frankfurt's special *Apfelwein* (apple wine). Among the most authentic are *Mutter Ernst* (12 Alte Rothofstr.; phone: 283822), which serves beer, *Apfelwein,* and such local fare as veal cutlets, wurst, and potato salad; *Zum Gemalten Hause* (67 Schweizerstr.; phone: 614559), which has a garden; *Apfelweinwirtschaft Wagner* (71 Schweizerstr.; phone: 612565); *Zur Germani* and *Zum Kanonesteppel* (16 Textorstr.; phone: 613336), together known as *Die Insel* (The Island); *Lorsbacher Tal* (in the center of Sachsenhausen, 49 Grosse Rittergasse; phone: 616459), which has its own apple winery; and, in the nearby suburb of Seckbach, *Zum Rad* (2 Leonhardsgasse; phone: 479128), a local favorite for its friendly ambience and attractive garden terrace.

Located 10 miles (16 km) north of the city, the *Spielbank Bad Homburg* casino (phone: 61-721-70170) in Bad Homburg's *Kurpark*, occupies a special place in European gaming history. The world's first gambling casino—established in 1841 under the aegis of the celebrated brothers Blanc, who went on to create the casino at Monte Carlo 20 years later—the glittering casino served as the setting of that famous novelette of compulsive gambling, *The Gambler*, whose author, the great Russian master Fyodor Dostoyevsky, managed to run through a nonfictional fortune of his own. There's gambling—plus dining and dancing—nightly. Another casino in the area is the *Spielbank Wiesbaden* (1 Kurhauspl.; phone: 611-536100) in Wiesbaden, 19 miles (30 km) west of Frankfurt.

Best in Town

CHECKING IN

Although Frankfurt has a total of 200 hotels and pensions, with over 20,000 beds, only the most confident traveler comes here without a reservation. Space always is tight, and empty hotel rooms are nearly nonexistent during the big trade fairs, when, incidentally, the highest prices normally prevail. At other times, however, hotels have plenty of empty rooms on weekends, and most offer cut-rate special packages for at least Friday and Saturday nights. Most of Frankfurt's major hotels have complete facilities for the business traveler. Those hotels listed below as having "business services" usually offer such conveniences as an English-speaking concierge, meeting rooms, photocopiers, computers, translation services, and express checkout, among others. Call thc hotel for additional information. At an expensive hotel, expect to pay from $250 to $350 a night for a double room. Moderate hotels charge from $150 to $250; places in the inexpensive category charge less than $150 a night. Hotel rooms have private baths and TV sets, unless otherwise indicated. Virtually all hotels in Frankfurt, regardless of price, share the German virtue of cleanliness. Be aware that most of the large luxury hotels no longer include breakfast in their rates; expect to pay about $20 per person for breakfast from the buffet. Smaller hotels generally still include breakfast in the price of the room. All telephone numbers are in the 69 city code unless otherwise indicated.

For an unforgettable experience in Frankfurt, we begin with our favorite, followed by our cost and quality choices, listed by price category.

ROOMS AT THE TOP

Gravenbruch Kempinski Advise the management of your flight arrival and they will send a limousine to whisk you to the pastoral sophistication of this elegant, 288-room hotel in a small town about 7 miles (12 km) outside Frankfurt. A perimeter of private parkland, graced by a willow-ringed pond, and a battalion of service staff will welcome you, and if there's a chill in the air, there's sure to be a well-stoked fire crackling in the lobby's hearth. Once settled in, you can decide between a wurst washed down by *Weizenbier* (light, fizzy beer made from wheat) in the homey, stone-and-wood *Tor Schänke,* or the finer fare of the *Forsthaus* served under wrought-iron chandeliers. There's also an outstanding, multi-course Sunday brunch. Business services are available. Neu Isenberg (phone: 610-25050; 800-426-3135; fax: 6102-505445).

EXPENSIVE

Arabella Grand With 378 spacious, modern rooms, this luxury property is conveniently located in the city center. Close to the Zeil, the main shopping street, the hotel has several restaurants, 24-hour room service, a pool, massage facilities, foreign currency exchange, and business services. 7 Konrad-Adenauer-Str. (phone: 29810; fax: 298-1810).

Frankfurt Inter-Continental One of the largest hotels in Germany, with American-style service and 849 luxuriously appointed rooms (ask for one on the river side). There are several restaurants, including the elegant *Rôtisserie.* Fitness facilities include a pool, a sauna, and a solarium. The hotel also offers 24-hour room service, foreign currency exchange, and business services. 43 Wilhelm-Leuschner-Str. (phone: 26050; 800-327-0200; fax: 252467).

Frankfurt Marriott The tallest hotel in Germany is near the fairgrounds, but its decor is more sophisticated than you might expect from a place that caters to conventioneers. There are 585 guestrooms, several restaurants, a small disco, and a seductive piano bar, *Die Bibliotheke.* There's even a bakery on the premises. Other amenities include 24-hour room service, foreign currency exchange, and business services. 2-10 Hamburger Allee (phone: 79550; 800-228-9290; fax: 795-52432).

Sheraton Frankfurt Walk right in from the airport's central terminal. An extension has made this one of Germany's largest hotels, with 1,050 rooms. There are three restaurants, including *Papillon,* with an extensive continental menu and a good wine list. There's also an indoor pool and a sauna. Other amenities include 24-hour room service, foreign currency exchange, and business services. Central terminal, *Flughafen Frankfurt Main* (phone: 69770; 800-334-8484; fax: 697-72230).

Steigenberger Frankfurter Hof Built in the tradition of grand European hotels, it was refurbished and restored to its prewar charm after serving as headquarters for the Allied occupation forces. Its 347 guestrooms are attractively furnished and feature plenty of luxury amenities. It's easy to find an attractive spot here where a waiter will bring a drink, a newspaper, or a message. International movers and shakers from the political and financial worlds dine in the elegant *Français* restaurant, while the less expensive *Frankfurter Stubb* has an extensive menu and offers excellent service (see *Eating Out* for both). Bicycle rental is available. Other amenities include 24-hour room service, foreign currency exchange, and business services. 17 Kaiserpl. (phone: 21502; 800-223-5652; fax: 215900).

MODERATE

Admiral In a nice location near the zoo, this 60-room hostelry offers good service, reasonable rates, and a restaurant. Business services are available. 25 Hölderlinstr. (phone: 448021; fax: 439402).

Am Berg Once a private villa and now a designated historical monument, this property offers 20 large rooms, rebuilt after World War II to their original 1900 style. There's no restaurant. 23 Grethenweg (phone: 612021; fax: 615109).

Am Dom Although in the historic downtown area, this smallish hostelry (25 rooms) is an oasis of quiet. There is no restaurant. 3 Kannengiessergasse (phone: 282141; fax: 283237).

Diana Near the city center, this small (24 rooms) place offers the standard comforts, but no extras. There's no restaurant. 83 Westendstr. (phone: 747007; fax: 747079).

Florentina Small (28 rooms), and in a pleasant neighborhood not far from the main train station. There's no restaurant. 23 Westendstr. (phone: 746044).

Frankfurt A motel in the city center is a rarity in Germany. This one, with 66 rooms, is convenient and offers good service and reasonable rates. There's also a restaurant. 204 Eschersheimer Landstr. (phone: 568010).

Maingau In Sachsenhausen, on the south bank of the Main River, this is a particularly reasonably priced 100-room hotel with a restaurant. Business services are available. 38-40 Schifferstr. (phone: 617001; fax: 620790).

Mozart This charming 35-room hostelry is next to the US military headquarters (the quieter rooms are in the back). There's a restaurant, and business services are available. 17 Parkstr. (phone: 550831).

INEXPENSIVE

Kautz Located on the Sachsenhausen side of the river, this small hotel has 15 comfortably furnished rooms and a restaurant. 17 Gartenstr. (phone: 618061; fax: 613236).

Weisses Haus This small, pleasant 32-room hotel is conveniently located just outside the city center. No frills here, but there is a restaurant on the premises, and the rooms certainly live up to German standards for comfort and cleanliness. 18 Jahnstr. (phone: 554605; fax: 596-3912).

EATING OUT

Though Frankfurt is not noted for its culinary artistry, local specialties are prepared just as well in restaurants as in private homes. The large population of foreign-born residents inspires a wide spectrum of European and Asian offerings. Lunch, often the main meal of the day, is served in most places between 11 AM and 3 PM. Restaurants then close until about 5:30 PM. Except in big hotel restaurants, it is difficult to just drop in anywhere for a late lunch. However, there is a late afternoon *Kaffee* ritual, at which Frankfurters fortify themselves with coffee and pastry or a snack at a *Konditorei.* All restaurants listed below are open for lunch and dinner unless otherwise noted. A local specialty that is a perfect nosh with beer or *Apfelwein* (apple wine) is *Handkäs mit Musik:* soft limburger cheese mixed with vinegar, oil, a bit of onion, and a few caraway seeds. And whether the frankfurter originated here or not, you still can buy the best franks in Frankfurt, on the freshest rolls, from a cart right outside the *Kaufhof* department store. For a three-course lunch or dinner for two, you'll pay between $160 and $225 at restaurants in the expensive category; $95 to $155 at places in the moderate range; and under $70 at inexpensive places. Prices do not include drinks, wine, or beer. Taxes and the tip are always included in the bill; however, it is customary to add a small extra amount for good service. All telephone numbers are in the 69 city code unless otherwise indicated.

EXPENSIVE

Bistro Rosa Owner Dinah Oehler has run this charming eatery for the last 10 years, and the decor reflects her fondness for pigs—there are lots of porcine paintings, prints, and sculptures, all in shades of *rosa* (pink). The menu changes seasonally, but no matter when you go, you can feast on such well-prepared delicacies as breast of duck in rhubarb sauce and marinated asparagus. Though the list of French wines is rather short, the vintages are a splendid complement to the food. Closed Sundays and holidays. Reservations necessary. Major credit cards accepted. 25 Grünebergweg (phone: 721380).

Bistrot 77 One of the city's top restaurants, it has been run by brothers Guy and Dominique Mosbach since 1977 and features excellent presentations of French fare in a simple, tasteful setting. The menu changes frequently, but possible entrées could include perch with lentils and duck prepared in several ways. The wine list features a number of Alsatian vintages from the Mosbach vineyard. Closed Sundays (except during trade fairs) and Saturday lunch. Reservations necessary. Major credit cards accepted. 1-3 Ziegelhüttenweg (phone: 614040).

Daitokai Formerly *Kikkoman,* this is an elegant Japanese restaurant. Open daily; dinner only on Saturdays and holidays. Reservations advised. Major credit cards accepted. Zoo Passage, 1 Friedberger Anlage (phone: 499-0021).

Erno's Bistro This place has been a Frankfurt favorite for 20 years. French, with checkered tablecloths and superior cooking, it offers such outstanding entrées as filet of beef in red wine sauce and salmon with a sesame crust. Be sure to leave room for the exquisite desserts (like the tarte tatin with ice cream) and fine cheeses that await at the end of the meal. There also is an excellent and extensive wine list. Even with a reservation in hand, you may have to wait for your table (the place can get crowded), but it's worth it. Closed weekends. Reservations advised. Major credit cards accepted. 15 Liebigstr. (phone: 721997).

Français Well-prepared game, French cuisine, and excellent service have made this one-Michelin-star dining room at the *Steigenberger Frankfurter Hof* a particular favorite of those used to eating the best. Closed Sundays, Mondays, holidays, and for four weeks during the summer. Reservations advised. Major credit cards accepted. 17 Kaiserpl. (phone: 21502).

Weinhaus Brückenkeller This restaurant, especially popular with international visitors, has been awarded two Michelin stars for its first-rate continental fare. The elegant dining room is tastefully decorated with antique furniture. Among chef Alfred Friedrich's most successful dishes are salmon and turbot roulade served with caviar sauce and baby goat with green and white asparagus. There's also an impressive wine list, and the service is impeccable. Open for dinner only; closed Sundays (except during trade fairs). Reservations necessary. Major credit cards accepted. 6 Schützenstr. (phone: 284238).

MODERATE

Alte Brückenmühle On the Sachsenhausen side of the river, this cozy eatery's decor is in the traditional, Old German style. The menu features the choicest cuts of veal, beef, pork, poultry, game, and fish—all prepared according to old Frankfurt recipes. Lunch specials are especially reasonable. Open daily; closed Saturday lunch. Reservations advised. Major credit cards accepted. 10 Wallstr. (phone: 612543).

Altes Zollhaus Travelers who could not make it through the Frankfurt city gates in time once found refuge for the night in this former customs house, dating from the 18th century. It's now a restaurant specializing in local dishes. Closed Mondays. Reservations advised. Major credit cards accepted. 531 Friedberger Landstr. (phone: 472707).

Frankfurter Stubb German specialties are beautifully prepared in this well-appointed cellar restaurant at the *Steigenberger Frankfurter Hof.* The decor is inspired by Goethe, including a window from his childhood house and framed anecdotes and prints depicting the great poet's life. During May, when *Spargel* (white asparagus) from the Schwetzinger area south of Frankfurt is in season, it is presented here in an imaginative array of dishes, served with wine chosen to complement its delicate flavor. Diners can also enjoy Franconian specialties such as boiled beef with green sauce and *Handkäs mit Musik.* Closed Sundays. Reservations advised. Major credit cards accepted. 33 Bethmannstr. (phone: 215679).

Gargantua Despite its name, this charming bistro is an intimate place that attracts diners who come for—and receive—first class continental fare at reasonable prices. The prix fixe menu, featuring four to six courses with fine wines, is an especially good deal, but dishes are available à la carte as well. Closed Sundays (except during trade fairs) and Saturday lunch. Reservations advised. Major credit cards accepted. 3 Friesengasse (phone: 776442).

INEXPENSIVE

Altes Café Schneider In business since 1906, this eatery/bakery has an Old World charm that sets it apart from other, more modern cafés in the city. Though especially popular for its sumptuous pastries (best enjoyed over a hot cup of coffee in the afternoon), the breakfast and lunch menus offer good local specialties at excellent prices. Open for breakfast and lunch only; closed Sundays and holidays. No reservations. No credit cards accepted. 12 Kaiserstr. (phone: 281447).

Da Pang This little Chinese restaurant is an ideal place to grab a quick, inexpensive lunch or snack. Menu items include various kinds of soup, spring rolls, and Szechuan-style meat and seafood dishes. *Note:* Since the neighborhood can get very rough after dark, it's best to come here for lunch. Open daily. Reservations advised. Major credit cards accepted. 17 Weserstr. (phone: 235483).

Harvey's A relatively recent addition to Frankfurt's restaurant scene, this café on the north side of the city offers good food and a quirky ambience that have quickly endeared it to locals. The highlight of the dramatic decor is the gilded bar and the striking modern murals on the walls; the menu offers a wide selection of seafood, meat, and vegetarian dishes. A good breakfast is served here, too. Open daily. No reservations. No credit cards accepted. 64 Bornheimer Landstr. (phone: 497303).

Klein Markthalle Located above the international food market hall, this restaurant is one of the best kept secrets in town. Locals flock here to partake of genuine home cooking in a friendly, homestyle setting. The fare, including veal cutlets, fried potatoes, and omelettes, is hearty and very tasty. Open for breakfast and lunch only; closed Sundays. No reservations. No credit cards accepted. 5 Hasengasse (phone: 293498).

Künstlerkeller Set in the cellar of a former Carmelite monastery dating from the 13th century, this place serves a menu of well-prepared local dishes. The convivial patrons will make you feel both comfortable and welcome. Closed Mondays. No reservations. Major credit cards accepted. 1 Münzgasse (phone: 292242).

Saladin Here is an informal eatery with a buffet of salads, soups, vegetarian entrées, and meat and seafood dishes, all freshly prepared and served cafeteria-style. Closed Sundays. No reservations. No credit cards accepted. 6 Adalbertstr. (phone: 779005).

Steinernes Haus This traditional beer hall, set in a rustic stone house built in the 15th century, serves up a menu of hearty specialties, including steak grilled tableside and liver dumplings with sauerkraut and mashed potatoes, along with a wide variety of beers and ales. Open daily. No reservations. No credit cards accepted. 35 Braubachstr. (phone: 283491).

Hamburg

Though it's a bit of a cliché, Hamburg's nickname—"the Venice of the North"—is an apt one. The city is honeycombed with canals and waterways spanned by 2,125 bridges (the most of any European city). Few urban locations are as picturesque: The downtown is enhanced by historic church spires, while the square in front of the Renaissance-style *Rathaus* (City Hall) evokes images of Piazza San Marco. The canals are rimmed by covered walkways with arches that create seemingly endless rows of Italianate loggias. A relatively recent addition, a network of glass-roofed shopping arcades, completes the picture of Germany's city beautiful. In terms of cosmopolitan flair, only Berlin compares.

Also known as "Germany's gateway to the world," Hamburg is the country's second-largest city (after Berlin), with a population of 1.65 million. Its natural harbor (and Germany's largest seaport) is located 65 miles from the North Sea at the confluence of three rivers—the Elbe, the Alster, and the Bille. Seagoing vessels take about six hours to negotiate this deep-water part of the Elbe. The Alster, a tributary of the Elbe, was dammed in the 12th century, creating two connected artificial lakes, Binnenalster and Aussenalster (Inner and Outer Alster). On one side of central Hamburg is the dockyard area, on the other, the Alster. Between them is the historic merchant city, with its five slender church spires.

Hamburg was an independent city-state in the Middle Ages—its original designation was the "Free and Hanseatic City of Hamburg"—and even today it exists administratively both as a city and a federal state. Residents have always been fiercely proud of their independence, a pride that was expressed most emphatically in 1871 when Kaiser Wilhelm I announced plans to elevate a Hamburg merchant to the nobility. The Mayor of Hamburg informed the startled kaiser, "It is impossible to raise the rank of a Hamburg citizen."

Hamburgians are quick to point out that the area the city now occupies has been inhabited continuously over the past 15,000 years (although permanent settlements can be traced back only 6,000 years). The first fortifications were built in 811 (probably by Charlemagne to defend against the Slavs), and although they were repeatedly pounded by fierce Viking raids, the town continued to grow. In 1189, Frederick Barbarossa (Holy Roman Emperor Frederick I—1155–90) granted Hamburg (then Hammaburg) a charter as a free city and port, thereby exempting its ships from paying duty. Not surprisingly, local merchants prospered greatly.

No trading power on earth equaled Hamburg during its years as a leading member of the Hanseatic League, a powerful federation of Northern European merchant cities that was established in the 13th century. The league, which controlled shipping in the Baltic and North Seas and virtu-

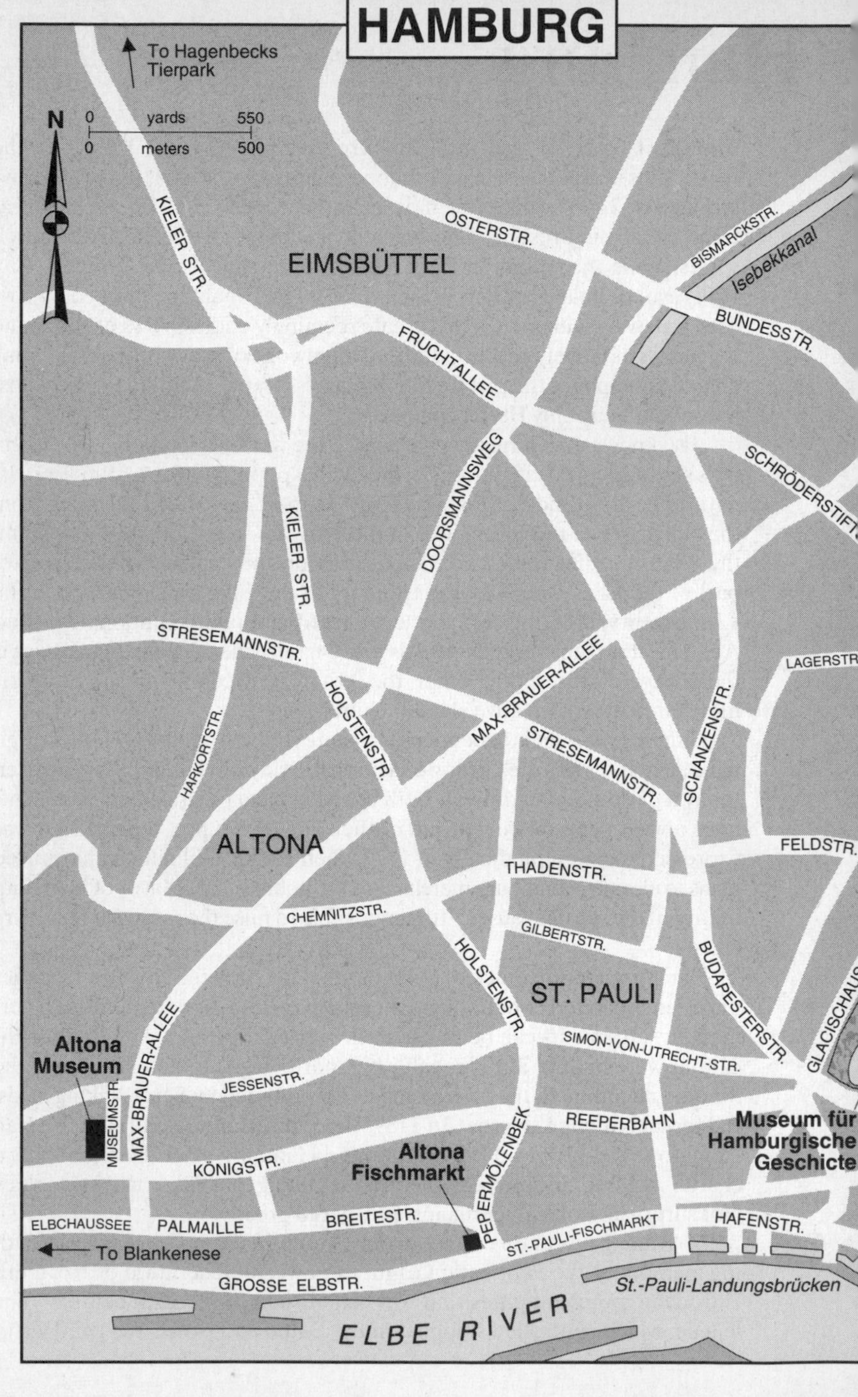
HAMBURG
To Hagenbecks Tierpark
N
0 yards 550
0 meters 500
KIELER STR.
OSTERSTR.
EIMSBÜTTEL
BISMARCKSTR.
Isebekkanal
BUNDESSTR.
FRUCHTALLEE
DOORSMANNSWEG
SCHRÖDERSTIFT.
KIELER STR.
STRESEMANNSTR.
HOLSTENSTR.
MAX-BRAUER-ALLEE
LAGERSTR.
HARKORTSTR.
STRESEMANNSTR.
SCHANZENSTR.
ALTONA
FELDSTR.
THADENSTR.
CHEMNITZSTR.
GILBERTSTR.
HOLSTENSTR.
BUDAPESTERSTR.
ST. PAULI
GLACISCHAUSS
Altona Museum
MAX-BRAUER-ALLEE
SIMON-VON-UTRECHT-STR.
JESSENSTR.
MUSEUMSTR.
REEPERBAHN
Museum für Hamburgische Geschicte
PEPERMÖLENBEK
KÖNIGSTR.
Altona Fischmarkt
ELBCHAUSSEE
PALMAILLE
BREITESTR.
ST.-PAULI-FISCHMARKT
HAFENSTR.
To Blankenese
GROSSE ELBSTR.
St.-Pauli-Landungsbrücken
ELBE RIVER

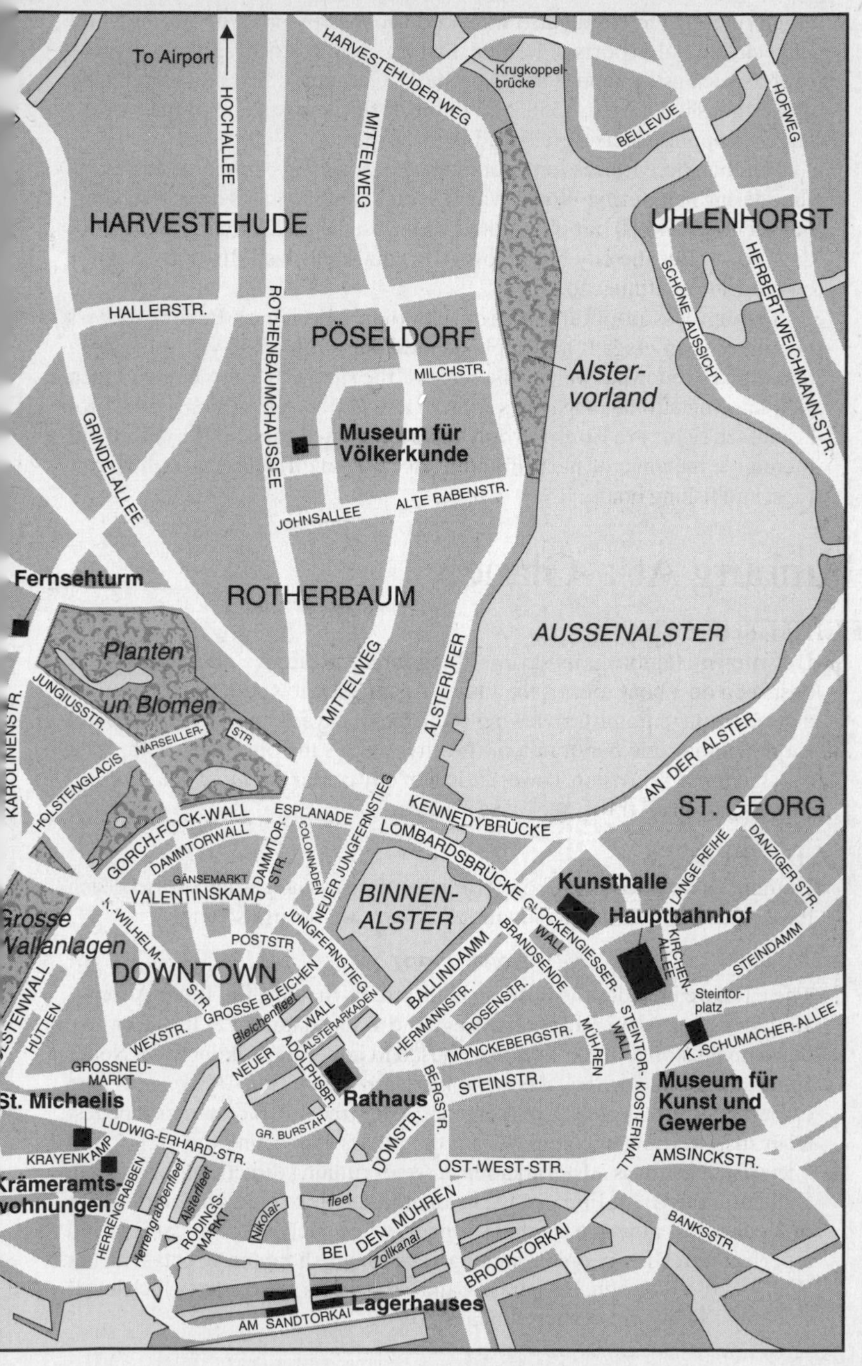

To Airport
HOCHALLEE
HARVESTEHUDER WEG
Krugkoppelbrücke
MITTELWEG
BELLEVUE
HOFWEG
HARVESTEHUDE
UHLENHORST
SCHÖNE AUSSICHT
HERBERT-WEICHMANN-STR.
HALLERSTR.
ROTHENBAUMCHAUSSEE
PÖSELDORF
MILCHSTR.
Alster-
vorland
GRINDELALLEE
Museum für
Völkerkunde
JOHNSALLEE
ALTE RABENSTR.
Fernsehturm
ROTHERBAUM
AUSSENALSTER
Planten
un Blomen
MITTELWEG
ALSTERUFER
JUNGIUSSTR.
KAROLINENSTR.
MARSEILLER-
STR.
HOLSTENGLACIS
AN DER ALSTER
NEUER JUNGFERNSTIEG
KENNEDYBRÜCKE
ST. GEORG
GORCH-FOCK-WALL
ESPLANADE
LOMBARDSBRÜCKE
DAMMTORWALL
DAMMTOR-
STR.
COLONNADEN
LANGE REIHE
DANZIGER STR.
GÄNSEMARKT
Kunsthalle
VALENTINSKAMP
BINNEN-
ALSTER
GLOCKENGIESSER-
WALL
Grosse
Wallanlagen
K.-WILHELM-
STR
Hauptbahnhof
POSTSTR.
JUNGFERNSTIEG
BALLINDAMM
BRANDSENDE
KIRCHEN-
ALLEE
DOWNTOWN
STEINDAMM
GROSSE BLEICHEN
Bleichenfleet
HERMANNSTR.
ROSENSTR.
Steintor-
platz
HÜTTEN
WEXSTR.
WALL
ALSTERARKADEN
STEINTOR-
WALL
MÖNCKEBERGSTR.
MÜHREN
K.-SCHUMACHER-ALLEE
GROSSNEU-
MARKT
NEUER
ADOLPHSBR.
Rathaus
STEINSTR.
BERGSTR.
KOSTERWALL
Museum für
Kunst und
Gewerbe
St. Michaelis
LUDWIG-ERHARD-STR.
GR. BURSTAH
DOMSTR.
KRAYENKAMP
OST-WEST-STR.
AMSINCKSTR.
Krämeramts-
wohnungen
HERRENGRABEN
Herrengrabenfleet
Alsterfleet
RÖDINGS-
MARKT
Nikolai-
fleet
BEI DEN MÜHREN
Zollkanal
BROOKTORKAI
BANKSSTR.
Lagerhauses
AM SANDTORKAI

ally monopolized trade, also included the nearby ports of Bremen and Lübeck, the Baltic ports of Bergen, Danzig, and Rostock, and inland trade centers such as Lüneburg and Augsburg. Germany's first stock exchange was established here in 1558, and in the 19th century some of the world's largest shipping fleets were based in its harbor.

Hamburg's centuries-long dominance of seagoing commerce came to a shuddering halt during World War II, when bombing raids devastated harbor facilities and all but obliterated its industrial area, along with most of downtown. But the city has recovered remarkably well. Its port complex on the Elbe continues to grow.

Though less popular with tourists than Munich or Berlin, today's Hamburg is an elegant and sophisticated city, with a 300-year-old opera house and a renowned vaudeville theater, the *Hansa.* It's also home to such well-known national magazines as *Stern* and *Der Spiegel.* Among its not-to-be-missed sights are Europe's only privately owned zoo and the harbor, an incredible mélange of pleasure craft, oceangoing freighters, coal barges, tugs, and fishing boats.

Hamburg At-a-Glance

SEEING THE CITY

Downtown Hamburg, its skyline dominated by the five church spires, is best seen on a boat tour of the Outer Alster. The tower of *St. Michaelis* is a good vantage point for viewing the Elbe dockyard and the Alster. And for a high-altitude panorama of the city, there's the observatory atop the *Fernsehturm* (Television Tower) north of city center at *Planten un Blomen.* For details on all three, see *Special Places.*

SPECIAL PLACES

Hamburg's downtown, harbor, Alsters, and parks and garden districts each have their own distinct personalities. All are well worth seeing.

DOWNTOWN

The city core includes the bustling main streets that line the Inner Alster—Jungfernstieg, Neuer Jungfernstieg, and Ballindamm. Exclusive shops, department stores, and offices are housed in imposing buildings. On Neuer Jungfernstieg, facing the lake, is the *Vier Jahreszeiten* (see *Checking In*), one of Europe's finest hotels. An interesting side street is Colonnaden, a pedestrian strip whose name comes from the pillars supporting the arches that enclose it. Nearby is Alsterarkaden, a street running directly along a canal. Built after the Great Fire of 1842 in an ornate style to emulate the romance of Venice, it is most pleasant in summer, when lively outdoor cafés afford a perfect perch for people watching. The major shopping streets—Neuer Wall, Grosse Bleichen, Poststrasse, and Mönckebergerstrasse (which locals call "the Mö")—are clustered near here.

RATHAUS (CITY HALL) A short stroll from the Jungfernstieg promenade, this palatial hall has an ornate tower, a green copper roof, and 647 opulently furnished rooms with glittering chandeliers suspended from gilt-edged coffered ceilings; exquisite tapestries hang on the walls, and paintings and murals depict Hamburg's past glories. Built near the end of the 19th century in a German Renaissance style, with gables and uniform rows of rectangular windows, the *Rathaus* offers guided tours (in English) of the reception area and major rooms hourly from 10:15 AM to 3:15 PM weekdays, to 1:15 PM weekends. The adjoining *Rathausmarkt*—with its modernistic glass and steel pavilions, shade trees, and a monument to poet Heinrich Heine—is a popular meeting place.

PASSAGEN This network of 12 covered arcades extending for a mile through the heart of downtown is perfect for window shopping, even in mid-winter. Lined with tasteful structures of marble and steel and set with statuary and tropical plants beneath curved glass domes, it includes the *Hanse-Viertel, Kaufmannshaus,* and *Galleria* shopping areas. Here are elegant shops selling designer clothing, antiques, rugs, jewelry, porcelain, household accessories, furniture, sweets, and delicacies. When you've browsed long enough, you can rest and grab a bite at one of the area's many fine restaurants and bars, such as *Mövenpick* (see *Eating Out*), a member of the Swiss chain of eateries that has become very popular throughout Europe; the Belle Epoque *Brasserie* in the Bleichenhof Passage; and the *Essen und Trinken Passage* (Eating and Drinking Passage) on Gänsemarkt, a food court with a wide variety of German and continental restaurants.

ST. MICHAELIS Popularly known as the *Michel,* this Protestant Baroque church is the best-known symbol of Hamburg. Its distinctive iron and brick tower contains Germany's largest tower clock—often consulted by sailors in the harbor. Built between 1751 and 1762, the church has been heavily damaged and restored twice—once after a 1906 fire and again after World War II. Faithfully restored to its original splendor, it has a sculpture of St. Michael above the main entrance and, inside, a sunburst-topped altar and Corinthian columns. The tower, with a platform at the top, offers panoramic views across the city center to the Alster lakes in one direction and the Elbe dockyards in the other. The tower (accessible by elevator as well as stairs) is closed Wednesdays. Admission charge to the tower. Englische Planke (no phone).

KRÄMERAMTSWOHNUNGEN Across from *St. Michaelis* are nine restored 17th-century houses whose interiors have been transformed into art galleries, gift shops, and restaurants, making this one of the most popular attractions in town. Originally homes of the widows of Merchants' Guild members, the buildings have been handsomely restored (with working gas lamps) and declared national monuments. One of the homes is now a museum (referred to simply as *Historic Home C;* 10 Krayenkamp; phone: 311-02624), with typical 17th-century furnishings, including fine wood paneling and silk fabrics and upholstery. The museum is closed Mondays; admission charge.

THE HARBOR

A relatively short walk from *St. Michaelis* (or take the *U-Bahn* No. 3 to *St. Pauli Landungsbrücken Station*), Hamburg's harbor is worth a visit, if only to watch the legions of ships pass by. More than 18,000 seagoing vessels a year sail the Elbe estuary from the North Sea to Hamburg, making that 65-mile strip one of the world's most active shipping lanes. Its annual cargo of 55 million tons keeps 160 tugs and 250 launches occupied, and 100,000 Hamburgians employed. A good vantage point is at the *Uberseebrücke,* a glass-enclosed restaurant seemingly suspended over the water at harborside (see *Eating Out*). There's also a harbor tour (see *Sightseeing Tours*).

ALTONA FISCHMARKT The open-air market at the harbor has been an institution since 1703. Generations ago fishermen used to sell their catches only before Sunday church services, but today the market has expanded both its hours and its stock in trade, selling everything from cut flowers to live rabbits. Stalls open at 5 AM on summer Sundays, somewhat later the rest of the year, with the activity at its most vibrant between 7 and 9:30 AM. Come for the experience, if not for the eclectic wares. On the Elbe walkway, a short stroll from the *Uberseebrücke.*

ELSEWHERE IN THE CITY

THE ALSTERS These two artificial lakes are best explored aboard boats that sail throughout the day from the Jungfernstieg quay (see *Sightseeing Tours*). Before or after embarking on a cruise, stop at the *Alsterpavillon* (see *Eating Out*), Hamburg's famed waterfront café. The Inner Alster affords dramatic views of downtown Hamburg—particularly of the skyline with its five church spires. Along the lakeshores are other charming cafés and numerous boat clubs where you can rent a sailboat, canoe, or rowboat. From the *Rabenstrasse U-Bahn Station,* enter *Alstervorland,* a park extending for several miles along the left bank of the Alster between Alte Rabenstrasse and Krugkoppelbrücke. A short distance from the park is the residential neighborhood of Pöseldorf; at its heart is Milchstrasse, a fashionable street restored as a quaint turn-of-the-century shopping area with narrow cobblestone passageways surrounded by converted stables and villas. Located here are designer boutiques, avant-garde art galleries, pricey antiques shops, bars, and posh cafés and restaurants.

PLANTEN UN BLOMEN (PLANTS AND FLOWERS) Close to the larger *Wallanlagen*—which includes the exotic plants and superb landscaping of the old botanical gardens—this compact green space is a favorite leisure-time destination. Attractions in the two parks include a greenhouse of tropical plants, the largest Japanese garden in Germany, several playgrounds, a roller skating rink (which is used for ice skating in winter), and cafés and restaurants.

There's a miniature railway (which children may ride on) that runs through the grounds. Every evening from April to mid-September, the fountains become the focus of a colorful light show accompanied by classical music; the show begins at 10 PM. Open daily. No admission charge. Main entrance is at the *Stephansplatz Station* of the *U-Bahn*.

FERNSEHTURM (TELEVISION TOWER) Located just beyond the western edge of *Planten un Blomen,* this tower offers the most panoramic views across the city and surrounding areas, and features a revolving restaurant that has reasonably priced afternoon *Kaffee und Kuchen* (coffee and cake). Open daily. Admission charge. Take the *U-Bahn* to *Messehallen Station.* 2-8 Lagerstr. (phone: 438024).

HAGENBECKS TIERPARK (HAGENBECK ZOO) Six generations of the Hagenbeck family have been involved in zoo-keeping. In operation since 1907, the zoo has long been one of Hamburg's favorite attractions. There are 2,500 animals representing 365 species from five continents living here in settings similar to their natural habitats: an attractive park-like environment of cliffs, rivers, and lakes. Open daily. Admission charge. It's located in the district of Stellingen, about 4 miles (7 km) northwest of the city center. Take the *U-Bahn* to *Hagenbecks Tierpark Station.* Hagenbeckallee (phone: 540-00147).

ENVIRONS

BLANKENESE Regarded by many as the most enchanting spot in the area, this former fishing village west of the city center, now a tony suburb and favorite holiday haven, is *the* destination of choice among well-to-do Hamburgians. If time allows (and energy endures), the best way to traverse the 6 miles (10 km) from downtown to Blankenese is on foot: The *Elbuferwanderweg* (Elbe Shore Walkway) follows the path of the historic river, meandering beneath towering shade trees to Blankenese via Hamburg's districts of Altona, Ovelgönne, Teufelsbrück, and Mühlenberg. (Note: It's a *long* walk, even if you stop at the pleasant cafés en route.) The half-hour trip by car (or city bus) along the tree-lined Elbchaussee affords its own pleasures, as it passes 19th-century estates of rich merchants, shipowners, and bankers. There's also ferry service twice daily from the St. Pauli piers; the trip takes about an hour. But if time is short, take the *S-Bahn;* it's only a 15-minute ride to *Blankenese Station.*

The village traces its roots to the 13th century when it sheltered pirates who attacked passing ships, but later gained respectability as home port for a deep-sea fishing fleet. In the 20th century retired sea captains made their homes here; today prosperous members of the city's advertising, publishing, and arts communities live here in splendid villas.

Pretty white houses line stairways leading to the top of Süllberg Hill, and the waterfront is dotted with thatch-roofed cottages, nautically outfitted seafood restaurants, and spacious open-air cafés. Stop to admire the colorful gardens, or enjoy the view from this side of the port while sipping a drink in a terrace restaurant overlooking the sea. *Sägebiels Fährhaus* (107 Blankeneser Hauptstr.; phone: 861514) is a good choice for German and Chinese food; history buffs may appreciate the fact that Kaiser Wilhelm II once celebrated his birthday here. The *Strandhof* (27 Strandweg; phone: 865236) serves excellent seafood dishes; it's closed Mondays and Tuesdays. Or try the riverside *Schifferhaus* (see *Eating Out*). You also can continue along the riverside walkway which stretches for several miles away from the hubbub of Hamburg.

HELGOLAND This tiny North Sea island off the coast is a historic haven that makes for a pleasant day trip from Hamburg. At various points in its life, it has been under the control of pirates, the Hanseatic League, the Danes, and the British; the latter traded the island to Germany in 1890 in exchange for Zanzibar. A longtime German naval base, Helgoland was further fortified during World War II. Not surprisingly, the Allies made it a key target, and the island's fortifications were totally destroyed. Today Helgoland is simply a striking formation of striated, 150-foot sandstone cliffs; its 2 miles of paths are ideal for the hiker and nature buff. The lone village on the island has a few small houses, an aquarium, a bird sanctuary, a few hotels, and several good seafood restaurants. In addition, there are duty-free shops offering perfume and designer clothing. Helgoland has a short strip of beach for swimming; you also can take a short boat ride to yet another small island with a swimming beach. *Jasper Reisebüro* (72 Colonnaden; phone: 343751; fax: 227-7595) arranges outings from Hamburg that begin with a 6:30 AM train ride to the coast town of Büsum; from there, a two-hour excursion by boat takes you to the island. After five hours or so on Helgoland, you return to Hamburg, arriving at about 9 PM. It's an unusual destination that's worth exploring.

Sources and Resources

TOURIST INFORMATION

Hamburg has five tourist information centers: the central office (on Burchardstr.; phone: 300510); at the *Hauptbahnof* (Central Railway Station; Kirchenallee exit; phone: 300-51230); at the arrival terminal of the airport (phone: 300-51240); in the *Hanse-Viertel* shopping arcade (Poststrasse entrance; phone: 300-51220); and at the harbor (St. Pauli Landungsbrücken, between Piers 4 and 5; phone: 300-51200). All are open on weekdays during normal business hours (though hours are sometimes shorter in winter), and some are open weekends and late at night as well; call before you go. Expect to pay minimal fees for brochures and maps.

LOCAL COVERAGE The monthly *Hamburg Vorschau* (in German and English)—on sale at tourist offices and hotel desks—has listings of attractions and special events. The English-language *Hamburger,* available free at hotels, lists museums, sports facilities, restaurants, and nightclubs. The *Hamburg Tourist Board*'s *Hamburg Tips from A to Z* (in English) includes a handy map of the city and public transportation routes. It's available (at minimal cost) from any of the tourist offices.

TELEPHONE The city code for Hamburg is 40.

GETTING AROUND

A vast, complex city, Hamburg is not a place you can "do" on your own. Your best bet is to get acquainted via a guided city bus tour followed by one of the popular harbor cruises (see *Sightseeing Tours* for both). And remember, though the distance between the Alster and the harbor is said to be only 1,000 steps (about 10 city blocks), the journey can be nerve-wracking because you'll be maneuvering over, under, or around a number of heavily traveled highways. Better to opt for the efficient public transportation system when leaving the shores of the Inner Alster and going crosstown.

AIRPORT Hamburg's international airport, which is now a supermodern, state-of-the-art facility, thanks to a recent $200-million expansion, is at Fuhlsbüttel, 6 miles (10 km) north of downtown. Improvements include additional parking facilities, a wide variety of duty-free shops, a more efficient baggage handling system, and easier access to the autobahn. The public transportation system offers express bus service and *S-Bahn* (S-1) or *U-Bahn* (U-1) service between the airport and city center. A private bus line, *Airport-City Express,* provides inexpensive service every 20 minutes between the airport and the *Hauptbahnhof.* In addition, a new rail connection between downtown and the airport, currently under construction, is scheduled to begin operating by 1998.

BUS, SUBWAY, TRAIN The quickest and easiest way to get around Hamburg is by using the *U-Bahn* (local subway) or the *S-Bahn* (rapid-transit train). This dense, efficient system (known as *HVV;* phone: 322911) works on the honor system: Passengers buy tickets from automatic dispensers and validate them themselves. Route maps of the system and individual lines are prominently posted; free maps are available from information offices, ticket counters, and hotels. Consider buying one of the low-cost tickets for unlimited rides—either a one-day ticket, a three-day pass, or the one- or three-day *Hamburg Card,* which includes unlimited travel on all public transportation, along with free admission to 11 museums, discounts on city tours, Alster cruises, and harbor tours. The card (one-day, 10 DM/about $6; 3-day, 18 DM/about $11; family plans available) is sold at tourist offices and all major hotels. Buses are preferable for scenic trips, such as the one to Blankenese.

CAR RENTAL All major rental agencies are represented in Hamburg and at the airport, including *Avis* (15 Drehbahn; phone: 341651); *Hertz* (34-36

Kirchenallee: phone: 801201); and *InterRent/Europcar* (156 Holstenstr.; phone: 389707). There's also *Autohansa* (52 Herderstr.; phone: 220-1188).

FERRY SERVICE The white fleet of the *Alsterschiffahrt* (Alsteranlege Jungfernstieg; phone: 341141 or 341145) plies the Inner and Outer Alster from April through October, offering ferry service between 10 stations. The fare is 1.50 DM (about 90¢). Passengers can board the motor launch at any stop along the way (and the ferry also takes bicycles at no extra charge). A farther reaching (but more expensive) alternative is the *HADAG Line* (phone: 311-70700), which also runs ferries around the city and other destinations along the Elbe (including Blankenese) during the day. The line's main departure point is No. 2 Brücke (Pier), St. Pauli Landungsbrücken. The fare is 12.50 DM (about $7.50).

SIGHTSEEING TOURS The hour-and-three-quarter guided bus tour of Hamburg goes around the Alsters, through the city center, then along the Reeperbahn and to the harbor. A two-and-a-half-hour tour covers a more extensive route along the harbor area and around the Elbchaussee into the attractive suburbs overlooking the Elbe. Another version combines the bus tour with a harbor cruise. For more information, contact the tourist office (see *Tourist Information*). For after-dark entertainment, *Hamburg by Night* (phone: 227-1060) conducts tours Tuesdays through Saturdays in season; Fridays and Saturdays only the rest of the year. Excursions include visits to several bars and a show at a Reeperbahn nightclub. All tours are conducted in both German and English, and leave from the Kirchenallee side of the *Hauptbahnhof,* across from the *Europäischer Hof* hotel.

Several boating excursions are also available. The *Alsterschiffahrt* (see *Ferry Service*) offers one-hour cruises of the Inner and Outer Alster, and two-hour trips through the waterways and canals of the old city between the Alster and Elbe. Cruises begin and end at Jungfernstieg quay. Schedules are posted at each station. Boats run from 10:45 AM until 6 PM April through October. The *HADAG Line* (see *Ferry Service*) arranges all-day cruises through the canal connecting the North Sea to the Baltic, arriving at Kiel in Schleswig-Holstein, and then returning to Hamburg by train. The company also offers evening tours with music and dancing, and more extensive Elbe cruises. All trips depart at No. 2 Brücke (Pier), St. Pauli Landungsbrücken.

TAXI There are cab stands at the *Hauptbahnhof* and all major hotels. Among the companies offering round-the-clock service is *Hansa Taxi* (phone: 211211).

SPECIAL EVENTS

In addition to a variety of trade fairs, Hamburg mounts numerous events, among them a trio of popular folk festivals named for the seasons: the *Frühlingsdom* (Spring Fun Fair) festival in March, the *Sommerdom* (Summer Fun Fair) in July, and the *Winterdom* (Winter Fun Fair) in November. All three fetes are similar to Munich's *Oktoberfest,* with music, plenty of food, and oceans of beer. April marks the annual *Hansepferdmesse* (Hansa Horse

Exhibition), where horses and equestrian equipment are shown at the *Messengelände* (Exhibition Grounds) across from *Planten un Blomen.* During the first weekend in May, the *Hafenfest* (Harbor Festival) along the Elbe River features fireworks, boat parades, and food and drink vendors; the festivities culminate in a performance of *Nabucco,* Giuseppe Verdi's opera about King Nebuchadnezzar. Also in May, the *German Tennis Open* takes center court in *Rotherbaum Park,* and runners test their endurance in the *Hanse Marathon.* Hamburg's *Sommerfest* (Summer Festival), featuring a folkloric show, plays, dance performances, concerts, and exhibits, runs for a month starting in late July; *Alstervergnügen* (Fun on the Alster), another folk music festival, occurs in late August. *Hanseboot,* the city's international boat show, is held during the last week in November; and the year closes with a *Weihnachtsmarkt* (Christmas Fair).

MUSEUMS

There are more than 50 museums in and around Hamburg—documenting everything from the history of milk, salt, brewing, and cast iron to dolls, butterflies, and ships in bottles. All museums listed below are closed Mondays and charge admission, unless otherwise indicated.

ALTONA MUSEUM This regional museum, located about 3 miles (5 km) from the city center, chronicles the evolution of commerce around Hamburg, including rural Schleswig-Holstein. Exhibits focus on shipping, farming, and fishing. Included are ship models, farmhouse interiors, and period costumes from past centuries. 23 Museumstr., Altona (phone: 380-7514).

KUNSTHALLE (HALL OF FINE ARTS) Hamburg's major art gallery features paintings by medieval masters of Germany and the Netherlands, as well as works by such renowned 19th-century Expressionist painters as Caspar David Friedrich, and several 20th-century artists including Munch, Picasso, and members of the German *Brücke* (Bridge) group. Of special note are the landscapes of Hamburg's surroundings by French artists Pierre Bonnard and Edouard Vuillard. Glockengiesserwall (phone: 248-62612).

MUSEUM FÜR HAMBURGISCHE GESCHICHTE (HAMBURG HISTORY MUSEUM) On display are several scale models showing the city's development from medieval times through the 1600s, ship models, and navigational instruments. 24 Holstenwall (phone: 350-423-6080).

MUSEUM FÜR KUNST UND GEWERBE (ARTS AND CRAFTS MUSEUM) Decorative arts collections with a major focus on Art Nouveau are featured; most notable is the gem-like *Paris Room,* an acquisition from the *1900 World Exhibition.* Also here is one of the world's most comprehensive faïence and porcelain collections. An unusual aspect is a room devoted to stage designs by Austrian Expressionist Oscar Kokoschka. *Destille,* a turn-of-the-century café with original lighting fixtures and a hand-carved dark-wood bar, serves light lunches and snacks. 1 Steintorpl. (phone: 248-862732).

MUSEUM FÜR VÖLKERKUNDE (ETHNOLOGY MUSEUM) One of Europe's most extensive collections of arts and artifacts; exhibits explore the daily lives of societies from around the world, including those in Africa, Indonesia, India, and Central Asia. Most of the items were collected over the last century by Hamburg merchants, shipowners, captains, and colonial officers on their travels. 64 Rothenbaumchaussee (phone: 441-95524).

SHOPPING

Except for the *Rathaus* and the canals, much of downtown Hamburg resembles a vast shopping mall. In addition to half a dozen streets devoted primarily to shopping, there are the 12 *Passagen* arcades (see *Special Places*). Merchants claim that the *Hanse-Viertel*—the so-called "Queen" of the arcades—attracts between 20,000 and 40,000 shoppers a day. For those who can afford the often steep prices, Hamburg is a shoppers' paradise, but even window shoppers can enjoy an afternoon's browse. A typical Hamburg *Einkaufsrummel* (shopping spree) starts along the Jungfernstieg—site of *Alsterhaus* (Nos. 16 to 20), the city's leading department store—and continues on to the Alsterarkaden boulevard. Turn right to reach Grosse Bleichen and Poststrasse, leading to the *Passagen.* Be sure to stop at one of the cappuccino cafés or champagne bars here. Another fashionable area is Pöseldorf, site of the original *Jil Sander* shop (8 Milchstr.; phone: 503-02173), where Germany's leading designer got her start. For standard shopping hours, see GETTING READY TO GO. Here is a sampling of shops worth checking out.

Antik-Center Here is a cluster of antiques shops selling primarily 19th- and 20th-century English furnishings and china. The Victorian period is particularly well represented; there also are many Art Deco pieces. 9-21 Klosterwall (no phone).

BOA Designer Biggi Stockhinger's limited editions of easy-to-wear women's clothing. 26 Jungfernstieg (phone: 474339).

Captain's Cabin Jaunty nautical clothing and other seafaring gear, including striped shirts, captain's hats, brass lamps, and charts. On the harbor at St. Pauli Landungsbrücken (phone: 316373).

Carl Tiefenthal Men's cashmere clothing and accessories. 43 Neuer Wall (phone: 367606).

Chici Mic The latest in designer women's clothing from Paris and Milan. 29 Hamburger Berg (phone: 319-1174).

Escada One of the big names in German design for women's fashions and accessories. 8 Grosse Bleichen (phone: 344550).

Haus des Osten Chinese imports, including tea sets, silks sold by the meter, handmade tablecloths, silk blouses, and dresses, all at reasonable prices. 7 Jungfernstieg (phone: 343680).

Helene Freund Exclusive fashions for women. 283 Alsterdorfer Str. (phone: 511-9323).

Laural Boutique Elegant clothes and matching accessories for women. 41 Neuer Wall (phone: 374-3270).

Leysieffe A confectionery shop that features the North German dessert specialty *Rote Grütze,* a pudding composed of raspberries, black currants, and cherries. 36 Grosse Bleichen (phone: 346899).

Monika Flec Famous for women's high-fashion hats. 15 Colonnaden (phone: 345437).

La Rochell International designer fashions for women. 36 Grosse Bleichen (phone: 345764).

Thomas-i-Punkt A leading designer of clothing and accessories for men. 24 Gänsemarkt (phone: 342009).

SPORTS AND FITNESS

A port city rich in green spaces, Hamburg is an ideal venue for sports enthusiasts.

BICYCLING Try the pathways around the Alster lakes. Bikes can be rented from *City Bike Fahrrad-Verleih* (2-4 Glacischausee; phone: 319-93131).

BOATING The large canal system, the Elbe, and the Inner and Outer Alster are perfect for waterway buffs. Canoes, rowboats, and sailboats can be rented at most ferry stops along the Alster. *Segelschule Hans Pieper* (1 Atlantic-Steg; phone: 247578) has a large selection of boats for rent and offers sailing instruction.

FITNESS CENTERS Among the best are *Body Affair* (186 Eppendorfer Weg; phone: 420-3370); *Club Vitatop* (16 Caffamacherreine; phone: 601-1210); and *Keep Fit* (20 Stahlwiete; phone: 850-2011).

GOLF Of the 14 golf courses in the Hamburg vicinity, we recommend the *Hamburger Golf-Klub Falkenstein* (59 In de Bargen; phone: 812177), in the Blankenese area (visitors may play only on weekdays); and the *Golf-Klub Treudelberg* (45 Lemsahler Landstr.; phone: 608220), in Lemsahl, about 45 minutes north of the city center. To play at either of these 18-hole courses, you must be a member of a golf club at home; it's a good idea to bring a letter from the pro or club president.

HORSEBACK RIDING For information on the city's numerous riding schools and their facilities, call *Landesverband der Reit- und Fahrvereine* (26 Neuer Wall; phone: 366606).

JOGGING Of the vast expanse of parks and gardens, the most popular venue for runners is the network of waterside paths in the *Alstervorland* park.

SOCCER Hamburg's professional *HSV* team plays in the *Volksparkstadion,* on Sylvesterallee. For tickets and information, contact *Hamburger Sportverein* (123 Rothenbaumchaussee; phone: 415-5141).

SWIMMING Although efforts are currently underway to clean up the polluted water in Hamburg's canals and the Alster lakes, swimming is still not allowed there. Instead, try *Alster Schwimmhalle* (21 Ifflandstr.; phone: 223012), with indoor and outdoor pools, as well as a sauna and a fitness center.

TENNIS Call *Hamburger TennisVerband* (20 Derbyweg; phone: 651-2973) for a list of city courts.

THEATER

Hamburg has some 40 theaters, including one of the largest and most important in Germany, and its popular offspring.

CENTER STAGE

Deutsches Schauspielhaus Ferdinand Fellner and Hermann Helmer, the architects behind the *Viennese Theater,* also designed this stage, which opened in 1900. The architecture shows Renaissance and Baroque influences, and the façade is decorated with busts of the great German poet/playwrights Goethe, Schiller, Lessing, and Kleist, as well as Shakespeare. Above these busts are sculptures of the Muses. The interior is opulent and comfortable; its most striking feature is a painting of Apollo and Harmonia on the ceiling by Munich artist Carl Marr. The *Schauspielhaus*'s heyday was from 1955 to 1963, when its productions directed by Gustav Gründgens made the theater one of the best in the German-speaking world. After closing for extensive renovation in the late 1970s, it reopened in 1984 with nearly 1,400 seats. Today, it presents prominent, large-scale performances of both classical and contemporary dramas, comedies, and musicals. 39-41 Kirchenallee (phone: 248713).

Kampnagelfabrik The vast and barren former armaments factory was intended to be only a temporary playhouse while the *Deutsches Schauspielhaus* was being renovated, but Hamburgians grew to love their culture factory, and it became a theatrical fixture with a loyal following. Home to one of Germany's avant-garde *Freigruppen* (theater groups who do not depend on government subsidies), the *Kampnagelfabrik* also hosts traveling shows and ambitious international projects by such outstanding directors as Peter Brook and Robert Wilson. Whatever is happening in contemporary theater, it's likely to be happening here. 20-26 Jarrestr. (phone: 297-91066).

Another significant venue in Hamburg is the *Piccolo Theater* (13-15 Juliusstr.; phone: 435348); with 50 seats, it is the world's smallest theater. For English-language performances, try the *English Theater* (14 Lerchenfeld; phone: 225543) and Germany's oldest music hall, *Hansa Theater* (17 Steindamm; phone: 241414). The *UFA-Palast Kino* (45 Gänsemarkt; phone: 343996), with 18 screens, sometimes shows films in English.

MUSIC

Hamburg's leading concert hall, *Musikhalle* (Karl-Muck-Pl.; phone: 346920), is home to both the *Hamburg Philharmonic* and *Hamburg Symphony. Hamburgische Staatsoper* (36 Grosse Theaterstr.; phone: 351721, box office; 35680, information) presents highly acclaimed opera productions and the *Hamburgisches Ballet* (Hamburg Ballet). *Operettenhaus* (1 Spielbudenpl.; phone: 270-75270) features both operettas and hit musicals, such as those by Andrew Lloyd Webber.

As any *Beatles* fan will tell you, the group made their international debut in Hamburg; today, the city remains receptive to new sounds in pop, rock, and jazz. *Logo* (5 Grindelallee; phone: 410-5658) is a popular student hangout that plays rock 'n' roll, and the *Markthalle* (49 Klosterwall; phone: 339491) also features rock music played loud and hard. Hamburg has a proliferation of Dixieland bands playing old-time jazz in dozens of clubs. To enjoy jazz—from vintage two-beat to fusion—there's *Birdland* (122 Gärtnerstr.; phone: 405277), *Cotton Club* (27 Alter Steinweg; phone: 343878), *Jazz-Forum* (13 Weidenbaumsweg; phone: 724-3661), *Fabrik* (36 Barnerstr., Altona; phone: 391565), and *Pöseldorfer Bierdorf* (141 Mittelweg; phone: 444188).

NIGHTCLUBS AND NIGHTLIFE

When it comes to after-dark activities, Hamburg has something for everyone—from elegant to downright seedy: For those who like their nightlife bawdy, the crossroads of the Reeperbahn and Grosse Freiheit in the St. Pauli district is the home of explicit sex shows, bars (mostly of the clip-joint variety), and ladies of the evening (they're registered with the city). For more upscale entertainment, try *Colibri* (34 Grosse Freiheit; phone: 313233) and *Safari* (24-28 Grosse Freiheit; phone: 315400), which also feature Sunday brunches with live music, starting around noon. Or take a *Hamburg by Night* tour (see *Sightseeing Tours*). *Café Keese* (19 Reeperbahn; phone: 310805) has dancing to big bands nightly until 4 AM—and the custom here is that the women ask the men to dance. Popular discos include *Alsterufer 35* (35 Alsterufer; phone: 418155) and *Top of Town,* on the top floor of the *SAS Hamburg Plaza* hotel (2 Marseiller Str.; phone: 350-23210). There's casino gambling—roulette, baccarat, and blackjack—daily at the *Inter-Continental* hotel (10 Fontenay; phone: 447044) from 3 PM to 3 AM; jacket and tie required. *Casino Reeperbahn* (94-96 Reeperbahn; phone: 310438) features blackjack, slots, and various electronic games from 4 PM to 4 AM daily. You must be at least 18 years old to enter a casino; passports must be presented at the door.

Best in Town

CHECKING IN

As might be expected in a major business city, Hamburg's hotel scene ranges from ultra-luxurious to comfortable to budget-minded. Prices at the high end are staggering—a suite at the *Vier Jahreszeiten,* for example, can run as much as $1,000 per night. In summer, particularly on weekends, most of Hamburg's luxury hotels offer discount packages; there are also special year-round *Happy Hamburg Days,* packages of one to three days offered through tourist offices with substantially reduced rates for accommodations (including breakfast), plus free public transportation, a city tour, a harbor cruise, and other extras. For more information contact one of the tourist offices (see *Tourist Information*). In season, expect to pay $250 to $350 or more for a double room at a hotel classified as expensive; $150 to $250 at a place in the moderate range; and less than $150 at those hostelries listed as inexpensive. As a rule, breakfast is not included in the room rate at luxury hotels. Unless otherwise indicated, all hotels listed below have private baths, TV sets, and phones in rooms. Most of Hamburg's major hotels have complete facilities for the business traveler. Hotels listed as having "business services" usually offer such conveniences as an English-speaking concierge, meeting rooms, photocopiers, computers, translation services, and express check-out, among others. Call the hotel for additional information. All telephone numbers are in the 40 city code unless otherwise indicated.

For an unforgettable experience in Hamburg, we begin with our favorites, followed by our cost and quality choices, listed by price category.

ROOMS AT THE TOP

Atlantic Kempinski A short walk from the train station, the elegant Jungfernstieg shopping area, and the theater and art districts, this neoclassical structure is a sparkling gem on Hamburg's hotel scene. The 243 guestrooms feature marble baths and are beautifully decorated either with 19th-century antiques or more modern furniture; ask for a room with a view of the city skyline and the boating activity on the Outer Alster. The public areas are equally grand: The lobby features a broad, sweeping staircase; the excellent *Atlantic* restaurant, serving both regional and French fare, has turn-of-the-century furnishings and chandeliers; and live piano music plays in the lounge in the afternoon and evening. In warm weather, the inner courtyard and garden is transformed into a café, and there is also the rustic *Atlantic-Mühle* tavern. Other amenities include a heated indoor pool, a sauna, a fitness room, a beauty salon, and business services. 72-79 An der Alster (phone: 28880; 800-426-3135; fax: 247129).

Vier Jahreszeiten An appealing combination of urban efficiency and polite refinement, this jewel built in the late 19th century has a lovely setting on the Inner Alster, but it is also conveniently close to shopping, theater, and the railway station. Because of its excellent service and facilities, it has been called "the best Swiss hotel outside Switzerland" by knowledgeable hoteliers. The 158 rooms and suites are individually decorated with antiques and feature plenty of luxury amenities, such as marble baths and mini-bars; ask for a lakefront room with a balcony. It has three restaurants: the elegant *Hearlin* and the rustic *Jahreszeiten Grill* for meals, and the *Condi Café* for snacks, coffee, and pastries. All around the property are flowered promenades, sleek yachts, and handsome villas. Business services are available. 9-14 Neuer Jungfernstieg (phone: 34940; fax: 349-4602).

EXPENSIVE

Europäischer Hof Facing the railroad station, this pleasant, traditional establishment boasts 320 well-appointed rooms. There is a good restaurant, and in the breakfast room, you can serve yourself from a marble fountain that spouts six different kinds of beverages—including champagne on occasion. There's also a pool and a sauna, and business services are available. 45 Kirchenallee (phone: 248248; 800-223-5652; fax: 2482-4799).

Garden Hotels Pöseldorf On a quiet side street in the elegant Pöseldorf district on the western side of the Alster, three turn-of-the century townhouses have been transformed into an ultramodern hostelry. The 57 rooms are equipped with every conceivable luxury, including marble baths, cable TV, VCRs, and hair dryers. It's a favorite of advertising executives, journalists, and radio, TV, and film people. Breakfast is served in the greenhouse-like winter garden. Business services are available. 60 Magdalenenstr. (phone: 414040; fax: 414-0420).

Hamburg Renaissance With 211 handsomely furnished rooms, Ramada's luxury property is housed in a magnificently restored 19th-century red brick building—part of the elegant *Passagen* shopping arcade complex—in the heart of historic Hamburg. An Art Nouveau interior features dark woodwork, polished brass, and ornate lighting fixtures. Business services and a fine restaurant offering French and German fare complete the picture. 36 Grosse Bleichen (phone: 349-18119; 800-2-RAMADA; fax: 349-18431).

Inter-Continental In a lovely garden setting near the Outer Alster, this 252-room member of the chain is somewhat inconvenient for downtown visits, but its amenities—indoor-outdoor pool, a sauna, a solarium, a rooftop restaurant with fabulous views, and a gambling casino—make it worth the trip. Bicycles are provided free of charge. There are special weekend rates year-round and special reduced-rate packages in summer. Business services are available. 10 Fontenay (phone: 414150; 800-327-0200; fax: 414-15186).

Prem Once a villa, this jewel of a small hotel, known as the "White House on the Alster," had been owned and managed by the Prem family since 1912. Happily, the dignified appearance of the salon and public rooms remain, as do the Louis XV–style furnishings of most of the 56 rooms. The front rooms overlook the Alster; those at the rear face a quiet garden. Like the hotel, its *La Mer* restaurant (see *Eating Out*) boasts the elegant furnishings of a palatial salon. The service is friendly. 9 An der Alster (phone: 241726; fax: 280-3851).

SAS Hamburg Plaza Beside the gardens of *Planten un Blomen* and only a short subway or bus ride from downtown is this modern-looking, 563-room airline-owned hotel. Amenities include a pool and a sauna; there's also a non-smoking floor and a Royal Club floor with complete business facilities. Upper-floor rooms have fine views of the gardens, the downtown skyline, the Alster, and the harbor. The 26th-floor *Top of Town* disco attracts the young and young at heart. There's also a restaurant; business services are available. 2 Marseiller Str. (phone: 35020; 800-221-2350; fax: 350-23333).

Steigenberger Hamburg Recently built, this red brick low-rise structure harmonizes well with the postwar buildings that also line the canals between the harbor and the Inner Alster. Conveniently located near the *Rathausmarkt* and the *Passagen* shopping arcades, this hotel features 234 rooms with cable TV, mini-bars, safes, and lovely views of the city. Other amenities include the *Calla* eatery, which serves generous Sunday brunches as well as breakfast, lunch, and dinner; a bistro café with outdoor seating in fine weather; and boat excursions from the hotel's own dock. Business services. 4 Heiligengeistbrücke (phone: 368060; 800-223-5652; fax: 368-06777).

MODERATE

Bellevue This converted townhouse with an adjoining modern addition is a family-run hotel that has long been popular with celebrities. Some of its 88 rooms have views of the Outer Alster; the newer wing offers the peace and quiet of a garden setting. *Pilsner Urquellstube,* the hotel restaurant, serves traditional German fare and beer in a casual setting. Business services are available. 14 An der Alster (phone: 248011; fax: 280-3380).

Elysée A more reasonably priced alternative to the city's grand hotels, it has 305 spacious rooms with king-size beds, marble bathrooms, and a lobby filled with tropical flowers. There's live jazz nightly at its *Bourbon Street Bar.* Other features include an Italian restaurant, a pool, a sauna, a fitness center, and business services. 10 Rothenbaumchaussee (phone: 414120; fax: 414-12733).

Hafen Hamburg Originally a seamen's home, this 252-room hostelry has a magnificent harbor view and a maritime motif. Rooms, although simply furnished, offer standard comfort. There is a restaurant, and business services are available. 9 Seewartenstr. (phone: 311130; fax: 319-2736).

Maritim Hotel Reichshof Across from the main railway station, it has an attractive, old-fashioned lobby, 288 pleasantly furnished rooms, and a fine restaurant. Business services are offered. 34-36 Kirchenallee (phone: 248330; 800-843-3311; fax: 248-33588).

Mellingburger Schleuse An idyllic forest setting enhances this rustic-looking, 37-room hotel. There's an outdoor swimming pool and a small restaurant. Business services are available. 1 Mellingburgredder (phone: 602-4001; fax: 602-7912).

INEXPENSIVE

Alster-Hof On a quiet side street near the *Vier Jahreszeiten,* this reasonably priced, 113-room hotel is efficiently run and nicely furnished. There is no restaurant. 12 Esplanade (phone: 350070; fax: 350-07514).

Baseler Hof Next door to the *Alster-Hof,* this family-run hotel with a restaurant and bar is another excellent choice for budget-conscious travelers. The 148 rooms are pleasant, but spartan. Business services are available. 11 Esplanade (phone: 359060; fax: 359-06918).

City House A small hotel (15 rooms) very close to the train station. There is no restaurant, but there are several in the area. 25 Pulverteich (phone: 280-3850; fax: 280-1838).

Ibis Hamburg Alster This member of the Ibis chain—just a few steps from the Outer Alster—offers exceptional value, including 165 bright, spacious rooms, business services, and a restaurant that offers reasonably priced buffet meals. 4-12 Holzdamm (phone: 248290; 800-873-0300; fax: 248-29999).

Pension Helga Schmidt Also near the Outer Alster, this modest, 15-room family-run townhouse has a no-frills lobby and simple, but pleasantly furnished rooms. There's no restaurant. 14 Holzdamm (phone: 280-2119; fax: 243705).

EATING OUT

One of the best things about Hamburg is its restaurants. A wide variety of food is available, from haute cuisine to local specialties such as *Rollmops* (pickled herring rolled in sour cream) and *Labskaus* (corned beef served with fried eggs, potatoes, beets, and pickles); the settings vary from the elegant crystal-and-china ambience of the top dining places to the earthier atmosphere of the *Imbiss* (waterfront snack bars). Because it's a port city, there are many fine ethnic restaurants as well. And though legend credits the city with the invention of the hamburger, Hamburg is best known for its fish—most espcially *Finkenwerder Scholle* (plaice), *Aalsuppe* (eel soup), and oysters, raw or baked with cheshire cheese. Expect to pay $200 or more for a three-course meal at restaurants in the very expensive category; $130 to $200 at expensive places; $85 to $130 at moderate restaurants; and less than $85 at inexpensive spots. Prices do not include drinks, wine, or beer, but they do include taxes and service charges. You should leave a small additional tip for good service. All telephone numbers are in the 40 city code unless otherwise indicated.

For an unforgettable dining experience, we begin with our favorite, followed by our culinary choices, listed by price category.

DELIGHTFUL DINING

Fischereihafen Ideally situated, this pricey dining place on the harbor is the best place to sample the freshest of catches—often reeled in only a few nautical miles away. There is great satisfaction to being this close to the source: At your window table you can enjoy herring within sight of the trawlers that netted it. The regional menu is especially appealing. Try the *Pfannfisch vom Steinbutt* (sautéed turbot) and *Grüner Hering gebraten auf Zwiebel-Tomaten-Butter* (grilled green herring served in an onion tomato butter). Open daily. Reservations necessary. Major credit cards accepted. 143 Grosse Elbstr. (phone: 381816).

VERY EXPENSIVE

Le Canard Built in the style of an ocean liner by a leading local architect, this is one of the city's most beautiful (and best) dining rooms; Michelin has given it one star. Picture windows afford magnificent Elbe River views, and in summer there's dining on an outdoor terrace. The menu includes seafood dishes, along with duck and other game (in season) and tempting desserts. Closed Sundays and holidays. Reservations necessary. Major credit cards accepted. 139 Elbchaussee, Altona (phone: 880-5057).

Cölln's Austernstuben Operating at the same city center site since 1883, this oyster cellar offers a limited menu—caviar, oysters, lobsters, and salmon—in exquisitely decorated salons. Its food has earned it one Michelin star. Closed weekends. Reservations necessary. Major credit cards accepted. 1-5 Brodschrangen (phone: 326059).

Landhaus Dill This converted country inn in the suburb of Nienstedten serves such well-prepared continental dishes as lobster salad and rack of lamb Provençal. Closed Mondays. Reservations necessary. Major credit cards accepted. 404 Elbchaussee, Nienstedten (phone: 828443).

Landhaus Scherrer A former brewery inn along the banks of the Elbe, this two-Michelin-star restaurant features caviar, truffle, and foie gras specialties, along with French nouvelle cuisine variations on traditional Hamburg themes. Typical specialties include stuffed oxtail, deer steaks *au jus* with sautéed cherries, and vegetable mousse. Closed Sundays. Reservations necessary. Major credit cards accepted. 130 Elbchaussee, Altona (phone: 880-1325).

La Mer In addition to superb service, elegant decor, and garden views, this dining room in the *Prem* hotel serves a memorable pot-au-feu and a wide range of seafood, including a marvelous turbot; Michelin has awarded it one star. Open daily; closed weekend lunch. Reservations necessary. Major credit cards accepted. 9 An der Alster (phone: 245454).

Schümanns Austernkeller The city's other historic oyster cellar (since 1884), this magnificent Belle Epoque–style place is divided into a series of intimate (and elaborately furnished) private salons. In addition to oysters, lobster, and salmon, there are lamb dishes. Impeccable service is another plus. Closed Sundays. Reservations advised. Major credit cards accepted. 34 Jungfernstieg (phone: 345328).

EXPENSIVE

Peter Lembcke This longtime institution occupies two floors of a townhouse and features down-to-earth (and sea) fare. Try the eel soup, herring, fish of the day, crayfish soups, *Labskaus,* and steaks. Closed Sundays and holidays. Reservations advised. Major credit cards accepted. 49 Holzdamm (phone: 243290).

Zum Alten Rathaus Great Gothic vaulted ceilings set the mood of this old-time restaurant, where the chef presents German nouvelle cuisine, including lamb and cabbage gratinée and salmon roulade in cabbage leaves. Fine wines and local beer complement the food nicely. Closed Sundays, holidays, and Saturday lunch. Reservations advised. Major credit cards accepted. 10 Börsenbrücke (phone: 367570).

MODERATE

Deichgraf Dating from 1763, this restaurant is situated in a gabled building on a short, narrow street that has the atmosphere of pre-war Hamburg. Its old-fashioned appearance is enhanced by antiques, heavy draperies, gilt-framed mirrors, an elaborate brass chandelier, and high, narrow windows. The real attention-grabber, however, are two stunning, three-foot-long models of 18th-century sailing schooners—one in the dining room and one over the bar. The menu offers superlative German and continental dishes such as *Hamburger Pannfish* (whitefish and potatoes cooked in wine sauce and served in an omelette). Closed Sundays. Reservations advised. Major credit cards accepted. 23 Deichstr. (phone: 364208).

Galerie Stuben Also known as *Zur Alten Kramerstube am Michel,* this atmospheric (and popular) spot in the historic *Krämeramtswohnungen* quarter (see *Special Places*) offers fine dining on two levels, looking out on the 17th-century cobbled courtyard in one direction and the green spire of *St. Michaelis* in the other. The menu features such continental dishes as chicken Cordon Bleu, lamb aspic with spinach, and fried flounder served with potato salad and bacon. Open daily noon to midnight. Reservations advised. Major credit cards accepted. 10 Krayenkamp (phone: 365800).

Ratsweinkeller One of Germany's most authentic *Rathaus* restaurants—great stone arches, ship models hanging from the ceiling, and dark wooden tables—it serves such dishes as *Labskaus,* eel soup, and lobster, with wine and beer. Prix fixe luncheons are an exceptional value. Closed Sundays and holidays. Reservations unnecessary. Major credit cards accepted. 2 Grosse Johannisstr. (phone: 364153).

Schifferhaus Nautically decorated, this old house on the riverside walkway in the charming village of Blankenese is an ideal dining stop. Sample the fish soup and eel dishes. Closed Mondays. Reservations unnecessary. Major credit cards accepted. 20 Strandweg, Blankenese (phone: 860385).

Uberseebrücke The main attraction of this plainly furnished restaurant in a box-like structure at St. Pauli is the close-up view through huge picture windows of boats in the harbor. Fresh seafood and traditional dishes are offered. Open daily. Reservations unnecessary. MasterCard and Visa accepted. Vorsetzen-Hafenrandpromenade (phone: 313333).

INEXPENSIVE

Alsterpavillon While Hamburg's most popular and most beautifully situated café overlooking the Inner Alster is known mainly as a place to enjoy afternoon coffee and cake and elaborate ice cream concoctions, there's also a limited luncheon menu offering salads, steaks, and veal cutlets. As you eat, enjoy the strains of Mozart and Strauss played by a string ensemble. Open daily. Reservations unnecessary. Major credit cards accepted. 54 Jungfernstieg (phone: 345052).

Alt Hamburger Aalspeicher A longtime favorite, this historic, canal-side pub is devoted almost exclusively to eel served in every conceivable form. The palate-pleasing, rich eel soup is regarded as the best in the city. Open daily noon to midnight. Reservations unnecessary. No credit cards accepted. 43 Deichstr. (phone: 362990).

Fischerhaus A big, popular eating place near the Elbe fish market, it specializes in absolutely perfect fish served in no-frills fashion in no-frills surroundings. Try the steamed turbot with horseradish sauce and boiled potatoes. Open daily. Reservations unnecessary. Major credit cards accepted. 14 St. Pauli Fischmarkt (phone: 314053).

Mövenpick At the lower level of the *Hanse-Viertel* shopping arcade, this complex includes an elegant sit-down place, a wine bistro, and several casual dining areas serving a variety of quick-and-easy meals at very reasonable prices.

Part of the famous Swiss chain of restaurants, it's popular with the downtown business crowd for lunch, but dinner is the best value here. Designing your own pizza is a popular choice: Pick one of three sizes of crusts, add toppings from a buffet boasting more than 50 ingredients—from anchovies to zucchini—and turn it over to the baker. There's also an all-you-can-eat salad bar. Open daily for breakfast, lunch, and dinner. Reservations unnecessary. Major credit cards accepted. 33 Poststr. (phone: 34100).

Nikolaikeller What *Alt Hamburger Aalspeicher* (see above) does for eel, this place does for herring—the menu offers it prepared in 20 different ways. Dishes are served in a traditional cellar setting. Closed Sundays. Reservations unnecessary. Major credit cards accepted. 36 Cremon (phone: 366113).

Old Commercial Room Located directly across from *St. Michaelis,* this tourist haunt's nautical decor is a bit overdone, but it serves authentic *Labskaus* with tall, cool glasses of carefully drawn Pils beer. Open daily. Reservations unnecessary. Major credit cards accepted. 10 Englische Planke (phone: 366319).

Heidelberg

It's not surprising to find a 375-year-old etching of Heidelberg in the window of a bookstore along this fabled city's main street. The surprise is how much the Heidelberg of today—one of Germany's most famous tourist centers—resembles its 17th-century ancestor.

In 1620, Heidelberg was a walled city along the southern shore of the Neckar River, with a sprawling castle on the slope of a small mountain, expansive gardens upon a plateau, a delicate-looking wooden bridge spanning the river, and orchards and woods in the distance. And even though the castle and sections of the walls today are in ruins, it doesn't take much imagination to see the old in the new. Alte Brücke (Old Bridge), also known as Karl-Theodor-Brücke, is much like its earlier counterpart, and the downtown area retains the beauty and architectural majesty of its former days. Perhaps the most noticeable differences are to be found in the architecture: Today's buildings are basically Baroque; 17th-century structures were Renaissance and Gothic in style. But the splendid backdrop hasn't changed. The 1,000-foot-high Königstuhl (King's Throne) and the Heiligenberg ("Mountain of the Saints"—one of the city's namesakes), topped by the remains of a 9th-century basilica, still dominate the scene; vineyards blanket slopes above the pristine river; and almond trees blossom in the spring.

More than any other place in Germany, Heidelberg embodies the country's fairy-tale charm and its dynamic cultural heritage. The Romantic movement flourished here, at Germany's oldest seat of learning, *Universität Heidelberg* (Heidelberg University), founded in 1386. Johann Wolfgang von Goethe wrote of Heidelberg; Robert Schumann and Carl Maria von Weber found inspiration here; J. M. W. Turner captured on canvas its ravishing sunsets; and Johannes Brahms composed his "Lullaby" while sitting by the Neckar River. The university also was the setting for some of the major religious reforms that swept through Germany and Europe in the 16th century. It was here, in a debate against Dominican friars in 1518, that Martin Luther advocated a split with Catholicism and defended his many attacks on the church, launching the Reformation; it was here that the Calvinist Profession of Faith was drafted 50 years later, deepening the schisms within Protestantism. Heidelberg quickly became known as a Calvinist citadel, earning the nickname "The German Geneva."

About three centuries later, the city won the favor of an especially discriminating 19th-century traveler, Mark Twain. In his popular *A Tramp Abroad,* Twain wrote fondly of his summer in Heidelberg (where he once served as a second in a pistol duel). Soon after, the city became a most sought-after vacation destination.

Germans have long regarded Heidelberg with an affection usually reserved for places along the Mediterranean. Indeed, the city has an Italianate character—its temperate climate, the translucent cast of its light, and the warm brick tones of its buildings evoke images of Florence.

The first evidence of human habitation in the Heidelberg area goes back 600,000 years. The *Kurpfälzisches Museum* (Palatinate Museum) displays a replica of the jawbone of *Homo erectus heidelbergensis* (Heidelberg Man), discovered in the vicinity in 1907 and since regarded as the earliest evidence of human life in Europe. Remains of a Celtic citadel on the Heiligenberg indicate habitation prior to the 1st century BC, and history records that in 40 BC the Romans built a settlement here. The name Heidelberg was first used in the 12th century, when the city was ruled by officials of the Holy Roman Empire called the *Kurfürsten* (Palatinate counts, or prince electors). By the 14th century, the *Kurfürsten* had become independent enough to establish their own domain, the Rhineland Palatinate, and they designated Heidelberg its capital.

Heidelberg's early period of glory lasted until 1622, when the Thirty Years War (1618–48) reached its gates. During the following years, armies from as far away as Sweden tried to capture this fortified settlement and finally, in the early 1690s, the French forces of Louis XIV blew up Heidelberg's castle and razed the city.

The reputation of modern-day Heidelberg can be traced to a sentimental play written in 1903 by Wilhelm Meyer-Förster, *Alt-Heidelberg* (Old Heidelberg). Based on Meyer-Förster's novel *Karl Heinrich,* it tells the story of a prince who attends the university and falls in love with a barmaid; almost instantly, the play was all the rage in Europe. In 1924, composer Sigmund Romberg set the story to music in his popular operetta, *The Student Prince.* Since its opening more than seven decades ago, the operetta has transformed Heidelberg into a kind of Brigadoon: Travelers invariably envision the city in terms of *The Student Prince*'s fanciful set designs, regarding the real thing as an extension of the make-believe rather than the other way around.

The look of today's Altstadt (Old City) does little to mar the storybook illusion. It is a place of spacious cobblestone squares, 17th-century churches, fountains and statuary, and picturesque homes with Madonnas, saints, and knights set into corner niches. Even downtown businesses—banks, bakeries, boutiques, butchers, cinemas, restaurants, taverns, and several department stores—are housed behind elegant 18th- and 19th-century façades. The area is closed to vehicular traffic, further enhancing the city's Old World atmosphere. And toward the river, gable-roofed row houses sit alongside barges and cruise liners. The Hauptstrasse, the main shopping district, extends beyond the Marktplatz to *Karlstor* (Karl's Gate), the remains of the former city gate, now at the end of the main street.

In addition to preserving its past, today's Heidelberg is in touch with its future. Not far from the city center are wide, traffic-filled boulevards with

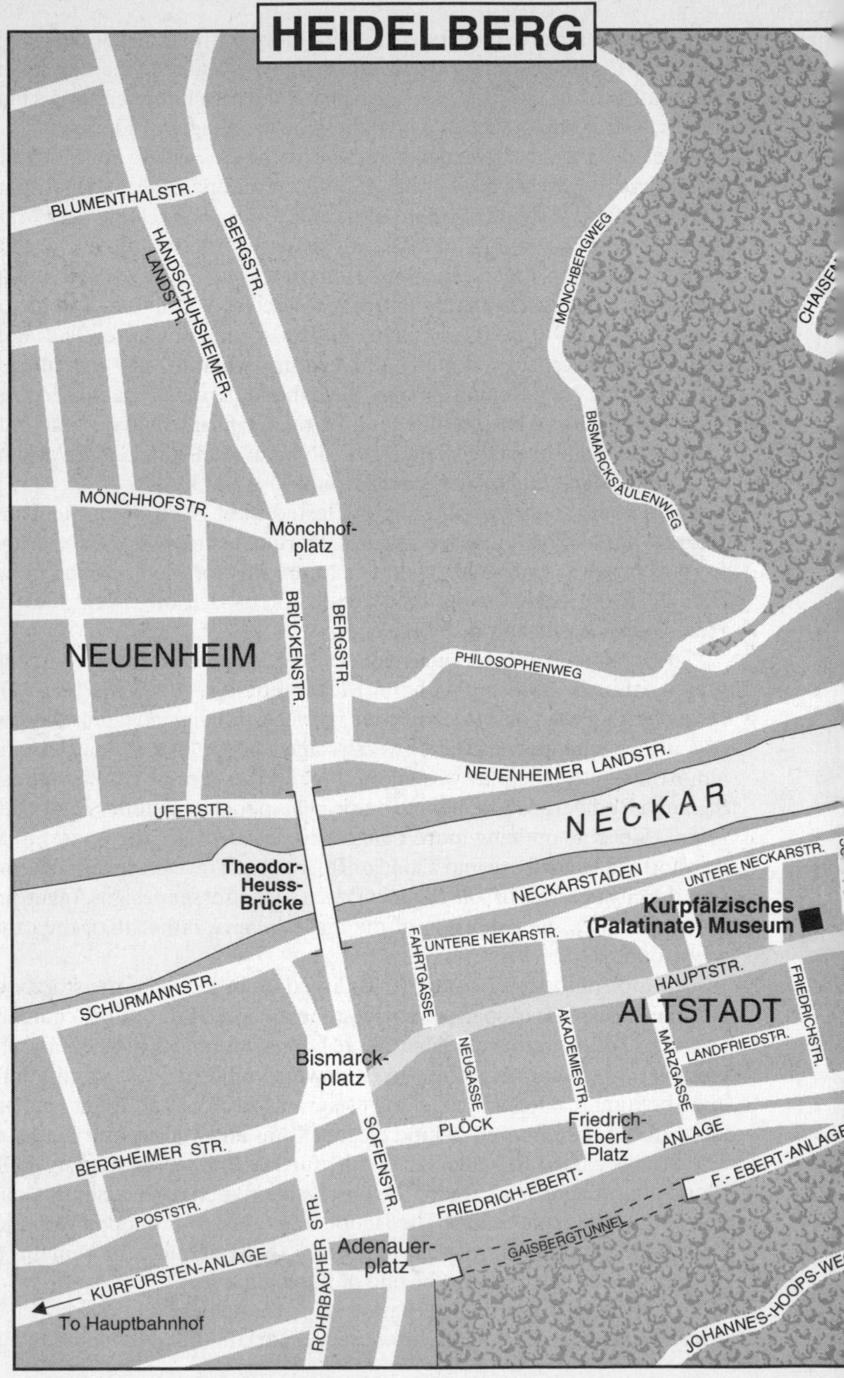
HEIDELBERG
BLUMENTHALSTR.
HANDSCHUHSHEIMER-LANDSTR.
BERGSTR.
MÖNCHBERGWEG
BISMARCKSÄULENWEG
MÖNCHHOFSTR.
Mönchhof-platz
BRÜCKENSTR.
BERGSTR.
NEUENHEIM
PHILOSOPHENWEG
NEUENHEIMER LANDSTR.
UFERSTR.
NECKAR
Theodor-Heuss-Brücke
NECKARSTADEN
UNTERE NECKARSTR.
Kurpfälzisches (Palatinate) Museum
UNTERE NEKARSTR.
FAHRTGASSE
SCHURMANNSTR.
HAUPTSTR.
FRIEDRICHSTR.
ALTSTADT
AKADEMIESTR.
MÄRZGASSE
LANDFRIEDSTR.
NEUGASSE
Bismarck-platz
SOFIENSTR.
PLÖCK
Friedrich-Ebert-Platz
ANLAGE
BERGHEIMER STR.
F.- EBERT-ANLAGE
FRIEDRICH-EBERT-
POSTSTR.
GAISBERGTUNNEL
ROHRBACHER STR.
Adenauer-platz
KURFÜRSTEN-ANLAGE
To Hauptbahnhof
JOHANNES-HOOPS-WEG

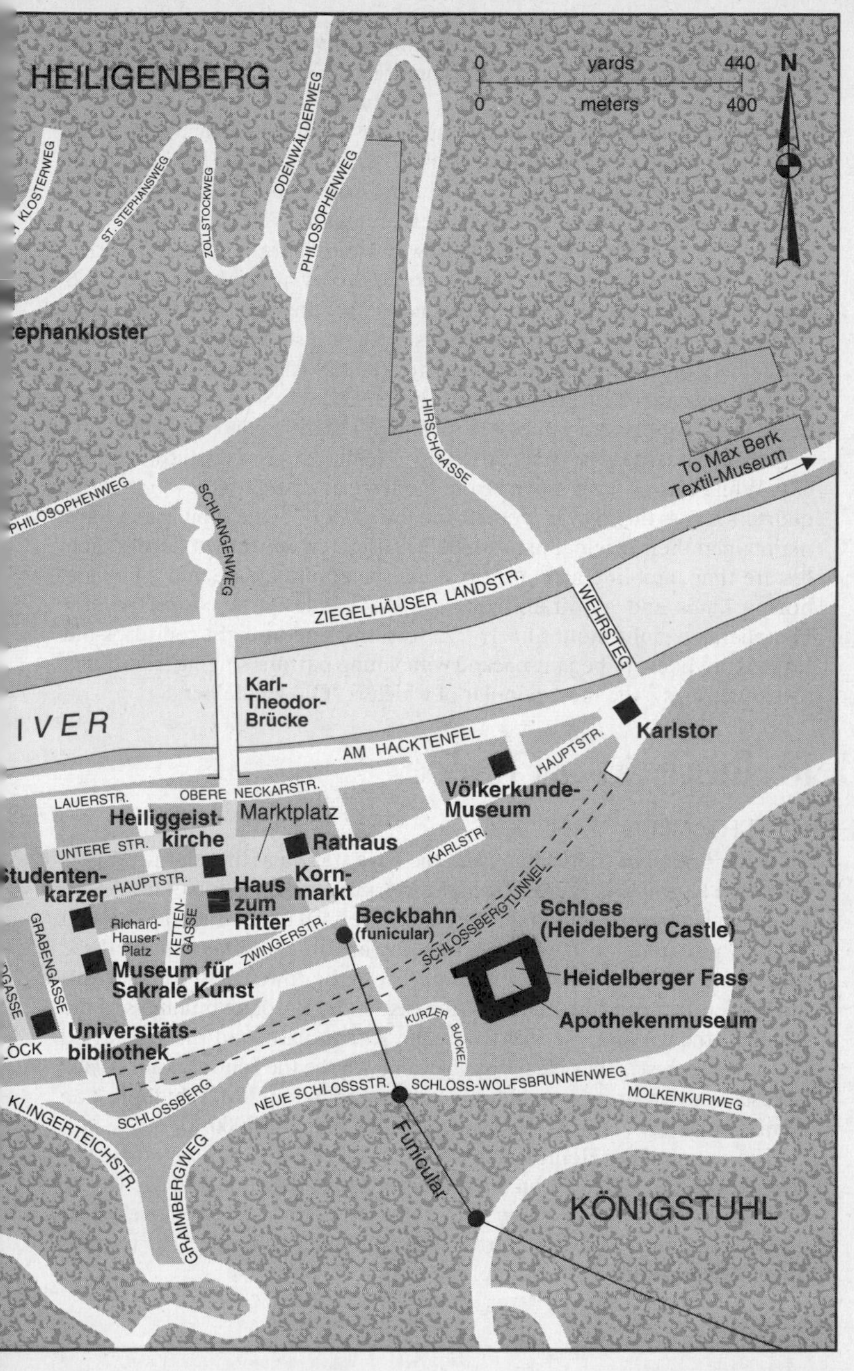
HEILIGENBERG
0 yards 440
0 meters 400
N
KLOSTERWEG
ST. STEPHANSWEG
ZOLLSTOCKWEG
ODENWÄLDERWEG
PHILOSOPHENWEG
Stephankloster
HIRSCHGASSE
To Max Berk Textil-Museum
PHILOSOPHENWEG
SCHLANGENWEG
ZIEGELHÄUSER LANDSTR.
WEHRSTEG
Karl-Theodor-Brücke
IVER
Karlstor
AM HACKTENFEL
HAUPTSTR.
LAUERSTR.
OBERE NECKARSTR.
Völkerkunde-Museum
Heiliggeist-kirche
Marktplatz
UNTERE STR.
Rathaus
KARLSTR.
Studenten-karzer
HAUPTSTR.
Haus zum Ritter
Korn-markt
GRABENGASSE
Richard-Hauser-Platz
KETTEN-GASSE
Beckbahn (funicular)
SCHLOSSBERGTUNNEL
Schloss (Heidelberg Castle)
ZWINGERSTR.
Museum für Sakrale Kunst
Heidelberger Fass
Apothekenmuseum
KURZER BUCKEL
Universitäts-bibliothek
PLÖCK
SCHLOSSBERG
NEUE SCHLOSSSTR.
SCHLOSS-WOLFSBRUNNENWEG
MOLKENKURWEG
KLINGERTEICHSTR.
GRAIMBERGWEG
Funicular
KÖNIGSTUHL

high-rise apartment complexes, suburban sectors, and industrial zones. In recent years Greater Heidelberg has emerged as a center of high technology. EURESCOM (the European Institute for Research Studies in Telecommunications) is located on a hillside estate overlooking the Altstadt, IBM has a research center on the banks of the Neckar, and the European Laboratory of Molecular Biology is nearby. Numerous international high-tech firms have offices in the Heidelberg Technology Park.

There are conflicting stories as to why Heidelberg was spared during World War II bombings: According to one theory, it was because the US Army planned to set up headquarters here after the war; another possible reason was that it was neither an industrial nor a strategic target. In fact, Heidelberg did become headquarters for the US Army in Europe, and as a result, accents of Brooklyn, the Midwest, and the South are still heard here. Most waiters and waitresses speak both German and English.

Thanks in large part to its university, Heidelberg is a youthful, vibrant city. While classes have moved from the historic district to new university quarters across the river in Neuenheim (only a few Altstadt buildings have maintained their original use), students still flock downtown during their leisure time, ambling arm-in-arm along the Hauptstrasse and its neighboring lanes and adjoining squares. On Sunday afternoons, several Hauptstrasse clubs mount lively jazz sessions, and at night centuries-old taverns are likely to be jam-packed with young patrons singing traditional drinking songs—the most popular of which is "Old Heidelberg."

Heidelberg At-a-Glance

SEEING THE CITY

Take the *Bergbahn* (funicular) from the base station at the southwest corner of the Kornmarkt (across from the Marktplatz) to the top of the 1,860-foot-high Königstuhl mountain; cars leave every 10 minutes spring through fall, every 20 minutes in winter. At the top are an amusement park, three restaurants, and an observation tower. From the tower platform, accessible by elevator, you can see it all—the castle, the Baroque buildings of the Altstadt, the winding Neckar River, the Rhine plain, and the Odenwald (Deserted Forest). On a clear day you can even see the Schwarzwald (Black Forest). The tower is closed mid-October through mid-March; there's an admission charge. For funicular information, call 573-2000.

The slopes of the Heiligenberg afford vistas of 19th-century red-roofed houses across the Neckar; on the southern side of the Heiligenberg are the ruins of the 11th-century *Stephanskloster* (St. Stephen's Monastery); its observation tower affords superb views of the river and town. The tower is open daily; no admission charge.

The *Scheffel Terrasse* (named for Heidelberg poet Viktor von Scheffel) at *Das Schloss* (Heidelberg Castle; see *Special Places*) offers a view of the Neckar and the Altstadt.

SPECIAL PLACES

The Altstadt, a pedestrian zone with the Marktplatz at its center, is so compact that you can stroll from one end to the other in less than an hour. A popular tourist destination, it can get crowded during the day at any time of the year, so try to get an early start. The map with English text issued by the city tourist office (see *Tourist Information*) includes a good self-guided walking tour.

HAUPTSTRASSE The Altstadt's main street and number one shopping area is the heart of town, a route that parallels the river and intersects with Marktplatz, the main square. It was a major thoroughfare from the 14th century until 1978, when it was converted into a pedestrians-only zone. Today elegant private residences in medieval and rococo styles sit alongside cafés, restaurants serving home-cooked meals, taverns that are favorites of university students, and all manner of shops. The street also is home to the city's best nightlife.

KURPFÄLZISCHES (PALATINATE) MUSEUM Also referred to as the *Stadtmuseum* (City Museum), this is worth a visit if only to see the building that contains it: the elegant early 18th-century *Palais Morass* (Morass Palace), the city's best-preserved example of Baroque architecture, with its grand staircase leading to top-floor rooms furnished in period pieces. The museum's two prize exhibits are a replica of the jaw of *Homo erectus heidelbergenesis* (prehistoric Heidelberg Man) and 16th-century woodcarver Tilman Riemenschneider's dazzling, late-Gothic *Windesheim Altar,* which depicts Christ and the Twelve Apostles. Also here are paintings spanning three centuries, from Dutch and Italian Masters to works of J. M. W. Turner. There's also a fine restaurant (see *Eating Out*). Closed Mondays. Admission charge. 97 Hauptstr. (phone: 583402).

STUDENTENKARZER (STUDENTS' PRISON) From 1712 until 1914, this Baroque university building was used to confine and discipline recalcitrant students. The guilty scholars were locked in narrow cells, living on nothing but bread and water for the first two or three days of their "sentences," which usually lasted from a few days to two to four weeks. Rather than being regarded as harmful to a student's reputation, a stint here was viewed as a mark of distinction, on a par with flesh wounds received during duels held in the traditional fencing clubs. Cell walls are covered with portraits in traditional silhouette style (only the students' caps are in color); inscriptions on the walls list the names and dates of incarceration of former occupants. Closed Sundays and Mondays. Admission charge. 2 Augustinergasse (phone: 542334).

UNIVERSITÄTSBIBLIOTHEK (UNIVERSITY LIBRARY) Included among the collection of one-and-a-half million books are illuminated manuscripts and some of the earliest printed works ever published, from the royal libraries of the electors who ruled Heidelberg between the 12th and 15th centuries. Of special note is a copy of the 14th-century *Manesse Codex,* an illustrated tome of medieval lyric poetry that was once set to music and sung by *Minnesänger* (medieval troubadours) in courts throughout Germany. Closed Sundays November through *Easter.* 107-109 Plöck (phone: 542380).

HAUS ZUM RITTER (KNIGHT'S HOUSE) Built in 1592 by a French cloth merchant, this was the only patrician dwelling to survive the city's destruction in 1693. Its name derives from the statue of St. George (of dragon-killing fame) that stands above the ornate Renaissance façade. For a decade (1695–1705) the building served as Heidelberg's town hall; in 1705 it was converted into an inn. Today it's the *Zum Ritter St. Georg* hotel (see *Checking In*). 178 Hauptstr. (phone: 20203 or 24272).

MARKTPLATZ With the *Rathaus* (Town Hall) on one side, the *Heiliggeistkirche* (Church of the Holy Ghost) on the other, and the *Herkulesbrunnen* (Hercules Fountain) at its center (where witches and heretics were burned at the stake in the 15th century), this spacious cobblestone square at the heart of Old Heidelberg is the city's most popular meeting place. Three times a day (at 11:55 AM and 1:55 and 6:55 PM), the bells in the *Rathaus* tower play folk melodies. The church, which boasts an impressive Gothic-vaulted interior, holds regular organ concerts (see *Music*). On Wednesday and Saturday mornings, an open-air market with stands stocked with food, clothing, and souvenirs sets up in front of the *Rathaus.* And the outdoor café scene—try *Café am Markt* (phone: 14444) or *Café Gundel* (phone: 20661)—is the best in town.

DAS SCHLOSS (HEIDELBERG CASTLE) The castle is the first stop on the Königstuhl funicular. You also can get here on foot (an arduous walk) or by car along the winding Neue Schlossstrasse (though private vehicles are prohibited on weekends and holidays). Few attractions in Germany are as popular, so be sure to come first thing in the morning or two hours before closing to avoid the crowds.

Construction of the walled castle, built to serve as the residence of the Palatinate electors and their families as well as to protect Heidelberg from attack, began in the early 14th century. As the work continued over the next 400 years, the original fortress was expanded into a vast complex of buildings, including several palaces in Gothic, High Renaissance, and Baroque styles. The oldest parts of the complex of buildings date from the 15th century. French troops blew up most of the castle in two raids during the Orleans War, the first in 1689 and the second in 1693. A reconstruction effort was started in the mid-18th century, but was abandoned after a lightning storm caused still more damage to the castle. The castle fell prey to scavengers and vandals, and the structure appeared to be condemned to ruin. Then, in 1810, an artist named Count Charles François de Graimberg stepped into the breach. Seeing potential in the romantic old castle, with its moats and turrets, he set out to save it. Graimberg had several rooms restored, moved in, and launched a publicity campaign. He created drawings and paintings of the castle in its previous glory and distributed them throughout the country. He also assembled a collection of castle artifacts, including coins, weapons, and statuary, which was put on display as well. A few years later, largely due to Graimberg's efforts, the government decided to open the complex as a public monument.

Today, although the castle is not completely restored, it remains an impressive sight. Huge courtyards are enclosed within sumptuous façades fitted with statues and topped by turrets and cupolas. Crumbling towers, along with delicate archways and portals, foster an eerie mood. Highlights of a castle visit include the Renaissance-style Friedrich wing, with its huge statues of Palatinate rulers on the façade. Still extant along the edge of the property is the massive *Torturm* (Gate Tower), with a moat and guardhouse. The *Elisabeth Tor* (Elizabeth Gate), designed in the form of a triumphal arch, leads into the flower-filled *Gun Park.* According to legend, the gate was built overnight in 1615 by Friedrich V (known as "The Winter King") as a gift for his teenage English bride, Elizabeth (who was the granddaughter of Mary, Queen of Scots). The castle is illuminated every night (with special light displays and fireworks several times a year—see *Special Events*); on most nights, you can get the best view by standing on the Alte Brücke across the way (see below).

In the castle's basement is the 18th-century *Heidelberger Fass,* a 57,200-gallon (220,000-liter) wine cask memorialized in the poetry of Heinrich Heine. It was the centerpiece of legendary palace revelry: As the story goes, Perkeo, a rowdy Italian dwarf who was the court jester, could drink many times his weight in wine, and once even managed to drain the cask of every last drop. Also included in the castle complex is the *Apothekenmuseum* (Pharmaceutical Museum). Spread through 10 subterranean rooms, it recalls an 18th-century apothecary, with period utensils, vessels, drug cabinets, and other artifacts. Guided tours (in German and English) of the castle and *Heidelberger Fass* are given every hour. The castle and *Heidelberger Fass* are open daily; the museum is closed weekdays November through March. Separate admission charges to the castle, *Heidelberger Fass,* and the museum; additional charge for the tour (phone: 53840, castle and museum; 165780, *Heidelberger Fass*).

ALTE BRÜCKE (OLD BRIDGE) Officially called Karl-Theodor-Brücke (after Prince Karl Theodor, the town elector who ordered it built), it was thought by Goethe to be the most beautiful bridge in the world. The fifth bridge to be erected here, this stone version was built in 1786 to replace the succession of wooden spans that had stood on this spot since medieval times. With its delicately curved arches, statues perched along its sides, and exquisite

Baroque towers, it is Heidelberg's most prominent reminder of the Romantic Age. During World War II, as part of its "scorched-earth policy" (choosing to destroy property rather than hand it over to the enemy), the German military blew up part of the bridge; it was later restored. Used by both vehicles and pedestrians, the Alte Brücke links the city to the Neuenheimer Landstrasse on the far side of the river, where a fairly steep footpath known as the Schlangenweg (Snake's Trail) leads part way up the slopes of the Heiligenberg. Located only a few minutes' stroll from the Marktplatz, the bridge is in the opposite direction of the castle on the narrow roadway, Steingasse.

PHILOSOPHENWEG (PHILOSOPHERS' WAY) This 1½-mile (2.5-km) path across the river from the Altstadt, beginning at Bergstrasse and stretching to the Alte Brücke, is considered by some to be one of the loveliest promenades in Europe; lined with flowering plants and trees, it is reminiscent of the Mediterranean. Philosophers Martin Heidegger and Hans-Georg Gadamer frequently walked along this trail, and it is still popular with intellectuals, who stroll by deep in philosophical conversation. A favorite time to come here is in the late afternoon, when the setting sun lends a romantic glow to the bridge, church towers, and castle. Other pathways connected to the Philosophenweg wend their way around the mountain, some into deep forests, others past vineyards, and still others along the river. Following a tradition that dates from the early 14th century, a fireworks display is held here on the first Saturday evening in June, July, and September (see *Special Events*).

THINGSTÄTTE Standing atop the Heiligenberg, this amphitheater was built by the Nazis in the 1930s as a nationalistic monument. Today it is an eerie reminder of fascism, though two concerts are held there in summer (for information, contact the tourist office—see *Tourist Information*). A shuttle bus operates between here and several points in the city on concert nights; other times, the *Thingstätte* is most popular as a hiking destination (it's a strenuous two-hour walk off the Philosophenweg). Open daily. No admission charge (no phone).

EXTRA SPECIAL

The scenic Neckartal (Neckar River Valley), one of Germany's premier wine districts, produces mainly red wines. Boat tours of the Neckar (see *Getting Around*) go past such medieval settlements as Neckargemund, perched on high ground overlooking the river; Dilsberg, a small fortress that successfully resisted attacks by the Bavarian army during the Thirty Years War; and Neckarsteinach, with several medieval castles. There are several good historic hotels in the area. For more information, see *The Neckar River Valley* in DIRECTIONS.

Sources and Resources

TOURIST INFORMATION

Tourist-Information, the main tourist office, is at *Hauptbahnof* (the central railway station; phone: 21341 or 27735); it is open daily. There's also another office at the castle (54 Neue Schlossstr.; phone: 21144); it is closed November through March.

LOCAL COVERAGE The English-language *Heidelberg This Week,* available for a small charge at tourist offices and hotels, offers detailed information on attractions and special events.

TELEPHONE The city code for Heidelberg is 6221.

GETTING AROUND

Since most visitors don't stray far from the traffic-free pedestrian zones of the Altstadt, the wooded trails of the Philosophenweg, or the gardens of the castle, the city is best explored on foot. For traveling farther afield, public transportation is first-rate and hassle-free.

AIRPORT The nearest international airports in Frankfurt and Stuttgart are each about an hour away by car or train. *TLS Transfer and Limousine Service* (426 Siemenstr.; phone: 770077) offers pick-up service via limousine or minibus between major hotels and *Flughafen Frankfurt Main* (Frankfurt-Main Airport). *Lufthansa Airlines* (phone: 69-690-30511 in Frankfurt) runs an airport shuttle bus service, with 17 round trips per day, between the *Renaissance* hotel in Heidelberg (see *Checking In*) and *Flughafen Frankfurt Main.*

BOAT *Rhein-Neckar Fahrgastschiffahrt* (phone: 20181) runs local boat tours and Neckar River Valley cruises from *Easter* to the end of October. The excursions, which last from 40 minutes to seven hours, depart from the docks below the *Stadthalle* convention center on the Neckar. Another cruise company offering frequent trips on the Neckar is *Personenschiffahrt Hornung* (phone: 480064).

BUS AND STREETCAR At Bismarckplatz, along the rim of the Altstadt, buses and streetcars depart regularly (every 10 to 20 minutes depending on the time of day) for trips to the *Hauptbahnof* (the central railway station) and into Neuer Heidelberg (New Heidelberg; those parts of the city not encompassed by the pedestrian zone). A single-ride ticket costs 3 DM (about $1.80). There is also a day pass that allows unlimited use of buses and streetcars throughout the metropolitan area; it costs 7 DM (about $4.20); the same pass, for the same price, also allows unlimited weekend travel. For more information about buses and streetcars, contact the *Verkehrsverbund Rhein/Neckar* (Rhine/Neckar Transit Authority; phone: 573-2000).

CAR RENTAL Major firms represented here include *Avis* (43 Karlsruher Str.; phone: 22215); *Hertz* (1 Kurfürsten-Anlage; phone: 23434); and *Europcar* (159 Bergheimer Str.; phone: 20845).

TAXI Taxis are available at Bismarckplatz or at the *Hauptbahnhof;* they also can be arranged through your hotel. For 24-hour service, call 302030.

TOURS *HSB-Stadtrundfahrt* (phone: 573-2000) conducts English-language guided bus tours from Bismarckplatz and the *Hauptbahnhof* twice daily May through October, once daily in April, and once on Saturdays only the rest of the year. The tourist office (see *Tourist Information*) sponsors guided walking tours of the Altstadt (in English) once a day on Thursdays, Fridays, and Saturdays in May through late October. Groups meet at the Löwenbrunnen (Lion's Fountain) on Universitätsplatz. Reservations are unnecessary. The price includes admission charges to museums visited during the tour.

TRAIN The luxurious *InterCity Express* (phone: 19419) offers hourly service from the *Hauptbahnhof* to Frankfurt and Stuttgart, where connections can be made to destinations throughout Germany and the rest of Europe.

SPECIAL EVENTS

Scores of cultural events are staged here each year, including one of the country's best music festivals.

A FAVORITE FETE

Heidelberg Schlossfest (Heidelberg Castle Festival) The setting is famous: the hilltop castle where ramparts, turrets, courtyards, and romantic ruins date from the 14th through 17th centuries. An opera is produced for each year's festival; there's also an annual revival of Heidelberg's own *The Student Prince,* complete with a horse and carriage processional. (The production is always performed in English, which makes it one of Germany's most accessible cultural events for Americans.) On the nights of the festival, the castle is illuminated with special lighting that casts a magical glow on the sandstone walls. The event, held late July through August, also includes solo, chamber group, and orchestral performances. For information and tickets, call the *Theater der Stadt* (Theater of the City; 4 Theaterstr.; phone: 583520).

In addition, *Karneval* (Carnival), with its colorful parades and other events, is celebrated on the Tuesday before *Fastenzeit* (Lent); church concerts are presented during *Osterwoche* (Easter Week); and the *Sommerszug* (Summer Procession), when children march through the streets of the Altstadt to celebrate the arrival of summer, is held on the third Sunday before *Ostersonntag* (Easter). Special floodlighting of the castle and a grand fireworks display—a tradition that dates back to June 1613 when Elector-Prince Friedrich V brought his new English bride, Elizabeth, back from their wedding in London—takes place on the first Saturdays of June and September. Classical and pop music performances take place in the castle courtyard every evening in summer; in foul weather, they are held in the castle's vast *Königshalle.* From June through August the *Heiliggeistkirche* hosts the public concerts of the *Internationales Sommer Organfest* (International Summer Organ Festival), which includes a *Bach Woche* (Bach Week) and a *Mozart Woche* (Mozart Week). On the first Saturday of June, July, and September, a fireworks display is held along the banks of the Neckar; it seems like the entire city turns out to picnic and watch the colorful celebration. The *Heidelberges Herbstfest* (Heidelberg Autumn Festival), held in various locations throughout the Altstadt during the last weekend in September, features fireworks, ballet performances, folkloric events, flea markets, wine tasting, and dancing.

MUSEUMS

In addition to those described in *Special Places,* these three museums are worth a visit.

MAX BERK TEXTIL-MUSEUM Housed in a former Protestant Baroque church and named for a wealthy local merchant, the collection features traditional German folk dress and embroideries and tapestries, along with an extensive collection of patchwork quilts from the US and Great Britain. Also on display are antique looms and early equipment used in printing, sewing, spinning, and weaving cloth. The museum is a 15-minute ride from the city on Bus No. 33 or 34. Open Wednesdays and weekends. No admission charge. 8 Brahmsstr., Heidelberg-Ziegelhausen (phone: 800317).

MUSEUM FÜR SAKRALE KUNST (MUSEUM OF SACRED ART) In the treasury of the Jesuit church, it has rare examples of gold and silver work by 18th-century Augsburg masters. Also on display are communion chalices, incense holders, water and wine vessels, bells, and altar cloths from the 17th, 18th, and 19th centuries. Closed weekdays November through May and Mondays year-round. Admission charge. 2 Richard-Hauser-Pl. (phone: 166393).

VÖLKERKUNDE-MUSEUM (ETHNOLOGY MUSEUM) Housed in the elegant, 18th-century *Palais Weimar* (Weimar Palace) and donated to the state of Baden-Württemberg by Viktor Goldschmidt, a university professor and statesman, the collection features ornamental masks, carvings, and craftwork from Africa, Oceania, Indonesia, and Tibet, plus Benin bronzes, gold weights from Guinea, and Chinese ceramics. Open Tuesdays through Fridays from 3 to 5 PM; Sundays from 1 to 5 PM. Admission charge. 235 Hauptstr. (phone: 22067).

SHOPPING

The town's main shopping mall, the Hauptstrasse, caters more to the needs of the local citizenry than to the visitor; it has the usual array of department stores, pharmacies, and other service-oriented shops. There's a branch of *Kaufhof* (24-28 Hauptstr.; phone: 5040), the major national department store chain, as well as *Horten* (on Bismarckpl.; phone: 9160), a local department store; both also have good, inexpensive restaurants (see *Eating Out*). Don't miss the open-air flea markets held at Marktplatz on Wednesdays and Saturdays and at Friedrich-Ebert-Platz on Tuesdays and Fridays. Flowers, fruits, vegetables, bread, and cheese are among the goods sold; even if you don't buy anything, it's a great way to soak up local color. There are some interesting bookshops, galleries, and antiques shops on the Plöck and several other small side streets behind the Kornmarkt. For standard shopping hours, see GETTING READY TO GO. Few shops are of special note, although the following are worth a peek:

Edmund von König Henckels and Solingen cutlery, Hummel figures, glassware, china, beer steins, and other souvenirs and gifts are featured here. 124 Hauptstr. (phone: 20929).

Gätsehenberger Two shops, both on Hauptstrasse: The branch at No. 42 specializes in fine linen, tablecloths, and bedspreads and coverlets, while the shop at No. 6 features women's lingerie and men's underclothing (phone for both: 22904).

J. Bernecker Antique books and graphics, including Baedeker guides dating from the 1800s and fine etchings of Heidelberg. 7B Gerberau (phone: 26137).

Kienscherff Handcrafted woodcarvings. 177 Hauptstr. (phone: 24255).

Leder-Meid High-quality leather goods, including wallets, handbags, and briefcases. 88 Hauptstr. (phone: 22570).

Muckels Maus Here is an extensivc collection of toys, including wooden blocks and figures, dolls, and puppets. 71 Plöck (phone: 23886).

Schafheutle As well as being a great café for sit-down snacking (see *Eating Out*), this place also offers a yummy selection of truffles, pastries, and cookies that can be boxed to take out. 94 Hauptstr. (phone: 21216).

Tischer A wide selection of glass, porcelain, and ceramics, both antique and contemporary pieces. 73 Hauptstr. (phone: 20709).

SPORTS AND FITNESS

With its mountain trails, miles of jogging paths along the Neckar, and boating, Heidelberg offers many options for the sports-oriented visitor.

BICYCLING There are about 93 miles (150 km) of cycling paths (some in better condition than others) on both sides of the Neckar, plus about 6 miles (10 km) of paths in the city itself. The *Deutsche Bundesbahn* (German Federal Railway; phone: 525343) has bikes for rent at the railway station April through September .

BOATING In good weather, paddle boats and rowboats can be rented at the Neckar pier next to the Karl-Theodor Bridge (no phone).

GOLF Major venues are the steep and very challenging 18-hole course at *Golf Club Lobenfeld* in the neighboring village of Lobenfeld (phone: 6226-40490); and another 18-hole layout, *Golfanlage Hohenhardter Hof* (in Wiesloch, a nearby town in the Baiertal district; phone: 6222-72081), which is on hilly but less difficult terrain.

HIKING The wooded trails of the Heiligenberg, leading off from the Philosophenweg, are ideally suited for casual walking. Along one of them are the ruins of a 9th-century basilica and monastery of St. Michael, located behind the remains of a Celtic wall dating from the 4th to the 1st century BC. Other easy hiking paths start at the cable car station on the Königstuhl.

JOGGING Both shores of the Neckar, paths around the Heiligenberg, and paths on both sides of the castle above the Altstadt are ideal for jogging.

SWIMMING A large outdoor pool at the *Tiergarten Schwimmbad* (Zoo Pool; 13 Tiergartenstr.; phone: 401174) is open daily May through September; to get there, take Bus No. 33 from Bismarckplatz. Fed by underground hot springs, the open-air *Heidelbergs Thermal Bad* (Heidelberg Thermal Pool; 4 Vangerowstr.; phone: 581966) is open daily April through September; take Streetcar No. 2 from Bismarckplatz. Indoor pools are at the *Darmstädter Hof Zentrum* (on the Bismarckplatz; phone: 581967) and *Kopfel* in *Sportzentrum Ziegelhausen* (32 Stiftweg; phone: 800622); all are open daily.

TENNIS There are 12 outdoor and three indoor courts at Kirchheimer Weg (phone: 12106), as well as four indoor badminton courts. The *Emmertsgrund Sports Center* (Otto-Hahn-Str.; phone: 382014) has four courts (three outdoor, one indoor).

THEATER

The main theaters are the *Zimmertheater* (118 Hauptstr.; phone: 21069); *Theater im Augustinum* (2 Jasperstr; phone: 3881); *Taeter-Theater* (147 Bergheimer Str.; phone: 163333); and the *Theater der Stadt* (4 Theaterstr.; phone: 583520); none offer productions in English. Other performances—including the perennial favorite, *The Student Prince*—are staged in the castle (see *Special Events*).

MUSIC

Concerts are presented throughout the year in theaters, churches, and the castle. Organ concerts are a regular feature at the *Heiliggeistkirche* (Marktplatz; phone: 21117) at noon on Sundays and holidays, and weekdays at 6 PM during the summer. For further information on musical performances, contact the church. The tourist offices (see *Tourist Information*) also have information on musical events.

NIGHTCLUBS AND NIGHTLIFE

Nightlife is concentrated primarily in the atmospheric student taverns, or *Lokale* (pubs). Menus of traditional *Lokale* include homemade goulash, salads, Matjes herring, various kinds of sausages, *Tellerfleisch* (boiled beef), schnitzel, sauerbraten, and rumpsteak. *Lokale* do not accept credit cards. *Zum Roten Ochsen* (217 Hauptstr.; phone: 20977), the city's most popular pub, has been run by six generations of the Spengel family. Its interior is of dark woodwork, and the surfaces of tables and benches (and even the walls) are carved with initials; guestbooks bear the signatures of such luminaries as Mark Twain and Otto von Bismarck. It is closed Sundays. Next door is *Zum Sepp'l* (213 Hauptstr.; phone: 23085), a tavern of similar style, open since 1634. This one is known for its loud (and sometimes boisterous) student patrons. Other old-time establishments include *Knösel* (20 Haspelgasse; phone: 22345) and *Schnookeloch* (see *Checking In*). *Brauerei Vetter* (9 Steingasse; phone: 15850), a rustic brewery tavern (copper tanks and tubing on site) on the narrow passageway leading from Marktplatz to the Alte Brücke, is lively from mid-afternoon to midnight. *Doctor Flotte* (130 Hauptstr.; phone: 20569) features taped jazz music in an atmosphere of old Berlin; in October through April, a Dixieland band plays on Sunday afternoons from 2 to 5 PM. *Alte Schmiede* (167 Hauptstr.; phone: 25189) and *Bierkrug* (147 Hauptstr.; phone: 12663) are popular beer bars, and *Café Journal* (162 Hauptstr.; phone: 161712) is a late-night gathering place for a hip, trendy crowd of all ages; offered here are newspapers and magazines from all over Europe and the US, and a diverse menu of snacks. A popular hangout for university students is the *Schwimmbad Musik Club* (13 Tiergartenstr.; phone: 470201). *Club 1900* (117 Hauptstr.; phone: 20176), open nightly until 3 AM, is the city's most popular disco. *Whiskey à Go Go* (10 Oberbadgasse; phone: 22661), the city's number one gay club, is open every night.

Best in Town

CHECKING IN

In Heidelberg—always a prime tourist destination and now an emerging high-tech business center—hotel space is often at a premium; it's best to reserve well in advance. Between mid-November and mid-March, discounts of at least 10% off regular rates are available. Especially popular is a vacation package offered by the tourist office in conjunction with several city hotels: "Three Romantic Days in Heidelberg" includes two nights' accommodations, daily breakfasts, one restaurant meal, a sightseeing tour, a museum pass, and other extras, at substantial savings over standard rates. Contact the tourist office (see *Tourist Information*) for information about this package, as well as about finding accommodations in modestly priced boarding houses and inns. Hotels in or close to the historic quarter of the

Altstadt offer greater convenience, but many of the larger and more modern chain members (Ramada, Rega) are located some distance away. For a double room with a private bath, TV set, and telephone, expect to pay $200 or more at hotels in the expensive category; from $115 to $200 at moderate places; and under $115 at inexpensive ones. Breakfast is generally included in the rate. All telephone numbers are in the 6221 city code unless otherwise indicated.

For an unforgettable experience in Heidelberg, we begin with our favorites, followed by our cost and quality choices, listed by price category.

ROOMS AT THE TOP

Der Europäische Hof Also known as the "Europa," Heidelberg's leading hotel since 1865 has been owned by several generations of the von Kretschmann family, who totally involve themselves in its day-to-day operations. Centrally located across from the *Stadtgarten* (City Garden), it's noted for its service (the concierge is a gem) and for the fine French food served in its *Kurfürstenstube* restaurant (see *Eating Out*). Each of the 135 rooms, eight junior suites, and six apartments is elegantly furnished; the decor ranges from Louis XVI period antiques and old-fashioned-looking plumbing fixtures to bold, modern fittings. The rooms in the original structure are especially spacious, with high ceilings and walk-in closets. All are equipped with plenty of modern amenities, including mini-bars. There are antique-filled public rooms, an outdoor terrace for summer dining, conference rooms, and a bar with a dance floor. 1 Friedrich-Ebert-Anlage (phone: 5150; 800-223-6800; fax: 515555).

Zum Ritter St. Georg For those who want to step back in time to Germany's Romantic Age, this is the place. A gem of 16th-century architecture, with antique furnishings, it was built in 1592 as the home of a French textile tycoon and has survived centuries of war and weather remarkably well. It is now an intimate hostelry with 39 rooms (12 are furnished with 19th-century antiques and decor; the others feature comfortable modern furnishings) and fine service. It offers plenty of atmosphere, as this precinct has long been a popular student haunt. Martin Luther once defended his credo in the area, and Goethe did a good deal of his writing here. Each day, it seems that most of the student population of Heidelberg saunters past; though it can be noisy (especially in the front rooms), many find the ambience very appealing. There's also a good restaurant. 178 Hauptstr. (phone: 20203 or 24272; fax: 12683).

EXPENSIVE

Hirschgasse This small family-run hotel (ca. 1472), a 10-minute walk from the Altstadt across the Neckar, is Heidelberg's oldest and most popular property. In the 19th century, student fencing clubs used the upper-floor halls for fighting duels. The 18 suites are furnished in contemporary English-country style; happily, the hotel's rustic, medieval exterior remains. There's a first-rate restaurant (*Le Gourmet;* see *Eating Out*) and a charming, tree-shaded terrace for breakfast. Reserve well in advance. 3 Hirschgasse (phone: 403-2160; fax: 403-32161).

Holiday Inn Crowne Plaza Located a five-minute walk from the city center, this member of the chain has 232 air conditioned, brightly furnished rooms; a fitness center with a pool, sauna, and solarium; and a good restaurant. Breakfast is not included. 1 Kurfürstenanlage (phone: 9170; 800-HOLIDAY; fax: 27007).

Prinz A fine Belle Epoque–style villa featuring rooms with modern comforts and conveniences, this small place (50 rooms) is located directly across the Neckar from the Altstadt near the Alte Brücke. For the best river views, ask for a top floor room. Facilities include a restaurant serving California-style fare, an indoor pool, a sauna, a whirlpool, and a steam bath with waterfall. Breakfast is not included. 5 Neuenheimer Landstr. (phone: 40320; fax: 403-2196).

Renaissance A big city–style place with features standard to the Ramada chain, this hotel on the banks of the Neckar has 251 spacious rooms, most with lovely river views. The decor is contemporary, and each room has the usual comforts such as a mini-bar and a VCR; video rental is also available. The hotel's main restaurant offers elegantly prepared German fare, while a pub serves more rustic dishes. There also is a business center, a pool, and a health club. Breakfast is not included. 16 Vangerowstr. (phone: 9080; 800-228-9898; fax: 22977).

MODERATE

Acor In a 19th-century neoclassical building, this hostelry has a beautifully arched entranceway leading to a grand circular staircase. The 18 rooms are furnished in a starkly modern, minimalist fashion. There is no restaurant, and amenities are few, but the hotel's location (a short walk from the Altstadt) is convenient. 55 Friedrich-Ebert-Anlage (phone: 22044).

Hackteufel The Scholl family has owned and operated this hotel for 30 years. Conveniently located in the Altstadt by the Alte Brücke, the 14 rooms and six apartments are comfortably furnished in contemporary fashion and offer the usual amenities. Several of the apartments feature beamed cathedral ceilings (ask for No. 12, which also has a great view of the river). Other pluses include a very good restaurant (see *Eating Out*) and parking. 7 Steingasse (phone: 27162; fax: 165379).

Holländer Hof This 19th-century house, located on the Neckar next to the Alte Brücke, has 40 pleasantly furnished rooms (one, simply called "the apartment," is a suite with an arched wooden beamed ceiling and great views of the Heiligenweg, the Neckar, and the Alte Brücke). There's also a popular restaurant and an open-air, riverside café. 66 Neckarstaden (phone: 12091; fax: 22085).

Parkhotel Atlantic Nestled in a quaint pastoral garden, this fine turn-of-the-century villa is located in the Neckar Valley near the castle. The 23 rooms have cable TV and mini-bars; several also have a lovely view of the river and the surrounding area. 23 Schloss Wolfsbrunnenweg (phone: 164051; fax: 164054).

Perkeo This place can be a bit noisy, but its 25 spacious rooms are attractively decked out with rustic woodwork and feature modern conveniences such as mini-bars. The hotel also has a good restaurant. The quietest rooms are in the back. 75 Hauptstr. (phone: 22255; fax: 163719).

Rega Hotel Heidelberg A relatively new addition, this high-rise chain member has 122 tastefully decorated rooms. Located a short stroll from the Altstadt, it features a popular bar and brasserie as well as a conference center and underground parking. 63 Bergheimerstr. (phone: 5080; fax: 508500).

Schönberger Hof A gem of a small hotel, with 15 clean and comfortable rooms and an excellent restaurant (see *Eating Out*), it faces the river along the edge of the Altstadt. It attracts a loyal clientele with its personalized, attentive service. 54 Untere Neckarstr. (phone: 24988; fax: 164811).

INEXPENSIVE

Am Kornmarkt A small, no-frills property, it is ideally located between the *Bergbahn* and the Altstadt. The 13 rooms are simply decorated, but clean and comfortable. There's no restaurant (but there is a breakfast room). 7 Kornmarkt (phone: 24325).

Bayrischer Hof Located just outside the Altstadt near Bismarckplatz, this family-run property has 43 fairly spacious rooms, many of which are decorated in a pleasant rustic style. There's no restaurant, but the breakfast room offers an extensive buffet. 2 Rohrbacherstr. (phone: 184045).

Molkenkur Deep in the forest about 3 miles (5 km) outside the city and perched 300 feet above the castle, this quiet and charming small hotel can be reached by car or cable car. The 12 guestrooms feature traditional decor, and the restaurant affords a stunning view of the castle from its terrace. Closed from December 12 through *New Year's Day.* 31 Klingenteichstr. (phone: 10894).

Schnookeloch This cozy hostelry, set in a 15th-century building in the Altstadt near the Neckar River, boasts 11 comfortable rooms equipped with the usual modern amenities (as well as a special treat—a complimentary half-bottle of local wine). The pub is a traditional student hangout. 8 Haspelgasse (phone: 22733; fax: 22377).

EATING OUT

Although not known for haute cuisine, Heidelberg's restaurants offer more than sauerbraten and Wiener schnitzel. Local cooking has French, Swiss, and Alsatian influences as well as German; it is colloquially known as "border cuisine." The *Simplicissimus* restaurant ranks among the best in the country for its Teutonic variation of nouvelle cuisine (*Neue Deutsche Küche*), earning a Michelin star. But for those who fancy local food, several restaurants serve generous portions of tasty home-cooked dishes at reasonable prices. In fact, dining in Heidelberg costs less than in other major towns in Germany. Expect to pay $100 or more for dinner for two at a restaurant listed as expensive; $65 to $100 in a moderately priced place; and less than $65 in an inexpensive one. Prices do not include drinks or wine; service charge and taxes are always included, but you should reward very good service with a small additional tip. Unless otherwise noted, the restaurants listed below are open for lunch and dinner. All telephone numbers are in the 6221 city code unless otherwise indicated.

EXPENSIVE

Le Gourmet Classic French cuisine, along with fine wines, are served in this beautifully decorated hotel restaurant. In summer the dining area extends out to a garden terrace affording memorable views of the Neckar and the castle. Open for dinner only; closed Sundays, holidays, and December 23 through January 7. Reservations necessary. Major credit cards accepted. In the *Hotel Hirschgasse,* 3 Hirschgasse (phone: 403-2160).

Kurfürstenstube Entering the main dining room of *Der Europäische Hof* is a little like stepping back into a 17th-century German inn, with its woodwork polished to a high gloss, dazzling copper chandeliers, and decorative copper, pewter, and ceramic wall ornaments. The menu includes lamb medallions with fresh tomato ragout, freshwater trout, and game in season. There is usually a three-course "meal of the day" which can be a good value. Open daily. Reservations advised. Major credit cards accepted. 2 Nadlerstr. (phone: 5150).

Schloss Weinstube Schönmehl Set in the former kitchen and bakery building of *Das Schloss,* this stately, Old World restaurant recently reopened under new ownership. There are several connected dining rooms, all elegantly furnished with unusual sculptures; the view of the castle in the moonlight is stunning. The menu offers local dishes prepared with a continental flair, including *Kartoffelsuppe* (potato soup) with truffles, goulash made with perch and pike and served with cilantro dumplings, and baked goose. Open for dinner only; closed Wednesdays. Reservations advised. Major credit cards accepted. Schlosshof (phone: 181084).

Simplicissimus Only a small sign at a corner house on a back street near Marktplatz marks Heidelberg's top dining place (one Michelin star). Owned by chef Hans Lummer and his wife, Melisse, it offers classic continental fare with nouvelle flourishes in a small, romantic setting with only 19 tables. Dishes include foie gras, salmon, lobster salad with avocados, smoked trout, breast of quail, sliced turbot, duck, filet of beef, rack of lamb, and saddle of rabbit. Or choose a prix fixe four- or five-course meal. Ingredients are shipped daily from the wholesale *Rungis* market near Paris. Open for dinner only; closed Tuesdays and three weeks from late July to mid-August. Reservations necessary. Major credit cards accepted. 16 Ingrimstr. (phone: 183336).

MODERATE

Kurpfälzisches Museum For the best in home-cooked food in the most opulent of settings, no place compares. The decor of this Baroque palace—which also houses the city museum—includes beamed ceilings and ornate columns, antiques, statuary, oil paintings, and stained glass windows. In summer there's alfresco dining in the garden. It's renowned for its fish dishes, homemade pasta, and succulent stews and ragouts. Excellent wines are served by the glass. Service is somewhat slow but attentive. Open daily. Reservations unnecessary. Major credit cards accepted. 97 Hauptstr. (phone: 24050).

Schönberger Hof This attractive and highly regarded dining room in the eponymous hotel is a favorite with locals looking for specialties from the Baden region—smoked pork ribs, pork cutlet, and potato-and-sauerkraut salad—along with top-rated local wines. The attentive service complements the elegant atmosphere. Open for dinner only; closed Saturdays and Sundays. Reservations advised. No credit cards accepted. 54 Untere Neckarstr. (phone: 22615).

Weinstube Zum Backofen Wolf Ziegs, the amiable owner of this place, makes diners feel as though they are visiting his home. The unpretentious ambience is complemented by the tasty local specialties, including *Marklosschesuppe* (clear bouillon with dumplings) and *Elsasser Flammkuchen* (a flat dish similar to pizza, served either with onions and sour cream or sugar and apples). There's also a good list of regional wines; Herr Ziegs will be glad to help you choose. Open for dinner only; closed Sundays and Mondays. Reservations advised. No credit cards accepted. 18 Haspelgasse (phone: 23847).

Zum Ritter The medieval-looking decor—a knight in armor in an alcove, ancient weapons, and pewter plates—provides a proper setting for the serving of such long-standing favorites as Matjes herring (garnished with a dressing made with sour cream, apples, and onions), boiled beef with horseradish, and schnitzel. There are first-rate beers on tap, and fine wines by the glass. Service can be erratic, at times indifferent, and the tour-group clientele off-putting, but the food is memorable and the price right. Open daily. Reservations unnecessary. Major credit cards accepted. 176 Hauptstr. (phone: 24272).

Zum Spriesel The former owner of the popular *Südpfanne* (which has closed) has moved on to open a restaurant in this historic *Gasthaus* (guesthouse) by the Alte Brücke. Overlooking the Neckar, this place offers a menu of continental specialties such as lamb's liver in cognac cream sauce, stuffed cabbage leaves with pan-fried potatoes, and roast French guinea fowl with sauerkraut, noodles, dried plums, and grapes. Open daily. Reservations necessary. No credit cards accepted. 66 Neckarstaden (phone: 23543).

INEXPENSIVE

Casablanca Traumsäfte The second word means "juice bar" in German, and that pretty much describes the place. It's a cozy, stand-up café that serves vegetable dishes, rice, noodles, salads, and soups, as well as fresh-squeezed fruit juices. Ideal for a quick lunch in the midst of a busy day of sightseeing. Closed Sundays. No reservations. No credit cards accepted. 164 Hauptstr. (phone: 26111).

Hackteufel On the narrow passageway leading to the Alte Brücke, this is a local favorite for simple meals—a place where chefs at fancier dining spots eat on their nights out. Home-style German cooking (try the *Maultaschen*—large filled raviolis) along with a variety of tap beers and fine wines are featured. Open daily for dinner only. Reservations advised. Major credit cards accepted. 7 Steingasse (phone: 27162).

Nordsee Meeresbuffet This informal, buffet-style eatery serves the freshest seafood at surprisingly reasonable prices. The menu changes daily depending on what the local fishermen have managed to pull in, but there is always a tasty fish soup and several grilled or broiled entrées served with potatoes or rice and vegetables. Closed Sundays. No reservations. No credit cards accepted. 20 Hauptstr. (phone: 22037).

Schafheutle Known locally as "the sweetheart of Heidelberg" because of its tasty pastries, this little bakery/café is a great place for a quick lunch or afternoon coffee and cake. In warm weather, tables are set up in a lovely outdoor garden. Open for breakfast, lunch, and afternoon coffee only; closed Sundays. No reservations. No credit cards accepted. 94 Hauptstr. (phone: 21316).

Schnitzelbank Hearty local dishes are served up at this warm, friendly place, along with a wide variety of regional wines and beers. Open daily for dinner only. No reservations. No credit cards accepted. 7 Bauamtsgasse (phone: 21189).

Zum Güldenen Schaf A historic, early-18th-century restaurant in the heart of the Altstadt, with a busy beer garden in the rear, it is known for its carefully drawn pilsener beer and tasty sausages with sauerkraut. Open daily for dinner only. Reservations unnecessary. No credit cards accepted. 115 Hauptstr. (phone: 20879; fax: 160409).

SHOP 'N' SUP

Both of the city's department stores, *Horten* (on Bismarckpl.; phone: 9160) and *Kaufhof* (24-28 Hauptstr.; phone: 5040), have good (and inexpensive) restaurants open during regular business hours Mondays through Saturdays. Neither place accepts reservations; major credit cards are accepted. They also have large food departments, including espresso and sandwich bars, and mini-restaurants serving seafood specialties, roast chicken, sausages, and hamburgers.

Leipzig

For the latter part of its 800-year history, this place that Goethe once called his "little Paris" has been one of the leading cultural and intellectual centers in Germany. The *Thomaskirche* (St. Thomas's Church), where Johann Sebastian Bach served as choirmaster, still claims one of the world's finest boys' choirs. And only Heidelberg's university, the country's oldest, has a more illustrious past than *Universität Leipzig* (Leipzig University). Goethe, Wagner, mathematician Gottfried Leibniz, composers Georg Philipp Telemann and Robert Schumann, poet-dramatist Gotthold Lessing, and philosopher Friedrich Nietzsche all studied here. Yet despite its long, distinguished past, the city has become best known in recent years as the spiritual home of Germany's reunification. It was here, in the second-largest city in the former German Democratic Republic (GDR), that the freedom revolution of 1989 got its start, through mass protest demonstrations that ultimately resulted in what became known as the "Leipzig Miracle." Beginning in the early fall of that year, more than 500,000 protesters gathered peacefully on Karl-Marx-Platz to call for the end of the hard-line Communist regime. To the surprise of all, the government soon capitulated, and national reunification was achieved the following October.

Leipzig has long been home to rebellious spirits. Here, in 1863, Ferdinand Lassalle founded the *General German Workers' Association,* one of the earliest antiestablishment Marxist-based unions, and about the same time Wilhelm Liebknecht and August Bebel made Leipzig a stronghold of the fitful German Social Democrats. Lenin secretly published his revolutionary newspaper, *Iskra,* in Leipzig in 1900, and Liebknecht's son Karl, along with Rosa Luxemburg, headed the radical Spartacus movement that became Germany's Communist Party after World War I.

A city of 565,000 people, Leipzig (whose name derives from *Lipsk*—"place of the lime tree" in Slavic) is one of the country's most important industrial and commercial centers. The trade fairs hosted by the city throughout the year attract exhibitors from up to 60 countries. Leipzig also is the site of a large printing industry; one of Europe's leading book-publishing centers since the mid-1700s, there were no fewer than 900 publishing-printing concerns in existence here by the early 1940s (nowadays, the number has dwindled to about 200). In addition, the city has a sports institute that has produced *Olympic* champions for four decades. It is also a place richly clothed in its past. For example, you can still eat and drink in *Auerbachs Keller,* the restaurant and tavern where the Devil met the title character of Goethe's *Faust.*

Located at the crossroads of two longtime mid-European trade and travel routes, Via Regia (King's Way) and Via Imperii (Imperial Way)—now bearing the unromantic designations F2 and F87, respectively—Leipzig prospered quickly after Margrave Otto von Meissen passed a charter in 1165 giving the town the right to hold three annual markets. From the street markets evolved today's specialized, heavily attended trade fairs, where goods ranging from shoes and books to forklifts and turbines are exhibited. You can't miss seeing the "M" logos that identify various *Messe* (market) areas on billboards, façades, and even atop a downtown skyscraper. During the GDR years, the fairs were vital sources of foreign hard currency and made Leipzig considerably more accessible and cosmopolitan than other East German cities.

Leipzig's musical credentials are extremely impressive. Germany's first professional orchestra made its concert debut here in the 1740s. The period of time that Bach spent here was his most creative (in more ways than one): During his 27 years in Leipzig, he composed many of his greatest works, including the *Magnificat, Mass in B Minor,* and *St. John Passion,* and sired a dozen children (out of a total of 20). In 1843, 93 years after Bach's death, the first German music conservatory was founded by composers Felix Mendelssohn and Robert Schumann. Richard Wagner, who was baptized in the *Thomaskirche* in 1813, inherited this rich tradition, one that maintains its high standards today with the performances of the outstanding *Gewandhausorchester* (Gewandhaus Orchestra) and *Thomanerchor* (Thomaner Choir), as well as those of *Oper Leipzig,* the city's fine opera company.

Universität Leipzig, which was called *Karl-Marx-Universität* (Karl Marx University, after the father of socialist ideology) from 1953 until Germany's reunification, dates back to classes held in the *Thomaskirche*'s refectory in 1409 and has exerted considerable influence ever since. The student population (currently numbering 16,000) was largely responsible for Leipzig's boldly satirical cabaret shows during the repressive GDR years and formed the driving force behind the mass demonstrations of 1989. Note the 468-foot-high administration building; constructed by the Socialist government and finished in 1968, it resembles an open book from some angles and a tooth from others. The bizarre 34-story silvery metal structure, an amazingly out-of-scale presence in a city center of restored churches and low-rise public buildings, has earned itself the nickname "the Wisdom Tooth." (Its construction caused much local controversy at the time: A beautiful, 13th-century Gothic church was torn down to make way for it.)

Leipzig was extensively damaged during World War II, and today the city center is a hodgepodge of banal Socialist-era structures and old buildings that are gradually being restored to their former elegance. Among the latter are the 16th-century *Altes Rathaus* (Old Town Hall); the *Neues Rathaus* (New Town Hall), which was built in the early 20th century on the edge of the neatly circumscribed Altstadt (Old City); and the *Thomaskirche,* whose origins date back to the early 13th century.

Post-reunification Leipzig has become something of a financial center. The city's 90-odd banks (only Frankfurt has more) are financing ren-

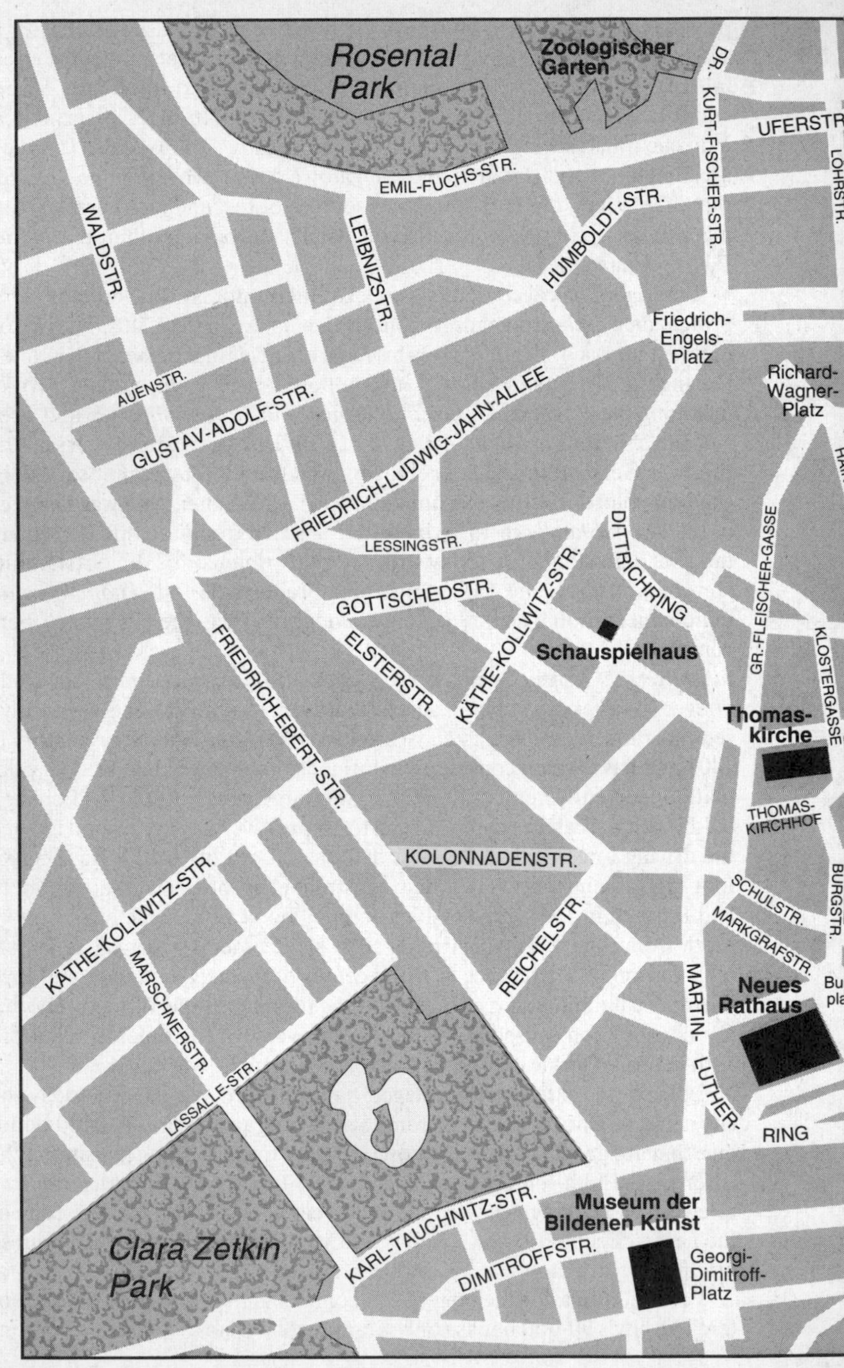

Rosental Park
Zoologischer Garten
DR.-KURT-FISCHER-STR.
UFERSTR.
LÖHRSTR.
EMIL-FUCHS-STR.
WALDSTR.
LEIBNIZSTR.
HUMBOLDT-STR.
Friedrich-Engels-Platz
Richard-Wagner-Platz
AUENSTR.
GUSTAV-ADOLF-STR.
FRIEDRICH-LUDWIG-JAHN-ALLEE
LESSINGSTR.
DITTRICHRING
GR.-FLEISCHER-GASSE
GOTTSCHEDSTR.
KÄTHE-KOLLWITZ-STR.
Schauspielhaus
KLOSTERGASSE
FRIEDRICH-EBERT-STR.
ELSTERSTR.
Thomas-kirche
THOMAS-KIRCHHOF
KOLONNADENSTR.
BURGSTR.
SCHULSTR.
MARKGRAFSTR.
KÄTHE-KOLLWITZ-STR.
MARSCHNERSTR.
REICHELSTR.
MARTIN-LUTHER-RING
Neues Rathaus
LASSALLE-STR.
KARL-TAUCHNITZ-STR.
Museum der Bildenen Künst
DIMITROFFSTR.
Georgi-Dimitroff-Platz
Clara Zetkin Park

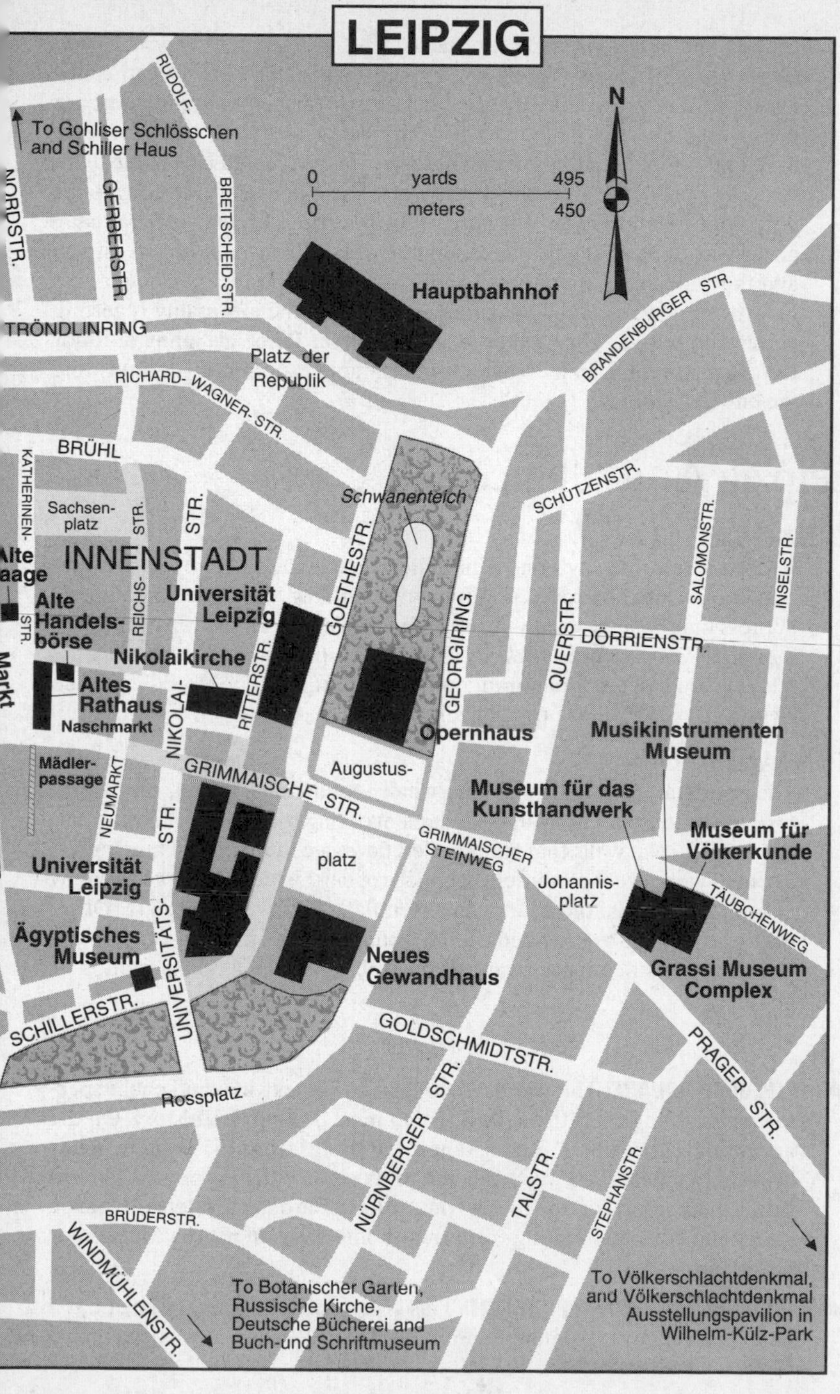

LEIPZIG
N
0 yards 495
0 meters 450
To Gohliser Schlösschen and Schiller Haus
RUDOLF-
NORDSTR.
GERBERSTR.
BREITSCHEID-STR.
TRÖNDLINRING
Hauptbahnhof
Platz der Republik
RICHARD-WAGNER-STR.
BRANDENBURGER STR.
BRÜHL
KATHERINEN-STR.
Sachsen-platz
STR.
Schwanenteich
SCHÜTZENSTR.
INNENSTADT
Alte Waage
Alte Handels-börse
Universität Leipzig
GOETHESTR.
GEORGIRING
QUERSTR.
SALOMONSTR.
INSELSTR.
DÖRRIENSTR.
REICHS-
Markt
Nikolaikirche
RITTERSTR.
Altes Rathaus
Naschmarkt
NIKOLAI-
Opernhaus
Musikinstrumenten Museum
Mädler-passage
NEUMARKT
GRIMMAISCHE STR.
Augustus-
Museum für das Kunsthandwerk
Museum für Völkerkunde
GRIMMAISCHER STEINWEG
platz
Universität Leipzig
Johannis-platz
TÄUBCHENWEG
Ägyptisches Museum
UNIVERSITÄTS-STR.
Neues Gewandhaus
Grassi Museum Complex
SCHILLERSTR.
GOLDSCHMIDTSTR.
PRAGER STR.
Rossplatz
NÜRNBERGER STR.
TALSTR.
STEPHANSTR.
BRÜDERSTR.
WINDMÜHLENSTR.
To Botanischer Garten, Russische Kirche, Deutsche Bücherei and Buch-und Schriftmuseum
To Völkerschlachtdenkmal, and Völkerschlachtdenkmal Ausstellungspavilion in Wilhelm-Külz-Park

ovation and new construction projects; scaffolding and *"Vorsicht: Frisch Gestrichen"* (Warning: Wet Paint) signs are facts of daily life. Occasionally, unexploded American or British bombs are unearthed as foundations are dug. Rusty, defunct streetcar tracks are being replaced, and 38 streets have undergone name changes (therefore, maps created before 1990 are virtually worthless). And one of the worst legacies of the GDR days—air pollution—is improving. With use of the notorious brown coal gradually giving way to natural gas, the enactment of land-conservation measures, and the wide-scale abandonment of the GDR's "Trabi" passenger cars in favor of newer, cleaner-burning alternatives, the air quality is getting better and better. This makes a stop at one of Leipzig's many outdoor terrace restaurants an increasingly pleasurable experience—as is visiting the city as a whole.

Leipzig At-a-Glance

SEEING THE CITY

Unfortunately, the city's one legitimate vantage point, the rooftop restaurant in *Universität Leipzig*'s administrative building, was closed indefinitely at press time. The best view currently available is from the top of the 300-foot-high *Völkerschlachtsdenkmal* (Battle of Leipzig Monument; see *Special Places*); you can see a panorama of the surrounding countryside, but the view of the city itself is unspectacular.

SPECIAL PLACES

The Innenstadt (Inner City) is barely half a square mile in area, and its historic attractions lie within an encirclement of ring roads that follow the pattern of medieval walls that were pulled down a century ago. Three public squares symbolize three different epochs of city history and serve as handy orientation points: the Markt, Sachsenplatz, and Augustusplatz. Other major attractions are located on the outer fringe of the ring-road, and a few more are still farther away but reachable via public transportation or by car.

INNENSTADT

MARKT (MARKET SQUARE) This was the heart and hub of activities and public spectacles, including executions, throughout most of Leipzig's history. On the north side is the gabled, Renaissance *Alte Waage* from 1555, where goods brought to the markets were weighed for taxation. On the opposite (south) side is the *Königshaus,* the former out-of-town Baroque residence of Saxon rulers and courtiers visiting from their home bases in nearby Meissen or Dresden.

THOMASKIRCHE (ST. THOMAS CHURCH) This ecclesiastical landmark began as a Romanesque-style Augustinian monastery in 1212, then was converted to a late Gothic high-roofed Saxon hall church in 1496. The octagonal tower was added in 1702, followed by Baroque interior alterations in 1721. Few churches contain so much history—both spiritual and temporal. From its pulpit, Martin Luther introduced his Reformation to Leipzigers in 1539; Bach conducted the *Thomanerchor* (Thomaner Choir) here 200 years later; in the late 18th century Wolfgang Amadeus Mozart played the church's organ; in 1813, Napoleon used the church as a stable and hospital; and Mendelssohn conducted Bach's *St. Matthew Passion* here in 1841. Bach lies buried beneath a bronze slab at the altar. A 6,300-pipe Sauer organ from 1889 dominates the choir loft, although a less august 1966 Schuke organ is better modulated to Bach's compositions. The *Thomanerchor,* successor to the boys' choir that Bach led, sings motets on Fridays at 6 PM, and motets and Bach cantatas on Saturdays at 3 PM. The choir also sings at the 9:30 AM Sunday service. (Exceptions are school vacation periods or when the group is on tour.) On the grounds is a statue of Bach with one of his pockets turned inside out, a wry reference to the constant money problems of a hardworking choirmaster raising 20 children. 18 Thomaskirchhof (phone: 287103).

BOSEHAUS Opposite the *Thomaskirche* is the former residence (ca. 1710) of merchant Georg Heinrich Bose, who with his close friend Bach played impromptu duets here. Reopened in 1985 in honor of the composer's 300th birthday, the elegant yellow house holds a small collection of Bach's personal and musical memorabilia and period instruments. Chamber concerts are scheduled from time to time in the upstairs *Bachsaal* salon, beneath a rococo ceiling fresco. Closed Mondays. Admission charge. 16 Thomaskirchhof (phone: 7866).

NIKOLAIKIRCHE (ST. NICHOLAS CHURCH) Larger than the *Thomaskirche* and older by a decade or so, the "Nikolai" is currently famous as the site of the peaceful gatherings that led directly to the "Leipzig Miracle." But there are strong Bach connections, too. Works he composed in his lodgings across town usually premiered here. The outside architecture and interior spaces were originally in the Romanesque style, but were changed to Gothic, Renaissance, then Baroque over the course of five centuries. Then came the current interior (designed in 1784), a flamboyant rendition of French classicism. The tops of the Grecian columns sprout green-and-pink "palm" flourishes near the diamond-patterned ceiling. St. Nicholas, the patron saint of merchants and traders, has long been the favored saint of Leipzig. The 6,000-pipe Ladegast organ, one of Germany's largest, was installed in 1857. Recitals are performed Wednesdays at 5 PM. The weekly tradition of Monday prayer and public discussions starts at 5 PM. 3 Nikolaikirchhof (phone: 200952).

ALTES RATHAUS (OLD TOWN HALL) Leipzig's Renaissance treasure, on the east side of the Markt, was built from scratch in an astonishing nine months between trade fairs in 1556. A wraparound inscription, reputedly the world's longest, proclaims the noble, civic achievements of Saxon margraves and electors. The building has sandstone arcades at street level and a tower with a sundial and blue and gilt clocks. The entire upstairs floor, including the grandiose *Festsaal* (banqueting hall), houses the *Stadtgeschichtiches Museum* (City History Museum; 1 Markt; phone: 70921), with the only accurate portrayal of Bach in existence (a 1746 painting by Haussmann), the first book printed in Leipzig (in 1481), and a large, meticulously detailed scale model of the walled city as it appeared early in the 19th century. There's also the *Felix-Mendelssohn-Zimmer* (Felix Mendelssohn Room), including musical and personal memorabilia from the composer-conductor's 12 years in Leipzig (1835–47). Closed Mondays. Admission charge to the museum.

ALTE HANDELSBÖRSE (OLD MERCHANTS' EXCHANGE) Located behind the *Altes Rathaus,* this little jewel box of a building with a Baroque porch and rooftop balustrades was used as a local merchants' guild hall when it opened in 1687. It was sublet 200 years later for use as a meeting place for the city council and for banquets, concerts, and costume balls; today, it is still used for special events. It overlooks the Naschmarkt, a small city square. A statue of Goethe as a dapper *Universität Leipzig* law student stands in the center.

SACHSENPLATZ Before World War II, this was a large, densely populated segment of the Innenstadt; after being destroyed by Allied bombing, it was converted to a public plaza. Today, the tourist office is on the north side of the square, while the east side is flanked by a graceless building block from the same Communist period. Flower beds and fountains provide aesthetic relief, and there are plenty of benches for people watching. Along Katharinenstrasse (on the west side) is a row of splendidly restored patrician townhouses designed in the Baroque and Renaissance styles.

MÄDLERPASSAGE The best-known of Leipzig's passageways is a skylit gallery that fans out in three directions from a central rotunda linking a pair of trade-fair buildings. Twenty-five Meissen porcelain chimes decorate one wall near the rotunda. Dating from 1914, it has recently been renovated, with upscale boutiques moving into storefronts along its marble corridors. Two larger-than-life black statues inside the main entrance depict devilish episodes from Goethe's *Faust.* They're here because he set a scene of his drama downstairs in *Auerbachs Keller* (see *Eating Out*), thus making the basement restaurant famous for more than its fine food. The passageway's main entrance, where the two statues loom above the restaurant's double stairway, is on Grimmaische Strasse. Side entrances are on Neumarkt and Petersstrasse.

NEUES RATHAUS (NEW TOWN HALL) A gloomy gray monster of bridge-connected buildings, the municipal council's complex has been undergoing extensive renovation and restoration. The Saxon rulers' *Schloss Pleissenburg* (Pleissenburg Castle) once occupied the site, at the southwest corner of the long-gone city walls. Completed in 1905, this city hall—the largest in Germany—was designed to appear impregnable, complete with a watch-tower rising from the castle tower's original foundation. The overall design is an eclectic jumble of styles—late medieval, neo-Renaissance, and 20th-century *Jugendstil*—with turrets, parapets, balconies, and statues galore. Downstairs is a good, typical *Ratskeller* restaurant (phone: 123-6202). Closed weekends. No admission charge. Main entrances are on Lotterstrasse.

AUGUSTUSPLATZ Well-known for the political upheavals that have occurred here in the recent past, this largest of Leipzig's public squares (once called Karl-Marx-Platz) is also the city's most visible showplace of high culture, especially dramatic when the nighttime floodlights click on. In addition, the square presents a broad-ranging panorama of 20th-century architecture, including the rather severe, neoclassical *Opernhaus,* which opened in 1960, and *Universität Leipzig*'s knife-like administration tower, nicknamed the "Wisdom Tooth." The sole 19th-century remnant is the 1886 *Mendebrunnen* (Mende Fountain). A gift to the city from a wealthy Leipzig widow, the splashing concoction is topped by an obelisk surrounded by goddesses, angels, and winged horses.

NEUES GEWANDHAUS In 1781, Leipzig's orchestra moved into the cloth merchants' Gewandhaus (guild hall). About a century later, it moved into its second home, an acoustically acclaimed concert hall also called the *Gewandhaus.* When that auditorium was destroyed by World War II bombing, the orchestra had to move to yet a third *Gewandhaus,* where it has been ever since. This building features a forward-tilting design and an absence of right angles. Music critics have lavished praise upon it, saying its acoustics match those of the former hall. Completed opposite the *Opernhaus* on Augustusplatz in 1981, it features Europe's largest ceiling painting—by Sighard Gille, inspired by Mahler's *Song of the Earth*—in the multilevel foyer. At night the well-lit mural is visible to passersby on the Augustusplatz. Music director Kurt Masur's world class symphony orchestra performs in the Great Hall beneath a 6,650-pipe Schuke organ and a slogan in Latin: "Res severa verum gaudium," meaning "To provide pleasure is a very serious matter." A polychromatic statue of Beethoven (1902), sculpted in bronze, alabaster, marble, and amber by Leipzig's Max Klinger, broods on a throne in the foyer of the smaller chamber music hall. A statue of Mendelssohn, portraying the musician in a bizarre-looking, avant-garde style, was placed in front of the building in 1993, commemorating his founding of the *Hochschule für Musik und Theater* (Conservatory of Music and Theater) 150 years earlier. Guided tours of the building (in German) are given at 6 PM on Thursdays when a concert is not scheduled. Admission charge. 8 Augustuspl. (phone: 71320).

KROCHHOCHHAUS Built between 1927 and 1928, this gray 11-story high-rise (on the Goethestrasse side of Augustusplatz) became the world's tallest freestanding carillon when it was crowned with a pair of 10-foot mechanical *Glockenmänner* (bell ringers). Every 15 minutes throughout the day and night, they swing hammers to ring the bell.

BEYOND THE INNENSTADT

CLARA ZETKIN PARK The largest, most beautiful park in the city center, it lies on both sides of the Hochflut canal southwest of the Innenstadt. Under ongoing renovation after years of neglect, it features pathways, ponds, gazebos, arched footbridges, and wooded glens.

ROSENTAL PARK Located northwest of the city toward the suburb of Gohlis, this green space offers meadows and nature trails winding through thick forests. Here, too, is the *Zoologischer Garten* (Zoological Garden). Founded by Ernst Pinkert in 1878, it has since become a world-renowned breeding facility for lions, a longtime symbol of Leipzig. The park also features an on-site aquarium restored in neo-Baroque style, and a shark pool. Both zoo and aquarium are open daily; separate admission charges for each. 29 Pfaffendorfer Str. (phone: 711-1500).

BOTANISCHER GARTEN DER UNIVERSITÄT LEIPZIG (BOTANICAL GARDEN OF LEIPZIG UNIVERSITY) This garden just outside the Innenstadt is one of the world's oldest (it was established in 1877). Featured here is a wide variety of plants, trees, and flowers from all over the world, including some tropical varieties. Closed Saturdays; the greenhouses are open on Sundays only. Admission charge. 1 Linnestr. (phone: 685-8285).

MUSEUM DER BILDENDEN KÜNSTE (MUSEUM OF FINE ARTS) Its façade pockmarked by bullets and darkened by pollution, Leipzig's major art museum is a massive stone structure of neo-Renaissance style; its main architectural features are its huge dome and a statue representing "Truth," a holdover relic from the building's past life as the *Reichsgericht* (Germany's Supreme Court). It was here that Leipzig native Karl Liebknecht was sentenced to a year in prison for his anti-militaristic writings. Here, too, was the arson trial of former Bulgarian Communist leader Georgi Dimitrov, falsely accused by the Nazis of setting fire to Berlin's *Reichstag* in 1933. (Dimitrov outsmarted chief prosecutor Hermann Göring with a courageously anti-Fascist defense and was acquitted—a damaging propaganda setback for the Nazis.)

Converted to a museum in 1952, the building now houses many works of the 17th-century Dutch masters and an impressive array of early German paintings, including Lucas Cranach the Elder's *Adam and Eve* and his portrait of Martin Luther, Cranach the Younger's *Crucifixion of Christ,* and 19th-century works by Caspar David Friedrich, Ludwig Richter, Adolph Menzel, Max Liebermann, and Max Klinger. Klinger's polychromatic sculptures of *Salome* (1893) and *Cassandra* (1895) are particularly popular. In addition, the museum frequently offers special exhibitions of contemporary art, both in its galleries and in a central courtyard. Closed Mondays. Admission charge. 1 Dimitroffpl. (phone: 313102).

VÖLKERSCHLACHTSDENKMAL (BATTLE OF LEIPZIG MONUMENT) During the Battle of Leipzig (also known as the Battle of Nations), a four-day siege in October 1813, Napoleon's army fought against a unified force of Prussian, Austrian, Russian, and Swedish troops on farmlands southeast of Leipzig. The French were decisively defeated, which eventually led to Napoleon's abdication and his exile to Elba. In 1913, a building made of 300,000 tons of granite was dedicated to commemorate the battle. The structure was built in heavy *Jugendstil,* with a crypt and a *Kuppelhalle* (Vaulted Hall) in the dank inner chambers. The high-ceilinged *Kuppelhalle,* resonating with a 15-second echo, is used for choral concerts on Sunday mornings (the groups sing slowly to accommodate the echo). A visible chunk was blasted out of the monument on the southwest side by an American attack in April 1945. Guided tours (in German only) are given at 10:30 AM, and at 1:30 and 2:30 PM. Open daily. Admission charge. Prager Str. (phone: 80471).

RUSSISCHE KIRCHE (RUSSIAN MEMORIAL CHURCH) Another centenary monument of the Battle of Leipzig, this one was built in remembrance of the 22,000 Russian soldiers who died fighting Napoleon's forces. The most prominent feature of the church's exterior is a white-and-gold onion-dome tower in old Russian Novgorod style. The interior is decorated in 18th-century icons, cossack standards, and plaques. Semmelweisstr. (no phone).

DEUTSCHE BÜCHEREI (GERMAN LIBRARY) A national repository of all German-language books published since 1913, with nine million tomes, brochures, pamphlets, and manuals stored in a complex of buildings. The main, original structure was designed in an unlikely mixture of styles—early Italian Renaissance and late German *Jugendstil.* The library itself is open by appointment and only for academic research, but for a quiet spot to read, visit the hushed *Lesesaal* (Reading Hall), decorated in dark woodwork, with balconies and a mural of nudes. A bridge connects the library with the *Buch- und Schriftmuseum* (Museum of Books and Letters; see *Museums*). The *Lesesaal* is closed Sundays. 1 Deutscher Pl. (phone: 227-1324).

SCHILLERHAUS In mid-1785, Goethe's friend and literary colleague, Friedrich von Schiller, stayed in a farmhouse in the rustic village of Gohlis, now a suburb north of Leipzig. During his five-month sojourn, Schiller wrote the second act of his drama *Don Carlos* and the first draft of "Ode to Joy," a poetic text used by Beethoven for the choral movement of his *Ninth Symphony.* The house is now a museum of literary memorabilia and papers maintained by Leipzig's *Schiller Society.* Closed Sundays, Mondays, and Thursdays. Admission charge. 42 Menckestr., Gohlis (phone: 583187).

GOHLISER SCHLÖSSCHEN Located near *Schillerhaus,* this small Baroque-rococo castle behind a wrought-iron fence and gate was built in 1758 for city councillor and merchant Caspar Richter. Murals and ceiling frescoes in the ballroom were painted by Adam Friedrich Oeser, who was Goethe's professor when the university law student minored in art here. The castle is a major repository of Bach archives, and the *Oesersaal* ballroom is the setting for occasional chamber music concerts. Open daily. Admission charge. 23 Menckestr., Gohlis (phone: 585-2979).

Sources and Resources

TOURIST INFORMATION

Leipzig Touristen Information (Leipzig Tourist Information Office; 1 Sachsenpl.; phone: 795-9322; fax: 281854) is conveniently located in the Innenstadt; it's closed Sundays. There's always at least one English-speaking staff member on duty at the central information desk. The office is a good source of maps, brochures, accommodations listings, and general information about Leipzig and the vicinity (most at a small charge). Guided city tours are regularly scheduled, and concert and theater tickets can be purchased here as well.

LOCAL COVERAGE There are no English-language newspapers in Leipzig. Two monthly guides, *Leipzig im* (insert name of month) and *Visa Leipzig,* feature schedules of events, accommodations information, sightseeing highlights, shopping hints, museum listings, and orientation maps (a few sections of *Visa Leipzig* are in English). *Leipzig zu Fuss* (Leipzig on Foot; Forum; 30.80 DM/about $18.50), a German-language book of walking tours, is available at local bookstores.

TELEPHONE The city code for Leipzig is 341.

GETTING AROUND

AIRPORT *Flughafen Leipzig-Scheuditz* (Leipzig-Scheuditz Airport; phone: 391365), in Scheuditz (9 miles/15 km northwest of the city), handles domestic and European flights, including such destinations as London, Paris, Zurich, and Budapest. A cab ride from the airport to downtown takes about a half hour. *Flughafenzubringer* (phone: 271589) offers bus service from the airport to the main railroad station every half hour from 7:45 AM to 11 PM, and from the railroad station to the airport every half hour from 6 AM to 9 PM. The fare is 5 DM (about $3) one way.

BUS AND STREETCAR Leipzig's *LBV* public transit network is Germany's second-most extensive (after Berlin's). From its hub at the *Hauptbahnhof* (main railroad station) at Platz der Republik, streetcars travel on 13 lines, going from downtown to the distant suburbs. An easy-to-follow map is available from the tourist office. Tickets can be purchased at vending machines at stations. Fares range from .50 DM (about 30¢) to 1.50 DM (about 90¢), depending on the length of the ride; an additional ticket is required for each transfer. The best value is a 24-hour, unlimited-use ticket, which costs 4 DM (about $2.40).

CAR RENTAL The major international firms—*Hertz* (phone: 224-1801), *Avis* (phone: 391-1132), and *Sixt-Budget* (phone: 224-1868)—staff counters at the airport. *InterRent Europcar* is located both at the airport (phone: 224-1820) and the main railroad station (phone: 718-9300). Many downtown hotels can arrange car rentals.

TAXI There are cab stands outside the main railroad station's West Hall, and taxis are usually waiting at or near the downtown hotel entrances. For a radio cab, call 7411 or 79555.

TRAIN Each day, 800 trains pass through the enormous *Hauptbahnhof* (main train station; facing Platz der Republik; phone: 7240), en route to destinations throughout Germany and Europe (including an overnight sleeper train to Paris). From 1915 until 1934, the Saxon and Prussian railroads ran separate, simultaneous operations here. The station itself is the second-largest in the world (exceeded in size only by New York City's Grand Central Terminal).

SPECIAL EVENTS

Gewandhausfesttage, an annual nine-day classical music festival in early October, features performances by the *Gewandhausorchester* (Gewandhaus Orchestra), visiting ensembles, and virtuoso soloists. For seven days from late November into early December, Leipzig's international *Dokfest* of documentary and animated films is held at the *Capitol* cinema on Petersstrasse and in the *Grassi Museum* complex. Leipzig's traditional *Weihnachtsmarkt* (*Christmas* Market), centered on the Markt, begins at the end of November and lasts until December 22.

MUSEUMS

In addition to those listed in *Special Places,* the following are worth a visit. Several are located in the *Grassi Museum* complex, a group of buildings containing museums, a movie theater, and art exhibitions. Unless otherwise specified, all are closed Mondays and charge admission.

AGYPTISCHES MUSEUM (EGYPTOLOGY MUSEUM) *Universität Leipzig*'s collection includes 600 artifacts and mummy cases spanning 5,000 years, from 4000 BC to AD 1000. Closed Saturdays and Mondays. 6 Schillerstr. (phone: 282166).

BUCH- UND SCHRIFTMUSEUM (MUSEUM OF BOOKS AND LETTERS) Located in a bland, windowless Communist-era building attached to the *Deutsche Bücherei* (German Library), this century-old city institution provides a 5,000-year perspective on the history of writing and bookmaking. 1 Deutscher Pl. (phone: 227-1324).

MUSEUM FÜR DAS KUNSTHANDWERK (ARTS AND CRAFTS MUSEUM) Domestic handicrafts and decorative art from the Middle Ages to today, with emphasis on Saxon decorative arts and needlepoint. In the *Grassi Museum* complex. 5-11 Johannispl. (phone: 291-5435).

MUSEUM FÜR VÖLKERKUNDE (ETHNOLOGY MUSEUM) Exhibited here are examples of arts and crafts of Asian cultures, including the Near East, India, and the Chinese Ming Dynasty. Russian, African, and Oceanic ethnic groups also are represented. In the *Grassi Museum* complex. 2 Täubchenweg (entrance on Johannispl.; phone: 291041).

MUSIKINSTRUMENTEN MUSEUM (MUSICAL INSTRUMENTS MUSEUM) *Universität Leipzig*'s seven-room collection has 3,000 European-made instruments, some dating as far back as the mid-16th century. Among those displayed are the former piano of composer Clara Wieck Schumann (1830), Bach-era organs, 19th-century grand and player pianos, harpsichords, glass harmonicas, music boxes, and hurdy-gurdies. In the *Grassi Museum* complex. 2b Täubchenweg; the entrance is on Dresdner Str. (phone: 294685).

STASI MUSEUM Displayed in the former headquarters building of Leipzig's Stasi (secret-service police force) is a collection of uniforms, dossiers, electronic surveillance equipment, and other reminders of the city's Communist past. Closed Mondays and Tuesdays. No admission charge. 24 Dittrichring (phone: 294405).

VÖLKERSCHLACHTSDENKMAL AUSSTELLUNGSPAVILLON (BATTLE OF NATIONS PAVILION) The collection, across the street from the gigantic granite memorial, includes early 19th-century weapons, uniforms, maps, decorations, portraits of the commanders, and other memorabilia. The biggest attraction is a diorama of 8,000 tin soldiers and miniature cavalry replicas that simulates the battlefield as it looked on October 18, 1813 (the third day of the siege). Open daily. 210 Prager Str. in Wilhelm-Kulz-Park (phone: 80471).

SHOPPING

It hasn't taken Leipzigers long to get into the swing of consumerism. Top-quality German-made products and international brand-name merchandise can readily be found. Prime shopping thoroughfares in the Innenstadt are Petersstrasse and its extension, Hainstrasse, and the Grimmaische Strasse pedestrian zone between the Markt and Augustusplatz. The two major department stores are *Karstadt* (on Petersstr.; phone: 71720) and *Horten* (on the Brühl at Richard-Wagner-Pl.; phone: 79270). There also are a number of covered shopping passageways, the most stylish being *Mädlerpassage* (see *Special Places*), an ideal route for foul-weather window shopping. There's also a busy food and flower market on the Sachsenplatz every Tuesday and Friday from 8 AM to 5 PM. For standard shopping hours, see GETTING READY TO GO. The following are the best stores in the Innenstadt:

Antiquitäten A small, stuffed-to-the-rafters antiques shop. 8 Hainstr. (phone: 291329).

Euro-Schach & Spiel Chess sets, board games, playing cards, and puzzles. 12 Burgstr. (phone: 298866).

Franz-Mehring-Haus The city's largest bookstore, on the first two floors of a building alongside Augustusplatz. 3-5 Goethestr. (phone: 292645).

Heinrich Schneider Leipzig's most prestigious jewelry, watch, clock, and silverware shop, it's been in business since 1888. In the *Altes Rathaus* arcade on the Markt (phone: 292531).

Joh. Seb. Bach Classical records and sheet music from J. S. Bach and others, as well as musicians' biographies. 9-19 Neumarkt (phone: 200068).

Kaffee Richter Dark woodwork and whirring coffee grinders are the hallmarks of this aromatic heaven, which has been in operation here since 1879. Exotic blends of coffee and tea, plus marzipan, stollen, and biscuits are sold; standup tables allow for on-site sipping. 43 Petersstr. (phone: 281583).

MCM The initials stand for *Michael Cromer München,* a leading Bavarian designer of fine luggage, handbags, and other leather items. 1 Nikolaistr. (phone: 289363).

Meissen Porcelain On Sachsenplatz, the local retail store for Saxony's best-known consumer product, Dresden china. 19 Katharinenstr. (phone: 204130).

Musikalien-Antiquariat Leipzig's biggest and oldest store specializing in records, sheet music, books, and complete musical scores. It's located across from the *Thomaskirche.* 15 Thomaskirchhof (phone: 289406).

Zechendorf Arts and crafts, including ceramics, textiles, carved toys and figurines, straw goods, and wooden *Christmas* items from southern Saxony's Erzgebirge region. 14 Neumarkt (phone: 204193).

SPORTS AND FITNESS

BOWLING In a modernistic building near the university, *Bowlingtreff Leipzig* (Wilhelm-Leuschner-Pl.; phone: 287402) features 14 bowling lanes, as well as a billiard room, a bar, and a café.

FITNESS CENTERS *Fitnessclub* (30 Bienitzstr.; phone: 491346) includes a fully equipped gym, a solarium, and saunas. Many hotels in town also have fitness centers.

FOOTBALL The *Leipzig Lions,* a franchise in a professional European league that plays American-style football, battle opponents in the *FC Sachsen Stadion* (phone: 621-2736), just northeast of the Innenstadt, from September through December.

HORSE RACING Leipzig's *Rennbahn Scheibenholz* course (4 Wundtstr; phone: 310424) has been holding horse races for 128 years; its season starts in early spring and ends in late autumn.

JOGGING In *Clara Zetkin Park,* footbridges across the Hochflut canal connect downtown with 3 miles (5 km) of parkland trails. Farther north, *Rosental Park*'s meadows and woodlands are intertwined with 6 miles (10 km) of paths.

SOCCER Leipzig's two pro teams, *VfB* and *FC Sachsen,* play in the 100,000-seat *Central Stadium,* the largest in Germany and part of the city's vast *Sportforum* athletic complex. The stadium entrance is on Friedrich-Ebert-Strasse. For tickets, call *Fussball-Club Leipzig* (phone: 84757).

SWIMMING The city has 14 public indoor pools. Closest to downtown is *Schwimmhalle Mitte* (Kirschbergerstr.; phone: 52640). Kulkwitzer See, a manmade lake constructed at the former site of a coal mine in Markranstädt, on the city's western Grunau outskirts, is popular for outdoor swimming.

TENNIS Court time can be arranged at two clubs: *Tennisclub RC-Sport* (4 Ziegeleiweg; phone: 470474) and *Tennisschüle Big Point* (76-78 Friedrich-Ebert-Str.; phone: 717-9315).

THEATER

The *Leipziger Schauspielhaus* (1 Bosestr.; phone: 79220) stages a wide range of productions, from classical Goethe and Schiller to modern dramas and farce. Downstairs in the *Opernhaus,* the *Kellertheater* (12 Augustuspl.; phone: 71680) specializes in musicals, as does *Musikalische Komödie* (30 Dreilindenstr.; phone: 475286). *Neue Szene* (16 Gottschedstr.; phone: 7651) and *Theater der Kirche* (7 Otto-Schill-Str.; phone: 275292) both focus on modern and experimental offerings. During Erich Honecker's authoritarian regime, Leipzig attracted a great deal of attention for cabaret theaters with a nightly repertoire of outspoken political satire. The audacity continues today, with jabs at opportunistic West Germans, crass materialism, and, as usual, big government. The best of them are *academixer* (6 Kupfergasse; phone: 200849); *Pfeffermühle* (16 Thomaskirchhof; phone 295887); and a cellar cabaret, *Leipziger Funzel* (12-14 Nikolaistr.; phone 200604).

MUSIC

Conductor Kurt Masur of the *Gewandhausorchester* became an international advocate against violence in 1989, when he stood in front of the *Neues Gewandhaus* on Karl-Marx-Platz (now Augustusplatz) and declared, "No guns against the people!" Soon afterward, he became the music director of the *New York Philharmonic* and now divides his time between Leipzig and New York City. The orchestra and chorus perform primarily in the *Neues Gewandhaus,* but on special occasions they also appear in the city's two landmark churches, the *Thomaskirche* and the *Nikolaikirche* (see *Special Places*). Tickets can be purchased at the tourist office and at the concert hall (8 Augustuspl.; phone: 71320; fax: 713-2200). The *MDR (Mitteldeutscher Rundfunk)* radio orchestra and chorus perform at various venues, including the *Neues Gewandhaus,* the *Nikolaikirche,* and in the *Festsaal* of the *Altes Rathaus.* Its "home hall," though, is north of the city center in the *Rundfunkhaus* (22-24 Springerstr.; phone: 51151). An Innenstadt ticket office for *MDR* events is located in the *Romanushaus* (23 Katharinenstr.; phone: 566-3552). Ask at the tourist office for the concert schedules of two classical music groups with distinguished histories: the *Hochschüle für Musik und Theater* and the university's *Pauliner Kammerchor.*

Staples at the acoustically fine *Opernhaus* (12 Augustuspl.; phone: 291036; fax: 716-8387) are bold productions of the *Ring* cycle and other Wagnerian standards, as well as Italian and Russian operas and ballet. You can get tickets at the tourist office or the box office of the *Opernhaus.* The *Thomaskirche* is the home of weekly *Thomanerchor* motets and cantatas; there also are organ recitals at the *Nikolaikirche.* Recital, chamber music, and choral venues include the *Bosehaus,* the *Alte Handelsbörse,* the *Altes Rathaus,* the *Gohliser Schlösschen*'s *Oesersaal,* and the *Kuppelhalle* inside the *Völkerschlachtsdenkmal* (see *Special Places* for all).

NIGHTCLUBS AND NIGHTLIFE

Leipzig's biggest and trendiest nightspot is *Tanzpalast Schauspielhaus* (1 Bosestr.; phone: 281023), whose two floors include a disco, six bars, a billiard room, and a restaurant—all open until 4 AM. For folk music, progressive rock, and Wednesday-night disco, the college crowd congregates in the underground vaults of *Moritzbastei* (9 Universitätstr.; phone: 292332), which once were part of the city wall fortifications. About 3 miles (5 km) west of the Innenstadt, *Boccaccio* (43 Kurt-Eisner-Str.; phone: 292828) features jazz, dance music, and cabaret acts. An Innenstadt dance club popular with all age groups is *Esplanade* (10 Richard-Wagner-Str.; phone: 282330); discos that are popular with university students include *Club 21* (20a Dittrichring; phone: 718-4203), *College Club* (16 Ritterstr.; phone: 292879), and *Manhattan Inn* (17 Elsbethstr.; phone: 52330). Intimate, quiet bars in the city center include *Bachstüb'l* (12 Thomaskirchhof; phone: 291062), *Bierstube* (11-13 Kolonnadenstr.; phone: 287924), *Pfeffermühlen Club* (16 Thomaskirchhof; phone: 292828), and *Tivoli* (13 Katharinenstr.; phone: 200323). There are casinos featuring roulette, baccarat, blackjack, and slot machines at the *Inter-Continental* (open daily from 7 PM until dawn) and at the *Stadt Leipzig* (open 1 PM until dawn); see *Checking In* for both. You must be at least 18 years old to gamble; a passport is required.

Best in Town

CHECKING IN

As is true throughout Eastern Europe, there are not enough high-quality and medium-range accommodations to meet the increasing demand that has followed the fall of Communism, so book well in advance. (Enterprising capitalists, however, are converting century-old flats in outlying areas into small properties.) Because trade fairs are held in the city throughout the year, there is virtually no low season. The tourist office (see *Tourist Information*) has information on room availability and can make reservations. Most of Leipzig's major hotels have complete facilities for the business traveler. Those hotels listed as having "business services" usually offer such conveniences as an English-speaking concierge, meeting rooms, photocopiers, computers, translation services, and express checkout, among others. Call the hotel for additional information. At hotels classified as expensive, expect to pay more than $185 per night for a double room (including breakfast, private bath, telephone, and TV set, unless otherwise indicated); $150 to $185 at moderate places; and less than $150 at inexpensive ones. All telephone numbers are in the 341 city code unless otherwise indicated.

EXPENSIVE

Deutschland A 281-room property that's made an impressive transition from its previous life as the *Am Ring* in the former GDR's *Interhotel* chain, this place is conveniently located across from Augustusplatz and the *Gewandhaus* concert hall. Though squarish and unromantic on the outside, its interior is attractive and comfortable. Each room has all the usual amenities, including a mini-bar; some have splendid views of the public square and city skyline. Parking is available for a modest per-night charge. The lobby area includes a bar, off of which is the skylit *Orangerie,* which is mainly used for group functions. The upscale *Serenade* grill attracts a cosmopolitan clientele. Business services are available. 5-6 Augustuspl. (phone: 21460; fax: 289165).

Inter-Continental This 450-room property is the leading modern luxury hotel in town. Features include an English-speaking concierge, a bar, lounges, and a gift shop. The high-ceilinged lobby gleams with cool Italian marble, and rooms are lavishly furnished and beautifully decorated, with marble bathrooms and mini-bars. There's a casino; a fitness club with an indoor pool, a solarium, saunas, and massage rooms; and a bowling alley. Prized among its four fine dining rooms is the *Brühl* (see *Eating Out*), while the top-floor *Club 27* has panoramic city views. Business services are available. 16 Gerberstr. (phone: 7990; 800-327-0200; fax: 799-1229).

Maritim Astoria For the best in terms of Old World gentility and comfort, this member of the upscale chain is favored by both trade-fair attendees and leisure travelers. Fortunately spared severe destruction during World War II bombing, the main six-story sandstone structure next to the railroad station was built early in this century; a postwar addition brought the room total to 323. Porcelain table lamps and lace curtains make the public areas elegant and attractive. Recent renovations include modern bathrooms with tubs and showers, up-to-date furnishings, and a fitness center, a solarium, and a sauna. In addition, all rooms have plenty of luxury amenities, including mini-bars. The *Galerie* dining room is first-rate (see *Eating Out*), while the street-front *City* restaurant features an exceptionally big breakfast buffet. There's also the atmospheric *Astoria-Club* bar. Other amenities include business services and garage parking. 2 Pl. der Republik (phone: 72220; 800-843-3311; fax: 722-4747).

Stadt Leipzig The only hotel located inside the ring-road loop is a 352-room holdover from the mid-1960s, when it catered mainly to tour groups from neighboring Eastern Bloc countries. Since then, facilities have been upgraded, and no property has a more central location. Pedestrian underpasses beneath Platz der Republik lead to the railroad station, and the *Opernhaus* and Sachsenplatz are a block away. Amenities include meeting rooms, a casino, a bar, a sauna, a whirlpool, and a solarium. The *Brogilius* restaurant serves well-prepared Saxon specialties. 1-5 Richard-Wagner-Pl. (phone: 214-5741; fax: 214-5300).

MODERATE

Corum Formerly the *Zum Löwen,* a drab GDR-era hotel, this property across from the railroad station has been completely renovated and reopened under a new name. The 121 rooms have been charmingly decorated with cherrywood furniture and pastel fabrics; amenities include mini-bars, in-room safes, marble baths, and hair dryers. There is also a health club, business services, a lobby bar, and the *Partout* restaurant, which serves light continental fare. 3 Rudolf-Breitscheid-Str. (phone: 125-1000; fax: 125-10100).

Deutscher Hof A good example of the private, small hotels that are blossoming in neighborhoods beyond the Innenstadt, this four-story, turn-of-the-century place offers 37 cozy rooms and a large suite, all well appointed with modern baths, tasteful furniture, radios, and windows looking out onto the tree-lined street. There's a good restaurant, an abundant breakfast buffet, and a pleasant cellar pub. The location, about 2 miles (3 km) northwest of downtown, is near Leipzig's sprawling *Sportforum.* The south side of *Rosental Park* is within easy walking distance. 31-33 Waldstr. (phone: 295050; fax: 286076).

Lindenau Another small hostelry in a building that's been restored inside and out, this four-story Best Western affiliate at a streetcar stop west of downtown has 38 well-furnished rooms—two with Jacuzzis. There are both smoking and nonsmoking rooms, and each has either a bathtub or a shower—not both. Other features include a sauna, a brightly colored breakfast room, and—an amenity rare in the renovated neighborhood spots—an elevator. The proprietor speaks English. Parking is in the rear. There's no restaurant, but the *Uhland Café* restaurant is across the street, as is a good bakery. 33 Georg-Schwarz-Str. (phone: 448-0310; 800-528-1234; fax: 448-0300).

Nestor Tucked away on a residential side street (across from a historic Lutheran church), this four-story modern property, built from scratch several years ago, is a rarity in a city of restored buildings. There are 81 modern rooms and suites, each with a tub and shower, and a mini-bar. Amenities include an elevator, a garage, and business services. Breakfast and dinner are served to guests only. Located about a mile (1.6 km) north of the city center. 15a Gräfestr. (phone: 59630; fax: 596-3113).

Zum Goldenen Adler Once a back-street 1906 tavern, this place has been transformed into a stylish hostelry with black-and-white Bauhaus-type furnishings and decor. The 19 large rooms are charmingly decorated with fresh flowers. The tiny lobby bar is popular with local residents, and the adjacent breakfast room is charming. There is no restaurant, however. Located about a mile (1.6 km) northeast of the city center. 10 Portlitzer Str. (phone: 688-0976; fax: 66326).

INEXPENSIVE

Bayrischer Hof A few blocks from the main railroad station, this economical choice lacks private baths (showers are down the hall), but few places are closer to the city center, or quieter at night. (It's located on the corner of a shopping strip that closes at sundown.) Housed in a 1920s building, the hotel has 45 clean and well-appointed rooms (if a bit small). The staff is friendly and helpful. Breakfast is served in the adjoining Italian restaurant, *Michele.* 13 Wintergartenstr. (phone/fax: 209251).

Continental Housed in a 1911 *Jugendstil* building with bulging curves and iron grillwork, this hotel, across the ring road from the railroad station's East Hall, offers 52 rooms with small balconies; some also have bay windows. Furnishings are bland, blond-veneer pieces from the mid-GDR period. Rooms have either tubs or showers, as well as radios. Public areas include a lobby bar with stained glass and much red plush, a lounge, and the *Arcata* restaurant. Two salons are available for private gatherings. 13 Georgiring (phone: 216590; fax: 216-59210).

Leipziger Vereinshaus What looks like a low-rise office building on a woebegone back street is actually a reasonably priced, pension-type, offbeat hotel. The 33 rooms are clean and fairly large, with light brown furniture, showers, and mini-bars. The restaurant is mediocre, but the breakfast buffets are good and ample. With its own movie theater and lounge and business services, it's a good place for both working and playing. Located southwest of the ring road, within walking distance of Augustusplatz. 5-9 Seeburgerstr. (phone: 287513; fax: 292125).

Plagwitz A small (17 rooms) hotel west of downtown, located off a main thoroughfare in a mixed residential-industrial district. Set in a restored building, the property has blond-wood furnishings in the guestrooms, a homey breakfast room (but no restaurant), and parking in front. 10 Weissenfelser Str. (phone: 479-6035; fax: 479-6055).

Schilling This mustard-colored 1911 building, Leipzig's first to be transformed into a private hotel after reunification, is close to a park and shops, cafés, and bakeries on nearby streets. All 33 rooms are equipped with the usual amenities; some also have mini-bars. In addition, there's a sauna and parking. All meals are served in the low-key *Alt Connewitz* restaurant. In the Connewitz district, about 3 miles (5 km) south of downtown via the No. 11 streetcar. 47A Meusdorfer Str. (phone/fax: 312364).

EATING OUT

While the business visitors attracted by the many trade fairs here made Leipzig an above-average restaurant city in the days of the GDR, the best food was found mostly in hotel dining rooms. This is no longer the case, as many exceptional private eateries have opened in the past few years. A popular local dish is *Leipziger Allerlei,* a blend of peas, carrots, cauliflower, asparagus, mushrooms, crayfish tails, dumplings, and bits of veal; other Saxony specialties include *Kartoffelsuppe* (potato soup) with sausages, bacon bits, and parsley, and *Quarkkeulchen,* a baked appetizer made from boiled potatoes, flour, sugar, and raisins, topped with cinnamon and served with a side dish of cream-topped applesauce. Reudnitzer is the main local beer, but certain establishments serve lighter, frothier Leipziger Gose beer as well. Dinner for two without drinks and wine (but including tax and service charge) will cost $75 or more in establishments classified as expensive, $35 to $75 at places described as moderate, and less than $35 at restaurants in the inexpensive category. Although the service charge is included in the bill, you should leave a few extra marks if you receive very good service. Unless otherwise noted, restaurants are open for lunch and dinner. All telephone numbers arc in the 341 city code unless otherwise indicated.

EXPENSIVE

Apels Garten Off the Innenstadt's beaten track, yet only a short walk west of the ring-road loop, this place serves some of the best Saxony specialties in town. The service is first-rate, the meals innovatively prepared, and the soft lighting and elegant decor create a romantic atmosphere. Open daily. Reservations necessary. Major credit cards accepted. 2 Kolonnadenstr. (phone: 285093).

Auerbachs Keller Leipzig's most famous restaurant has been a university students' cellar hangout ever since it opened in 1530. One of these scholars, Goethe, set a *Faust* episode here, in which the bedeviled doctor and Mephistopheles first meet, engage in a debate, then zoom out astride a wine barrel. Murals illustrating scenes from the drama decorate the walls, and the cellar's original appearance has been faithfully reconstructed. Specialties include regional German dishes. A good Sunday brunch is served. Open daily.

Reservations advised. Major credit cards accepted. 2-4 *Mädlerpassage* (phone: 216-1040).

Brühl Chef Frank Baumbach of the *Inter-Continental* hotel's prized dining room is renowned for his innovative regional and continental fare, including fried saddle of venison, simmered in red wine sauce, accompanied by sautéed pears and potato croquettes. The decor is modern, chic, and elegant, with dark wood paneling, plants, and chandeliers. The wine list—Leipzig's longest—offers vintages from the Napa Valley, France, Spain, and Italy. Open daily. Reservations necessary. Major credit cards accepted. 16 Gerberstr. (phone: 7990).

Erdener Treppchen Flowery arbors arch over the center row of tables, and delicate tiles that resemble Delft cover the back wall of this corner restaurant. Homemade soups, clear oxtail among them, are a mainstay. The most popular choices are breast of duck with blackberries, followed by a Saxon dessert specialty: cream-smothered *Pflaumenkuchen* (plum cake). Open daily. Reservations unnecessary. Major credit cards accepted. 26 Neumarkt (phone: 209560).

Galerie The first-rate dining room of the *Maritim Astoria* hotel is well known for its fine preparations of meat, especially rack of lamb cooked in a delicate herb sauce; the menu includes vegetarian offerings as well. The classic decor of Chippendale furniture, oil paintings in gilt frames, and beaded crystal chandeliers creates an elegant atmosphere. Open daily for dinner only. Reservations necessary. Major credit cards accepted. 2 Pl. der Republik (phone: 72220).

Gasthaus des Meeres Despite their city's landlocked location, Leipzigers crave well-prepared seafood, and this downtown establishment caters to that need. The menu features exceptional presentations of prawns, North German Matjes herring, and freshwater perch, trout, salmon filets, and *Steinbutt* (turbot), which are flown in fresh each morning. Open daily. Reservations unnecessary. Major credit cards accepted. 1 Pfaffendorfer Str. (phone: 291160).

Paulaner-Palais What used to be an ordinary-looking place with a downstairs tavern has been glamorously reborn as the focal point of a major restoration project. The restaurant now occupies the street-level floors of two attached buildings—one in Biedermeier style, the other a 1753 Baroque beauty painted yellow with white trim. Menu choices offer heaping portions of Bavarian, Saxon, Austrian, and Italian specialties; try the pork medallions in a wild mushroom sauce. Open daily; brunch served on Sundays. Reservations advised. Major credit cards accepted. 3-5 Klostergasse (phone: 211-3115).

Pfeiffer's Weinstuben Not just another local wine restaurant, this place steers clear of Saxon dishes in favor of Alsatian and Swabian recipes such as *Maultaschen* (oversize raviolis with various types of fillings) and *Spätzle* (short, thick noodles usually served as a side dish). For a real change of pace, try the spicy Mexican filet of beef with rice and kidney beans. Open daily. Reservations advised after 8 PM. No credit cards accepted. 6 Dittrichring (phone: 281323).

Stadtpfeiffer (City Piper) Favored by musicians and concertgoers, this pricey place in the west wing of the *Gewandhaus* features unusual delicacies such as calf's tongue with lentil salad and medallions of sturgeon with white wine sauce. The wine list includes German, French, and Italian vintages. Closed Sundays. Reservations necessary (book well in advance if you want a pre-theater dinner). Major credit cards accepted. 8 Augustuspl. (phone: 286494).

Thüringer Hof With carved Gothic doors, arched ceilings, blackened woodwork, and ornamental wrought-iron details, the decor is in stark contrast to the simple, yet bountiful meals. The menu includes sauerbraten with red cabbage and dumplings (Thuringian-style), and pork sausages with onions, hash brown potatoes, and vegetables. Open daily. Reservations advised. Major credit cards accepted. 19 Burgstr. (phone: 209884).

MODERATE

Café am Brühl Located in a restored 18th-century building with a classical façade, this place is both a pastry café and a family-run restaurant. Salads are excellent, and a house specialty is fish potpourri, blending salmon, halibut, and shrimp. For dessert: chocolate tortes and creamy éclairs. Open daily. Reservations unnecessary. Major credit cards accepted. 1 Richard-Wagner-Pl. (phone: 291424).

Goldener Drache The Chinese food is typical, but the special ambience—candlelight in a little glass pavilion—makes this place unusually intimate and romantic. Particularly good dishes are the chicken or beef chop suey; there's also a friendly bar. Open daily. No reservations. Major credit cards accepted. Am Hallischen Tor (phone: 211-5094).

Libretto The alfresco terrace of this brasserie-bistro at the rear of the *Opernhaus* overlooks the swan lake and park. Chicken dishes and steaks are good and affordable and the bar is a pre- and post-performance gathering place. Open daily. Reservations advised. Major credit cards accepted. 12 Augustuspl. (phone: 716833).

Medici Leafy potted plants give a Mediterranean feel to this small, casual spot next to the *Nikolaikirche.* The menu offers tasty Italian specialties; one of the best dishes is *saltimbocca alla Romana* (veal and ham braised in wine). Open daily. Reservations advised. Major credit cards accepted. 5 Nikolaikirchof (phone: 211-3878).

Mövenpick The upscale Swiss chain arrived in Leipzig three years ago. Housed in a 15th-century building, this informal eatery offers pasta, sandwiches, salads, and pastries. The breakfast buffet is one of the best in town. You can help yourself at a counter or be served at a table. Open daily. No reservations. Major credit cards accepted. 1-3 Naschmarkt (phone: 211-7722).

Neptun A small, clean, seafood place with a nautical blue-and-white color scheme and a predominantly local clientele. It's worth the short trek from the Innenstadt on the streetcar. Open daily. Reservations advised. Major credit cards accepted. 4B Eisenbahnstr. (phone: 694982).

Ohne Bedenken A thoroughly old-style tavern in a 1905 building in suburban Gohlis, this place is best known as the "home" of Leipzig's light Gose beer and for its big, hearty helpings of Saxon dishes. In warm weather, its backyard beer garden offers outdoor seating and "oom-pah" music. It's very popular with trade-fair attendees. Open for dinner only; closed October through April. Reservations necessary. Major credit cards accepted. 5 Menckestr. (phone: 55734).

Pastarella Near the railroad station and Sachsenplatz, this popular Italian eatery adorned with potted plants and fake Tiffany lamps serves flavorful pasta, along with cups of espresso and cappuccino. Open daily. Reservations unnecessary. Major credit cards accepted. 10 Richard-Wagner-Str. (phone: 281438).

Plovdiv Bulgarian fare, most notably goulash with brussels sprouts and potatoes, is served here; there's also a convivial bar. Ask to be seated in the rear dining area, which is quieter than the main room. Open daily. Reservations advised. Major credit cards accepted. 17 Katharinenstr. (phone: 209227).

Regina Weinstuben Warmed by a tile stove in winter, this cozy spot in a central location is one of the city's oldest and most charming wine restaurants. Weekend piano music is featured, as are east German wines from Saxony and Saxony-Anhalt. Open for dinner only; closed Sundays. Reservations advised. Major credit cards accepted. 14 Hainstr. (phone: 282052).

Varadero A bona fide Cuban restaurant, with palms, straw wall hangings, ceiling fans, Havana travel posters, and photos of Fidel Castro. Try the *camarones fritos* (fried shrimp) for an appetizer, then *pavo* (turkey) garnished with fruit and ginger for the main course. Open daily. Reservations advised. No credit cards accepted. 8 Barfussgässchen (phone: 281686).

Zill's Tunnel Hannelore Melitzer runs a reasonably priced, long-established *Bier- und Weinstuben* at street level, below a small wine restaurant that serves a traditional *Leipziger Allerlei.* Saxony's Elbtal vintages dominate the wine list. Open daily. Reservations advised. Major credit cards accepted. 9 Barfussgässchen (phone: 200446).

Zwiebelchen A bustling, casual presence on the Innenstadt restaurant scene, it offers sandwiches, soup, and full-course Saxon meals with wine. Open daily. No reservations. No credit cards accepted. In the heart of the shopping district. 1-3 Petersstr. (phone: 211-4571).

INEXPENSIVE

Milchbar Pinguin Italian-style ice cream (similar to gelato) is popular all over Germany, and this very popular *Milchbar* (ice-cream parlor) serves 24 different flavors of it, as well as a variety of beverages. Open daily. No reservations. No credit cards accepted. 4 Katharinenstr. (phone: 241808).

Nordsee und Nudelmacher *Nordsee,* a cafeteria-style eatery, is the best value downtown for delicious seafood, cooked to order. Try the paella, which mixes Alaska salmon with clams, chicken, and rice. *Nudelmacher,* a pizza-pasta emporium, shares the same space. Both are open daily. No reservations or credit cards accepted at either place. 37 Petersstr. (phone: 211-7772).

Zum Goldbroiler A bistro-style eatery on a narrow shopping street near the Brühl, it serves fresh fish, fowl, and meat dishes with smooth Saxon Ur-Krostitzer beer. Closed Sundays. Reservations unnecessary. Major credit cards accepted. 17-19 Hainstr. (phone: 281964).

KAFFEE KLATCHES

Given to making frequent stops for *Kaffee und Kuchen* (coffee and cakes), Leipzigers live up to their nickname, "the coffee Saxons." Among the sinfully delicious delights offered at local coffeehouses are *Leipziger Lerchen* (Leipzig larks) marzipan sweets, gingerbread cakes, *Alt Leipzig* praline confections, *Bienenstich* ("bee sting") honey almond tortes, and *Blätterteiggebäck* (puff pastries). Most of these places also offer inexpensive light meals. Favorite coffee spots include *Cather* (15 Katharinenstr.; phone: 200243); *Centra* (26 Petersstr.; phone: 281726); *Colonnade* (22 Kolonnadenstr.; phone: 287621); *Concerto* (13 Thomaskirchhof; phone: 204343); *Corso* (2 Neumarkt; phone: 282233); *de Saxe* (11-15 Markt; phone: 293717); *Mephisto* (in the *Mädlerpassage;* phone: 2165-1082); and *Ring-Galerie* (4 Dittrichring; phone: 216-2015).

The city's oldest and most famous coffeehouse has got to be *Zum Kaffeebaum,* at 4 Kleine Fleischergasse; founded in 1694, it counted the likes of Bach, Goethe, Schiller, Richard Wagner, Franz Liszt, and Robert and Clara Schumann among its regular customers. Unfortunately, the little eatery has gone out of business amid complications over its ownership. At press time, however, there was continuing speculation that it might reopen. It's definitely worth checking, if only to see *Zum Kaffeebaum*'s trademark sculpture of a turbaned Turk lounging beneath a *Kaffeebaum* (coffee tree), which still adorns the doorway of the building.

Munich

Bavaria is a place apart from the rest of Germany; gayer, more rosy-cheeked, less Teutonic. And Munich, the principal city of this southern region in the lap of the Bavarian Alps, is one of the jolliest cities in all Europe. It is renowned for two of the wildest, noisiest, fun-filled festivals anywhere. During *Oktoberfest* each year (which begins in September, oddly enough), hundreds of thousands of Germans and tourists celebrate the wedding of Crown Prince Ludwig to Princess Therese von Sachsen-Hildburghausen. The fact that the wedding took place in 1810 doesn't deter the crowd's enthusiasm one bit. Then, about four months later, *Müncheners* go on another binge, called *Fasching.* Traditionally, all sorts of bizarre behavior is acceptable—and usually takes place—during this carnival season, preceding *Lenten* abstinence.

Even when there is no formal festival taking place, this is the beer capital of the world. Germans guzzle more beer than the people of any other country: 150 liters per person per year. But the Bavarians do even better, downing 280 liters apiece annually.

The thing that makes Munich so special, however, is that it is able to combine this earnest lust for life with modern sophistication. There is a pleasing blend of elegance and rustic charm, the naughty and the nice, here. Bavarian beer gardens and folk art coexist with high fashion, grand opera, and astrophysics, giving rise to such nicknames as "Village of a Million," and "Metropolis with a Heart."

A cultural and intellectual center, Munich has produced the largest number of German Nobel Prize winners; it is the home of the respected *Bayerische Staatsoper* (Bavarian State Opera), more than 60 legitimate theaters and cabarets, and important scientific institutes; and it is the second-largest university city in Germany, with more than 100,000 students in residence.

Statistics show that only one in three of Munich's 1.3 million citizens was born here, and one in 10 come from outside Germany. But it's not surprising that this cosmopolitan center that manages to retain such a strong Alpine village flavor would be so attractive to outsiders.

During the past 830-odd years, Munich has grown up along the banks of the Isar River, which flows down from the Bavarian Alps through forest and farmland before cutting a determined path through the eastern part of the city on its way to meet the Danube. On very clear days, the Alps, some 50 miles away, provide a stunning backdrop for the city.

Munich (München in German) takes its name from the monks, *Munichen* in Middle High German, who founded a Benedictine monastery in this area in the 9th century. The city itself was established beside the Isar River in 1158 by Henry the Lion, Duke of Saxony, who had been ceded part of

Bavaria by Emperor Friedrich Barbarossa. But in 1180 Barbarossa replaced Duke Henry with the Palatine Count Otto von Wittelsbach. From that time, the House of Wittelsbach was linked closely to Bavaria's and Munich's fortunes until the monarchy was replaced by a republic after World War I.

Toward the middle of the 19th century, Bavarian King Ludwig I put much of his energy into making Munich the most beautiful city in Europe. It was during his reign that many of the city's great buildings were erected and Ludwigstrasse was built. However, the king was forced to abdicate in 1848 when the scandal of his liaison with Lola Montez, a Spanish dancer, lent fuel to a revolutionary movement. His grandson, Ludwig II, who became king in 1864 at the age of 18, carried out an even more grandiose building scheme. He ordered the construction of three extravagant castles and commissioned an array of phantasmagoria ranging from a boat in the shape of a huge shell to furniture, porcelain, and robes. Often called "the Dream King" and "Mad King Ludwig," Ludwig II was much loved by his subjects, but court doctors declared him to be in an "advanced stage of mental disorder" and he was stripped of his powers shortly before he died by drowning at the age of 40; whether his death was accident, suicide, or murder remains a mystery.

After Germany's defeat in World War I, Munich was the center of the Nazi movement. Adolf Hitler and his National Socialists made an abortive attempt to seize power here in 1923 during the infamous Beer Garden Putsch. In 1938, Mussolini, Chamberlain, and Daladier met here with Hitler and agreed to let Germany annex the Sudetenland.

Much of the city was destroyed in bombing raids during World War II, but unlike some of its sister cities, Munich eschewed the modern and reconstructed its past. Except for the space-age architecture of the suburban *Olympiapark* (Olympic Park), built for the 1972 summer games, and the *Gasteig* cultural center, Munich looks like a typical old European city. In some cases, original plans were used in the reconstruction or restoration of Munich landmarks. Today the city's public buildings reflect the many styles in which they were built over the centuries: late Gothic, Venetian Renaissance, neoclassical, rococo, and Baroque. Church spires and bell towers, rather than high-rise office buildings, dominate the skyline.

Modern Munich is many things: an Old World city; a center of culture and sophistication; a city of gaiety; an intellectual center; and, with all its beer, wurst, and *Gemütlichkeit* (good cheer), a carnival of life.

Munich At-a-Glance

SEEING THE CITY

An exceptional view of Munich and the Bavarian Alps is available from the *Olympiaturm* (Olympic Tower), located just northwest of the city at *Olympiapark.* The 951-foot television tower was erected to facilitate tele-

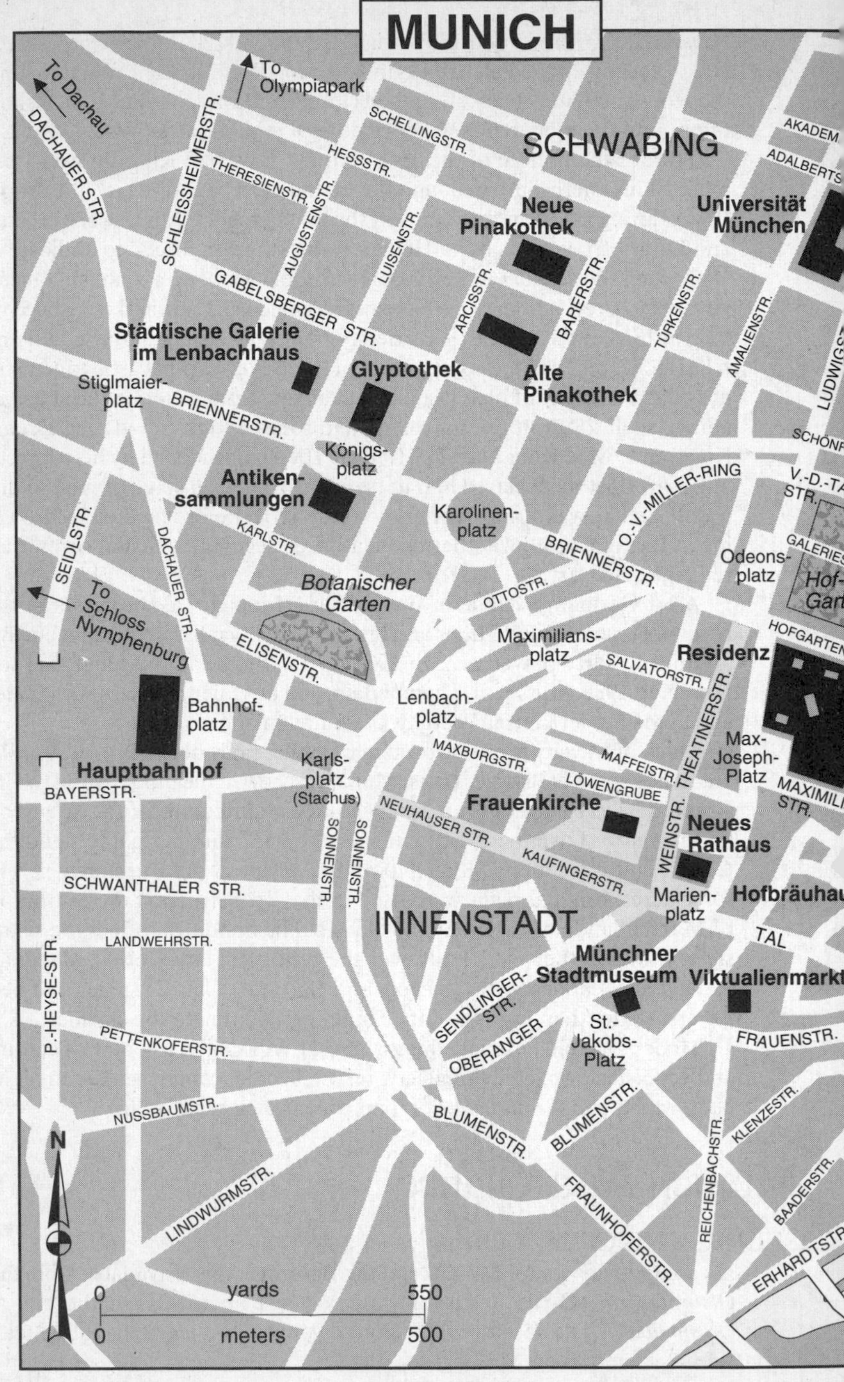
MUNICH
To Dachau
To Olympiapark
DACHAUER STR.
SCHLEISSHEIMERSTR.
THERESIENSTR.
HESSSTR.
SCHELLINGSTR.
SCHWABING
AKADEM
ADALBERTS
AUGUSTENSTR.
LUISENSTR.
Neue Pinakothek
Universität München
GABELSBERGER STR.
ARCISSTR.
BARERSTR.
TÜRKENSTR.
AMALIENSTR.
LUDWIGS
Städtische Galerie im Lenbachhaus
Glyptothek
Alte Pinakothek
Stiglmaier-platz
BRIENNERSTR.
Königs-platz
SCHÖNF
Antiken-sammlungen
O.-V.-MILLER-RING
V.-D.-TA STR.
Karolinen-platz
KARLSTR.
SEIDLSTR.
DACHAUER STR.
BRIENNERSTR.
Odeons-platz
GALERIES
Hof-Gart
Botanischer Garten
OTTOSTR.
To Schloss Nymphenburg
ELISENSTR.
Maximilians-platz
HOFGARTEN
Residenz
SALVATORSTR.
Bahnhof-platz
Lenbach-platz
THEATINERSTR.
Max-Joseph-Platz
MAXBURGSTR.
MAFFEISTR.
Hauptbahnhof
Karls-platz (Stachus)
LÖWENGRUBE
MAXIMILIA STR.
BAYERSTR.
Frauenkirche
NEUHAUSER STR.
WEINSTR.
Neues Rathaus
SONNENSTR.
KAUFINGERSTR.
SCHWANTHALER STR.
Marien-platz
Hofbräuhau
INNENSTADT
LANDWEHRSTR.
TAL
P.-HEYSE-STR.
Münchner Stadtmuseum
Viktualienmarkt
SENDLINGER-STR.
St.-Jakobs-Platz
PETTENKOFERSTR.
OBERANGER
FRAUENSTR.
NUSSBAUMSTR.
BLUMENSTR.
KLENZESTR.
N
REICHENBACHSTR.
LINDWURMSTR.
FRAUNHOFERSTR.
BAADERSTR.
ERHARDTSTR.
0 yards 550
0 meters 500

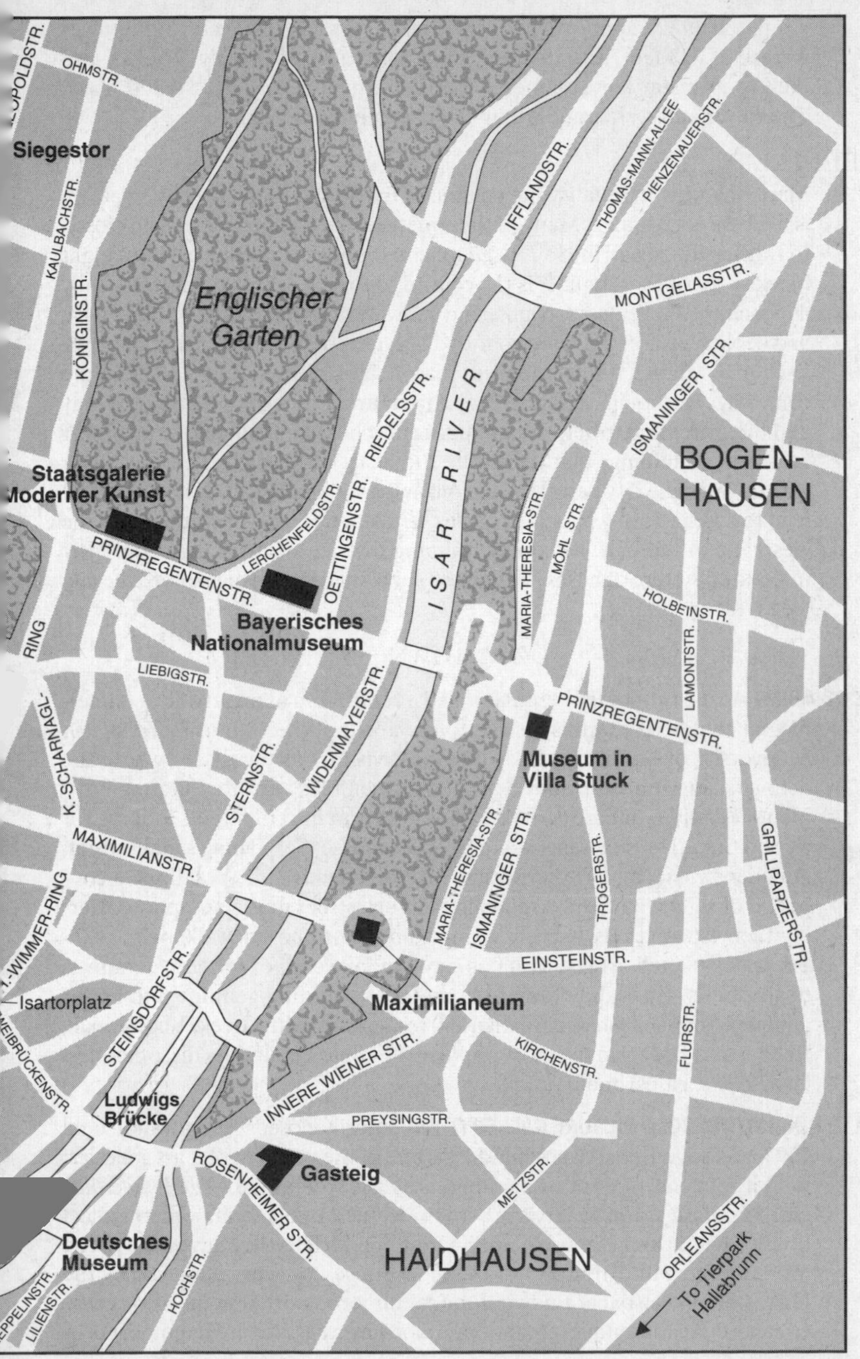
OHMSTR.
Siegestor
KAULBACHSTR.
KÖNIGINSTR.
Englischer
Garten
IFFLANDSTR.
THOMAS-MANN-ALLEE
PIENZENAUERSTR.
MONTGELASSTR.
ISMANINGER STR.
RIEDELSSTR.
ISAR RIVER
BOGEN-
HAUSEN
Staatsgalerie
Moderner Kunst
LERCHENFELDSTR.
OETTINGENSTR.
MARIA-THERESIA-STR.
MÖHL STR.
PRINZREGENTENSTR.
HOLBEINSTR.
Bayerisches
Nationalmuseum
RING
LIEBIGSTR.
LAMONTSTR.
K.-SCHARNAGL-
WIDENMAYERSTR.
PRINZREGENTENSTR.
Museum in
Villa Stuck
STERNSTR.
MAXIMILIANSTR.
MARIA-THERESIA-STR.
ISMANINGER STR.
TROGERSTR.
GRILLPARZERSTR.
STEINSDORFSTR.
EINSTEINSTR.
Isartorplatz
Maximilianeum
INNERE WIENER STR.
KIRCHENSTR.
FLURSTR.
Ludwigs
Brücke
PREYSINGSTR.
ROSENHEIMER STR.
Gasteig
METZSTR.
Deutsches
Museum
HAIDHAUSEN
ORLEANSSTR.
To Tierpark
Hallabrunn
HOCHSTR.
LILIENSTR.

vising the *1972 Summer Olympics.* An elevator will take you to the tower terrace at 623 feet, with its impressive panorama of the city. There's also the *Tower* restaurant (phone: 308-1039), which revolves for a 360° view. The tower and restaurant are open daily; admission charge.

SPECIAL PLACES

Marienplatz, with its tall white column of the Virgin Mary, the city's patron, is the heart of Munich. Many of the streets leading from it have been closed to traffic and turned into a *Fussgängerzone* (pedestrian zone). About eight blocks west of Marienplatz is the central square, Karlsplatz, known locally as Stachus, where buses, trams, and subways to all parts of the city arrive and depart. Visitors often are confused because street names change abruptly in central Munich for no apparent reason. You always can get back to the center again, though, because there are numerous signs pointing the way and the spires and towers of landmark churches stand out above the lower red-roofed buildings that constitute the heart of Munich. The Isar River cuts through the city's eastern section, and a walk north along its banks will lead to a huge, lovely park, the *Englischer Garten* (English Garden). On the west side of the park lies the Schwabing district. Munich has a superbly integrated system of buses, trams, and subways to help you explore the city (see *Getting Around*).

DOWNTOWN

SCHWABING At the turn of the century, it had a reputation as an artistic and intellectual center. Today this district to the north of the *Universität München* (University of Munich) is known to most visitors as the place "where the action is" in Munich. By day Schwabing resembles any other German residential district, but around 6 PM people swarm into its streets looking for a good time. The sidewalks along Leopoldstrasse, Schwabing's main street; Amalienstrasse; and Türkenstrasse take on a festive air. You'll see a confusion of sights: painters displaying their art, street musicians, poets offering their latest verses, barbers giving haircuts on the sidewalk, palm readers, quick-sketch artists. You can buy sandals, copper jewelry, ceramics, beads, belts—just about anything, in fact, including genuine and bogus antiques. Schwabing has more than 200 restaurants, with Greek, Yugoslavian, Italian, and Bavarian the most popular. There are countless discotheques, jazz *Kellers,* cafés, and boutiques.

ALTE PINAKOTHEK (OLD PICTURE GALLERY) Temporarily closed for renovation until 1997, this huge Renaissance building is one of the world's great art galleries; until it reopens, most of its paintings are displayed at the *Neue Pinakothek* (see *Museums*). The gallery's artworks include large and important collections of Dutch and Flemish painting from the 14th to the 18th century. The museum was built from 1826 to 1836 to house paintings gathered by the Dukes of Wittelsbach. Ludwig I made numerous other acquisitions that enhanced the museum's reputation. Among its treasures are major works by

Albrecht Dürer and Peter Paul Rubens, as well as *Battle of Issus* by Albrecht Altdorfer and *Saint Erasmus and Saint Maurice* by Matthias Grünewald.

DEUTSCHES MUSEUM (GERMAN MUSEUM) Considered the largest technical museum in the world, it sits on Isarinsel (Isar Island) in the Isar River southeast of the city center. Included among its massive displays are the original 139-foot U-boat built in 1906, locomotives from the *Bavarian State Railway,* a collection of antique pianos and organs, a Messerschmitt 267 jet fighter from 1944, a planetarium, salt and coal mining exhibits in actual caverns, and an aeronautical and space center (including a full-size model of a lunar module). A treat for kids of all ages, this is really an oversize chest full of games, with plenty of buttons to push, levers to pull, and strange-colored, fizzy liquids to watch. This adult toy collection includes a miniature church tower that gets struck on command by a well-placed bolt of lightning, a sleekly menacing original V-2 rocket (the missile that flopped as Hitler's secret weapon), and a sort of oversized, motorized tricycle that is the great-grandfather of today's Mercedes-Benz. Unfortunately, detailed descriptions are available only in German, but it's still very much worth a visit. Closed *New Year's Eve* and *New Year's Day.* Admission charge. Reached by subway (*Isartor* station) or by walking across one of several bridges connecting the island with the city. Isarinsel (phone: 21791).

GASTEIG High on the right bank of the Isar River, just 400 yards from the *Deutsches Museum,* this cultural center is one of Munich's newest attractions. It unites under one roof a philharmonic hall, two smaller concert halls, the *Richard Strauss Musikschule* (Richard Strauss Music Conservatory), and the municipal library. The $130-million building has an ultramodern design, a sharp contrast to the surrounding neighborhood. Open daily. 5 Rosenheimer Str. (phone: 480-98614).

ENGLISCHER GARTEN (ENGLISH GARDEN) This 18th-century garden, one of the oldest landscaped parks on the Continent, is a favorite meeting place. It has lakes, pavilions, riding trails, a site frequented by nude sunbathers, a Japanese teahouse, and a *Chinesischer Turm* (Chinese Tower). At the base of the tower is the city's largest beer garden, where the favorite pastime is quenching one's thirst with a liter of beer while enjoying the passing scene. If you want to splurge, take a pleasant (but pricey) carriage ride. The park is northeast of the city's center, between Schwabing and the Isar River.

FRAUENKIRCHE (CATHEDRAL OF OUR LADY) The onion domes atop two 325-feet symmetrical towers have made this late Gothic cathedral Munich's most distinctive landmark. Its dull red brick façade was damaged extensively during air raids in 1944, but the exterior has been completely restored to its original appearance. The cathedral contains a rich depository of religious works of art, relics, sacred tombs, and the mausoleum of Emperor Ludwig IV. An elevator takes passengers to the top of the south tower, from which there is a good view of the city. 1 Frauenpl.

RESIDENZ (PALACE) Although damaged during World War II, the royal palace has regained much of its glory. Built for the Dukes of Wittelsbach, the palace has been extended over the centuries to form a complex of buildings with seven inner courts. There are state rooms and royal suites decorated in Renaissance, rococo, and neoclassical styles, and displays of royal treasures. Closed Mondays. Admission charge. Entrance at 3 Max-Joseph-Pl. (phone: 290671).

BAYERISCHES NATIONALMUSEUM (BAVARIAN NATIONAL MUSEUM) The vast array of art and historical memorabilia from the Middle Ages to the 19th century on display here should give you an excellent introduction to Bavarian culture. The museum has what may be the most extensive collection of arts and crafts in the world. Along with its tapestries and woodcarvings, the museum is best known for its unique *Krippenschau Collection* of *Christmas* crèches (nativity scenes). Closed Mondays. Admission charge. 3 Prinzregentenstr. (phone: 211241).

HOFBRÄUHAUS (BEER HALL) This immense structure is a dance palace, a restaurant, and a national monument to the good life. In the beer garden, you'll be part of a scene people around the world associate with Munich: cheerful waitresses and waiters in peasant costumes—often carrying as many as 10 steins of beer at once—moving through a noisy crowd selling pretzels stacked on long sticks, or white *Radis* (radishes) cut into fancy spirals—both suitably salty to help you work up a thirst. It's not expensive, and is a must on any visitor's sightseeing agenda. Open daily. 9 Am Platzl (phone: 221676).

NEUES RATHAUS (NEW CITY HALL) Built in the 19th century, Munich's *Neues Rathaus* dominates Marienplatz. Each day throngs of people peer up at its famous *Glockenspiel,* waiting to see the mechanical knights and their squires joust while the carillon signals to the city that it is 11 AM. It is a delightful diversion, not to be missed. This is also the site of the city's annual *Christkindlesmarkt* (Christmas Market)—another must-see, even if you don't buy any of the trinkets, ornaments, or tasty food items for sale. Marienpl.

VIKTUALIENMARKT (VICTUALS MARKET) In this open-air market, farmers, butchers, bakers, and other purveyors of food specialties set out their wares Mondays through Saturdays. It's the perfect place to browse, take pictures, and buy a snack or picnic fixings. Located a few blocks south of Marienpl.

SUBURBS

OLYMPIAPARK (OLYMPIC PARK) Built for the *1972 Olympic Games,* it also was the scene of the terrorist kidnapping of Israeli athletes. The modern sports complex includes swimming pools, tracks, and gymnasiums. The park also has an 80,000-seat stadium—under an extraordinary skin-like roof—and an artificial lake. The Olympic Village, which housed the *Olympic* athletes and officials, is now a major residential suburb. Guided tours are available in German (and in English for groups by prior arrangement), and you even can swim in one of the pools that Mark Spitz made famous in his successful pursuit of seven gold medals back in 1972. The park can be reached easily by bus or subway. Admission charge. Oberwiesenfeld (phone: 3067-2424).

SCHLOSS NYMPHENBURG (NYMPHENBURG PALACE) Just west of the city limits stands a splendid 495-acre park with lakes, hunting lodges, and *Schloss Nymphenburg,* once the residence of the Bavarian kings. The great hall of the palace is decorated with frescoes by Johann Baptist Zimmermann, and the *Marstallmuseum* in the south wing of the palace houses state carriages and sleighs. The *Porzellanarbeitsschutzgesetz Nymphenburg* (Nymphenburg China Factory), with showrooms open to the public, is on the north crescent of the grounds. Outdoor concerts are presented here during summer months, and it is a particularly lovely spot to visit when the rhododendron are in bloom from May through June. Closed Mondays. Admission charge. Entrance from Menzingerstrasse (phone: 179080).

TIERPARK HELLABRUNN (HELLABRUNN ZOO) The nearby city of Hellabrunn keeps its extensive collection of animals in Europe's largest zoo, a 173-acre natural setting of forestland and rivers. It's famous for breeding rare animals and for its anthropoid ape section. There is regular bus and subway service from Marienplatz. Guided tours (in German) are given on Wednesdays; tours in English are available to groups by reservation. Open daily. Admission charge. Four miles (6 km) south of Munich at 30 Tierparkstr. (phone: 625080).

DACHAU Though the town itself is an attractive place near a misty heath, its name has evoked nothing but horror since this first Nazi concentration camp was built in 1933. During World War II, some 200,000 prisoners and deportees were imprisoned here, and an estimated 32,000 of them died or disappeared. The old administration building is now used as a museum where photos, memorabilia, and exhibitions document the camp's cruel history. Also see *Memorable Monuments and Museums* in DIVERSIONS. Closed Mondays, *Christmas Eve,* and the afternoons of *New Year's Eve* and *Shrove Tuesday.* No admission charge. Dachau, 14 miles (22 km) northwest of Munich, can be reached by the Petershausen commuter train *(S-2)* from the *Hauptbahnhof* (main railway station). There is a direct bus (No. 722) from the station to the camp; get off at the Robert Bosch stop (phone: 8131-1741).

EXTRA SPECIAL

It's said that over 650 kinds of beer are brewed in Bavaria, including those made privately. Munich is the home of six of Germany's major producers; one of them, Spaten (which alone makes nine different labels), will arrange tours (by advance appointment only). During a half-hour walk through the plant, accompanied by an English-speaking guide, guests learn the vari-

ous steps of beer making—from germination of the barley to bottling the brew. The tour is an essential preliminary to enlightened imbibing. Admission charge. 48 Marsstr. (phone: 51220 for reservations).

Sources and Resources

TOURIST INFORMATION

The *Munich Tourist Office* has information counters at the *Hauptbahnhof* (Bayerstr.; entrance 2; phone: 239-1256) and at the *Flughafen Franz Josef Strauss* (Franz Josef Strauss Airport; phone: 975-92815; also see *Getting Around,* below). Both offices are open daily until late evening. For information in English on museums and other sights, call the tourist office at 239162 or 239172.

LOCAL COVERAGE The twice-weekly *Munich Times* and the monthly *Munich Found* are English-language newspapers. The tourist office publishes an official monthly program, *München,* that lists theater, museum, and concert schedules, special exhibitions, hotels, restaurants, camping facilities, and other useful information, but it is published only in German. However, many hotels provide literature in English focusing on Munich's activities and entertainment programs.

TELEPHONE The city code for Munich is 89.

GETTING AROUND

Munich has an integrated rapid-transit system; the tickets that you buy from the blue dispensers at stations, streetcar stops, and on those vehicles bearing a white-and-green "K" sign can be used on buses, streetcars, subways, and local trains. You can cancel the tickets yourself in automatic canceling machines at the barriers of stations and in streetcars and buses bearing a yellow-and-black "E." A single ride costs 2.50 DM (about $1.50) or more, depending on how many zones you're traveling through; however, there is a reduced-rate ticket for about 10 DM ($6) that permits unlimited transport in a 24-hour period. These special tickets are sold at the tourist offices and all ticket offices.

AIRPORT The *Flughafen Franz Josef Strauss,* 18 miles (28 km) northeast of downtown Munich, is the terminus for all domestic and international flights into Munich. A rapid-transit train line *(S-8)* connects the city center with the airport, and leaves approximately every 20 minutes from the *Hauptbahnhof.* Buses also leave from the *Kieferngarten* subway station every 40 minutes for the airport; the trip takes approximately 25 minutes. For airport flight information, call 975-21313.

BUS AND STREETCAR The Karlsplatz is the main junction for Munich's streetcars, and the *Ostbahnhof* (East Railway Station) across the Isar from central Munich is the terminal for many of the city's blue-and-white buses.

CAR RENTAL There are international and local rental firms in downtown Munich and at the airport. If you do drive, you should know that in some areas of Munich traffic-light poles contain two sets of lights: one on top for cars and a bottom set for bicycles. Munich also employs "motorbike" women, easily recognized by their light blue jumpsuits, who patrol the highways to aid lost or stranded motorists. Fluent in several languages, these women carry maps, tourist information, and other helpful material.

SUBWAY AND TRAIN The subway, called the *U-Bahn,* crosses the city in a north-south direction and has its central stops at Marienplatz and the *Hauptbahnhof.* Like most European underground rail systems, the *U-Bahn* is clean, modern, and efficient. The *S-Bahn,* which connects with the *U-Bahn* at Marienplatz and *Hauptbahnhof,* is the interurban express line. It runs underground across the city in an east-west direction. Outside the city, it branches out over the whole national railway network. For information on *S-Bahn* trains, call 557575. For information on trains to other parts of the country, call 19419 (schedules) or 55414 (fares).

TAXI Munich's taxis are expensive. It will cost you about 5 DM ($3) just to have the driver flip down the arm of the meter. Taxis can be hailed on the street, or you can get one radio-dispatched by dialing 21610 or 19410.

SPECIAL EVENTS

In addition to *Oktoberfest,* Munich is famous the world over for its annual bow to operatic excellence.

FAVORITE FETES

Munich Opera Festival In July, while most of Europe's opera houses have their summer siesta, Munich sets out a month-long musical feast. The rich diet of Wagner is washed down with sparkling Donizetti, and bubbling *bel canto*—as *Figaro* weds, *Carmen* beds, *La Traviata* dies, and *Rigoletto* has the last sob. Most performances by the *Bayerische Staatsoper* (Bavarian State Opera) take place in the monumental *Nationaltheater* (Max-Joseph-Pl.; phone: 221316), but a few are held in the *Cuvilliés Theater,* an ornate 18th-century venue inside the *Residenz* (1 Residenzstr.; phone: 290671).

Oktoberfest No self-respecting lager lover should miss *Oktoberfest;* celebrated from late September through the first Sunday in October, it is 16 riotous days of beer drinking, sausage eating, and merrymaking at *Theresienwiese* (Theresa's Meadow), a fairgrounds where local breweries set up gaily decorated beer-garden buildings, brass bands oom-pah-pah continuously, and oxen are roasted on open spits. Unbelievable quantities of beer are drunk: Some 750,000 kegs are tapped.

Fasching—another longtime tradition which has been celebrated in Munich since the 14th century—hints more of indulgence in forbidden pleasures of the flesh (there is a traditional agreement that husbands and wives overlook one another's indiscretions during *Fasching*), but it, too, is characterized by lots of drinking and endless fun-seeking. The nonstop street reveling is all the more colorful for the outlandish costumes the celebrants don for fancy balls and an enormous parade through the city. Also see *Quintessential Germany* in DIVERSIONS.

MUSEUMS

Besides those mentioned in *Special Places,* notable museums in Munich include the following:

ANTIKENSAMMLUNGEN (ANTIQUES COLLECTION) Classical art, including Joseph Loeb's collection of Etruscan gold and silver. Closed Mondays. Admission charge. 1 Königspl. (phone: 598359).

BMW-MUSEUM Cars, motorcycles, and airplane engines of the Bavaria Motor Works. Open daily. Admission charge. 130 Petuelring (phone: 389-53307).

GLYPTOTHEK Greek and Roman sculpture. Closed Mondays. Admission charge. 3 Königspl. (phone: 286100).

JÜDISCHES MUSEUM (JEWISH MUSEUM) Exhibits devoted to Jewish history, culture, and traditions. Closed Fridays through Mondays and on Jewish holidays. No admission charge. 36 Maximilianstr. (phone: 297453).

KUNSTHALLE (ART GALLERY) Its space is used to show temporary, visiting exhibitions of paintings and sculpture. Open daily. No admission charge. 15 Theatinerstr. (phone: 224412).

MÜNCHENER STADTMUSEUM (CITY MUSEUM) Exhibits here cover Munich's history since the Middle Ages. Closed Mondays. Admission charge. 1 St.-Jakobs-Pl. (phone: 233-22370).

MUSEUM IN VILLA STUCK Turn-of-the-century and contemporary art are displayed. Closed Mondays. Admission charge. 60 Prinzregentenstr. (phone: 455-5510).

NEUE PINAKOTHEK A collection of 19th- and early 20th-century art; in addition, this gallery displays most of the paintings from the *Alte Pinakothek* (which is closed until 1997; see *Special Places*). Closed Mondays. Admission charge. 29 Barerstr. (phone: 238-05195).

STAATSGALERIE MODERNER KUNST (STATE MUSEUM OF MODERN ART) This recently renovated museum houses a collection of 20th-century sculpture and painting. Closed Mondays. Admission charge. 1 Prinzregentenstr. (phone: 292710).

STÄDTISCHE GALERIE IM LENBACHHAUS (MUNICIPAL GALLERY IN THE LENBACH HOUSE) Kandinsky and the Blue Rider School are featured. Closed Mondays. Admission charge. 33 Luisenstr. (phone: 233-0320).

VALENTIN MUSEUM Dedicated to one of Munich's legendary entertainers, Karl Valentin. Open daily. Admission charge. Gate Tower, Isartorpl. (phone: 223266).

SHOPPING

Munich is such an elegant shopping city that some visitors confess to losing all sense of proportion once turned loose in the pedestrian zone. Shops tempt you with Bavarian beer steins, wonderful antiques, marvelous German porcelain, and items of German steel as well as Parisian fashions. Munich's most elegant shops can be found along Maximilianstrasse and Briennerstrasse and the small streets between Marienplatz and Odeonsplatz. Most of the antiques shops are concentrated in Neuturmstrasse, near Marienplatz. The city's leading department stores are *Oberpollinger* (off Karlspl.; phone: 290230), which is affiliated with the national *Karstadt* chain of stores, and *Kaufhof* (Marienpl.; phone: 269072). For standard shopping hours, see GETTING READY TO GO. *Auer Dult* is a wonderful flea market for secondhand goods, antiques, and curiosities, set up three times a year—usually in May, July, and October at 2 Mariahilfplatz, across the Isar in the southeastern district of Au.

Alois Dallmayr A world-famous fancy food store. 14-15 Dienerstr. (phone: 21350).

Anglia English Bookstore The biggest selection of English-language paperbacks in southern Germany. 3 Schellingstr. (phone: 283642).

Beck Famous for textiles, womenswear, and Bavarian handicrafts. 11 Marienpl. (phone: 236910).

Biebl Solingen carving sets and other items made of this renowned German steel. 25 Karlspl. (phone: 597936).

Dieter Stange-Erlenbach Pelze Famed for its timeless and fashionable furs—for him and for her. 21 Maximilianstr. (phone: 535974).

Dirndlkönigin An interesting display of Bavarian handicrafts, including the best selection of Bavarian folk costumes in Munich. 18 Residenzstr. (phone: 293804).

Kunstring Contemporary and antique dinnerware. 4 Briennerstr. (phone: 281532).

Loden-Frey Men's and women's loden coats. 7-9 Maffeistr. (phone: 236930).

Ludwig Mory A huge and varied stock of interesting beer steins, as well as a collection of pewter objets d'art. 8 Marienpl. (phone: 224542).

Maendler High fashion for women. 7 Theatinerstr. (phone: 291-3322).

Moderne Creation München (MCM) The latest in chic fashion accessories. 11 Nicolaistr. (phone: 331096).

Moshammer's Clothing for men. 14 Maximilianstr. (phone: 226924).

Obletter Germany's largest toy store. 11-12 Karlspl. (phone: 231-8601).

Pini The city's largest store for cameras and allied equipment. Am Stachus (phone: 594361).

Rosenthal Home of the marvelous china, crystal, and cutlery. 8 Theatinerstr. (phone: 220422 or 227547).

Staatliche Porzellan Manufaktur (State Porcelain Factory) The main distributor of Nymphenburg porcelain. 1-2 Odeonspl. (phone: 172439 or 282428).

Wallach Haus Bavarian furniture, dirndls, and peasant dresses. 3 Residenzstr. (phone: 220871).

Walter Leather clothing for men and women. 9 Amalienstr. (phone: 282294).

Wesely Ornately decorated wax candles typical of this region. 1 Rindermarkt (phone: 264519).

SPORTS AND FITNESS

The excellent facilities built for the *1972 Summer Olympics* are used by a variety of professional teams in Munich, providing visitors with an opportunity to see everything from European soccer and basketball to ice hockey and track and field events. Sports schedules are listed in the monthly tourist office program, *München* (see *Local Coverage*).

BICYCLING Bikes can be rented at the entrance to the *Englischer Garten* (at the corner of Königinstrasse and Veterinärstrasse; phone: 529943); the garden is a very pleasant place to cycle through. *Park & Bike* (18 Häberlstr.; phone: 539697); *Radius Touristik* (9 Arnulfstr.; phone: 596113); and *City Hopper Tours* (95 Hohenzollern Str.; phone: 272-1131) also rent bicycles.

FITNESS CENTERS The *Sportstudio* (16 Hansastr.; phone: 573479) is a gym that is open to non-members.

JOGGING Try the *Englischer Garten,* which stretches north from Prinzregentenstrasse and is easily accessible from downtown.

SOCCER *Bayern München,* one of Europe's top soccer teams, plays its home games year round (except January, June, and July) at the *Olympiastadion* (Olympic Stadium). For information and tickets, contact *Olympiapark* (see *Special Places*) or the tourist office.

SWIMMING The *Olympia Schwimmhalle* (Olympic Swimming Hall) in *Olympiapark* (see *Special Places*) is open to the public daily.

THEATER

Munich has been known for centuries as a theater city. You can see everything from Greek tragedy to classical ballet to modern experimental drama in the numerous theaters here. The chief theaters are the *Residenz Theater* (1 Max-Joseph-Pl.; phone: 225754) and the *Münchener Kammerspiele* (Munich Chamber Theater) in the *Schauspielhaus* (26 Maximilianstr.; phone: 237-21328). Other venues include the *Cuvilliés Theater* in the *Residenz* (1

Residenzstr.; phone: 290671); *Theater in Marstall* (Marstallpl.; phone: 225754); *Prinzregententheater* (Prince Regent's Theater; 12 Prinzregentenpl.; phone: 221316); the *Münchener Marionettentheater* (Munich Puppet Theater; 29A Blumenstr. at Sendlinger-Tor-Pl.; phone: 265712); and the *Münchener Theater für Kinder* (Munich Theater for Children; 46 Dachauer Str.; phone: 595454 and 593858).

MUSIC

Opera has been performed in Munich since 1650, and the names of Wagner, Mozart, and Richard Strauss (Strauss was born in Munich) are linked closely with the *Bayerische Staatsoper* (Bavarian State Opera), which performs in the *Nationaltheater* (Max-Joseph-Pl.; phone: 221316).

The *Munich Opera Festival,* with performances held at the *Nationaltheater* and the *Cüvilliés Theater* (see *Special Events*), is the highlight of the city's summer opera offering; opera also can be heard at the *Staatstheater am Gärtnerplatz* (3 Gärtnerpl.; phone: 201-6767). Hardly a day passes without a classical concert at one of the halls at the *Gasteig* (see *Special Places*).

NIGHTCLUBS AND NIGHTLIFE

Nightlife and Schwabing are almost interchangeable terms. You can dance over an aquarium filled with sharks at *Hamlet Light* in the *Holiday Inn Crowne Plaza* (see *Checking In*); disco at *Cadillac* (1 Theklastr.; phone: 266974) and at *Charly M.* (5 Maximilianspl.; phone: 595272); or rock the night away at *Nightclub* in the *Bayerischer Hof–Palais Montgelas* (2-6 Promenadepl.; phone: 212-0994). Music and other entertainment is offered at *Clip* (25 Leopoldstr.; phone: 394578), and *Domicile* (19 Leopoldstr.; phone: 399451) offers jazz and rock. There's usually an interesting program of live music or cabaret-style satire on tap at *Nachtcafé* (5 Maximilianspl.; phone: 595900), as well as at the *Riem Airport* (400 Töginger Str., Riem; phone: 906322), housed (as its name implies) in the city's former airport terminal. A disco that appeals to trendy *Müncheners* is *Bubbles* (25 Oskar-von-Miller-Ring; phone: 281182); *Sunset* (69 Leopoldstr.; phone: 390303) is another popular dance spot. At *Harry's New York Bar* (9 Falkenturmstr.; phone: 222700) you can gawk at celebrities while imbibing one of 500 different drinks.

Biting humor and satire are the offerings at the literary cabaret *Lach- und Schiessgesellschaft* (Ursulastr.; phone: 391997); and don't miss the vocal renditions of Gisela (who only goes by one name, à la Cher or Madonna) at her bistro, *Schwabinger Gisela* (38 Herzog-Heinrich-Str.; phone: 534901). Jazz can be heard at clubs such as *Saint Thomas* (302 Tegernseer Landstr.; phone: 690-5456) and *Unterfahrt* (96 Kirchenstr.; phone: 448-2794). For rock and pop, try *Music Hall Epikero* (2 Detmoldstr.; phone: 351-0869) and *Schwabinger Podium* (1 Wagnerstr.; phone: 399482). *Waldwirtschaft Grosshesselohe* (3 Georg-Kalb-Str.; phone: 795088) offers great Bavarian beer as well as live jazz. On Monday evenings you can hear some of the best Irish and British folk music at the *Irish Folk Pub* (9 Fraunhofer Str.; phone: 679-2481).

If you'd like to test your luck, take the *Garmisch Casino's Blitz Bus* or one of the other buses the casinos run to bring players from Munich to the Garmisch area at the foot of the Alps, 54 miles (87 km) away. The buses leave from the north side of the *Hauptbahnhof* at 5 PM on weekdays and at 2 PM Sundays. They leave Garmisch at 11 PM for the return trip to Munich. The trip takes about an hour and 35 minutes each way. For information, contact the tourist office at the *Hauptbahnhof* (see *Tourist Information*).

Best in Town

CHECKING IN

Except during *Oktoberfest* and *Fasching,* there is plenty of hotel space in Munich. Top hotels will cost a minimum of $150 a night for a double, and most of their rooms go for much higher prices; moderate-priced hotels charge between $90 and $140 a night; and anything below $90 must be considered inexpensive. The hotels listed below have a bath or a shower in every room, and in almost every case the rooms have telephones; room rates do *not* include breakfast unless specified. Be sure to make reservations well ahead if you're coming for *Oktoberfest* or *Fasching.* Munich also has many delightful, inexpensive pensions. They don't have all the conveniences of a modern hotel, such as private baths, but they do have *Gemütlichkeit*—the typical warmth and geniality that is one of the best reasons to visit Munich. Most of Munich's major hotels have complete facilities for the business traveler. Those hotels listed as having "business services" usually offer such conveniences as an English-speaking concierge, meeting rooms, photocopiers, computers, translation services, and express checkout, among others. Call the hotel for additional information. All telephone numbers are in the 89 city code unless otherwise indicated.

For an unforgettable experience in Munich, we begin with our favorites, followed by our cost and quality choices of accommodations, listed by price category.

ROOMS AT THE TOP

Bayerischer Hof–Palais Montgelas Overlooking the verdant, flower-filled Promenadeplatz, this stately 442-room property has maintained its reputation for excellent service and high standards ever since once of its early guests, King Ludwig I, came here to bathe (the royal palace didn't have bathtubs). But the *Bayerischer* is more than mere bathtubs—much more. The bustle in the lobby is reminiscent of a movie set; the elevator whisks you to the rooftop swimming pool with an unforgettable view of the city; and in the basement, *Trader Vic's* offers spareribs and Polynesian cocktails—an unexpected treat in this traditionally German city. The *Garden* restaurant is an idyllic oasis in summer (see *Eating Out*), while the baronial lounge—with its fireplace—is a warm refuge in winter. The guestrooms are equipped with plenty of amenities, including mini-bars; other features include 24-hour room service, foreign currency exchange, and business services. 2-6 Promenadepl. (phone: 21200; 212900, reservations from within Germany; 800-223-6800; fax: 212-0906).

Rafael This elegant establishment occupies a remarkable 19th-century building that formerly housed ballrooms and then the *Antik Haus* art galleries. The 74 rooms and suites, as well as the public rooms, are decorated in a luxurious, late 19th-century style. *Mark's* is the intimate dining room. There is a rooftop swimming pool with a sweeping view of the Bavarian capital. Other amenities include 24-hour room service, foreign currency exchange, and business services. 1 Neuturmstr. (phone: 290980; fax: 222539).

Vier Jahreszeiten Kempinski In the mid-19th century, king and urban-planner Maximilian II mapped out the broad boulevard that now bears his name and commissioned this jewel of a hostelry for the wayside. The king bankrolled an entrepreneurial waiter with whom he played cards; his reward was this grand, 325-room hotel (now part of the Kempinski chain), which today would still satisfy the whims of any sovereign. The *Vier Jahreszeiten*, whose name is German for "Four Seasons," is so close to Munich's theaters and opera that you can be wiping off the shaving cream as the house lights dim and still make it to your seat before the curtain goes up. After the show, join the cast for a drink in the basement bar, where the spectacle of people watching makes the *Jahresezeitenkeller* Munich's true center for the performing arts. Its restaurant is among the best in the city (see *Eating Out*). Other amenities include 24-hour room service, foreign currency exchange, and business services. 17 Maximilianstr. (phone: 230390; 800-426-3135; fax: 230-39693).

EXPENSIVE

Grand Hotel Continental Formerly the *Continental Royal Classic,* this 145-room property is a favorite of those who know the city well. Close to the center of town, it's still known affectionately as the *"Conti."* Filled with flowers and priceless antiques, the hotel is part of a group of buildings known as the *Kunstblock,* the center of the Munich art and antiques market. Other amenities include two restaurants, 24-hour room service, foreign currency exchange, and business services. 5 Max-Joseph-Str. (phone: 551570; fax: 551-57500).

Hilton Park Close to the picturesque *Englischer Garten,* this 500-room hostelry is designed to meet the particular needs of the international business traveler. There are several restaurants, a pool, a sauna, a shopping arcade, and a massive underground garage. Other amenities include 24-hour room service, foreign currency exchange, and business services. 7 Am Tucherpark (phone: 38450; 800-HILTONS; fax: 384-51845).

Holiday Inn Crowne Plaza A 360-room hotel on Schwabing's main thoroughfare, it's the home of the *Hamlet Light* disco (see *Nightclubs and Nightlife*), as well as a restaurant. Other amenities include 24-hour room service, foreign currency exchange, and business services. 194 Leopoldstr. (phone: 381790; 800-HOLIDAY; fax: 381-79888).

Königshof Despite its central location, this traditional and comfortable 132-room establishment is quiet. It also boasts one of Munich's best hotel restaurants, which has a great view of busy Karlsplatz. Other amenities include 24-hour room service, foreign currency exchange, and business services. 25 Karlspl. (phone: 551360; fax: 551-36113).

Penta Part of a European chain and designed to cut down on rapidly soaring hotel prices, this huge 740-room property caters to a predominantly business clientele. Guests carry their own baggage to their rooms. A unit in each room dispenses drinks, snacks, and even continental breakfast. There is an extensive shopping arcade and restaurant complex under the hotel, which is near the *Deutsches Museum.* Other amenities include 24-hour room service, foreign currency exchange, and business services. 3 Hochstr. (phone: 48030; fax: 4488-8277).

Platzl On the site of an old historic mill, this 170-room hotel has been modernized, with conveniences such as phones and mini-bars in all the guestrooms and a large parking garage. Other amenities include 24-hour room service, foreign currency exchange, and business services. There's no restaurant, however. It's located in the center of the Altstadt, across the street from the *Hofbräuhaus* (see *Special Places*). 1 Platzl (phone: 237030; fax: 237-03800).

Queen's Idyllically set on the right bank of the Isar River, near some of Munich's lushest greenery, this property offers 150 tastefully furnished rooms and a restaurant. Other amenities include 24-hour room service, foreign currency exchange, and business services. 99 Effnerstr. (phone: 927980; fax: 983813).

Sheraton East of the center of town, this 650-room link in the international chain is clearly geared to the convention trade. There's a restaurant, as well as 24-hour room service, foreign currency exchange, and business services. 6 Arabellastr. (phone: 92640; 800-334-8484; fax: 916877).

MODERATE

Biederstein Probably Munich's quietest hostelry, this charming 32-room place is on the fringe of Schwabing, next to the *Englischer Garten.* There's no restaurant, but there is 24-hour room service. Other amenities include foreign currency exchange and business services. 18 Keferstr. (phone: 395072; fax: 348511).

Daniel Here are 85 plain but clean and comfortable guestrooms. The hotel offers good value, as well as a great location near train and subway stations and within walking distance of most shopping areas in the city. There's no restaurant, but foreign currency exchange and business services are available. 5 Sonnenstr. (phone: 554945; fax: 553420).

Englischer Garten A homey guesthouse with 27 cheerfully decorated rooms, its location—overlooking a canal on one side and the beautiful *Englischer Garten* on the other—and its very reasonable rates make it popular with tourists. Amenities include foreign currency exchange and business services, but there's no restaurant. 8 Liebergesellstr. (phone: 392034; fax: 391233).

Intercity This comfortable 260-room hotel is in the *Hauptbahnhof,* but it's surprisingly quiet. There's no restaurant, but 24-hour room service, foreign currency exchange, and business services are offered. 10 Bayerstr. (phone: 545560; fax: 596229).

Leopold This 80-room hotel, on the fringe of Schwabing, is in an old 19th-century house. The back wing is quieter and faces a garden. There's no restaurant. Amenities include 24-hour room service, foreign currency exchange, and business services. 119 Leopoldstr. (phone: 367061; fax: 893-67061).

Lettl Centrally located, this hostelry has 35 rooms (ask for one in the newer wing). Breakfast is included in the room rate (there's a breakfast room, but no restaurant). Other amenities include 24-hour room service, foreign currency exchange, and business services. 53 Amalienstr. (phone: 283026; fax: 280-5318).

Mariahilf A particular favorite with English tourists, this 25-room pension is in a quiet sector of the city across the Isar from central Munich. Amenities include 24-hour room service, foreign currency exchange, and business services. There's no restaurant. 83 Lilienstr. (phone: 484834; fax: 489-1381).

Splendid Alongside the calm Isar River, this pleasing little hotel is also close to the theater, museum, and shopping district. All 40 rooms are well equipped and unusually quiet. There's no restaurant, but 24-hour room service is available. Other amenities include foreign currency exchange and business services. 54 Maximilianstr. (phone: 296606; fax: 291-3176).

Uhland A charming little 37-room hotel in a lovely old building on a street near *Theresienwiese* (Theresa's Meadow). Amenities include 24-hour room service, foreign currency exchange, and business services. There's no restaurant. 1 Uhlandstr. (phone: 539277; fax: 531114).

INEXPENSIVE

Mariandl This charming pension near *Theresienwiese* has 25 quiet rooms and a restaurant famed for its classical music in the evenings. Amenities include an English-speaking concierge and foreign currency exchange. 51 Goethestr. (phone: 534108 or 535158).

Theresia Very close to the museums, this well-run establishment has 24 rooms. Amenities include an English-speaking concierge and foreign currency exchange. There's no restaurant. In Schwabing, 51 Luisenstr. (phone: 523-3081 or 521250; fax: 532323).

EATING OUT

Bavarian cuisine is hearty and heavy, and most of it seems created to make you consume inordinate amounts of beer. *Leberknödel* (liver dumplings) are the most famous of more than four score Bavarian dumplings. *Leberkäse* translates as liver cheese but is neither; it's a baked pâté of beef and bacon. *Schweinswürstl mit Kraut* (pork sausages and sauerkraut) is another unforgettable local dish. Munich is the wurst (sausage) capital of the world. *Weisswurst,* a veal-based white sausage, is sold throughout the city by street vendors as well as in beer gardens. You'll also want to taste some of the local pretzels and salt rolls and sticks sold under such names as *Brez'n, Römische,* and *Salzstangerl.* Another specialty here is a large, tasty white *Radi* (radish), cut in spirals and sold with plenty of salt. If all of this makes you very thirsty, order *ein Mass Bier;* that's a liter. Otherwise, *eine Halbe* (a half liter) should suffice. If you need a break from Bavarian fare, you can choose from a wide variety of other ethnic foods, especially in the conglomeration of foreign restaurants in Schwabing, some of them the best in Germany.

Dining out can be expensive in Munich; even beer-hall fare, once the staple of budget-minded students, can add up quickly to $15, $18, or more. At expensive restaurants expect to pay a minimum of $85 for a meal for two, not including drinks or wine; $40 to $85 at places in the moderate price range; and less than $40 at the eateries we describe as inexpensive. Prices include taxes and tip, though you should leave an extra mark or two for good service. Unless noted otherwise, the restaurants listed are open for lunch and dinner. All telephone numbers are in the 89 city code unless otherwise indicated.

For an unforgettable dining experience we begin with our culinary favorites, followed by our cost and quality choices, listed by price category.

DELIGHTFUL DINING

Austernkeller If you're marooned in landlocked Bavaria with a longing for seafood, descend into the vaulted Oyster Cellar. Here you'll find oysters of every type and temperature, smoked salmon, bouillabaisse, spits of grilled king prawns, lobster casseroles—probably even mackerel sherbet. The setting is Nautical Deco, the atmosphere is animated, almost raucous, and the place is great fun. If you have a play or a plane to catch, there's an oyster bar near the entrance where you can always grab six quick *fines de claire* and a glass of Muscadet. Closed Mondays. Reservations advised. Major credit cards accepted. 11 Stollbergstr. (phone: 298787).

Tantris A thick aroma of truffles—scattered in paper-thin slices over a salad of scallops and leeks—hovers in this shrine of high-art cookery. The sleek decor is the perfect setting for the newest of nouvelle cuisine, streamlined dishes artfully composed from the day's market harvest by chef Hans Haas. Keeper of the wine cellar Paula Bosch, who presides over the annual gathering of Munich's nobly robed Knights of the Brotherhood of Bordeaux Wines, will also help you select the perfect accompaniment to your dinner. Closed Sundays and Mondays. Reservations advised. Major credit cards accepted. 7 Johann-Fichte-Str. (phone: 362061 or 362062; fax: 361-8469).

Vier Jahreszeiten Kempinski Everything about this restaurant is tastefully discreet, from its half-lit glow to its creamy decor and hushed carpeting. The dining room in the *Vier Jahreszeiten Kempinski* hotel offers Bavaria's most elegant and sophisticated fare, and when you've had the *Lachsforelle mit Kerbelsahne glaciert* (salmon trout glazed with chervil cream) or the *Kalbsfilet und Morcheln in Blätterteig* (filet of veal and morels in puff pastry in broccoli cream), you'll forget all about the last time you saw Paris. Closed Saturdays, Monday lunch, and August. Reservations necessary. Major credit cards accepted. 17 Maximilianstr. (phone: 230390).

EXPENSIVE

Boettner A tiny wine restaurant in a high-ceilinged, paneled room behind a caviar-lobster shop, it has only about 10 tables and always is crowded. The specialty here is lobster. Closed Saturday evenings, Sundays, and holidays. Reservations necessary. Major credit cards accepted. 8 Theatinerstr. (phone: 221210).

Garden This elegant hotel dining room offers continental fare with Alsatian accents—onion quiche, baked scallops, smoked salmon lasagne in vermouth sauce, wurst and sauerkraut, and roasted venison in red pepper sauce. Open daily. Reservations necessary. Major credit cards accepted. *Hotel Bayerischer Hof–Palais Montgelas,* 2-6 Promenadepl. (phone: 212-0993).

Kaferschänke What started out as a corner grocery store has worked itself up to one of Europe's largest delicatessens and Germany's biggest catering service, and now includes a popular restaurant upstairs over the sprawling store. You can get anything from *Presskopf* (homemade head cheese) to bass from the Mediterranean. Closed Sundays. Reservations advised. Major credit cards accepted. 73 Prinzregentenstr. (phone: 41680).

Sabitzer A favorite of Munich's beautiful people, decorated all in white with turn-of-the-century art hung on the walls, this fine, small spot serves nouvelle cuisine. Closed Sundays. Reservations advised. Major credit cards accepted. 21 Reitmorstr. (phone: 298584).

MODERATE

Bistro Terrine The latest culinary vogue in Munich is the bistro, and this one is in the middle of swinging Schwabing. Its continental fare is complemented by the heady Mediterranean atmosphere. Closed Sundays and holidays. Reservations advised. Major credit cards accepted. 89 Amalienstr.; entrance is on Türkenstr. (phone: 281780).

Goldene Stadt Bohemian dishes are served in the four adjoining dining rooms here. A photomural of the Charles Bridge in Prague dominates the main dining room. Closed Sundays. Reservations advised. Major credit cards accepted. 44 Oberanger (phone: 264382).

Halali Not far from Schwabing, this eatery serves high-quality nouvelle cuisine with a hearty Bavarian touch at remarkably reasonable prices. Well-prepared game dishes are the house specialty. Closed Sundays. Reservations advised. Major credit cards accepted. 22 Schönfeldstr. (phone: 285909).

Mifune Ever since actor Toshiro Mifune opened this place, it's been a must for lovers of Japanese food. Closed Sundays; lunch only on Saturdays. Reservations advised. Major credit cards accepted. 136 Ismaninger Str. (phone: 987572).

Spatenhaus A fine example of a typical Bavarian *Gaststätte* (inn), with its whitewashed walls, pine tables and chairs, and many cozy niches. A delicious dinner here might include roast duck, suckling pig, or hare with mushrooms in cream sauce; dessert could be the flaky apple strudel or crisp apple fritters. Open daily. No reservations. No credit cards accepted. 12 Residenzstr. (phone: 290-7060).

Spöckmeier This popular *Gasthaus*—which some say serves the best veal sausages in town—has two dining rooms: The vast, whitewashed and raftered hall downstairs bustles with shoppers and sightseers, and the smaller, paneled room upstairs hums with the quiet conversation of elegant drinkers. Closed Sundays from June through August. No reservations. No credit cards accepted. 9 Rosenstr., just off Marienpl. (phone: 268088).

Weisses Bräuhaus Perhaps the most traditional of Munich's restaurants, this inn has been serving hearty food and wheat beer at the same site for over 400 years. A best bet is the roast pork with dumplings. Open daily. No reservations. No credit cards accepted. 10 Tal (phone: 299875).

Zum Alten Markt Just a stone's throw from the colorful *Viktualienmarkt,* this downtown eatery is a must for lovers of good, but reasonably priced, continental fare. The emphasis is on fish and veal dishes. Closed Sundays and *Christmas* through mid-January. Reservations advised. No credit cards accepted. 3 Dreifaltigkeitspl. (phone: 299995).

INEXPENSIVE

Alte Börse Nestled in a quiet passageway between two busy streets is this rare German hybrid—a café/restaurant that serves pastries and coffee or full-course dinners. True, it closes early and the menu is solidly German, but the pastries are heavenly continental concoctions. Try their famous Russian punch cake. Closed after 6 PM and Sundays. Reservations unnecessary. No credit cards accepted. Entrances on 3 Maffeistr. and 17-18 Schäfflerstr. (phone: 226795).

Bratwurstherzl Around the corner from the *Viktualienmarkt* (see *Special Places*), this is one of the last truly Bavarian establishments in swinging Munich. It serves only lunch—and be sure to be seated by 11 AM, since its traditional local specialties are very popular with *Müncheners.* Closed Sundays. No reservations. No credit cards accepted. 3 Heiliggeiststr. (phone: 226219).

Donisl A visit here is a Munich must: This centuries-old beer hall is where many *Müncheners* come for their daily brew and sausage ration, usually in the late morning. Open daily. No reservations. Major credit cards accepted. Next to the *Neues Rathaus.* 1 Weinstr., at Marienpl. (phone: 220184).

Mariannenhof At the edge of downtown Munich, this unpretentious place offers good food at reasonable prices in a comfortable atmosphere. Both continental and traditional Bavarian fare is served. Attached to the restaurant are a bar and a tavern. Open daily; dinner only on weekends. No reservations. No credit cards accepted. 1 Mariannenstr. (phone: 220864).

Pfälzer Weinprobierstube This tradition-laden wine cellar, located in the *Residenz* (see *Special Places*), features vintages from the Pfalz (Palatinate) region. The hearty food is also from that former part of Bavaria. Open daily. No reservations. No credit cards accepted. 1 Residenzstr. (phone: 225628).

Sofia Grill Somewhat off the beaten path—south of downtown and near the wholesale meat market—this friendly, casual eatery is well worth the trip. Though many of the dishes have a Bulgarian flavor—*shopska* salad with sheep's cheese, for example—the extensive menu also includes Balkan and Viennese entrées—Wiener schnitzel, goulash, and *rasniçi* (meat kebabs). Closed Mondays. Reservations unnecessary. No credit cards accepted. 157 Lindwurmstr. (phone: 775717).

BIERGÄRTEN

One of the pleasures of summertime Munich is the garland of beer gardens strung out across the city—cool and companionable oases in the middle of the urban oven. Tree-shaded, open-air dining spaces with long wooden tables and benches, these reasonably priced establishments offer everything from just plain beer and pretzels to grilled chicken and barbecued spareribs. The air is redolent with eucalyptus and bratwurst, and *Müncheners* will loll in these places for hours, nursing a single stein of beer. Among the most characteristic: *Königlicher Hirschgarten* (1 Hirschgarten; phone: 172591); *Taxisgarten* (12 Taxis; phone: 156827); *Augustiner* (on Neuhauser Str., near the *Hauptbahnhof;* no phone); and the sprawling *Menterschwaige Garten* (4 Menterschwaigstr.; phone: 640732), located outside of town on the banks of the Isar river.

Nuremberg

The most vivid images associated with Nuremberg are connected with Nazi Germany: massive rallies here during the 1930s, with Adolf Hitler proclaiming the supremacy of the Third Reich; the Nuremberg Laws, which labeled German Jews as second class citizens and officially denied them civil rights; and the international tribunal held in the city after World War II, where many of the party's leaders were sentenced to death for war crimes. But this city on the Pegnitz River in Franconia (formerly a duchy in Austrasia, the kingdom ruled by the Franks in the 6th, 7th, and 8th centuries) has a distinguished history that stretches back centuries before the Second World War. A major trading post in the Middle Ages, Nuremberg went on to become the center of the German Renaissance, nurturing many artistic and scientific innovators of that age. Well known the world over for its *Lebkuchen* (gingerbread) and exquisite hand-crafted toys, the city is also a growing industrial metropolis of half a million people (second in size in Bavaria only to Munich).

Nuremberg is first mentioned in writing in the year 1050, in a document signed by Emperor Henry II emancipating a local bondswoman. Known at that time as Nourenberc, the burgeoning town's location between Italy and northern Europe made it a convenient trading point. It quickly grew in size and prominence, receiving a charter in 1219 and being designated a Free Imperial City by the end of the 13th century; by then it was being called by its present name. Emperor Charles IV visited often, sometimes staying for months at a time. It was Charles who decreed in the Golden Bull of 1356 that each newly elected Holy Roman Emperor would hold his first Imperial Diet (meeting of rulers) in Nuremberg.

The city's wealth and status increased during the 15th and 16th centuries, when it developed into a major center for art, culture, and science. Albrecht Dürer, the first German painter to achieve international renown, was born here in 1471 and produced many of his best known works in a house on the Tiergärtnerplatz in the Altstadt (Old City). The house, where he lived from 1509 until he died in 1528, is one of Nuremberg's major tourist attractions. Other local artists who achieved great prominence were sculptors Veit Stoss (1445–1533) and Adam Krafft (1455–1509). Examples of works by all three can be seen here today, particularly in the *St. Lorenzkirche* (Church of St. Lawrence) and the *St. Sebalduskirche* (Church of St. Sebaldus). Another famous native of Nuremberg was Hans Sachs (1494–1576), a 16th-century *Meistersinger* (a member of a guild devoted to creating and performing poetry and music). The city was also the site of several important inventions during this period, including the pencil, the pocket watch, and the geographical globe.

The advent of the Thirty Years War in 1618 abruptly ended Nuremberg's glory days. Damaged during the battles, the city fell on hard times: Its trade

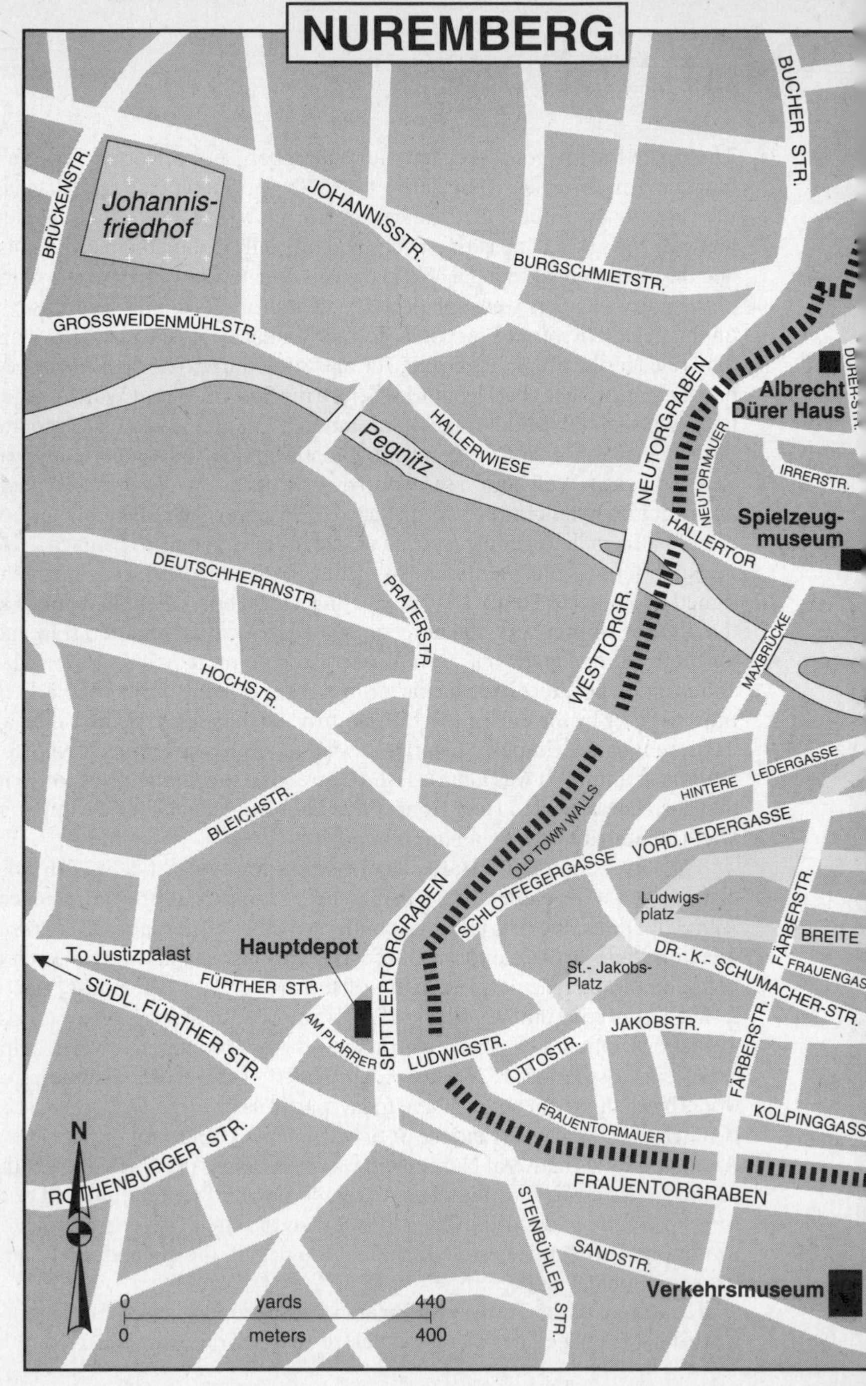
NUREMBERG
BUCHER STR.
BRÜCKENSTR.
Johannis-
friedhof
JOHANNISSTR.
BURGSCHMIETSTR.
GROSSWEIDENMÜHLSTR.
NEUTORGRABEN
Albrecht
Dürer Haus
Pegnitz
HALLERWIESE
NEUTORMAUER
IRRERSTR.
Spielzeug-
museum
HALLERTOR
DEUTSCHHERRNSTR.
PRATERSTR.
WESTTORGR.
MAXBRÜCKE
HOCHSTR.
HINTERE LEDERGASSE
BLEICHSTR.
OLD TOWN WALLS
VORD. LEDERGASSE
SCHLOTFEGERGASSE
SPITTLERTORGRABEN
Ludwigs-
platz
FÄRBERSTR.
BREITE
Hauptdepot
DR.- K.- SCHUMACHER-STR.
To Justizpalast
FRAUENGAS
St.- Jakobs-
Platz
FÜRTHER STR.
SÜDL. FÜRTHER STR.
AM PLÄRRER
JAKOBSTR.
LUDWIGSTR.
OTTOSTR.
FÄRBERSTR.
KOLPINGGASS
FRAUENTORMAUER
N
ROTHENBURGER STR.
FRAUENTORGRABEN
STEINBÜHLER STR.
SANDSTR.
Verkehrsmuseum
0 yards 440
0 meters 400

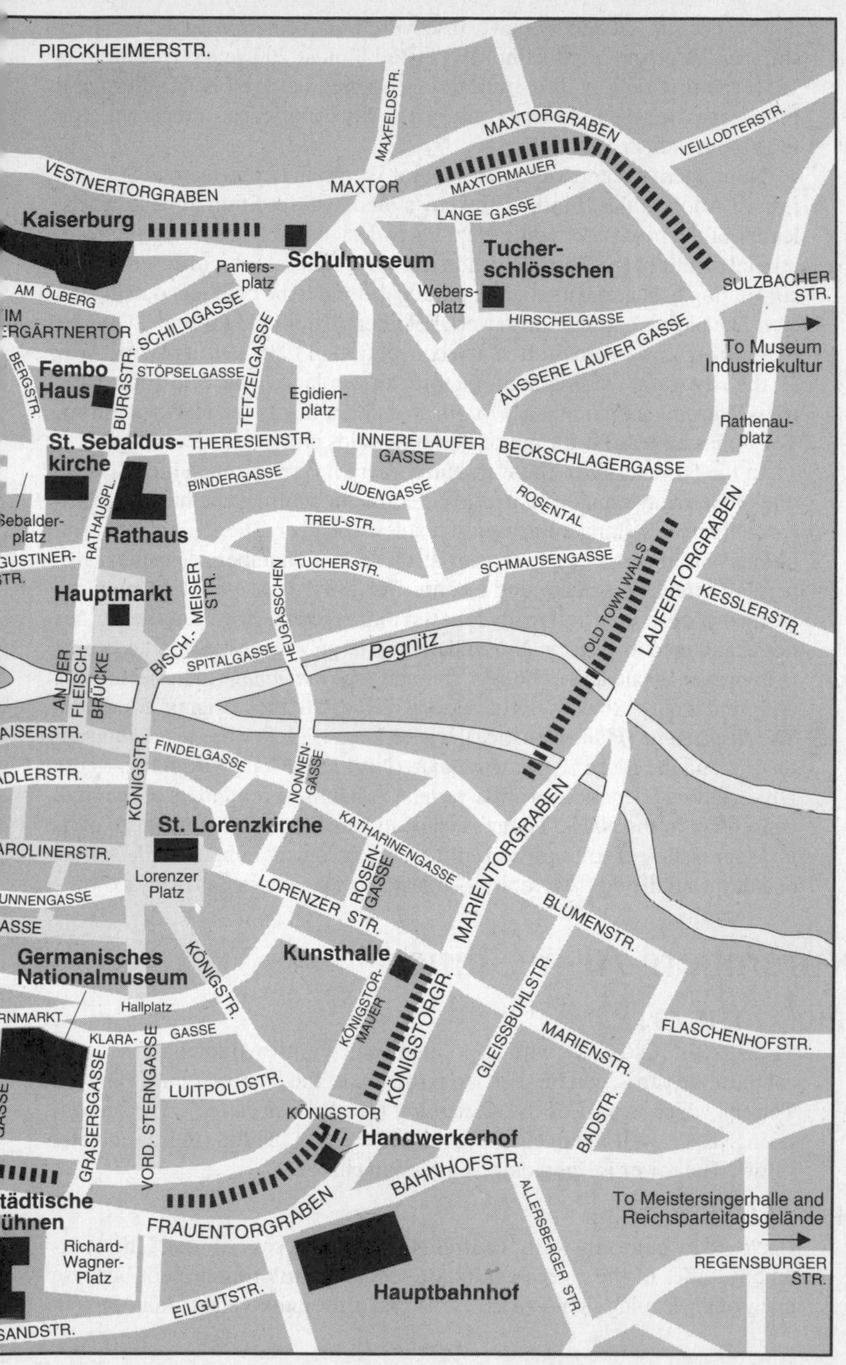

PIRCKHEIMERSTR.
MAXFELDSTR.
MAXTORGRABEN
VEILLODTERSTR.
VESTNERTORGRABEN
MAXTOR
MAXTORMAUER
LANGE GASSE
Kaiserburg
Schulmuseum
Paniers-
platz
Tucher-
schlösschen
Webers-
platz
AM ÖLBERG
SULZBACHER
STR.
HIRSCHELGASSE
To Museum
Industriekultur
SCHILDGASSE
TETZELGASSE
ÄUSSERE LAUFER GASSE
BERGSTR.
Fembo
Haus
STÖPSELGASSE
BURGSTR.
Egidien-
platz
Rathenau-
platz
St. Sebaldus-
kirche
THERESIENSTR.
INNERE LAUFER
GASSE
BECKSCHLAGERGASSE
BINDERGASSE
JUDENGASSE
ROSENTAL
RATHAUSPL.
Rathaus
TREU-STR.
LAUFERTORGRABEN
Sebalder-
platz
TUCHERSTR.
SCHMAUSENGASSE
MEISER
STR.
HEUGÄSSCHEN
OLD TOWN WALLS
KESSLERSTR.
Hauptmarkt
BISCH.-
SPITALGASSE
Pegnitz
AN DER
FLEISCH-
BRÜCKE
FINDELGASSE
NONNEN-
GASSE
KÖNIGSTR.
MARIENTORGRABEN
St. Lorenzkirche
KATHARINENGASSE
ROSEN-
GASSE
Lorenzer
Platz
LORENZER STR.
BLUMENSTR.
Germanisches
Nationalmuseum
KÖNIGSTR.
Kunsthalle
KÖNIGSTOR-
MAUER
KÖNIGSTORGR.
GLEISSBÜHLSTR.
Hallplatz
KLARA-
GASSE
MARIENSTR.
FLASCHENHOFSTR.
GRASERSGASSE
VORD. STERNGASSE
LUITPOLDSTR.
KÖNIGSTOR
Handwerkerhof
BADSTR.
BAHNHOFSTR.
Städtische
Bühnen
FRAUENTORGRABEN
ALLERSBERGER STR.
To Meistersingerhalle and
Reichsparteitagsgelände
Richard-
Wagner-
Platz
REGENSBURGER
STR.
EILGUTSTR.
Hauptbahnhof
SANDSTR.

dominance superseded by newly discovered maritime routes, Nuremberg suffered an economic decline that lasted almost 200 years. But then, in 1835, the first railway link in Germany opened between Nuremberg and Fürth, and over the following century, the city experienced a regrowth, this time as an industrial center.

Nuremberg's reemergence as a major Bavarian city attracted the attention of Adolf Hitler. Finding the city's medieval tradition appealing, the leader of the newly ascending Nazi Party designated Nuremberg the ceremonial center of the Third Reich in the early 1930s. Hitler ordered a large convention hall, grandstand, and parade ground to be built just outside the city. The party's annual rallies were held here from 1933 through 1938; the Nuremberg Laws were drafted at a convention in 1935. During World War II, the city was a leading manufacturer of airplane, tank, and submarine parts. Nuremberg paid dearly for its prominent link to the Nazi war effort: The Allies targeted it for major bombing raids and nearly decimated it.

In the 50 years since the war, Nuremberg has risen yet again. It is now one of Germany's major industrial cities, manufacturing chemicals, electrical equipment, writing implements, textiles, and beer. The 48 fairs and exhibitions Nuremberg hosts each year attract a large number of business visitors, and the city is becoming a center for tourism as well. In a reunited Germany, it is poised and ready for even more growth. However, the city has not abandoned its history: Nuremberg was largely reconstructed according to its prewar layout, and its houses, churches, the *Kaiserburg* (Imperial Castle), and 3 miles of the town walls have been restored to their original condition. The *Justizpalast* (Hall of Justice), where Nazi leaders were tried and sentenced, and the *Reichsparteitagsgelände* (Nazi Party Rally Grounds), where Hitler addressed massive crowds, remain as haunting reminders of the city's connection to the Nazis. Today's visitor to Nuremberg can get a taste of its 900-year history of triumph and cultural advancement mingled with conflict and devastation and then rebirth—a history that mirrors Germany's own.

Nuremberg At-a-Glance

SEEING THE CITY

The Altstadt (Old City), with its pointed gables, timber-framed houses, and cobblestone yards, can be seen from the top of the *Sinnwellturm* (Sinnwell Tower), which is part of the *Kaiserburg* (see *Special Places*). The breathtaking vista is well worth climbing the 113 steps to the top (there is no elevator). The tower is open daily; admission charge.

SPECIAL PLACES

Enclosed by huge city walls, central Nuremberg is easy to tour. The areas on both sides of the river Pegnitz are ideal for exploring on foot because many of the leading sights—such as the castle, the marketplace, and Albrecht

Dürer's house—are within walking distance of each other. The cemetery where Dürer and Veit Stoss are buried can be found on Johannisstrasse, a charming street lined with little Baroque-style houses outside the walled part of the city. It can be reached on foot, by car, or by tramway. The *Reichsparteitagsgelände* and the *Justizpalast* are both accessible by public transportation.

DOWNTOWN

HANDWERKERHOF West of the *Königstor* (King's Gate), this medieval craftsmen's courtyard is situated directly behind the old city wall (the massive tower next to it was built in 1388). Today the courtyard is filled with the workshops of potters, glassblowers, carvers, doll makers, and other artisans; there also is a stall that sells gingerbread and a little eatery offering Franconian specialties. Closed Sundays and from late December through mid-March. No admission charge.

ST. LORENZKIRCHE (CHURCH OF ST. LAWRENCE) A short distance from the *Königstor,* down the pedestrian area of Königstrasse, is this Protestant church, which also lends its name to the area south of the Pegnitz. Dating from about 1250, the church was destroyed by bombing in 1945, but has been painstakingly restored to its original splendor. The structure is distinguished by twin Gothic steeples; its hunchbacked look is created by the raised choir (a space behind the altar where the clergy stand). The interior is equally splendid, containing Stoss's hanging sculpture *Engelsgruss* (Angel's Greeting), among other fine works of art. In summer, be sure to look at the Renaissance-style *Tugendbrunnen* (Virtues Fountain) in front of the church; the female figures spurt water from their breasts—a most unusual sight. Services are still conducted here on Sundays. On Lorenzer Pl., near Königstr. and Lorenzstr. (phone: 209287 or 209288).

HAUPTMARKT This marketplace stands on the site of a former Jewish ghetto, which was burned to the ground by townspeople as part of an anti-Semitic pogrom in 1349. During the weeks before *Christmas,* Germany's most famous *Christkindlesmarkt* is held here (for details, see *Special Events*). The rest of the year, a fruit, vegetable, and flower market takes place daily—a colorful spectacle with dozens of vendors loudly extolling their wares and negotiating prices in idiomatic German. A dominant feature in the marketplace is the *Schöner Brunnen* (Beautiful Fountain), an elegant, 60-foot-high Gothic fountain from the late 14th century. Try to be here at noon, when the clock in the gable of the adjoining *Frauenkirche* (Our Lady's Church) puts on a show called the *Männleinlaufen:* As the clock strikes the hour, seven exquisitely carved miniatures of noblemen dressed in red come out to pay homage to Emperor Charles IV. Located off Rathauspl., just north of An der Fleisch-Brücke.

RATHAUS (TOWN HALL) The grandeur of this structure, built in the 1620s to replace a 14th-century hall, reflects Nuremberg's importance as a trading place and conference site for the emperor in the 17th century. Destroyed during World War II, it was subsequently restored to its original state. Today, the building's medieval prison cells and *Lochgefängnis* (torture chamber) can be explored. Open daily. Admission charge. Rathauspl. (phone: 231-2690).

ST. SEBALDUSKIRCHE (CHURCH OF ST. SEBALDUS) Like its twin, *St. Lorenzkirche* (above), this church was devastated in attacks during World War II but has been faithfully restored to its former glory. Although not as richly endowed with artwork as *St. Lorenzkirche,* it contains the shrine of St. Sebald, a Gothic cast-bronze housing by Peter Fischer, a triptych of *Christ's Passion and Resurrection* by Adam Krafft, and woodcarvings by Veit Stoss. Sebalderpl. (phone: 224572).

ALBRECHT-DÜRER-HAUS Dürer, the renowned German Renaissance painter, moved into this respectable-looking four-story house at the corner of Tiergärtnerplatz in 1509, and lived and worked here until his death in 1528. The 16th-century architecture remains, both inside and out: The exterior features half-timbering and gables, and the kitchen and parlor have been faithfully restored. In the square, 50 yards or so from the house, sits an unusual sight: a modern bronze figure that depicts a huge rabbit bursting out of a crate and squashing a man. The artwork, created in 1984 by sculptor Jürgen Görtz, parodies Dürer's *Resting Hare;* the rabbit's position exactly replicates that of the one in the famous painting. Closed Mondays. Admission charge. Tiergärtnerpl. (phone: 231-2568).

KAISERBURG (IMPERIAL CASTLE) Every German emperor between 1050 and 1571 held court in this huge palace joined to the northwest corner of the city wall, though none lived there. All the furniture and trappings were "leased" while the rulcrs held court; for that reason, the *Kaisersaal* (Imperial Hall) and the *Rittersaal* (Knights' Hall) stand empty today. There also is the *Palaskapelle* (Palas Chapel), with simple, Romanesque architecture; a 164-foot well; and the *Sinnwellturm* (Sinnwell Tower), which affords a great view of the Altstadt. There are guided tours (available in English by prior arrangement); also, a leaflet in English detailing a self-guided tour is available at the *Sinnwellturm.* Open daily. Admission charge. Located off Tiergärtnerplatz (phone: 225726).

SPIELZEUGMUSEUM (TOY MUSEUM) Set in a Renaissance-style building with several modern additions, this is one of the most delightful museums in Germany. Among its exhibits is an extensive collection of dollhouses, all with meticulous reproductions of typical rooms such as kitchens and drawing rooms. Other exhibits include antique books, dolls, and other playthings. Closed Mondays. Admission charge. 13-15 Karlsstr. (phone: 231-3260).

GERMANISCHES NATIONALMUSEUM (GERMANIC NATIONAL MUSEUM) The largest museum of art and culture in Germany, it is set in a former monastery.

Exhibits date from the Stone Age to the 19th century and include antique armor and weapons, musical instruments, paintings and other art (including works by Dürer), and the world's first geographical globe (made in 1491). Closed Mondays. No admission charge on Sundays and holidays. 1 Kornmarkt (phone: 13310).

FEMBO HAUS Built in the 16th century, this is one of the few merchants' houses that survived World War II. Its interior, including the wood paneling and rich stucco ceilings, is still intact. Now a museum, the house contains furniture and paintings dating from the 17th century to the present. Closed Mondays. Admission charge. 15 Burgstr. (phone: 231-2595).

ENVIRONS

REICHSPARTEITAGSGELÄNDE (NAZI PARTY RALLY GROUNDS) In the southeastern part of the city, this area is the most significant reminder of the Nazi era in Nuremberg. When Adolf Hitler chose Nuremberg as the site for ceremonial Nazi rallies, he ordered the construction of a parade ground, a stadium, a *Zeppelintribüne* (grandstand), and a convention hall fashioned after the Colosseum in Rome. His grand plans were interrupted by the war; some construction had begun, but only the *Zeppelintribüne* was completed. Echoes of what was and what could have been ring in the otherwise empty space—in use only during the annual *Norisring Rennen* (Norisring Car Race). The *Kaiserburg* can be seen on the horizon, which to Hitler symbolically linked the Third Reich to the glorious days of the German Empire. An exhibition on the Nazis and their history can be viewed in the *Goldenesaal* (Golden Hall) of the *Zeppelintribüne.* Guided tours of the area (in German) are given on weekends at 2 PM starting at the *Luitpoldhain* tram stop; English-language tours can be arranged for large groups. Closed Mondays and November through June. Admission charge for tours only. Take the *U-Bahn* No. 1 or No. 11 to Aufsessplatz, and then take either tram No. 4 to Dutzendteich or No. 9 to Luitpoldhain. From either place, it's a short walk to the *Zeppelintribüne.* At the *Zeppelinfeld* (phone: 231-2519).

JUSTIZPALAST (HALL OF JUSTICE) Here, in courtroom 600, many of the Nazi leaders were tried for war crimes in late 1945. The prisoners were held in underground cells during the trials. Ten of the defendants, including Joachim von Ribbentrop, Julius Streicher, Martin Bormann (in absentia), and Hermann Göring, were sentenced to death (although Göring committed suicide in his cell before he could be executed). Today, the hall still holds trials. Tours in English are available by prior arrangement. Closed weekends. No admission charge. To get here, take the *U-Bahn* No. 1 to Bärenschanze. Fürther Str. (phone: 32101).

JOHANNISFRIEDHOF (JOHANNIS CEMETERY) Albrecht Dürer and Veit Stoss are among the famous Germans buried in this churchyard on Johannisstrasse, laid out in 1518. The surrounding area is dotted with quaint old houses and small cafés. The houses at Nos. 13 and 47 Johannisstrasse have attractive little gardens, complete with boxwood border beds and sculptures, that are open to the public during the day (no admission charge). Take tram No. 6 to Brückenstrasse; from there, it's a short walk to the entrance on Johannistrasse.

Sources and Resources

TOURIST INFORMATION

The *Nürnberg Verkehrsverein* (Nuremberg Tourist Board) has offices in the central hall of the *Hauptbahnhof* (main railroad station) and, during summer, in the *Rathaus* at the *Hauptmarkt* (phone: 233-6110 for both). They can provide information, maps, brochures, and hotel and restaurant listings, and will arrange accommodations and guided tours. Both offices are closed Sundays.

LOCAL COVERAGE The monthly *Das Aktuelle Monats Magazin* and *Plärrer* magazines (both in German only) are the major local publications. No English-language newspapers or magazines are available in the city. However, the *Colour City Guide,* available at museum shops and the tourist office, is a short guide in English of the Altstadt, including a map. Another handy guidebook is *Rundwege Nürnberg* (Bayerische Verlagsanstalt; 12 DM/about $7.20), which describes several walking tours of the city in German and English. It can be purchased at local bookstores.

TELEPHONE The city code for Nuremberg is 911.

GETTING AROUND

AIRPORT *Flughafen Nürnberg* (Nuremberg International Airport), 4 miles (6 km) outside the city center, has flights to most major European cities, including Frankfurt, from which you can catch international flights to the US and other non-European destinations. The taxi ride to the airport takes about 20 minutes. Bus No. 20 connects the airport to Nuremberg; it makes the trip every 30 minutes from 5 AM to 11 PM. For information, call 350-6240.

BUS AND SUBWAY Nuremberg has a small and comprehensive underground system (three lines) as well as buses and tramways. Tickets, which can be used on all forms of public transportation, are available at automatic dispensers located throughout the city. A single ride costs 2.20 DM (about $1.20); passes allowing unlimited use for a day (6.90 DM/about $4.15), a weekend (9 DM/about $5.40), and a week (23.50 DM/about $14.10) are available. The main bus, tram, and subway depot is on Am Plärrer, on the southwest tip of the Altstadt.

CAR RENTAL The major international firms are represented at the airport. Companies in town include *Avis* (139 Allersberger Str.; phone: 49696);

Hertz (25 Unter Grasersgasse; phone: 209086); and *Sixt Budget* (966 Witzchelstr.; phone: 318-8888).

TAXI Cabs can be hailed in the streets; there also are taxi stands at the *Hauptbahnhof,* Hallplatz, Lorenzplatz, Jakobsplatz, *Hauptmarkt,* and Laufer Platz. To call ahead for a taxi, contact *Taxi Central Nürnberg* (phone: 19410).

TOURS *Reba Eno Travel* (phone: 204444) offers guided city bus tours in German and English. The trips, which include the castle, *Johannisfriedhof,* the *Reichsparteitagsgelände,* and the *Justizpalast,* leave Hallplatz daily at 9:30 AM from May to October and during *Christkindlesmarkt.* Tickets can be purchased on the bus. Tours also can be arranged through the tourist office (see *Tourist Information*).

TRAIN *InterCity* and *InterCity Express* trains run every hour between the *Hauptbahnhof* and Hamburg, Cologne, Frankfurt, and Munich (phone: 19419).

SPECIAL EVENTS

The highlight of Nuremberg's calendar occurs at *Christmas,* when the city seizes the opportunity to put on a very special celebration.

A FAVORITE FETE

Christkindlesmarkt Each year, more than two million visitors from Germany and the rest of the world come to Nuremberg for this market, held daily throughout December in the *Hauptmarkt.* Similar festivities are held across Germany, but this one is the country's oldest, dating from the early 17th century. On the first Friday in December, the market is opened in a ceremony featuring a teenaged girl (wearing a gold wig, unless she is naturally blonde) representing the *Christkind* (Christ Child). (The tradition of having a young girl play the *Christkind,* which began shortly after World War II, stems from the German notion of Christ as a blonde angel.) The *Christkind,* selected in a beauty contest similar to the Miss America pageant, stands on the parapet of the adjoining *Frauenkirche* (Our Lady's Church) and recites a poem to officially begin the market. From then on, the *Hauptmarkt,* gaily decked out for the occasion with *Christmas* decorations, is filled with vendors selling toys, pastries (including the ubiquitous gingerbread), and other holiday items. One of the festivity's highlights is a procession on *Lucientag* (St. Lucia's Day, December 13), when thousands of children bearing lighted paper lanterns march through the city streets from the Fleisch-Brücke to the castle. Also see *Quintessential Germany* in DIVERSIONS.

Most other events in Nuremberg happen during the summer; for information on specific dates and places, contact the tourist office (see *Tourist*

Information). In odd-numbered years, the *Internationales Figurentheater Festival* (International Puppet Theater Festival) is held in May at various locations in Nuremberg and in the nearby cities of Fürth and Erlangen. The *Volksmusik in St. Katherina* (Folk Music Festival in St. Katharina), with folk, jazz, and classical concerts performed at various venues throughout the city, occurs from May through October; there also are dance and theater performances. The *Jazz-Ost-West* festival, featuring performances by international musicians, is held at various venues during the first three weeks of August in even-numbered years. The *Norisring Rennen* (Norisring Car Race) is held in the *Norisring* at the *Zeppelinfeld* over two days in June. In celebration of *Internationale Orgelwoche* (International Organ Week), Europe's leading festival of sacred music, organ concerts are performed in Nuremberg's main churches for a month in early summer. During the *Bardentressen* (Minstrels' Gathering) in July, musicians perform in the streets throughout the city; the spectacle attracts visitors from around the world. July also marks the annual *Internationales Marathon* road race.

MUSEUMS

In addition to those mentioned in *Special Places,* Nuremberg has a number of other interesting museums, most of them within walking distance of each other.

KUNSTHALLE (ART MUSEUM) Features exhibitions by contemporary German artists. Closed Mondays. Admission charge. 8 Marientorgraben (phone: 231-2403).

MUSEUM INDUSTRIEKULTUR (MUSEUM OF INDUSTRIAL CULTURE) Set in a former factory, this museum has displays focusing on Germany's history as an industrial nation—among them, steam engines, a gypsum mill, and re-creations of typical street scenes from the 19th century, including middle class homes and shops. Closed Mondays. Admission charge. 62 Aussere Sulzbacher Str. (phone: 231-3648).

SCHULMUSEUM (SCHOOL MUSEUM) Examines the history of education in Germany from the Middle Ages to the present. Closed Saturdays. Admission charge. 37 Panierpl. (phone: 208387).

TUCHERSCHLÖSSCHEN (TUCHER'S LITTLE CASTLE) Built in 1533 as the residence of a local aristocrat, this house contains 16th-century German and Italian furnishings. Open for guided tours only (in English by prior arrangement), given Mondays through Thursdays at 2, 3, and 4 PM and Fridays at 9, 10, and 11 AM. Admission charge. 9 Hirschelgasse (phone: 231-2371).

VERKEHRSMUSEUM (MUSEUM OF TRANSPORT) Exhibits about the history of the railway and postal service, including a model of the first German locomotive (from 1835), vintage stamps, original 19th-century trains, and the luxurious royal carriage of King Ludwig II of Bavaria. Open daily. Admission charge. 6 Lessingstr. (phone: 219-2428).

SHOPPING

Though Nuremberg isn't really a shopper's city, there are some unique and often interesting places worth checking out. In the area near the *Kaiserburg* are small, often family-run stores with miniature dollhouse furniture (including some exquisite—and pricey—pieces), tin figures, antique pewter, and pottery. More conventional antiques shops and a few art galleries are found in the lanes behind *Unschlitthaus of 1490,* a huge sandstone building at Unschlittplatz formerly used as a warehouse for tallow (*Unschlitt*) and grain.

Karstadt The city's major department store, with a variety of men's and women's clothing, furnishings, and housewares. 14 Königstr. (phone: 213490).

Kistner Antique books and engravings, some of which date from as early as 1460. 6 Weinmarkt (phone: 203482).

Lebkuchen Frauenholz Tasty, fresh-baked gingerbread and honey sold in a reproduction of a half-timbered, 18th-century building. 1 Bergstr. (phone: 243464).

Obletter Toys and model trains. 2 Königstr. (phone: 20775).

Villeroy & Boch Exquisite porcelain trinkets, as well as paper napkins with fanciful designs. 13 Königstr. (phone: 223182).

Weihnachtstruhe/Puppenhaus Dolls, dollhouses, and other playthings. 16 Albrecht-Dürer-Str. (phone: 243303).

Zinn Menna Tin soldiers, both antique and new. 3 Bischof-Meiser-Str. (phone: 227481).

Die Zinnfigur A large variety of beautifully crafted tin figures, including (but not limited to) soldiers. 54 Obere Schmiedgasse (phone: 226546).

SPORTS AND FITNESS

BICYCLING There are good cycling paths along the Pegnitz River. *Bicycle Rent* (17 Bielingstr.; phone: 397337) is open Mondays through Saturdays; your hotel may also be able to arrange rentals.

GOLF In one of the city's neighborhoods outside the walls, *Golfclub am Reichswald* (100 Schiestlstr., Nürnberg-Kraftshof; phone: 391288) has an 18-hole public course open mid-March through October.

SOCCER The local soccer team, *FC Nürnberg* (known simply as "the club"), plays on Saturdays mid-February through April in the *Frankenstadion* near the *Zeppelinfeld.* Tickets can be purchased at the *Amtliches Bayerisches Reisebüro* (Bavarian Travel Bureau; at the *Hauptbahnhof;* phone: 20100) or at *Karstadt* department store (see *Shopping,* above).

SWIMMING *Hallenbad Langwasser* (25 Breslauer Str.; phone: 803979) has both indoor and outdoor pools. There are indoor pools at *Hallenbad Süd* (120 Allersberger Str.; phone: 443884); *Palm Beach* (29 Albert-Magnus-Str.; phone: 688-7980); and *Hallenbad Nord-Ost* (85 Elbinger Str.; phone: 515025).

Outdoor pools are at *Freibad West* (41 Wiesentalstr.; phone: 330262); *Naturgartenbad* (20 Schlegelstr.; phone: 592545); and *Sportbad Langsee* (25 Ebenseestr.; phone: 543516).

TENNIS *Foldina Tennis* (at Messezentrum; phone: 819900) has 19 indoor and 12 outdoor courts.

THEATER

The *Städtische Bühnen* (City Theater; 2-10 Richard-Wagner-Pl.; phone: 231-3808), a massive 19th-century building with an ornate interior, is Nuremberg's main venue, presenting both classic and new works in theater and opera. Experimental, avant-garde productions are performed at the *Theaterhalle Tafelwerk* (60 Aussere Sulzbacher Str.; phone: 540730), a factory that was converted into a theater in 1986. Though the outside still looks industrial, the interior is attractive and comfortable.

Cabaret-style shows are presented at the *Loni-Ubler-Haus* (60 Marthastr.; phone: 541156), and puppet shows for children are staged at the *Marionetten-Theater* (in a gazebo at *Cramer-Klett-Park,* just outside the city walls; phone: 890538). Every summer, open-air theater productions are performed at the ruins of *Katharinenkloster* (Katharinen Monastery), just inside the wall near the river. Tickets can be ordered through *Kulturamt* (phone: 2310).

MUSIC

A wide variety of music—from classical and rock to avant-garde and folk—can be heard in Nuremberg. Regular concerts by the *Nuremberg Philharmonic Orchestra* and the *Nuremberg Symphonics* take place in the *Meistersingerhalle* (21 Münchener Str.; phone: 492011). Opera is performed at *Städtische Bühnen* (see *Theater*). The excellent choirs that perform at *St. Sebalduskirche* and *St. Lorenzkirche* are always a treat to hear. Rock concerts are held at the *KOMM* (Communication Center; 93 Königstr.; phone: 223647). For more details about musical events throughout the city, contact the tourist office (see *Tourist Information*).

NIGHTCLUBS AND NIGHTLIFE

For such a quaint, sleepy-looking town, Nuremberg has a surprisingly brisk nightlife. The pubs in the Weissgerbergasse area near the *Kaiserburg* attract a lively crowd of university students, as does the *Kettensteg* beer garden (just beyond the chain bridge across the Pegnitz; phone: 221081). Good dance clubs include *Don't Panic,* in the *KOMM* (93 Königstr.; phone: 221463) and *Mach 1* (1-9 Kaiserstr.; phone: 203030). *Kon Tiki* (10-14 Untere Wörthstr.; phone: 722-1139) is a Polynesian-style cocktail bar located on the banks of the Pegnitz. *Schmelztiegel* (21 Bergerstr.; phone: 203982) is a jazz club offering live bands every Tuesday and recorded music on other evenings. The most recent addition to the nightlife scene is *LGB* (16 Burgstr.; phone: 471973), with live music, a bar, and a cinema showing mainly movies in German.

Best in Town

CHECKING IN

Throughout the year, Nuremberg gets deluged with both vacationers and businesspeople attending the numerous trade fairs held here, so it's a good idea to book well in advance. However, if you arrive in town without a confirmed reservation in hand, the tourist office at the *Hauptbahnhof* (see *Tourist Information*) can help you get a room. Due to open early this year is the *Mövenpick Cadettt,* a 148-room establishment across from the airport which will have a fitness center, a sauna, business services, and conference rooms, as well as a branch of *Mövenpick,* the popular Swiss restaurant chain that owns the property (for more information, call 711-94930 in Stuttgart). Most of Nuremberg's major hotels have complete facilities for the business traveler. Those hotels listed as having "business services" usually offer such conveniences as an English-speaking concierge, meeting rooms, photocopiers, computers, translation services, and express checkout, among others. Call the hotel for additional information. Expect to pay more than $200 a night for a double room (including breakfast, private bath, TV set, and phone, unless otherwise noted) at a hotel listed as very expensive, $140 to $200 at places described as expensive, $80 to $120 at hotels in the moderate category, and under $70 at places listed as inexpensive. All telephone numbers are in the 911 city code unless otherwise indicated.

VERY EXPENSIVE

Grand Close to the station, this late-19th-century hotel with 186 rooms offers such luxury amenities as a sauna and a fitness room. The *Brasserie* (see *Eating Out*) is one of the city's best continental restaurants; *Die Kanne* tavern serves good Franconian fare. Business services are available. 1-3 Bahnhofstr. (phone: 23220; fax: 232-2444).

Maritim The unprepossessing exterior of this building hides a first class hotel—the most exclusive and luxurious in town. Conveniently located near the *Hauptbahnhof* and the Altstadt, this modern property has 316 well-appointed rooms and suites with marble baths. Other amenities include two restaurants (including the elegant *Die Auster;* see *Eating Out*), a piano bar, an indoor pool, a sauna, and business services. 11 Frauentorgraben (phone: 23630; 800-843-3311; fax: 236-3836).

Scandic Crown Located in a charming, picturesque, and upscale neighborhood on the east side of town, this modern 152-room hotel offers both a quiet atmosphere and relative proximity to the city center's tourist attractions, shopping, and restaurants. The ambience is almost palatial, with marble floors in the public areas and tasteful, contemporary decor in the guestrooms. Facilities include a pool, a sauna, a fitness center, and a tanning salon, as well as conference rooms and business services. The dining room serves continental and Franconian fare. 200 Valznerweiherstr. (phone: 40290; fax: 404067).

EXPENSIVE

Altea Hotel Carlton This grand 130-room hotel, built in 1939 and modernized and refurbished, has managed to retain some of its original charm. The *Golf Bar* restaurant features live music into the small hours. Its location near the railway station is convenient, albeit a bit noisy. Business services are available. 13-15 Eilgutstr. (phone: 20030; fax: 200-3532).

Atrium Set in a park near *Meistersingerhalle,* this comfortable establishment offers 187 well-appointed rooms, a solarium, a bar, a French restaurant, and business services. 25 Münchener Str. (phone: 47480; fax: 474-8420).

Dürer Next to *Albrecht-Dürer-Haus* in the Altstadt, this quiet, modern property offers 105 rooms, a bistro, a bar, and a full fitness center with a solarium. There's also a convenient underground parking lot. 32 Neutormauer (phone: 208091; fax: 223458).

Nestor The design of this 75-room hostelry innovatively combines a 19th-century patrician house with a modern addition featuring a lobby, a solarium, a conference room, and a good restaurant. It's conveniently located on the tramway route and a short walk from the city center. Business services are available. 125 Bucher Str., Nürnberg-Buch (phone: 34760; fax: 347-6113).

MODERATE

Burghotel A small, 47-room hotel near the castle, it fills up fast year-round due to its quiet, convenient location, so be sure to reserve well in advance. The cozy interior is decorated in traditional Franconian style. There's no restaurant. 3 Lammsgasse (phone: 204414; fax: 223458).

Hotel am Jakobsmarkt Modern and quiet, this property with 70 standard rooms and a few apartments with kitchenettes is very close to the city center. There is a fitness center, but no restaurant. 5 Schottengasse (phone: 241434; fax: 22874).

Merian A cozy, historic alternative to the modern establishments in town is this 20-room inn set in an 18th-century house. Many of the rooms offer a lovely view of a cobbled square surrounded by other 18th-century houses and trees; the *Opatija* restaurant is on the ground floor. 7 Unschlittpl. (phone: 204194; fax 221274).

Weinhaus Steichele This small, charming hostelry just outside the city wall near Jakobsplatz features 45 rooms and a restaurant that has attractive decor, good Franconian fare, and an excellent wine list. 2-8 Knorrstr. (phone: 204377; fax: 221914).

Zirbelstube In a country setting near the canal, about 6 miles (10 km) outside the city, is a beautiful historic house (protected by the National Trust) built in the 18th century. There are six individually decorated, cozy rooms and one of the best restaurants in town (see *Eating Out*). It is inconvenient to public transportation, however, so a car is essential. Closed for two weeks in February and three weeks during summer holidays (which change from year to year). 1 Friedrich-Overbeck-Str., Nürnberg-Worzeldorf (phone: 998820).

INEXPENSIVE

Jugendgästehaus Nürnberg Underneath the huge roof of the *Kaiserburg*'s imperial stables, this hostel provides basic accommodations at very reasonable rates—ideal for travelers on a tight budget. There are 72 rooms with two to six beds each, and four rooms with 15 beds each; all have shared baths. The establishment has a cafeteria, a disco, table tennis, and a TV room with a VCR. 2 Burg (phone: 221024; fax: 22040).

Jugend und Economy Here are 139 rooms with few frills (though all have at least a shower and some have TV sets and private baths) just outside the city walls. A full buffet breakfast is included in the rate. There's also a cafeteria that serves simple Franconian fare. 47-49 Gostenhofer Hauptstr. (phone: 92620; fax: 926-2130).

EATING OUT

Nuremberg is the place to sample traditional Franconian specialties—particularly bratwurst (roasted sausages). Street vendors downtown often sell bratwurst wrapped in a crisp roll and garnished with a bit of mustard for informal munching; numerous restaurants also serve many versions of the spicy food. Another local specialty is fresh carp, prepared in various ways. Continental fare is offered in the city's more elegant dining places (these are usually open for dinner only). Many of the city's inexpensive eateries are closed in the evenings. Expect to pay $100 to $150 for a three-course meal for two (not including drinks or wine) at a restaurant listed as expensive, $60 to $90 at moderate places, and under $60 at inexpensive places. Taxes and service charges are included in the bill, but you should leave a small additional tip for good service. Unless otherwise noted, restaurants are open for lunch and dinner. All telephone numbers are in the 911 city code unless otherwise specified.

For an unforgettable dining experience, we begin with our culinary favorite, followed by our cost and quality choices, listed by price category.

DELIGHTFUL DINING

Essigbrätlein Like Germany itself, the restaurant in this Franconian inn built in 1550 has outlasted all its different managements and names without sacrificing a bit of its charm. The rustic look of its wood walls and tables is softened by elegant modern touches—

crisp napery, fine china, and gleaming silver. Every morning, the chef visits the local markets, sifting through produce as if he were panning for gold. The menu offers a limited number of Franconian and French dishes with chicken, beef, and fresh seafood, all exquisitely prepared. The dining experience may be pricey, but it's well worth it. It's very popular, so make your reservations early. Closed Sundays, Mondays, and Saturday lunch. Reservations necessary. Major credit cards accepted. 3 Am Weinmarkt (phone: 225131).

EXPENSIVE

Die Auster The classy restaurant at the *Maritim* hotel offers first-rate continental fare in surroundings that are ornate to the point of being a bit flashy. Open for dinner only; closed Sundays and during August. Reservations advised. Major credit cards accepted. 11 Frauentorgraben (phone: 236-3812).

Brasserie Tastefully decorated with sandstone walls, Tiffany glass, and wood furnishings, the dining room of the *Grand* hotel combines Old World elegance with Art Deco style. The menu features excellent presentations of both Franconian and continental fare; typical dishes include steaks, cutlets, *Ratsherrenteller* (beef or pork served in a mushroom sauce), liver dumpling soup, and wurst prepared in various ways. On Friday evenings, there is an all-you-can-eat buffet. The quintessentially German *Kaffee und Kuchen* (coffee and cake) is served here in the afternoons. Open daily. Reservations advised. Major credit cards accepted. 1-3 Bahnhofstr. (phone: 23220).

Im Goldenen Posthorn Across from *St. Sebalduskirche,* this restaurant is set in a historic building dating from 1498. The place used to be a stop for mail delivery in the Middle Ages; its name—which roughly translates as "At the Golden Post-Bugle"—refers to the fact that mail carriers used to blow a bugle to announce their arrival in a town. Here, authentic regional fare is served in appropriately Franconian surroundings: The decor is simple and rustic, with wooden benches and bull's-eye windows. Try the fresh carp (offered in the winter) either baked or fried; another choice is wurst prepared with a mixture of onions and vinegar. One of the restaurant's most famous patrons was artist Albrecht Dürer; the mug he used to drink his beer from is on display. Closed Sundays. Reservations advised. MasterCard and Visa accepted. An der Sebalduskirche (phone: 225153).

Schwarzer Adler A few minutes' drive from the city, this beautiful 19th-century inn offers Old World atmosphere and first-rate fare. Try the red snapper with ginger or breast of duck with Calvados; for dessert, the white chocolate mousse served with frosted pears is a sinful treat. There is a delightful garden in the rear. Closed from late December to the beginning of January. Reservations advised. Major credit cards accepted. 166 Kraftshofer Hauptstr., Nürnberg-Kraftshof (phone: 305858).

Zirbelstube In the hotel of the same name, this intimate, romantic dining room overlooking a canal serves light, perfectly prepared continental fare featuring fresh seafood, lamb, and veal; its wine list is exemplary. Open for dinner only; closed Sundays and Mondays, two weeks in February, and three weeks during the summer. Reservations advised. Major credit cards accepted. 1 Friedrich-Overbeck-Str., Nürnberg-Worzeldorf (phone: 998820).

MODERATE

Fischküche The decor of this seafood eatery harkens to the 1960s, and the service and atmosphere are friendly and casual. The menu is exclusively seafood—including fresh carp, lobster, oysters, and salmon served in generous portions. It is often crowded, especially during trade fairs. Open daily. Reservations necessary. Major credit cards accepted. 63 Pirckheimer Str. (phone: 351003).

Peppino You might not expect to find first-rate Italian food in Germany, but here it is—ravioli, spaghetti, and a wide selection of pizza. The excellent cooking, friendly service, and moderate prices make up for the rather pedestrian atmosphere. Closed Sundays and Mondays. No reservations. No credit cards accepted. 16 Maffeipl. (phone: 440137).

INEXPENSIVE

Amaranth Located on a side street near the pedestrian zone, this buffet-style vegetarian restaurant offers a choice of more than 20 salads, several specials, and fresh-squeezed fruit and vegetable juices. The menu changes frequently, but typical dishes include vegetable lasagna and celeryroot schnitzel (a version of Wiener schnitzel made with celeryroot, a large, ball-shaped green vegetable, and served with sauerkraut and mashed potatoes). The place is dominated by an eye-catching two-story granite fountain built into a wall. Open daily; no lunch on weekends. 11 Färberstr. (phone: 243724).

Confiserie Neef This café is a good place for afternoon coffee and fresh baked pastries. Closed Sundays. No reservations. No credit cards accepted. 29 Winklerstr. (phone: 225179).

Karstadt Feinkoststadl In the *Karstadt* department store, this eatery serves fresh oysters and seafood, along with delicatessen-style sandwiches. Open for breakfast and lunch; no breakfast on weekends. No reservations. No credit cards accepted. 14 Königstr. (phone: 213490).

Lederer Garten Traditional Franconian fare is served at this friendly beer garden; live bands sometimes play in the evenings. Open daily. No reservations. Major credit cards accepted. Located just outside the Bärenschanze stop of the *U-Bahn* (no phone).

Lotos A casual snack bar serving vegetarian and macrobiotic dishes, as well as some Indian and Thai specialties. Open daily for lunch only. No reservations. No credit cards accepted. 1 Unschlittpl. (phone: 243598).

Stuttgart

Few metropolitan areas have become so thoroughly identified with big-name industrial enterprise as Stuttgart. The world knows this city on the Neckar River, with a population of around 580,000, as a major business center—the headquarters of the Daimler-Benz and Porsche automobile companies, IBM Germany, Kodak Europe, the Siemens communications firm, and Bosch, the electrical equipment manufacturer. Symbols of industry dominate the downtown skyline: A revolving three-pointed Mercedes silver star atop the railroad station's 190-foot tower faces off against a red neon Bosch logo atop another tower across the way. Along with being a center of high-tech industry, Stuttgart is the governmental and cultural capital of the federal state of Baden-Württemberg. Its citizens are largely unpretentious and practical. Even the city's rather gutteral name contributes to its unromantic, almost stereotypical, working class image.

Like most stereotypes, however, this one tells only a small part of the story. In a lovely setting surrounded by the wooded Swabian Hills, Stuttgart has a bucolic, old-fashioned quality. More than half the urban area is devoted to parks, gardens, and forests, and a vineyard slopes right into the middle of downtown, near the railroad station. Dozens of stairways climbing to the hilltops from the lower town give the city something of a San Francisco atmosphere. Slicing through central Stuttgart is the *Schlossgarten* (Palace Garden), a stretch of public greenery so extensive that it's divided into three segments. The vast, beautiful *Rosenstein Park* abuts the *Schlossgarten,* and another large green space, the *Höhenpark,* includes Killesberg Hill on the northern outskirts of the city.

In addition, Stuttgart has an enduring reputation as an intellectual and cultural center: *Universität Stuttgart* (Stuttgart University) and the *Deutsches Institut für Auslandsbeziehungen* (Institute for International Relations) have nurtured such distinguished figures as poet Friedrich von Schiller, and the city boasts world class theater, opera, symphonic and chamber music, and art.

Stuttgart also has long been known for bold architecture, particularly for structures built during the Bauhaus movement of the 1920s and 1930s. Striking examples of this style include the city's first skyscraper, the 18-story *Tagblatt Turm* (built in 1928), which has been declared a historic monument; and the *Weissenhofsiedlung* (Weissenhof Colony; see *Special Places*). Other noteworthy buildings include the *Altes Schauspielhaus,* a *Jugendstil* (similar to Art Nouveau) theater built in 1909; and the Art Nouveau–style *Markthalle.* And although much of the downtown area was rebuilt in a rather bland modern style after being leveled by bombing in World War II, the reconstruction was mainly done using travertine marble and local sandstone, and as a result, the buildings have a pleasantly light and airy quality. Many of the postwar structures continue Stuttgart's tradition of architectural innovation. The Schulstrasse, Germany's first pedestrian mall, was finished in 1953; the impressive *Neues Rathaus* (New Town Hall), a neo-Bauhaus building featuring a glockenspiel that plays Swabian folk songs three times a day, was completed in 1956; and the *Fernsehturn* (Television Tower), also built in 1956, was the first of its kind in the world. But the city retains Old World elements as well. Part of the downtown area has been laid out in a crisscross pattern of charming pedestrian zones that are grouped around several plazas dating from the 16th to the 19th centuries.

In fact, Stuttgart's architecture offers an intriguing portrait of the city's history and its destiny. On Schillerplatz, the venerable *Stiftskirche* dates from the mid-15th century. The *Altes Schloss* (Old Palace) blends 14th-century Gothic and 16th-century Renaissance motifs, and the *Königsbau* (King's Building) on Schlossplatz (Palace Square) has changed little since it was first erected in the mid-19th century. In contrast is the starkly modern, asymmetrical appearance of the *Liederhalle* cultural and convention center near the town center, designed in 1956 by Adolf Abel and Rolf Gutbrod. The world-famous *Staatsgalerie* (State Gallery) is another blend of old and new: The original, neoclassical building has been combined with a modern addition, the *Neue Staatsgalerie* (New State Gallery), which opened only 11 years ago.

Once a sleepy outpost on the Neckar, Stuttgart owes its emergence as a city (as well as its name) to—of all things—a stud farm. In AD 950, the local Count of Swabia, concerned that Hungary might choose the area to launch an invasion of Germany, established the Stutengarten (literally, "mares' garden") in order to breed strong, agile horses and prepare a cavalry. (This part of Stuttgart's history is reflected in its coat of arms, which shows a prancing black horse on a gold background within a red frame—an image that is reflected today in the Porsche logo.) The next few centuries saw a period of slow but steady growth for the settlement. Exactly when the establishment received its current name is unknown, but the first reference to it as "Stuttgart" occurred in a document dated 1160. It was chartered as a market town in the 13th century. In 1320, the Counts of Swabia officially designated Stuttgart as their base and built the *Altes Schloss;* and in 1495, when the state of Württemberg was established, Stuttgart became its capital. Besides the *Altes Schloss,* several other royal residences were built in the area over the years, such as the 18th-century Baroque palace in nearby Ludwigsburg.

In the 19th century, Stuttgart's fate was irrevocably altered by the Industrial Revolution—in particular, the advent of the automobile. In the late 1800s, Karl Benz (1844–1929), a German engineer who lived and was educated here, pioneered the first internal combustion engine set on wheels—the first car. At around the same time, another local engineer named Gottlieb Daimler (1834–1900) managed to perfect the technology—and was able to get the jump on Benz. In 1890, Daimler founded the world's

STUTTGART

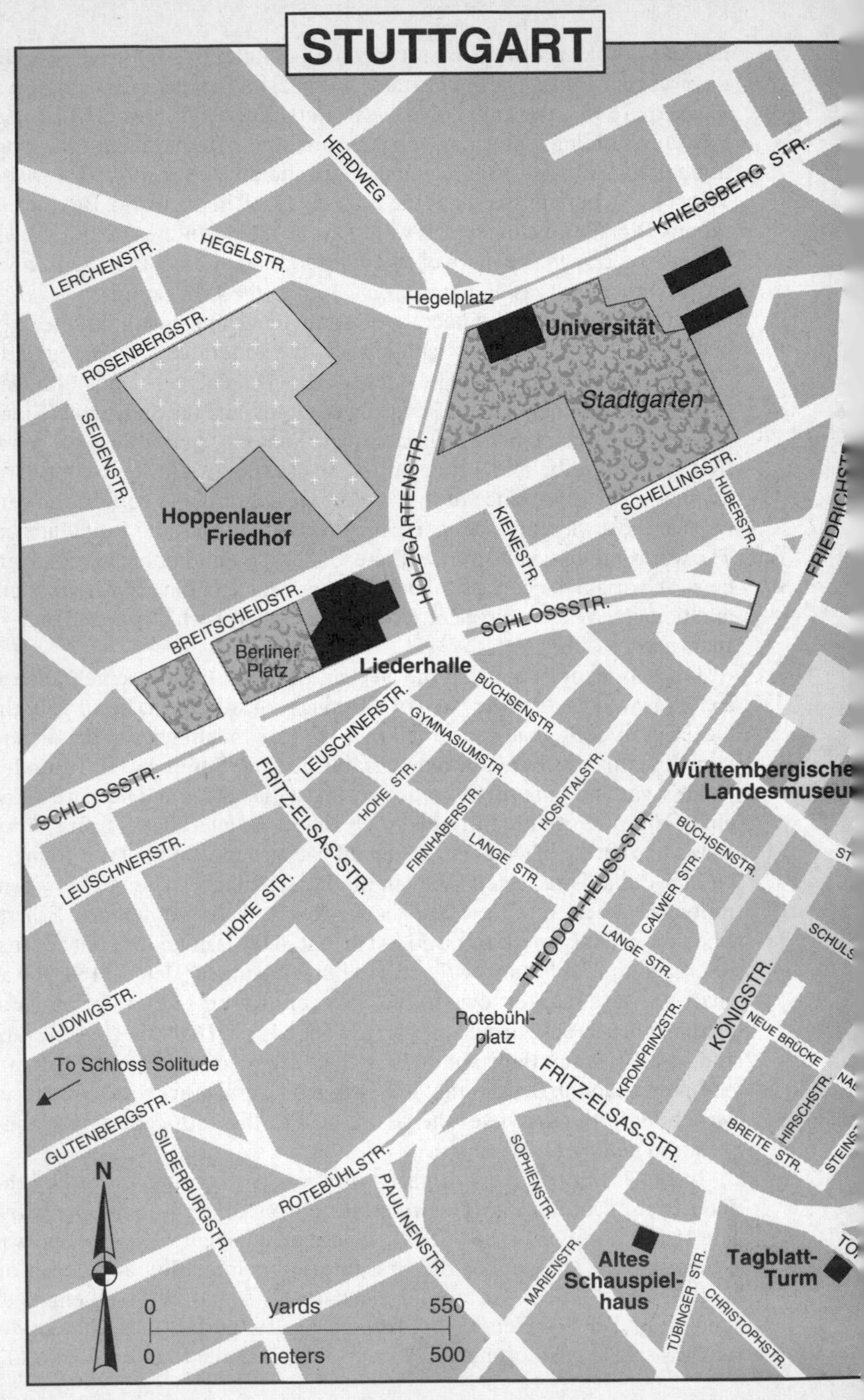

HERDWEG
KRIEGSBERG STR.
LERCHENSTR.
HEGELSTR.
Hegelplatz
Universität
ROSENBERGSTR.
Stadtgarten
SEIDENSTR.
HOLZGARTENSTR.
SCHELLINGSTR.
HUBERSTR.
Hoppenlauer
Friedhof
KIENESTR.
FRIEDRICHSTR.
BREITSCHEIDSTR.
SCHLOSSSTR.
Berliner
Platz
Liederhalle
BÜCHSENSTR.
LEUSCHNERSTR.
GYMNASIUMSTR.
Württembergische
Landesmuseum
SCHLOSSSTR.
FRITZ-ELSAS-STR.
HOHE STR.
HOSPITALSTR.
FIRNHABERSTR.
LEUSCHNERSTR.
LANGE STR.
THEODOR-HEUSS-STR.
BÜCHSENSTR.
CALWER STR.
HOHE STR.
LANGE STR.
SCHULS
LUDWIGSTR.
Rotebühl-
platz
KÖNIGSTR.
NEUE BRÜCKE
To Schloss Solitude
KRONPRINZSTR.
FRITZ-ELSAS-STR.
HIRSCHSTR.
GUTENBERGSTR.
SILBERBURGSTR.
SOPHIENSTR.
BREITE STR.
ROTEBÜHLSTR.
PAULINENSTR.
N
MARIENSTR.
Altes
Schauspiel-
haus
TÜBINGER STR.
Tagblatt-
Turm
CHRISTOPHSTR.
0 yards 550
0 meters 500

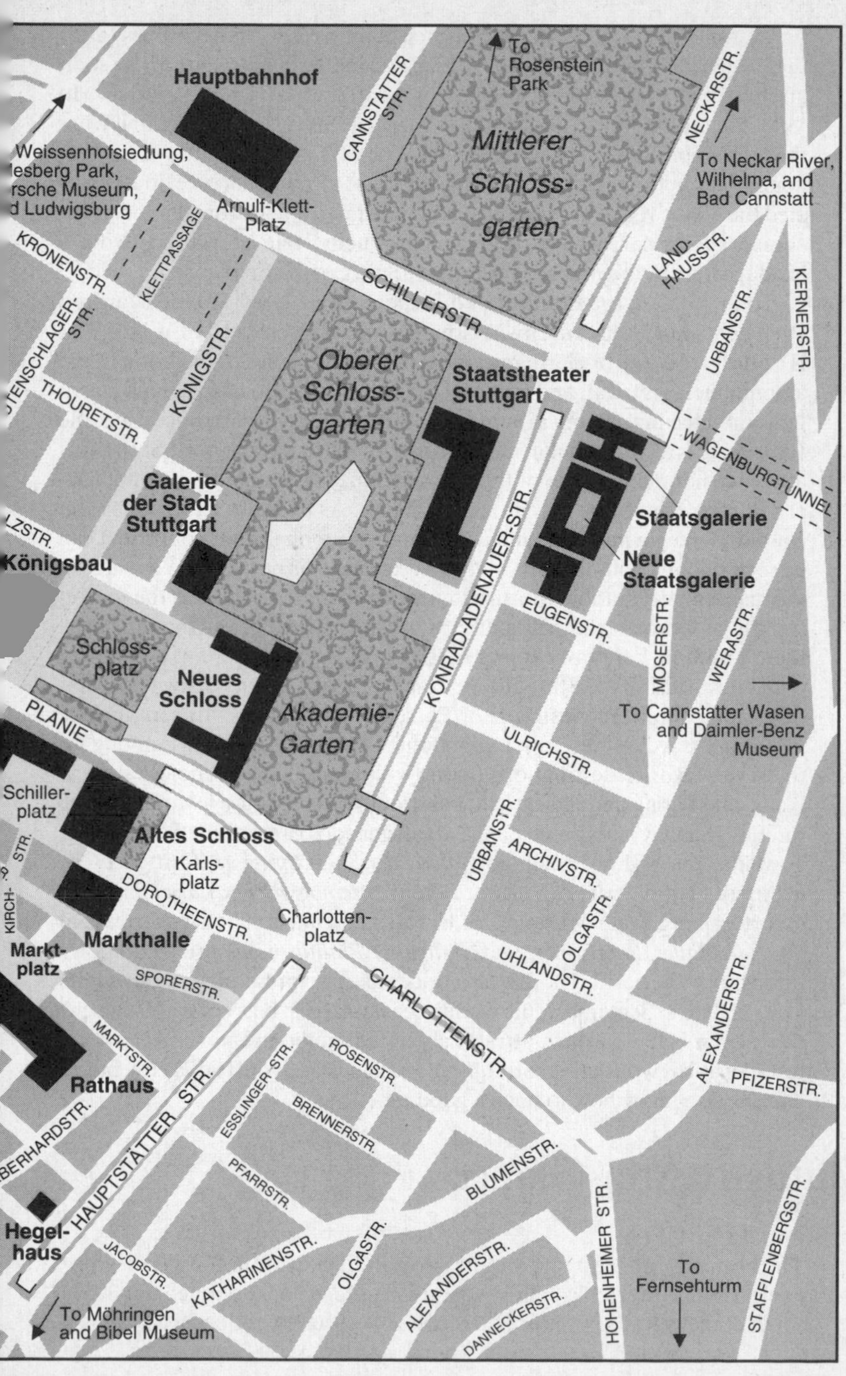
Hauptbahnhof
To Rosenstein Park
Mittlerer Schloss-garten
To Neckar River, Wilhelma, and Bad Cannstatt
Arnulf-Klett-Platz
Oberer Schloss-garten
Staatstheater Stuttgart
Galerie der Stadt Stuttgart
Königsbau
Staatsgalerie
Neue Staatsgalerie
Schloss-platz
Neues Schloss
Akademie-Garten
To Cannstatter Wasen and Daimler-Benz Museum
Schiller-platz
Altes Schloss
Karls-platz
Charlotten-platz
Markt-platz
Markthalle
Rathaus
Hegel-haus
To Möhringen and Bibel Museum
To Fernsehturm
CANNSTATTER STR.
NECKARSTR.
SCHILLERSTR.
KRONENSTR.
KLETTPASSAGE
KÖNIGSTR.
THOURETSTR.
LAND-HAUSSTR.
URBANSTR.
KERNERSTR.
WAGENBURGTUNNEL
KONRAD-ADENAUER-STR.
EUGENSTR.
MOSERSTR.
WERASTR.
ULRICHSTR.
PLANIE
ARCHIVSTR.
OLGASTR.
DOROTHEENSTR.
UHLANDSTR.
CHARLOTTENSTR.
SPORERSTR.
MARKTSTR.
ROSENSTR.
ESSLINGER STR.
BRENNERSTR.
ALEXANDERSTR.
PFIZERSTR.
HAUPTSTÄTTER STR.
BLUMENSTR.
PFARRSTR.
JACOBSTR.
KATHARINENSTR.
HOHENHEIMER STR.
STAFFLENBERGSTR.
DANNECKERSTR.

first automobile factory, naming his first commercial cars Mercedes (after the daughter of his top salesman). Benz opened a similar enterprise soon afterward; in 1926, the two companies merged to form Daimler-Benz. In 1948, the automobile again made its mark on Stuttgart. Still reeling from the heavy bombing it received during World War II, the city got an economic shot in the arm when Ferdinand Porsche (who had previously created the Volkswagen at Hitler's behest) designed a teardrop-shaped, rear-engine sports car, which he began producing and marketing from a headquarters in the northern suburb of Stuttgart-Zuffenhausen.

Today, under the enlightened leadership of Lord Mayor Manfred Rommel (son of General Erwin Rommel, the "Desert Fox" of World War II), Stuttgart is one of Germany's most prosperous cities. In addition to the automobile, electrical, and computer industries, it also has become a center for publishing, chemical engineering, textiles, and food processing; the *Liederhalle* is also a popular site for conventions and trade fairs. Stuttgart's affluence has made it one of the cities of hope for people from southeastern Europe, who come here in search of jobs. As a result, immigrants from Bosnia-Herzegovina, Romania, and Turkey (among other countries) can be seen selling goods at stalls in the marketplace or hawking their wares at the main railway station. Stuttgart is on occasion referred to as the forgotten city of German tourism, perhaps because potential vacationers think there's nothing here but car factories. (In fact, locals joke that the bulk of out-of-town visitors to Stuttgart are coming to take factory delivery of their new cars from Mercedes-Benz or Porsche.) But in the 19th century, the inveterate traveler Alexander von Humboldt ranked Stuttgart among his top seven favorite destinations (along with more obvious choices such as Rome and Paris), and the city still has a lot to offer. Nature lovers can stroll through its many lush, green parks; art aficionados can visit the *Staatsgalerie,* as well as the highly acclaimed *Galerie der Stadt Stuttgart* (Stuttgart City Gallery); history buffs can explore the *Württembergisches Landesmuseum* (Württemberg State Museum) of historical artifacts. The city's excellent *Stuttgart Ballet, Staatsoper,* and *Stuttgarter Philharmonie* are well known throughout the world. The city also prides itself on presenting the *Cannstatt Volksfest* late in September, the world's second-largest beer festival (Munich's *Oktoberfest* is first), which attracts about five million visitors a year. True to its Swabian work ethic, Stuttgart certainly is an industrious city, but its citizens also know how to have a good time.

Stuttgart At-a-Glance

SEEING THE CITY

The best view of Stuttgart and its surroundings is from the *Fernsehturm* (Television Tower; 124 Jahnstr., Stuttgart-Degerloch; phone: 288-3037), south of the city atop Bopser Hill (accessible either by car or on a bus tour).

Built in 1956, it has an observation platform 712 feet above ground level and the *Turmrestaurant,* serving good German food at an altitude of 498 feet. Open daily; admission charge to the tower. The hill itself also offers great views across the city, with the wide Neckar flowing along its eastern rim.

SPECIAL PLACES

Many of the city's historical landmarks, museums, and galleries are within walking distance of the central Schlossplatz. Attractions outside the downtown area, such as the auto plants (including the *Daimler-Benz Museum* in Untertürkheim) and sites in Ludwigsburg and Bad Cannstatt, are conveniently accessible via *U-Bahn, S-Bahn,* streetcars, and buses.

SCHLOSSPLATZ (PALACE SQUARE) Studded with 19th-century fountains, an Alexander Calder mobile, and rows of shade trees, this square is a favorite place for a stroll or a rest after a morning's sightseeing. Formerly the property of the rulers of Württemberg, its regal trappings remain in the neoclassical, colonnaded *Königsbau* (King's Building), which was erected in 1860 for formal balls and concerts; restored in the 1950s, today it is the seat of the Baden-Württemberg Stock Exchange. At the center of the square stands a monument that was erected in 1841 to commemorate the 25th anniversary of Wilhelm I's rule.

ALTES SCHLOSS (OLD PALACE) Originally built in 1320 as a residence for the counts of Württemberg, this moated castle is a lovely relic of the city's past; in the 16th century, a magnificent Renaissance-style inner courtyard was added. In medieval days, jousts were regularly held here; today, the castle houses the *Württembergisches Landesmuseum* (Württemberg State Museum; see below). Though the towered and turreted castle was heavily damaged by bombing during World War II, a faithful restoration has preserved its previous appearance. Today, it is a venue for concerts during the summer; and opening ceremonies for the annual *Weinachtsmarkt* (Christmas Market) are conducted here in late November. In Schillerplatz, alongside the castle, stands an 1839 statue of Friedrich von Schiller, second in importance only to Goethe in German literature. Schiller (1759–1805), who studied in Stuttgart, was originally a lyric poet but is best known for his romantic dramas based on historical themes, most notably *Die Jungfrau von Orleans* (The Maid of Orleans) and *Wilhelm Tell.* Closed Mondays. No admission charge. 6 Schillerpl. (no phone).

WÜRTTEMBERGISCHES LANDESMUSEUM (WÜRTTEMBERG STATE MUSEUM) Exhibits of this collection in the *Altes Schloss* include objects unearthed from the tomb of a Celtic prince; provincial Roman relics, including a cameo of Jupiter; and such medieval items as stained glass windows, Baroque altarpieces, elaborately decorated gowns, and the Württemberg crown jewels. Also here are a costume and textile collection, antique timepieces, musical instruments, and coins. Closed Mondays. No admission charge. 6 Schillerpl. (phone: 279-3400).

NEUES SCHLOSS (NEW PALACE) Like the *Altes Schloss* across the street, this castle once served as a royal residence. Built between 1746 and 1807, it was designed to resemble Versailles on a smaller scale; a complete reconstruction in the 1960s restored its magnificent, Baroque architecture. A three-story structure with two wings surrounding a large main plaza, the main entrance is off the Schlossplatz. A second square, Karlsplatz, also adjoins the *Neues Schloss.* Originally a garden for ladies of the court, the space was redesigned as a public square in the 18th century, and in 1898 an equestrian statue of Emperor Wilhelm I was erected.

MARKTHALLE Near the *Schlosspark* (Palace Park), on Dorotheenstrasse between the *Rathaus* and Schillerplatz, this is a vast, Art Nouveau–style covered market with a frescoed façade built between 1912 and 1914. Fresh flowers, fish, meat, fruit, and vegetables are sold here daily during regular business hours. A small wine bar on an upper gallery overlooking the *Markthalle* offers fine views of the colorful scene as vendors haggle over prices with potential buyers.

SCHLOSSGARTEN (PALACE GARDEN) Stretching for 2½ miles (4 km) from the city center to the Neckar at Bad Cannstatt, the grounds have lovely lakes and several palaces, including the partially restored ruins of a 16th-century castle that was destroyed by fire in 1902, and *Villa Berg,* a 19th-century country house built as the residence for a Crown Prince of Württemberg. Laid out between 1806 and 1818 by order of King Friedrich of Württemberg, this green space is linked with many of the city's other parks and gardens.

GALERIE DER STADT STUTTGART (STUTTGART CITY GALLERY) With one of the most important collections of 19th-century and early 20th-century German art, this museum on the Schlossplatz is one of the city's best. Built in 1913 and located in the *Kunstgebäude* (Art Building), the low-rise, copper-domed structure topped with a gilded stag boasts Italianate arcades, plus nine rooms of paintings, drawings, and sculpture ranging in style from classical to Expressionist. Among the collection's most prized pieces are several paintings by Otto Dix (1891–1969), a German Expressionist artist whose canvases convey the defeated Germany during the postwar 1920s. (Accused of plotting to kill Hitler, Dix was imprisoned in 1939.) Chief among his work is the spectacular *Grossstadt* (Big City) triptych, which displays savage images of pre-Hitler Germany. Closed Mondays. No admission charge. 2 Schlosspl. (phone: 112938).

STAATSGALERIE (STATE GALLERY) Located across from the *Schlossgarten,* this museum is actually two linked facilities: Works of the Old Masters are housed in a neoclassical building, while modern art is displayed in the connected *Neue Staatsgalerie* (New State Gallery; see below). Designed by architect Georg Gottlob Barth and opened by King Wilhelm I in 1843, the original building was expanded beyond its horseshoe shape 40 years later. During World II, the museum was extensively damaged by bombing, but it has been restored to its original splendor. Its collection features artists from the Middle Ages to the 19th century and includes important works by such great German artists as Lucas Cranach the Elder, Hans Baldung Grien, and Hans Holbein the Elder. Flemish and Dutch masters—Memling, Rubens, Rembrandt, and Hals, among others—are also represented, and the French section includes works by Bonnard, Braque, Cézanne, Gauguin, Manet, Monet, Renoir, and Corot. There also is a famed collection of about 350,000 graphics (including 2,000 lithographs by Honoré Daumier) and what is regarded as the most important collection of European drawings and 20th-century prints in Germany. Closed Mondays. No admission charge. 3032 Konrad-Adenauer-Str. (phone: 212-5050).

NEUE STAATSGALERIE (NEW STATE GALLERY) Designed by Scottish architect James Stirling, this offshoot of the *Staatsgalerie* was hailed at its opening 11 years ago as the city's most spectacular architectural achievement in decades. Reflecting a range of architectural influences, from the designs of 19th-century classicist Karl-Friedrich Schinkel to those of modernist Le Corbusier, the long, low structure nestles against a sloping hillside. The postmodern building has a natural stone façade, colonnades, massive curved windows, steel and plastic ornamentation, and bright blue and red tubing snaking throughout. Although a visit here is often combined with a visit to the *Staatsgalerie,* this institution is a fine museum in its own right. Housed here is the largest and most important collection of Picassos in Germany, along with works of such masters of modern art as Braque, Chagall, Dix, Kandinsky, Klee, de Chirico, Dalí, and Mondrian. There are also works by other modern artists, including Pollock, Rauschenberg, and Warhol. Also displayed are sculptures by Henry Moore, Rodin, Maillol, and Giacometti. Closed Mondays. No admission charge. 3032 Konrad-Adenauer-Str. (phone: 212-5050).

LIEDERHALLE The asymmetrical *Liederhalle* (also known as *Kultur- und Kongresszentrum Liederhalle*—Culture and Convention Center Music Hall) is considered the second-greatest contemporary structure in town, after the *Neue Staatsgalerie.* Completed in 1956 by architects Adolf Abel and Rolf Gutbrod, the exterior is a unique blend of austere concrete, mosaics, glazed brick, and quartz. Inside are three concert halls with outstanding acoustics, along with convention facilities. Located a few miles west of the town center, its concert halls have a total seating capacity of 5,300. 1 Berliner Pl. (phone: 258-9712).

ENVIRONS

BAD CANNSTATT Producing more mineral water a day (almost 480,000 gallons) than any other spa center in Europe except Budapest, this suburb of Stuttgart was once an important camp of the Romans, who established the first bathhouses here. In the 19th century, it became a favorite vacation haunt for royalty, who would come from all over Europe to "take the waters" in this pastoral setting on the far side of the Neckar. Today that spirit lives on at the classically designed *Kursaal* (Spa Center; 1 Königspl.; phone: 216-7108), built in 1837; its mineral baths recently reopened after a complete renovation. Open-air concerts and jazz performances are held in the courtyard in summer. The *Stadtmuseum* (City Museum; 71/1 Marktstr.; phone: 564788), in a former cloister stable, houses Celtic and Roman relics and permanent displays chronicling the evolution of the baths. The museum is open Wednesday afternoons and weekends; no admission charge. To get to the town from the center of Stuttgart, take suburban railway *S-Bahn* 1 or 3, or tram lines U1, U2, or U13.

GOTTLIEB-DAIMLER-GEDÄCHTNISSTÄTTE (GOTTLIEB DAIMLER MEMORIAL) More than 100 years ago in a little workshop in Bad Cannstatt, Gottlieb Daimler perfected the gasoline-powered, internal combustion engine, which soon led to his Daimler Motor Company—the world's first automobile factory. The nearby villa where he lived at the time was destroyed during World War II bombing raids, but the workshop remained intact. The original workroom, once a greenhouse in Daimler's garden, now displays models of early Daimler vehicles—a motorcyle, a motor carriage, a motorboat—plus papers and documents relating to the engineer's work. Closed Mondays and holidays. No admission charge. 13 Taubenheimstr., Bad Cannstatt (phone 172-2578). From downtown, take tram line 2 or *U-Bahn* (subway) Nos. 1 or 13.

DAIMLER-BENZ MUSEUM On the grounds of the world's oldest automobile factory, located in the eastern suburb of Stuttgart-Unterturkheim, this is arguably Stuttgart's most popular attraction. A huge exhibition space displays some 100 Mercedes-Benzes, from the first crude car to the latest luxury models, along with "Silver Arrow" racers; restored, preserved antiques; and Mercedes-Benz engine-powered boats, airplanes, and motorcycles. Visitors can listen to detailed commentary in English on headphones as they move from section to section. Videos chronicle the history of the venerable firm, including such tidbits as celebrities who have owned Mercedes-Benzes and the cars' performance in auto racing. A gift shop offers all sorts of items on the Mercedes theme—books, model cars, posters, and accessories—and a café serves light meals and snacks. Closed Mondays and holidays. No admission charge. 136 Mercedesstr., Stuttgart-Untertürkheim (phone: 172-2578). From downtown take Bus No. 56 (marked "Stadion"), *S-Bahn* 1 to the *Neckarstadion* stop, or Line 5 from the central train station.

PORSCHE MUSEUM Though smaller than the *Daimler-Benz Museum,* this collection is similar in spirit, offering several examples of Porsche's high-performance race cars, which dominated auto racing in the 1970s, and the legendary sports coupes that are still sold today. The museum is set in the company's factory, which has been manufacturing Porsche automobiles since 1948. Open daily. No admission charge. 42 Porschestr., Stuttgart-

Zuffenhausen (phone: 827-5685). From downtown, take the No. 6 *S-Bahn* to the *Neuwirtshaus* stop or Bus Nos. 52, 90, or 99 to the *Porsche* stop.

WEISSENHOFSIEDLUNG (WEISSENHOF COLONY) Back in the 1920s, 16 European architects, including Bauhaus proponents Ludwig Mies van der Rohe, Le Corbusier, and Walter Gropius, were asked to build a cluster of 21 model homes. The result was the *Werkbund Ausstellung* (Werkbund Exhibition), a group of residential buildings notable for their stark modern design. A decade later the Nazis declared the project an example of "degenerate art" and planned to raze the structures, but then decided to turn them into offices instead. World War II bombings destroyed a good part of the settlement, but 11 of the buildings were restored and stand as milestones in modern residential architecture. Located on Am Weissenhof, about 3 miles (5 km) northeast of the city center, the homes are mostly privately owned and not open to the public; one, however, houses the *Weissenhofsiedlung Information* (Weissenhof Information Center; 20 Am Weissenhof; phone 257-9187), which features an exhibition and a video program about the settlement, as well as brochures and pamphlets. Free tours are led by an English-speaking guide on Saturdays at 11 AM. Closed Mondays. No admission charge. From downtown, take Bus No. 43 to the *Kunstakademie* stop.

WILHELMA One of Europe's most extensive combinations of botanical and zoological gardens, this former summer estate of Kaiser Wilhelm I rates as one of Baden-Württemberg's most popular attractions. The zoo accommodates 8,000 animals, and there are tropical greenhouses as well as plants and trees from all over the world. It's located about 2 miles from the city center, in *Rosenstein Park* (an extension of the *Schlossgarten*) across from Bad Cannstatt. Open daily. Admission charge. Neckarstr. (phone: 54020). From downtown, take tram U14.

SCHLOSS SOLITUDE Located on a hilltop in a wooded area a few miles west of downtown, this 18th-century rococo palace was built between 1763 and 1769 as the main summer residence for the dukes of Würtemberg. Designed in the Hellenic style by the French court architect Phillipe de la Guépière, the castle is set on an arcaded base with a central rotunda. Rooms in the main house are furnished in grandiose period style, and one wing has been turned into a residence for visiting artists. Also here is the *Schloss* restaurant (phone: 699-0745; closed Sundays and Mondays), offering a highly regarded menu of traditional German fare and fine wines. Closed Mondays. Admission charge. Wildparkstr. (phone: 696669). From downtown, take Bus No. 92. By car, take Rotenwaldstrasse 6 miles (9 km) toward Leonberg.

LUDWIGSBURG This small city 10 miles (16 km) north of Stuttgart is the site of the *Residenzschloss* (Schlossstr.; phone: 7141-186440), the splendid Baroque castle built in 1704 by Duke Eberhard Ludwig, who ruled Württemberg for 27 years, for Countess Wilhelmina von Grävenitz (his mistress). The town,

Europe's first planned community, was laid out in a neat geometrical grid of streets centered around the palace. The 18th-century houses, with pale stone façades and red-tile roofs, have a strikingly similar appearance. There's a tourist office (10 Wilhelmstr.; phone: 7141-910252; fax: 7141-910774), which is open daily.

If Stuttgart's *Neues Schloss* is Versailles in miniature, the *Residenzschloss* is a full-scale model; in fact, it is nicknamed "the Swabian Versailles." The complex is composed of 18 buildings with 432 rooms, enclosed within the great, formally designed gardens of the *Schlosspark* (Palace Park). Its attractions include displays of fine, locally made porcelain and barrels holding almost 24,000 gallons of wine. Children will be particularly interested in the theme garden centered around the fairy tales of the Brothers Grimm; it features scenes from the stories enacted by mechanical figures, as well as live performances. The *Schlosspark* and the theme garden are open daily from late March to mid-October; admission charge. Access to the castle is by tours only, which are given in English at 1:30 PM weekdays, at 2:30 PM Saturdays, and at 11 AM and 1:30 and 3:15 PM Sundays and holidays. The palace is closed December; admission charge.

Two other castles in Ludwigsburg, also in the *Schlosspark,* are *Schloss Favorite,* a hunting lodge built in 1723, with a wildlife park and nature reserve; and *Schloss Monrepos,* a lakeside palace erected between 1760 and 1764. *Schloss Favorite* is open daily and charges admission; *Schloss Monrepos* itself is closed to the public, but the grounds, including the lake and gardens, are open (no additional admission charge). For more information about both castles, contact the *Schlossverwaltung* (Castle Tourist Office; phone: 7141-186440). With its several fine hotels, including the *Schlosshotel Monrepos* on the palace grounds (see *Checking In*), the town also is a pleasant (and more bucolic) base for exploring Stuttgart. From the main railroad station, take the No. 4 *S-Bahn.*

Sources and Resources

TOURIST INFORMATION

The *Stuttgart Tourist-Info* (Stuttgart Tourist Office) has a walk-in information center (indicated by a sign reading "I-Punkt") opposite the main railway station (1A Königstr.; phone: 222-8243). It's open daily. Room reservations can be made here, and maps and brochures are available, usually at a minimal charge.

LOCAL COVERAGE *Stuttgarter Monatsspiegel* is a monthly English-language publication featuring lists of restaurants, hotels, attractions, and coming events. There's also *Stuttgart News,* a free monthly paper published in German and English. Both are available at many hotels and the tourist office.

TELEPHONE The city code for Stuttgart is 711.

GETTING AROUND

AIRPORT *Flughafen Stuttgart-Echterdingen* (Stuttgart-Echterdingen Airport) is located along the southern rim of the city at Stuttgart-Echterdingen, 8 miles (13 km) from the city center. There is an *S-Bahn* connection between the main railway station and the airport. Although there are international and some transatlantic flights in and out of the airport, better connections can be made through the airport in Frankfurt. The *Lufthansa Airport Express* offers *Lufthansa* passengers nonstop train service between the Stuttgart railway station and *Flughafen Frankfurt Main* (Frankfurt-Main Airport) four times a day; the trip takes 85 minutes. There's also bus service every 25 minutes between *Flughafen Stuttgart-Echterdingen* and the *City-Air-Terminal* (14 Lautenbergergasse; no phone), located downtown near the railroad station and several hotels. The half-hour trip costs 7 DM (about $4).

BOAT From late March through October, the *Neckar-Personen-Schiffahrt* (phone: 541073) offers two-hour cruises on the Neckar. Ships leave from the dock at Wilhelma, Bad Cannstatt.

BUS, SUBWAY, SUBURBAN TRAIN, TRAM The public transport system, *Verkehrs- und Tarifverbund Stuttgart* (*VVS*), includes subways (*U-Bahn*), trams, rapid-transit trains to outlying areas (*S-Bahn*), and mass transit buses. Tickets can be purchased for 1.50 DM (about $1) per ride; there also are one-day passes for 16.50 DM (about $10) that allow unlimited use of all *VVS* transport. For further details, call *VVS* at 660-6233.

CAR RENTAL The major firms include *Avis* (18 Katharinenstr.; phone: 241441); *Hertz* (23 Schillerstr.; phone: 226-2921); *InterRent Europcar* (78 König-Karl-Str., Bad Cannstatt; phone: 561801); and *Sixt-Budget* (17 Leonhardspl.; phone: 243925).

TAXI Cabs can be hailed, picked up at taxi stands (primarily at the airport, the main railroad station, and major hotels), or contacted by calling a general dispatch number (phone: 566061). Few taxis are found downtown due to the preponderance of traffic-free streets.

TOURS Two- and three-hour guided city tours leave from in front of the *Hotel am Schlossgarten* at 10 AM, noon, and 2 and 5 PM daily from May through September; at 2 and 4 PM weekdays and 10 AM, noon, and 2 and 4 PM Sundays in April and October; and 2 and 4 PM Saturdays and 10 AM and noon Sundays the rest of the year. Tickets are available at the tourist office's walk-in center (see *Tourist Information*). The center also arranges free two-hour walking tours (with a German-speaking guide) that leave from the Altes Schloss on Saturdays at 10 AM and 2 PM.

TRAIN Located on Arnulf-Klett-Platz, the *Hauptbahnhof* (main station; phone: 19419) is part of the *Deutschen Bahnen* (German Railways) system that connects all major cities in Germany and cities throughout Europe. *InterCity Express* (*ICE*) offers the fastest train service to Frankfurt (about an hour and 22 minutes).

SPECIAL EVENTS

A sports-conscious city, Stuttgart hosts several professional tennis tournaments: the *Stuttgart Classics,* two week-long competitions held in February and October; and a nine-day tournament in July officially called the *Mercedes Internationale Weissenhof ATP Tennis-Turnier* (though the locals just call it the *Mercedes Cup*). The one-day *Stuttgarter Jazz-Tage* (Stuttgart Jazz Open-Air Festival) takes place in *Killesberg Park* in July. In odd-numbered years, the *Internationale Bachakademie* (International Bach Academy) sponsors a five-week *Europäisches Musikfest Stuttgart* (Stuttgart European Festival of Music) starting in early August. Another musical event in August is the week-long *Internationale Festtage Alter Musik* (International Early Music Festival). The most popular annual attraction is the so-called *Weindorf* (Wine Village), a two-week fair on the Schillerplatz that starts in late August. Vintners display 350 different wines from around Baden-Württemberg, and food booths feature Swabian specialties. *Jazz Tage* (Jazz Days), a week-long festival of jazz music, takes place in early September; and the 16-day *Cannstatt Volksfest* (Cannstatt Folk Festival) is a popular beer and regional food bash with music, dance, and fireworks held in the *Cannstatter Wasen* park (about 2 miles/3 km northeast of the city center) from late September into October. From mid-November into the beginning of December is the *Stuttgarter Buchwochen* (Stuttgart Book Weeks), one of the city's most popular trade fairs. A *Christkindlesmarkt* featuring handicrafts, hot *Glühwein* (mulled wine), and gingerbread runs from late November until *Christmas* along Kirchstrasse and in the Marktplatz and Schillerplatz.

In nearby Ludwigsburg, the best-known event is *Blühendes Barock,* a horticultural show and cultural festival with displays of plants as well as performances of music, dance, and theater. It is held from mid-March through mid-October in the *Schlosspark* on the grounds of the *Residenzschloss.*

MUSEUMS

In addition to those described in *Special Places,* the following museums are worth visiting. None charges admission.

BIBELMUSEUM (BIBLE MUSEUM) The printing and publishing of the Bible have been linked to Stuttgart since 1812. A permanent exhibition, "The Bible Yesterday, Today, and Tomorrow," provides information on the history of the printing of the Bible. Also displayed are pictures, manuscripts, woodcuts by Lucas Cranach, and valuable editions from the 15th century. Closed weekends. 31 Balinger Str. in the suburb of Stuttgart-Möhringen (phone: 71810).

BRAUHAUS MUSEUM (BREWERY MUSEUM) The 5,000-year history of beer, including technological developments in the brewing process, is depicted. Antique drinking mugs and beer-making equipment are on display. Closed Mondays. 12 Robert-Koch-Str. in the suburb of Vaihingen, 6 miles (10 km) from the center of Stuttgart (phone: 737-0201).

HEGELHAUS Philosopher Georg Wilhelm Friedrich Hegel, a pioneer in metaphysics, was born in this house in 1770. The ground-floor exhibit, "Stuttgart in Hegel's Day," features household items and antique articles detailing the city's history between 1770 and 1831. Upper floors display objects linked to Hegel's life and work. Closed Mondays. 53 Eberhardstr. (phone: 216-6733).

WEINBAUMUSEUM (VITICULTURE MUSEUM) Practiced in this area for more than 750 years, wine-growing has been an integral part of Stuttgart's development. Among the features in this wine museum, set in a half-timbered building, are a fully equipped cooper's workshop, ancient winepresses, oversize barrels, and antique goblets. Wine tasting also is available, and there's a wineshop. Open Saturday afternoons, Sundays, and holidays April through October. 4 Uhlbacher Pl. in the suburb of Uhlbach (phone: 325718).

SHOPPING

With their strong working class heritage, Stuttgarters are less style-conscious than their counterparts in Berlin, Düsseldorf, Hamburg, and Munich. However, the general affluence here has resulted in an abundance of fine shops. The vast *Klett Passage* underground shopping complex in front of the railroad station incorporates pedestrian malls and covered arcades. Several good downtown shopping streets are the Königstrasse past the Schlossplatz, Kirchstrasse, Eberhardstrasse, and Stiftstrasse. Another tempting area is Calwer Strasse and the adjacent *Calwer-Passage,* with more shops mingled with half-timbered houses from the 18th and 19th centuries. Alongside the Marktplatz is *Breuninger* (Karlspassage; phone: 257750), the city's best and biggest department store, carrying a wide variety of clothing, furniture, housewares, and cosmetics. In addition, a popular flea market selling used furniture, books, and household items is held on Karlsplatz on Saturday afternoons. For standard shopping hours, see GETTING READY TO GO; note, however, that the *Klett Passage* is open until 10 PM weekdays—much later than any other store or shopping mall in Germany.

Savvy shoppers can get especially good deals at the factory outlet shops in the nearby suburbs, which are accessible by train. Two of the best are *Hugo Boss* (Kanalstr., Metzingen; phone: 7123-41361), south of the city center, with men's clothing by the internationally famous local designer; and the *Salamander* shoe outlet (Bahnhofstr., Kornwestheim; phone: 7154-150), just north of the city. A list of other factory outlet shops is available from the tourist office. The following are other shops worth exploring:

Hans Rehn High-quality pens manufactured in Germany (including the locally made Lamy brand), as well as leather wallets, notepads, stationery, and other items. 3 Stiftstr. (phone: 226-2361).

Hennecke A trendy boutique offering fashionable womenswear, both casual and dressy. 4 Kirchstr. (phone: 236-9492).

Holy's One of the city's top places for the latest styles in menswear; among the names represented are Armani and local designer Hugo Boss. 54A Königstr. (phone: 221872).

Kurtz Toys, games, puzzles, dolls, and other charming *Spielwaren* (playthings). 10 Am Marktpl. (phone: 244149).

Pavillon A downtown boutique offering fine crystal, silver, jewelry, and paintings from the 19th and early 20th centuries. 31-33 Eberhardstr. (phone: 243134).

Süsi This little shop sells a variety of chocolate confections, as well as scrumptious *Lebkuchen* (gingerbread). 1 Königstr. (phone: 226-4115).

Tritschler In business since 1723, this place offers a wide selection of fine china, ceramics, and decorative housewares. Am Marktpl. (phone: 291582).

Wittwer The biggest bookshop in the city, with tables for sit-down browsing and a large foreign-language section with titles in English, French, Spanish, and Italian. 30 Königstr. (phone: 25070).

SPORTS AND FITNESS

FITNESS CENTERS Stuttgart's health clubs include *Fitness Center Weilimdorf* (9 Holderäckerstr.; phone: 866-1376) and *Fitness Center Löwentor* (38 Löwentor; phone: 851545).

GOLF Visitors can play during the week on the 18-hole course at *Stuttgart Golfclub Solitude* (phone: 7044-5852) in the suburb of Mönsheim, about 20 miles (32 km) northwest of the city.

HORSEBACK RIDING Mounts are available by the hour from *Reitverein Denkendorf* on Hohnstrasse in the nearby town of Denkendorf (phone: 346-1286).

JOGGING Miles of interconnected paths link the city center with the *Schlossgarten, Rosenstein Park,* and six bridges that cross the Neckar into Bad Cannstatt.

SOCCER *VfB Stuttgart,* the city's first-division *Bundesliga* soccer team, plays on Saturdays from October through April at *Gottlieb-Daimler-Stadium,* formerly known as *Neckar Stadium,* on Mercedesstrasse. The *Stuttgart Kickers,* a second-division team, meet rivals in the large *Waldau* sports complex near the *Fernsehturm* in Stuttgart-Degerloch, among other venues. For tickets and schedule information, contact the tourist office (see *Tourist Information,* above).

SPAS There are two facilities with hot springs in Stuttgart itself: *Mineralbad Leuze* (Koenig-Karls-Brücke; phone: 283224) and *Mineralbad Berg* (9 Am

Schwanenpl.; phone: 261060). In addition, the *Kursaal*'s mineral springs at Bad Cannstatt have reopened after an extensive renovation (see *Special Places*).

TENNIS There are 18 outdoor courts available on the Cannstatten Wiesen (Cannstatt Meadows), near *Gottlieb-Daimler-Stadium* (phone: 216-4181), and seven indoor courts and 57 outdoor courts at *Tennis-Ski-und-Sportschule* (Tennis Ski and Sport School; 73 Emerholzweg, Stuttgart-Stannheim; phone: 801025).

THEATER

The internationally renowned *Stuttgart Ballet,* directed by Marcia Haydée, features such dramatic John Cranko–choreographed classics as *Swan Lake, Romeo and Juliet, Carmen, Eugene Onegin,* and *Taming of the Shrew.* Ballet, dramas, experimental theater, and *Die Staatsoper* (State Opera) performances are presented in the *Staatstheater Stuttgart* (Stuttgart State Theater; 6 Oberer Schlossgarten; phone: 20320). The city also has some 30 other venues, including the *Renitenz-Theater* (65 Eberhardstr.; phone: 297075), which puts on highly regarded satirical cabaret; and the area's oldest playhouse, the *Wilhelma Theater* (9 Neckartalstr., Bad Cannstatt; phone: 543984), which is used for student productions of the *Hochschule für Musik und darstellende Künste* (Stuttgart College of Music and Performing Arts).

MUSIC

Musical life is centered on the spacious *Liederhalle* (1 Berliner Pl.; phone: 258-9712), a pitch-perfect venue of three concert halls; it is home to the *Stuttgarter Philharmonie* and hosts visiting artists as well. Stuttgart is also well known for its choral groups, most notably the *Gächinger Kantorei* and *Bach Collegium* ensembles, which perform oratorical works at the *Internationale Bachakademie* (1 Johann-Sebastian-Bach-Pl.; phone: 619210).

NIGHTCLUBS AND NIGHTLIFE

The city is proud of its local wines, and for many of its citizens, a few convivial hours in a friendly *Weinstube* (tavern) constitutes a night out on the town. Some good ones to try are *Hirsch Weinstube, Weinstube zur Kiste,* and *Zur Weinsteige* (see *Eating Out* for all three). *Dixieland Hall* (3B Marienstr.; phone: 226-2832) is the place to go for Dixieland and modern jazz. *Monument* (31 Calwer Str.; phone: 226-1607) is a popular disco attracting a young, trendy clientele. The *Longhorn* (6 Heiligenwiesen; phone: 426838) features live performances of country-and-western music. There also are "international-style" nightclubs featuring live music, dancing, and a floor show, usually including striptease. Popular with conventioneers and trade-fair visitors, the top clubs of this type are *Four Roses* (24 Leonhardspl.; phone: 242737) and *Moulin Rouge* (58 Königstr.; phone: 294707). Many visitors take the "Stuttgart by Night" guided tour run on Wednesday, Friday, and Saturday nights by the tourist office (see *Tourist Information*). The trip, which begins in early evening and ends around 1:30 AM, includes a light dinner and visits to several area clubs.

Best in Town

CHECKING IN

In keeping with its down-to-earth character, Stuttgart has no grand, super-deluxe hotels. Accommodations are comfortable, functional, and often reasonably priced (particularly on weekends, when many hotels offer discounted rates). The tourist office (see *Tourist Information*) has information on dozens of small, inexpensive hotels and guesthouses, in both the city and the surrounding area. All rooms in the hotels listed below have private baths or showers. Most of Stuttgart's major hotels have complete facilities for the business traveler. Those hotels listed below as having "business services" usually offer such conveniences as an English-speaking concierge, meeting rooms, photocopiers, computers, translation services, and express checkout, among others. Call the hotel for additional information. For a double room (including breakfast, private bath, a phone, and a TV set unless otherwise indicated), expect to pay between $200 and $300 per night at hotels listed in the expensive category; $120 to $200 at moderate hotels; and under $120 at inexpensive places. All telephone numbers are in the 711 city code unless otherwise indicated.

EXPENSIVE

Hotel am Schlossgarten This property is among Stuttgart's most luxurious. Although the modern, box-like building looks unimpressive from the outside, the interior decor exudes a conservative elegance (bordering on stuffiness), and the service is attentive and efficient. The 125 guestrooms feature modern, stylish furnishings and amenities such as color TV sets and mini-bars; some also boast lovely views of the adjacent *Schlossgarten.* The hotel has two excellent restaurants, including the *Zirbelstube* (see *Eating Out*). Its central location, on a far corner of the square in front of the railway station, is yet another asset. Business services are available. 23 Schillerstr. (phone: 20260; fax: 202-6888).

Inter-Continental Known locally as the "Inter-Conti," this five-year-old establishment faces the *Schlossgarten,* a short distance from the city center. There are 277 well-appointed rooms, and amenities include the excellent *Les Continents* restaurant (see *Eating Out*), a pool, and a fitness club. Business services are available. 60 Neckarstr. (phone: 20200; 800-327-0200; fax: 202012).

Maritim Stuttgart Close to the *Liederhalle* convention center, this luxurious hotel is especially popular with business travelers and concertgoers. The design of the building is low-slung and angular, with balconies wrapped around a multilevel reception area and shopping arcade. Attached to the complex is a historic, round *Reithalle* (equestrian riding hall) built in 1885, which is used for group functions. The 555 guestrooms are handsomely appointed and feature such amenities as mini-bars and fax hookups. Other facilities include the formal *Rôtisserie* dining room, a more casual bistro, a piano bar, and a health club with a gym, pool, sauna, and solarium. Business services are available. 2 Forstr. (phone: 9420; 800-843-3311; fax: 942-1000).

Steigenberger Graf Zeppelin Like the *Hotel am Schlossgarten,* this place has a rather unprepossessing exterior—austere and purely functional. However, its central location across from the railway station makes it an ideal base from which to tour the city, and the 280 rooms and suites are tastefully furnished and feature such amenities as color TV sets, mini-bars, in-room safes, and soundproofed windows. Its four restaurants serve food ranging from regional specialties at the *Zeppelin Stüble* to the ambitious continental fare of the *Graf Zeppelin* (see *Eating Out* for both). Other facilities include a pool, sauna, and massage room. Business services are available. 7 Arnulf-Klett-Pl. (phone: 204-8542; 800-223-5652; fax: 204-8542).

MODERATE

Fontana An impressive high-rise in Vaihingen, a suburb about 6 miles (10 km) south of the city, this 250-room hotel is particularly popular with conventiongoers. Guestrooms are bright and cheerfully decorated; service is brisk and efficient. Amenities include two restaurants, a pool with a bar, a steambath, a sauna, and a massage room. Business services are available. 5 Vollmoellerstr., Vaihingen (phone: 7300; fax: 730-2525).

Kongresshotel Europa This property near the convention center has 114 rooms featuring mini-bars, as well as a restaurant and a fitness center. Business services are available. 26 Siemensstr. (phone: 810040; fax: 854082).

Messehotel Europa Under the same management as the *Kongresshotel Europa* across the street (see above), this is another pleasant and centrally located property. The 114 rooms are attractive and offer mini-bars; there is also a restaurant serving local specialties. Business services are available. 33 Siemenstr. (phone: 814830; fax: 814-8348).

Relexa Waldhotel Schatten In a country setting outside the city center between the *Liederhalle* convention center and *Schloss Solitude,* this property offers 144 well-appointed rooms, a good restaurant, a fitness center, and business services. Magstadterstr. (phone: 68670; fax: 686-7999).

Royal The striking, contemporary decor, 100 spacious rooms, and a convenient location near the city center make this a good choice for both business travelers and vacationers. There's also a restaurant serving regional specialties. Business services are available. 35 Sophienstr. (phone: 625050; fax: 628809).

Schlosshotel Monrepos Billed as a "castle hotel" (the literal translation of *Schlosshotel*), this establishment is in reality a fairly plain building on the grounds of a splendid Baroque castle in nearby Ludwigsburg. But its garden setting provides a welcome respite from the busy, urban atmosphere of Stuttgart. The 71 rooms, with lovely castle or garden views, are decorated with modern furnishings and bright colors; amenities include minibars and large baths. The stylish *Bugatti* restaurant serves good Italian fare; a more informal choice is the rustic *Gutsschenke,* offering reasonably priced regional specialties. There is a lake on the grounds, and boating and other water sports are available to guests. Business services are offered. Monrepösstr., Ludwigsburg (phone: 7141-320; 800-528-1234; fax: 7141-3220).

Unger Convenient to the railroad station and the *City Air Terminal,* this clean, recently renovated establishment offers 80 well-appointed rooms, a conference center, and on-site parking. The friendly staff makes guests feel right at home. A breakfast buffet is included in the rate; there is no restaurant. 17 Kronenstr. (phone: 20990; fax: 209-9100).

INEXPENSIVE

InterCity Located inside the main railroad terminal at the heart of the city, this 100-room hotel is serviceable and clean, if rather plain. There is no restaurant. 2 Arnulf-Klett-Pl. (phone: 299801; fax: 226-1899).

Mack This small hotel owned and managed by a friendly local family is near the train station. There are 50 rooms, which are pleasantly decorated but feature few amenities. There's no restaurant. 5-7 Kriegerstr. (phone: 292942; fax: 293489).

Pflieger Under the same ownership and management as the *Mack* (above), this 37-room property across the street provides basic, friendly accommodations with few amenities. There's no restaurant. 9-11 Kriegerstr. (phone: 221878; fax: 293489).

Rieker A small, modest hotel with 63 rooms centrally located near the railway station. There is no restaurant. 3 Friedrichstr. (phone: 221311; fax: 293894).

EATING OUT

Stuttgart could be considered one of the last bastions of authentic regional fare in Germany. Swabian food tends to be hearty, home-style cooking. Among the specialties are *Maultaschen* (large ravioli with various types of fillings), *schwäbischer Rostbraten* (braised beef, usually served with sauerkraut), *Linsen mit Saiten* (lentil stew with sausages), *Spätzle* (short, thick noodles), and *Schupfundeln* (spicy noodles). *Gaisburger Marsch* (a stew containing beef, potatoes, and *Spätzle*), Stuttgart's favorite local dish, was originally created at *Bäckerschmide* (see below). Swabian wines, though not as well known as those from the Rhine or Moselle regions, rank among the best in Germany, and the locally brewed Dinkelacher beer is also good. The best dining is usually in hotel restaurants, which are patronized as much by locals as by visitors. Expect to pay $120 to $160 for a three-course meal for two (not including drinks or wine) at restaurants classed as expensive; $85 to $120 at moderate places; and less than $85 at inexpensive eateries. Prices include taxes and service charges, but leave a small additional tip to reward good service. Unless noted otherwise, restaurants are open for lunch and dinner. All telephone numbers are in the 711 city code unless otherwise indicated.

EXPENSIVE

Alte Post Much favored among locals, this one-Michelin-star dining spot in a traditional Swabian inn tempers its rustic atmosphere with elegant touches and impeccable service. Offered here are Swabian dishes and such classic French fare as *langouste* in white wine sauce and *poularde* with green-pepper cream sauce. The wine list offers a wide selection of modestly priced vintages. Closed Sundays and holidays, Monday and Saturday lunch, and two weeks in July. Reservations necessary. MasterCard and Visa accepted. 43 Friedrichstr. (phone: 293079).

Les Continents This elegant dining room at the *Inter-Continental* hotel offers both classic French fare and regional dishes in a sophisticated setting. A prix fixe, seven-course "tasting" menu is offered at dinner, and the weekday "Business Lunch Buffet" is a real bargain. Open daily. Reservations advised. Major credit cards accepted. 60 Neckarstr. (phone: 20200).

Graf Zeppelin One of Germany's top hotel restaurants, this first-rate eatery offers such continental specialties as lamb filet with rosemary sauce and rack of venison with cassis sauce. The service is unusually attentive but not intrusive. Open for dinner only; closed weekends and holidays. Reservations necessary. Major credit cards accepted. In the *Steigenberger Graf Zeppelin Hotel,* 7 Arnulf-Klett-Pl. (phone: 299881).

Hirsch Weinstube Owned and operated by the friendly and energetic Heiderose Frietsch, this place in a nearby suburb presents innovative regional dishes in a typically Swabian atmosphere. The menu changes daily, depending on the whim of the chef, but usually features both traditional Swabian dishes and continental fare. Closed Sundays, holidays, Monday and Saturday lunch, and *Easter* week. Reservations necessary. Major credit cards accepted. 3 Maierstr., Möhringen (phone: 711375).

MODERATE

Brasserie Flo A branch of the popular chain that includes Paris's *La Coupole,* it re-creates the quintessential French restaurant in the shopping arcade of the *Breuninger* department store. An informal atmosphere, cheerful service, and a reasonably priced menu featuring well-prepared seafood direct from the main Paris markets and mammoth servings of *choucroute* (a French version of sauerkraut) have quickly endeared this place to the locals. It's a good idea to come here for dinner; the crowds at lunch can be formidable. Closed Sundays. No reservations. Major credit cards accepted. Karlspassage (phone: 211-1661).

Goldener Adler Regional Swabian dishes—such as *Maultaschen, Spätzle,* and fresh mussels—are the specialties of this downtown dining spot. Also, try a bottle of red wine from Baden-Württemberg. Closed Mondays and July. Reservations advised. Major credit cards accepted. 38 Böheimstr. (phone: 640-1762).

Der Zauberlehrling The name means "The Sorcerer's Apprentice," and that may well be a fit description of Andreas Müller, the chef at this cozy eatery on the edge of downtown. Müller's distinctive and innovative versions of Swabian delicacies, such as *Maultaschen* and *Spätzle,* have the locals clamoring for more. Closed Sundays. Reservations necessary. No credit cards accepted. 38 Rosenstr. (phone: 237-7700).

Zeppelin Stüble Well-prepared Swabian specialties, including *Maultaschen, Rostbraten,* and *Apfelküchle* (apple fritters with sugar and cinnamon), are presented in a country-style setting at the *Steigenberger Graf Zeppelin* hotel. Open daily. Reservations unnecessary. Major credit cards accepted. 2 Lautenschlagerstr. (phone: 226-4013).

Zirbelstube The main dining room of *Hotel am Schlossgarten* is beautifully decorated in an elegant but rustic style, with oak-paneled walls and ceiling, a great tile stove, and antiques. The menu offers both international and regional specialties; there's also a wide variety of fine wines. In warm weather, diners may eat on the terrace, which overlooks the *Schlossgarten.* Closed July. Reservations advised. Major credit cards accepted. 23 Schillerstr. (phone: 20260).

Zur Weinsteige In the *Wörtz* hotel, this atmospheric *Weinstube* features beautiful woodcarvings, wrought-iron accents, and an outdoor garden sheltered beneath a grape arbor. The menu offers regional specialties prepared with the freshest local seafood, lamb, and game. The wine list is fine as well. Closed weekends as well as from mid-December to mid-January. Reservations advised. Major credit cards accepted. 30 Hohenheimer Str. (phone: 240681).

INEXPENSIVE

Bäckerschmide This oh-so-traditional *Weinstube* invented *Gaisburger Marsch* in the 19th century. It's still on the menu, along with many other regional specialties. Open daily; closed Sunday and holiday dinners. No reservations. Major credit cards accepted. 42 Schurwaldstr. (phone: 466035).

Bernies Kachelofen Charmingly decorated with antiques, this cozy *Weinstube* serves Swabian specialties along with local wines. Open for dinner only; closed Sundays. No reservations. Major credit cards accepted. 10 Eberhardstr. (phone: 242378).

Der Besen Right in the heart of the city center is this country-style *Weinstube* decorated with a timbered ceiling and old farm equipment. Swabian specialties are featured on the menu. Open daily for dinner only. No reservations. No credit cards accepted. 38 Rosenstr. (phone: 233265).

Café Königsbau On the second floor of the *Königsbau,* overlooking the Schlossplatz, this is one of Stuttgart's favorite cafés. It's a perfect spot to enjoy coffee and cake and fancy ice-cream concoctions in the morning and afternoon; there's also a limited lunch menu. Open daily for breakfast and lunch only. No reservations. No credit cards accepted. 28 Königstr. (phone: 290787).

Paulaner Biergarten am Killesberg A vast outdoor beer garden set amidst lush greenery. It serves a menu of pub grub and snacks, along with Bavarian beer and Swabian wines. Open daily during warm weather. No reservations. No credit cards accepted. 39 Stresemannstr. (phone: 251848).

Weinhaus Stetter An unpretentious place popular with Stuttgarters, it presents delicious regional food and wines. Closed Sundays and weekday lunch. No reservations. No credit cards accepted. 32 Rosenstr. (phone: 240163).

Weinstube Schellenturm Popular for its well-prepared Swabian specialties (such as *Maultaschen, Rostbraten,* and *Spätzle*), this eatery has a casual, relaxed atmosphere and friendly service. Open for dinner only; closed Sundays. Reservations advised. American Express accepted. 22 Weberstr. (phone: 236-4888).

Weinstube zur Kiste One of the oldest and most famous of Stuttgart's *Weinstuben,* this 19th-century eatery occupies two floors of a tavern. Its down-home, regional cooking and fine wines have ensured its continuing popularity over the years—so expect it to be crowded most of the time. No reservations. No credit cards accepted. 2 Kanalstr. (phone: 244002).

Diversions

Unexpected Pleasures and Treasures

Quintessential Germany

Given Germany's long history of fragmentation and internal conflict, it may seem strange to refer to any particular set of places or experiences as emblematic of the entire country and its people—as "quintessentially German." But even before it officially came together again in 1990, Germany had its own unique character—emphasizing pride, orderliness, and love of beauty—and a richly varied cultural heritage. Fortunately, both are quite accessible to visitors today. We think the suggestions listed below—including both well-known and obscure delights—are a good place to begin an exploration of Germany's personality.

HARVESTTIME IN MOSEL-RHINE COUNTRY Roaming the vineyard-laden hills sloping down to the Mosel and Rhine Rivers is an intoxicating experience (pun intended). Every corkscrew turn from Trier to Koblenz, and the broad bend flowing downstream toward Mainz and Worms, cradles a fabled wine village. In Bernkastel, Rüdesheim, and Nierstein, the nectar of the grape is aged in oak vats and then bottled; there are plenty of wineries (often housed in lovely historic castles) to tour and vintages to sample. Throughout the area, these villages often hold *Weinfeste* (wine festivals), where you can taste a variety of vintages and get to know the local people at the same time. Even if you're a teetotaler, a day cruise along either river is a delight. As you sail on the Rhine by the massive stone cliffs, home to the legendary Teutonic siren Lorelei, the haunting song that once supposedly lured sailors to their deaths on the rocks still seems to echo here. Although most of the area's vineyards can be visited year-round, try to be on these rivers at harvesttime (from late August until mid-October), when their banks take on tawny hues of ocher and burnt sienna, and workers, armed with pruning shears and buckets, fan out into the disciplined braids of vines. For weeks, the air is filled with the tantalizing smell of newly pressed wine.

LOUNGING ON THE ISLAND OF SYLT A vacation spent on Sylt, a scrap of land in the North Sea, will forever dispel the stereotype that an island getaway must always involve lots of palms and piña coladas. Jutting out from the North Frisian coastline, its rough edges abraded over the centuries by the gentle ebb and flow of the sea, Sylt offers an entirely different island experience. The island is accessible by rail from Niebüll on the mainland; the train takes cars as well as people. The surroundings here are a wistful combination of lofty lighthouses, sand dunes, whipping winds, and cirrus clouds. At a moment's notice, the weather can turn cold, even in summer (Syltians often can be seen strolling on the sand in mink—yes, mink!—coats), but the beach is beautiful even then. While sitting in one of the ubiquitous, three-sided *Strandkörben* (wicker beach armchairs big enough for two), you may see a fellow beachcomber fling off his or her coat and run naked into the icy water—this is one of the few nudist beaches in Germany. There are several good hotels in Sylt's two main towns, Westerland and Kampen; among the best are the *Stadt Hamburg* (2 Strandstr., Westerland 25980; phone: 4651-8580; fax: 4651-858220) and *Walters Hof* (on Kurhausstr., Kampen 25999; phone: 4651-4490; fax: 4651-45590). While away the hours watching the boldly changing cloud formations and children building sand castles on the beach. Or cycle along the wide beachside promenades of Westerland, or down one of the many paths lined with wild roses. Time seems to stand still on Sylt, and most of its inhabitants don't mind a bit.

ALPINE TRAILS OF THE ZUGSPITZE Strap on a backpack, lace up your sturdy boots, and pocket your souvenir Puma lockback knife: You're ready for a jaunt into the wilderness. In the shadow of the Zugspitze, the country's highest mountain and only real altitude, you'll experience a world mercifully free of traffic gridlock and smog alerts, a world of white mountain peaks lined with evergreen trees, bracing air, and flora that appears to grow out of the rock itself. Around the summit of this 9,840-foot peak, accessible by cog railway and cable car, are a cluster of broad plateaus and smaller peaks, all veined by miles of well-marked and well-kept hiking trails with rustic huts that serve as resting places and overnight accommodations. Stand on an open hillside in the warming sun, listen to the far-off cowbells, and look across the crevasse to glittering glaciers. The people you'll meet along the way run the gamut from elderly (but extremely fit) grandmothers to rugged men wearing *Lederhosen,* brightly colored shirts, and felt hats sporting the typical *Gamsbart* (a tuft of chamois hair resembling a shaving brush). Here and there you'll see a simple wooden cross marked with a name and date—a grim reminder of the potential treachery of these paths. At the end of a long day of trekking, you can warm your toes in front of a giant, tile-covered stove in your hut, trade tales of mountain goats and fog banks with your fellow adventurers, and enjoy simple but tasty food. When you turn in, your wooden bunk will feel as sumptuous as the eiderdown-blanketed beds at the *Vier Jahreszeiten;* and by morning, you'll be ready to start all over again.

REMNANTS OF EAST GERMANY: THE BRANDENBURG GATE AND THE BERLIN WALL The seam where Germany was split apart and sewn back together again, the *Brandenburger Tor* (Brandenburg Gate) has been the backdrop to some of the most spine-chilling images in modern history: Hitler's elite police goose-stepping through it by night in the early 1930s, torches blazing; the 1953 suppression of a rebellion against the Communist regime; and the

1961 construction of that huge, monstrous monument to the Cold War: the *Berlin Wall.* Scenes from the more recent past, however, are more cheerful, even exhilarating: At the gate, as well as at several other checkpoints, thousands of newly liberated Ossies (East Germans) were hugged and wildly cheered by Wessies (West Germans) as the Wall teetered and fell in late 1989. Along the Mühlenstrasse, you can still see remnants of the Wall, the largest section of which is now painted with colorful murals and called the *East Side Gallery.* A new museum that will display exhibits about the Wall and its history is currently under construction near the *Bernauerstrasse U-Bahn* station—the spot where, over 30 years ago, the first person was shot trying to cross the border between East and West Berlin. And at the *Brandenburger Tor* itself, stand under the copper sculpture of the *Goddess of Victory* in a horse-drawn chariot and look around: The guard posts have been leveled, the electric grids dismantled, and most of the Wall finally bulldozed. *Checkpoint Charlie,* for decades steeped in espionage lore, finally has come in from the cold.

KARNEVAL IN THE RHINELAND Germany's *Karneval* (called *Fasching* in Bavaria) theoretically begins on November 11, gets more intense by the beginning of February, and reaches its peak during the week leading up to *Aschermittwoch* (Ash Wednesday). The festivities, traditionally the last fling before the austere 40 days of *Fastenzeit* (Lent), shake any remaining vestiges of decorum and restraint from the usually staid German persona and set ordinary social conventions aside. The carnival is a yearly binge of boisterous parades and masquerade balls, streamers and balloons, painted faces and stolen kisses. Oompah music is heard everywhere, even in office buildings, and inhibitions are lost in a spray of beer foam. The epicenter of the turbulence is in the Rhineland, notably in Mainz and Cologne, and rippling out to Aachen and Düsseldorf in the north and Freiburg in the south. Finding a party is easy; just head for the neighborhood tavern and join a crowd of revelers indulging in the traditional German custom of *schunkeln* (linking arms and swaying to band music). On *Fastnachdonnerstag* (Shrove Thursday, also known as *Weiberfastnacht*—Ladies' Night), frenzied women armed with scissors roam pedestrian zones, offices, and coffeehouses and snip off the ties of any men foolish enough to wear them. The wayward revelry comes to an abrupt close at dawn on *Aschermittwoch* during the traditional breakfast of herring (supposedly a hangover remedy), when the prim German lifestyle reasserts itself for another year. *Ach du lieber*. . . .

THE OLD MARKET SQUARE OF SAARBRÜCKEN For centuries, the Saarland was the rope in a Franco-German tug-of-war. Today, it provides residents and visitors alike with an intriguing blend of two rather dissimilar cultures. In Saarbrücken, the capital of Saarland, you can shop for both Baden and Bordeaux wines at the corner mom-and-pop establishment (known here as "Tante Emma" shops) and listen to either the *chansons* played on French radio stations or the *Fussball* scores favored by German broadcasters. The cobblestoned St. Johanner Marktplatz is encircled by lovingly restored Baroque buildings, clothing boutiques, jewelry shops, and outdoor cafés. It's also the center of much cross-cultural activity, including a biweekly outdoor produce market; the summer *Perspective du Théâtre* (Theater Perspective), which is the only festival in Germany that presents French theater in French; the *Altstadt Festspiele* (Old Town Festival), also held in summer; a pair of autumn wine fetes; and a *Weihnachtes Volksfest* (Christmas Folk Festival). In addition, a monthly flea market is held in the *Bürgerpark*. The whir of bicycle wheels, the murmur of voices, and the chiming of nearby church bells mix with the mellow jazz piped from the square's many *Kneipen* (taverns). The raised central fountain, a bubbling relic of the 18th century, is likely to be mobbed with local teenagers—it's the Saarbrücken version of an American shopping mall.

THE ARTISTS' COLONY OF WORPSWEDE On the flat, sodden marshland in the north known as Teufelheidemoor (Devil's Moor) lies the still-pristine artists' haven of Worpswede. The colony, begun in 1889, was founded as an escape from the stifling straitjacket of bourgeois life—a German Haight-Ashbury. Its original residents, a handful of painters, poets, architects, and sculptors, were drawn by the dense greens of the landscape, the whites of the birches and windmills, and the peaty browns of the moor canals. The roll call for the Worpswede School reads like a Prussian Establishment dropout list: Otto Modersohn, Paula Becker-Modersohn, Fritz Mackensen, Hans am Ende, and Fritz Overbeck. Writer Rainer Maria Rilke lived here for a time with sculptor Clara Westhoff, fathering a child with her before moving on to Paris. The works of the Worpswede Generation can be seen in local museums, farmhouses, and—most memorably—the *Zionskirche* (Church of Zion), whose walls are splashed with fanciful paintings of flowers done by Becker-Modersohn. (She did not do the work voluntarily: It was her penalty for waking the entire village by ringing the church bell in the middle of a night of revelry.) Today, the resident artists still focus on their work, leaving worries about the sinking mark, the profit margin of Daimler-Benz, and the future of the European Economic Community to their less aesthetic countrymen. Here, you can watch a potter working in clay or a weaver creating rough cloth. Or just hang out at *Café Verrückt* (Café Crazy; 3 Lindenallee; phone: 4792-1028), a favorite bohemian haunt, and enjoy freshly steeped East Frisian tea and wild raspberry pie—or perhaps some buckwheat cake, a local specialty. *Note:* In 1895, a Munich exhibition of works by Worpswede artists brought the colony to the attention of the art world; this year, the town is celebrating the centennial of that event with a series of gallery exhibitions, concerts, and literary readings held in various locations.

A SUMMER EVENING IN A MUNICH BIERGARTEN It's 6 PM in Munich, and the main thoroughfares are deserted. You may think everybody's taken off to the beaches of Spain, but think again. A few random rights and lefts off the

Maximilianstrasse and Kapuzinerstrasse reveal legions of parked cars and bikes, and, beyond them, the city's many beer gardens. Munich, at the buckle of the Bavarian beer belt, has developed a unique way to enjoy (and promote) its local specialty. *Königlicher Hirschgarten, Taxisgarten, Augustiner,* and the base of the *Chinesischer Turm* (Chinese Tower) in the *Englischer Garten* (English Garden) are just a few of the sprawling, open-air drinking halls where *Müncheners* gather to consume good beer and good food (which they often bring with them in picnic hampers). The pebbled floors are sprinkled with white acacia blossoms; trellises, hedges, and crisscross fences separate one place from another; and lanterns strung between trees provide a warm glow. The prevailing mood is jovial—much tamer than during *Oktoberfest* (see *Special Events* in *Munich,* THE CITIES), but jolly nonetheless—with children cavorting late into the evening, avid courting worthy of a singles bar, and toasting of eternal *Brüderschaft* (brotherhood, friendship).

KURFÜRSTENDAMM, Berlin One of Berlin's major boulevards, the posh Kurfürstendamm is a glittering circus, bustling with activity. Once a royal bridle path for Brandenburg's Prince Elector on his jaunts to the *Grunewald Jagdsitz* (Grunewald Hunting Lodge), today's "Ku'damm" is a lively gathering place for artists, students, and other members of the avant-garde. At what has become an East-West crossroads, Slavic street vendors and German-owned shops coexist in the shadow of the *Kaiser Wilhelm Gedächtniskirche* (Kaiser Wilhelm Memorial Church), a 19th-century house of worship that was destroyed by World War II bombing and left largely unrepaired as a remembrance of the horrors of war. On a languid *Spaziergung* (promenade) down the street, you may see an open-air rock concert, a street carnival, or a political demonstration against the injustice of the moment. In the background are a motley crew of bongo drummers, straggling string quartets, and mimes and other street performers offering impromptu art in exchange for a few coins. If your feet get tired or hunger strikes, there are plenty of sidewalk cafés where you can reenergize yourself without missing a single moment of the action. At the café terrace of the *Bristol Kempinski* hotel (where Sally Bowles savored caviar and champagne in *Cabaret*), you can listen to the music of the *Drehorgel,* Berlin's traditional street instrument, and witness the beginning of a capital's rebirth.

NUREMBERG'S CHRISTKINDLESMARKT Of the hundreds of outdoor *Christmas* feasts, fetes, and fairs in Germany, the *Christkindlesmarkt* in Nuremberg is certainly the brightest. Under the spires of the *Frauenkirche* (Our Lady's Church) in the heart of the walled inner city, a giant *Christmas* tree sits in the middle of the *Hauptmarkt,* lighted candles delicately balanced on its boughs. The market's opening ceremony, held the first Friday in December, features a teenage girl in a gold wig (unless she happens to already be blonde) representing the *Christkind* (Christ Child—Germans traditionally depict Christ as a blond cherub). After the *Christkind* recites a poem from a parapet of the *Frauenkirche,* trumpets blow a fanfare and the bells of *St. Sebalduskirche* (Church of St. Sebaldus) and the *Lorenzkirche* (Church of St. Lorenz) play *Christmas* carols, which can be heard all over the city. From then until *Christmas,* the aroma of cinnamon wafers, *Lebkuchen* (gingerbread cookies), tangerines, and sugar-roasted almonds fills the crisp, cold air around the *Hauptmarkt.* Wrap up warmly and join the locals in browsing through the log stalls displaying the signature gifts of Nuremberg: *Zwetschgenmännla* (prune cookies shaped like men), angels of tinsel and gold foil, tin figures, hand-whittled dollhouses, and glass-blown decorations. Sip *Glühwein,* a heated, spicy wine, and warm your hands over the fragrant smoke of a chestnut stand while strains of Bach from a brass ensemble flood the square. Try not to miss the traditional candlelight procession on *Lucientag* (St. Lucia's Day, December 13), when thousands of children march through the streets carrying lighted paper lanterns. On a Sunday evening in late December, there's a special service in the *Frauenkirche* that features the Upper Palatinate region's oldest and most traditional carols. (If you want to attend, arrive early—the church fills up fast.) During this *Christmas* fair, the nights are anything but silent.

THE CORNER IMBISS STUBE, Anywhere in Germany Looking like white sentry boxes, *Imbiss Stuben* (snack stands) send out their tantalizing aromas from what seems to be every other corner in German cities large and small. Germans tend to eat their evening meal rather late, and during the seemingly endless hours between lunch and dinner the *Imbiss Stube* is one of the best places to stave off hunger with a stand-up shish kebab. Other specialties served at these little stands include several different types of wurst (sausage); *Bouletten,* a meat patty similar to a hamburger; and bushels of *Pommes* (pronounced *Pum*-mess), the curiously un-German term for French fries. Some of the larger stands offer an even wider variety of choices—goulash soup, corn on the cob, fried chicken, and even eggrolls. At an *Imbiss Stube,* informality reigns and class distinctions disappear: The people you'll find here at any given time may include matrons taking a break from shopping, club-cruising punk rockers, and couples in fashionable evening dress grabbing a bite on their way to the opera. Hours vary from one stand to the next, and some remain open until quite late at night, so there's a good chance that no matter what time it is, you can get a cup of coffee (and maybe a hot dog to go with it) at the corner *Imbiss Stube.*

Best Hotels

Germany has no shortage of prime accommodations for its visitors—from modern luxury properties with hundreds of rooms to charming little guesthouses set in the midst of the Alpine wilderness to castle-hotels redolent with history. For descriptions of the best inns and hotels in the major German cities, see the individual chapters in THE CITIES; listed below are our choices of outstanding properties in smaller cities and towns and rural areas. Most of these hotels combine Old World ambience with all the amenities we've come to expect in modern times—and although their locations are often a bit out of the way, we've found them well worth the trip. Entries are listed alphabetically by location.

MÖNCHS POSTHOTEL, Bad Herrenalb, Baden-Württemberg Hubert and Gabriele Mönch have a long-standing family history to maintain: Mönchs have been accommodating guests in this gabled, half-timbered Black Forest house since 1863. The 34 guestrooms are spacious and attractive; ask for one with a view of the garden. There are flowers everywhere—grand arrangements that match the floral bedspreads, single blossoms to accompany room-service breakfast, and cheerful sprays on the tables of *Klosterschänke* restaurant, which offers excellent presentations of French and local fare (if it's on the menu, try the saddle of venison). In summer, when the wide windows of the *Locanda*—a charming restaurant featuring light dishes inspired by the Piedmont region of Italy—are open to the garden, the heady scent of roses mingles with the bouquet of Barolo wine. Later, you can walk off those excess calories on several hiking trails nearby. Information: *Mönchs Posthotel,* 2 Dobler Str., Bad Herrenalb 76332 (phone: 7083-7440; fax: 7083-74422).

HOTEL RÖMERBAD, Badenweiler, Baden-Württemberg In a regal setting within the cosmopolitan triangle formed by Freiburg, Basel, and the Alsatian city of Colmar, this hostelry affords the height of luxury to those who can afford its sky-high rates. Hidden behind the building's mansarded, *Louvre*-like façade are the conduits for the hot-spring water that's piped into the baths in the 84 guestrooms and one of the two swimming pools. Eavesdrop on poolside conversations and you might hear the grumbling of an exiled monarch or a toast to a billion-dollar merger. The art of the deal is balanced with the sound of music when world class concerts are held in the hotel's octagonal salon. There is also a good restaurant serving both regional specialties and continental fare. Information: *Hotel Römerbad,* 1 Schlosspl., Badenweiler 79410 (phone: 7632-700; fax: 7632-70200).

PARK HOTEL, Bremen, Bremen Minutes from the industrial rumble of the Bremen docks, the château-like hostelry sits wrapped in a mantle of woods and greenery, the 500-acre *Bürgerpark;* there's also a lake on the property. Foliage-filtered sunlight dapples the property's bicycle paths and permeates the 150 guestrooms, enhancing the pastel colors and understated charm of the decor. Every room has a view of the park, and some overlook the lake. Even the bathtubs have great views, so you can bird watch while you luxuriate in the steamy water. Have tea by the fire in the domed colonnade or a nightcap in the *Jugendstil* bar. The hotel has two restaurants, as well as a chic café where in warm weather patrons can dine on an open-air terrace with a great panoramic view of the lake. Information: *Park Hotel,* Postfach 102667, D2800 Bremen 1 (phone: 421-34080; 800-223-5652; fax: 421-340-8602).

PARK HOTEL ADLER, Hinterzarten, Baden-Württemberg Under the same family's management for 15 generations, this playground complex in the middle of the Black Forest has expanded gradually since it opened in 1446. In 1770, Marie Antionette slept here on a trip from Vienna to Paris. The original 17th-century building has been enhanced by such amenities as indoor and outdoor tennis courts, a swimming pool, a deer park, and stables that can even accommodate guests' horses. Each of the hotel's 78 rooms and suites is individually decorated (some with antiques, some with more contemporary furnishings) and there are seven dining rooms clustered beneath the low, sloping roof of the main house. Among them is the 17th-century *Stube,* offering primarily seafood in an atmospheric room with rustic woodwork, a beamed ceiling, and antiques. The tiled stove in the *Stube* is the kind that once jutted out into every kitchen in Bavaria, thawing chilled hikers and drying wet socks; here it gives the dining area a warm, convivial glow. There's also a French dining room featuring classical continental fare, such as breast of pigeon and foie gras in a pastry shell with morel sauce, steamed turbot with lobster hollandaise, and fine wines. Information: *Park Hotel Adler,* 3 Adlerpl., Hinterzarten 79856 (phone: 7652-1270; fax: 7652-127717).

WASSERBURG ANHOLT, Isselburg, North Rhine–Westphalia When you drive across the moat into the majestic central court of this turreted red brick castle-hotel and hoist the drawbridge behind you, you'll be well protected from the stress of modern-day life. What you do here is entirely up to you: You can enjoy leisurely meals in the waterside outdoor café, amble through a lovingly tended French garden, putt around on an 18-hole golf course, or view the art collection of the hotel's German proprietor. The 28 antique-filled guestrooms have goose-down comforters, so you're guaranteed to have a great night's sleep. Information: *Wasserburg Anholt,* Klever Str., Isselburg 46419 (phone: 2874-4590; fax: 2874-4035).

SCHLOSSHOTEL KRONBERG, Kronberg im Taunus, Hessen Once the residence of a lonely widow, Victoria, Queen of Prussia and Empress of Germany, who came here after the death of her husband, Emperor Friedrich III, in 1888, this splendid palace is still fit for a monarch. The opulent details—shimmering chandeliers, burnished antiques, gilt-framed family portraits, lamps with hunting-horn motifs, and richly designed Oriental carpets—reflect Victoria's royal tastes. The elegant furnishings extend to the 58 guestrooms and the grand salons and reception halls, perfect for business conferences. The superb restaurant serves classic fare with a light touch, such as rose-shaped portions of petal-thin smoked salmon slices. Information: *Schlosshotel Kronberg,* Postfach 1326, Kronberg im Taunus 61476 (phone: 6173-70101; fax: 6173-701267).

HOTEL BAD SCHACHEN, Lindau im Bodensee, Bavaria Since the 18th century, people have been coming to this old-fashioned 130-room mountain resort for the hot springs, the fresh, bracing air, the paths through the thickly wooded grounds, and the soothing views of the cobalt-blue lake ringed by the Alps. At this preserve on the banks of the Bodensee (Lake Constance), parasol-twirling ladies, and gentlemen wearing white suits and Panama hats would not seem out of place. The healing regime is traditional—and taken quite seriously: The expert staff coordinates your fitness program, supervising and administering facials, massages, body wraps, exercise routines, and baths in bubbling water infused with aromatic herbs. You also can exercise your body on the hotel's two tennis courts or in the two swimming pools. Or simply relax and enjoy the beautiful natural surroundings—you can even have breakfast in bed if you wish. The dining room serves tasty (and healthful) preparations of Bavarian and continental dishes. Open April through mid-October. Information: *Hotel Bad Schachen,* 1 Bad Schachen, Lindau 881311 (phone: 8382-2980; fax: 8382-25390).

SONNENALP, Ofterschwang über Sonthofen (Allgäu), Bavaria The ideal spot for a sporting vacation. No matter what the season, this resort can arrange a strenuous activity to match, whether it's whitewater rafting, hiking through a green Alpine meadow, or skiing down a steep mountain slope. After a day's exercise, you can slow the pace and swim in the heated pool or take a ride in a horse-drawn sleigh. Other sports facilities include a second heated pool (this one outdoors), eight tennis courts, and an 18-hole golf course. The hotel offers 220 charmingly furnished rooms and suites, all with geranium-filled boxes under windows that afford postcard-perfect views of the Allgäuer Alps. The walls are lined with knotty pine and the furnishings are of rugged-looking wood, giving the rooms a rustic, country-house charm. Dining options include the formal *Silberalistel* restaurant (dinner only), the Italian *Seepferd'l* (lunch only), a large breakfast buffet, and a tavern. Information: *Sonnenalp,* Ofterschwang über Sonthofen (Allgäu) 87527 (phone: 8321-2720; fax: 8321-272242).

HOTEL EISENHUT, Rothenburg-ob-der-Tauber, Bavaria Nothing much has changed in this most pristine medieval city in Germany—not even the namesake steel helmet at this hostelry's door. Inside, the decor is much the same as it was in the 16th century, when Rothenburg's most distinguished citizens lived in these two houses: Everywhere you look are crossed halberds, stone arches, wrought-iron chandeliers hanging from coffered ceilings, and chairs upholstered in studded leather and brocade. The main building has 54 rooms; the separate *Gast Haus* (guesthouse) has 25. Excellently prepared international dishes are served in the restaurant. The banquet rooms, whose walls are lined with carved and painted wooden saints, are available only by special arrangement. Information: *Hotel Eisenhut,* 3 Herrngasse, Rothenburg-ob-der-Tauber 91541 (phone: 9861-7050; fax: 9861-70545).

ROMANTIK HOTEL FASANERIE, Zweibrücken, Rhineland-Palatinate Tucked into a forested corner of the Pfälzer Wald, this secluded gingerbread house is the ideal place for roughing it in style. The 50-room hotel gets its name from its pastoral setting in the former pheasant-breeding grounds (*Fasan* is the German word for pheasant) of an exiled 18th-century Polish king. The larger-than-life murals on the walls of the breakfast room, painted in 1941 by local artist Hermann Croissant, show a wartime Germany's wistful fantasy of idyllic courtly life—a life that you can now experience here. After a day of cantering on horseback through the lovely, deep forest, the house-style pheasant is de rigueur for dinner. The hotel also has a pool, and guests can play golf and tennis nearby. Information: *Romantik Hotel Fasanerie,* Zweibrücken 66482 (phone: 6332-9730; fax: 6332-97311).

WALD- UND SCHLOSSHOTEL FRIEDRICHSRUHE, Zweiflingen, Baden-Württemberg One of the best country inns in Germany, this 18th-century Baroque castle once served as a hunting lodge for Emperor Johann Friedrich I. Nowadays, however, the game here tends to be golf (on an 18-hole course on the hotel's six square miles of forested grounds) or tennis rather than venison or bear. The 51 rooms, with rich, polished mahogany paneling and decorated with comfortable furniture and eiderdown quilts, are distributed between two buildings: the original castle and a more modern structure. The property also boasts three tennis courts (two indoor, one outdoor), a pool, a sauna, a whirlpool bath, and two restaurants. The main dining room has earned two Michelin stars for its French cooking (see *Best Restaurants* in this section), and the more rustic *Jägerstube* features regional dishes featuring pigeon, pike, and veal. Our favorite rooms are No. 66, in a corner, with a huge mahogany bed and the plushest eiderdown comforter that's ever warmed our toes; and No. 55, with two beds and an overstuffed sofa. It's all enough to make one believe that the good life is still alive and well—at least here. Information: *Wald- und Schlosshotel Friedrichsruhe,* Zweiflingen 74639 (phone: 7941-60870; fax: 7941-61468).

Best Restaurants

Although the French defined and refined the concept of haute cuisine, Germany has more than its share of restaurants serving fine continental fare; a few have been awarded Michelin stars for their pains. And don't forget the wide range of excellent wines produced in vineyards all over Germany (for more about these, see *Visitable Vineyards* in this section). In this country, eating is a ceremony to be savored, and Germans are congenial, obliging hosts who are always eager to initiate newcomers to the wonders of their cooking. We have described the best dining spots in major cities in the individual chapters in THE CITIES; below is a list of several equally fine places off the beaten path, most specializing in superbly prepared international dishes. Though the restaurants that follow are set in more remote areas, they are just as distinguished as their urban counterparts. Entries are listed alphabetically by location.

RESIDENZ HEINZ WINKLER, Aschau im Chiemgau, Bavaria One of Germany's designer restaurants, this three-Michelin-star dining spot is housed in a cloister-like building that has been a hotel since the late 15th century. Heinz Winkler, for years the gastronomic guru of Munich's *Tantris* restaurant, has led his faithful followers to the mountaintop village of Aschau, and daily performs culinary miracles in his kitchen. The 40-minute trip from Munich or Salzburg is a scenic prelude to an evening-long gastronomic event. Winkler was made an honorary member of the clique of chefs who cook for heads of state, and his roster of well-fed celebrities includes King Juan Carlos of Spain, Jean-Paul Belmondo, and a jet-setting conductor or two. Among his delightful concoctions are ravioli stuffed with sweetbreads and coated with a white truffle sauce, lobster medallions with saffron on black noodles, and saddle of venison in port wine and pistachio sauce. Open daily. Reservations necessary. Major credit cards accepted. Information: *Residenz Heinz Winkler,* 1 Am Kirchpl., Aschau im Chiemgau 83229 (phone: 8052-17990; fax: 8052-179966).

SCHWARZWALDSTUBE, Baiersbronn, Baden-Württemberg The 18th-century *Kur- und Sporthotel Traube-Tonbach,* set in the heart of the Schwarzwald (Black Forest), evolved slowly from a way station for loggers into a sports playground—and its superb three-Michelin-star dining room proves that the way to visitors' hearts is definitely through their stomachs. The decor is in a charming rustic style, with traditionally carved wooden furnishings and a coffered wooden ceiling; there are only 10 tables, so patrons are assured a private, intimate dining experience. Ask to sit by the window so you can take in the glorious view of the surrounding forest. The varied and frequently changing menu, which has been presided over by chef Harald Wohlfahrt for the past 18 years, presents such exquisitely prepared continental dishes as veal medallions in goose liver sauce, lobster cassoulet, vegetable *Charlotte Russe* served with goose liver and truffles, and lamb ribs with shallots and herbs baked in basil sauce. Closed Thursday and Friday lunch and most of July. Reservations necessary (for a Saturday night, reserve three *months* in advance). Major credit cards accepted. Information: *Schwarzwaldstube, Kur- und Sporthotel Traube-Tonbach,* 237 Tonbachstr., Baiersbronn 72270 (phone: 7442-492665; fax: 7442-492692).

RESTAURANT DIETER MÜLLER, Bergisch Gladbach, Rhineland-Westphalia Culinary celebrity Dieter Müller has adopted the kitchen of the secluded *Schlosshotel Lerbach* as his private domain. The restaurant that bears his signature approaches the German ideal of *Gesamtkunstwerk*—a total work of art; Michelin has awarded it two stars. The pale rose and off-white hues and antique fountain of the *Wintergarten* and the rustic wood furnishings and iron cabinets of the *Altes Speisezimmer* are effective backdrops for the main attraction: the food. Müller gives such traditional continental dishes as roast breast of duck an exotic flair by marinating it in lavender-scented honey and herbs from Provence and serving it with a garnish of spring vegetables. There's even a split-level suite in the tower, so you don't have to eat and run. Closed Sundays and Mondays. Reservations necessary. Major credit cards accepted. Information: *Schlosshotel Lerbach,* Lerbacher Weg, Bergisch Gladbach 51469 (phone: 2202-2040; fax: 2202-204940).

RATSKELLER, Bremen, Bremen A wine cellar in the basement of a city's municipal building is a common—and curious—German institution. Thus it could be argued that the most important document in the Gothic, gabled *Rathaus* (Town Hall) in Bremen's central square is the exhaustive wine list. This honor roll boasts a selection of 600-odd German wines, ranging from rieslings to Bernkastels. Not to be outdone, the kitchen offers such fine regional specialties as chicken in cognac sauce, steamed filet of cod, and duck in orange sauce—perfect accompaniments to the wine. Open daily. Reservations advised. Major credit cards accepted. Information: *Ratskeller,* Am Markt, Bremen 28195 (phone: 421-321676).

VOSS HAUS, Eutin, Schleswig-Holstein This historic establishment, one of the best restaurants in the entire state of Schleswig-Holstein, is nearly three centuries old. Part of a 15-room village inn, the dining room has a cozy and welcoming interior, with dark paneling, carved wooden doors, beamed ceilings, antique prints and lithographs on the walls, and a vintage North German tile fireplace. The menu offers outstanding preparations of such regional specialties as pan-fried filet of plaice served with halibut, tiny shrimp, and buttery potatoes; Holstein potato soup with croutons; and *Rote Grütze* (a pudding made from fresh-picked berries cooked in fruit juice and steeped in cream) for dessert. Finish off your meal with a hot cup of *Pharisaer* (coffee with rum and sugar, topped with cream). This place is a must-stop for anyone traveling through northern Germany. Open daily. Reservations advised except in winter. Major credit cards accepted. Information: *Voss Haus,* 6 Vosspl., Eutin 23701 (phone: 4521-1797).

ULRICHSHÖHE, Nürtingen-Hardt, Baden-Württemberg You'll feel as if the green carpet of the Swabian Jura beneath the terrace here has been rolled out just for you. The menu of this one-Michelin-star establishment features such continental dishes as cutlet of dove in brioche with truffle sauce, and sole and lobster fricassee. Owner Annegret Bub-Schilling, an award-winning hostess, welcomes her guests with consummate grace, while the waiters seem to appear exactly when you need them and then disappear discreetly into the background. Inside, the elegant decor (cherry wood furnishings, porcelain, fine silver, and abundant bouquets of fresh flowers) is matched only by the presentation of the meal. Closed Sundays, Mondays, and January. Reservations advised (especially for dinner). Major credit cards accepted. Information: *Ulrichshöhe,* 14 Herzog-Ulrich-Str., Nürtingen 72622 (phone: 7022-52336).

HOTEL-RESTAURANT SCHWEIZER STUBEN, Wertheim, Baden-Württemberg The grounds of this geranium-decked 16-room resort hotel on the banks of the Main surround no fewer than three great restaurants. The crown jewel, the French-style restaurant that bears the hotel's name, has been awarded two Michelin stars. The combination of knotty pine walls and silky vanilla upholstery in the dining room is a pleasant blending of the style of a Parisian drawing room and a Nordic ski chalet. The food is merely spectacular: langoustines bathed in lemon-ginger sauce and braised goat with olive oil and anchovies are only two of the specialties. The Italian *Taverna la Vigna* (one Michelin star) has whitewashed walls, tiled floors, and wrought-iron grilles; its menu features such delicacies as Venetian-style calf's liver with polenta and braised duck served with savoy cabbage. The Swiss *Landgasthof Schober* has beamed ceilings and the type of heavy-set furniture one expects to find in the kitchen of an Alpine home. The menu here goes far beyond fondue; try the steak tips with ratatouille and roasted potatoes. Take our advice: Rather than agonizing over which place to choose, stay in the area long enough to try all three. The *Restaurant Schweizer Stuben* is closed Mondays, Tuesdays, and the first three weeks of January; the *Taverna la Vigna* is closed Sundays, Mondays, and the first three weeks of February; and the *Landgasthof Schober* is closed Wednesdays, Thursdays, and the first three weeks of January. Reservations advised. Major credit cards accepted. Information: *Hotel-Restaurant Schweizer Stuben,* 11 Geiselbrunnweg, Wertheim-Bettingen 97877 (phone: 9342-3070; fax: 9342-307155).

WALD- UND SCHLOSSHOTEL FRIEDRICHSRUHE, Zweiflingen, Baden-Württemberg The isolated luxury of this 18th-century hunting lodge is still much as it was during the time when the evening menu depended on what the guests had bagged that day. The ornate decor of the hotel extends to its elegant two-Michelin-star restaurant: plush carpeting, shimmering chandeliers, satin-lined walls, and heavy red drapes. *Taubenbrüstchen mit roter Bete und marinierten Steinpilzen* (pigeon breast with beets and marinated mushrooms) and *Seeteufel mit Meerrettichbutter gratiniert auf Bohnenragout* (monkfish served with a sharp horseradish sauce and beans) are just two of the innovative continental dishes offered here. Closed Mondays and Tuesdays. Reservations necessary. Major credit cards accepted. Information: *Wald- und Schlosshotel Friedrichsruhe,* Zweiflingen 74639 (phone: 7941-60870; fax: 7941-61468).

Shopping Spree

In the past, shopping in Germany promised the possibility of buying something for far less than you would pay for the same item at home—if you could even find it. Nowadays, due to galloping inflation and waltzing currencies, good buys are harder to find. Also, more and more German goods are being exported (a trend that is likely to grow even more popular now that the country is reunified), so you're often better off picking up an import at your hometown corner store rather than enduring the hassle of customs regulations and too-full suitcases. (And don't bother with duty-free shops, either: It's hardly worth the effort of weeding through all the overpriced merchandise to find the few bargains.) The moral of the story is this: View shopping as another part of the *experience* of travel. Buy because it brings you into contact with people and places, customs and creation. Shop for high-quality items that you will use often, things that will remind you of those people and places when you are back home. Then your purchase becomes an expensive snapshot, and the pleasure of the experience lingers.

Germany is a world leader in the production of several types of goods, most of which can be found in a variety of stores in major cities such as Berlin and Munich. If the city you're visiting is covered in THE CITIES, check "Shopping" in the respective chapter for a detailed listing of shops in that area. What follows is an item-by-item guide to what to buy.

CAMERAS Leica, Rollei, and Zeiss are the leading German brands of cameras and photographic equipment. You'll find their products in large cities; however, any given item may be available in the US for a lower price, so comparison shopping is essential.

CHINA AND PORCELAIN Germany (especially Dresden) has been producing fine china and porcelain for centuries. In particular, look for the names Meissen, Rosenthal, and KPM.

CLOCKS The Black Forest region is well known for its intricately carved wooden cuckoo clocks, which make fine souvenirs and gifts. High-quality precision timepieces are also a good buy and can be found throughout the country.

CLOTHES AND ACCESSORIES Men's and women's clothes by the leading international names (including German designers Jil Sander, Ursula Conzen, Guido Boehler, and Reimer Clausen) are available in most major cities. Michael Cromer München (known as MCM for short) is renowned for excellent leather goods, including wallets, luggage, and handbags. For a touch of local flair, purchase a sweater or overcoat made of loden wool; the rustic look of these fashions has become chic throughout Europe.

CUTLERY J. A. Henckels and WMF (which stands for Württembergische-Metalwaren-Fabrik) are two leading German manufacturers of knives and fine silverware. Their products are available in department and specialty stores in most major cities.

FOODSTUFFS AND LIQUOR Gingerbread, sausages, jam and marmalade, and honey make tasty reminders of your visit to Germany. The beer produced in Bavaria is among the world's best, and schnapps is another popular drink.

HANDICRAFTS Fine woodcarvings are available in most rural areas of Germany, but the best place to go is the village of Oberammergau, on the Alpine Road. The cities of Bremen and Lübeck are well known for producing exquisite ships in bottles.

OPTICAL PRODUCTS Highly calibrated, precise telescopes, microscopes, and binoculars are a German specialty that can be found in most major cities.

PEWTER AND TIN Nuremberg is the place to look for exquisite items made of pewter and tin, particularly antique tin soldiers, vases, and dishes.

TOYS Again, Nuremberg has some of the finest playthings that Germany has to offer, including hand-carved wooden blocks and figures, and nutcracker soldiers.

VIOLINS If you're in the market for a truly first class violin, head for Mittenwald on the Austrian border, nicknamed "The Village of a Thousand Violins."

Visitable Vineyards

Wine making is one of Germany's oldest traditions, dating back to Roman times. Driving leisurely through the country's vine-patterned hills, sampling vintages, and selecting some favorites to take home is far more appealing than a hasty browse through the duty-free shop at the airport. When you serve wine produced by vineyards you've actually visited, you'll be able to describe the grounds (and often the historic buildings on the premises), the cask-lined cellar, and the fresh aroma of the actual grape. Touring vineyards can easily take up an entire vacation; a particularly good time for a wine-themed trip is during the harvest season, from late August until mid-October, when many villages hold *Weinfeste* (wine festivals) on weekends from about 11 AM until midnight or later. These events are tailored for the avid oenophile, who can wander from one awninged stand to another, sipping a riesling (white wine) or a *weissherbst* (rosé) and striking up conversations with other samplers.

High-quality vineyards can be found all over Germany. You can taste your way up the Rhine or down the Mosel, a winding waterway that flows from France and empties into the Rhine at Koblenz; or you can organize your travels around the Neckar or Main River. The most scenic stretch of the Middle Rhine is located in a narrow winding valley of the Rhine between the towns of Bingen and Koblenz—at about 1,700 acres, it's one of the smallest wine regions in the country. But despite the valley's small size, the names of its vineyard castles grace the labels of some fine riesling wines; much of the planting and harvesting work here is done by hand. In the Rheingau, between Rüdesheim and Wiesbaden, the late-ripening riesling yields elegant wines with a bouquet redolent of apricots and peaches.

The Pfalz, extending from near Worms to the border of Alsace at Schweigen, is Germany's most wine-saturated terrain—a six-mile-wide and

50-mile-long strip of purple and green. The exceptionally warm climate is especially good for grape growing; in fact, every fifth bottle of the country's wine comes from the Pfalz. If you order a glass of wine here, you may well get more than you bargained for: the typical wineglass holds almost a full pint! The region is traversed by the Deutsche Weinstrasse (German Wine Road), a lush, grape-laden route popular among day-trippers out to combine hiking with wine tasting.

Mosel wine is the hands-down favorite of many connoisseurs—its taste is light, flavorful, and often more delicate than wines produced in the Rhine region. The *Bernkasteler Doctor* vineyard in this region produces the country's most distinguished (and expensive) wines; the word "Doctor" in its name comes from a local legend that Archbishop Bömund II once recovered from an illness by drinking the wine. The elbling grape, cultivated for centuries in the upper Mosel, has a tartness that lends itself exquisitely to sparkling wines.

The Neckar River Valley in Württemberg produces about 10% of the German harvest each year, with much of the vineyard area concentrated near Stuttgart. The wines made here are diverse: the trollinger, light red and fruity (and exclusive to this area); the schwarzriesling (which literally translates to "black riesling," though it is no relation to the riesling grape); and the dark, almost violet lemberger. Among the whites, robust, hearty rieslings make up the greatest percentage (almost a quarter of the entire vineyard surface).

Flat green or brown bottles called *Bocksbeutel* are the signature of Franken, one of the easternmost of Germany's wine-growing regions. Wines produced in this area along the Main River—particularly those from the region's classic grapes, silvaner and müller-thurgau—are dry and fruity, with an unmistakable earthy flavor. Baden's celebrated vineyards stretch 250 miles from the Taubertal (Tauber River Valley) in the north to the Bodensee (Lake Constance) in the south; many growers in this region produce dry wines that go well with food. The area's largest wine growing district is the Kaiserstuhl. Here and elsewhere in Baden, the burgundy (also called pinot) varieties are popular, including spätburgunder, grauburgunder, and weissburgunder.

Below is a selection of Germany's prime wine regions, with the best vineyards in each listed alphabetically by town. You will most likely need a car to do extensive touring, although some areas are accessible by train or bus from major cities. There also are some pretty hiking trails that take in vineyards en route. Though you can drop in on some wineries without an appointment, it's always a good idea to call them ahead of time; many are small, family-run operations and may need time to prepare for your visit. Wear sensible, rubber-soled shoes for negotiating slippery floors, and bring a sweater or light jacket (even in summer).

THE RHEINGAU

For information on the Rheingau, contact *Gesellschaft für Rheingauer Weinkultur,* Im Alten Rathaus, Geisenheim 65366 (phone: 6722-8117; fax: 6722-6643).

KLOSTER EBERBACH/VERWALTUNG DER STAATSWEINGÜTER, Eltville The viticultural tradition started by the Cistercian monks in this 12th-century cloister continues uninterrupted to this day. *Kloster Eberbach* (Eberbach Monastery) now serves as the administrative headquarters of the Hessian State Wine Domain's 350 acres of riesling and spätburgunder vines (many of which have been sold for record prices at auction). On Sunday afternoons in summer, you also can enjoy a concert in the Romanesque basilica. A restaurant on the grounds serves good food along with the wines. Tours and tastings are available daily; the *Jugendstil* press house at the *Staatsweinkellerei* (State Wine Cellar) is closed Sundays. Information: *Verwaltung der Staatsweingüter,* 56-62 Schwalbacher Str., Eltville 65343 (phone: 6123-61055; fax: 6123-4366).

DOMDECHANT WERNER'SCHES WEINGUT, Hochheim The generic nickname for Rhine wines, "hock," was derived from the village of Hochheim, situated on the bank of the Main River, just a few miles east of its confluence with the Rhine. Here, Oda and Franz Werner Michel cultivate 30 acres of riesling vines. Dry riesling and sparkling wines are specialties. In addition to beautiful vaulted cellars with traditional, aged oak casks, the family has a small wine museum. Their neoclassical manor house, built in 1780, is also worth seeing. Tastings and cellar visits are offered weekdays and Saturdays, or by appointment on Sundays. Ring the house doorbell. Information: *Domdechant Werner'sches Weingut,* 30 Rathausstr., Hochheim am Main 65239 (phone: 6146-2008; fax: 6146-61153).

FÜRST VON METTERNICH-WINNEBURG'SCHES DOMÄNERENTAMT, SCHLOSS JOHANNESBURG, Johannisburg This world class wine estate's viticultural tradition dates from 1097. During the 18th century, *Schloss Johannesburg* (Johannesburg Palace) and extensive cellars were built, and the vineyards were planted exclusively with riesling grapes, which were harvested late in the season in order to produce very rich, fruity wines. Cellar visits are by appointment only, but the vintages can be sampled in the *Weincabinet* shop and a wine pub on the premises. The shop is closed Sundays in November and weekends mid-December through February; the pub is closed Tuesdays and January through February. Information: *Schloss Johannesburg,* Geisenheim-Johannisberg 65366 (phone: 6722-70090; fax: 6722-700933).

WEINGUT GEORG BREUER, Rüdesheim In 1984, proprietor Bernhard Breuer, one of the area's most dynamic personalities, cofounded the Rheingau region's *CHARTA* group, which produces superb, dry-style Rheingau rieslings. Breuer's 53 acres of steep vineyards include some of Rüdesheim's best sites (particularly the individually owned *Rauenthaler Nonnenberg* vineyard in the eastern portion of the region). Besides riesling dinner wines, other Breuer specialties include riesling dessert wines, barrique-aged pinot varieties (blanc, gris, and noir), and brandies. All can be sampled during tasting tours, in the on-premises *Vinothek* shop, in the *Berg Schlossberg* bistro next door, or at *Rüdesheimer Schloss,* the family's hotel and wine restaurant on the Drosselgasse in town. Tastings and cellar visits are offered daily *Easter* through mid-November; at other times, ring the doorbell. Information: *Weingut Georg Breuer, Vinothek,* 8 Grabenstr., Rüdesheim 65385 (phone: 6722-1027; fax: 6722-4531).

WEINGUT SCHLOSS VOLLRADS, Winkel Set at the edge of the forested Taunus Hügeln (Taunus Hills), about a mile north of Winkel, is a magnificent castle overlooking 125 acres of riesling vineyards. Numbering among the handful of German castles permitted to use its name as a wine appellation, *Schloss Vollrads* (Vollrads Castle) is also one of the world's oldest wine estates, dating from 1211; it has been in the same family for 27 generations. Wine tastings are conducted (by appointment only) in the period rooms of the 17th-century palace, and a wine pub in the historic cavalier's house (closed Tuesdays and Thursdays in winter and the entire month of January) offers a less formal sampling of the estate's wines with food. Formal tastings are offered weekdays year-round; an open-air tasting stand in the courtyard is open every afternoon from May through mid-October. Information: *Schloss Vollrads,* Oestrich-Winkel 65375 (phone: 6723-660; fax: 6723-1848).

THE NAHE

For information on the Nahe, contact *Weinland Nahe,* 6 Dessauer Str., Bad Kreuznach 55545 (phone: 671-27563; fax: 671-27568).

WINZERGENOSSENSCHAFT RHEINGRAFENBERG, Meddersheim Despite its distance from the Nahe region's better-known estates, the *Rheingrafenberg* cooperative winery is worth visiting because it offers good value for the money, particularly for the house specialty Eiswein. The 100 members collectively cultivate 370 acres of grapes for the production of wine, sparkling wine, brandy, and grape juice. The powerful, fragrant riesling wines from the area's best sites, *Rheingrafenberg* and *Altenberg,* are available from dry to lusciously sweet varieties. Tastings and cellar visits are available weekdays and Saturdays. Information: *Winzergenossenschaft Rheingrafenberg,* 63 Naheweinstr., Meddersheim 55566 (phone: 6751-2667; fax: 6751-6101).

PRINZ ZU SALM-DALBERGISCHES WEINGUT, SCHLOSS WALLHAUSEN, Wallhausen Descendants of the Knights of Dalberg number among Germany's oldest wine-growing families, with viticulture documented as early as 1200. The present 25-acre grounds are situated in the rustic village of Wallhausen, at the foot of the Soon Forest, and produce a wide variety of traditional grapes, notably riesling, silvaner, and the spätburgunder and grauburgunder pinots. Visitors are welcome to sample the wines and visit the cellars at the castle in Wallhausen. Just ring the bell next to the "Weinverkauf" sign weekdays and every second Saturday of the month. Information: *Prinz zu Salm-Dalbergisches Weingut, Schloss Wallhausen,* Wallhausen 55595 (phone: 6706-289; fax: 6706-6017).

THE PFALZ

For information on the Pfalz, contact *Pfalzwein,* 3 Chemnitzer Str., Neustadt 67433 (phone: 6321-912328; fax: 6321-12881).

WEINGUT FITZ-RITTER, Bad Dürkheim The beautiful manor house was built in 1785, the year this 54-acre estate was founded. Hearty riesling wines are its forte, but the winery also produces spicy gewürztraminer and dry grauburgunder, weissburgunder, and spätburgunder pinots. Rosé, red, and white sparkling wines are available, several with antique labels, as well as brandies and grape juice. A lovely garden with rare and exotic trees borders the vineyards. There's a small museum with wine-related artifacts dating from Roman times, as well as a gift shop where you can purchase the estate's vintages and wine accessories. Visitors are welcome weekdays and Saturdays, or by appointment on Sundays. Information: *Weingut Fitz-Ritter,* 51 Weinstr. N., Bad Dürkheim 67098 (phone: 6322-5389; fax: 6322-66005).

WEINGUT LINGENFELDER, Grosskarlbach This 37-acre estate in Grosskarlbach, less than 4 miles (6 km) southeast of Grünstadt, produces riesling, scheurebe, dornfelder, and spätburgunder (pinot noir). The vaulted red sandstone cellars house stainless steel tanks, aged oak casks, and barriques (for the red wines). Specialties include dry reds with great structure and complexity; elegant dry rieslings; and superb dessert wines from the scheurebe grape. Brandies and homegrown apples also are available. Visitors are welcome to tour the cellars and taste the wines weekdays and Saturdays, or by appointment on Sundays. Information: *Weingut Lingenfelder,* 27 Hauptstr., Grosskarlbach 67229 (phone: 6238-754; fax: 6238-1096).

WEINGUT KOEHLER-RUPRECHT, Kallstadt Kallstadt, on the Weinstrasse, is home to one of the Pfalz's finest vineyards and a tasty local specialty made of minced pork, potatoes, and spices cooked and served in a sow's stomach: Both are named *Saumagen* (pronounced *Zow*-mah-gen, it literally means "sow's stomach"). For outstanding versions of both the dish and the wine produced at the vineyard, visit the Philippi family's half-timbered winery and hotel-restaurant. The 20-acre estate, founded in 1680, specializes in dry rieslings as well as rich, full-flavored dessert wines. The spätburgunders also are highly prized. Park across the street from the estate and ring the doorbell of the house on the left as you enter the courtyard. Cellar visits and tastings are offered weekdays and by appointment on weekends. The *Hotel-Restaurant Weincastell zum Weissen Ross* is closed Mondays, Tuesdays, and January. Information: *Weingut Koehler-Ruprecht,* 84 Weinstr., Kallstadt 67169 (phone: 6322-1829; fax: 6322-8640).

THE AHR

For information on the Ahr, contact *Touristik-Service Ahr, Rhein, Eifel, Bäder-, Wein- und Wanderland,* 11 Markt, Bad Neuenahr–Ahrweiler 53474 (phone: 2641-97730; fax: 2641-977373).

WEINGUT J. J. ADENAUER, Ahrweiler Family-owned and -run for 500 years, the 17-acre estate is the last on the Ahr that exclusively produces red wine, 80% of which is spätburgunder, with small quantities of portugieser and dornfelder. Deep in color, fragrant, and flavorful, the *Adenauer* reds are highly prized. Sparkling wine and brandies also are available. Visitors are welcome to see the cellars and sample the wines on weekdays and Saturdays. Information: *Weingut J. J. Adenauer,* 8 Max-Planck-Str., Bad Neuenahr–Ahrweiler 53474 (phone: 2641-34473; fax: 2641-37379).

WEINGUT TONI NELLES, Heimersheim Less than 15 miles (25 km) south of Bonn—where the tiny Ahr River flows into the Rhine—the steep, south-facing slope of the Ahrtal (Ahr Valley) is the site of Heimersheim's excellent vineyards, *Landskrone* and *Burggarten,* and where most of the Nelles estate's 12 acres are planted. The family's viticultural tradition dates from 1479. Harmonious dry reds from portugieser and spätburgunder grapes and piquant rieslings are the estate's finest wines. Sparkling wine and brandies also are available. Cellar visits and tastings are held weekdays and Saturdays. Information: *Weingut Toni Nelles,* 13a Goeppinger Str., Bad Neuenahr–Ahrweiler 53474 (phone: 2641-24349; fax: 2641-79586).

MOSEL-SAAR-RUWER

For information on the Mosel-Saar-Ruwer, contact *Mosel-Saar-Ruwer Wein,* 12a Gartenfeldstr., Trier 54295 (phone: 651-76621 or 651-45967; fax: 651-45443).

WEINGUT DR. PAULY-BERGWEILER, Bernkastel Dr. Peter Pauly and his wife are the owner-managers of this estate and of the *Weingut Peter Nicolay* in Urzig. Under cultivation are 45 acres of primarily riesling vines in the most important middle Mosel villages from Erden to Brauneberg and a portion of the famed *Doctor* vineyard in Bernkastel. Overlooking the river, the Paulys' 1893 villa is fashioned of local Mosel slate and is a fine example of *Jugendstil* architecture. The tasting room, in an old cask cellar below the house, is open Mondays through Saturdays mid-May through late October (other times by appointment only). Information: *Weingut Dr. Pauly-Bergweiler,* 15 Gestade, Bernkastel-Kues 54470 (phone: 6531-3002; fax: 6531-7201).

WEINGUT FREIHERR VON SCHLEINITZ, Kobern Just minutes from Koblenz are some of the world's steepest vineyards. Konrad Hähn and his American wife, Laurel, are among the few growers still willing to tend vines on these near-perpendicular slate hills, a tradition in this region since 1650. Here, as throughout the area, the riesling is the finest grape, but sparkling wine and brandy also are available. Tastings and visits to the vaulted cellars are offered (preferably by appointment) weekdays and Saturdays. Information: *Weingut Freiherr von Schleinitz,* 15 Kirchstr., Kobern-Gondorf 56330 (phone: 2607-268; fax: 2607-8204).

WEINGUT REICHSGRAF VON KESSELSTATT, Trier In the heart of what is considered to be Germany's oldest town is the Baroque *Schloss Kesselstatt* (Kesselstatt Palace), home of one of the country's great private wine estates. The 160 acres of riesling vineyards, located throughout the valleys of the Mosel, Saar, and Ruwer rivers, have been cultivated for more than a century. *Kesselstatt* has won more awards for outstanding wine making than any other estate in Germany. This is one of the few places where high-quality riesling wines from the entire region can be tasted and compared. Ask to see the historic cellars. The vintages can be sampled in the wine shop or in an on-premises pub (both open daily). There also is a first-rate restaurant in the palace which features fine German food and the estate's wines; closed Sundays, Mondays, and February. Information: *Weingut Reichsgraf von Kesselstatt,* 9-10 Liebfrauenstr., Trier 54290 (phone: 651-75101; fax: 651-73316).

BADEN

For further information on Baden, contact *Weinwerbezentrale Badischer Winzergenossenschaften,* 5 Kesslerstr., Karlsruhe 76185 (phone: 721-557028; fax: 721-557020).

WEINGUT KARL H. JOHNER, Bischoffingen Since they started their estate in 1985, Karl Heinz and Irene Johner have built a striking, modern cellar and acquired 20 acres of steep, terraced vineyards planted mostly with pinot varieties. The estate's wines are dry and powerful, aged in small oak casks. Tastings and cellar visits are offered weekdays; call ahead to make sure someone is home. Information: *Weingut Karl H. Johner,* 20 Gartenstr., Vogtsburg-Bischoffingen 79235 (phone: 7662-6041; fax: 7662-8380).

MARKGRÄFLICH-BADISCHES WEINGUT SCHLOSS STAUFENBERG, Durbach The Margraves of Baden, vintners since the 14th century, are major vineyard owners, with estates near the Bodensee (Lake Constance), Baden-Baden, and Durbach. The impressive setting for their Durbach estate is the 11th-century *Schloss Staufenberg* (Staufenberg Castle), purchased by the family in 1832. Riesling (known as klingelberger in this part of Baden) is the estate's primary grape, but there are several pinot varieties as well. The castle terrace affords visitors a magnificent view over the estate's 67 acres, and there is a wine pub and shop on the premises. Cellar visits are by appointment only; visitors may taste the wines daily, however. Information: *Markgräflich-Badisches Weingut Schloss Staufenberg,* Durbach 77770 (phone: 781-42778; fax: 781-440578).

WEINGUT STIGLER, Ihringen Ihringen, Baden's largest wine-growing community, is less than 4 miles (6 km) from Breisach on the Rhine. Andreas Stigler's great-grandfather founded this estate in 1881; today, it has grown to nearly

20 acres in Ihringen, Oberrotweil, and Freiburg. Stigler's full-bodied, dry silvaner wines are a house specialty; also noteworthy are the rieslings, available either very dry or as sweet dessert wines. Visitors in the summer can sample the wines outdoors, beneath a beautiful grape-laden pergola. Cellar visits and tastings are offered weekdays, or by appointment on weekends. Information: *Weingut Stigler,* 29 Bachenstr., Ihringen 79241 (phone 7668-297; fax 7668-94120).

WEINGUT REICHSGRAF UND MARQUIS ZU HOENSBROECH, Michelfeld The Marquis of Hoensbroech's wine estate is situated in the open countryside near Michelfeld. Since Hoensbroech established himself in the Kraichgau area in 1968 (a relative newcomer), he has built up the Baden estate to 42 acres and developed an excellent reputation for his dry, food-compatible wines, particularly from the weissburgunder (pinot blanc) grape. Riesling, grauburgunder, and the red spätburgunder are the other main varieties. At a festival held here in mid-August, guests can ride through the vineyards in replica turn-of-the-century coaches, and picnic while enjoying the estate's wines. Cellar visits and tastings are given weekdays and Saturdays. Information: *Weingut Reichsgraf und Marquis zu Hoensbroech,* Angelbachtal-Michelfeld 74918 (phone: 7265-381; fax: 7265-7998).

WEINGUT SALWEY, Oberrotweil The Salwey family has been making wine since 1720. Most of their 40 acres of vines are planted on the weathered volcanic and mineral-rich soil of the Kaiserstuhl, but some are in the gneiss and granite soil in the heart of the Schwarzwald (Black Forest). To discover the influence of different soils on a wine's bouquet and flavor, visitors can compare Salwey's excellent spätburgunder *weissherbst* (rosé) wines from both areas. Other vintages produced on the estate are silvaner and pinot whites and luscious dessert wines from the ruländer grape. Cellar visits and tastings are held weekdays and Saturdays. Information: *Weingut Salwey,* 2 Hauptstr., Vogtsburg-Oberrotweil 79235 (phone: 7662-384; fax: 7662-6340).

TAUBERFRÄNKISCHER BOCKSBEUTELKELLER, Wertheim-Reicholzheim The 700 members of this cooperative winery in Reicholzheim, a small village just south of Wertheim near the Tauber and Main Rivers, cultivate nearly 700 acres of hillside vineyards. Powerful, dry white rieslings predominate, supplemented by several pinot varieties. Tastings and cellar visits are welcome weekdays and Saturdays. Information: *Tauberfränkischer Bocksbeutelkeller,* 1-3 St.-Georg-Str., Wertheim-Reicholzheim 97877 (phone: 9342-29000; fax: 9342-290080).

WÜRTTEMBERG

For information on Württemberg, contact *Werbegemeinschaft Württembergischer Weingärtnergenossenschaften,* 6 Raiffeisenstr., Möglingen 71696 (phone: 7141-241411; fax: 7141-241461).

SCHLOSSGUT HOHENBEILSTEIN, Beilstein The Dippon family founded this wine estate in 1906 and are the sole owners of the 25-acre *Schlosswengert* vineyard. In addition to the red varieties typically found in Württemberg, such as trollinger, lemberger, and spätburgunder, proprietor Hartmann Dippon cultivates a small amount of the rare samtrot (a mutation of pinot meunier) and the spicy muskattrollinger. His finest white wines are the rieslings. Tastings and cellar visits are offered weekdays and Saturday mornings. Nearby is a signposted hiking trail through the vineyards. Information: *Schlossgut Hohenbeilstein,* Beilstein 71717 (phone: 7062-4303; fax: 7062-22284).

WEINGUT SONNENHOF, Gündelbach This estate is at the foot of vine-covered hills that encircle it like a bowl. Charlotte and Albrecht Fischer cultivate 72 acres of very steep, partially terraced vineyards planted mainly with red varieties such as lemberger, dornfelder, and the rare muskattrollinger. There are also spicy white wines, including gewürztraminer and muskateller. Most unusual are the estate's red dessert wines made from frozen trollinger and lemberger grapes. Visitors are welcome to sample the wines and tour the cellars weekdays and Saturdays. Information: *Weingut Sonnenhof,* Vaihingen-Gündelbach 71665 (phone: 7042-21038; fax: 7042-23894).

WEINGÜTER UND SCHLOSSKELLEREI GRAF VON NEIPPERG, Schwaigern Schwaigern and Neipperg are located in hilly, rural countryside less than 10 miles (16 km) west of Heilbronn. Since 1248, the Counts of Neipperg have cultivated nearly 80 acres of vines. Today, the estate and its historic cellars are housed in a rococo palace next to the Gothic church in Schwaigern. The red lemberger grape (which the Neipperg family imported from Austria in the 18th century) is a house specialty. The estate's red pinots and white wines also enjoy a loyal following. Tastings and cellar visits are given weekdays and Saturday mornings. The wines can be sampled with food at *Zum Alten Rentamt,* the historic restaurant next to the palace (closed January). Information: *Weingüter und Schlosskellerei Graf von Neipperg,* Schwaigern 74193 (phone: 7138-5081; fax: 7138-4007).

FRANKEN

For information on Franken, contact *Frankenwein-Frankenland, Haus des Frankenweins,* 1 Kranenkai, Würzburg 97070 (phone 931-12093; fax: 931-17175).

FÜRSTLICH CASTELL'SCHES DOMÄNENAMT, Castell Tucked in the Steigerwald is the small village of Castell, home of one of Germany's oldest wine-growing dynasties, the Princes of Castell. Many of their present vineyards are mentioned in documents dating from 1258. Aside from the sweet dessert wines, most of the wines produced on this 175-acre estate are very dry; 11 white and three red varieties are available. The rieslaner, a cross between silvaner and riesling, is a house specialty, and brandies and sparkling wines are also produced. In mid-July, a wine festival takes place in the gardens of the Castell's 17th-century palace. Tastings and cellar visits are offered weekdays and Saturdays. Information: *Fürstlich Castell'sches Domänenamt,* 5 Schlosspl., Castell 97355 (phone: 9325-60170; fax: 9325-60185).

WEINGUT HANS WIRSCHING, Iphofen Dr. Heinrich Wirsching is the 14th generation of the family to run this 143-acre wine estate in the medieval village of Iphofen, a few miles south of Castell. Full-bodied, dry silvaner wines are their specialty, but their riesling, müller-thurgau, and scheurebe wines also have won high praise. One of the most famous samplers of this estate's vintages was Pope John Paul II—he was served Wirsching wine during his trip to Germany in the 1980s. Visitors are welcome to visit the vaulted cellars beneath the 400-year-old house and sample the wines weekdays and Saturday mornings. Information: *Weingut Hans Wirsching,* 16 Ludwigstr., Iphofen 97346 (phone: 9323-3033; fax: 9323-3090).

STAATLICHER HOFKELLER, Würzburg The cellars beneath the Baroque *Residenz* palace are among the most splendid in the world. Since the 18th century, they have housed the wines of the *Staatlicher Hofkeller,* acquired by the Bavarian state after church properties were turned over to secular owners in the early 19th century. The 420 acres, scattered throughout Franken in top-rated sites, are planted primarily with riesling, müller-thurgau, and silvaner vines. Cellar visits are by appointment only, but the wines can be sampled at the shop, which is located in the building to the left of the palace (closed Sundays). The building on the right of the *Residenz* is the *Hofkeller-Weinstuben,* which serves good food and the estate's wines (closed Mondays and Sunday dinner). Information: *Staatlicher Hofkeller,* 3 Residenzpl., Würzburg 97070 (phone 931-305-0923; fax: 931-305-0966).

WEINGUT BÜRGERSPITAL ZUM HEILIGEN GEIST, Würzburg Founded in 1319 as a charitable foundation, the *Bürgerspital* continues to fund a home for the elderly with the proceeds from wine sales. Most of its 350 acres of vineyards are in or near Würzburg itself, and it owns the largest portion of the Stein vineyard, the city's most famous and best site. The *Bürgerspital* was bottling its *Steinweine* in *Bocksbeutel* as early as 1726. Its dry, full-bodied riesling and silvaner wines are prized worldwide. Tastings and cellar visits are offered weekdays and Saturday mornings. A wine store is also on the premises; it's closed Saturday afternoons and Sundays. In addition, the wines are served at the Bürgerspital's *Weinstube* (wine pub); the pub is closed Tuesdays and August. Information: *Weingut Bürgerspital zum Heiligen Geist,* 19 Theaterstr., Würzburg 97070 (phone 931-350-3441; fax: 931-350-3444).

RHEINHESSEN

For information on Rheinhessen, contact *Rheinhessenwein,* 33-35 An der Brunnenstube, Mainz 55120 (phone: 6131-681058; fax: 6131-682701).

WEINGUT KÜHLING-GILLOT, Bodenheim This winery could be described as a young wine estate with a long tradition. *Kühling-Gillot* dates from 1970, when Gabi

Kühling married Roland Gillot, thus merging their two 18th-century family estates. Known primarily for dry, flavorful rieslings, the estate also offers "blanc de noir" sparkling wine and highly acclaimed dessert wines. Visitors should ring the house doorbell, but if the gate is open, just go around to the park in back of the lovely *Jugendstil* villa. Cellar visits and tastings are offered weekdays and Saturday mornings. From mid-June to mid-September, you can enjoy the wines with light fare in the park on Friday, Saturday, and Sunday evenings. Information: *Weingut Kühling-Gillot,* 25 Oelmühlstr., Bodenheim 55294 (phone: 6135-2333; fax: 6135-6463).

WEINGUT J. & H. A. STRUB, Nierstein It's a few steps from Nierstein's market square to the *Strub* estate, situated here since 1864. Proprietor Walter Strub and his family live in the half-timbered house across the small courtyard from the cellars. The estate, consisting of 45 prime acres, produces distinctively fruity, crisp wines; the finest whites are the rieslings and silvaners. Because the wines are usually bottled early in spring, they often retain a touch of natural spritz. The courtyard is turned into an outdoor tasting room during Nierstein's colorful wine festival in late July. Visit the cellars and sample the wines weekdays or by appointment on weekends. Information: *Weingut J. & H. A. Strub,* 42 Rheinstr., Nierstein 55283 (phone: 6133-5649; fax: 6133-5501).

WEINGUT WITTMANN, Westhofen Günter and Elisabeth Wittmann's 18th-century estate in Westhofen, just off of Autobahn 61 between Alzey and Worms, has long been a well-kept secret. Its spacious gardens and vaulted cellars are attractive and inviting; the estate devotes a third of its 40 acres to riesling grapes, but silvaner and several pinot varieties are grown here too. Wittmann's dessert wines also are excellent, with exotic fruit aromas and flavors; sparkling wine and brandies are available as well. Cellar visits and tastings are offered weekdays and Saturdays, or by appointment on weekends. (The Wittmanns suggest calling ahead anyway to make sure someone is home.) Information: *Weingut Wittmann,* 19 Mainzer Str., Westhofen 67593 (phone: 6244-7042; fax: 6244-5578).

Taking the Waters: Spas

The spa tradition in Germany is lengthy and well established. For almost 2,000 years (dating to Roman times), travelers have flocked to spa towns like Baden-Baden and Wiesbaden, whose mineral-rich waters were thought to have miraculous healing powers. Many of the people who visited these spots were of royal birth, rich and famous, or both: frequent spa-goers included such luminaries as Charlemagne, Kaiser Wilhelm I, Brahms, Wagner, Nietzsche, Empress Maria Theresa of Austria, and Czar Nicholas I of Russia. These places gradually became flourishing cities with the spa as their raison d'être; in short order, canny developers added a wide range of upscale hotels, restaurants, golf courses, tennis courts, racetracks, gambling casinos, and elegant shops. "The cure" remains popular today—and while the experience does not come cheap, you don't have to be a king or a film star to visit a spa city. At Germany's more than 350 resorts and health farms, you'll find baths of every tint and temperature, power showers, steamrooms and saunas, whirlpool baths and sprays, masseuses, mud tubs, paraffin packs, salt and honey rubs, infrared and ultraviolet treatments, facilities for vapor inhalations, and aerobic exercise programs. You can even drink the mineral water—but bear in mind that while the effect may be beneficial, the taste is often less than appealing (read: awful). Most spa centers in Germany have been recognized by the government with "Staatsbad" (state bath) status. You can either make arrangements with a spa or arrange for a spa package with a hotel. Expect the atmosphere to be more formal than at most US spas—here, taking the waters is serious business. And you will probably be required to have a checkup by a local doctor before being submerged, steamed, and pummeled. Whether or not you believe in the healing power of a spa vacation, you will undoubtedly emerge feeling rejuvenated and pampered. Information about the temple of indulgence that is Baden-Baden, including area attractions, hotels, and restaurants, is listed in *Baden-Baden,* THE CITIES; listed alphabetically below are several other choice spa destinations throughout Germany.

BAD KISSINGEN The Franconian River flows through this town, located in northern Bavaria near Frankfurt and Würzburg. In addition to taking the waters here, visitors can enjoy the town's romantic medieval architecture, casino, and parks and gardens. The primary spa building is the *Kurhaus;* facilities include six different springs for bathing and drinking, mud baths, seawater Jacuzzis, and saunas. Our favorite hotel here is the *Steigenberger Kurhaushotel* (3 Am Kurgarten; phone: 971-80410; 800-223-5652; fax: 971-804-1597), a posh, 100-room property with its own spa facilities and direct access to the *Kurhaus.* Its restaurant serves French haute cuisine (which can be modified to meet individual dietary needs). Information: *Staatliche Kurverwaltung,* 1 Am Kurgarten, Bad Kissingen 97688 (phone: 971-80480; fax: 971-804840).

BAD ORB Located 28 miles northeast of Frankfurt near the Taunus region, and famous for its plentiful hot mineral springs and its treatments for circulatory disorders, this small health resort offers therapy bath pools, steam inhalation, mineral water for drinking, and electrotherapy treatment. The main public spa is the ultramodern *Leopold-Koch-Bad;* its large mineral water pool maintains temperatures in the 90s F to allow swimming year-round. Information: *Kurverwaltung,* 1 Kurparkstr., Bad Orb 63619 (phone: 6052-830; fax: 6052-4780).

BAD REICHENHALL The springs here are purportedly the most saline in Europe; the water is used in the treatment of respiratory ailments. The town is quite attractive, with tulips in the *Kurgarten* and the Bayerischen Alpen (Bavarian

Alps) forming a dramatic backdrop; its air and water quality are protected by laws that prohibit heavy industry in the region. Facilities include several heated saltwater pools (three indoor, one outdoor), tennis in summer, and ice skating and skiing in winter. Bad Reichenhall has a particularly good reputation for the treatment of respiratory problems, rheumatism, and skin ailments—not to mention the simple stresses of everyday life. Information: *Kurverwaltung,* 15 Wittelsbacherstr., Bad Reichenhall 83435 (phone: 8651-6060).

BAD WÖRISHOFEN The famous German treatment called *Kneippkur,* which is now administered at spa centers across the country, was developed here in the 19th century by Sebastian Kneipp, a local clergyman. Extensive use of hydrotherapy, attention to proper diet, and mental and emotional relaxation exercises are the cornerstones of the plan. The town, in a lovely pastoral setting ringed by the Alps, has more than 200 spa establishments offering massage, exercise programs, herbal therapy, and nutrition counseling, as well as swimming, golf, and tennis. Information: *Kurverwaltung,* Postfach 1443, Bad Wörishofen 86817 (phone: 8247-350255 or 8247-350256).

WIESBADEN This world-famous spa town, sheltered between the Rhine and the Taunusberg (Taunus Mountains) but only a 20-minute drive from metropolitan Frankfurt, dates back to Roman times. Public spa facilites include one of the finest open-air thermal pools in the country and thermal baths that include indoor and outdoor pools, massage rooms, solariums, a sauna, and a gym. Hot mineral water gushes from 26 springs, so you can "take the cure" even when it's snowing. Excellent hotels abound; one of our favorites is the stately *Nassauer Hof* (3 Kaiser-Friedrich-Pl.; phone: 611-1330; fax: 611-133632), which has 210 guestrooms and several restaurants (including *Die Ente vom Lehel,* whose continental fare rates a Michelin star), gardens, and a pool fed by the hotel's own mineral spring, as well as a full-service beauty salon and spa. Information: *Kurbetriebe der Laundeshauptstadt Verkehrsbüro,* 15 Rheinstr., Wiesbaden 65183 (phone: 611-172-9780; fax: 611-172-9799).

Cruising Germany's Waterways

Germany's history has always been closely linked to its waterways—a network of rivers and canals that connects almost every corner of the country. The most important and famous German river is the Rhine; less well known is the fact that a cool trickle of water arising in the Schwarzwald (Black Forest) is the beginning of the legendary Danube's long run to the Black Sea. (The Danube is the second-longest of all European rivers—the Volga is first.) And a popular shortcut for ships traveling between the Baltic and North Seas is a canal that begins at Kiel, a port in northern Germany.

In the Middle Ages, the cities that gained prominence were usually ports. For instance, Hamburg, Bremen, and Lübeck became members of the powerful Hanseatic League due to their favorable position along the North Sea and Baltic routes. Along with the other members of the league, these cities dominated European trade for centuries. Later, several inland river ports took their place as major trading centers: Düsseldorf, on the Rhine; Frankfurt, on the Main; Mannheim, at the confluence of the Rhine and the Neckar; and Passau, on the Danube. Berlin, originally a port on the Spree River, is still a major shipping depot, with freighters transporting goods to and from both the Baltic and North Seas. Other rivers, like the Elbe, Mosel, Saar, and Weser, move commercial boats across the heart of the Continent today.

But the traffic is not all commercial. Excursion ships and cruise liners carry vacationers and day-trippers along these rivers, as well as across Germany's many lakes. In Germany you can take a cruise of almost any length, from a few hours to weeks at a time. Resorts on most lakes also offer opportunities for renting rowboats and sailboats by the hour, day, or week. Unless otherwise specified, the excursions described below are offered from April through October. Here are our favorite water-based getaways.

GERMANY'S GREAT RIVERS

DANUBE *Klinger Personenschiffahrt* (8 Werftstr., Regensburg 93059; phone: 941-52104) offers several excursions on the Danube leaving from Regensburg, including a trip to *Walhalla,* the Greek-style shrine to heroes of Nordic mythology and German history; the round trip takes three hours with a one-hour stop at the monument. (For more information about *Walhalla,* see *Memorable Monuments and Museums* in this section.) Those interested in taking a more leisurely cruise should take the nine-hour sail (available on Sundays only) that wends its way from Regensburg between forested hills to the charming town of Passau, situated on a spit of land at the confluence of the Danube and Inn Rivers.

ELBE Since the reunification of Germany in 1990, cruising enthusiasts have discovered the pleasures of traveling on the Elbe, which flows northward through the former East Germany to Hamburg. The river passes through gently rolling wooded terrain that provides pleasant scenery, but the real attraction of an Elbe cruise is the opportunity to visit several historic cities that were formerly inaccessible to Westerners. Among these are Magdeburg, the "Cathedral City of the Elbe"; Dessau, home of the *Bauhaus* (also see *Memorable Monuments and Museums* in this section); the famed porcelain city of Meissen; and Dresden, the capital of Saxony. *KD River Cruises of Europe,* with two offices in the US (2500 Westchester Ave., Purchase, NY 10577; phone: 914-696-3600 or 800-346-6525; and 323 Geary Street, Suite 619, San Francisco, CA 94102; phone: 415-392-8817 or 800-858-8587), offers many different itineraries on this river, including several that feature stops in Prague as well as Meissen and Dresden. We recommend you take advantage of the comfortable accommodations on *KD*'s boats, since eastern Germany still lacks a sufficient number of good hotels to meet the increase in tourism.

MAIN Sometimes referred to as "The Equator of Germany," the Main is the symbolic borderline between the northern and southern parts of the country. From the river, you can see the magnificent skyline of Frankfurt; east of Frankfurt the scenery becomes bucolic, with grassy hills dotted with small, pretty villages, including Mittenberg, an old market town with half-timbered houses. Cruises from Frankfurt along the Main are organized by *Primus Line* (36 Mainkai, Frankfurt 60311; phone: 69-281884; fax: 69-284798); and excursions from Würzburg that travel along the loveliest stretch of the Main and pass through the Main-Donau Kanal (Main-Danube Canal) are given by *Fränkische Personenschiffahrt* (1a Juliuspromenade, Würzburg 97070; phone: 931-51722; fax: 931-13313).

NECKAR From the famed university city of Heidelberg, this river meanders through a landscape of orchards and vineyards. As the Neckar flows downstream toward Mannheim and meets with the Rhine, the activity becomes more commercial, with numerous freighters and barges. Excursions and cruises of varying lengths from Heidelberg along the Neckar are organized by *Rhein-Neckar Fahrgastschiffahrt* (17 Untere Neckarstr., Heidelberg 69117; phone: 6221-20181; fax: 6221-20211).

RHINE and MOSEL One of Europe's most popular cruising waterways has long been the passage along the Rhine between Amsterdam and Basel, Switzerland. German cities along this river are Cologne, Frankfurt (where the Rhine meets the Main), and Trier; the stretch between Frankfurt and Trier takes in some of the Rhine's most romantic scenery. The Mosel, which meets the Rhine at Koblenz, passes through lovely wine country, with rolling green hills and vineyards (also see *Visitable Vineyards* in this section). *KD German Rhine Line* (15 Frankenwerft, Cologne 50667; phone: 221-20880; fax: 221-208-8229) offers several trips along the Rhine and Mosel, including a route along the Middle Rhine that passes the dramatic cliffs where the legendary Lorelei lured sailors to their deaths with her siren song. *KD* cruises also can be booked through *KD River Cruises of Europe* (see the *Elbe* entry) or *Bernkasteler Mosel Personenschiffahrt* (52 Goldbuch Str., Bernkastel-Kues 54470; phone: 8222-4023). All-day cruises on the Mosel between Trier and Bernkastel are run by *Fahrgastschiffahrt Martin Kolb* (13 Schanzstr., Bernkastel-Kues 54470; phone: 2673-1515; fax: 2673-1510).

LAND OF LAKES

The Alp-ringed area of Bavaria south of Munich is generously dotted with lakes that make popular weekend and vacation destinations, particularly in warm weather. People come from all over Germany to sail on the Bodensee, Chiemsee, Ammersee, Starnberger See, Königsee, Kochelsee, Tegernsee, and Forggensee.

BODENSEE Germany's largest lake, the Bodensee (known in English as Lake Constance) is 40 miles long and 8 miles across at its widest point—almost an inland sea. Its eastern tip is in Bavaria, while the rest is in Baden-Württemberg; its southern shore borders Austria and Switzerland. *Bodensee Schiffsbetriebe* (6 Hafenstr., Konstanz 78462; phone: 7531-281398; fax: 7531-281373) runs 18 excursion boats that offer regular service between the island of Lindau and the city of Konstanz; they stop in Friedrichshafen, Meersburg, and other German lakeside ports, as well as in Bregenz, Austria, and Rorschach, Switzerland. The same company also offers theme cruises and Saturday night dinner cruises with dancing. On Lindau, boats can be rented at the Seebrücke (Lake Bridge) and at the *Inselhalle* (Island Hall) next to the fishing boat harbor from *Hodrius Bootvermietung* (phone: 8382-4285). In Konstanz, boat rentals can be arranged by *Huber Sport und Boote* (32 Gottlieber Str.; phone: 7531-22879). For more information about Lake Constance, including accommodations and sights in the area, see *The German Alpine Road and Lake Constance* route in DIRECTIONS.

CHIEMSEE One of the largest Alpine lakes in Germany, the Chiemsee presents a vast expanse of still, clear blue water; tiny, charming villages dot the shores, and the magnificent Alps are in the background. Lake excursions are run by *Chiemsee Schiffahrt Ludwig Fessler* (108 Seestr., Prien 83209; phone: 8051-6090; fax: 8051-62943).

FORGGENSEE This artificial lake offers plenty of beautiful Alpine views. The sight of the Lech River cascading from the mountains to the south and Füssen's picturesque skyline, dominated by a charming old castle, are particularly special. Forggensee excursions are operated June through September by *Staatliche Forggensee Schiffahrt* (3 Lechhalde, Füssen 87629; phone: 8362-6221).

KÖNIGSEE The enormous stone crest of Mt. Watzmann is the eye-catching scenic feature of this blue-green ribbon of water, the most beautiful of all the Alpine lakes. Also look for the rounded red domes of the little *Bartholomökirche* (Church of St. Bartholomew), visible from the lake. You can cruise these waters on quiet electric boats, which can be rented from *Staatliche Schiffahrt Königsee* (55 Seestr., Schönau am Königsee 83471; phone: 8652-4026; fax: 8652-64721).

TEGERNSEE Since Tegernsee's *Benediktineres Kloster* (Benedictine Cloister) became a summer residence for nobility in 1817, summer visitors have flocked to the shores of this beautiful lake. Though the crowds can sometimes be formidable, the panoramic view of the Alps, the sparkle of sunlight on the water, and the colorful resort life on the shore (with villas, hotels, and plenty of people watching) are worth the sail. *Tegernsee Staatliche Schiffahrt* (70 Seestr., Tegernsee 83684; phone: 8022-4760) coordinates trips on the Tegernsee; you also can rent rowboats and sailboats on your own from *Bootverleih* (44 Seestr., Rottach-Egern 83700; phone: 8022-24093).

Great Ski Slopes

Skiing is one of the most memorable activities any downhiller can enjoy during a German vacation. In the first place, no other mountains in the world are quite like the Alps. America has peaks as high, but the valleys in Germany (as in the rest of Europe) are generally lower, so that the ski runs tend to be longer and more diverse. It's a good idea to avoid skiing at *Christmastime* if you possibly can. Not only are the lift lines miserably long and the days very short, but the weather conditions are also unreliable enough that you might well end up learning how to make parallel turns on grass and mud. If you have no choice about when to go, at least try to get your skiing in before December 26, while German families are still sitting around their *Christmas* trees, or in late January, which usually offers the best combination of good snow, slightly longer sunny days, off-peak prices, and relatively uncrowded slopes. Another good tip for avoiding hordes of fellow skiers: Ski during lunchtime, when most Germans will be taking their midday meal.

But no matter when you go, always ask about avalanche warnings and don't stray from the beaten trail. Each winter dozens of free-range skiers become avalanche casualties, but there are seldom any victims on marked ski runs. Good hotels are easy to find, and even the most modest little *Gasthaus* usually offers cozy pine-paneled rooms, fluffy eiderdowns, and handsome Tyrolean furniture. Listed below are our two favorite German downhill ski areas.

GARMISCH-PARTENKIRCHEN Americans first got to know this Alpine ski resort back in the days when it was chiefly the US military that occupied the powdery slopes and a few dollars bought all the snow you could ski. The town itself is large, modern, and busy, and offers a whole range of winter sports activities, including curling and bobsledding. High above is the 9,840-foot Zugspitze, Germany's tallest mountain, whose peak, miraculously, is accessible by cog railway and cable car. There is a fine assortment of lifts and trails for every grade of skier, and the facilities are scrupulously maintained by a large local staff. A good hotel in the area is the *Dorint* (59 Mittenwalder Str.; phone: 8821-7060; fax: 8821-706618), a 425-room property with a good restaurant, a beer garden, an indoor pool, and a sauna. Information: *Verkehrsamt,* Richard-Strauss-Pl., Garmisch-Partenkirchen 82467 (phone: 8821-1806; fax: 8821-18055).

REIT IM WINKL A picturesque Bavarian town almost astride the Austrian border in the middle of a wide-open valley, and with a base elevation of 2,296 feet, this is not the kind of place you're likely to see represented on bumper stickers and ski parka patches. Yet, with more than a dozen tows and chair lifts fanned out on a cluster of broad plateaus and mild peaks under 6,560 feet, it's ideal for beginners and intermediates; skiing in the basin between

Winklmoos-Alm and Kammerköhr-Steinplatte is immensely satisfying and only of medium difficulty. There is a 2½-mile toboggan trail, with a smaller version for children, and a fleet of horse-drawn sleighs for drives in the country, *Doctor Zhivago*–style (that is, with fur blankets wrapped around your knees). Evenings, sausage and sauerkraut are piled into small mountains on your dinner plate at any of the nearby restaurants. Hotels in the area include the 72-room *Unterwirt* (2 Kirchpl.; phone: 8640-8010; fax: 8640-801150), with a restaurant, indoor pool, and sauna; *Altenburger Hof* (3 Frühlingstr.; phone: 8640-8994; fax: 8640-307), with 13 rooms, an indoor pool, and a sauna (but no restaurant); and *Edelweiss* (1 Am Gruenbuehel; phone: 8640-1651), a traditional Bavarian-style property with 20 rooms and a restaurant. Information: *Verkehrsamt, Rathaus,* Reit im Winkl 83242 (phone: 8640-80020).

Memorable Monuments and Museums

Inspired by their classical education and by their national respect for history, it was Germans who pioneered the discipline of archaeology and the scholarly study of art and culture. German art historians, archaeologists, curators, and collectors were among those who discovered the ancient civilizations of the Mediterranean. They unearthed Pompeii, dismantled the Greek city of Pergamon, and shipped whole sections of their finds back to Berlin. If they couldn't take the originals with them, they replicated them in gleaming modern versions, like *Walhalla* and the *Brandenburger Tor* (Brandenburg Gate). Germany's museums also are blessed with some of the world's greatest works of art, thanks to the princes, barons, dukes, and other royal philanthropists who generously bequeathed their collections to the public. In addition, Germany has a number of historical monuments that serve as vivid reminders of the country's turbulent history. For descriptions of the most significant historic monuments and most outstanding museums in Germany's major cities, consult the individual chapters in THE CITIES; listed below are some additional sites that are a bit out of the way but well worth the trek. Entries are listed alphabetically by location.

DACHAU CONCENTRATION CAMP, Dachau, Bavaria A visit to Dachau will make you ponder the mystery of how the savagery of the Holocaust could have taken place in the supposedly civilized 20th century. The contrast between this town of quaintly terraced buildings, where farmers once tilled the earth and landscape artists painted, and the Nazis' evil activities here is truly mind-boggling. It is difficult to imagine the pall of human ashes from the infamous ovens soiling the misty green Bavarian hills in the distance. Today, Dachau is a medium-size city that has gone on with its life while still acknowledging the grim reality of its past. The *KZ* (*Konzentrationslager*—concentration camp) itself has been (mercifully) sanitized, but a stark reminder of the agonies suffered here remains: In front of the concrete office buildings where the paperwork that fueled the "Final Solution" was completed, there is a memorial sculpture depicting spindly, gnarled bodies intertwined like knots in a barbed-wire fence. The ovens also are on display, as are two reconstructed shacks where the prisoners slept; a 22-minute documentary (in English) about the history of the camp is shown daily at 11:30 AM and 3:30 PM. This is not a place for the fainthearted, but it tells a story that the world must always remember. Closed Mondays, *Christmas Eve,* and the afternoons of *New Year's Eve* and *Shrove Tuesday.* No admission charge. Information: *KZ Gedenkstätte,* 75 Alterulmer Str., Dachau 85221 (phone: 8131-1741).

BAUHAUS, Dessau, Saxony-Anhalt In the 1920s, dazzled by visions of a brave new world in which everyone, rich or poor, would live simple, spartan lives, architect Walter Gropius founded this visionary institute as a school and workshop for a group of his disciples. The *Bauhaus,* a large complex of buildings, was meant to be the crucible of a thorough fusion of industry, arts, and crafts. The main focus of the Bauhaus movement, whose members went on to revolutionize the skylines of Chicago and New York City, was to create architecture that reflected Gropius's creed of bare-bones functionalism: The front and back of this style of building are identical, and the transparent, pure glass walls are uncluttered by friezes, moldings, pilasters, or any other trappings. Partially destroyed by bombing during World War II, the complex has been completely restored to its original appearance. Displayed inside are photos, architectural drawings, and other exhibits chronicling the history of the Bauhaus movement. Closed Mondays. Admission charge. Information: *Bauhaus Dessau,* 38 Gropiusallee, Dessau 06846 (phone: 340-613159).

WALHALLA, Donaustauf (near Regensburg), Bavaria This is the monument of monuments: a Greek temple to German genius, named for the resting place of the slain heroes of Norse mythology (which also was featured prominently in Richard Wagner's *Ring* cycle). With its Olympian view of the Donautal (Danube River Valley), its rows of Doric columns, and its busts of prominent Germans, including Luther and Goethe, *Walhalla* expresses Germany's veneration for the classical world, for nature, and for itself. The long cascade of marble stairs in the front presents a most challenging climb; if you want to avoid this, there is another more easily accessible entrance in the back of the monument. Open daily. Admission charge. Information: *Donaustauf Verwaltungsgemeinschaft,* 5 Woerther-Str., Donaustauf 93093 (phone: 9403-95020).

MUSEUM GUTENBERG, Mainz, Rhineland-Palatinate This place (named after the founding father of the printed page) is the lodge of an ancient brotherhood of readers who love books not just for what they say, but for their physical presence—their comforting weight and inky smell, the grain of their lustrous leather bindings, and the texture of their finely woven pages. Book publishing for the masses began in Mainz in 1440, when Johannes Gutenberg invented moveable type and began churning out books on his printing press. Here, faithfully reproduced as it looked in the 15th century, is the inventor's workshop; one of the prize exhibits is a rare first edition of the famed Gutenberg Bible. Closed Mondays. Admission charge. Information: *Weltmuseum der Druckkunst,* 5 Liebfrauenpl., Mainz 55116 (phone: 6131-122644 or 6131-122640).

THE ROMAN RUINS OF TRIER, Rhineland-Palatinate During the Roman Empire, Trier was an outpost of sophistication in a desolate northern Europe still mired in the Iron Age. The Romans poured a great deal of energy and resources into making Trier a beautiful city, constructing many lovely buildings using the dark sandstone that was plentiful in the area. One impressive remnant of that era still stands today: the *Porta Nigra,* a triple row of exquisitely crafted stone arches that have guarded the entrance to downtown for over 16 centuries. Other surviving Roman edifices are the spare and cavernous *Basilica* (which now doubles as a Protestant church), the stately ruins of the *Imperial Baths,* and the charming moss-covered *Amphitheater.* The *Porta Nigra,* the *Imperial Baths,* and the *Amphitheater* are all closed Mondays November through March, as well as throughout December. Admission charge. Information: *Tourist-Information Trier,* Porta-Nigra-Platz, Trier 54292 (phone: 651-48071).

VIKING COUNTRY, Schleswig-Holstein The entire area of what is now the state of Schleswig-Holstein was prime Viking territory; the Nordic warriors found it a convenient base for sea voyages between here and Scandinavia. Here, at the northernmost tip of Germany, the Vikings built a port called Haithabu (also known as Haddeby), well sheltered by a fjord. Today, the town of Schleswig has two renowned museums about Viking life and lore. A collection of artifacts associated with these Nordic seamen, including their hand-crafted broadswords, armor, and ships, is displayed in the *Wikingermuseum* (Viking Museum) in Haitabu, just southeast of town. Exhibits at the *Archäologisches Landesmuseum* (State Archaeological Museum), in *Schloss Gottorf* (Gottorf Castle), include a ship excavated from the Nydam marshes in the 19th century and several 5th-century corpses exhumed from the bogs. Both museums are closed Mondays and December; admission charge. Information: *Wikingermuseum,* 76 An der Bundesstr., Schleswig 24837 (phone: 4621-81330); *Archäologisches Landesmuseum, Schloss Gottorf,* Schleswig 24837 (phone: 4621-813222).

Germany's Best Festivals

The concert halls, theaters, and opera houses in Berlin, Dresden, Frankfurt, Hamburg, Leipzig, and Munich are justifiably famous for their splendid productions of classical music and epic dramas, and these cities also host a variety of excellent arts festivals (for details, consult the individual chapters in THE CITIES). However, you don't have to go to a big city to take in a Monteverdi opera or to listen to the best international jazz artists; plenty of first-rate fetes are held in small towns all over the country. The festivals held throughout Germany each year number in the hundreds. Their settings range from town squares and courtyards to historic churches, castles, and stately gardens. The offerings are equally varied—opera, classical music, jazz, country-and-western music, film, and theater, to name just a few. All told, these celebrations allow visitors to sample Germany's cultural riches on a small, intimate scale. Entries are listed alphabetically by location.

MUSIC FESTIVALS, Bad Hersfeld, Hessen This riverside spa town between Kassel and Fulda is notable for several annual events, all held in the ruins of Bad Hersfeld's 12th-century Romanesque abbey. An organ festival and *Bach Tagen* (Bach Days) both take place over *Easter* weekend; and the *Bad Hersfeld Festkonzerten* (Bad Hersfeld Festival Concerts), featuring operas, symphonies, and concertos, are held June through August. Information: *Arbeitskreis für Musik,* 9 Nachtigallenstr., Bad Hersfeld 36251 (phone: 6621-15005).

RICHARD WAGNER FESTIVAL, Bayreuth, Bavaria The best-known, fanciest (and most costly) of European music festivals, this event dates from 1876. Founded by Wagner himself as a showcase for his works, the inaugural production was *Das Rheingold.* In the spirit of his ideal of *Gesamtkunstwerk*—the complete, multimedia work of art—Wagner not only created the scores and lyrics for his "music dramas" but also shaped the productions and even the theater itself. The festival, held late July through August in the Franconian town where the composer built his *Villa Wahnfried,* ordinarily features five Wagnerian operatic classics in the *Fest Theater* (Festival Theater) on the northern edge of Bayreuth. The musicians are secreted in a camouflaged pit, so that the leitmotifs seem to seep from the theater's walls. Wagner's grandson Wolfgang runs the festival today. Information: *Richard Wagner Festival,* Postfach 100262, Bayreuth 95402 (phone: 921-20221).

BODENSEE FESTIVAL, along the Bodensee, Baden-Württemberg Germany's largest lake, whose south shore is Austrian and Swiss territory, is the beautiful setting for an annual series of concerts, ballet, theater, and recitals held from May through early June. An international Who's Who of guest orchestras and solo musicians come here to share the stage with Baden-Baden's *Südwestdeutsche Philharmonie* (Southwest German Philharmonic); past performers have included the *Wiener Staatsoper* (Vienna State Opera), the *Kiev State Opera Orchestra,* and pianist Emanuel Ax. The festival takes place in towns and small cities along the German shore, mainly Friedrichshafen, Konstanz, Lindau, Meersburg, and Uberlingen, plus the "garden island" of Mainau and the nearby Swiss town of St. Gallen. Information: *Bodensee*

Festival, 21 Olgastr., Friedrichshafen 88045 (phone: 7541-92320) or 3 Spanierstr., 78467 Konstanz (phone: 7531-52016).

MUSIKTAGE, Donaueschingen, Baden-Württemberg Held the third weekend in October, this festival of new music is a forum for exploring new areas of musical composition and performance. The young composers featured here are from all over the world, including Germany, Latvia, and South Korea, and they are as likely to write a sonata for electric guitar and personal computer as for a classical or chamber music ensemble. The *Symphonie Südwestfunk* (Southwest Radio Symphony Orchestra) performs here as well. Information: *Städtisches Kultur- und Verkehrsamt,* Donaueschingen 78166 (phone: 771-857221).

HÄNDEL FESTIVAL, Halle, Saxony-Anhalt Since 1951, this industrial city, the birthplace of *Messiah* composer Georg Friedrich Händel, has celebrated his works with an annual festival. Over five days in early June, the *Halle Opera* presents one of Händel's 46 operatic compositions, the *Halle Philharmonie Orchester und Chor* (Halle State Philharmonic and Chorus) perform one of his major oratorios, and various guest ensembles play Händel's chamber music. Venues for the performances include the Baroque mansion on Grosse Nikolaistrasse, where the composer was born in 1685. Information: *Händel Festival,* 51 Grosse Ulrichstr., Halle 06108 (phone: 345-23277).

PASSAU EUROPÄISCHE FESTWOCHEN (PASSAU EUROPEAN FESTIVAL WEEKS), Passau, Bavaria On a point of land where the Danube and Inn Rivers meet, Passau has presented this multifaceted celebration, featuring opera, symphony and chamber music, ballet, organ recitals, and drama, since 1952. Performances are held from June through July. Information: *Passau Europäische Festwochen,* 22 Dr.-Hans-Kapfinger-Str., Passau 94032 (phone: 851-33038).

MAX-OPHULS FILM FESTIVAL, Saarbrücken, Saarland This festival proudly eschews the high-stakes, high-blood-pressure world of box-office blockbusters and bombs in favor of the cinematic fringe. The event, with far less hoopla and haggling than the Venice and Cannes festivals, is the only major showplace for the work of young German-language filmmakers. During festival week in late January, a loft-like space known as *Die Garage* (named for the auto showroom it once was) is converted into *Lola's Bistro,* a combination coffeehouse and screening room. Movies are screened—and then intensely analyzed for meaning and symbolism in informal conversations afterward. Information: *Verkehrsverein Saarbrücken,* Am Rathaus, Saarbrücken 66127 (phone: 681-36901 or 681-35197; fax: 681-390353).

SCHLESWIG-HOLSTEIN MUSIK FESTIVAL, Schleswig-Holstein This marvelous attraction begun in 1988 is held from late June through mid-August at various locations throughout Germany's northernmost state. Concerts are staged not only in the bigger cities of Kiel, Flensburg, and Lübeck, but also in towns, villages, and even country barns, between the North Sea and the Baltic. (The festival goes a bit farther afield, too, to Hamburg and locales in Lower Saxony.) The *Festorchester* (Festival Orchestra), featuring 120 musicians from all over the world, was organized by Leonard Bernstein; today it is led by such top-name guest conductors as Yehudi Menuhin and Sir Georg Solti. Major international orchestras also participate, as do chamber ensembles and instrumental and vocal soloists; past performers have included the *Leipzig Gewandhaus,* the *London Philharmonic,* and the *Orchestre de Paris.* Information: *Kartenzentrale des Schleswig-Holstein Musik Festival,* Postfach 3840, Kiel 24037 (phone: 431-567080).

MUSIC FESTIVALS, Schwetzingen, Baden-Württemberg This small town near Heidelberg is renowned for its rococo castle, built in the early 18th century, and its formal *Schlossgarten.* From the end of April through May, the castle's *Rokokotheater* (Rococo Theater) and several other venues in town host the *Schwetzingen Festspiele* (Schwetzingen Festival), with operas and concerts of classical music. Also held in the castle's theater for three weekends in September is the *Mozartfest,* a series of performances that mainly feature the great composer's works. Information: *Verkehrsverein Schwetzingen,* Postfach 1924, Schwetzingen 68709 (phone: 6202-4933).

THÜRINGER BACH WOCHE (THÜRINGEN BACH WEEKS), Thuringia This event, held from March through early April, takes its inspiration from the fact that Johann Sebastian Bach was born in the town of Eisenach in west Thuringia. Music composed by members of the Bach family—both J. S. himself and some of his sons—is presented in Eisenach and several other towns in the region, including Weimar, Mühlhausen, Arnstadt, Gotha, and Erfurt. Information: *Thüringer Bach Woche,* Bachhaus, 21 Frauenplan, Eisenach 99817 (phonc: 3691-203714).

INTERNATIONALES MAIFEST (INTERNATIONAL MAY FESTIVAL), Wiesbaden, Hessen The venerable little spa city, a short distance west of Frankfurt, hosts this well-known gala, usually spanning a three-week period from late April through May. Held in Wiesbaden's neoclassical *Hessisches Staatstheater* (Hessen State Theater), the program is wide-ranging, encompassing grand opera, theater, and avant-garde musical performances that feature top-level international companies. Information: *Internationales Maifest, Staatstheater Wiesbaden,* Wiesbaden 65185 (phone: 611-333014).

RHEINGAU MUSIK FESTIVAL, Wiesbaden, Hessen This festival, held July through August, is yet another reason to visit the vineyard country in Hessen, along the east bank of the Rhine. The emphasis is on German classics, from Bach, Händel, and Telemann to Beethoven, Brahms, and Richard Strauss. Wiesbaden is the site of numerous festival concerts, but events are also featured in smaller, folksier Rheingau towns, plus the medieval *Kloster Eberbach* monastery, and the 18th-century *Schloss Johannisberg.* Information: *Rheingau Musik Festival,* 5b Zehntenhofstr., Wiesbaden 65201 (phone: 611-260465).

MUSIC FESTIVALS, Würzburg, Bavaria The most opulent landmark in this Franconian wine city on the river Main is its 18th-century Baroque *Residenz* palace. A *Barokfest* takes place here for three days in late May, followed by the hugely popular *Mozartfest,* a three-week event in June that has been held since 1932. In November, the town sponsors the *Würzburg Jazz Fest,* held in the nearby suburb of Grombühl. Information: *Kulturamt der Stadt Würzburg,* Haus zum Falken am Markt, Würzburg 97070 (phone: 931-37336).

Churches, Castles, and Palaces

Over the last millennium or so, the part of Europe now called Germany has been unified, splintered, and cobbled back together innumerable times. War and religion were often intertwined: With every shift in boundary between the turf of a fervent prince and that of a hawkish bishop, there would be a new subdivision of authority. Local rulers and aristocrats, eager to create concrete reminders of their lofty position in life, would build themselves grand cathedrals and palaces. Throughout this book, we have described notable churches and palaces in Germany's major metropolitan centers in the individual chapters in THE CITIES; listed below are some exceptional edifices to be found in smaller towns off the beaten track. Entries are listed alphabetically by location.

KAISERDOM (EMPEROR'S CATHEDRAL), Aachen, Rhineland-Westphalia Today a provincial spa town, Aachen was once the center of the world. Charlemagne made the city his headquarters in the 8th century, during his campaign to Christianize and unify northern Europe into an empire. This Byzantine-style chapel is one of the few remnants of that period in Aachen's history. The oldest part of the structure, now surrounded by Gothic additions, is the central octagonal basilica, which Charlemagne had designed to resemble the Church of San Vitale in Ravenna, Italy. Throughout the chapel's interior are lofty, multicolored marble columns, which were made in Italy and then brought here. On the upper floor of the basilica is the massive but plain stone *Throne of Charlemagne,* where the great leader sat during church services and where subsequent Holy Roman Emperors were crowned. Don't miss the gem-stocked treasury, with its gorgeously wrought gold-and-silver bust of Charlemagne, or Charlemagne's marble sarcophagus. Admission charge to treasury. Information: *Verkehrsverein Bad Aachen,* Postfach 2007, Aachen 52022 (phone: 241-180-2960 or 241-180-2965; fax: 241-180-2931).

WARTBURG, Eisenach, Thuringia The hilltop cluster of reddish stone and half-timbered houses here, joined by a massive wall and dominated by a parapeted tower, has graced this land since 1067. The great banquet hall looks much as it did when it hosted the marathon *Sängerkrieg* music contests that featured the great *Minnesänger* (members of a guild of poets, singers, and songwriters) of the Middle Ages. In the paneled *Lutherstube,* Martin Luther painstakingly translated the Bible from Greek into German. One of the walls has a stain on it; according to legend, the blotch was caused when Luther threw a pot of ink at a vision he thought was the devil. Also within the complex is a museum of Reformation-era artifacts and paintings, a courtyard, and the *Südturm,* a tower affording a great panoramic view of the forested Thuringian hills and the entire town of Eisenach. In the 19th century, this stolid bastion was the site of demonstrations by students who wanted a united German nation. Open daily. Admission charge. Information: *Die Wartburg Stiftung,* Wartburg, Eisenach 99817 (phone: 3691-3001, 3691-3002, or 3691-3004).

VILLA HÜGEL, Essen, Rhineland-Westphalia The Krupp family château dates to the early 1870s, when Otto von Bismarck backed his foreign policies with the help of this family's weaponry. The mansion, set in a private park and designed in the restrained style of an Italian Renaissance palazzo, has an air of serenity and peace that seems curiously incongruous with the war machinery that made its creators and owners so rich. Nevertheless, it was here, in these wood-paneled salons, that powerful men gambled in secret with the lives of millions. Today, the villa is open to the public. During the summer, it is the site of rotating art exhibits. Closed Mondays. Admission charge. Information: *Villa Hügel,* 15 Hügel, Essen 45133 (phone: 201-188-4837).

BURG GUTTENBERG, Hassmersheim, Neckar Valley, Baden-Württemberg On a hill over the Neckar River, protected by medieval walls six feet thick, this is one of only a few medieval castles to survive the vicissitudes of German history. It is home to the Baron of Gemmingen-Guttenberg, whose family has lived here since the 15th century, when the castle was already several centuries old. Here you can see the well-stocked arsenal of broadswords and suits of armor, as well as the birds of prey that live here, some by the castle moat, others tethered to perches outside. Several times a day, there are demonstrations in the art of falconry. Closed mid-November through mid-March. Admission charge. Information: *Burgschenke Burg Guttenberg,* Hassmersheim 74855 (phone: 6266-228; fax: 6266-1697).

ST. MICHAELISKIRCHE (ST. MICHAEL'S CHURCH), Hildesheim, Lower Saxony This fortress-like Benedictine church, standing atop a hill, recalls Hildesheim's position as an outpost of Christendom on the eastern border of the Ottonian realm in the 11th century. The building is an outstanding example of Romanesque basilican architecture; the outside has a row of graceful arches and Gothic-style windows, while the most striking feature inside is the 13th-century painting of angels on the ceiling just above the nave. If the abbey church was a defense against paganism, it was also an example of the era's distinct lack of separation between church and state. During much of the Middle Ages, political and religious leaders were locked in a bear hug of mutual distrust and forced cooperation. The prince and the bishop coexisted warily right here in the church—the biggest building around. The secular administration was quartered in the *Westwerk,* the bulky widening of the nave at the other end of the church, away from the spiritual domain of the altar. Information: *Verkehrsverein Hildesheim,* 1c Am Ratsbauhof, Hildesheim 31134 (phone: 5121-15995; fax: 5121-31704).

SCHLOSS SANSSOUCI, Potdsam, Brandenburg In the 18th century, while the people of the garrison city of Potsdam were forced to share their already crowded homes with army soldiers, the Hohenzollerns lived in comfort and luxury in this airy compound in *Sanssouci Park* on the edge of town. Frederick the Great had the palace built as a place of respite from the burdens of power. He called it *Schloss Sanssouci* (derived from a French phrase meaning "without care") and between matters of state spent his time ambling its graveled lanes and dallying in rococo rooms glowing with gilded stucco. The ruler also dotted the grounds with ancillary buildings, including a picture gallery with works by Rubens, Van Dyck, Tintoretto, Caravaggio, and other 17th-century Old Masters; a pea-green teahouse, designed in Chinese Baroque style; a mansionette for guests; and, at the other end of the estate, a second castle called the *Neues Schloss* (New Palace). Built in 1769 and never actually lived in, it was intended to demonstrate the Prussian state's unbroken might after the Seven Years' War. In August 1991, Frederick's remains, which for many years had been in *Burg Hohenzollern* in Hechingen, southeast of Stuttgart, were reinterred at the palace. Closed the first and third Mondays of the month. Separate admission charges for all attractions. Information: *Potsdam-Information,* 5 Friedrich-Ebert-Str., Potsdam 14469 (phone: 331-21100; fax: 331-23012).

THE KÖNIGSSCHLÖSSER (SCHLOSS HOHENSCHWANGAU and SCHLOSS NEUSCHWANSTEIN), near Schwangau, Bavaria These castles, among the best-known attractions in Germany, are indelibly associated with Ludwig II (the infamous "Mad King Ludwig"). *Schloss Hohenschwangau* (Hohenschwangau Castle) was built in 1832 by Ludwig's father, Crown Prince Maximilian (one of the Wittelsbachs and later King of Bavaria), on the ruins of a 12th-century fortress that had been demolished in 1809 during a battle against Napoleon. The Tudor-style structure's interior was decorated in the ornate fashion typical of the Wittelsbach dynasty. The young Prince Ludwig spent his formative years in *Hohenschwangau,* often in the company of composer Richard Wagner. Wagner stayed here as a long-term houseguest, introducing Ludwig to music, theater, and mythology, and they formed a lasting friendship, though it was closer to adoration on Ludwig's part. (Wagner, however, probably had an ulterior motive: Ludwig proved to be a lucrative meal ticket for the composer.) On the second floor of the castle is the music room, which still has the piano on which both Ludwig and Wagner played. The ceiling of King Maximilian's bedroom is dotted with bright lights, so that it resembles a star-filled sky. When he became king in 1864—at the age of 18—Ludwig II threw himself into creating extravagant fantasy castles, one of which was the neo-Gothic *Schloss Neuschwanstein.* In 1869, Ludwig had a stage designer draw up plans for the spectacular feudal fortress of this castle, which took 17 years to build. The castle's interior looks more like a series of stage sets than a residence, and Wagner connections abound: a grotto from *Tannhäuser, Lohengrin* swan motifs, and depictions—in paintings and murals—of stagings of *Parsifal, Tristan und Isolde,* and *Siegfried.* The balcony of the unfinished throne room offers views across two lakes to *Hohenschwangau.*

Ludwig's castle projects, which occupied an ever-increasing amount of his energy and attention, were ultimately his undoing. In June 1886 the government, nearly bankrupted by the king's extravagance, had him declared insane. He was dethroned and banished to a minor family castle on the Starnberger See under the care of a doctor. Three days later, both the king and his doctor were pulled from the lake—dead. The exact circumstances of their deaths remain a mystery to this day. But in spite of his tragic, ignominious end, Ludwig is still held in high esteem in Bavaria today.

Both castles, which may be visited only on 35-minute guided tours, are closed *All Saints' Day* (November 1), *Christmas Eve,* and *New Year's Day;* admission charge. Information: *Schloss Hohenschwangau* or *Schloss Neuschwanstein,* Schwangau 87645 (phone: 8362-81128 for Hohenschwangau; 8362-81035 for Neuschwanstein).

EXTERNSTEINE, Teutoburger Wald, Rhineland-Westphalia Just a mile or so from the village of Horn-Bad-Meinberg, secluded in a forest, is the German equivalent of Stonehenge. Indeed, like Stonehenge, this craggy rock formation was originally a pagan shrine. It rises out of the ground like a stage set for the *Ring of the Nibelungen.* In the Middle Ages, the tallest of the stone pillars reminded pilgrims of Golgotha, and replicas of Jerusalem's holiest Christian shrines were carved into spaces in the rock. A 12th-century relief of the Deposition (Christ's descent from the cross) is carved into the limestone wall of one of the grotto chapels; this is a rare example of Byzantine influence in German Romanesque art. Also here is a stone replica of the Holy Sepulchre. Closed November through March. Admission charge to visit the chapels. Information: *Städtisches Verkehrsamt, Rathaus,* Lange Str., Detmold 32756 (phone: 5231-9770; fax: 5231-767299).

MÜNSTER (CATHEDRAL), Ulm, Baden-Württemberg The 530-foot spire of Ulm's cathedral (the world's tallest) looms over the pitched roofs of this city's half-timbered homes. Its foundations were laid in 1377, but the structure wasn't finished until the late 19th century. Despite the fact that it was built over a period of 500 years, the architecture is congruent and pleasing. The Renaissance-style doors are framed by three arcades and crowned by a statue of a man in mourning created by Hans Multscher in 1472. The "Ulm Sparrow," a symbol of the town, perches on the roof. The interior features stunning stained glass windows, sculptures, and stone filigree; take particular note of Jörg Syrlin the Elder's famous choir stalls, decorated with carved representations of biblical characters as well as historical figures. The view from the top of the spire (a heart-taxing climb of 768 steps) is a sweeping panorama that takes in Ulm and the surrounding countryside all the way to the Alps. Inside, there is a massive organ whose thundering music almost shakes the building to its foundations; try to attend one of the hour-long organ concerts given daily at 11 AM. Information: *Verkehrsverein Ulm,* 51 Münsterpl., Ulm 89073 (phone: 731-64161; fax: 731-64173).

RESIDENZ, Würzburg, Bavaria One of the most elaborate palaces in Europe and a fine example of Baroque architecture, this castle was built between 1719 and 1744. The centerpiece of the interior is the *Treppenhaus,* a grand staircase ascending to the largest ceiling painting in the world, a magnificent work by artist Giovanni Battista Tiepolo. The painting portrays Tiepolo's rather fanciful idea of heaven, which blends historic events with purely imaginary scenes. The same artist also furnished the elaborate frescoes of the *Kaisersaal* (Emperor's Hall). Another room, the *Weissersaal* (White Hall), features lovely stucco walls, and the *Gartensaal* (Garden Hall) has more ceiling paintings, this time by Johannes Zick. The rococo-style *Paradenzimmer* (Parade Rooms) are also worth a look. On the grounds, there is a beautifully landscaped *Hofgarten* (Court Garden) with a fountain and a topiary, as well as a restaurant (closed Mondays and Sunday dinner). The palace is also the setting of several music festivals throughout the year (see *Best Festivals* in this section). The palace is closed Mondays. Admission charge. Information: *Residenz Verwaltung,* 2 Residenzpl., Würzburg 97070 (phone: 931-355170).

Directions

Introduction

After two world wars, crushing defeat, foreign occupation, and division into two hostile halves, there is again a united Germany at the geographic center of the Continent. *Wiedervereinigung* (reunification), the dream that postwar Germans for so long could only hope might be realized some distant day, suddenly came true in October 1990 with the absorption of the former German Democratic Republic in the east into the Federal Republic of the west.

The two parts of Germany remain, however, very different. The east, long touted as the "socialist workers' paradise" of the Communist bloc, remains underdeveloped and inefficient by most Western standards. The economy here has a long way to go before it catches up with the prosperous "other Germany." Pollution continues to be a problem in the heavily industrialized areas south of Berlin; however, the process of converting from coal to natural gas heating has accelerated greatly in recent years and several antiquated factories that used to spew noxious fumes into the air have closed. The task of rebuilding the infrastructure in the east also is proving to be far more formidable (and expensive) than anticipated. Despite a crash construction effort, it is expected to be at least five (and probably closer to 10) years before the highway network in the east is on a par with the superb autobahns and secondary routes in the west. Meanwhile, the number of traffic accidents in the east has risen sharply with the arrival from the west of drivers in high-powered cars, accustomed to burning up speed-limitless autobahns. Eastern drivers, accustomed to a pre-unification limit of 100 kilometers per hour (62 mph), are similarly a hazard in the west (although most have replaced their tinny little Trabants in favor of more efficient, cleaner-burning cars).

Except in the largest cities, travel services also are in short (but gradually increasing) supply in what was East Germany. At the time of reunification, the number of hotel beds in the east was estimated at 75,000, compared with 3.5 million in the west. There are several truly international class hotels—built by the former Communist government mainly to accommodate foreign guests paying in hard currency—in Leipzig, Dresden, and the former East Berlin. Elsewhere, however, choices remain limited, although many hotels in eastern Germany are being privatized, and some have become affiliated with US and other Western hotel chains. The best properties in eastern Germany are the ones that had been operated by a government agency, *Interhotel,* which entered into a leasing arrangement with the German *Steigenberger* chain soon after reunification. (For information in the US, contact *SRS Hotels Steigenberger Reservation Service,* 40 E. 49th St., New York, NY 10017; phone: 212-593-2988.)

But eastern Germany does have many attractions for travelers. While the former West Germany became rapidly modernized after World War II, the GDR was in effect locked in a time warp. As a result, the small towns and villages that escaped bombing during the war still retain a genuine Old World look and feel that has yet to be superceded by commercial development. Visitors to this part of the country often feel as though they're traveling backward through time.

Today's Germany, although considerably smaller than its prewar size, again is one of the larger countries in Europe; with 137,740 square miles, it is slightly smaller than the state of Montana. The landscape, however, is one of Europe's most diversified. Most of the renowned areas—the castle-crowned Rhine, the Black Forest, the Bavarian Alps and lakes, festive Munich, and lovely, riverfront Heidelberg—are in the west. Except for the wooded Thuringian highlands, the Harz Mountains in Sachsen-Anhalt, and the Erzgebirge (Ore Mountains) of Saxony, the east is largely flat, the beginning of the great Northern European plain that extends eastward through Poland and Russia to the Ural Mountains.

Everywhere in Germany you encounter history as well as scenery. The Germanic culture goes back to at least the 7th century BC, when this heavily forested land was home to numerous tribes such as the Bavarians, Franconians, Frisians, Saxons, Thuringians, and Swabians, whose names survive as regional place names. In AD 9, these so-called "Barbarians" scored one of the most decisive victories in history when they defeated three Roman legions in the Teutoburg Forest, southeast of the modern city of Bielefeld, thus ending Roman expansion northward. The Rhine and Danube Rivers became the empire's border for the next four centuries, and the Germanic tribes avoided becoming "Latinized," never adopting the Roman culture and language as did most other peoples of Western Europe. They were, however, gradually converted to Christianity (from the 5th through the 9th centuries).

In the 9th century, the separate tribes were somewhat united when they came under the sway of Charlemagne (Karl der Grosse in German), ruler of the Franks, a kindred people who had migrated westward across the Rhine into present-day France. Although Charlemagne's empire soon disintegrated, the Germans perpetuated its memory until almost modern times in the Holy Roman Empire—a political fiction that supposedly united them but which the French philosopher Voltaire bitingly dismissed as "an agglomeration" that was "neither holy, nor Roman, nor an empire." He was right on the mark. In fact, feudalism reigned supreme. Germany was a bewildering patchwork of squabbling principalities and duchies lorded over by petty nobles who were often not much more than landed bandits, constantly in conflict with each other and with many foreign foes, including the pope in Rome.

While the rest of Europe was consolidating into nation-states, Germany remained divided, initially by politics and then, in the 16th century, by religion. The Reformation began here when Martin Luther (1483–1546), a priest and professor of theology, rejected what he viewed as a corrupted Roman church and refused to renounce his belief that individual salvation could be achieved through faith alone. His excommunication in 1521 only exacerbated the conflict. Luther's forceful preaching and writing drew many in Germany (and elsewhere in Europe) to the Protestant cause. The movement grew and spread, and eventually the situation erupted into the Thirty Years War, which raged from 1618 to 1648.

The image of Germany in modern times is of an aggressive country threatening its neighbors. For much of their history, however, the Germans have suffered from the aggressions of others, as French, Spanish, English, Swedish, and other foreign armies used German territory as their battleground. This was particularly true during the Thirty Years War; records dating from after that conflict describe vast areas of Germany as virtually depopulated wastelands. Germany was again a battleground during the Napoleonic Wars (1803–15), after which its map was redrawn, eliminating the majority of its smallest states and preparing the way for a long-delayed unification.

Austria-Hungary, the heir to the Holy Roman Empire (which had finally been obliterated by Napoleon), vied for leadership in Germany with Prussia, a militaristic semi-kingdom on the northeastern frontier that had developed into a particularly powerful entity. A series of wars culminated in Prussia's victory over the German *"Erbfeind"* (hereditary enemy), France, in 1870. A German Empire uniting all states except Austria was proclaimed, with the Prussian ruler installed as kaiser. At first, Germany exerted a stabilizing influence in Europe. Prince Otto von Bismarck, the imperial "Iron Chancellor" and architect of unity, sought to maintain the status quo through a network of alliances with other powers that effectively isolated the old adversary, France, still smarting from its defeat. This was also a period of rapid industrial growth, economic expansion, and social development. Although the government was autocratic, with little power delegated to an elected *Reichstag* (Parliament), it enacted the most advanced body of social legislation in any country of that day. The Bismarckian system remains the basis of the social welfare system of today's Germany. The period leading up to 1914 is still looked back upon by most Germans as a golden age.

But with the advent of a new emperor, Wilhelm II, in 1888, Bismarck was dismissed and a policy of colonial expansion led to friction with other powers, especially Britain, that culminated in World War I. Defeated, the empire collapsed and was succeeded by a republic, proclaimed in the university town of Weimar and since known to history as the Weimar Republic. It was unable to cope with the severe economic problems of the postwar years and was paralyzed by the rivalry of its many small political parties. Disunity and despair brought Adolf Hitler and his Nazi Party to power in 1933. His Third Reich (the first having been the Holy Roman Empire, the second Bismarck's German Empire) quickly brought on another war, and after six years of horrendous bloodshed, genocide, and devastation, another absolute German defeat. In 1945, the victorious Allies met at Yalta and Potsdam and divided Germany into four zones of occupation—British, French, American, and Soviet.

Rising tensions between East and West, aggravated by the Soviet blockade of Berlin in 1948–49, resulted in the division of Germany into "East" and "West." The three Western allies soon merged their zones, turning over most powers to a new German government in 1949, which established a temporary capital in the university town of Bonn, in the Rhineland. The next two decades saw the *Wirtschaftswunder* (economic miracle) that not only rebuilt but transformed the country—actually, only the western half of the former country—into the strongest economy in Europe and the third among all industrial democracies, after the United States and Japan.

A very different Germany emerged in the Soviet-occupied territories. A Communist state, the German Democratic Republic was established in 1949 in response to the merger of the western zones. It also made economic progress, especially after the construction of the Berlin Wall in 1961 and the fortification of the entire zonal border between the two Germanys, which cut off the defection of large numbers of East Germans to the West. The GDR became the showcase of the Communist bloc, with a gross national product second only to that of the Soviet Union. East Germany was regarded as the most stable of the Warsaw Pact satellites, and enjoyed the highest standard of living.

But in 1989, the Wall sprang some leaks. The process of change began when Hungary opened its border with Austria. East Germans took advantage of the opportunity to defect by detouring through a "brotherly socialist state." More sought to exit through what was then Czechoslovakia. Then antigovernment street demonstrations broke out in East German cities, especially Leipzig, and the Berlin Wall was breached by crowds from both sides. Events could no longer be controlled. Elections in the GDR led to an interim government, and with the approval of the four World War II powers, a decision to unite the two Germanys sooner rather than later. The West German deutsche mark (DM) became the common currency in June 1990, formal unification was declared in October, and the first all-German parliamentary election since 1933 took place in December 1990.

Germany has been the cradle of heroes and villains. It is the land of such giants such as Bach, Brahms, Beethoven, and Wagner in music; Hegel, Kant, and Heidegger in philosophy; and Goethe, Schiller, and Thomas Mann in literature. Karl Marx and Friedrich Engels were the originators of modern Communist ideology, just as Einstein was the pioneer of modern physics. Paradoxically, it also was in Germany that Hitler came to power, and it was here, not so long ago, that this contradictory populace nurtured the cancerous growth of Nazi fascism.

Many people fear a recurrence of the Nazi nightmare in Germany, and the increase of sporadic neo-Nazi incidents fuels that concern. The task of melding two regions that have had such very different experiences for almost half a century into one country is formidable, and there are many questions still to be answered. The division of the haves in the "west" and the have-nots in the "east" has spawned troubling new economic and sociological friction, which the reunified Germany is struggling to address.

One of the focal points of the transition to a united Germany is movement of the capital city. After 43 years as the "provincial capital," Bonn has officially been replaced by Berlin (the historic capital) as the seat of the federal government. However, the *Bundestag* (lower house of Parliament) and other government agencies are not scheduled to move to Berlin before the turn of the century, and Bonn will not become a ghost town even then, as the *Bundesrat* (upper house of Parliament) will remain there, along with nearly half the federal ministries and two-thirds of the civil servants.

These are particularly exciting times in which to visit Germany and witness the rebuilding of a great nation, set to benefit from the newly integrated European economy. The future of the now-depressed eastern region can be seen today in the west: War-ravaged cities and towns have long since been rebuilt in modern style, but where possible the best of the old has been retained, or in many cases lovingly reconstructed. *Kölner Dom* (Cologne Cathedral), virtually unscathed in World War II, towers over the ancient Rhineland city that began as a Roman frontier post. Vibrant and exciting Berlin, no longer a divided city, contains some of the world's greatest art treasures. Munich is not only one of the world's most festive cities, but may well be the most livable. According to a poll some years back, two out of three Germans would prefer to live in the Bavarian capital if given the choice.

The former East Germany also has its showcase cities. Dresden, the capital of the Saxon prince electors and lavishly embellished by them over the years, was considered the most beautiful of Europe's Baroque cities before World War II. It was virtually leveled by British and American air raids near the very end of the war, but its most impressive architectural treasures have been reconstructed gradually over the past few decades. Leipzig, another important Saxon city, was once the home of Johann Sebastian Bach and still claims one of the world's finest boys' choirs. The Baltic Sea coast, a favorite prewar vacation area that includes Rügen Island, does not yet have the facilities for large numbers of visitors, but can be expected to be an attraction again as redevelopment progresses.

The myriad sights and sites to be found in Germany's major metropolises are covered in THE CITIES. In addition, the extraordinary variety of the German countryside, its historic towns and small hamlets, can be explored by following our 10 driving routes. In the north, a traveler can visit the four most important members of the former Hanseatic League (Bremen, Hamburg, Lübeck, and Rostock), explore several cities in the state of Mecklenburg–West Pomerania (including Wismar, Stralsund, and the state capital, Schwerin), and relax in the lake country of Holsteinische Schweiz

(Holstein Switzerland) or on a beach such as at Travemünde on the Baltic Sea. The short, pleasant route from Frankfurt to Heidelberg follows the charming Main River Valley through the gentle wooded hills of the historic Odenwald and Spessart areas. Westphalia, land of ham and pumpernickel, castle-hotels and wayside inns, can best be seen in a circular route that begins in Dortmund. Castles, vineyards, and dramatic vistas mark the fabled Rhineland, which includes the area from Mainz to Koblenz, but can be extended to Cologne and Düsseldorf. Germany's Burgenstrasse (Castle Road) meanders along the Neckar River Valley, passing more than a dozen palaces on the way from Heidelberg to Heilbronn. Rolling hills and thick forests characterize the Black Forest region, which extends from Basel, in Switzerland, to the exclusive German spa city of Baden-Baden. The lovely Romantische Strasse (Romantic Road) runs from Würzburg on the Main River to Füssen in the Alpine foothills, and passes through Bavaria's fabulous old Baroque towns. The Alpine Road and Lake Constance route, which for many represents the essence of Germany with the fanciful *Königsschlösser* (King's Castles) built by "Mad" King Ludwig II, picturesque medieval villages, and bustling spa and lakeshore towns, ends up at Germany's borders with Switzerland and Austria. The eastern route begins in Potsdam and traces the road west across gently rolling hills to Magdeburg, over the Harz Mountains southward to the foothills of the Thuringian Forest, and then back north to Naumburg.

No matter where you choose to explore in this still-evolving country, with its beautiful scenery, historical atmosphere, and striking architecture, the trip is bound to be a fascinating voyage of discovery.

Northern Germany

Two separate seacoasts account for northern Germany's long nautical history. The North Sea meets Lower Saxony's shoreline, while the Baltic Sea ("Ostsee" on German maps) has had considerable influence in the eastern state of Mecklenburg–West Pomerania. Between these two regions is the northernmost state of Schleswig-Holstein, extending from the Elbe River estuary up to the Danish border.

The dominant force along both coasts early in Germany's history was the Hanseatic League, established in the mid-13th century as a free association of medieval towns and cities that concentrated on trade. The most prominent (and richest) members of the league were the city-states of Bremen, Hamburg, and Lübeck, as well as Rostock, Wismar, and Stralsund on the Baltic. Since they were self-governing and did not have to pay taxes to any larger power, these mercantile centers grew extremely prosperous and became a powerful force in commerce within Germany, as well as in trade with such foreign powers as England, Sweden, the Netherlands, Norway, Poland, and Russia.

Although the Hanseatic League faded away three centuries ago, the effects of its affluence and prestige are still discernable today. For example, Hamburg and Bremen remain full-fledged city-states on a political par with the other states comprising the German Federal Republic. The residents of the entire region feel a fierce sense of pride. In fact, people here often identify themselves as citizens of the city they live in (saying they are Hamburgians, Bremians, or Lübeckers, for example) before saying they are Germans. The league's legacy of wealth and distinction also is evident in the region's sturdy-looking, richly embellished buildings. Northern Germany boasts numerous beautiful structures that either escaped destruction during World War II or have been carefully restored; the chance to view them is one of the major incentives to travel here.

Thanks to national reunification, the whole of northern Germany is now accessible to travelers. Visitors can choose from among a wide variety of destinations and itineraries: They can focus on the North Sea, the Baltic Sea, or the two coastlines combined; explore the lovely, relaxing lake districts a short distance inland from both coasts; visit significant seaports; tour such smaller, relatively undiscovered towns as Stade, Schleswig, and Bad Doberan; or enjoy the beaches and resorts of Travemünde (near Lübeck in the west) or Warnemünde (near Rostock in the east).

The northwest route described below, taking in Bremen, Lübeck, and part of Schleswig-Holstein, covers a distance of about 225 miles (360 km) and can be traveled by car in three to four days. People who want a first-hand look at current living conditions in what was formerly the GDR can return to Lübeck and continue on through the northeastern state of

Mecklenburg–West Pomerania, stopping in Schwerin, Wismar, Rostock, and Stralsund. This northeast route will add about 185 miles (306 km) and an additional three days to the trip. Those who choose to travel through eastern Germany should be prepared for inconveniences and difficulties: fewer people speak English, the choice of accommodations is narrower, and drivers will often encounter detours and slowdowns caused by road repairs and improvements.

For general information and maps about the northwest, contact the *Fremdenverkehrsverband* (Tourist Office; Nordsee-Niedersachsen-Bremen, 19020 Bahnhofstr., Oldenburg 26122, Germany; phone: 441-921710; fax: 441-921-7190). For information and maps about the northeast, contact the *Landesfremdenverkehrsverband* (Government Tourist Office; Mecklenburg-Vorpommern e.V., 1 Platz der Freundschaft, 0-2550 Rostock 1, Germany; phone: 381-725261; fax: 381-752260).

Hotel prices vary a great deal along both the western and eastern routes; costs are generally higher in the larger cities, especially Hamburg. A double room (with private bath or shower, TV set, and breakfast included, unless otherwise indicated) will cost more than $200 a night in hotels listed as very expensive; $150 to $200 in hotels described as expensive; $100 to $150 at places in the moderate category; and less than $100 at places described as inexpensive. A meal for two (not including wine, drinks, or tip) will cost $45 to $55 at restaurants listed as expensive; $30 to $45 at moderate restaurants; and $15 to $30 at inexpensive places. Restaurants are open for lunch and dinner unless otherwise noted. For each location, hotels and restaurants are listed alphabetically by price category.

NORTHWEST GERMANY

BREMEN Germany's oldest seaport (having been a market port since AD 965) is the natural starting point for any tour of the northwestern coast. Before setting out, stop at Bremen's tourist information office (29 Bahnhofspl.; phone: 421-308000), in front of the main train station. Open daily, it offers maps, brochures, a booklet describing a walking tour, and information about hotels and pensions.

Like many European cities, Bremen is best seen on foot. The compact heart of the city is the Altstadt (Old Town) surrounding the Marktplatz. Latter-day Bremen, including the 19th-century Schwachhausen neighborhood of terraced houses, has grown around this central core. Bremen used to be enclosed by a high wall, but the wall has since been replaced by gardens following its original zigzag pattern. A delightful pastime for visitors and locals alike is to stroll along the *Wallanlagen* (Rampart Walk), with its moat and windmill.

Bremen's huge market square (which residents affectionately call their *gute Stube*—parlor) is worth a visit, if for nothing more than the delicious smell of coffee from the sidewalk cafés and the lovely colors and shapes of fresh fruits and vegetables. It's a favorite local hangout, with plenty of activity during the day. The flamboyant, 15th-century *Rathaus* (Town Hall), facing the market square, typifies a regional style of architecture called Weser Renaissance; it houses the *Ratskeller,* an excellent cellar restaurant with the largest list of local wines in Germany (see *Best en Route*). Another noteworthy sight on the Marktplatz is an imposing statue of the knight Roland, who served under Charlemagne and was immortalized in the medieval *Chanson de Roland.* A symbol of the separation of church and state, the 30-foot figure defiantly faces the twin-steepled *Dom St. Petri* (St. Peter's Cathedral).

While in Bremen, don't miss the old Schnoor quarter, with its narrow streets, tiny courtyards, half-timbered houses, taverns, tea rooms, galleries, and craft shops. Some tempting deals on handmade goods can be found here. Or take a stroll down Böttcherstrasse, a 100-yard-long alleyway that has been transformed into a brick-paved pedestrian zone; because of its out-of-the-way location, its tiny size, and its popularity, locals affectionately call Böttcherstrasse Bremen's "secret main street." Thirty bells made of Meissen porcelain in the step-gabled *Haus des Glockenspiels* (Carillon House; 7 Böttcherstr.) chime three times daily: at noon and at 3 and 6 PM.

Another popular attraction in Bremen is the *Bremer Landesmuseum für Kunst und Kulturgeschichte* (Bremen Museum of the History of Art and Civilization; 240 Schwachhauser Heerstr.; phone: 421-496-3575). Popularly known as the *Focke-Museum,* it has a fine collection of historical artifacts. The museum is closed Mondays; admission charge.

For people who have the urge to set out to sea, boat tours of the Weser River and Bremen's harbor area leave the Martini jetty four times each day.

Bremerhaven, Bremen's much younger sister city, is well worth a side trip. Located 35 miles (56 km) farther north on the A27 autobahn, it ranks as Europe's largest container facility and Germany's second-largest port (after Hamburg). Interestingly enough, it is because of Bremen that Bremerhaven exists at all. In the early 17th century, the merchants of Bremen noticed that their precious port was becoming clogged with silt accumulating from the Weser River. Dredging operations then were not what they are now, so the facilities simply moved a short distance downstream to Vegesack. Eventually, Vegesack too became clogged with mud, so in 1827 the merchants moved still farther downstream and established a deep-sea port at Bremerhaven. The city's *Deutsches Schiffahrtsmuseum* (German Maritime Museum; Van-Ronzelen-Str.; phone: 471-44048) is the largest of its kind in the country. The museum is closed Mondays; admission charge.

Another interesting side trip is to the quaint artists' colony of Worpswede (about 17 miles/28 km northeast of Bremen), with some 300 resident painters, sculptors, potters, weavers, and silversmiths displaying their work (also see *Quintessential Germany* in DIVERSIONS). Take the unnumbered road out of Bremen toward the village of Lillenthal and follow the signs to Worpswede.

Park Bremen's leading hotel is in the lovely Bürgerpark. It has 150 charming guestrooms, spacious, cheerful public areas, a heated garden terrace, and a fine restaurant. Also see *Best Hotels* in DIVERSIONS. Im Bürgerpark, Bremen (phone: 421-34080; 800-223-5652; fax: 421-340-8602). Very expensive.

Alte Gilde This popular cellar restaurant is set in a 17th-century townhouse with authentic Hanse atmosphere. The menu specializes in well-prepared seafood dishes such as crab soup and haddock in mustard sauce. Open daily; closed Sunday dinner. Reservations advised. Major credit cards accepted. 24 Ansgaritorstr., Bremen (phone: 421-171712). Expensive to moderate.

Landhaus Louisenthal A few miles north of the city center, in the suburb of Horn, this charming 1835 hotel with 60 rooms and a sauna is noteworthy for its quiet country-style atmosphere. 105 Leher Heerstr., Horn (phone: 421-232076; fax: 421-236716). Expensive to moderate.

Ubersee This pleasant 124-room hotel is near the market square. In addition to the usual amenities, it offers conference facilities. 27-29 Wachtstr., Bremen (phone: 421-232076; fax: 421-236716). Moderate.

Ratskeller In the 500-year-old *Rathaus,* this place has lots of atmosphere and also serves good food. It's popular with the local folk, who meet here to sample some of its 600 German wines. Also see *Best Restaurants* in DIVERSIONS. Open daily. Reservations advised. Major credit cards accepted. Am Markt, Bremen (phone: 421-321676). Moderate.

Café Knigge A thoroughly Germanic *Konditorei* (pastry café) with an outdoor terrace in a pedestrians-only lane, it has been a Bremen institution since 1889. A good, reasonably priced choice for light lunches, salads, and *Kaffee und Kuchen* (coffee and cake). Open daily. No reservations. No credit cards accepted. 42 Sögestr., Bremen (phone: 421-13068). Inexpensive.

En Route from Bremen Bremen and Hamburg are only 75 miles (120 km) apart—little more than an hour's drive along the speedy E22 autobahn. If you want a more leisurely trip that includes a stop at the little town of Stade along the way, you can choose to take a series of country roads. The scenic route is well worth the extra time, as it meanders through open moors and alongside thatch-roofed cottages and half-timbered barns—common sights in this part of Germany. The prettiest way is to take Route 74 northeast via Osterholz-Scharmbeck and Bremerwörde, passing through a stretch of the gorgeous orchard country of Lower Saxony; the distance to Stade is about 50 miles (80 km).

STADE This historic town, another member of the Hanseatic League, lies in the midst of an orchard district called *Das Alte Land* (the Old Country), which is particularly lovely in springtime. Virtually unknown to most tourists, placid little Stade has many impeccably maintained and restored houses and shops, all crammed together in a style typical of medieval times. Be sure to take a look at *St.-Cosmae-Kirche* (St. Cosmas Church), with an onion-dome spire, as well as the Flemish-style *Rathaus* (City Hall) and the *Alte Stadtwaage* (Old Weighing House) in the harbor basin, where goods were weighed to determine the appropriate duty. At one end of the fish market is the *Schwedenspeicher* (7 Wasser West; phone: 4141-3222), a Swedish storehouse that was built between 1692 and 1705 to serve as a supply depot for the Swedish troops that occupied the region at that time. Today, it serves as a regional museum for Lower Saxony, with exhibits on Stade's Hanseatic history and the area's years as a Swedish domain. The museum is closed Mondays; no admission charge.

En Route from Stade Take Route 73 via Buxtehude and then the autobahn north through the Elbe tunnel, which leads straight into central Hamburg. The total distance covered is about 19 miles (30 km) and can be driven in well under an hour.

HAMBURG For a detailed report on the city and its hotels and restaurants, see *Hamburg* in THE CITIES.

En Route from Hamburg The direct route from Hamburg to Lübeck is only 41 miles (66 km) along the E47 autobahn. However, for those taking a more leisurely tour, Ratzeburg (31 miles/50 km away) is a pleasant stop. To get there, take the E26 autobahn east to Route 207, then continue north.

RATZEBURG An island town (it sits in the middle of a lake), Ratzeburg is a lovely place to stay for a weekend, with plenty of swimming, boating, and fishing. The affluent town has such an easygoing atmosphere that it's hard to believe that the border with East Germany, with its forbidding watchtowers, fences, and mine fields, used to be less than 2½ miles (4 km) away. By all means see the *Ratzeburger Dom* (Ratzeburger Cathedral) on the east edge of town; one of the largest brick churches in northern Germany, it has an interesting altar triptych. Ratzeburg's tourist office (9 Am Markt; phone: 4541-2727) is open daily. Mölln, 6 miles (10 km) south of here, is the mythical burial place of Till Eulenspiegel, the mischievous German folk hero. Besides its place in German legend, the town features an attractive step-gabled town hall that's worth a look.

BEST EN ROUTE

Der Seehof This low-key hotel, with 65 rooms, a garden, a sauna, and a boat dock, is directly on the lake. You would be hard pressed to find a more charming place to spend a night or weekend. Even the restaurant is a bargain. 1-3 Lüneburger Damm, Ratzeburg (phone: 4541-2055; fax: 4541-7861). Moderate.

En Route from Ratzeburg Take Route 208 west out of town, then rejoin Route 207 and continue north to Lübeck; the total distance traveled is about 16 miles (25 km).

LÜBECK The administrative and judicial capital of the Hanseatic League for more than 300 years, Lübeck retains the flavor of a medieval town, complete with seven signature church steeples marking the skyline of the Innenstadt (Inner City). The mighty, double-barreled gate at the city's entrance—the *Holstentor*—hardly can fail to impress a visitor. Built between 1464 and 1478 as part of the fortifications, the gate serves as the symbol of Lübeck and is pictured on 50 DM banknotes. It also houses the *Museum im Holstentor,* a museum of municipal history (phone: 451-122-4129); closed Mondays; admission charge. Along the gateway is a uniform row of 16th-century warehouses that were used to store salt shipped from Lüneberg during the Hanseatic era.

Lübeck has several other museums, each a minor gem. *St.-Annen-Museum* (St. Anne's Museum; 15 St. Annenstr.; phone: 451-4137) is a former convent that now houses a collection of ecclesiastical art, including a 15th-century altarpiece by Hans Memling. The *Bernhaus und Drägerhaus* museums (9-11 Königstr.; phone: 451-122-4148), occupying two adjacent patrician residences, give visitors an excellent understanding of how people lived during the height of the Hanseatic League. The *Bernhaus* also exhibits 19th- and 20th-century artwork. All three museums are closed Mondays; admission charge.

The *Rathaus* (Town Hall), on two sides of the Marktplatz, is one of Germany's oldest and most ornate town halls, incorporating styles ranging from Gothic to Renaissance. Note the portholes punctuating the roofline. The *Marienkirche* (St. Mary's Church), an enormous red brick structure, is both a 13th-century, Gothic house of worship and a 20th-century war memorial. On *Palm Sunday,* 1942, the church was bombed, and the two giant bells in the south tower came crashing down; the remains are still embedded in the broken stone floor today. The white Baroque *Buddenbrookhaus* (4 Mengstr.; phone: 451-136258) was the home of Thomas Mann's grandparents and the inspiration for the novelist's *Buddenbrooks* saga about the rise and decline of a Lübeck mercantile family. The house is closed Mondays; admission charge.

One of the products for which Lübeck is most famous is its luscious marzipan candy, made from almond paste and powdered sugar. It comes in myriad shapes, and you often see Lübeckers strolling along the streets, happily munching on a marzipan pig, pear, or apple. The best place in Lübeck (if not the world) to buy marzipan is the two-story *I. G. Niederegger Konditorei-Café* (89 Breite Str.; phone: 451-530070), across from the *Rathaus.* Here you can enjoy both a sinfully sweet piece of marzipan and a delicious cup of coffee to go with it; the café is open daily. A package of marzipan is the perfect gift from Lübeck—either for friends or for yourself.

Like most other German cities, Lübeck has an excellent tourist office (Am Markt; phone: 451-122-8106), which can provide information and maps and for a small fee will help arrange a room for the night. It is closed Sundays.

BEST EN ROUTE

L'Etoile A chic, intimate dining place set in the Jugendstil home of a young Lübecker couple. Delicious and attractive presentations of nouvelle cuisine with a European touch are featured. The soft lighting is especially romantic. Open daily. Reservations necessary. No credit cards accepted. 8 Grosse Petersgrube, Lübeck (phone: 451-76440). Expensive.

Senator Lübeck Penta The finest hotel in the city is on a canal overlooking the Altstadt (Old Town), just a few steps away from the *Holstentor.* Its 225 spacious guestrooms are tastefully furnished, and most feature views of Lübeck's breathtaking skyline. The *Trave* restaurant offers excellent dining, while *Bierstube Kogge* is a vibrant after-hours spot. An indoor pool, a sauna, a fitness center, conference facilities, and underground parking round out the picture. 7 Lastadie, Lübeck (phone: 451-1420; 800-225-3456; fax: 451-142-2222). Expensive.

Schiffergesellschaft Popular with American visitors, this historic shipmasters' guild house dates from 1535 and features nautical decor. A broad range of traditional German fare is served here, including hearty meat and seafood dishes and luscious desserts. This is the ideal place to try *Labskaus,* a beef-and-potato hash mixed with onions and served with a fried egg on top. Closed Sundays. Reservations advised. No credit cards accepted. 2 Breite-Str., Lübeck (phone: 451-76776). Moderate.

Wullenwever In a former brewery, this fine, 16th-century restaurant is one of Lübeck's best. Light, well-prepared food is served courteously in a setting of understated elegance. Closed Sundays and Mondays. Reservations advised. Major credit cards accepted. 71 Beckergrube, Lübeck (phone: 451-704333). Moderate.

Alter Speicher A folksy, family-run hotel centrally located in the Altstadt, it has 57 rooms, a cozy restaurant that serves only breakfast, and parking. Quiet and comfort are the watchwords here. 91-93 Beckergrube, Lübeck (phone: 451-71045; fax: 451-704804). Inexpensive.

En Route from Lübeck At Lübeck, you have two choices: Either turn northwest toward Kiel and Schleswig and continue touring northwest Germany, or turn east, branching off into northeast Germany (for details on this leg of the trip, see *Northeast Germany,* below). If you decide to continue on the northwest route, the drive from Lübeck to Kiel (approximately 51 miles/83 km) goes through an area that the Germans call the

Holsteinische Schweiz (the Switzerland of Holstein) because of its 140 lakes and numerous forests. The area also looks a lot like Wisconsin. Take Route 207 out of Lübeck and turn onto Route 76, which leads to Kiel via Eutin and Plön. If it's a beach day, detour a few miles east to Travemünde, on the Baltic Sea; it's a fashionable resort with a casino. If not, stop at either Eutin, Carl Maria von Weber's home town, with 18th-century brick houses and lots of antiques shops, or Plön, which is on the Plöner See, Schleswig-Holstein's largest lake.

KIEL The 19th-century Kiel Canal, which connects the North Sea with the Baltic and with a harbor that opens onto a fjord, makes Kiel a busy port and yachting center. This mid-size metropolis also is the capital of Schleswig-Holstein. Most of Kiel was destroyed by bombing during World War II, and the city has been rebuilt in a bland modern style. However, the Jugendstil tower of the *Rathaus,* built in 1911, still survives, and the city's bustling fish market is lively and colorful. Several large parks fringe the canal (the world's busiest), and the *Hindenburgufer* (Hindenburg Quay) is a 2-mile, tree-shaded promenade along the fjord.

BEST EN ROUTE

Voss Haus This restaurant, the dining room of a charming (and moderately priced) 15-room inn, is nearly 300 years old. The dark woodwork, beamed ceilings, and tiled fireplace create a homey atmosphere, and the menu offers excellent preparations of fish caught fresh from Eutin's lake. It is one of the best restaurants in the entire state of Schleswig-Holstein. Also see *Best Restaurants* in DIVERSIONS. Open daily. Reservations advised. Major credit cards accepted. 6 Vosspl., Eutin (phone: 4521-1797; fax: 4521-1357). Expensive.

Landhaus Hahn North of Plön, in the village of Schellhorn, this comfortable hostelry has 22 rooms and a good restaurant. Am Berg, Schellhorn (phone: 4342-86001; fax: 4342-24211). Moderate to inexpensive.

En Route from Kiel Continue northwest along Route 76 another 31 miles (50 km) to Schleswig.

SCHLESWIG Founded by the Vikings, Schleswig is the oldest town in Schleswig-Holstein. For many years, it was a Viking stronghold; from here they plundered and looted the towns to the south, such as Hamburg and Bremen. Be sure to see the *Schleswiger Dom* (Schleswig Cathedral; Essenstr.); built in 1100, it features the incredibly delicate *Bordesholm Altar,* carved in oak by Hans Brüggeman between 1514 and 1521.

In Haitabu, just southeast of town on Route 76, is the *Wikingermuseum* (Viking Museum; Haddebyer Noor; phone: 4621-81330), which contains some of Schleswig-Holstein's best-known artifacts from that society. It's closed Mondays and December; admission charge. The area's other big attraction is the *Nydam* boat, an Anglo-Saxon vessel dating from the 4th century. The boat is on display at the *Archäologisches Landesmuseum* (State Archaelogical Museum) in *Schloss Gottorf* (Gottorf Castle; phone: 4621-813222), on an island surrounded by a moat about a half mile from the center of Schleswig. The museum also contains fine exhibitions of folklore, art, and handicrafts. It's closed Mondays and December; admission charge. For more information, see *Memorable Monuments and Museums* in DIVERSIONS. The castle also has a good, inexpensive cellar restaurant (phone: 4621-32990).

BEST EN ROUTE

Waldhotel On the grounds of *Schloss Gottorf,* this small hotel sits in a placid woodland setting. It offers nine pleasantly furnished, well-maintained rooms and a good restaurant. 1 Stampfmühle (phone: 4621-23288; fax: 4621-23289). Moderate to inexpensive.

En Route from Schleswig Our tour of the northwest ends here; travelers who want to visit the rest of northern Germany can take Route 76 the 62 miles (99 km) back to Lübeck, the jumping-off point for our northeast route.

NORTHEAST GERMANY

Although this area of the country, like the rest of the former East Germany, is undergoing rapid modernization and evolution, visitors here can still get the sense of being pioneers exploring a completely new frontier. At present, most hotels and restaurants still operate on a cash-only basis, although the number of places that accept at least some credit cards is increasing. It's always a good idea to check with the hotel when making room reservations.

En Route from Lübeck From Lübeck, take Route 104 southwest into the state of Mecklenburg–West Pomerania. Crossing over what used to be the infamous borderline separating the two Germanys, drive through Rehna, Gadebusch, and Lützow to reach Schwerin, located about 42 miles (67 km) from Lübeck.

SCHWERIN The capital of Mecklenburg–West Pomerania, Schwerin lies comfortably nestled among a cluster of lakes and ponds. One of the prime attractions here is the *Schweriner Schloss* (Schwerin Castle; 1 Lennestr.; phone: 385-812865), built in the 19th century for Duke Friedrich Franz II. The castle, adorned with pinnacles, turrets, spires, belfries, and gilded domes, sits on an attractively landscaped island in the Schweriner See. Its many rooms and galleries can be seen only on a guided tour, which can be arranged by the tourist office (see below). The castle is open daily; admission charge. There's a café serving light meals and snacks on the premises.

On the mainland, the *Staatliches Museum* (State Art Museum; Am Alten Garten; phone: 385-57581) has a collection of paintings by Dutch, Flemish, and German artists, including *Bildnis einer Jungen Frau* (Portrait of a Young Lady) by Paulus Moreelse and several works by renowned modern painter Max Liebermann. It's closed Mondays; no admission charge. Other places of interest include the Marktplatz, connected to several narrow pedestrian lanes; a 13th-century, Baltic-style Gothic cathedral (on Bischofstr. near the Marktplatz); and the neoclassical *Staatstheater* (Am Alten Garten; phone: 385-882222), where operas and plays are performed. The tourist office (11 Am Markt; phone: 385-812314; closed Sundays) provides information about accommodations, attractions, and restaurants; from April through October it also arranges boat excursions on the area's many waterways.

BEST EN ROUTE

Café Prag The genteel Old European ambience and authentic regional fare (including fish soup and other seafood dishes) make this casual restaurant popular with both locals and visitors. Open daily. Reservations unnecessary. No credit cards accepted. 17 Schlossstr., Schwerin (phone: 385-864095). Moderate to inexpensive.

Nordlicht This small hotel (five rooms) is situated in the Altstadt (Old Town) center of the city. Nearby is a pond called the Pfannenteich, which is surrounded by walkways for strolling; the marketplace is also close. 2 Apothekerstr., Schwerin (phone: 385-864747; fax: 385-557-4383). Inexpensive.

En Route from Schwerin Continue 18 miles (28 km) north on Route 106 alongside the west bank of the Schweriner See to Wismar on the Baltic coast.

WISMAR Don't be put off by the rather dull, socialist-style apartment buildings that dot the environs of this venerable city. Once you've made your way through the heavy traffic to the Innenstadt (Inner City), you'll find the charming Marktplatz; the largest market square in Germany, it is surrounded by a slew of patrician townhouses and distinctive public buildings. The types of architecture here run the gamut from 14th-century North German Gothic to 19th-century neoclassical. The centerpiece of the Marktplatz is a Dutch, wrought-iron water pump from 1602. For more information on the city, check with the tourist office (Am Markt; phone: 3841-2958), which is closed Sundays.

En Route from Wismar Head east on Route 105, a two-lane highway, toward the Hanseatic cities of Rostock and Stralsund; Rostock is about 36 miles (58 km) away. The road meanders through several Baltic coastline communities dotted with attractive little houses and shops and featuring convenient access to nearby beaches. The prettiest of these are Bad Doberan, Kröpelin, Neubukow, and Ribnitz-Damgarten.

In Bad Doberan, there is a huge red brick church that originally was the *Münster* (minster) of a Cistercian monastery. Built in 1368, its interior features an impressive high altar with a 45-foot crucifix. The town's tourist office (1 Goethestr.; phone: 38203-3001) is open daily. The *Molli,* a narrow-gauge steam train that has been running since 1886, takes passengers on a 10-mile (16-km) scenic ride from Bad Doberan to the Baltic resort villages of Heiligendamm and Kühlingsborn; it departs on the 40-minute journey several times daily from a little station on Goethestrasse near the tourist office. Heiligendamm is particularly appealing, with its 19th-century white cottages and villas, a neoclassical *Kurhaus* spa center, and a nice stretch of beach. A noteworthy landmark in Ribnitz-Damgarten, a provincial town about 15 miles (24 km) east of Rostock, is its *Rostocker Tor,* a medieval gate tower.

ROSTOCK Mecklenburg–West Pomerania's largest city and seaport, Rostock (pop. 250,000) has a medieval gate tower of its own, the steepled *Kröpeliner Tor.* This gate is the entry point to the inner core of the city, which began developing in the 13th century and flourished during the golden era of the Hanseatic League. The wide, bustling Lange Strasse in the inner city is a commercial and residential street that was laid out from 1953 to 1959 during postwar reconstruction; running parallel to it is Kröpeliner Strasse, a charming pedestrian zone. *Universität Rostock* was Northern Europe's first university (established in 1419); its neo-Renaissance main hall stands on Universitätsplatz. Neuer Markt, the market square, is lined with a row of gabled Gothic and Baroque buildings, but its highlight is the 13th-century *Rathaus* (City Hall; 22 Neuer Markt; phone: 381-23577), with seven pointed towers. A vaulted restaurant in the cellar of the *Rathaus* is noted for offering a wide variety of exotic teas, as well as good local fare. The *Marienkirche* (St. Mary's Church), on Am Ziegenmarkt, a tiny side street off Lange Strasse, is also well worth seeing. The interior features a Baroque 18th-century organ whose pipes reach clear to the lofty ceiling, and an immense astronomical clock that has gauged the time of day, month, year, and position of the planets since 1472. Rostock's tourist office (13-14 Schnickmannstr.; phone: 381-459-0860) is closed Sundays October through April.

In warm weather, take a side trip to Warnemünde, 9 miles (14 km) from Rostock on Route 103. This little fishing village offers a long stretch of beach and grassy dunes, as well as shops, outdoor cafés, villas, and cottages facing the Alter Strom waterway.

BEST EN ROUTE

Neptun This 350-room high-rise was once popular among GDR bigwigs. Recently renovated, it is now spacious, brightly lit, and comfortable; service is efficient and courteous. It boasts a prime location on the beach, as well as two dining rooms and a fitness center. 19 Seestr., Warnemünde (phone: 381-5460; 800-223-5652; fax: 381-54023). Expensive.

Warnow Rostock's largest hostelry, with 345 rooms, is smack dab in the city center. The well-appointed guestrooms feature mini-bars and balconies; other amenities include a restaurant serving regional specialties, conference facilities, and parking. 40 Lange Str., Rostock (phone: 381-4590; fax: 381-459-7800). Expensive.

Mond und Sterne This eatery is a standout among Rostock's many fish-and-steak restaurants. The food is well prepared and delicious, and the decor is traditional Hanse-style, with brass light fixtures and beams of rough-cut timber. Open daily. Reservations advised. No credit cards accepted. 85 Strandstr. (phone: 381-459-0344). Moderate.

Perle am Bodden Here is a thoroughly modern property with 14 rooms, an appealing restaurant, and a glassed-in pavilion. The location, in a lakefront village east of Rostock, is especially attractive. 14-15 Fritz-Reuter-Str., Ribnitz-Damgarten (phone: 3821-2148; fax: 3821-811846). Moderate.

En Route from Rostock From Rostock, continue west on Route 105 another 44 miles (71 km) to Stralsund.

STRALSUND Like Rostock, this town has a strong connection to the Hanseatic tradition. It also features a red brick *Marienkirche* (on Neuer Markt) and a North German Gothic *Rathaus* (on Alter Markt). But the Altstadt (Old City) here is completely hemmed in by bays, coves, and ponds, so its maritime past is more obvious than Rostock's. Also, more of its 18th- and 19th-century timber buildings have survived intact. Walking through Stralsund's winding, narrow streets gives a real sense of experiencing life as it was in the Middle Ages—and that impression is likely to be further enhanced once the public squares, long neglected by the GDR administration, are restored to their former glory. The tourist office (Alter Markt; phone: 3831-252251) has more information about the town; the office is closed Sundays.

Stralsund is also the jumping-off point for an excursion to Rügen, Germany's largest island. For many years, Rügen has been a popular destination for European vacationers who want to get away from it all. Here are fine, sandy beaches, dramatic chalk cliffs, villages of thatch-roofed houses, and windswept vistas; if some of them look familiar, it's probably because you've seen the romantic landscapes of Caspar David Friedrich, who painted here a century ago. *Note:* Nude sunbathing and skinny-dipping are prevalent on the beaches here, as they are on nearly every Baltic beach in Germany.

BEST EN ROUTE

Getreidebörse This vintage Stralsund establishment, which reopened recently after a complete refurbishment, combines a convenient central location with fine regional fare, including *Griebenroller* (a casserole of potatoes, eggs, and bacon) and fish soup. On the upper level is the *Artus-Hof,* an intimate, cheerful café. Open daily. Reservations unnecessary. No credit cards accepted. 8 Alter Markt, Stralsund (phone: 3831-251203). Moderate to inexpensive.

Norddeutscher Hof *Gemütlichkeit* (warm hospitality) and charm permeate this romantic little inn, ideally situated in the Altstadt. The 14 rooms and restaurant are attractively decorated in an old-fashioned style. 22 Neuer Markt, Stralsund (phone/fax: 3831-293161). Moderate to inexpensive.

Frankfurt to Heidelberg

If you drive the 59 miles (94 km) from Frankfurt am Main to Heidelberg on the autobahn, the trip will take about an hour, but you won't see much more than the backs and sides of huge high-speed trailer trucks. There's a lovely alternate route, however, that wriggles its way south along the Maintal (Main River Valley), through charming old river towns with half-timbered houses, historic churches and abbeys, romantic castles, gentle wooded hills, and fertile green valleys.

Without any side trips, the Main River Valley route from Frankfurt to Heidelberg covers about 107 miles (171 km); pleasant detours can add half again as much to that distance. The whole route easily can be driven in a single day, but it's far more pleasant to give yourself at least a day and a half.

The areas you'll be driving through are known as the Odenwald and the Spessart. Prehistoric peoples lived along the banks of the Main, but there was no real development until about AD 800, when many monasteries, like the one still standing in Seligenstadt, were established, and the monks began the region's agricultural development.

Although plans are vague and seem far in the future, the Main River is slated to become part of an overall Rhine-Danube international waterway system. At present, however, its banks are still relatively quiet and peaceful, even in Frankfurt and in the other highly populated industrial areas, and the area is not touristy in any way. Visitors to the Main Valley usually are vacationers from Frankfurt and other German cities who are not partial to discos or pizza parlors. The valley's small towns—such as Michelstadt, with its lovely old Marktplatz, or Wertheim, with its red sandstone castle—are unspoiled. And Heidelberg may well be the most beautiful city in Germany.

For maps, pamphlets, and information about the Frankfurt area, contact the tourist office in Wiesbaden, *Kurbetriebe der Landeshauptstadt Verkehrsbüro* (15 Rheinstr., Wiesbaden 65185; phone: 611-172-9780; fax: 611-172-9799); for the Heidelberg vicinity, contact *Verkehrsverein Heidelberg* (Pavillon am Hauptbahnhof, Heidelberg 69117; phone: 6221-10821; fax: 6221-167318); both are closed Sundays.

Prices along this route vary; they're significantly higher in the larger cities, so that you'll have to pay more for everything in Frankfurt and Heidelberg. Plan to spend $200 to $300 (more in Heidelberg) per night for a double room (with a private bath and TV set, unless otherwise indicated) in hotels we have classified as expensive; $100 to $190 in moderate hotels; and less than $90 in inexpensive places. Rates usually include breakfast. A dinner for two without wine will cost $100 to $190 in restaurants listed as expensive; $75 to $95 in moderate restaurants; and $25 to $65 in inexpensive places. Taxes and service charges are included, but you might want to add an extra tip to reward good service. All restaurants are open for lunch and dinner unless otherwise indicated. For each location, hotels and restaurants are listed alphabetically by price category.

FRANKFURT For a detailed report on the city and its hotels and restaurants, see *Frankfurt* in THE CITIES.

En Route from Frankfurt Take Route 43 out of Frankfurt toward Offenbach. You might want to stop in Offenbach (about 4 miles/7 km from Frankfurt) to see the *Deutsches Ledermuseum* (German Leather Museum; 86 Frankfurter Str.; phone: 69-813021), containing leather objects from all over the world. The museum is open daily; admission charge. Leave Offenbach via Route 43, heading for Hanau. In Kesselstadt, just before you reach Hanau, is the Baroque *Schloss Philippsruhe* (Philippsruhe Castle; on Rte. 43; phone: 6181-295510). This striking structure is nestled in the heart of the fairy-tale country that inspired the Brothers Grimm, who grew up in the area. *Schloss Philippsruhe* is closed December through March; admission charge. At Hanau (10 miles/16 km from Offenbach), you can visit the hometown of the celebrated storytelling brothers. The house they were born in is closed to the public, but there is a monument dedicated to them in the market square. An interesting museum of local jewelry called *Goldschmiederhaus* (Goldsmith's House; Altstädter Markt; phone: 6181-295430) is also in Hanau. It's closed Mondays; no admission charge.

From Hanau, continue another 6 miles (10 km) to the intersection of Routes 43 and 45 and then drive another 3 miles (2 km) on Routes 8 and E42 to Seligenstadt. Park before you reach the center of town (parking usually is not permitted in the centers of small villages in Germany).

SELIGENSTADT The principal attraction here is a magnificently maintained former Benedictine abbey founded in AD 825 by Einhard, the biographer of Charlemagne. However, the town itself is much older. It was a fortified castle on the *limes*—the wall built by the Romans through most of central Germany until they were driven from the country by the Alemanni in AD 260. Guided tours (in German only) of the abbey, which is located in the center of town, are conducted year-round every day except Mondays. Don't let the language barrier put you off; you'll understand more than you think you will.

Seligenstadt is a good place to see the various architectural styles and periods of German history. The abbey itself has undergone many remodelings in a thousand years, and with each remodeling, the building acquired elements of the style characteristic of the time.

From the abbey, walk toward the Main River. Then turn left and head for the ruins of the *Kaiserpfalz,* known also as the *Palatium* or the *Jagdsitz* (Hunting Lodge). The castle was built about 1235 for Holy Roman Emperor

Frederick II, who led a fascinating life that included no fewer than three excommunications.

Walk to the Marktplatz along the narrow Palatiumstrasse. All along the way and around the Marktplatz itself you will see some outstanding examples of the famous German *Fachwerkhäuser* (half-timbered houses).

BEST EN ROUTE

Klosterstuben Next to the abbey and the convent garden, this restaurant features excellent German cooking. It also serves a locally brewed beer (becoming increasingly rare in Germany as big breweries take over). Closed Sundays and Mondays. Reservations advised. No credit cards accepted. 7 Freihofpl., Seligenstadt (phone: 6182-3571). Moderate.

En Route from Seligenstadt Leave Seligenstadt via the same road you entered by (Route E42) and drive 4 miles (7 km) to Aschaffenburg.

ASCHAFFENBURG Chosen by the electors of Mainz as one of their residences, Aschaffenburg has beautiful parks, a large Renaissance castle, and an interesting church. *Schloss Johannisberg* (St. Johannisberg Castle; Am Schlosspl.; phone: 6021-22417), built in 1605–14 for the powerful Archbishops of Mainz, is most impressive; it is shaped like a hollow square. See the palace and walk through its gardens to the *Pompeianum,* a reproduction of the Castor and Pollux house at Pompeii, built for the capricious Ludwig I of Bavaria. The palace and gardens are closed Mondays; admission charge. Then walk along the Landingstrasse behind the palace to the *Stiftskirche,* a 10th-century church that is an interesting mixture of Baroque, Gothic, and Romanesque styles of architecture. The church's real attraction is its exceptional art: There is a Grünewald altarpiece and a Resurrection scene by Lucas Cranach the Elder (1520). While you're in Aschaffenburg, be sure to walk through *Schönbusch Park,* on the outskirts of town (follow the signs from Löherstrasse). This 18th-century green space is one of Germany's most charming, with pools, islands, and a country house built for the archbishops in 1780. The house is closed Mondays; admission charge.

BEST EN ROUTE

Post Not far from the *Schloss Johannisberg,* this 71-room hotel has a beautiful traditional decor and an ambience of friendliness and comfort. The restaurant offers good continental food with a broad range of choices; other amenities include a pool and a fitness center. 19 Goldbacherstr., Aschaffenburg (phone: 6021-21333; fax: 6021-13483). Expensive to moderate.

En Route from Aschaffenburg Leave Aschaffenburg via an unnumbered road that runs parallel to the Main River and Route 469 and continue 8 miles (13 km) to Miltenberg. (If you want to save a bit of time and don't mind traveling a less scenic road, Route 469 also leads to Miltenberg; the distance is about the same, but it's a faster highway.)

MILTENBERG Again, park your car in the first convenient parking lot; don't try to drive in or through the town center. (You won't need your car—the walk from one end of Miltenberg to the other takes about 15 minutes.)

The town showplace is its Marktplatz; it's triangular, relatively small, and surrounded by exceptional half-timbered houses. From the marketplace walk along the main street, the Hauptstrasse, which also is lined with fascinating houses.

Miltenberg was little more than a wide spot in the Roman wall until the 13th Legion was ousted by the Germanic tribes in AD 260. The *Gasthaus zum Riesen* is not as old as Miltenberg, but files in Mainz, Munich, and Würzburg prove that the inn was open and operating in the 12th century. A whole string of Holy Roman Emperors have lodged here, beginning with Frederick Barbarossa, who stayed in 1158 and 1168. During the Thirty Years War, the inn housed VIPs from both sides—depending on who was in control at the moment. It's still an ideal overnight stopping place (see *Best en Route*).

The *Städtisches Verkehrsamt* (Tourist Office) in the *Rathaus* (Town Hall; 69 Engelpl.; phone: 9371-400119; fax: 9371-67081) has an excellent walking guide to Miltenberg; the office is closed Sundays. Though in German only, it is so clearly arranged that you can walk in sequence from one spot of interest to the next with no trouble.

BEST EN ROUTE

Gasthaus zum Riesen In operation since the 12th century, this place with 14 guestrooms purports to be Germany's oldest hostelry (though *Zum Roten Bären* hotel in Freiburg makes the same claim). Based on authenticated guest lists, the owner and restorer, W. Jöst, has furnished a series of bedrooms after the period of some famous visitors—Queen Christina of Sweden, for example. All furnishings are genuine antiques. There is a restaurant. Open mid-March through mid-December. Reservations necessary—especially for the "name" rooms. 97 Hauptstr., Miltenberg (phone: 9371-2582; fax: 9371-67176). Moderate.

En Route from Miltenberg A worthwhile side trip is the 18-mile (29-km) jaunt to Wertheim along the same unnumbered road you took to Miltenberg. The road parallels the Main River all the way. If you want a break from driving, leave your car in Miltenberg and take the ferry to Wertheim. The boat leaves Miltenberg at 9:30 AM on Tuesdays, Thursdays, and Saturdays; the return trip leaves Wertheim at 6 PM.

WERTHEIM The Main and Tauber Rivers meet at Wertheim, and the town is dominated by a castle constructed of red sandstone, a building material characteristic of the Odenwald and Spessart areas. An English-language guidebook is available from the *Wertheim Fremdenverkehrsgesellschaft* (Wertheim Tourist Office) in the *Rathaus* (Town Hall; Am Spitzen Turm; phone: 9342-1066); the office is closed Sundays. The Marktplatz is worth seeing, with a Renaissance monument known as the *Engelsbrunnen* (Angel's Fountain) at one end. The *Stiftskirche* (Am Marktpl.) has a number of unusually beautiful, well-preserved tombstones and memorials from the 16th century. You'll have to climb to the top of a hill to see the old castle, but the view of Wertheim and the rivers is worth a little puffing. Don't miss the opportunity to dine at *Schweizer Stuben* (see *Best en Route*), one of Germany's best restaurants.

BEST EN ROUTE

Schweizer Stuben Follow the signs to this truly excellent restaurant (two Michelin stars), featuring the finest continental and German fare in comfortable surroundings. It's part of a hotel that has 16 beautifully appointed rooms and two other excellent dining rooms. Closed Mondays, Tuesdays, Thursday lunch, and the first three weeks of January. Reservations necessary. Major credit cards accepted. Also see *Best Restaurants* in DIVERSIONS. 11 Geiselbrunnweg, Wertheim (phone: 9342-3070). Expensive.

En Route from Wertheim Return to Miltenberg, then pick up Route 469 and continue 5 miles (8 km) to Amorbach.

AMORBACH You're sure to notice the red sandstone towers of the abbey church that dominates Amorbach. It was built between 1742 and 1747 on the site of an earlier Romanesque church. The interior of this now-Baroque abbey is worth seeing. Its chancel screen is one of the finest in Germany, and it has a justifiably well-known organ; concerts are held here during the high tourist season (April through October).

BEST EN ROUTE

Der Schafhof What was once a Benedictine monastery is now a romantic 14-room hotel. It has an excellent restaurant, noteworthy for its lamb dishes, as well as a lovely garden. 1 Schafhof, Otterbachtal, 2 miles (3 km) west of Amorbach (phone: 9373-8088; fax: 9373-4120). Expensive to moderate.

En Route from Amorbach Take Route 469 west. After about 3 miles (5 km), pick up Route 47 (the Nibelungenstrasse) and continue another 3 miles (5 km) to Michelstadt.

MICHELSTADT Here is the heart of Wagner country, where all the mythical action of his great operas was set. This is where the Nibelungen, evil guardians of a magic hoard of gold, are supposed to have done their hunting, and where, somewhat farther south, the great hero Siegfried went on the royal hunt during which Hagen killed him. Whether you are a true believer or not, the gently sloping countryside is beautiful.

Michelstadt has what may be the most enchanting Marktplatz in the Odenwald, with a 16th-century fountain, a charming *Rathaus* (Town Hall), and many remarkable half-timbered houses. Notice especially the unusual design of the two bay windows in the *Rathaus.*

En Route from Michelstadt At this point, you can go either to Worms (42 miles/67 km west along Route 47) or to Heidelberg (38 miles/61 km southwest on Route 37).

WORMS This city is so packed with history and interest that visitors will want to take time to see as much as possible. It was destroyed in 436 by Attila the Hun, and in 1521 it was the scene of the famous Imperial Diet that passed judgment on Martin Luther. Worms became a Protestant city in 1525 and, as a result, was subject to heavy reprisals during the Thirty Years War. It was almost totally destroyed by the French in 1689, deprived of its free city status when annexed by France in 1801, and was returned to German rule by the Congress of Vienna in 1815. History is written on its streets, its buildings, and on every corner.

The *Verkehrsverein* (Tourist Office; 14 Neumarkt; phone: 6241-25045) has a great deal of helpful material and information in English; it is closed Sundays. Look for it just opposite *Dom St. Petri* (St. Peter's Cathedral), which is one of Germany's finest examples of 13th-century Romanesque architecture. The high altar is by Balthasar Neumann, a famous 18th-century master of German Baroque architecture.

Worms is one of the oldest centers of Jewish culture in Germany and has the oldest synagogue in the country, founded in the 11th century. Services are no longer held here (the city's Jewish community is gone), but the synagogue can be visited daily. The ancient Jewish cemetery, just behind the Worms cathedral, was founded in the 11th century and also is worth a visit.

HEIDELBERG For a detailed report on the city and its hotels and restaurants, see *Heidelberg* in THE CITIES.

En Route from Heidelberg After visiting Heidelberg, you might choose to explore the scenic Neckartal (Neckar Valley) to the east, its gorge surrounded by high, thickly forested hills; see *The Neckar River Valley* in this section.

Westphalia

Though well liked by Germans and other Europeans, Westphalia, a dreamy area of castles, country inns, half-timbered houses, windmills, forests, hills, and mineral spas, has been little explored by Americans. (The proprietor of the noted *Schütte* hotel-restaurant in Oberkirchen claims that until last year, he had never had any American guests.) Perhaps Americans have shunned Westphalia because it contains part of the great industrial Ruhrtal (Ruhr Valley); in fact, Dortmund, Westphalia's principal city, is one of the major cities of the Ruhr. However, a good part of this area is picturesque, peaceful countryside—an excellent refuge for well-heeled Ruhr residents (as well as visitors from other parts of Germany) who want to relax in a rural retreat.

In the northern part of Germany, Westphalia extends from the Rhine to the Weser River. It's a region of small, hedged-in farms that form a checkerboard pattern across the landscape. Strict regional laws keep the villages small, the forests intact, and the air unpolluted here. The castle-hotels and wayside inns have turrets and half-timbered exteriors, with baronial interiors and open fireplaces; yet they also have indoor plumbing, central heating, and 20th-century mattresses. In Westphalia you'll see none of that rundown look found in Europe's more remote and poorer country areas. For maps and information about the region, contact the *Landesverkehrsverband Westfalen* (Westphalia Tourist Office; 3 Friedenspl., Dortmund 44135; phone: 231-527506 or 231-527507; fax: 231-524508); it's closed Sundays.

The name "Westphalia" first appears in connection with a section of the duchy of Saxony in the 10th century. In the later Middle Ages, its major towns of Münster, Paderborn, Bielefeld, and others were prosperous members of the Hanseatic League (an association of mercantile city-states). The Peace of Westphalia, which was signed in Münster in 1648 to end the Thirty Years War, gave Prussia a foothold in the area, which it maintained—except for the brief Napoleonic reign in 1808–13—until 1945.

Westphalia is noted for its hearty food, which is among the most distinctive in Germany. A traditional beer-hall nosh starts with an ice-cold *Steinhäger,* a gin-like schnapps drink from the town of Steinhagen near Bielefeld; when served, the drink is often poured from a stoneware bottle into one of the deep pewter spoons Westphalians use as shot glasses. Then comes a chaser of cool Westphalian beer from Dortmund, which is second only to Munich as a German brewing city. Finally, there's pumpernickel—also Westphalian in origin—with butter, and justly famous Westphalian ham, served on a wooden board. But you needn't feel your dining options are limited; this area has plenty of restaurants that offer good continental fare as well.

You can enjoy the culinary and visual riches of Westphalia by touring the area in a circular route that begins and ends in Dortmund. The round trip is about 405 miles (675 km), including side trips.

Visitors to Westphalia will delight in the many charming hotels and inns to be found in the smaller towns; prices here also tend to be lower than in the larger, more-frequented city areas. In an expensive hotel, a double room (with private bath and TV set, unless otherwise noted) will cost about $100 to $200 per night; in a moderate hotel, $60 to $90; and in an inexpensive place, less than $50. Breakfast is generally included in the room rate. Dinner for two without wine will cost $60 to $90 in expensive restaurants; $30 to $50 in moderate establishments; and under $25 in inexpensive places. Prices include taxes and service charges, but if you're happy with the service, leave a small additional amount. Restaurants are open for lunch and dinner, unless otherwise noted. For each location, hotels and restaurants are listed alphabetically by price category.

DORTMUND Like all the cities in the Ruhr, Dortmund was leveled in World War II and rebuilt along coldly modern lines that are rather devoid of character. It is not dirty, however; the whole Ruhr has strict air pollution laws. Have a look at the *Westfalenpark,* with its *Rosarium* (1,500 varieties of roses, half a million plants) and its TV tower topped by a revolving restaurant. Dortmund is best known as a beer-producing center; if you want to visit a brewery, contact the *Verband Dortmunder Bierbrauer* (3 Ostenhellweg; phone: 231-525532). The *Westfalenhalle* (200 Rheinlanddamm; phone: 231-230-4666) often hosts concerts of pop and rock music. There's also an elegant casino, *Spielbank Hohensyburg* (200 Hohensyburger Str.; phone: 231-77400 or 231-774-0210). Formal dress, though not mandatory, is strongly advised. You must be 18 or older to enter; bring your passport as proof of age and identity.

En Route from Dortmund Head east into Westphalia proper, toward the Sauerland, an unspoiled region of woods and lakes to the east and south. The autobahn gets you out there quickly. Take the Sauerland Line (A45) for 50 miles (80 km), following the signs to Siegen and Frankfurt. At Olpe, take Route 55 north another 12 miles (20 km) to Lennestadt.

At this point you may wish to take a short side trip. Turn onto the B236 and continue another 3 miles (5 km) to Attendorn, a place of lakes, a huge stalactite cave, and remarkable rock formations. The cave, called *Attahöhle* (to get there, follow the signs to Tropfsteinhöhle), is open daily; admission charge. Return to Lennestadt and take the scenic Route B36 another 34 miles (55 km) to Winterberg, one of the biggest German winter sports areas outside the Alps, via the beautiful little village of Oberkirchen. At Winterberg, drive north on Route B480 19 miles (30 km) to Olsberg.

BEST EN ROUTE

Burghotel Schnellenberg This 13th-century castle in the middle of the woods has a commanding view of Attendorn. Many of the 42 rooms are in the towers. You can dine in the rustic *Rittersaal Salon,* where game and fish dishes are especially recommended. Recreational opportunities here include tennis, hiking, and fishing in several nearby lakes. Open mid-January through *Christmas.* Located about 2 miles (3 km) east of Attendorn (phone: 2722-6940; fax: 2722-6946). Expensive.

Gasthof Schütte Run by the Schütte family since 1774, this half-timbered former coach house is in the middle of Oberkirchen, a Sauerland village of 800 inhabitants. The hotel offers 59 well-appointed rooms, indoor and outdoor pools, horseback riding, and a sauna. An 18-hole golf course is in nearby Schmallenberg. The restaurant's Westphalian food specialties include ham and *Pfefferpotthast,* a very spicy stew. The game dishes are excellent: Try venison with red wine. The typically Westphalian interior is rustic, with an open fireplace. 2 Eggeweg, Schmallenberg-Oberkirchen (phone: 2975-820; fax: 2975-82522). Expensive to moderate.

OLSBERG *Schloss Gevelinghausen* (Gevelinghausen Palace; phone: 2962-2834) is the starting point for Gypsy wagon tours of the Sauerland on "two horse-power," which are offered May through October. The wagons come complete with sleeping facilities for two to six people, blankets, linen, a stove, dishes, pots and pans, gas lanterns, and a gas heater. During the trip, which lasts up to eight days, you follow a prescribed route and stop each night at a farm where they stable the horses.

En Route from Olsberg Continue on Route B480 about 7 miles (11 km) to Brilon (nicknamed "the most forested town in Westphalia"), drive 25 miles (41 km) more to Paderborn, then take Routes B1 and B239 for another 22 miles (35 km) to Detmold.

DETMOLD You now are in the middle of the Teutoburger Wald (Teutoburg Forest), another popular Westphalian district, which went down in German history as the place where the Romans were stopped in their northward march, in an epic battle in AD 9. Germanic tribesmen dealt them a stunning defeat, and the Roman Empire never extended any farther north in continental Europe. A towering, 175-foot statue to the tribal chief Hermann, who led the battle, commands a hill just 4 miles (6 km) outside the city at the village of Heiligenkirchen. Not to be missed is *Adlerwarte,* a sanctuary for birds of prey at nearby Berlebeck (phone: 5231-47171). The eagles, vultures, and other big birds fly freely at 11 AM and 2:30 PM daily. The sanctuary is open daily; admission charge. Other attractions at Detmold include *Fürstliches Residenzschloss* (Princely Castle; phone: 5231-22507), whose architecture shows Baroque and Renaissance influences (open daily; admission charge); the *Lippisches Landsmuseum* (4 Ameide; phone: 5231-25231), a museum of local history (closed Mondays; admission charge); and the *Westfälisches Freilichtmuseum* (Westphalia Open-Air Museum; phone: 5231-7060), the largest museum of its kind in Germany, displaying historical buildings and typically Westphalian farmhouses (closed Mondays and November through March; admission charge).

En Route from Detmold Drive 17 miles (28 km) on Routes B239 and B66 to Bielefeld.

BIELEFELD One of Westphalia's larger cities, Bielefeld is starkly modern for the most part, but some fine patrician houses remain and there's also *Schloss Sparrenburg* (Sparrenburg Castle; 1 Am Sparrenberg; no phone), whose tower affords a good view of the Teutoburg Forest. Both castle and tower are closed November through March; admission charge.

En Route from Bielefeld From here, take Route B61 for 27 miles (43 km) to Minden via Herford. On the way, the road passes the Porta Westfalica, where the Weser River suddenly emerges spectacularly out of the mountains from between two hills, and flows on to the broad North German plain. One of the hills is topped with a monument to Kaiser Wilhelm. Along the way, you might want to stop in Bad Oeynhausen to visit its *Motor-Museum* (25 Weserstr.; phone: 5731-9960); its collection of vintage motorbikes is the largest in Europe. The museum is open daily; admission charge.

MINDEN Minden is a good place to board one of the old paddle boats that ply the Weser. Also be sure to see the outstanding Romanesque cathedral with its 11th-century crucifix and a 1480 painting of the Crucifixion by a Westphalian master. There's a bridge here where the Mittelland Kanal (Mittelland Canal) passes over the Weser. Also interesting is the Schachtschleuse (Great Lock), just north of town; 279 by 33 feet long, it links the Mittelland Canal with the Weser.

BEST EN ROUTE

Schloss Petershagen In Petershagen, 6 miles (9 km) north of Minden, a moated castle (built in 1306) on the Weser River houses a small hotel (12 rooms) and an elegant restaurant featuring international fare. The building is in an appealing location surrounded by meadows and parks. It's not the place for Westphalian specialties, although it does feature fish from the Weser in some dishes, such as smoked eel and trout soup. This palace also offers a "knightly banquet" for groups only, with waiters dressed in medieval costumes, live music of the period, and menus offering old recipes. There's a bar in the cellar, and the surrounding park has tennis courts and a heated swimming pool. 5 Schloss Str., Petershagen (phone: 5707-346; fax: 5707-2373). Expensive to moderate.

En Route from Minden Proceed along Route B65 another 12 miles (20 km) to Lübbecke. Along the route in this area, you'll see an abundance of old windmills dotting the landscape. From Lübbecke, take Route B239 south to Löhne, a distance of about 7 miles (12 km), then drive west on the autobahn 29 miles (46 km) to Osnabrück. From here, continue south on Routes B51 and B475 another 24 miles (39 km) to Warendorf.

WARENDORF This is the horse capital of Germany, site of a state-operated stud farm, an important riding school, and the headquarters of the *Deutsches Olympia-Komitee für Reiterei* (German Olympic Equestrian Committee). There are plenty of rental horses here and lots of riding paths; it is a good place to book a vacation in the saddle. Contact the local tourist office for more information on riding (1 Markt; phone: 2581-54222); it is closed Sundays. There are big parades here on the last Saturday in September and the first Saturday in October, when horses are led by saddle masters in elegant uniforms.

BEST EN ROUTE

Im Engel Established in 1557, the hotel has been in the hands of the Leve family, the present proprietors, since 1692. It is right in the center of the Altstadt (Old City) and has the usual rustic interior, with oak furniture, carved beams, pewter, old pictures, and an open fireplace. The restaurant serves continental dishes featuring lamb and duck, as well as refined versions of such Westphalian specialties as *Pfefferpotthast* (a spicy beef stew). Facilities include a pool, sauna, and solarium. Closed three weeks in summer. 35-37 Brünebrede, Warendorf (phone: 2581-93020). Expensive to moderate.

En Route from Warendorf Take Routes B64 and B51 west 16 miles (25 km) to Münster.

MÜNSTER Westphalia's historic capital, which evolved from a humble monastery near the small settlement of Mimigernaford in the 8th century, today is the site of *Westfälische Wilhelms-Universität Münster* (Westphalian University of Munster), one of Germany's largest universities. Students make up one-fifth of the city's total population of 270,000. In 1648, the Treaty of Westphalia was signed here, ending the Thirty Years War. The *Friedenssaal* (Hall of Peace), set in the historic *Rathaus* (Town Hall; Prinzipalmarkt; phone: 251-492-2724), has various exhibits about the treaty and the war. The *Friedenssaal* is open daily; admission charge. The *Rathaus* also is home to the tourist office (phone: 251-510180; open daily) and is the starting point for a guided 90-minute tour of the city (in English) given every Saturday May through October. The Prinzipalmarkt, the oldest and busiest street in town, is lined with Renaissance-era houses with elegant arcades and façades.

Also on Prinzipalmarkt is the Gothic *Sankt Lamberti* (Church of St. Lambert), built between 1375 and 1450. Hanging from the steeple are several steel cages, which have a gruesome connection to a bit of local history. In the year 1534, a fanatically religious, quasi-socialist group called the *Wiedertäufer* (Anabaptists), led by a Dutchman named Jan van Leiden, took over Münster and briefly attempted a national revolution. Van Leiden proclaimed himself king and established a reign of terror; among his edicts were compulsory rebaptizing of adults and community ownership of all property. Anyone who defied or criticized him or the movement was executed. When the government recaptured the town in 1535, bringing the "empire" to a bloody end, van Leiden and two other leaders of the *Wiedertäufer* were tortured and killed, and their mutilated corpses were displayed for several weeks in the cages you see today.

On nearby Bogenstrasse is the *Kieperkerl,* a statue of a porter in traditional medieval garb carrying a *Kiepe* (wicker basket) on his back. This entire area is picturesque and lively, chockablock with sidewalk cafés and restaurants where university students come to socialize. Another popular attraction in Münster is the *Schloss,* a Baroque castle on the eastern outskirts of the city. Inside the building is a small café with a pretty garden terrace that's perfect for outdoor dining in good weather. The castle is surrounded by the *Schlossgarten,* a park and botanical gardens. The castle's interior is closed to the public; the park and gardens are open daily; no admission charge.

The historic city center is surrounded by the Promenade, a tree-lined, 3-mile trail ideal for walking and bicycling. Bikes can be rented from *Hansen* (7 Hörsterstr.; phone: 251-44998; closed Sundays) or at the main railway station (open daily). The trail follows the outline of the former city walls, passing a park with sculptures by such great modern artists as Henry Moore and Donald Judd, the *Schlossgarten,* and a lake. On the far side of the water are two other attractions: *Allwetter-Zoo,* a small zoo (315 Sentruper Str.; phone: 251-89040); and the *Mühlenhof* (223 Sentruper Str.; phone: 251-82074), an open-air museum devoted to history and architecture, which features a 17th-century windmill. Both are open daily and charge admission.

St. Paulus Dom (St. Paul's Cathedral), a low-lying Romanesque building on Domplatz, is typically Westphalian, with its astronomic clock in the ambulatory and a glockenspiel that plays daily at noon. The Domplatz is liveliest on Wednesday and Saturday mornings, when an open-air market is held in front of the church. During the *Christmas* season, Münster holds a special *Weihnachtsmarkt* (Christmas Market) here and at several other locations around the city center.

The lush, green plains surrounding Münster are known for their moated medieval castles and fortified houses where local nobles once lived (unfortunately, most of these are closed to the public). A particularly interesting sight near Lüdinghausen, 19 miles (30 km) from the city via the A43 and B235, is the 13th-century *Schloss Vischering* (Vischering Castle; phone: 2591-3621). Set on its own island, the castle features an attractive interior, a historical museum, and a prison beneath. It is open daily; admission charge. Two other castles in the area are worth a quick visit. *Hülshoff* (near Havixbeck, 3 miles/5 km west of the city; phone: 2534-1052) has a museum commemorating poet Annette von Droste-Hülshoff, who was born here in 1797. It is closed in January and February; admission charge. The stately

Nordkirchen (about 8 miles/13 km from Münster) is now owned by the university. Its nickname, "The Westfalian Versailles," somewhat overstates the case, but it is an impressive 18th-century building and the largest palace in Westphalia. *Nordkirchen* itself is closed weekdays, but the lovely, landscaped grounds are always open; no admission charge. The region also can be conveniently explored by bicycle, as there are numerous marked trails throughout.

BEST EN ROUTE

Romantik-Hotel Hof zur Linde A half-timbered farmhouse 5 miles (8 km) from downtown in the village of Handorf, this 48-room hostelry has a tranquil location and an excellent restaurant. 1 Handorfer Werseufer, Münster (phone: 251-32750; fax: 251-328209). Expensive.

Schloss Wilkinghege This 14th-century castle surrounded by a moat was converted to an elegant hotel in 1955. Located 4 miles (6 km) from Münster, it offers 33 comfortable, well-appointed rooms and suites overlooking a golf course. There's also a good restaurant, and tennis courts are nearby. 374 Steinfurter Str., Münster (phone: 251-213045; fax: 251-212898). Expensive.

Waldhotel Krautkrämer About 4 miles (6 km) from the center of town, this modern 70-room hotel is on its own lake. It provides a rare combination of comfort, hospitality, sublime surroundings, and one of Germany's best restaurants. Paul McCartney, José Carreras, and Leonard Bernstein are only a few of the celebrated guests who have signed the large book in the lobby. 173 Am Hiltruper See, Münster (phone: 2501-8050; fax: 2501-805104). Expensive.

Kleines Restaurant im Oer'schen Hof This dining spot combines Southern hospitality (owner Ann Shook Bradford hails from Alabama) and refined French cuisine—an unusual mix anywhere, let alone in Germany. The menu offers classic French dishes using local game, meat, and produce in a stylish but relatively informal atmosphere. There's also a short but excellent wine list. Closed Sundays. Reservations advised. No credit cards accepted. 42 Königstr., Münster (phone: 251-42061). Expensive to moderate.

Uberwasserhof Here are 62 simply furnished guestrooms (but featuring all the usual amenities) ideally located in the center of Münster's lively university quarter. There's also a restaurant. 3 Uberwasserstr., Münster (phone: 251-41770; fax: 251-417-7100). Moderate.

Gasthof Stuhlmacher This restaurant set in a 15th-century house near the *Rathaus* has typical Westphalian decor and cooking, with 11 famous beers on tap. The interior is elaborately carved in wood and has stained glass windows, leather seats, and old pictures. Specialties include homemade *Sülze* (pickled meat in aspic) and Westphalian ham. Open daily. Reservations advised. Major credit cards accepted. 6 Prinzipalmarkt, Münster (phone: 251-44877). Moderate.

Drübbelken Hearty local fare is the specialty of this eatery set in a picturesque half-timbered building. Diners can enjoy grilled meat, pancakes, fried potatoes, omelettes, or seafood; an open fireplace gives the dining room an appealing glow of warmth. Open daily. Reservations advised on weekends. No credit cards accepted. 14 Buddenstr., Münster (phone: 251-42115). Moderate to inexpensive.

Pinkus Müller At this 19th-century student hangout, tourists, professors, and students sit side by side at long wooden tables on which every inch of surface has been carved with the initials of generations. Each regular customer has his own mug with his name on it, which hangs from a peg on the wall. The decor is German "schmaltz," with stained glass windows, overhead beams with painted mottoes in Low German, an open fireplace, and even a cannon. (Don't be afraid to ask for help in interpreting the menu—it's in Low German, which even natives have trouble understanding.) Several beers are on tap; if you're feeling adventurous, try *Altbierbowle,* a sweet cocktail made with beer and fresh fruit. You may want to begin with a schnapps served from a deep spoon. Full meals can be had, but the fare is mostly snacks that go well with beer, such as *Töttchen,* a small dish of veal and mustard, or *Potthast,* a Westphalian stew of smoked meat and sausages. Closed Sundays. Reservations advised. No credit cards accepted. 4-10 Kreuzstr., Münster (phone: 251-45151). Moderate to inexpensive.

En Route from Münster The most direct route from Münster to Bochum is to drive 43 miles (70 km) on the A43 autobahn. But the longer route is far more scenic, and there are a few noteworthy attractions along the way. Continue along Route B51 16 miles (25 km) to Dülmen; the estate of the Duke of Croy on the west side of town is the only wild horse sanctuary (with 200 horses) in Europe. The local event of the year is the annual roundup on the last Saturday in May. The sanctuary (phone: 2594-4045) is open weekends March through October; admission charge. From Dülmen, continue on Route B51 20 miles (33 km) to Recklinghausen and visit the *Ikonen-Museum* (Icon Museum; 2 Kirchpl.; phone: 2361-587396), where more than 600 icons are exhibited thematically. The museum is closed Mondays; admission charge. In May and June, Recklinghausen is the site of the annual *Ruhr Festival* of music, theater, opera, and art exhibitions. From Recklinghausen, take the autobahn (Rte. A43) about 9 miles (15 km) south to Bochum.

BOCHUM This is the site of another unique museum, the *Bergbaumuseum* (Museum of Mining; 28 Am Bergbaumuseum; phone: 234-51881). The big attraction is an actual coal mine below the building, with nearly 2 miles of tunnels you can explore. It is closed Mondays; admission charge. The city also boasts *Planetarium Bochum* (67 Castroper Str.; phone: 234-910369), Germany's best-known public observatory and planetarium, which is only accessible by guided tours (in German only) given at 2 PM Tuesdays and Thursdays,

7:30 PM Wednesdays and Fridays, and 1:30, 3, and 4:30 PM on weekends. There's an admission charge. Bochum has a wealth of theatrical and musical venues; plays are presented at the *Schauspielhaus* (15 Königsallee; phone: 234-33330), and the *Zeche* (50 Prinz-Regent-Str.; phone: 234-72003) features pop and rock concerts. The Andrew Lloyd Webber musical *Starlight Express* is performed nightly at the *Starlight Express Halle* (Stadionring; phone: 234-777666).

En Route from Bochum From here, take the autobahn (Rte. A40) about 9 miles (15 km) west to Essen.

ESSEN This major metropolis of the Ruhr Valley is not the gritty industrial city a visitor might expect. The *Münster* (cathedral) here is one of Germany's oldest churches, dating back to the 9th century; its interior has some notable stained glass of a later date and a treasury of medieval artifacts (the treasury is closed Mondays; admission charge). The *Folkwang Museum* (41 Goethestr.) houses a collection of artworks ranging from Impressionist paintings to avant-garde sculpture. It is closed Mondays; admission charge. On the city's southern outskirts is the *Villa Hügel,* the baronial former residence of the Krupp steel and arms dynasty. Resembling an elegant railroad station more than a home, it offers a somewhat grim glimpse of how the uppermost classes once lived. The villa is closed Mondays; admission charge (also see *Churches, Castles, and Palaces* in DIVERSIONS). Another must-see is the *Alte Synagoge* (Old Synagogue; 29 Steeler Str.; phone: 201-884643), a magnificent domed structure housing an exhibition about the lives of Jews in Germany before and during the Holocaust. It is closed Mondays; no admission charge.

BEST EN ROUTE

Schloss Hugenpoet In the village of Kettwig, off Route A52 (the autobahn) just south of Essen, this hotel and its restaurant are among the most charming in Germany. Its "poetic" name means "Toad Pool" in the Low German dialect. There have been castles on this site since AD 778, but the present building dates back only to the mid-17th century. The residence of a succession of noble families, it was converted into a luxurious hotel in 1955, with 18 individually decorated rooms and a suite. The property is surrounded by a moat, with parking in the courtyard, which is reached by crossing a bridge and going through a gatehouse. The main dining room is in a glassed-in terrace overlooking the water and formal gardens, and other amenities include a tennis court and a private park. 51 August-Thyssen-Str., Kettwig (phone: 2054-12040; fax: 2054-120450). Expensive.

En Route from Essen To return to Dortmund, continue east on the A40 another 22 miles (35 km).

The Rhineland

Long before the autobahn and the jetport, and before the rail lines stitched the continent into a whole, the Rhine River was Europe's main street and prime commercial thoroughfare. The river was also a fertile ground for the artistic spirit, inspiring some of Germany's greatest writers (Goethe and Heinrich Heine) and musicians (Wagner set age-old Rhine myths to music in his epic *Ring* cycle), as well as painters both from Germany and the rest of Europe (including J. M. W. Turner, who captured riverside settings on canvas). Karl Baedeker, father of the modern travel guide, established himself in Koblenz to research and write his first book, a guide to the Rhine, published in 1834. And by the time Mark Twain arrived here on his second European visit in 1878 (an experience he would recount in *A Tramp Abroad*), this river ranked among Europe's most popular tourist destinations.

Today the Rhine is still a busy and important shipping route, linking dozens of inland ports such as Ludwigshafen and Duisburg to the North Sea and the oceans beyond. The majestic river remains a major tourist attraction as well—part playground, part historical monument, and part natural wonder.

Fed by melting Alpine snows in Switzerland and sharing frontage with France and the Netherlands, the Rhine is 820 miles long. But the section that is the source of the river's romantic image and lore is the stretch that flows (northward) through Germany. By common consensus, "the Rhineland" encompasses only the 50-mile Rhine gorge between Mainz and Koblenz. It is this section of the river—with its castles, vineyards, steep banks, dangerous whirlpools, and tales of heroes, Rhine maidens, and Lorelei—that most captures the imagination.

But while the Rhine's legends and magnificent scenery have their attractions, one cannot forget that the Rhineland is also wine land. By most accounts, Germany's best wine district is the Rheingau, extending roughly from Wiesbaden to the mouth of the Lahn River near Kamp, only a few dozen miles downstream. Along this short stretch, a southern exposure ripens noble riesling grapes to perfection. For the confirmed wine connoisseur, a trip down the Rhine gorge is something of a pilgrimage. For the neophyte sipper, a few well-chosen stopovers here will provide a succinct introduction to the white wines many experts claim are the best in the world. The sparkling wines produced in this region are also worth sampling. For information about German wine, write to the *German Wine Information Bureau* (79 Madison Ave., New York, NY 10016; phone: 212-213-0909). See also *Visitable Vineyards* in DIVERSIONS.

Perhaps it's the wine that gives the people in this region their easygoing and fun-loving nature. Whatever its source, the relaxed and joyous outlook on life found here is particularly evident among hoteliers and restaurateurs: Visitors often find that Rhinelanders cultivate their guests as attentively as they do their vines. The central tourist office for the region has two branches: *Landesverkehrsverband Rheinland* (69 Rheinallee, Bonn 53173; phone: 228-362921) and *Fremdenverkehrsverband Rheinland-Pfalz* (103-105 Löhrstr., Koblenz 56068; phone: 261-31079); both are closed Sundays.

The route presented here follows the river north from Mainz through the Rhineland and on to Düsseldorf, passing the cities of Bonn and Cologne (Köln) along the way. The entire trip covers about 143 miles (229 km) one way, but you'll want to spend at least two or three days in this glorious region. As there are myriad ways to travel this much-trafficked route, the destination points described are accessible by car, by rail, or by excursion boat. If you are traveling by car, you will see from maps that this stretch of river is flanked by several major roads. The auto traveler can easily cross the Rhine at one of several bridges at Koblenz and make a round trip by returning along Route 42 on the east bank. Rail lines also parallel the river on both sides (although the west bank affords the best scenery and the most interesting stops). In addition, many *Köln-Düsseldorfer (K-D)* or *Bingen-Rüdesheimer* river steamers ply this route. For information about boat trips, contact *K-D Schiffsagentur* (15 Frankenwerft, Köln; phone: 221-20880; or Am Rathaus, Mainz; phone: 6131-224511) or *Bingen-Rüdesheimer* (10 Rheinkai, Bingen; phone: 6721-14140). Multilingual bus tours also are available; for these, contact the *Deutsche Zentrale für Tourismus* (German National Tourist Office; 69 Beethovenstr., Frankfurt am Main 60325; phone: 69-75720; closed Sundays); or stop at one of the city tourist offices—often labeled *Verkehrsamt* or *Verkehrsverein*—along the Rhine route. They also provide maps and tourist information.

Travelers also may opt to combine several modes of transportation along this route. The bearer of a Eurailpass, for example, can make as many stops as desired along the way to, say, Koblenz, and then use the pass at no extra charge on one of the river steamers for a pleasant return trip. And at several points car ferries, called *Autofähre,* will provide transportation across the river for a nominal fee.

The Rhineland has been prime tourist country for over a century. Good hotels abound (Rüdesheim and the surrounding area alone have over 60), though in the wine villages the best were built in an age when guests arrived with servants and steamer trunks. Today they are like faded aristocrats and seem somewhat overpriced by American standards. Hotel restaurants can be excellent, however, and a continental breakfast—often augmented by eggs or sausage—invariably is included in the overnight price. Good double rooms may be found all along the river at prices ranging from $30 to $50 and up—though private bathrooms are not always available, so make sure you get what you want before booking. Our advice is to arrive early and head for the city tourist office, whose multilingual personnel can help you find a room. In the Rhenish cities, the top hotels meet the highest international standards and command prices to match; here, English is the second language. Below, we list just a few of the top hotels, but modest *Gasthäuser* and pensions are plentiful everywhere, and there also are many campgrounds along the river on both sides.

We have classified hotels that charge more than $100 per night for a double room (with private bath and TV set, unless otherwise indicated) as very expensive; $75 to $95, expensive; $60 to $75, moderate; and less than $60, inexpensive. A dinner for two without wine, but including tax and tip, will cost $70 to $120 in an expensive restaurant; $40 to $65 in a moderate place; and $20 to $35 in an inexpensive spot. Although the tip is included in the bill, you should leave a small additional amount to reward good service. Restaurants are open for lunch and dinner, unless otherwise indicated. For each location, hotels and restaurants are listed alphabetically by price category.

MAINZ This 2,000-year-old city founded by the Romans is most notable for its favorite son, Johannes Gutenberg, who invented movable type here in 1440. In the *Museum Gutenberg* (5 Liebfrauenpl.; phone: 6131-122640) you can see an original Gutenberg Bible and a replica of the famed printer's press, as well as an exhibition on the history of printing through the centuries. The museum is closed Mondays; no admission charge (also see *Memorable Monuments and Museums* in DIVERSIONS). Mainz is the scene of a boisterous *Karneval,* climaxing in the *Rosenmontag* (Rose Monday) parade on the last Monday before *Aschermittwoch* (Ash Wednesday). *Mainzer Dom* (Mainz Cathedral), though not architecturally impressive, is worth visiting for its art treasures, particularly the medieval sculpture by the Master of Naumburg in its *Bischöfliches Dom- und Diözesanmuseum* (Cathedral and Diocesan Museum; 3 Domstr.; phone: 6131-253344). The museum is closed Sundays; no admission charge.

En Route from Mainz Take Route B455 to Wiesbaden, where the road intersects with Autobahn A66. Drive to the western end of A66, where it becomes Route B42, and continue to Rüdesheim (a total distance of 22 miles/35 km).

RÜDESHEIM It's downright touristy—and packed with visitors in the summer and fall. Head straight for the Drosselgasse, a narrow, cobblestone alley lined with restaurants, wine taverns, and souvenir shops. Pick a pub where the oompah band isn't too loud, order yourself a *Römer* (a wine goblet with a bottle-green pedestal) of the local product, and get a taste of what the Rhineland is all about. This small city boasts rousing wine festivals in May and August and also has one of Germany's best wine museums, in *Schloss Brömser* (Brömser Castle; phone: 6722-2348), along Route 42 at the west end of town. Here you can browse through 28 display rooms containing wine presses and various viticultural artifacts showing the 6,000-year history of wine making. A free brochure is available upon request. The castle is closed December through February; admission charge. If you stop here, carry a jacket or sweater with you, for the cellar-like rooms are cool even in summer. To find a room or to collect a handful of brochures describing the sights ahead, contact Rüdesheim's city tourist office (16 Rheinstr.; phone: 6722-2962), where English-speaking personnel will answer all your questions; the office is closed Sundays. Another Rüdesheimer attraction is the curious *Siegfrieds Mechanisches Musikkabinett* (Siegfried's Mechanical Music Cabinet; 29 Oberstr; phone: 6722-49217), a collection of self-playing musical contraptions of the past, housed just off Drosselgasse. It is closed December through February; admission charge.

Rüdesheim is a good place to catch a *K-D* river steamer. The trip to St. Goarshausen and back makes a nice afternoon jaunt, allowing plenty of time for wine sipping and a leisurely meal in the ship's surprisingly good restaurant.

BEST EN ROUTE

Kronenschlösschen Nestled in the quiet village of Hattenheim, about 6 miles (9 km) east of Rüdesheim, this hostelry offers a tranquil place to unwind after a day's sightseeing. The 18 rooms and suites are decorated in a luxuriously romantic style. Facilities include a good restaurant and a bar with a garden terrace. Rheinallee, Hattenheim (phone: 6723-640; fax: 6723-7663). Expensive.

Waldhotel Jagdschloss Niederwald Here's a true *Schloss* hotel high on the Rhine hills, 3 miles (5 km) northwest of Rüdesheim. The restaurant features wine tastings and game in season—as well it should, for this was part of the former hunting lodge of the Archbishop of Mainz. There is also a large swimming pool, four tennis courts, and a sauna. Open spring through fall. Auf dem Niederwald (phone: 6722-1004; fax: 6722-47970). Expensive to moderate.

En Route from Rüdesheim Before crossing to Bingen and the more scenic left bank of the river, you might want to take a 9-mile (14-km) side trip north on Route 42 to Assmannshausen by way of Niederwald Hügel (Niederwald Hill). Just north of Rüdesheim, you'll pass the grim-visaged Amazon that is the *Niederwalddenkmal* (Germania Monument), built on Niederwald Hill in the 1870s to commemorate the unification of Germany. You also can get to the hill from Rüdesheim by bus or by a funicular (mid-April through November only), which transports passengers from the center of the village up the steep, vine-bearing slopes of the hill for spectacular views and picture taking.

Assmannshausen is an oddity because it produces only red wine (called "spätburgunder"), which comes from the burgundy-type (pinot noir) grape;

however, only a local vintner with an exaggerated view of his own product would rank Assmannshausen red anywhere near the noble white rieslings from the surrounding area.

There are short daily boat excursions from Rüdesheim to Assmannshausen that stop at an island in the middle of the river. The island is the site of the *Mäuseturm* (Mouse Tower), built centuries ago by the wicked Archbishop of Mainz as a stronghold for extracting tolls from passing ships. According to legend, when the nasty archbishop ordered his henchmen to wipe out a band of beggars who came pleading for handouts, an army of mice rose up to avenge the slain beggars, chased the archbishop into the tower, and gobbled him up alive. One can readily see how the Brothers Grimm found plenty of fairy-tale material in Germany!

From Rüdesheim, take the car ferry to Bingen, picking up Route 9 on the other side.

BEST EN ROUTE

Krone Overlooking the Rhine in Assmannshausen, this lovely 400-year-old inn has a museum in the second-floor lounge, with letters and manuscripts by famous people who have stayed here. The spacious bedrooms have traditional furniture (our favorites are No. 71 and No. 77) and the public rooms are oak-paneled and full of antiques. The food in the restaurant is outstanding; try the turtle soup, fresh salmon, or eel. Breakfast is not included in the room rate. Open spring through fall. 10 Rheinuferstr., Assmannshausen (phone: 6722-4030; fax: 6722-3049). Expensive.

BINGEN In itself, this little town of 24,000 people is not especially interesting. But in common with nearby villages, it shares the typically relaxed Rhineland ambience. After a fine meal with wine, there's no better place in Germany for an evening stroll than through Bingen's narrow brick and cobblestone streets or along the riverfront of this most delightful Rhineside town.

BEST EN ROUTE

Römerhof Across the narrow Nahe River, in the suburb of Bingerbrück, is this charming, tranquil hotel with 25 guestrooms. The view is bewitching, and the site historic. Among the features are a garden and a lovely Rhenish wine tavern. The restaurant is closed Saturdays. Open spring through fall. 10 am Rupertsberg, Bingerbrück (phone: 6721-32248). Moderate.

En Route from Bingen This stretch of road is justly celebrated for its dramatic scenery, romantic castles, and legendary landmarks. There are more castles in the area than one could comfortably see in a week, so don't feel bad about passing up most of them. The easiest and most direct route, which also offers some pleasant views along the way, is to stay on the B9 the entire 40 miles (65 km) between Bingen and Koblenz. (Another option, if you're an adventurous driver, is to take the Rheingoldstrasse, a narrow steep road that winds up into the vine-laden hills and affords truly spectacular vistas. However, bear in mind that this route actually incorporates several different roads and is not well-signposted, so it is very easy to get lost.) Just north of Bingen, several castles on the hills to the left invite you to do a little historical poking around. Especially worthy is *Burg Reichenstein,* set in a valley. It's useful to know the difference between the German words *Burg* and *Schloss,* both translated as "castle" by most dictionaries. A *Burg* is a fortified medieval structure, today often in ruins. Its military aspect is obvious. A *Schloss,* on the other hand, is more of a palace and is usually lavishly decorated and furnished. Many of these historical buildings, such as *Burg Reichenstein,* now offer guest accommodations (see *Best en Route*).

On the right, about 15 miles (24 km) from Bingen, are the Rhine gorge's two most distinctive landmarks—one might even say trademarks. *Die Pfalz* (The Palatinate) is a squat, dome-roofed, whitewashed medieval toll station in the middle of the current between Bacharach and Oberwesel. In the romantic past, *Die Pfalz* had chains stretched across the river to stop passing ships, and cannons were leveled at stubborn river captains. This fortified structure did a brisk business until an international agreement in 1868 eliminated all such extortion on the Rhine. Try to get a photo of *Die Pfalz* when an especially colorful river barge is passing in the foreground or background. Seven miles (11 km) downstream from *Die Pfalz,* on the east side of the river, is the legend-haunted Lorelei, a sheer outcropping of rock forever immortalized by the poem of Heinrich Heine. According to the sagas, a blonde maiden—a Germanic version of the sirens in Greek mythology—lured sailors to their deaths with song from her perch on this rock. As *K-D* excursion boats pass this point, strains of Schumann melodies are played on a sound system, and the Germans on board suddenly look very reverent—understandably so, because the Lorelei is as characteristically German as Old Faithful is American. It's a "must" stop, and today a road runs to the top.

From *Die Pfalz* and the Lorelei, it's another 3 miles (5 km) to St. Goar and St. Goarshausen.

BEST EN ROUTE

Burg Reichenstein Here are 12 simple but comfortable guestrooms set in a beautiful medieval fortress. There's also a restaurant. In the village of Trechtingshausen, 4 miles (6 km) from Bingen (phone: 6721-6101; fax: 6721-6198). Moderate.

ST. GOAR AND ST. GOARSHAUSEN These twin towns face one another across a broad, lake-like expanse of the Rhine. Near St. Goar is *Burg Rheinfels* (47 Schlossberg; phone: 6741-7753), a castle/fortress perched on a rock. Its

Heimatmuseum has exhibits about local history. The castle and museum are closed weekdays November through March; admission charge. It also offers several guestrooms (see *Best en Route*).

The St. Goar tourist office (closed Sundays) is on Heerstrasse (No. 86; phone: 6741-383; fax: 6741-7209). A few steps beyond is *Doris Mühl* (phone: 6741-7128), a shop that offers an incredible array of cuckoo clocks, beer steins, high-quality glassware, and Hummel figurines. Three decades of American GIs have helped this shop thrive, and its English-speaking proprietors gladly welcome Americans.

You can take the car ferry (which operates daily except Saturdays year-round) across to St. Goarshausen, which is as delightful as its sister village on the left bank. Travelers with children may find the carnival rides set up near the *K-D* steamer dock a welcome distraction. St. Goarshausen is the scene of the majestic *Rhein in Flammen* (Rhine in Flames) fireworks and spotlight extravaganza on the third Saturday in September; the spectacle is best seen from St. Goar across the river. St. Goarshausen is just north of the Lorelei.

BEST EN ROUTE

Schlosshotel auf Burg Rheinfels Tucked in the picturesque ruins of a medieval castle, this 57-room establishment looks out over St. Goar and the Lorelei rock. It has an open-air terrace with a spectacular view, an indoor pool, a sauna, a museum, a conference room, and a restaurant specializing in venison. 47 Schlossberg, St. Goar (phone: 6741-8020; fax: 6741-7652). Expensive.

Zum Goldenen Löwen Overlooking the Rhine, this small hotel (12 rooms) has a restaurant with an outdoor terrace where the view is excellent. Open April through December. 82 Heerstr., St. Goar (phone: 6741-1674; fax: 6741-2852). Moderate.

Hauser With a lovely view of St. Goarshausen across the river, this small, modest hotel offers 19 guestrooms, a café, and a terrace. 77 Heerstr., St. Goar (phone: 6741-333; fax: 6741-1464). Inexpensive.

En Route from St. Goar Continue north on B9. The steep-sided Rhine gorge ends beyond the village of Boppard, a residential valley town with a particularly pleasant promenade, aptly, but not too imaginatively, named the *Rheinallee* (Rhine Promenade). Proceed to Koblenz, about 22 miles (36 km) from St. Goar.

KOBLENZ Here the Rhine is joined by the Mosel River, a famous wine river route well worth a side trip (see *The Mosel River and Its Valley* in this section). However, Koblenz itself, which was almost totally annihilated during World War II, is a modern city with very few attractions of interest.

En Route from Koblenz Though less dramatic than the stretch between Bingen and Koblenz, the area north of Koblenz has many intriguing features. Take Route B9 from Koblenz toward Bonn, which is about 37 miles (60 km) to the northwest. Along the way, visit the *Abtei Maria Laach* (Abbey of Maria Laach); a Benedictine monastery near the left bank of the Rhine, it boasts a Romanesque basilica. It's a short detour of 9 miles (14 km) west of the river at Andernach. The abbey is most interesting for its location on the Laacher See, the largest of the volcanic lakes in the Eifel plateau, a peaceful, wooded area.

Farther north along the Rhine are the ruins of *Burg Rheineck* (Rheineck Castle), with a view of the surrounding valley. Still farther, on the slope of a former volcano, is *Rolandsbogen* (Roland's Arch), the ruins of the castle of the knight Roland, hero of the *Chanson de Roland.*

Southeast of Bonn, on the right bank (there's a car ferry from Bad Godesberg to Königswinter), is the Drachenfels (Dragon Cliff), a romantic, rocky summit with a ruined tower and a panoramic view that includes the Eifel plateau, Bonn, and Cologne. The Drachenfels was named for the legendary dragon slain by Siegfried, the hero who became invincible by bathing in its blood. Excursions for Drachenfels (15 minutes by cog railway) leave from Königswinter at frequent intervals. The cliff is in the *Siebengebirge* (Seven-Mountain Range) national park, whose low summits, once crowned with castles, now are crowned with forests.

BONN In June 1991, Bonn (pop. 296,000) lost its status as Germany's "provisional" capital to Berlin, the historic capital 350 miles (560 km) to the east. The postwar Germans must have wanted the capital of the new Germany in a place where nothing exciting ever happens, for after its spirited pre-Lenten street carnivals on *Weiberfastnacht* and *Rose Monday* (the dates vary each year), the city goes back into hibernation. Its loss as Germany's capital will be partly offset by the fact that when the move takes place (it began last year and is scheduled to be completed by the turn of the century), nearly half the federal government ministries and offices will remain here. And Bonn retains two further claims to fame that will endure forever: Ludwig van Beethoven was born and spent his early years in this Rhineside city, and Robert and Clara Schumann lived here. The *Beethoven-Haus* (Beethoven House; 20 Bonngasse; phone: 228-632500) deserves a stop. (At press time, however, it was temporarily closed for renovations, so call ahead to check on its status before visiting.) The *Schumann-Haus* (182 Sebastianstr.; phone: 228-773658) is also worth a visit for its memorabilia about the famous family of composers. It is closed Tuesdays and Saturdays; no admission charge. In addition, see the *Alter Zoll,* a bastion with a view of the Rhine, and stroll along the promenade on the banks of the river, past the *Bundestag,* where the Parliament still meets. Other attractions in town include the *Münster* (Cathedral; Münsterpl.), built between the 11th and 13th centuries; the *Kunstmuseum Bonn* (Bonn Fine Arts Museum; 2 Friedrich-Ebert-Allee; phone: 228-776262), featuring a collection of German Expressionist paintings (closed Mondays; admission charge); the adjacent *Bundeskunsthalle*

(Federal Gallery of Fine Arts; 4 Friedrich-Ebert-Allee; phone: 228-917-1200), with temporary exhibitions of contemporary art (closed Mondays; admission charge); and the *Rheinisches Landesmuseum* (Rhine Country Museum; Colmantstr; phone: 228-72941), with such historical and cultural exhibits as the skull of the first Neanderthal man, which was discovered in the nearby Neandertal (Neander Valley), Roman artifacts, and German and Dutch art from the 17th to the 19th centuries (closed Mondays; admission charge).

BEST EN ROUTE

Steigenberger Venusberg Bonn's most luxurious hotel is on a hill overlooking the city and the Rhine Valley. Designed in the style of a French country mansion, this luxurious hostelry has 80 rooms and six suites, as well as two restaurants. 1 An der Casselsruhe, Bonn (phone: 228-2880; fax: 228-288288). Very expensive.

Ibis This link in the French-based chain of hotels offers 185 guestrooms, a good restaurant, a pleasant garden, and parking. 33 Vorgebrigstr., Bonn (phone: 228-72660; 800-873-0300; fax: 228-7266405). Moderate.

Königshof Situated on the Rhine not far from the city center, this modern hotel offers comfort and convenience. The 140 rooms are well appointed, and other amenities include a restaurant, a bar, and a pretty terrace. 9 Adenauerallee, Bonn (phone: 228-26010; fax: 228-260-1529). Moderate.

En Route from Bonn Take the A3 autobahn and continue another 22 miles (35 km) to Cologne.

COLOGNE (KÖLN) For a detailed report on the city and its hotels and restaurants, see *Cologne* in THE CITIES.

En Route from Cologne From here, Düsseldorf is just over 30 miles (48 km) farther north on A57.

DÜSSELDORF For a detailed report on the city and its hotels and restaurants, see *Düsseldorf* in THE CITIES.

The Neckar River Valley

This route along the meandering Neckar River follows Germany's Burgenstrasse (Castle Road) from Heidelberg to Heilbronn. More than a dozen castles and strongholds can be found along this road, some of which housed aristocratic families during the Middle Ages. Many of the princely feudal dwellings are in ruins; others are intact and have been restored as museums, hotels, inns, and wine taverns. *Schloss Zwingenberg* (Zwingenberg Castle), for example, still is inhabited by royalty—by relatives of Britain's Prince Philip—but *Schloss Hirschhorn* and *Schloss Hornberg* now are hotels.

One of Germany's wine districts, producing mainly red wines, the scenic Neckartal (Neckar River Valley) is surrounded by high, forested hills crowned with castles, fortresses, and quaint old towns. Beginning in Heidelberg, this one- or two-day drive runs 50 miles (80 km) southeast to the wine producing town of Heilbronn, where the Castle Road ends. From here it's an additional 32 miles (51 km) south through the Schwäbische Hügel (Swabian Hills) to the major industrial and cultural center of Stuttgart. Finally, you can drive yet another 27 miles (43 km) south to see Tübingen, a charming old university town nicknamed "the Athens of Germany" because it once was home to so many of the country's greatest poets, philosophers, scientists, and other cultural figures, including astronomer Johannes Kepling, philosophers G. W. F. Hegel and Friedrich Schelling, and poet Johann Uhland.

Well-marked hiking trails connect towns and castles in this region, and the forested castle areas generally are honeycombed with quiet, scenic trails. Boat trips leave from many locations on the Neckar; passenger and car ferries can transport you to interesting sites on the opposite bank. For more information on the ferries and boat trips, call *Neckarpersonenschiffahrt* (phone: 711-541073 in Stuttgart). A bicycle lane also runs along most of the route. The valley has plenty of health spas and resorts for the recreation-minded. For maps and further information about the region, contact the *Landesfremdenverkehrsverband Baden-Württemberg* (Baden-Württemberg Tourist Office; 3 Lautenschlagerstr., Stuttgart; phone: 711-22280) or *Fremdenverkehrsverband Neckarland-Schwaben* (Neckarland-Swabia Tourist Office; Marktpl., Heilbronn; phone: 7131-562270; fax: 711-222-8270); both are closed Sundays.

On Germany's Castle Road, hotels and inns—even those in the castles—are surprisingly reasonable. The most expensive places are in the larger cities such as Stuttgart. A double room with private bath will cost $100 to $180 per night in hotels listed as expensive; $75 to $90 at places in the moderate category; and under $70 at inexpensive places. Rates include tax and service, and usually breakfast as well. Many of the restaurants along this route are in the hotels and inns. A dinner for two, without wine but including taxes and tips, will cost $75 to $120 in an expensive restaurant; $50 to $70 in a moderate place; and less than $40 in an inexpensive spot. Although the tip is included, you should leave a few extra deutsche marks (DM) to reward good service. Restaurants are open for lunch and dinner unless otherwise noted. For each location, hotels and restaurants are listed alphabetically by price category.

HEIDELBERG For a detailed report on the city and its hotels and restaurants, see *Heidelberg* in THE CITIES.

En Route from Heidelberg Located about 3 miles (5 km) from Heidelberg on Route 45, Neckargemünd, a 1,000-year-old town by the winding Neckar, features old inns such as *Zum Ritter,* which has open-air terraces overlooking the valley (see *Best en Route*). A church steeple rises over half-timbered houses and the old *Rathaus* (Town Hall) on Rathausplatz. From here Dilsberg is a short detour of 3 miles (5 km) on Route 158.

DILSBERG A fortified hamlet high above the Neckar River, Dilsberg resisted Imperial General Tilly and his Bavarian men during the Thirty Years War. The stout ramparts and lookout towers of this walled city are visible from both banks. If you park your car outside the walls and enter the town on foot, you can explore the fortress, with its mysterious subterranean tunnel (closed mid-October through March; admission charge), and the *Burgruine* (Castle Ruins; open summers only; admission charge), whose tower, with almost 100 stairs, offers a panoramic view of the river.

BEST EN ROUTE

Zum Ritter In Neckargemünd, this charming inn was built in 1286. It offers 37 rooms, a terrace with an extraordinary view, and a good restaurant. The lilac tree standing in the inner courtyard is 200 years old. 40 Neckarstr., Neckargemünd (phone: 6223-7035; fax: 6223-73339). Moderate.

En Route from Dilsberg Return by the same route to Neckargemünd. Then take Route 37 about 4 miles (7 km) to the north bank, and drive the 3 miles (5 km) to Neckarsteinach. You'll spot castle ruins on the ridge as you approach the town.

NECKARSTEINACH Also known as the Vierburgeneck (Four-Castle Corner), this town boasts four medieval citadels built in the 12th and 13th centuries. On the left side of Route 37, shortly before you reach the town, a parking area marks the start of a wooded trail that connects the four castles: *Vorderburg, Mittelburg, Hinterburg,* and *Schadeck.* The walk takes about 45 minutes and ends in the town itself, not far from the parking area. During the *Vierburgfest* (Four-Castle Festival), held on several evenings throughout the summer, the castles are illuminated and fireworks are exploded. Neckarsteinach's center is carefully preserved, so you also may want to stroll along the old town walls. The 15th-century Gothic church (on Kirchenstr.) is particularly noteworthy.

En Route from Neckarsteinach Follow Route 37 to Hirschhorn, approximately 5 miles (8 km) away.

HIRSCHHORN This well-preserved medieval town, filled with lovely half-timbered houses, is dominated by its impressive castle fortress, *Schloss Hirschhorn* (Hirschhorn Castle), which now is part of the *Schloss-Hotel* (see *Best en Route*). The towered defenses were built in the 13th century, but the castle itself dates from the 16th century. For a small fee you can climb the 121 steps of the tower, which lead to a magnificent view of the sharp Hirschhorn bend in the river. There is also a castle monastery and a lovely Gothic church (open daily). The tourist office is in the *Haus des Gastes* (2 Alleeweg; phone: 6272-1742); it is closed Sundays. Below the castle, the walled village still holds the remains of a deep moat. The *Ersheimer Kapelle* (Ersheimer Chapel), said to be the oldest church in the Neckar Valley (dating from 773), is across the river; from there you can get a good view of the castle.

BEST EN ROUTE

Schloss-Hotel A hilltop castle-hotel with 15 rooms, it overlooks the Neckar River Valley and the small town below. Dining facilities include indoor restaurants and an outdoor terrace with an excellent view. Accommodations in the guesthouse annex are less expensive than those in the castle. Open February through November. Auf der Burg Hirschhorn, Hirschhorn (phone: 6272-1373; fax: 6272-3267). Moderate.

En Route from Hirschhorn Continue along Route 37 up the north bank of the river for about 7 miles (11 km) to Eberbach.

EBERBACH This ancient imperial city has fortress ruins that date from the 11th century. Four powerful towers attest to its medieval beginnings. The old Deutscher Hof (German Court), the medieval center of town, is alive with colorful inns, half-timbered houses, and cobbled streets. In the Altmarkt (Old Market Square), the town's eventful history is recorded in 14 scenes painted on a front wall of the *Karpfen* hotel. You can see other engraved murals on the oldest inn in the city, the 16th-century *Gasthaus zum Krabbenstein* (13 Obere Badstr.), and at the Heumarkt (Hay Market).

After a walk in the Altstadt (Old City), stop at the large red and white *Viktoria Café* (5 Friedrichstr.; phone: 6271-2018) and choose from an immense assortment of confections, candies, and other desserts (a house specialty is an orange wine cream pie created to honor Queen Victoria). The town also has a health resort park, large forested reserves, indoor and outdoor swimming pools, and tennis courts.

BEST EN ROUTE

Alte Badhaus Formerly a medieval bathhouse (hence its name), this hotel in the center of town has 10 comfortably furnished rooms and an elegant restaurant serving well-prepared continental dishes. On the Lindenpl., Eberbach (phone: 6271-71057; fax: 6271-7671). Moderate.

En Route from Eberbach Continue on Route 37 for 7 miles (11 km) to Zwingenberg.

ZWINGENBERG Follow signs to the *Bahnhof* (Train Station) and park your car. A short distance up the road, a paved path leads to *Schloss Zwingenberg* (Zwingenberg Castle); one of the most magnificent palaces on the Castle Road, it is the residence of the Battenbergs, relatives of Britain's Prince Philip. The interior is open to the public Tuesdays, Fridays, and Sundays from 2 to 4:15 PM in May through September; admission charge. The fortress has been spared the damage of wartime bombings and is almost untouched by renovation. The Lords of Zwingenberg, its first owners in the 13th century, supplemented their income by imposing customs fees on shipping on the Neckar River. Two more castle ruins—*Stolzeneck* and *Minneburg*—can be seen across the river.

En Route from Zwingenberg Take Route 37 out of Zwingenberg and drive about 50 miles (80 km) to Neckarzimmern.

NECKARZIMMERN Follow the signs to the *Burg Hornberg* (Hornberg Castle), now a hotel (see *Best en Route*). Overlooking vineyards sloping to the river's bank, the castle was once the home of the Knight of the Iron Fist, Götz von Berlichingen, who wore an artificial hand after losing his right hand in the Bavarian War of 1504. You can explore the ruins of some of the castle buildings, visit the museum with its medieval armor and implements, and climb the watchtower (almost 140 wooden steps) for a commanding view of the Neckar Valley. The castle was first mentioned in a document in 1184. Since that time it has changed hands several times; it has been sold, given away, and even pawned during its colorful history. It is closed December through February; admission charge.

BEST EN ROUTE

Burg Hornberg High above the river, this castle-hotel has 24 stylishly decorated rooms and a terrace with a view of the river valley. The castle's former stable has been converted into a restaurant serving regional specialties (don't miss the mushrooms) and wines from the castle vineyards below. The atmosphere is informal. Open March through November (phone: 6261-4064 or 6261-4065; fax: 6261-18864). Expensive to moderate.

En Route from Neckarzimmern Continue on Route 37 the 4 miles (6 km) to Gundelsheim. From here, take Route 27 about 3 miles (2 km) over the bridge across the Neckar to Neckarmühlbach, and continue another mile (1.6 km) on an unnumbered road parallel to the river to *Burg Guttenberg* (Guttenberg Castle), one of the very few medieval German castles that have never been destroyed; it is, in fact, still a residence.

Dating from the 12th century, *Burg Guttenberg* offers more than just historical and architectural interest. It also houses an extensive collection of live birds of prey, many uncaged, from all over the world. Here, amidst the stately castle fortifications, perch eagles, vultures, and other predators. The birds entertain visitors during a show in which vultures swoop down over the heads of the audience. Housed in the castle is the *Burg Guttenberg Museum* (phone: 6266-228), which displays such historical artifacts as medieval books and documents, instruments of torture, woodcuts, engravings, copper etchings, jewelry, kitchenware, porcelain, and glass. An old spiral stairway provides access to the different floors of the museum and leads to a door marked "zum Turm" (to the tower). If you decide to climb the more than 100 steps to the open top, you'll be rewarded with a sweeping view of the countryside. The museum is closed December through February; admission charge. There's also a good restaurant (see *Best en Route*).

For more information about the area's attractions and accommodations, contact the local tourist office in Neckarmühlbach (45 Theodor-Heuss-Str.; phone: 6266-7910; fax: 6266-79140); closed Sundays.

From *Burg Guttenberg,* continue on the unnumbered road alongside the river about 4 miles (7 km) to Bad Wimpfen.

BEST EN ROUTE

Burgschenke Burg Guttenberg Within the castle grounds, this fine restaurant offers game dishes such as venison, good desserts, and local wines. The view of the valley is memorable. Closed Mondays, Tuesdays, and December through mid-March. Reservations advised. MasterCard and Visa accepted. *Burg Guttenberg* (phone: 6266-228; fax: 6266-1697). Moderate.

BAD WIMPFEN This royal city of the Castle Road was the imperial residence of the Hohenstaufens in the 13th century. Bad Wimpfen am Berg, as the older part of Bad Wimpfen is called, is distinguished by the towers, spires, and red tile roofs that crown its half-timbered structures. The skyline of this older part of town, marked with stately towers, is especially impressive when seen from the right side of the Neckar.

A short walking tour of the old section takes about an hour and is highly recommended. Most of the buildings were erected in the 13th century. You can see the market square, with its lovely *Rathaus* (Town Hall); the Romanesque *Steinhaus* (no phone), built around 1200 and now housing a museum about Bad Wimpfen's history (closed Mondays and November through March; admission charge); the *Blauturm* (Blue Tower; Blauturmgasse; no phone), which is closed Mondays and mid-October through March (no admission charge); and the 13th-century *Roteturm* (Red Tower), which was the emperor's refuge in times of danger (not open to the public). A walk down Klostergasse in the newer part of town passes many charming half-timbered houses with gardens and the *Ritterstiftskirche St. Peter im Tal* (Knights' Church of St. Peter-in-the-Valley; phone: 7063-8546), which has a 10th-century façade and an overall French Gothic design. Authentic Gregorian chants can be heard during Sunday services. Also on Klostergasse are several buildings dating from 1543 which were bathhouses in the 16th and 17th centuries.

BEST EN ROUTE

Schloss Heinsheim In Heinsheim, a town near Bad Wimpfen on the left bank of the Neckar, this Baroque manor and guesthouse has its own palace chapel, a pool, gardens, and a vineyard. Indoor and outdoor dining and a classic drawing room provide the final touches. It has excellent service, a friendly atmosphere, and good food. 36 Gundelsheimerstr., Heinsheim (phone: 7264-1045; fax: 7264-4208). Expensive to moderate.

En Route from Bad Wimpfen For an interesting side trip from Bad Wimpfen, take the unnumbered road along the river another 2 miles (3 km) farther to Bad Friedrichshall.

BAD FRIEDRICHSHALL This small spa town also has salt mines that are still worked today. You can arrange a tour of the saltworks or visit the local castle-hotel, *Schloss Lehen* (see *Best en Route*). Then drive along the right bank to nearby Neckarsulm, a town with two attractions that will interest automobile and motorcycle buffs: the Audi automobile factory (1 Christian-Schmidt-Pl.; phone: 7132-312868), which can be toured weekdays at 9 and 11 AM and 1 and 3 PM (reservations required); and the *Zweiradmuseum,* which literally means "Two-Wheel Museum" (Urbanstr.; phone: 7132-35271). Set in the former *Deutschordenschloss* (Castle of the Teutonic Order), *Zweiradmuseum* exhibits chronicle the development of original models of bicycles and motorcycles. It's closed on *Christmas;* admission charge.

BEST EN ROUTE

Schloss Lehen A quiet, elegant house set back from the road on the edge of town, this hostelry is surrounded by greenery and gardens. Built in the 1400s, it offers a home-like atmosphere, 28 nicely decorated guestrooms, and a good restaurant. 2 Hauptstr. Bad Friedrichshall (phone: 7136-4044; fax: 7136-20155). Expensive.

En Route from Bad Friedrichshall At Bad Friedrichshall, cross the river and take Route 27 south along the riverbank another 6 miles (10 km) to reach Heilbronn.

HEILBRONN In the midst of forests and vineyards, this is one of Germany's major wine producing towns. You can sample the fine wines at the *Heilbronne Ernte* (Heilbronn Harvest), a traditional wine festival in early September; *Weindorf* (Wine Village), a festival centered around the *Rathaus* (Town Hall), also held in September; or at any time in any of Heilbronn's inns such as the *Insel* (see *Best en Route*).

Formerly a free imperial city, Heilbronn has many interesting buildings. The 1315 tower of the *Kilianskirche* (Church of St. Kilian) was Germany's first Renaissance structure. Also in the city center are the 15th-century *Rathaus* (Town Hall) with its ornamental clock, made in 1580, and the 14th-century Gothic *Käthchenhaus,* a patrician dwelling in the market square (closed to the public).

BEST EN ROUTE

Insel In the heart of the city, this 120-room hotel with its own park actually is on a small island in the middle of the Neckar. The modern hotel has a café terrace, a restaurant offering Swabian specialties, and a French restaurant. Most of its rooms have balconies, and there is an outdoor swimming pool. Friedrich-Ebert-Brücke, Heilbronn (phone: 7131-6300; fax: 7131-626060). Expensive.

En Route from Heilbronn If you have additional time, you may choose to continue along the right bank of the Neckar, taking Route 27 for 32 miles (51 km) to Stuttgart. This road passes through gently rolling vineyards and small, picturesque medieval towns such as Lauffen, Kirchheim, and Besigheim. You might want to stroll along some of the streets in these old towns.

STUTTGART For a detailed report on the city and its hotels and restaurants, see *Stuttgart* in THE CITIES.

En Route from Stuttgart Continue another 27 miles (43 km) south on Route 27 to Tübingen, a lovely old university town.

TÜBINGEN The campus of *Universität Tübingen* (Tübingen University), founded in 1477, surrounds the town's Renaissance castle, whose terraces, bastions, and gardens offer a fine view of the Neckar and the Altstadt (Old City). Nearby is the Marktplatz, which is especially colorful on market days—Mondays, Wednesdays, and Fridays—when you sometimes can see peasants in regional dress selling produce. Don't miss the famous Platanenallee, an avenue of plane trees on a manmade island in the Neckar, a pleasant place both day and night. The Platanenallee can be reached by the

Eberhardbrücke (Eberhard Bridge). Both the bridge and the island offer excellent views of the town, with its river, its old houses, and its willow trees.

BEST EN ROUTE

Krone With tasteful traditional furnishings, modern facilities, and a good restaurant with an international menu, this 51-room hotel fits well into the atmosphere of the old university town. 1 Uhlandstr., Tübingen (phone: 7071-31036; fax: 7071-38718). Expensive.

Hotel am Schloss Just outside the gate of the castle that looks out over on the town, this small hotel has 23 rooms, some furnished with antiques; window boxes overflowing with flowers; and an excellent small restaurant serving Swabian specialties. 18 Burgsteige, Tübingen (phone: 7071-21077; fax: 7071-52090). Expensive to moderate.

The Black Forest

The Schwarzwald (Black Forest) lies in southern Germany, bounded roughly by a rectangle made by the cities of Rastatt, Basel, Schaffhausen, and Pforzheim. It is inappropriately named, as the forests are no darker or blacker here than any other forests in Germany; in fact, the whole area receives considerably more sunshine than the overall average for the rest of the country. It is a bright, open land of tree-covered mountains, rolling hills, and intermittent pine and birch forests. There are ski resorts and spas here, as well as ordinary mountain towns that are small, rustic, colorful, and often tucked away in valleys of stunning serenity and beauty. Some of the larger cities, such as Baden-Baden and Freiburg, are renowned as cultural centers, but many of the small towns are quaintly provincial in their outlook—in fact, some of the people still wear their regional costumes.

Throughout its history, the Black Forest region has clung tenaciously to its own identity. During the Thirty Years War, the area passed from the hands of the Austrians to the French and then to the Bavarians. The French took control again in 1679, then the Austrians returned in 1697 and brought the area back under the Austrian sphere of influence. The region became part of the German Duchy of Baden and the Kingdom of Württemberg in 1815, which were brought together to form the state known as Baden-Württemberg over a century later. All of this turbulent history has given the Schwarzwälders a strong sense of self; indeed, they revel in their distinctive customs and manners.

There's hardly a section of the Black Forest that is lacking in beauty and charm. If you take the autobahn from Basel to Baden-Baden, the distance is 102 miles (163 km); our longer, but incomparably more scenic route climbs over the 4,898-foot Feldberg Mountain peak and runs along the renowned Schwarzwälder Tälerstrasse (Rte. 294), just to name two of its highlights. The tour could be made in as little as one day, but you'll probably prefer to spend two or three. To hurry through an area like the Schwarzwald is to miss such delights as staying in half-timbered little *Gasthäuser* (inns) with warm, smoky dining rooms where the locals drink their nightly beer and *Kirschwasser,* a fiery local distillation made from cherries. The speedy traveler would also miss such regional specialties as *Schwarzwälder Schinken,* a smoked ham sliced so thin it is transparent; or the luscious taste of fresh mountain trout, cooked with almonds, with heaps of boiled salted potatoes as the perfect side dish. Brochures, maps, and information about the region are available from the *Fremdenverkehrsverband Schwarzwald* (Black Forest Tourist Office; 14 Rotteckring, Freiburg; phone: 761-31317 or 761-31318), which is closed Sundays.

In the Black Forest, a double room (with private bath and a TV set, unless otherwise indicated) at hotels in the expensive category will cost $160 or more per night; at places the moderate range, from $110 to $150; and at hotels in the inexpensive category, less than $100. Room rates generally include breakfast. Dinner for two (without wine, but including taxes and tips) will run $90 to $150 in expensive restaurants; $60 to $90 in moderate places; and less than $50 in inexpensive spots. Restaurants are open for lunch and dinner, unless otherwise stated. For each location, hotels and restaurants are listed alphabetically by price category.

En Route from Basel (Switzerland) Starting from the southwest corner of the Black Forest, near the Swiss border city of Basel, it is only a short, 6-mile (9-km) drive north to Lörrach on Route 317. There are some interesting ruins above Lörrach called *Burg Rötteln* (no phone; closed Mondays; admission charge) and the town's *Museum am Burghof* (Am Burghof; no phone) contains many fine examples of Black Forest handiwork, such as ceramics, sculptures, woodcarving, clocks, and religious figurines from the 17th century to the present. The museum is closed Mondays; admission charge.

Continuing on Route 317, it is a 25-mile (40-km) drive to the village of Todtnau, at an altitude of 2,169 feet. The air here is so clean and pure that Todtnau has been recommended as a resort for people with respiratory ailments. There are not many manmade attractions in the area, but there still is plenty to do. In the winter, the area is renowned for its skiing (both downhill and cross-country), and in the summer, hikers come out in droves to tramp through the woods and valleys surrounding the town. Other summer activities include swimming (both indoor and outdoor pools are available), miniature golf, and open-air concerts.

From Todtnau, Route 317 (here known as the Feldbergstrasse) continues east to Titisee via the route over the Feldberg, the highest mountain peak in the Black Forest (4,898 feet). The Feldberg offers the best skiing in the Black Forest, and during the summer the views from this mountain area are unequaled in the entire region. The Titisee is a gem of a mountain lake, with a picture-postcard village that is one of the Black Forest's most popular summer resorts. From Titisee, take Route 31 west for 5 miles (8 km) to Hinterzarten.

HINTERZARTEN A year-round southern Black Forest resort, in winter it is one of Germany's leading cross-country ski centers, with some 60 miles of marked trails fanning out over hills to the neighboring forest. From spring into fall, hikers can traverse the network of hiking trails that lead through the woods. Little known outside of the country, this is basically a low-key, family-style resort, but one worth discovering. Situated on a dead-end road, with no through traffic to shatter the stillness or pollute the crisp mountain air, the town also boasts the first class *Park Hotel Adler* (see *Best en Route*).

Park Hotel Adler Established in 1446, this elegant hostelry boasts 78 beautifully appointed rooms with marble baths in a vast parkland setting. The complex includes an oversize indoor pool, a beauty salon, and other sports facilities. There are also seven restaurants. Also see *Best Hotels* in DIVERSIONS. 3 Adlerpl., Hinterzarten (phone: 7652-1270; fax: 7652-127717). Expensive.

Schwarzwaldhof A small, family-run country hotel located near the railway station, its 39 rooms are decorated in typical rustic style, with down comforters on the beds even in mid-summer. The big drawing card here is the restaurant, featuring such traditional German home-cooked specialties as boiled beef and roast veal served with dumplings—and huge salads. The restaurant is closed Tuesdays. Reservations advised. Visa accepted. 2 Freiburger Str., Hinterzarten (phone: 7652-12030; fax: 7652-1413). Inexpensive.

En Route from Hinterzarten From Hinterzarten, Route 500 heads north through the picturesque market towns of St. Margen and St. Peter, each graced with its own hilltop church. The road winds through a pastoral landscape over the hills through two charming towns, Kandel (24 miles/38 km from Hinterzarten) and Waldkirch (7 miles/12 km farther); from here, it's a scenic 40-mile (64-km) drive along Route 294 to Freiburg im Breisgau. A far more direct (but less scenic) road is Route 31, only 19 miles (30 km) to Freiburg. Originally dubbed the Höllental (Hell Valley) and now a main route, this historic passage was once a rickety coach road installed in 1770 to accommodate the 15-year-old daughter of the Empress Maria Theresa of Austria when she journeyed from Vienna to Paris to marry the dauphin, Louis XVI. The future Queen Marie Antoinette of France traveled with an entourage of officials and servants in a caravan of 50 horse-drawn carriages.

FREIBURG IM BREISGAU A modern, bustling university city of 200,000 along the edge of the Black Forest, Freiburg maintains its sense of Old World charm as surely as an aged Schwarzwälderin with her round *Bollenhut* on her head. For a fine view of the city and its surroundings, take a cable car to the top of the Schlossberg; it leaves from a station in the valley several times daily year-round (except for three weeks in November when it is closed for inspection).

Founded in 1120 as a market and trading town, Freiburg was badly damaged during bombing raids in World War II, yet today all of the damage has been repaired. Affectionately referred to by Freiburgers as "Germany's smallest big town," it boasts rare medieval landmarks: the *Schwabentor,* 13th-century gates at the entrance to the city; an ornately decorated *Rathaus* (Town Hall; on Rathauspl.); and its most glorious attraction, a splendid Gothic cathedral (on Münsterpl.) that is the equal of any other church in Europe. Begun in the 12th century, this is the only Gothic cathedral in Germany that was totally completed during the Middle Ages. (The cathedrals in both Cologne and Ulm were not finished until the 19th century.) Its main architectural features are a 386-foot tower, flying buttresses, and pinnacles; the interior contains spectacular stained glass windows, a Hans Bildung Grien high altar, and artworks by Hans Holbein.

You could easily spend an hour just wandering the traffic-free historic core, where water runs in narrow canals along cobbled passageways inlaid with split stones from the Rhine. (As you stroll around, though, watch out for the roughly 30,000 students commuting to and from classes on their bicycles.) A lively market is set up on the Münsterplatz, the square adjoining the cathedral, on most mornings, even in winter. In summer and fall, farmers come from the surrounding countryside to sell their homegrown fruits and vegetables, as well as wild honey. Year-round, stands dispense the ubiquitous local spicy sausages, best eaten on the spot.

Opposite the south side of the cathedral stands the 16th-century *Kaufhaus,* originally erected as a merchants' hall but now used as a festival hall on special occasions. (Its shocking orange hue makes it stand out from the rest of the buildings in the Münsterplatz.) Nearby is the Rathausplatz, which contains the unusual *Rathaus,* formed by joining two old patrician houses that stood beside each other. Other important sights in the city are the *Haus zum Walfisch* (Whalehouse) near the *Rathaus,* and the *Augustiner Museum* (Am Augustinerpl.; phone: 761-201-2527), a Gothic house built in 1516 that contains medieval and Baroque art of the Upper Rhine region. The museum is closed Mondays; admission charge.

Because of its proximity to France and Switzerland, the area's local cooking offers a blend of international influences; it is colloquially known as "border cuisine." Freiburg also is known for its *Weinstuben,* cozy little wine taverns, many of which dispense vintages made locally from grapes cultivated within the city limits. For a good local wine, try a Freiburger Schlossberg (though perhaps the best wine in the entire Baden region is made a few miles to the west in the village of Ihringen, where the Doktorgarten and Winklerberg are both considered excellent vineyards). Get a taste of the region's excellent beers at the *Feierling Brewery Café* (46 Gerberau; phone: 761-26678).

BEST EN ROUTE

Colombi On the edge of the Altstadt (Old City) opposite a park is Freiburg's top hotel, with fine service, an excellent restaurant, a tearoom, and a popular wine bar (the bartender has worked here for the past 25 years). Many of the 92 rooms have balconies; there's also a pool, a sauna, and beauty facilities. Of the several restaurants, the best is the one-Michelin-star *Falkenstube,* offering filet of turbot stuffed with lobster and salmon and wrapped in spinach leaves, and medallions of venison in green pepper sauce. 16 Rotteckring, Freiburg (phone: 761-21060; fax: 761-31410). Expensive.

Enoteca Ristorante and Trattoria Here is a modern restaurant featuring a menu of Italian specialties, including pasta dishes and entrées prepared with meat and seafood. Service is friendly and attentive, but a bit slow, so don't eat here if you're in a hurry. There's also a large wine list. The trattoria across the street at 6 Schwabentorplatz (under the same management) offers a similar but more limited menu at lower prices. Open daily. Reservations necessary. Major credit cards accepted. 19-23 Gerberau, Freiburg (phone: 761-30751). Expensive to moderate.

Zum Roten Bären Directly on the *Schwabentor,* this is one of the oldest *Gasthäuser* in Germany (founded in 1120, it's as old as the city itself). Run by the Hansen family for generations, its 25 charmingly decorated rooms (appointed with plenty of modern amenities) and its excellent food at moderate prices are hard to beat. 12 Oberlinden, Freiburg (phone: 761-387870; fax: 761-387-8717). Expensive to moderate.

Oberkirchs Weinstuben The place for regional cooking. It's on a little square adjoining the lovely old *Kaufhaus* department store. The restaurant is an old, dark-paneled place with rustic wooden chairs. Try the game dishes—pheasant, wild boar, deer, and rabbit—all deliciously prepared. There are also 26 comfortable guestrooms. Closed Sundays. Reservations unnecessary. Major credit cards accepted. 22 Münsterpl., Freiburg (phone: 761-31011). Moderate.

Zum Storchen A popular local hangout serving snacks, simple meals, and Sunday brunch. Good regional wines and beers, too. Open daily. No reservations. No credit cards accepted. 7 Schwabentorpl., Freiburg (phone: 761-34970). Inexpensive.

En Route from Freiburg From here, drive about 25 miles (40 km) on the B3 and the B294 via Waldkirch to the turnoff for Route 500 (north); Furtwangen is about 2 miles (3 km) farther along Route 500. This stretch of road is called the Deutsche Uhrenstrasse (German Clock Road) in honor of the Black Forest's most famous product, the cuckoo clock. Examples of this kitschy specialty are on display and for sale throughout the region as well as in a museum in Furtwangen (see below). There are several scenic overlooks along this road, each one of them worth a stop. During the summer, the tiny mountain villages, many of them nothing more than a handful of houses with barns attached, are set off by meadows rife with little white and blue flowers; it all seems too perfect to be real.

FURTWANGEN This small town is worth a stop because of its excellent *Uhrenmuseum* (Clock Museum; 11 Gerwigstr.; phone: 7723-656117). Here, virtually anything that can be made to tell time is displayed. There are cuckoo clocks of every shape, size, and description, from a tiny clock that would fit into the palm of a hand and gives off a cuckoo like a canary with laryngitis, to a monstrous old hanging clock with a cuckoo that also sounds like a canary with laryngitis. There are grandfather clocks, grandmother clocks, and clocks that are simply grand. The museum is closed December through March; admission charge.

BEST EN ROUTE

Ochsen A quiet place to spend the night. The Keller family offers friendly hospitality, 34 clean, simple rooms, and inexpensive food, served in truly gargantuan portions. 9 Marktpl., Furtwangen (phone: 7723-2016; fax: 7723-2716). Inexpensive.

En Route from Furtwangen Continue along Route 500. Just before the road winds its way down into Triberg (about 11 miles/18 km from Furtwangen), there is a turnoff with a magnificent view of the surrounding valley. This also is the entrance to the Triberger Wasserfall (Triberg Waterfall); at 492 feet, it's the highest one in all of Germany. An interesting walk begins at the top of the waterfall and continues down the path alongside it to the town of Triberg, a distance of about 3 miles (5 km), all on carefully manicured trails with handrails. Sections of the waterfall are beautiful, but don't expect anything on the scale of Niagara or Victoria Falls.

TRIBERG The tiny town of Triberg itself is both pretty and interesting. Its primary attraction—a must-see for any visitor—is the *Heimatmuseum* (Home Museum; 4 Wallfahrtstr.; phone: 7722-4434), a collection of local handicrafts and woodcarvings. There also is a fine assortment of clocks; a collection of old mechanical musical instruments, including player pianos and an old pipe organ that still plays with the loudest racket imaginable; and a room completely decorated with woodcarving—walls, ceiling, benches, everything. Children of all ages will be entranced by the moving characters in the mechanical band. The museum is open daily; admission charge.

BEST EN ROUTE

Park Hotel Wehrle One of the finest hotels in the Black Forest (set in a lovely park), this stately property offers good service, 54 well-appointed rooms, indoor and outdoor pools, a sauna, a solarium, and *Zum Goldenen Ochsen,* an excellent restaurant known for its trout dishes (20 different kinds are listed on the menu). There's also comfortable period furniture and lots of atmosphere. 4 Gartenstr., Triberg (phone: 7722-86020; fax: 7722-860290). Expensive.

En Route from Triberg Just outside the town, Route 500 intersects Route 33. Turn onto Route 33 and continue north toward Freudenstadt (22 miles/35 km from Triberg). Along the way, in the village of Niederwasser, there is an excellent restaurant, the *Gasthaus Rössle* (see *Best en Route*). Directly across the road from the restaurant is a gift shop selling everything from cuckoo clocks to hand-carved wooden plates, all at prices much lower than at the main tourist centers in Germany (and it accepts major credit cards, a rarity in this part of Germany). Neither the restaurant nor the gift shop can be missed, as they are the *only* things on the road near Niederwasser. From there, continue along Route 33. At Hausach, the road intersects Route 294, the famous Schwarzwälder Tälerstrasse, which continues up to Freudenstadt. Along the way, it passes through the charming village of Alpirsbach, with its Benedictine monastery, built in 1095.

BEST EN ROUTE

Gasthaus Rössle Set in a tiny village, this excellent and reasonably priced restaurant specializes in fresh fish and tender veal steaks served with fresh peas and carrots. There also are 25 guestrooms. Closed Wednesdays. Reservations advised. MasterCard and Visa accepted. 26 Freiburger Str., Niederwasser (phone: 7808-2272; fax: 7808-3668). Inexpensive.

Löwen Post In the market square of a charming village, this is a comfortable and pleasant 13-room hotel with a good restaurant. 12 Marktpl., Alpirsbach (phone: 7444-2393). Inexpensive.

FREUDENSTADT Freudenstadt has one of the most elegant new market squares in all of Germany. The original market square was destroyed during the war, but the reconstruction has been well done. Aside from the Marktplatz, there is little to see in Freudenstadt, but it is an excellent town for shopping for such things as clocks and woodcarvings. There also are more than 560 miles of hiking trails leading through the woods and valleys around the town.

BEST EN ROUTE

Kurhotel Sonne am Kurpark This small hotel, in a park opposite a spa center, not only offers comfortable accommodations in its 47 rooms, but also boasts one of the Black Forest's best restaurants, featuring regional dishes. In addition, there's a swimming pool, sauna, and solarium. 63 Turnhallestr., Freudenstadt (phone: 7441-6044; fax: 7441-6300). Expensive.

En Route from Freudenstadt From here, the scenic Schwarzwald Hochstrasse (Black Forest High Road) affords spectacular vistas, passing the Mummelsee, a mountain lake, and opening onto views across the Rhine plains to France on the far side of the river. The road follows Route 28 from Freudenstadt to Zuflucht for a distance of 10 miles (16 km) and then

Route 500 for another 28 miles (46 km) to Baden-Baden. An alternative route to Baden-Baden is a continuation of the Schwarzwälder Tälerstrasse (Black Forest Low Road; Rte. 462). About the same length, it is an easier drive (fewer curves and hills), albeit a bit less scenic one. Along the second route is Baiersbronn, where the first-rate *Schwarzwaldstube* restaurant is well worth a visit (see *Best en Route*).

BEST EN ROUTE

Schwarzwaldstube The irresistible combination of excellent food and rustic splendor, as well as a fine French menu, make this one of Germany's most acclaimed and highly regarded restaurants (three Michelin stars). Being part of the elegant 18th-century *Kur- und Sporthotel Traube-Tonbach* doesn't hurt, either (it has 182 lavishly appointed guestrooms). Also see *Best Restaurants* in DIVERSIONS. Closed Thursday lunch, Friday lunch, and most of July. Reservations necessary (for a Saturday night, reserve three *months* in advance). Major credit cards accepted. 237 Tonbachstr., Baiersbronn (phone: 7442-492665; fax: 7442-492692). Expensive.

BADEN-BADEN For a detailed report on the city and its hotels and restaurants, see *Baden-Baden* in THE CITIES.

The Romantic Road

The so-called Romantische Strasse (Romantic Road) runs south through Bavaria, from the imperial city of Würzburg on the Main River to the mountain frontier town of Füssen in the foothills of the snow-clad Bayerischen Alpen (Bavarian Alps). It truly lives up to its romantic name, not for any dramatic scenery on the road itself, which traverses gentle, wooded hills and quiet valleys, but for its glorious medieval towns, some of which are 2,000 years old, and many of which have survived much as they appeared in the Middle Ages.

The wealth of sights along this route almost defies belief. In Würzburg and some of the other towns a visitor can see the incomparable works of Tilman Riemenschneider, the Master of Würzburg, a 16th-century Gothic woodcarver and sculptor with a very distinctive style. There's also Rothenburg ob der Tauber, Germany's best-preserved medieval city, with its walls, fountains, and gabled patrician houses, and Augsburg, once the richest city in Europe, with elegant avenues, lovely fountains, and mansions of the rich, as well as what is probably the world's oldest extant housing project for the poor, dating from 1519. Also not to be missed are the *Wieskirche* (Church in the Meadow), the rococo masterpiece of Dominikus and Johann Baptist Zimmermann, set in the midst of meadows near the tiny town of Wies, near Landsburg, and Germany's two most magnificent castles, located at Schwangau, where the Romantic Road crosses paths with the Alpine Route. During the summer, the area has folk festivals, open-air operas, castle concerts, and traditional centuries-old plays.

This 215-mile (344-km) route begins in Würzburg, then heads south on A81 to Tauberbischofsheim and Route 290 to Bad Mergentheim. It hooks up with Route 19 and follows the Tauber River through Weikersheim and Creglingen to Rothenburg, continues on Route 25 through central Bavaria, shifts to Route 2 to Augsburg, and then proceeds on Routes 17a and 17 to Füssen in the Alpine foothills.

Although much of the route follows principal highways, some portions are on small, winding, two-way roads that pass through tiny villages. Look out for signs, because the route is not always clearly marked. In the towns, narrow, cobblestone streets make driving difficult, so you may want to look for a parking area (marked with a large, white *P* on a blue background), and then walk into the Altstadt (Old City) areas. Since there aren't many gas stations along this route, keep an eye on your gas gauge and fill up whenever you can.

For information and maps of the region, contact the *Touristik Arbeitsgemeinschaft Romantische Strasse* (Romantic Road Tourist Office; Am Marktpl., Dinkelsbühl; phone: 9851-90271; fax: 9851-90279); it is closed Sundays.

The popularity of the Romantic Road as a tourist destination is reflected in its hotel and restaurant prices. If you don't mind sharing a bath, you'll find you can get accommodations at much lower rates. For a double room (with private bath unless otherwise indicated), expensive hotels on this route will charge $175 to $200 per night; moderate places, $125 to $175; and inexpensive places, less than $125. Service and breakfast are included in the rates.

A dinner for two, not including drinks or wine, will cost $90 or more in an expensive restaurant; $60 to $90 in a moderate one; and less than $60 in an inexpensive place. Taxes and tips are included in the bill, but you should leave a small additional amount for good service. Restaurants are open for lunch and dinner unless otherwise noted. For each location, hotels and restaurants are listed alphabetically by price category.

WÜRZBURG Set amid the vine-clad hills of the Franconian wine country, this is Germany's outstanding Baroque city. Though bombed heavily during World War II, it has been completely restored. Würzburg, which remained staunchly Catholic throughout the Reformation, is known as the "city of the Madonnas," for more than 300 statues of the Virgin stand in front of its houses. The early history of the town was dominated by the prince-bishops who lived there, first in the *Marienberg* fortress and later in the *Residenz* palace, both of which still are standing. Würzburg also is famous for its art treasures, most of which are the creations of two men: the 16th-century Gothic sculptor Tilman Riemenschneider, known as the Master of Würzburg, and the 18th-century German Baroque architect Balthasar Neumann, court architect to the prince-bishops.

The fortress and the palace, on opposite banks of the Main River, are the major sights in the city. High above the town, the *Marienberg* fortress now houses the fine *Mainfränkisches Museum* (Franconian Museum of the Main; phone: 931-43016), with its extraordinary sculptures by the Master of Würzburg. It is closed Mondays; admission charge. Near the fortress is the *Käppele,* a Baroque chapel with rococo decorations and a lovely view of the town, river, and fortress. Cross the Mainbrücke (Main Bridge), dating from the 15th century and decorated with statues of 11 saints, to the *Residenz* (2 Residenzpl.; phone: 931-355170), where you can see the court gardens, the *Kaisersaal* (Imperial Hall), the *Hofkirche* (Court Church), and the grand *Treppenhaus* (staircase). You also can visit the wine cellars underneath the palace (by appointment only) or sample the vintages on sale at the adjacent wine shop. The palace, wine cellar, and shop are closed Mondays; admission charge to the palace. For more information about the palace, see *Churches, Castles, and Palaces* in DIVERSIONS; for additional details on the wine cellar, see *Visitable Vineyards,* also in DIVERSIONS.

Other noteworthy Würzburg structures are the *Dom St. Kilian* (Cathedral of St. Kilian), a Romanesque church with sculptures by Riemenschneider, and such secular Baroque buildings as the *Haus Zum Falken;* both are near the Marktplatz on the palace side of the river.

While in this city, stop in one of the restaurants or wine taverns offering Franconian wine and *Meefischli* (little fish from the Main River).

BEST EN ROUTE

Rebstock Once a palace, now a modern hotel with 81 rooms, it has a neoclassical façade and is furnished with a harmonious mixture of traditional and modern pieces. The rooms are comfortable, and there's also an attractive terrace and two restaurants. 7 Neubaustr., Würzburg (phone: 931-30930; fax: 931-309-3100). Expensive.

Schützenhof This attractive, popular eatery is set in a 19th-century house with a garden terrace on a hill that overlooks Würzburg and the Maintal (Main Valley). The menu offers Franconian specialties prepared with a light touch, such as roast goose and boiled beef with noodles and horseradish, as well as a selection of unusual wines pressed from berries rather than grapes. Its wonderful view of the valley makes it a popular spot for dining alfresco in the summer. Closed December through February. Reservations advised. No credit cards accepted. 268¼ Mainleitenweg, Würzburg (phone: 931-72422). Moderate.

Bürgerspital Weinstube This traditional wine tavern is a must. The wines are almost impossible to find elsewhere, and Franconian dishes like *Bratwurst mit Kraut* provide hearty accompaniment. Closed Tuesdays and mid-July through mid-August. No reservations. No credit cards accepted. 19 Theaterstr., Würzburg (phone: 931-350-3441). Inexpensive.

En Route from Würzburg Take the A3 autobahn out of town toward Frankfurt, then take the A81 to Tauberbischofsheim; the total distance is 23 miles (37 km).

TAUBERBISCHOFSHEIM A lovely little town with a 1,200-year history, Tauberbischofsheim has several focal points: the *Kurmainzische Schloss mit Türmerstrum* (Palace of the Prince Electors of Mainz and Manor House; on Schlosspl.; no phone) which is closed Mondays and from November through *Easter* and charges admission; the double Gothic *Sebastianuskapelle* (Chapel of St. Sebastian), on St. Liobaplatz; and the Baroque *Liobakirche* (Church of St. Lioba), on Marktplatz. Half-timbered buildings and Baroque courtyards lend this valley township the tranquil atmosphere of the past. The town has garnered fame as a center for fencing enthusiasts.

En Route from Tauberbischofsheim Leave the town via Route 290 and drive 11 miles (18 km) farther to Bad Mergentheim.

BAD MERGENTHEIM This small town is both an international spa resort and a historical center. The Order of Teutonic Knights was based in the magnificent Renaissance *Schloss Mergentheim* (Mergentheim Palace) from 1525 until it was dispossessed by Napoleon in 1809. Founded in 1128, during the Crusades, this religious and military order wielded considerable political power in the surrounding area (as well as significantly influencing German history through its conquest of Prussia). You might want to take a look at the palace with its noteworthy Baroque church, which was redesigned by Balthasar Neumann during the 18th century. The palace is located at 16 Schlossplatz (phone: 7931-52212). It is closed Mondays and *Christmas Eve* through *New Year's Day;* admission charge.

BEST EN ROUTE

Victoria This 84-room hotel-spa has bath, massage, and swimming facilities, as well as an excellent restaurant, *Zirbelstuben.* Guests also can dine on the attractive garden terrace. Rooms feature glassed-in balconies. 2 Poststr., Bad Mergentheim (phone: 7931-5930; fax: 7931-593500). Expensive.

En Route from Bad Mergentheim Continue on Route 290 to Route 19 for a total of 9 miles (14 km) to Weikersheim, where the Renaissance *Schloss Weikersheim/Stammsitz des Hauses Hohenlohe* (Castle of the Princes of Hohenlohe; phone: 7934-8364) is worth a stop for its remarkable 16th- to 18th-century furniture, tapestries, porcelain, and sculptures of emperors and empresses. It is closed December through February; admission charge. Continue from Weikersheim on an unnumbered road another 9 miles (14 km) to Creglingen and its *Herrgottskirche* (Church of Our Lord), about half a mile outside the town on the Blaufelden Road. This little church in the countryside, completed in 1389, contains many art treasures, among them the altar of the Virgin Mary, the masterpiece of woodcarver Tilman Riemenschneider, the Master of Würzburg. It's 14 miles (22 km) on the same road from here to Rothenburg. To get in the right mood for this medieval walled town, park outside the walls and walk through a gate into the medieval fortress.

ROTHENBURG Overlooking the steep, beautiful Taubertal (Tauber River Valley), Rothenburg ob der Tauber is the best-preserved example of a medieval town in Germany. It's also very popular with tourists, especially during the summer and at *Christmastime.* This former imperial residence has remained intact largely because of its failure to recover economically from the Thirty Years War; it remains a typical 16th-century town, its gabled houses retaining their steep Gothic roofs and oriel windows. Its huge encircling fortress walls and watchtowers are straight out of a fairy tale, and the town inside the walls is intriguingly medieval as well, with its narrow, cobblestone streets and graceful, flowing fountains. Historic inns here display skillfully crafted wrought-iron signs, and horse-drawn carriages still carry visitors through the central area of the city.

According to legend, Rothenburg was saved from destruction during the Thirty Years War by the drinking prowess of its leading citizen. When Tilly, commander of the Imperial Army, threatened to destroy the town, the burgomaster, Nusch, offered him a cup of the best local wine, after which Tilly agreed to spare the town if someone could quaff six pints all at once. Nusch obliged. This tale is reenacted seven times a day when the clock on the *Ratstrinkstube* (City Councillors' Tavern) in the market square strikes 11 AM, noon, and 1, 2, 3, 9, and 10 PM. The doors on each side of the clock open to reveal the disbelieving figure of General Tilly as he watches the town mayor empty a more than three-liter bumper of wine in one draught.

The *Rathaus* (Town Hall), also in the market square, has two sections, one of which is 14th-century Gothic and the other 16th- and 17th-century Renaissance. You can climb its tower for a spectacular view of the city fortifications, which form the outline of a wine goblet. The tower is open daily; admission charge. From the *Rathaus* you can walk to the Herrngasse, the widest street in the city, which begins at the market square. The Herrngasse is lined with stately patrician houses, which are decorated with a variety of gables. Nearby is the *Kriminalmuseum* (Criminal Museum; 3 Burggasse; phone: 9861-5359), which displays instruments of medieval torture. It is open daily, but hours change seasonally; it's best to call ahead and check before you go. There's an admission charge. From the museum it's a short walk to the city's oldest and mightiest gate tower, the *Burgtor,* which leads into the *Burggarten,* a lovely public garden with a view of the Tauber bend, the curious medieval two-tier bridge called the Topplerschlösschen, and the village of Detwang. Within the city's walls, countless streets and alleyways beckon you to explore shops, galleries, restaurants, taverns, and museums.

There are festivals here on *Whitsuntide* (seven Sundays after *Easter*) and in September, and throughout the year the community sponsors cultural events, concerts, and historical plays. Information about such events usually is posted in the market square, or contact the tourist office (2 Marktpl.; phone: 9861-40492), which is closed Sundays. There is much to see and do in Rothenburg, so this is a good place to spend at least one night.

BEST EN ROUTE

Eisenhut A colorful, historical inn, this luxurious 80-room property is actually several medieval patrician houses joined together. This also is the site of Rothenburg's top restaurant, with prices to match. Excellent international cuisine and wine can be enjoyed in the richly paneled, galleried dining hall or on the garden terrace overlooking the Tauber River. Try the trout specialties in season. The restaurant is closed January. Reservations advised. Major credit cards accepted. 3-7 Herrngasse, Rothenburg (phone: 9861-7050; fax: 9861-70545). Expensive.

Goldener Hirsch In a quaint section of the city, this 80-room hotel is a remake of a 17th-century inn. A comfortable establishment with traditional decor and good service, it features the *Blaue Terrasse* restaurant, with a panoramic view of the river valley. 16 Untere Schmiedgasse, Rothenburg (phone: 9861-7080; fax: 9861-708100). Expensive.

Burg-Hotel A large half-timbered house at the city wall, this 14-room hostelry offers a good view for somewhat lower prices than those charged at the hotels noted above. Charmingly set in a small garden with a pool, it is attractively decorated and offers friendly service. 1 Klostergasse, Rothenburg (phone: 9861-5037). Expensive to moderate.

Baumeisterhaus Right off the market square in a patrician residence built in 1596, this restaurant has a beautiful courtyard, good German food, and reasonable prices. Open daily. Reservations advised. Major credit cards accepted. 3 Obere Schmiedgasse, Rothenburg (phone: 9861-3404). Moderate.

Ratsstube Also on the market square and very popular, this tavern-style restaurant features such regional dishes as blood sausages with sauerkraut and Bavarian mixed grill. Don't miss the white asparagus dishes in season (May and June). Open daily. No reservations. No credit cards accepted. 6 Marktpl., Rothenburg (phone: 9861-5511). Inexpensive.

Zur Höll A wine tavern in the town's oldest house (1222) on the town's oldest street, it's well worth a visit, both for its Franconian wines and its regional dishes. Open for dinner only; closed Tuesdays. No reservations. No credit cards accepted. 8 Burggasse, Rothenburg (phone: 9861-4229). Inexpensive.

En Route from Rothenburg Take Route 25 out of Rothenburg and drive 17 miles (28 km) to Schillingsfürst, where you might want to see the excellent *Heimatmuseum* (Home Museum) in the *Brunnenhaus* (Fountain House; phone: 9868-5889), which has a fine folklore collection, including Franconian costumes, crafts, and furniture. It's closed Mondays; admission charge. From here, continue another 8 miles (13 km) on Route 25 to Dinkelsbühl.

DINKELSBÜHL Here is yet another beautifully preserved medieval city, complete with walls, towers, and gateways—all mirrored dreamily in the green waters of the town moat.

This is a sleepy 16th-century town, except during a week-long festival in mid-July known as *Kinderfest* (Children's Festival). The celebration honors the children of the town, who during the Thirty Years War induced the Swedish invaders to spare Dinkelsbühl. Other summer highlights include an outdoor theater, performances by the Dinkelsbühl *Jungenband* (Boys' Band), and a night watchman who makes his rounds throughout the Altstadt (Old City).

Take the time to wander around the Altstadt; its unpaved medieval streets are lined with 15th- and 16th-century houses decorated with hand-carved signs and flower-festooned balconies. Segringer Strasse and Nördlinger Strasse are particularly interesting, as is the *Deutsches Haus* (German House) on Weinmarkt, with its elaborate Renaissance decorations. The *Georgkirche* (St. George's Church), on Marktplatz in the center of town, is a 15th-century Gothic structure with remarkable carvings and a Romanesque tower. For information about the area's attractions and accommodations, consult the tourist office (Marktpl.; phone: 9851-90240; fax: 9851-90279), which is closed Sundays.

BEST EN ROUTE

Deutsches Haus A half-timbered house dating from 1440, this 13-room inn, decorated with richly painted designs and woodcarvings, is elegantly furnished. The restaurant serves local specialties. 3 Weinmarkt, Dinkelsbühl (phone: 9851-6059; fax: 9851-7911). Moderate.

Goldene Rose In the heart of town, this pretty, six-story inn dates from 1450. The 33 rooms are modernized, but they are charmingly furnished with antiques, and the hotel offers a homey atmosphere at a reasonable rate. It also has a good restaurant. Open March through December. 4 Marktpl., Dinkelsbühl (phone: 9851-831; fax: 9851-6135). Moderate.

En Route from Dinkelsbühl It's about 19 miles (30 km) from here to Nördlingen im Ries on Route 25.

NÖRDLINGEN IM RIES Nicknamed the "living medieval city," this fortified town has retained not only its ancient buildings and city walls, but many of its medieval customs and costumes as well. In the Rübenmarkt in the center of town, the peasants still wear traditional dress on market days (Wednesday and Saturday mornings). A circular town, Nördlingen is circumscribed by roofed parapet walks that pass by the wall's many towers and gates. A watchman still surveys the town, calling out at night from the top of the tower of the late-Gothic *Georgkirche* (St. George's Church) in the center of town. The 15th-century church, with its tower of volcanic rock, its 15-foot bell (christened Daniel), and its lavishly decorated interior, is worth seeing; the lovely painted altarpiece by Friedrich Herlin, however, is in the *Stadtmuseum* (1 Vordere Gerbergasse; phone: 9081-84120). This museum also houses a collection of exhibits about the town's history, including geological displays, minerals, and paintings. It is closed Mondays; admission charge. The tourist office (closed Sundays) is on Marktplatz (No. 2; phone: 9081-4380; fax: 9081-84102).

BEST EN ROUTE

Kaisershof Hotel Sonne Next to the *Rathaus* (Town Hall) and the cathedral, this Old World inn, dating from 1477, has been modernized. It offers 40 comfortable rooms, good service, and four dining rooms (closed Wednesdays) that serve Swabian specialties and other local fare. 3 Marktpl., Nördlingen (phone: 9081-5067). Moderate.

En Route from Nördlingen It's 11 miles (18 km) on Route 25 to Harburg, where a castle stands guard over a lovely hamlet on the Wörnitz River. *Schloss Harburg* (Harburg Castle; phone: 9003-1268), right in the center of town, is worth a stop for the art treasures in its museum—illuminated manuscripts, engravings, Gothic tapestries, and woodcarvings by the incomparable Riemenschneider. The castle is closed Mondays and November through mid-March; admission charge. At Donauwörth, yet another medieval town 6 miles (10 km) farther on Route 25, the Wörnitz River meets the Danube; from here, take Route 2 and continue along the Lech River for 27 miles (43 km) to Augsburg.

AUGSBURG Historical buildings of every style and epoch grace this city, Bavaria's third-largest and the oldest on the Romantic Road. Founded in 15 BC, Augsburg was a Roman provincial capital for 450 years and a free imperial city for 500 more. Two fabulously wealthy families, the Fuggers and the Welsers, dominated Augsburg during the 15th and 16th centuries, making it a major trading and banking center. The Fuggers, financiers of the Hapsburg dynasty, wielded enormous power and influence; the Welsers once owned most of Venezuela.

During and after its Renaissance heyday, Augsburg attracted artists and humanists. Both Holbeins were born here, as was the architect Elias Holl, who created the *Rathaus* (Town Hall), built in 1620, and other Renaissance structures. Later, Leopold Mozart, father of the great composer, was born here, and his house still stands as a museum, *Mozart Haus* (30 Frauentorstr.; phone: 821-324-2898). It's closed Tuesdays; admission charge. Not far from here, on a side street off Leonhardsberg Strasse, is the house in which the late German playwright Bertolt Brecht was born in 1898. It, too, is now a museum, *Brecht Haus* (7 Auf dem Rain; phone: 821-324-2779), which is closed Mondays; admission charge.

Start at the huge *Rathaus* on Rathausplatz; in front is the impressive *Augustusbrunnen* (Fountain of Augustus), created in 1594. Walk south on the beautiful, wide Maximilianstrasse, the main street, decorated with fountains and lined with mansions built by the wealthy Renaissance burghers. Behind the lovely *Herkulesbrunnen* (Hercules Fountain) is the very attractive *St.-Ulrich- und St.-Afra-Kirche* (Church of St. Ulrich and St. Afra), built in 1500. Since the 1555 Peace of Augsburg between German Catholics and Protestants, it has contained two churches—Catholic and Protestant.

Also worth seeing is the town cathedral, north of the *Rathaus,* which has 11th-century bronze doors, the oldest stained glass windows in Germany (12th century), and paintings by Hans Holbein the Elder. *Schloss Schaezler* (Schaezler Palace; 46 Maximilianstr.; phone: 821-324-2175) contains a magnificently decorated rococo banqueting hall, and the *Deutsche Barockgalerie* (German Baroque Gallery; phone: 821-502070), with works by such German masters as Holbein the Elder and Dürer, and by non-Germans such as Rembrandt, Rubens, and Veronese. The palace and gallery are closed Mondays and November through February; separate admission charges for each. East of the town center is the Fuggerei, a housing project for the poor built by the Fugger family in 1519 and still inhabited today; it includes four gates, a church, eight streets, and 66 gabled houses.

For useful information about Augsburg, contact the *Verkehrsverein* (Tourist Office; 7 Bahnhofstr.; phone: 821-502070), which is closed Sundays.

BEST EN ROUTE

Drei Mohren Combining contemporary with traditional decor, this 110-room hotel, famous since 1723, was destroyed in an air raid in 1945. Rebuilt in a somewhat overly opulent style, it still offers first class accommodations. Its formal dining room serves international dishes and features such specialties as venison and filet of sole with white wine sauce. It also has an attractive garden terrace. 40 Maximilianstr., Augsburg (phone: 821-50360; fax: 821-157864). Expensive.

Fuggerkeller In vaulted, cave-like rooms below street level in the former Fugger residence, this eatery is noted not only for its setting, but for its fine local food and drink. The strong, dark Fugger beer is an experience. Closed Sunday dinner and August. Reservations advised. Major credit cards accepted. 38 Maximilianstr., Augsburg (phone: 821-516260). Moderate to inexpensive.

Ratskeller This restaurant in the *Rathaus* has particularly good, solid German food at reasonable prices. Open daily. Reservations advised. Major credit cards accepted. 2 Elias-Hall-Pl., Augsburg (phone: 821-154087). Moderate to inexpensive.

Arcade/Bis This no-frills hostelry with 104 rooms is popular with business travelers because of its efficient service, its reasonable prices, and its convenient location behind the train station. There is also a restaurant and bar. 25 Halderstr., Augsburg (phone: 821-50160; fax: 821-501-6150). Inexpensive.

7 Schwaben Its name translates as "Seven Swabians," but you'll find many more than seven people in this traditional *Gasthaus*—it's popular with both locals and tourists. The hearty local specialties served here include baked spinach-cheese strudel, several varieties of *Spätzle* (noodles), and *Maultaschen* (a German form of ravioli stuffed with meat). Closed *Christmas* and *New Year's Day*. Reservations unnecessary. Major credit cards accepted. 12 Bürgermeister-Fischer-Str., Augsburg (phone: 821-314563). Inexpensive.

En Route from Augsburg Leave Augsburg via Route 17a and drive about 24 miles (38 km) to Landsberg, where there are many works of brothers Johann Baptist and Dominikus Zimmermann, two 18th-century master architects. Their rococo creations include the *Rathaus* (Town Hall), the *Johanniskirche* (St. John's Church), and the *Ursulinenkirche* (St. Ursula's Church). Also take a look at the lovely Hauptplatz (Main Square), with its fountain and its 1425 *Bayertor* (Bavarian Gate), adorned with turrets and sculptures.

From Landsberg, continue on Route 17a (which becomes Route 17 as you leave town). As you head toward Füssen, about 68 miles (110 km) farther along, be sure to stop in Wies (on a tiny side road to the left, 17 miles/27 km from Landsberg off Route 17) and see yet another masterpiece by the brothers Zimmermann: the marvelous *Wieskirche* (Church in the Meadow), acknowledged as the greatest achievement of rococo art in Germany. Set in the meadows, surrounded by woods, this magnificently ornamented structure, erected between 1746 and 1754, was so lovingly built that Dominikus Zimmermann spent the last 10 years of his life nearby, unwilling to leave his finest creation. The simple exterior stands in marked contrast to the rich interior, with its oval cupola, elaborate woodcarvings, paintings, frescoes, and giltwork—all beautifully lit by many well-placed windows. Time has taken its toll, however, and the church has been renovated, but the original look has been retained.

About 2 miles (3 km) before Füssen (66 miles/106 km from Landsberg), take a left onto a little side road off Route 17 to Schwangau and Hohenschwangau, the homes of the two most impressive castles in all Germany, *Hohenschwangau* and *Neuschwanstein.* Also known as the *Königsschlösser* (Royal Castles), they were both the residences of Ludwig II, also known as "Mad King Ludwig," and contain original furnishings and decorations. Both castles may be visited only on 35-minute guided tours (available in English). *Neuschwanstein* (phone: 8362-81035) and *Hohenschwangau* (phone: 8362-81128) are closed *All Saints' Day* (November 1), *Christmas Eve,* and *New Year's Day;* admission charge. (For additional details about *Hohenschwangau* and *Neuschwanstein,* see *Churches, Castles, and Palaces* in DIVERSIONS.) From the castles, return to Route 17 and continue to Füssen.

FÜSSEN This mountain frontier town, once the summer residence of the Augsburg bishops, includes a 13th-century palace and an 18th-century church high above the river Lech. A majestic wall of Alps provides a fitting backdrop for this spa and winter-sports resort. The medieval stone buildings of the town lend a picturesque quality to this, the final stop on the Romantic Road. From here, you can cross through mountain passes into the Austrian portion of the Alps. The tourist office (2 Augsburgerstr.; phone: 8362-7077) is open daily.

Hirsch This 48-room hotel has a central location, a restaurant, a terrace, and parking. Open mid-February through November. 4 Schulhaussstr., Füssen (phone: 8362-541308; fax: 8362-508113). Expensive.

Sonne Also in the center of Füssen, this hostelry has 32 comfortable, rustic rooms and a café. 37 Reichenstr., Füssen (phone: 8362-6061; fax: 8362-6064). Moderate.

Pulverturm In the idyllic *Kurhaus* spa center, it serves both continental and regional dishes. You can dine indoors or on the pleasant terrace. Open daily. Reservations advised. Major credit cards accepted. 1 Schwedenweg, Füssen (phone: 8362-6078). Moderate to inexpensive.

The Harz Mountains

During the 40 years prior to the reunification of Germany, the Harz Mountain region was a microcosm of the country; both were split down the middle into eastern and western sections by the border established in 1949. The region, covered with forests, pocked by limestone caves, and shaped by high, rugged hills, is dotted with numerous castles, churches, and fortresses built during the Middle Ages. Our route through and beyond the Harz runs through several significant cities: Potsdam, a residence of Frederick the Great during the 18th century as well as the site of the conference in which Churchill, Stalin, and Truman decided the fate of postwar Germany; Eisenach, birthplace of Johann Sebastian Bach; and Weimar, the home of Goethe and Schiller and namesake of the short-lived republic that fell with the rise of Hitler. Near Weimar is the site of Buchenwald, one of the most notorious World War II concentration camps.

The route begins in Potsdam, then goes to Magdeburg and the Harz Mountain towns of Quedlinburg and Wernigerode. From Wernigerode it continues southwest to Eisenach, after which it swings eastward to Erfurt and Weimar. After turning northward to Naumburg, you can go on to Leipzig. In general, we purposely have steered clear of the autobahns, as these show travelers so much less of the countryside than the quieter country roads. *Note:* Due to extensive road-improvement projects in the area, expect to run into many *Umleitung* (Detour) signs along this route; allow plenty of driving time between points.

Maps, brochures, organized tours, and other information are available from the tourist offices in each of the cities and some of the towns. In Berlin, inquire at the *Europäischer Reisebüro* (European Travel Agency; 5 Alexanderpl.; phone: 2-215338 or 2-153565).

Although the situation is slowly improving, obtaining hotel accommodations in the former East Germany remains difficult. The better hotels often are fully booked by visiting businesspeople and government officials for weeks in advance. Even more frustrating is the inadequate telephone service in eastern Germany, which makes telephone reservations difficult. Be aware, too, that prices for the most appealing places equal those in western Germany, although room standards seldom measure up to their western counterparts. Many hotels are undergoing extensive renovations to bring them up to par, and new ones are being built, but it will take several more years before significant signs of improvement are seen. The *Allgemeine Deutsche Zimmer Reservierung* (German General Room Reservation Service; phone: 69-740767) in Frankfurt can help make reservations (for a small booking charge) in eastern Germany. In addition, local tourism offices maintain lists of hotels, guesthouses, and private rooms. The lists are available for a small fee.

On this route, the cost per night of a double room (with private bath, unless otherwise indicated) at a hotel listed as very expensive will be more than $170; at an expensive property, it will range from $105 to $160; at a place described as moderate, from $80 to $105; and at an inexpensive hotel, $55 to $80. Dinner for two, with drinks and wine, will cost $55 or more at expensive restaurants, between $25 and $50 at places in the moderate range, and under $25 at inexpensive places. Tips are included in the bill. All restaurants are open for lunch and dinner unless otherwise indicated. For each location, hotels and restaurants are listed alphabetically by price category.

POTSDAM Most people know Potsdam as the place where the four victorious powers of World War II—Russia, Britain, the US, and France—officially ratified the 1945 agreements (reached at Yalta a few months earlier) that split Germany and Berlin into four zones of occupation. But Potsdam, which celebrated its millenium in 1993, has been an important city since 1660, when the Princes of Hohenzollern chose it as their country residence and began a palatial building program that ended only in the late 19th century. The 18th century saw the city develop as the military center of Prussia, boasting at one time a ratio of 8,000 soldiers to just 17,000 inhabitants. Since World War II, shapeless modern architecture and now-regretted demolition programs have marred some of Potsdam's old charm, but the palaces and the parks still are as delightful as ever. Potsdam was prewar Germany's Hollywood, producing feature films at its famous Universum Film Aktiengesellschaft (UFA; Universal Film Company) studios in adjacent Babelsberg.

You might start with a walk round the Altstadt (Old City), centering on Brandenburger Strasse, now Potsdam's primary pedestrian street, with small cafés and shops. A nearby information bureau (at 5 Friedrich-Ebert-Str.; phone: 331-21100; fax: 331-23012) is accessible via Am Alten Markt, a smaller pedestrian lane. From Brandenburger Strasse, it's an easy walk along the Allée nach Sanssouci to Potsdam's main attraction, *Sanssouci Park,* site of the Baroque *Schloss Sanssouci* (Sanssouci Palace; phone: 331-22051), which was built on Frederick the Great's orders from 1745 to 1747. Also on the park grounds are a picture gallery, an ornate Chinese teahouse, statues, shrubbery, and another creation of Frederick's 46-year reign, the *Neues Palais* (New Palace). To avoid crowds, it's a good idea to arrive at the park before 11 AM. The entire complex is closed the first and third Monday of the month; separate admission charges for all attractions. Also see *Churches, Castles, and Palaces* in DIVERSIONS.

In the northeastern part of town, the *Schloss Cecilienhof* hotel (see *Best en Route*), built in 1913 in the style of an English country mansion, is where the 1945 conference took place. The *Schloss Cecilienhof* also houses an interesting museum devoted to the conference, which includes the original furniture. The museum is closed the second and fourth Monday of the month; admission charge to non-guests (phone: 331-969-4245). As if to remind visitors of the consequences of that meeting, a stretch of the Berlin Wall once stood just 200 yards away, in full view of anyone standing at the bottom of the garden.

BEST EN ROUTE

Hotel Mercure Potsdam This large high-rise hotel, at the entrance to town nearest Berlin, is one of the most prestigious in the east, with prices to match. It has 211 rooms, a sauna, dancing, entertainment, a restaurant, and a bar. Lange Brücke, Potsdam (phone: 331-23141; fax: 331-22498). Expensive.

Schloss Cecilienhof Set in a 20th-century version of an English country house, this historic building, though smaller and less luxurious than the *Hotel Mercure Potsdam,* has 42 guestrooms, a restaurant, a café, and a pleasant outdoor terrace overlooking the Havel River. *Neuer Garten,* Potsdam (phone: 331-37050). Expensive.

Klosterkeller In business since 1736, this popular, old-fashioned restaurant offers decent local food. You can wash down your meal with a pint of Potsdam's own Rex Pils beer, with a portrait of Frederick the Great on the label. Open daily. No reservations. No credit cards accepted. 94 Friedrich-Ebert-Str., Potsdam (phone: 331-21218 or 331-23669). Inexpensive.

En Route from Potsdam Route 1, part of the main trans-European artery (begun by Hitler in the 1930s) that links Paris and Berlin, leads out of town into the farmland along the Havel River. If you are here in spring, the cherry blossoms on either side of the two-lane highway are breathtaking. Brandenburg, 25 miles (40 km) along the route, was the capital of the Prussian state for centuries, but it declined as Berlin took over the role of administrative center. Another hour's drive along the tree-lined Route 1 brings you via sleepy villages to Magdeburg, on the Elbe about midway between Berlin and the Harz Mountains.

MAGDEBURG The heavy machine works and steel mills in Magdeburg, the capital of the federal state of Saxony-Anhalt, are historically connected to one of the city's most influential citizens, former mayor Otto von Guericke (1602–86). In 1650, von Guericke proved the power of vacuum and invented the "Magdeburg Hemispheres" to demonstrate the principle of air pressure. Other noteworthy men from Magdeburg are Baron Friedrich Wilhelm von Steuben (1730–94), who became a hero fighting with the colonies during the American Revolution, and composer Georg Philip Telemann (1681–1767). Sadly, Magdeburg has had a history of destruction. It burned down almost totally during an attack in 1631, and more than 90% of the rebuilt inner city was razed by Allied bombing in January 1945. Only parts of the city center have been reconstructed as they once were. The tourist office (9 Alter Markt; phone: 391-31667) has brochures, maps, and lists of attractions and accommodations; it's closed Sundays. Begin your tour at the *Rathaus* (Town Hall). You'll notice the famous 13th-century statue of the *Magdeburger Reiter* (Magdeburg Rider) on his horse facing the building from the square. It's actually just a copy of the original statue, sculpted in 1240, which is now in the *Kulturhistorisches Museum* (Museum of Cultural History; Otto-von-Guericke-Str.; phone: 391-32645). The museum is closed Mondays; admission charge. A 10-minute walk through what's left of the Altstadt (Old City) leads to the mainly 12th-century *Kloster Unser Lieben Frauen* (Cloister of Our Dear Lady), possibly one of the best-restored architectural ensembles in the country. Next door is the cathedral, with quaint cloisters around the side entrance; first recorded as a place of worship in 955, it is the oldest church in eastern Germany. In the northern transept a group of six wooden figures by Ernst Barlach, a highly regarded 20th-century Expressionist sculptor, memorializes starkly and impressively the dead of World War I. The Nazis had the figures removed from the cathedral in 1933, but they were reinstalled in 1957.

BEST EN ROUTE

Maritim Formerly the *Interhotel International,* this big, centrally located hotel (353 rooms) has a restaurant, a café, and a solarium. Some might consider it modern and characterless, but that's the case with many of the better hotels in the country's eastern region. 87 Otto-von-Guericke-Str., Magdeburg (phone: 391-3840; 800-843-3311; fax: 391-554140). Expensive.

En Route from Magdeburg The most direct route to Quedlinburg is to take Route 81 out of Magdeburg towards Halberstadt about 31 miles (50 km), and then take Route 79 southeast approximately 4 miles (6 km). However, for a taste of small country roads that are almost completely free of traffic, bear right on the outskirts of Magdeburg and take Route 81 south as far as Egeln. From there, follow Route 180 to Aschersleben and then take Route 6 to Quedlinburg via Hoym. You'll travel along rural roads through typical German provincial towns, hardly changed since World War II. This more scenic route covers about 41 miles (66 km).

QUEDLINBURG Hardly hit by the war, the town of Quedlinburg still boasts hundreds of picturesque half-timbered houses, many with the old signs of their former owners. Head for the marketplace, where restorers have done an impressive job on the Renaissance-style *Rathaus* (Town Hall) and on the colorful woodcarvings on the façades of the surrounding 16th-century houses. Beyond the *Rathaus* is the *Schlossberg,* crowned by *Stiftskirche St. Servatius* (Church of St. Servatius), whose 19th-century towers rest on a medieval base. In 1945, several of the church's treasures, including pieces of rock crystal from medieval times and a richly ornamented shrine, were stolen by a soldier from Texas; the items were recovered only last year, and are now on display. Guided tours of the cathedral are given daily on the half hour until 3:30 PM; they are available in English on request during the summer. From the balustrade of the *Schloss* (castle) there's a stunning view of Old Quedlinburg, with its tiled roofs tilting at all angles. The *Schlosskrug* restaurant (see *Best en Route*) is a good place for lunch or a snack. The tourist office is at 12 Markt (phone: 3946-2633); it's closed Sundays.

BEST EN ROUTE

Schlosskrug Set in the castle forecourt, this restaurant serves good lunches (outside if the weather's good) and afternoon coffee. Closed Mondays. No reservations. No credit cards accepted. 1 Schlossberg, Quedlinburg (phone: 3946-2838). Expensive to moderate.

Pension Theophano In a fully restored half-timbered house dating from the 17th century, this hotel makes an ideal base for exploring the area. It's right on Quedlinburg's old market square; the 16 rooms feature private showers, TV sets, pine furnishings, and even fax hookups. There's a cozy wine bar and a restaurant. 13-14 Markt, Quedlinburg (phone: 3946-96300; fax: 3946-963036). Moderate.

Gambrinius This brightly lit, centrally located café offering tasty, light fare (sandwiches, soup, salads) is a good place to stop if you need a break from sightseeing. Open daily. No reservations. No credit cards accepted. 7 Karlspl., Quedlinburg (phone: 3946-72739). Moderate to inexpensive.

En Route from Quedlinburg Continue to drive along the northern fringe of the Harz Mountains, taking the minor road through Weddersleben and Thale. After Thale you pass through Blankenburg; stop briefly at the dramatic ruins of *Burg Regenstein* (Regenstein Fortress) just out of town to the right. Chiseled from sandstone, the building was first used as a stronghold in the 5th century. Nine miles (14 km) farther on is Wernigerode.

WERNIGERODE This is the most photogenic town in the eastern part of the Harz vacation area. Its colorful and half-timbered 16th-century *Rathaus* (Town Hall), at the crossing of Marktstrasse and Breite Strasse, looks like something out of a fairy tale by the Brothers Grimm. Unfortunately, 40 years of neglect by the former East German authorities allowed many of the town's quaint buildings to deteriorate. Much of the town center looks as if it had been bombed, even though Wernigerode emerged largely unscathed from World War II. There is an unusual feudal museum in the medieval castle that overlooks the town; its exhibits include furniture and objects illustrating daily life in the Middle Ages and the history of the Harz region. The museum is closed Sundays; admission charge (phone: 32856-23303). Wernigerode is also the northern terminus for the *Harzquerbahn,* a narrow-gauge steam railway that links the northern and southern Harz. If you have time, take a trip (it costs only a few pfennigs) up through Drei-Annen-Hohne and past the Brocken, which at 3,747 feet is the highest peak in the Harz. It was chosen by Johann Wolfgang von Goethe for the witches' *Walpurgisnacht* scenes in *Faust.*

En Route from Wernigerode Drive on Route 244 toward Elbingerode, where it intersects with Route 27. Then take Route 27 east to Rübeland. Before you get to Rübeland, you may want to take a brief detour off Route 27 to the left, where there are some impressive limestone caves worth seeing—if you have the patience to wait in a long line. From the caves, continue through Rübeland on Route 27, and then take rural Route 6 through the northern foothills of the Harz Mountains to Goslar via Ilsenburg and Bad Harzburg. (At the intersection of Route 27 and Route 6 is the town of Blankenburg; trivia lovers will be interested to learn that the first kindergarten was established here by Friedrich Fröbel in 1840.) The total distance covered is about 28 miles (45 km).

GOSLAR Set in what was the West German region of the Harz Mountains during the years when the country was divided, Goslar has long been a distinguished city. It had particularly high stature during the era of the Holy Roman Empire, as indicated by the imperial *Kaiserpfalz* (Emperor's Palace; 6 Kaiserbleek; phone: 5321-704358). Built between 1009 and 1056 and greatly expanded over the next 700 years, it is the world's largest purely Romanesque building. The palace is open daily; admission charge. The town's wealth, derived from silver mines in the nearby Rammelsberg highlands, found expression in the resplendent, late-Gothic *Rathaus* (Town Hall), built in 1450, and the rows of half-timbered houses with elaborately carved cross beams and window frames surrounding the market square. Two-thirds of all the buildings in the Altstadt (Old Town) date from before World War I; 168 were erected before 1550. *Goslar-Hahnenklee Tourist-Information* (7 Markt.; phone: 5321-2846) has plenty of information about local attractions, shops, accommodations, and restaurants; it's closed Sundays.

En Route from Goslar Return to Bad Harzburg and pick up Route 4 heading south. This road travels through the heart of the Harz Mountains to Route 81. Take Route 81 south and continue to Nordhausen via Hasselfelde. The total distance from Goslar to Nordhausen is about 46 miles (74 km).

NORDHAUSEN The southern terminus of the railway from Wernigerode, Nordhausen produces Germany's famous schnapps, Echter Nordhäuser Doppelkorn. First bottled in 1507, it is available in local liquor stores.

Five miles (8 km) northwest of Nordhausen is the memorial to the Dora concentration camp, which once stood on the site. Inmates here were forced to work in atrocious conditions in underground factories, building the V2 rockets Hitler used to blitz England in the latter part of World War II.

The Kyffhäuserberg (Kyffhäuser Mountain), 15 miles (24 km) southeast of Nordhausen, rises 1,565 feet out of the north Thuringian plain, and is shrouded in local lore. One legend has it that Emperor Friedrich Barbarossa was asleep in his underground cave here until the time came to unite the German people. With the proclamation of the united German Reich in 1871, composed of the 24 previously independent German states, Kaiser Wilhelm I had a monument erected on the Kyffhäuser Mountain peak, representing himself as a glowering and mighty Barbarossa in red sandstone. In good weather, the view from the top of the mountain is breathtaking, extending northward over the Harz and westward past the former border between East and West Germany.

En Route from Nordhausen Now continue along Route 81 to Bad Frankenhausen, take Route 85 to Sachsenburg, and then pick up Route 86 to Eisenach via Straussfurt—a total of 54 miles (86 km).

EISENACH An automobile manufacturing center since the turn of the century, Eisenach is better known as the site of the *Wartburg,* a bastion dating from 1067 atop a 600-foot hill. Now housing several museums, this fortress complex was the home of the medieval *Minnesinger* minstrels (immortalized by Richard Wagner in his opera *Tannhäuser*) and served as Martin Luther's retreat in the 16th century, when he translated the Bible from Greek into German. The *Wartburg* is open daily; admission charge (phone: 3691-3001, 3691-3002, or 3691-3004). For more information about the fortress, see *Churches, Castles, and Palaces* in DIVERSIONS. The composer Johann Sebastian Bach was born in Eisenach, and the family home (21 Frauenplan; phone: 3691-3714) houses a fascinating collection of musical instruments and Bach family memorabilia. It's open daily; admission charge.

BEST EN ROUTE

Fürstenhof This 51-room property, built in high-turreted Wilhelmine style, was originally a spa resort when it opened in 1902, but during the days of the GDR it was converted into a rather drab hotel called the *Stadt Eisenach.* Since then, the place has undergone a complete renovation and has reclaimed its original name (but only a few of its spa facilities). The location combines proximity to the town's attractions with lovely views of the *Wartburg.* Other amenities include a restaurant and ample parking. 11-13 Luisenstr., Eisenach (phone: 3691-7780; fax: 3691-203682). Expensive to moderate.

Auf der Wartburg Recently renovated and more attractive than ever, this 15-room hostelry perches on a slope alongside the walls of the *Wartburg.* The dining room features good food and an outdoor terrace with lovely views of the town and the surrounding forested hills. Eisenach (phone/fax: 3691-5111). Moderate.

Glockenhof At the foot of the *Wartburg*'s hill, this woodsy restaurant offers traditional Thuringian specialties in a charming, Old German atmosphere. There are also 23 modest guestrooms upstairs. Open daily. No reservations. No credit cards accepted. 4 Grimmelgasse, Eisenach (phone: 3691-2340; fax: 691-234131). Inexpensive.

En Route from Eisenach Route 7, with views of the Thuringian hills on the right, takes you 34 miles (54 km) east to Erfurt. On the way, a half-hour excursion southeast to Arnstadt is very rewarding (turn onto the autobahn and head for Gotha). First mentioned in 704, Arnstadt is one of the oldest towns in this part of Germany. Bach began his career as an organist here from 1703 to 1707. Besides a beautifully restored marketplace, Arnstadt also has a 200-year-old *Mon Plaisir* doll collection in the *Neue Palais* (New Palace; phone: 3628-2932), which is closed Mondays; admission charge. From here, Erfurt is a 20-minute drive north.

ERFURT A provincial capital and major industrial center, Erfurt is the only sizable town in central Germany that was not largely destroyed in World War II. It was liberated by the Americans in April 1945, but was handed over to the Russians under the agreements reached at Yalta and Potsdam that divided Germany into occupied zones. Dominating Erfurt are two Catholic churches side by side on the Domberg (Cathedral Hill). The walls of the *Dom* (Cathedral) and those of the *Severikirche* (both finished by the 15th century) lie just a few feet apart at their closest point. In town, a walk down the Marktstrasse leads to the Krämerbrücke, a 14th-century ensemble of houses on a bridge over the Gera River. Formerly traders' houses, they were restored in the 1960s as delightful little antiques shops, bookstalls, and cafés. This is a good place to find that unusual souvenir.

BEST EN ROUTE

Erfurter Hof Opposite the railroad station is one of the best-kept and most distinguished hotels in what was East Germany. It has plenty of modern conveniences and the excellent *Kellerrestaurant,* serving interesting culinary inventions. The rooms in the back are quieter than those facing the station. 1 Willy-Brandt-Pl., Erfurt (phone: 361-5310; fax: 361-646-1021). Expensive.

Bürgerhof Centrally located, this 49-room hostelry with a restaurant is as comfortable as it is unpretentious. Be forewarned, however, that there are no private baths. 35 Bahnhofstr., Erfurt (phone: 361-642-1307). Moderate.

Thuringian This 156-room hotel is set on the eastern edge of the inner city, a particularly convenient location. There are also parking facilities—an advantage in the often-crowded town of Erfurt—and a restaurant. 126-127 Yuri-Gagarin-Ring, Erfurt (phone/fax: 361-646-5512). Moderate.

Gildehaus Set in the city's former merchants' guild house, this dining spot has been a local favorite for many years. The menu offers homestyle preparations of Thuringian specialties, particularly sausages and soups; the ambience is charming and old-fashioned. Open daily. Reservations advised. Major credit cards accepted. 13-16 Fischmarkt, Erfurt (phone: 361-643-0692). Moderate to inexpensive.

En Route from Erfurt From Erfurt, continue east on Route 7 another 13 miles (21 km) to Weimar.

WEIMAR This town of just 65,000 people is one of the country's most important centers of German history and culture. Goethe and Schiller both wrote some of their greatest works in Weimar in the 18th and early 19th centuries. In 1919, the first German Republic, historically known as the Weimar Republic, proclaimed its constitution in the town's now reconstructed *Deutsches Nationaltheater* (German National Theater; Theaterpl.; phone: 3643-755301; 3643-755334, box office). The Weimar Republic fell during the world economic crisis in the early 1930s, when the ferociously nationalistic Nazi Party rose to power. The theater offers concerts, as well as classical and contemporary plays and operas in German. The *Schillerhaus* (12 Schillerstr.; phone: 3643-62041) is where the famous dramatist lived from 1802 to 1805; it is full of personal mementos and costumes from productions of *Wilhelm Tell* and his other works. The house is closed Thursdays; admission charge. The *Goethe National Museum* (1 Am Frauenplan; phone: 3643-62041) is set in the house where Goethe lived from 1782 until his death in 1832. Visitors can explore 14 of the rooms; among the exhibits are the writer's collections of minerals and artworks, and the library, with about 5,000 books. There is also a pleasant café. The museum is closed Mondays; admission charge. A short walk from Goethe's house past the *Elephant* hotel (see *Best en Route*) brings you to a park where the poet used to walk, which is now named after him. Across the river is the *Gartenhaus* (Garden House; Im Park der Ilm; phone: 3643-2472) that Goethe used in the summer (he wrote *Iphigenie* here, among other things); it contains a collection of his drawings. The house is open daily; admission charge.

BEST EN ROUTE

Weimar Hilton This 295-room establishment has an idyllic location opposite the *Goethepark.* The atmosphere is quiet, dignified, and historical. Among the many modern facilities are three restaurants, a swimming pool, a health club, and a sauna. 25 Belvederer Allee, Weimar (phone: 3643-7220; 800-HILTONS; fax: 3643-722-7412). Very expensive.

Elephant Centrally located, this place dates from 1696, but has most of the facilities you could want plus some extras, such as a garden terrace and a cozy lounge with a fireplace. The *Elephantkeller* is an excellent, vaulted restaurant in the basement. 19 Am Markt, Weimar (phone: 3643-61471; fax: 3643-65310). Moderate.

BUCHENWALD Before leaving the area, take a detour to Buchenwald, 3 miles (5 km) northwest. Now run as a national memorial, it's the site of one of Hitler's most notorious concentration camps, opened in 1937. Here 56,000 people, including Jews, Communists, and prisoners of war, died before the surviving inmates were freed by the Americans in April 1945. The contrast between the barbarities once perpetrated here and the humanistic ideals of nearby Weimar is chilling. It is closed Mondays; admission charge (phone: 3643-67481).

En Route from Weimar Route 7 takes you toward Jena, but turn left at Route 87 and head past Apolda to Naumburg; the total distance traveled is about 22 miles (35 km).

NAUMBURG This town, in the midst of beautiful orchard country known as the *Blütengrund,* was a major trading and religious center in the Middle Ages. Although you may think you've had your fill of medieval architecture after Magdeburg and Erfurt, the cathedral here should be seen. The *Naumburger Dom* (Naumburg Cathedral), which is dedicated to Saints Peter and Paul, has been beautifully preserved; its earliest parts date from 1210. Inside are realistic and humorous carved figures of ordinary folk of the time, installed in the late 13th century. Before you leave Naumburg, visit the *Ratskeller* in the *Rathaus* (Town Hall; Wilhelm Pieck Pl.; phone: 3445-202063; no credit cards accepted). Here you can sample the very dry wine produced by local vineyards in the Saale and Unstrut River Valleys. Try it; it's little known outside this part of the country and it's excellent.

En Route from Naumburg From here, the university city of Leipzig is a 31-mile (50-km) drive along Route 87. For a detailed report on the city and its hotels and restaurants, see *Leipzig* in THE CITIES.

The German Alpine Road and Lake Constance

This passage through the Bavarian Alps makes for one of the most scenic drives in all of Europe. For some 300 miles (485 km), between Berchtesgaden in the east (a scant dozen miles from the Austrian festival city of Salzburg) and Lindau on Lake Constance in the west, Die Deutsche Alpenstrasse (the German Alpine Road) wends its way among grand mountains, shimmering lakes, deep forests, and high-altitude castles and resorts. The Alps here are dominated by the Zugspitze, at just under 10,000 feet Germany's highest mountain.

Our suggested itinerary is composed of two connected auto tours. One follows the dramatic Alpine Road; the other is an extension of that drive beyond Lindau, to the Lake Constance region. Though only 30 miles (50 km) farther, it gives an added (and worthwhile) dimension to the journey. With occasional detours, the drive covers about 375 miles (600 km). You could easily spend a week or more in what is generally recognized as one of the loveliest and most interesting parts of Germany.

The routes can be followed in either direction; the suggested itinerary goes east to west since many travelers are likely to combine the drive with a Munich visit. Traveling through villages that look morc likc stagc scts from 19th-century operettas, the route reveals a world of cobblestone streets lined with colorful old wooden houses whose bright frescoes, carved doorways, and dark balconies are set off by windowsills rimmed with bursts of brilliant flowers. Also along the way are Baroque churches with high, white onion domes and towers. Oberammergau, of *Passion Play* fame, is on this route, as are several famous spa and lake resorts and the spectacular *Königsschlösser* (Royal Castles)—two fantastic, fairy-tale palaces that are probably already familiar to people who have visited *Walt Disney World* and *Disneyland.*

Note: In winter, the scenery along the Alpine Road, with its snow-covered mountains and pastures, is breathtaking, and the area also offers plenty of recreational possibilities, including skiing. However, driving can be extremely perilous. Mountain passes are often closed, and those roads that do remain open can be hazardous. We suggest that you travel this route during the winter only if you are thoroughly familiar with driving over snowy roads, have a car in good mechanical condition, and are well prepared for emergency situations. If you want to ski here, contact travel authorities for alternative transportation suggestions. The driving is best from spring through fall, but the roads can be dangerous no matter what the weather: There are hairpin turns and steep ascents and descents (if at all possible, rent a car with front-wheel drive)—and a lot of drivers who think of this stretch as Germany's answer to *Le Mans.*

Accommodations are generally in smaller resort hotels or country inns at relatively reasonable prices compared to the rest of Germany. For a double room (with private bath and TV set, unless otherwise noted), expect to pay $175 or more in a hotel listed as very expensive; $140 to $175, expensive; $110 to $140, moderate; and less than $110, inexpensive. Rates include full breakfast and service charges unless otherwise indicated; most resort hotels also charge an additional spa tax. Prices listed are during high season; rates drop considerably at other times. Between June and mid-October and during the *Christmas* season, advance reservations are always a good idea. A three-course meal for two, including tax and service charge, will cost $90 or more at restaurants in the expensive category; between $60 and $90 at moderate restaurants; and less than $60 at inexpensive places. For each location, hotels and restaurants are listed alphabetically by price category.

THE GERMAN ALPINE ROAD

En Route from Munich Drive south on the high-speed autobahn A-8. Even from this main road, you will have views of the Alps and the lakelands of Upper Bavaria like the Chiemsee. Once off the highway, turn south to Route B-20, which follows narrow country roads that pass through tunnels of trees, venturing deep into the Alps. The distance between Berchtesgaden and Munich is 95 miles (154 km).

BERCHTESGADEN The ancient market town of Berchtesgaden, surrounded by three mountain chains, is near Germany's second-highest peak, the Watzmann (about 9,000 ft.). Berchtesgaden was Adolf Hitler's favorite retreat. In the 1930s, high up on the slopes of the Obersalzberg, he built his famous *Kehlstein* (also known as "Eagle's Nest"), a mountain villa with a spectacular Alpine view. A vast subterranean fortress built into the mountainside beneath the villa served as a Nazi headquarters where Hitler held high-level staff meetings to plot the course of the war. But Berchtesgaden was a popular vacation haunt long before the Führer's time. Members of the Wittelsbach dynasty, who ruled Bavaria from Munich from 1250 until 1918, claimed the town as their own personal summer hideaway in 1810; their sumptuous palace remains a major sightseeing attraction.

Today, Berchtesgaden still ranks as one of Germany's most popular year-round mountain resorts. As a ski destination it is second only to Garmisch-Partenkirchen, farther along this route. In summer, hiking trails lead through some of the loveliest territory in the Alpine chain. A variety of athletic activities can be pursued, including mountain biking and white-water rafting. Not surprisingly, Berchtesgaden is very crowded on weekends during the summer, with the town center all but impossible to navigate by car. Park near the railway station; from behind the station you can take the stairs, bridge, or hillside paths to explore the heart of the town on foot.

The tourist office (closed Sundays October through February) is located across from the railway station in the *Kurdirektion des Berchtesgadener Landes* (Spa Headquarters; 2 Königseer Str.; phone: 8652-9670). Here you can pick up detailed maps of the region, along with information about accommodations, including bed and breakfast establishments, attractions, and excursions in and around town.

The main in-town sight is *Schloss Wittelsbach* (Schlosspl.; phone: 8652-2085), a former Augustine monastery that the Wittelsbach family converted into a royal palace. Now a museum, it features antique furnishings from the 18th and 19th centuries, a Romanesque cloister, and impressive collections of art, arms, porcelain, and tapestries. On the grounds, the 12th-century abbey church is graced by sacred artwork, including fine wood sculptures by two German masters of the medium, Tilman Riemenschneider and Veit Stoss. The museum can be viewed only on guided tours, given at 11 AM and 2 PM. It's closed Saturdays year-round and Sundays from October through *Easter;* admission charge.

There are several ways to reach the area's scenic heights. A cable lift in Obersalzberg, 2½ miles (4 km) from Berchtesgaden, rises to a height of about 3,300 feet above the town. Another option is to take the last cable car stop to the upper reaches of Mt. Jenner, where a terrace 6,000 feet in the air affords truly stupendous views. Finally, a shuttle bus connects Obersalzberg to the base of *Kehlstein,* Hitler's "Eagle's Nest." From the stop, a tunnel into solid rock leads to what remains of the former Nazi complex, where you can take an elegant brass-lined elevator 407 feet through the heart of the mountain to the villa. You can drive as far as Obersalzberg, or take the public bus from the post office (next to the railway station). *Kehlstein* bus service runs from mid-May to mid-October. The round-trip takes at least an hour and a half.

Located 3 miles (5 km) south of town on Route B-20 is one of the major highlights of the Alpine Road: the Königsee, a ribbon of blue-green water wedged between the almost vertical Watzmann on one side, and Kahlersberg on the other. Lake cruises visit the tiny island of St. Bartholomö, which is named after its delicate, red-roofed miniature chapel. Cars must be left in the municipal parking lot (for a fee) at the end of the road by the lakehead, where boats leave frequently on two-hour cruises. Cruises run from early morning until early evening year-round except when the lake is frozen. Tickets can be bought near the cruise pier, where rowboats also can be rented.

BEST EN ROUTE

Geiger Once a country farmstead, it was converted to a luxury hotel by the Geiger family, who have operated it since the 19th century. The chalet-style property, which is a member of the Relais & Châteaux group, is set amidst ravishing Alpine scenery in the Stanggass neighborhood of Berchtesgaden. Victorian antiques decorate the interior, and 40 of the 50 rooms have balconies with mountain views. The restaurant offers excellent local specialties and a panoramic view of the lovely surroundings. There also are two pools. Closed mid-November through mid-December. Visa only accepted. 103-115 Berchtesgadener Str., Stanggass (phone: 8652-9653; fax: 8652-965400). Expensive.

En Route from Berchtesgaden From here the Alpine Road heads west and then north on Route B-20 to Bad Reichenhall, a distance of 12 miles (20 km).

BAD REICHENHALL One of Germany's most renowned spas (see *Taking the Waters: Spas* in DIVERSIONS), Bad Reichenall is in a relatively flat area within a bend of the Saalach River. Though it is far older than Berchtesgaden (dating back to Celtic times), the town appears more modern, built around the attractive *Kurpark* with its spa center. There is little that is rustic, quaint, or even "Alpine" about Bad Reichenhall, yet it offers fine hotels in all price ranges, good places to eat, no parking problems, and minimal crowds.

BEST EN ROUTE

Steigenberger Axelmannstein In a former castle surrounded by exquisitely landscaped grounds, its 151 rooms—some modern, some more traditional—are equipped with mini-bars. Facilities include a spa, a restaurant, and a bar with dancing in the evenings. 4 Salzburger Str., Bad Reichenhall (phone: 8651-7770; 800-223-5652; fax: 8651-5932). Very expensive.

Kirchberg-Schlössl Traditional fare is featured at this one-Michelin-star restaurant decorated in tasteful Baroque style; menu specialties include pike with sauerkraut and beer sauce, lamb with thyme, and Bavarian salads. Closed Wednesdays, two weeks after *Karneval* (February), and the three weeks after *Pentecost* (usually from May into June). Reservations advised. Major credit cards accepted. 11 Thumseestr., Bad Reichenhall (phone: 8651-2760). Expensive.

Bayerischer Hof Though its modern building lacks atmosphere, this hotel is conveniently located (across from the railway station) and comfortable. The 60 rooms are bright and cheerful, with pale wood furnishings. There's a big indoor pool and a sauna. Rooms in the rear are quieter and have sunny balconies overlooking attractive gardens. The restaurant serves regional fare and fine wines. Closed January through mid-February. 14 Bahnhofspl., Bad Reichenhall (phone: 8651-6090; fax: 8651-609111). Moderate.

Kurhotel Alpina This 65-room Bavarian hostelry has a restaurant serving continental fare to guests only. Closed November through January. No credit cards accepted. 5 Adolf-Schmidt-Str., Bad Reichenhall (phone: 8651-2038; fax: 8651-65393). Moderate.

En Route from Bad Reichenhall From Bad Reichenhall, take the Alpine Road—now Route 312—for 6 miles (10 km); turn onto Route 306 north for another 6 miles (10 km), and then west on Route 172 for 16 miles (25 km) to Reit im Winkl.

REIT IM WINKL Dominated by a fine Baroque church, the town is dotted with traditional Alpine-weathered wooden farmhouses topped with graceful bell towers. Usually crowded with visitors in Tyrolean hats and britches, this is a quintessential German mountain resort. Also see *Great Ski Slopes* in DIVERSIONS.

BEST EN ROUTE

Altenburger Hof A family-owned and -operated country inn in the center of town, this small chalet has flower-laden balconies with striking Alpine views. The 13 spacious rooms feature modern decor, antique rugs, and amenities such as mini-bars; there's an indoor pool, a sauna, and fitness equipment. The dining room (for guests only) serves Bavarian home cooking. Closed November. No credit cards accepted. 3 Frühlingstr., Reit im Winkl (phone: 8640-8994; fax: 8640-307). Moderate.

En Route from Reit im Winkl Head west 16 miles (25 km) on Route 172 to Oberaudorf; then take the unmarked road 6 miles (10 km) to its intersection with Route 307. Continue on Route 307 for 18 miles (30 km) to the bucolic town of Miesbach, where Route 307 joins with Route 472. Go west on 307/472 for 6 miles (10 km); turn left (south) onto 307/318 for 5 miles (8 km) to Gmund, on the northern shore of the Tegernsee, one of the most beautiful spots in southern Germany.

TEGERNSEE The settlements around this lake receive more than two million visitors each year; this relatively small area—only 10 road miles (16 km) in circumference—holds a wealth of interesting sights. Tegernsee's former Benedictine monastery (8th century) later served as a residence for one of the ruling Wittelsbachs; today, it is the *Bräustüberl* (1 Schlosspl.; phone: 8022-4141), a cavernous, rustic beer-hall restaurant, but it retains its medieval appearance. At the southern tip of the lake, Rottach-Egern is Bavaria's answer to St. Moritz, with luxury hotels, restaurants, and shops. It is set at the base of 5,800-foot Mt. Wallberg, whose summit can be reached by cable car. Excursion boats leave from the resort town of Tegernsee.

BEST EN ROUTE

Bachmair am See The most luxurious spot in this most fashionable area, its 282 elegantly appointed rooms are distributed among several Bavarian-style buildings around the Tegernsee. The *Gourmet,* an upscale restaurant serving well-prepared French fare, is worth a visit even if you don't stay here (dinner only; closed Tuesdays; reservations advised; American Express accepted); there's also the *Bayerische Stub'n,* a more casual and modestly priced eatery. Breakfast and dinner are included in the rate. Other amenities include an indoor pool and a sports center. 47 Seestr., Tegernsee (phone: 8022-2720; fax: 8022-292790). Very expensive.

Zur Post A family-run hotel with 45 pleasantly furnished rooms, it offers home-style, affordable lodgings. The beer-garden restaurant on the premises is popular with both visitors and locals. Visa and MasterCard only accepted. 17 Hauptstr. (phone: 8022-66780; fax: 8022-667-8162). Inexpensive.

En Route from Tegernsee From Gmund at the northern end of the lake, take Route 307 north for 2 miles (4 km) and then Route 472 west for 8 miles (12 km) to Bad Tölz.

BAD TÖLZ Another of Bavaria's leading spas, this one specializes in treatments for heart and circulatory ailments with its iodine-laced spring waters. It is also what is known as a climatic health resort, due to the health-giving properties of the pure mountain air. Like Bad Reichenhall, Bad Tölz doesn't offer extraordinary sights, but the town has a wide range of reasonably priced hotels. In the spa quarter, the *Kurverwaltung* (tourist office; 11 Ludwigstr.; phone: 8041-70071) can arrange accommodations. It is closed Sundays. The neighboring *Alpamare* (13 Ludwigstr.; phone: 8041-509334) is a leisure center with thermal baths, indoor and outdoor swimming pools, a wave pool, a sauna, a solarium, a steambath, and a fitness center. It's open daily.

BEST EN ROUTE

Tölzer Hof With 86 balconied rooms in three modern buildings, this spa hotel has a separate wing with a pool, sauna, fitness center, and massage facility. Public areas are decorated in typical Bavarian style. The restaurant (for hotel guests only) serves regional fare. 21 Rieschstr., Bad Tölz (phone: 8041-8060; fax: 8041-806333). Moderate.

En Route from Bad Tölz From here continue on Route 472 west for 5 miles (8 km) to Bad Heilbrunn, another spa; in another 4 miles (7 km) is Benediktbeuern, with the oldest Benedictine monastery in Upper Bavaria, dating from 739; and 4 miles (7 km) farther is Kochel am See, with a wall of mountains to the east, and marshland to the west. From here, take Route 2 for 20 miles (32 km) to Mittenwald on the Austrian border.

MITTENWALD Described by Goethe as "a living picture book," this ancient town ranks among Bavaria's major showplaces. The old Roman road between Augsburg and Verona ran through this high mountain pass, hemmed in by the sheer rock wall of the Karwendel range separating Bavaria from Austria. During the Middle Ages, goods shipped on the international trade route up from Italy through the Brenner Pass and Innsbruck passed through Mittenwald, and the successful merchants of that time built the splendid homes that still stand here today.

Mittenwald is also known as "The Village of a Thousand Violins." Starting around 1685, after the trade route had been shifted to another pass, the art of violin making was introduced to Mittenwald by a native son who had studied with a master violin maker in Cremona. The creation of exquisite violins, violas, and cellos using spruce and maple wood from neighboring forests became the specialty of a school of Mittenwald craftsmen. The violins of Mittenwald gained international renown, and were exported to many parts of the world. The traditions of playing and making violins continue to this day. The historic *Geigenbau Museum* (Violin Museum; 3 Ballenhausgasse; phone: 8823-2511) shows the step-by-step process of violin making within the setting of a working craftsman's studio. It is closed November through mid-December; admission charge.

Mittenwald can be explored leisurely in a couple of hours. In addition to the *Geigenbau Museum,* the town boasts a wealth of splendid medieval homes with brilliantly painted façades lining the main street, Obermarkt, and its northern extension, Ballenhausgasse. On Ballenhausgasse is the 18th-century *Petrus- und Pauluskirche* (Church of Saints Peter and Paul), a notable rococo structure with a Gothic tower and murals of the saints. In addition to its excellent network of hiking trails, Mittenwald is a top ski destination. Year-round, the Karwendelbahn cable car transports passengers to 7,825 feet, where there is a summit terrace café with expansive views of the surrounding mountains. The *Kurverwaltung* (tourist office; 3 Dammkarstr.; phone: 8823-33981) is closed weekends October through May.

BEST EN ROUTE

Bichlerhof Although the exterior is modern, the interior of this 26-room hostelry has a rustic, homey atmosphere. All rooms have balconies and mini-bars. Amenities include a restaurant (for guests only), a pool, a sauna, and a whirlpool bath. 5 Adolf-Baader-Str., Mittenwald (phone: 8823-5053; fax: 8823-4584). Expensive to moderate.

Berggasthof Gröblalm Overlooking the town, this comfortable country house has 30 guestrooms, many of which offer a sweeping panoramic view of Mittenwald, scenic pastures, and the Karwendel range. There's also a wraparound terrace with equally glorious views. Other amenities include three restaurants (all serving Bavarian fare), a sauna, and a whirlpool. Closed late October through early December. No credit cards accepted. It's located near the Luttensee Mountains, a 10-minute walk from the center of town (phone: 8823-5033; fax: 8823-82481). Moderate.

Pension Hofmann Many of the 22 rooms face the mountains or the hotel garden. Some have balconies, and all have private showers. The pension offers breakfast, but there's no restaurant. No credit cards accepted. Located just five minutes from the town center. 25 Partenkirchnerstr., Mittenwald (phone: 8823-1318; fax: 8823-4686). Moderate.

Post Centrally located in a historic building with painted façade, this charming 87-room hotel is decorated in traditional Bavarian style, with a popular terrace café, a cozy wine tavern, and the rustic *Poststüberl* restaurant, where old-time regional favorites are served by a friendly staff. 9 Obermarkt, Mittenwald (phone: 8823-1094). Moderate.

Postkeller Traditional regional cooking and, on some nights, music and dancing are dished out in this enormous room that accommodates 450 diners. Beer from the brewery next door is on tap here. Open daily. Reservations advised. No credit cards accepted. 13 Innsbrucker Str., Mittenwald (phone: 8823-1729). Moderate.

Alpenrose Originally a 13th-century cloister and now a small (19-room) inn, its chapel remains part of the property. The decor is traditional Bavarian style. There's a restaurant which features game dishes as well as fish in season, and a *Weinkeller* (wine cellar) that offers food and drink and, occasionally, music. 1 Obermarkt, Mittenwald (phone: 8823-5055). Moderate to inexpensive.

En Route from Mittenwald Drive northwest for 12 miles (19 km) on Route 2 to Garmisch-Partenkirchen, two towns that have been combined into one.

GARMISCH-PARTENKIRCHEN One of the winter sports capitals of Germany, Garmisch (the more familiar name of the two towns) hosted the *Winter Olympics* in 1936, when Europe was on the brink of war. Now one of the continent's best-outfitted ski resorts, it has some 40 ski lifts and cable cars, a network of 70 miles of downhill runs, and excellent cross-country skiing. The charm of Garmisch-Partenkirchen, a good-size modern city, lies in its surroundings—meadows, pastureland, and pine woods running to the slopes of mountains—and the hundreds of trails that run through them. Cable cars carry passengers to the more-than-a-mile-high peak of Wank mountain; the sun terrace at the top affords some spectacular views. The *Bayerische Zugspitzbahn* (27 Olympiastr.; phone: 8821-7970), an electric cog railway, leaves every hour for the 75-minute ride most of the way up the 9,721-foot Zugspitze, Germany's highest peak, to the *Sonn Alpin,* an informal, self-service restaurant. From there, a cable car travels to the summit terrace. The trip up the Zugspitze can also be made by cable car, leaving from the Eibsee station outside Garmisch. Always wear warm clothing (even in summer a thick sweater and windbreaker are sometimes needed), along with sunglasses and sunscreen. Also see *Great Ski Slopes* in DIVERSIONS.

In addition to sports, Garmisch also has a fairly active nightlife, including casino gambling. For more information about attractions and accommodations, contact *Verkehrsamt der Kurverwaltung* (Tourist Office; Richard-Strauss-Pl.; phone: 8821-1806); it is open daily.

BEST EN ROUTE

Posthotel Partenkirchen One of Europe's legendary mountain resort inns and a member of the prestigious Chaîne de Rôtisserie group, this property was a stagecoach stop in the 18th century. The rococo building has a gaily frescoed façade and 60 antique-filled rooms. There are three Bavarian-style restaurants—the main dining room, another that opens during high season, and a third that serves breakfast only. 49 Ludwigstr., Garmisch-Partenkirchen (phone: 8821-51067; fax: 8821-78568). Expensive.

En Route from Garmisch-Partenkirchen From here, the Alpine Road heads north (on Rte. 2) to Oberau, then on Routes 2 and 23 to Oberammergau, for a total of 12 miles (19 km). Along the way you pass through Ettal; visible on the south (left) side are the high walls of the huge *Kloster Ettal,* the monastery founded by Emperor Ludwig the Bavarian in 1330. It now serves as a school run by Benedictine monks. The original church was redecorated in the 18th century and stands as a prime example of Bavarian rococo style architecture.

OBERAMMERGAU A town of great beauty, where the cattle are still led through the streets on their way to and from pasture, Oberammergau is best known as the site of the *Passion Play,* depicting the last days of Christ. Now mounted on a vast open-air stage once a decade (the next production will be held in the year 2000), the play was first performed in 1634 in a far shorter version than today's 16-act, daylong marathon. Originally, the townspeople put on the play as a token of gratitude to God for sparing them from the Black Plague in 1633, the year it swept through most of Bavaria. Today, about one-third of the town's 5,200 inhabitants participate in the summer spectacle, and about 4,700 people attend each performance. By the end of the season (May through September), 500,000 people from all over the world have seen it.

Oberammergau is also renowned for its woodcarving, largely on religious themes. Artisans can be viewed at work at the *Holzschittschule* (Woodcarving School; 3 Ludwiglangstr.; no phone) on Tuesdays and Fridays; many of their pieces are sold in local shops. Historic carvings, including a collection of 18th-century *Christmas* crèches, are on display at the *Heimatmuseum* (8 Dorfstr.; phone: 8822-32256). It is closed Mondays mid-May through mid-October; the rest of the year, it's open Saturday afternoons only. There's an admission charge. The open-air theater where the *Passion Play* is performed can be visited year-round; there is also an exhibition about the spectacle in an attached building. It is closed Mondays, mid-November through mid-December, and the last three weeks of January; there is an admission charge.

Of the many homes with beautifully painted façades, the *Pilatushaus* (Ludwig-Thoma-Str.), built in 1750, rates as the finest. The *Pfarrkirche* (parish church; Ettalerstr.) is a beauty, too, with its clock tower topped by an onion dome, and a dazzling interior with fine frescoes and rococo altarpieces. The town's Old World charm, however, has been somewhat corrupted by the onslaught of tourism. Buses disgorge hordes of sightseers daily; many are day-trippers, though, so a relative peace returns by the late afternoon. There are a number of fine hotels here, such as the *Parkhotel Sonnenhof* (see *Best en Route*). The *Verkehrsbüro* (tourist office; 9 Eugen-Pabst-Str.; phone: 8822-1021) is open daily.

BEST EN ROUTE

Parkhotel Sonnenhof A country hotel at the edge of town, it overlooks the Ammer River and the lovely *Pfarrkirche.* With 72 spacious, balconied rooms, the hotel is a short walk from the town center. Amenities include a pool, a sauna, a cocktail bar, and two restaurants. 12 König-Ludwig-Str., Oberammergau (phone: 8822-1071; fax: 8822-3047). Moderate.

Café-Restaurant Zum Lois Down the road from the *Sonnenhof* hotel, this eatery is decorated in rustic style, with antlers hanging on the wood-paneled walls and an old-fashioned tiled stove. The menu offers down-to-earth Bavarian specialties (game, sausages), beer on tap, and wine. Closed Wednesdays. No reservations. No credit cards accepted. 39 König-Ludwig-Str., Oberammergau (phone: 8822-3917). Inexpensive.

En Route from Oberammergau Continue north on Route 2-23 to Echelsbacher Bridge across the Ammer River, a distance of 10 miles (17 km), where there is a worthwhile detour. Turn left onto an unnumbered road and continue 4 miles (7 km) to the magnificent *Wieskirche* (Church in the Meadow), the masterpiece of architect Dominikus Zimmermann. Built between 1746 and 1754, it is considered the finest of Bavaria's rococo churches. Though simple on the outside, its interior is decorated with luminous ceiling frescoes and a gilt-adorned high altar. Two miles (3 km) farther along this unnumbered road is Steingaden; here the road intersects with Route 17. Take Route 17 for 11 miles (17 km) to Schwangau, home of the famed *Königsschlösser* (Royal Castles), which figured prominently in the life of Ludwig II (the infamous "Mad King Ludwig").

SCHWANGAU The Alpine Road and the Romantic Road (see *The Romantic Road* route in this section) meet at a point dominated by the fairy-tale, neo-Gothic *Schloss Neuschwanstein* (Neuschwanstein Castle). Perched on a rocky pinnacle at the edge of a lake, its towers and turrets seem to touch the sky. Also here is the Tudor-style *Schloss Hohenschwangau* (Hohenschwangau Castle), another architectural masterpiece. Both castles may be visited only on 35-minute guided tours (available in English as well as German).

Neuschwanstein (phone: 8362-81035) and *Hohenschwangau* (phone: 8362-81128) are closed *All Saints' Day* (November 1), *Christmas Eve,* and *New Year's Day;* admission charge.

To view the *Königsschlösser* up close, you will have to leave your car in one of the private parking lots in Schwangau. From the area where the lots are, it is a short walk up village streets lined with souvenir stands and sausage vendors to *Schloss Hohenschwangau.* There are several ways to get to *Neuschwanstein,* about a mile from Schwangau: a half-hour walk (up a steep hill); a shuttle bus from the *Lisl* hotel across from *Hohenschwangau* to the end of the road, from which it's a 10-minute walk to the castle; or a horse-drawn carriage departing from the *Müller* hotel (16 Alpseestr.; phone: 8362-81990).

Both castles are prime tourist destinations for more than eight million people a year; be warned that on summer weekends the traffic can be backed up for miles, and the wait to see the castles can be two hours or longer. Try early morning, preferably on a weekday, to avoid the crush.

Concerts of classical music are presented at *Neuschwanstein* from time to time on September evenings. For more information about "Mad King Ludwig" and his *Königsschlösser,* see *Churches, Castles, and Palaces* in DIVERSIONS. For more information about accommodations and other attractions in the area, contact the *Kurverwaltung Rathaus* (tourist office; 2 Münchener Str.; phone: 8362-81980); it is open daily.

BEST EN ROUTE

Schlosshotel Lisl Located between the two royal castles, this villa-style property boasts 56 high-ceilinged rooms (some with views of *Neuschwanstein* and *Hohenschwangau*), a pool, and a popular restaurant. Closed January to mid-March. 1 Neuschwansteinstr., Schwangau (phone: 8362-8870; fax: 8362-81107). Expensive to moderate.

En Route from Schwangau About 2 miles (4 km) farther along Route 17 is Füssen (see *The Romantic Road* route, in this section). The journey from Füssen to Lake Constance is a circuitous one, zigzagging through verdant valleys along the way. From Füssen, go 11 miles (18 km) northwest on Route E532 to the town of Neselwang; then southwest for 12 miles (20 km) on the unmarked road to Immenstadt. From Immenstadt go northwest for 24 miles (40 km) on Route 308 to just north of Lindenberg; from there take Route E54 southwest for 12 miles (20 km) to Lindau, the first town on Lake Constance.

LAKE CONSTANCE

Lake Constance (its name in German is Bodensee) is like an inland sea. Germany's largest lake, it is also the third-largest in Europe, after Lake Balaton in Hungary and Lake Geneva in Switzerland. Some 40 miles long, and about 10 miles across at its widest point, it is bordered by Switzerland and Austria. The Rhine passes into the lake's eastern end along the Austrian-Swiss frontier, leaving it again near the city of Constance (Konstanz) at the opposite end.

Despite heavy water traffic between the lake's border countries, Constance remains an idyllic, balmy setting—an expanse of lake with flowers planted all around its shores and the Alps forming a jagged snow-capped horizon in the distance. Its tiny, historic towns also have the worn cobblestone streets, red-roofed houses, and ancient towers usually associated with the chillier towns of the high mountains. An ideal place to begin a tour is the island of Lindau.

LINDAU Its full name is Lindau im Bodensee—literally, "Lindau in Lake Constance." Lindau is connected to the mainland by a narrow bridge for cars, bicycles, and pedestrians at one end and a long causeway for trains at the other—a Swabian version of Venice, but without the canals.

Lindau achieved prestige during the Middle Ages due to its strategic position on a major trade route between northern Europe and Italy. It was an imperial city of the Holy Roman Empire between 1275 and 1803. As with Mittenwald, Lindau's fame and fortune depended on its merchant traffic; however, its period of affluence lasted far longer, until the advent of the railroad between northern and southern Europe in the late 19th century made the Lindau connection obsolete.

Though the railroad took away one avenue of business, it created another: It made Lindau accessible to the rest of Europe, marking its birth as a vacation destination. Developers moved in, building large and impressive hotels where defensive walls had once stood. By 1900, the little town was one of Europe's top summer resorts. Lindau's heyday as a resort was between the two world wars, although it is still a popular tourist destination today. Its harbor entrance is guarded by the huge stone lion of Bavaria on one side, and the "new" lighthouse (from the 19th century) on the other. (On the inner bank of the harbor is the "old" lighthouse; graceful as a Venetian campanile, it is the only vestige of its 13th-century seaside fortifications.)

The town's shoreline promenade is flanked with open-air terrace cafés, with lovely, old-fashioned hotels in the background; during afternoons in high season, an orchestra plays lilting melodies on a terrace adjoining the promenade.

Behind the hotels are pedestrians-only thoroughfares connected by alleyways, creating a charming Old World ambience. The whole island can easily be explored on foot in a little over an hour, taking in the patrician, gable-roofed houses, some with vaulted arcades; and the flamboyant 15th-century *Rathaus* (City Hall; Ludwigstr.), with brilliant murals across its front depicting dignitaries who came to the city for an imperial conference in 1496. Perhaps the top attraction, however, is the *Haus Zum Cavazzen,* whose round *Thieves' Tower,* with a steeply pointed spire crowned by equally sharp turrets, is a town landmark. Rebuilt in 1730 as a Baroque mansion, it now houses the *Städtisches Museum* (Municipal Museum; Am Marktpl.; phone: 8382-275405) with mechanical musical instruments and exhibits chronicling the area's history. The museum is closed Mondays and from November through March; admission charge. Next door, the 11th-century *Petruskirche* (St. Peter's Church) is Lindau's oldest standing structure, with interior frescoes believed to have been painted by Hans Holbein the Elder.

The town has fine hotels and restaurants in a variety of price ranges (see *Best en Route*). Sports facilities are plentiful, too, including bicycle, rowboat, and sailboat rentals, and there's casino gambling at the *Spielbank* (2 Oskar-Groll-Anlage; phone: 8382-5200). During July and August, the lakeside *Bregenz Music Festival* (phone: 8382-3015), featuring classical music played on an open stage built out on the lake, is held in Bregenz, Austria, only a 6-mile (10-km) drive (or a short boat ride) away. For more information on area attractions and accommodations, contact *Tourist Information am Hauptbahnhof* (phone: 8382-260030; fax: 8382-260026), across from the railway station; closed Sundays.

BEST EN ROUTE

Bayerischer Hof The exterior of this grand resort hotel (ca. 1854) hasn't changed since its heyday in the 1920s and 1930s. The 104 guestrooms, however, are luxuriously appointed with plenty of modern amenities and large baths. Several of the upper rooms have a marvelous view of the lake and the Alps in the distance. The excellent restaurant serves Bavarian fare prepared with such local ingredients as trout caught in Lake Constance and fresh mushrooms. Open *Easter* through October. MasterCard and Visa only accepted. Bahnhofpl., Lindau (phone: 8382-5055). Very expensive.

Hotel Bad Schachen This is a resort for the truly health-conscious: Its hot springs, hiking paths, and fresh air have a revitalizing effect on its guests. The 130 rooms are attractively decorated in a rustic style. Amenities include a good restaurant serving local and international fare, two pools, tennis courts, and a "wellness center" offering massages, manicures, and facials. For more information, see *Best Hotels* in DIVERSIONS. Closed mid-October through March. 1 Bad Schachen, Lindau (phone: 8382-2980; fax: 8382-25390). Expensive.

Reutemann-Seegarten Under the same ownership and management as the pricier *Bayerischer Hof* next door (see above), this property offers 64 clean, comfortable rooms, some with stunning lake views. There's a popular terrace café on the lakeside promenade as well. On the Seepromenade, Lindau (parking lot entrance on Ludwigstrasse; phone: 8382-5055). Expensive.

Gasthaus zum Sünfzen Opened in 1358, this restaurant in a historic building at one end of the pedestrian zone was originally an exclusive dining spot for local nobility. Nowadays, it is Lindau's most popular eating place. (Its name literally means "Guesthouse for Groaning"—a witty reference to the groans of pleasure uttered by diners after a good meal.) In a rustic dining room with mellow woodwork, specialties from Bavaria and neighboring Baden-Württemberg (including seafood from Lake Constance and local game) are served along with generous mugs of beer and regional wine. In warm weather, you can dine on the cobblestone terrace. Closed February. Reservations unnecessary. Major credit cards accepted. 1 Maximilianstr., Lindau (phone: 8382-5865). Moderate to inexpensive.

Insel This small, modest hotel on Lindau's main pedestrian street offers 28 attractive rooms. There's a bar-café and a breakfast room, but no formal restaurant. An exceptional value compared to the more expensive lakeside hotels. 42 Maximilianstr., Lindau (phone: 8382-5017). Inexpensive.

En Route from Lindau From here, Route 31 continues along the lakeside, first to Wasserburg, a former island fortress that resembles Lindau, but on a smaller scale. Totally traffic-free (cars are forbidden by law on the island), it has fine old houses, a 14th-century castle that is now the *Schloss Wasserburg* hotel, and a church erected in the same period, with a Baroque tower built partially on 10th-century fortifications. Nonnenhorn, a nearby neighbor to the west, is a charming fishing village surrounded by vineyards. Even farther west, in Langenargen, is the medieval castle of the Counts of Montfort, which was converted into a faux-Oriental palace in the 19th century; today it serves as the tourist office (phone: 7543-30292; closed Sundays). Orchards line the lakeside, and nestled in the hills are several renowned wine towns, among them Hagnau, Immenstaad, and Nonnenhorn. About 15 miles (24 km) from Lindau, the coast road reaches Friedrichshafen, the largest town on the northern side of the lake.

FRIEDRICHSHAFEN Since Friedrichshafen was the only place on Lake Constance that was bombed in World War II (the town was a center for aircraft production), it appears much more modern than its neighbors. It was from here, on July 2, 1900, that the first engine-driven airship was launched. Invented by Graf von Zeppelin, this famous cigar-shaped dirigible served as the prototype for later models. By the 1920s, zeppelins were regarded as the wave of the future for mass air transportation. In 1929, the LZ 127 *Graf Zeppelin* went around the world. Soon thereafter, regular transatlantic service was set up between Friedrichshafen and Lakehurst, New Jersey, until the *Hindenburg* disaster in 1937, when the dirigible burst into flames in mid-flight. By then, however, Friedrichshafen was ready to replace zeppelins with another aeronautical industry: the Dornier flying boats, a fleet of passenger-carrying transatlantic seaplanes.

Today, Friedrichshafen's major attraction is the *Zeppelin Museum* (1 Adenauerpl.; phone: 7541-203441), with displays of the dirigibles' engines, navigational equipment, and passenger compartments, as well as many photographs of the airships. Located on the second floor of the *Rathaus* (City Hall), the museum is closed Mondays and during February; admission charge. The tourist office (1 Friedrichstr.; phone: 7541-21729) has leaflets and brochures about area attractions and accommodations; it's closed Sundays.

En Route from Friedrichshafen Route 31 continues along the lake, passing through Immenstaad, Kirchberg, and Hagnau, three pretty wine town/summer resorts with half-timbered houses, old churches, and a few castles. Meersburg is about 11 miles (18 km) from Friedrichshafen. Although over-endowed with quaint shops and often jammed with tourists, this little village is still worth a stop.

MEERSBURG This medieval town, enclosed within high ramparts overlooking the lake, is a true Lake Constance showpiece. Arched entrances set into the base of ancient towers, dating from the early 7th century, lead into rough cobblestone lanes lined with three- and four-story half-timbered houses. Of the two castles here, the *Altes Schloss,* with its *Dagobert's Tower,* is the oldest occupied castle in Germany, dating from the seventh century. *Neues Schloss,* from the mid-1700s, is a masterpiece by architect Balthazar Neumann, with a splendidly ornate interior that serves as the setting for evening concerts on Saturdays from late June through August. *Altes Schloss* (near Steigstr.; phone: 7532-6441) is open daily. *Neues Schloss* (on Schlosspl.; phone: 7532-82385) is closed November through *Easter.* Both castles charge admission. The 16th-century *Rathaus* (City Hall; Am Marktpl.) is outfitted with a cavernous *Ratskeller* (no phone), which serves regional specialties with local wines. It's closed Wednesdays. For more information, visit the *Verkehrsamt* (tourist office; 4 Kirchstr.; phone: 7532-431111); closed weekends and holidays.

En Route from Meersburg Car ferries frequently cross the lake from Meersburg to Constance year-round; the trip takes 25 minutes. Follow signs (marked with the silhouette of a boat) to the dock. The fare is collected on board (phone: 7531-8031).

CONSTANCE Constance (Konstanz in German) is the largest city on the lake; its size and location give it cosmopolitan and international flair. Spreading along the lakefront and the banks of the Rhine, the city is lined with carefully preserved medieval lanes and rows of patrician houses from the 14th and 15th centuries, some built around cobblestone courtyards. From spring through fall, Constance's character is energetic and sprightly, with sailboats and windsurfers zipping back and forth across the harbor beneath a wide expanse of blue sky. From the lake the view is of dense greenery (including palm trees) and the red-roofed houses typical of the region, backed by towers and spires from the 14th and 15th centuries. Along the Rhine sit massive, 19th-century stone mansions, with gables and cupolas, Art Nouveau façades, statuary, and ornate decoration around the doors and windows.

Once a Celtic fishing port, Constance later developed into a Roman fortification, named Constantia to honor the 3rd-century emperor Constantius Chlorus. In 1414, the Christian Reform Council convened here to resolve a quarrel over rival claims to the papacy. The election here of Pope Martin V in 1417 was the only time a pope has ever been selected on German soil. The remodeled *Konzilgebäude* (Council Building) now serves as a modern festival and convention hall.

Another historic structure in town began as a 13th-century Dominican monastery. Abandoned by the order 550 years later, it served as a factory until the 19th century, when the Zeppelin family moved in and converted it into a mansion. Graf von Zeppelin, inventor of the airship, was born here in 1838; in 1875 he converted the property into the *Insel* hotel (see *Best en Route*). No visit to Constance would be complete without enjoying afternoon coffee and cake at the *Insel*'s lakeside terrace café.

The old inner city, with pedestrian zones and cobblestone alleys rimmed with medieval buildings, is a short walk from the *Insel.* Major points of interest include the 11th-century Romanesque *Münster* (basilica), with a high altar given to the city by a member of the wealthy Fugger family from Augsburg. The top of the spire affords an extensive panoramic view of the lake and the Alps. *Jan Hus Haus* (64 Hussenstr.; phone: 7531-29042) serves as a memorial to the Bohemian religious reformer summoned here from Prague by the Council of Constance to stand trial for heresy. He was imprisoned in this low frame structure before being burned at the stake in July 1415. The house is closed Mondays; no admission charge. The *Rosgarten Museum* (3-5 Rosgartenstr.; phone: 7531-284246), set in a stately Gothic house, contains a fine collection of medieval art and handicrafts. The museum is open Tuesdays through Saturdays in May through September; no admission charge. Constance also has casino gambling in the elegant *Spielbank* (21 Seestr.; phone: 7531-5408), which also has a first-rate restaurant serving international fare and a popular terrace café. The tourist office (13 Bahnhofpl.; phone: 7531-284376) publishes a self-guided walking tour (in English) of Constance. The city is a good base for enjoying the entire lake region; cruises travel from here to other ports such as Friedrichshafen and Lindau in Germany, Breyenz in Austria, and Romanshorn in Switzerland. You also can sail into the western extension of the lake that juts like a finger into the greenery surrounding the Untersee.

One of the most interesting side trips from the city is to the island of Mainau. The island is reachable by boat (excursion steamers run between Constance and Mainau April through October); visitors also may choose to drive 5 miles (8 km) from Constance on Route 2 to a mainland parking lot, from which they can cross a bridge to Mainau.

MAINAU Known as "the Flower Island," Mainau is blessed with an abundance of greenery—and an equally huge number of tourists (there's an admission charge to the island itself). Its splendid 110-acre garden is the work of the present owner, Count Lennart Bernadotte of Sweden. The flowers on display include 280 species of rhododenron, 1,300 types of roses, hundreds of varieties of fuchsia, and more than a million tulips, plus orchids, hyacinths, narcissi, pansies, and dahlias. Palm, banana, orange, and lemon trees also thrive here (some in greenhouses) alongside the 18th-century castle that is Count and Countess Bernadotte's home (closed to the public). Guided tours are offered in German daily; they are also available in English to large groups with advance notice. Mainau is open daily year-round; the best time to visit the garden is April through October.

If possible, come early on a weekday, and count on spending the day. There are four restaurants, including the highly regarded *Schwedenschenke* and the *Comturey Keller* (see *Best en Route*). For more information about Mainau, call the tourist office (phone: 7531-3030).

BEST EN ROUTE

Halm When this establishment across from the railway station opened in 1874, it enjoyed a sterling reputation as a top luxury hotel. In 1914, however, it lost its luster and closed. In 1991, the property was acquired by the Leibrand family, given a complete face-lift, and reopened, restored to its former glory. Along with 102 spacious guestrooms, it has a grand stairway and two restaurants: the formal *Maurischer Saal,* set in a Moorish great hall, and the lively *Brasserie.* 6 Bahnhofpl., Mainau (phone: 7531-1210; 800-447-7462; fax: 7531-21803). Very expensive.

Insel Formerly a 13th-century Dominican monastery, this hotel retains parts of the original structure, including a vaulted chapel in the ballroom, arches and pillars, frescoed walls, and leaded-glass windows. The more modern public areas are decorated with wood-paneled walls, ornate tile stoves, and rustic furniture. Situated on a small island connected to the mainland by bridge, the property's 100 spacious and elegant guestrooms offer all manner of luxury amenities; many have lake views. The *Dominikaner Stube* offers the finest regional cooking in town and the more formal *Seerestaurant* features an ambitious continental menu. There also is a lakeside terrace café and a bar where the local elite come to be seen. Closed January through February. 1 Auf der Insel, Mainau (phone: 7531-1250; 800-223-5652; fax: 7531-26402). Very expensive.

Schwedenschenke The best restaurant on the island serves a menu of Swedish dishes and fresh seafood in a comfortable country-style setting. Open daily. Reservations unnecessary. Major credit cards accepted. Mainau (phone: 7531-303156). Moderate.

Comturey Keller Set in a former wine cellar, this dining spot still has a 25,000-liter wine barrel as its centerpiece. It offers a menu of regional specialties, draught beer, and local wines. Open daily for breakfast, lunch, and early dinner only. Reservations unnecessary. Major credit cards accepted. Mainau (phone: 7531-303156). Moderate to inexpensive.

En Route from Constance From here, Route 13 continues about 40 miles (65 km) to the Black Forest (see *The Black Forest* route in this section).

The Mosel River and Its Valley

Everyone knows about the stately, noble Rhine; steeped in legends, its siren's call still drifts above the waters and echoes through the trees. The passage through the Mittel Rheintal (Middle Rhine Valley) between Koblenz and Rüdesheim is probably the continent's most famous river route. By comparison, the adjoining Mosel (which meets the Rhine at Koblenz) is far less known, considered little more than a minor extension of the Rhine, a mere side trip from the main attraction, and a relatively minuscule passage in a land of such giant waterways as the Rhine and Danube. But read on: Though on a smaller and more intimate scale and lacking in myths and legends, the Mosel is every bit as attractive as the Rhine, if not more so. Scenery is the key here: Vistas embrace everything from lush forests to vineyard-covered slopes, and though the view that opens at every serpentine turn begs a second look, rest assured—there's plenty more ahead.

The source of the Mosel River is high in the Vosges Mountains of France. The river cuts north across the *département* of Moselle, then goes on for about 22 miles (35 km), forming the border between Luxembourg and Germany. On this last stretch, the road on the German side of the river—the Mosel Weinstrasse (Mosel Wine Road)—passes through wine country dense with vineyards and dotted with charming wine villages. (For information on specific vineyards in the region, see *Visitable Vineyards* in DIVERSIONS.) From the Luxembourg border the river continues another 10 miles (16 km) to Trier; from there until it reaches the Rhine at Koblenz, the Mosel follows a route full of hairpin turns and breathtaking scenery.

Grapes have been cultivated in the Moseltal (Mosel River Valley) since pre-Roman times. When the Romans settled in Trier more than 2,000 years ago they found wild grapes growing in profusion on slopes along the river; by the 3rd century these grapes were replaced with cultivated varieties brought in from Italy and planted by expert viticulturists under the aegis of Emperor Probus. *Mosella,* a poem by Decimus Magnus Ausonius written in the 4th century, deals with the delights of a journey on this "river of sweet-scented wines." During that time, extravagant villas served as summer homes for emperors and other members of the noblity. But except for those in Trier, most relics of Roman times have all but disappeared from the area. Today, medieval villages straight out of storybooks, turreted castles dating from the 11th to the 15th centuries, and seemingly endless rows of vines line both sides of the river.

The following 125-mile (200 km) drive along the Mosel between Koblenz and the ancient city of Trier is best done at a leisurely pace, allowing time to take to the water on one of a number of river cruises between Koblenz and Trier during high season (from mid-May to mid-October). This route should take three days—spend at least one night in Trier, and perhaps another in Bernkastel-Kues.

Accommodations along the Mosel are generally found in smaller resort hotels or rustic country inns, at relatively reasonable rates. The exception is Trier, which has several big city hotels at big city prices—as well as a few moderately priced ones. Rates in the wine towns along the Mosel can vary considerably from season to season, with high season (and high rates) in effect from late August through October. For a double room (with private bath and a TV set, unless otherwise noted) in those hotels we have listed as expensive, expect to pay between $125 and $150 per night; from $90 to $125 at places in the moderate category; and less than $90 in inexpensive places. Room rates generally include breakfast.

For a three-course dinner for two, not including drinks (local wines served by the glass or pitcher are good value), expect to pay $75 or more at restaurants in the expensive category; between $60 and $75 at places in the moderate range; and less than $60 at inexpensive eateries. Taxes and tips are included; however, you might want to leave a small additional amount to reward very good service. Restaurants are open for lunch and dinner, unless otherwise indicated. For each location, hotels and restaurants are listed alphabetically by price category.

KOBLENZ The name Koblenz comes from the Latin *confluentia,* referring to the junction (or confluence) of the Rhine and Mosel Rivers. All but destroyed during World War II, Koblenz was rebuilt as a modern city, offering few attractions.

En Route from Koblenz Set out from the Neue Moselbrücke (New Mosel Bridge) at the southern end of the city along Route 49, which follows the eastern bank of the river.

For the first 32 miles (52 km) between Koblenz and Cochem, the route passes broad valleys and undulating hills dotted with an occasional castle; barges, steamers, and car ferries ply the river in what looks like a water-bound rush hour. Farther along, bridges connect the two riverbanks.

About 10 miles (15 km) south of Koblenz, at the first major curve in the river, is the medieval village of Winningen, its attractive half-timbered houses set on a vine-covered hillside. In another 6 miles (10 km) is Alken, another gem of a wine town set under the watchful gaze of the hilltop *Schloss Thurant* (Thurant Castle). At this point, a bridge, one of several along the route, spans the river. Cross to the opposite side and continue south on Route 416 for 6 miles (10 km) to Moselkern, a pretty wine village located where the narrow Eltz River flows down out of the hills through the wild forested Eltztal (Eltz Valley) to the Mosel. In the area of Treis-Karden, another 3 miles (5 km) along, is the 800-year-old *Burg Eltz* (Eltz Castle;

phone: 2672-1300), a romantic edifice replete with towers and turrets. (Its picture appears on the 500 DM banknote.) One of Germany's lesser-known, yet best-preserved medieval castles, it boasts some splendid Gothic furnishings and an impressive collection of armor and weapons. Guided tours (in German only) of the castle are conducted daily April through October; there's an admission charge. In Ries, a small village a few miles farther along the river, is *Burg Pyrmont* (Pyrmont Castle; phone: 2672-2345), another famous medieval structure. Standing next to a scenic waterfall, the castle dates to 1225 and has been well preserved. Guided tours are given daily, and a slide show chronicles the castle's history (both are available in English). There's also a pleasant café. The castle is closed Mondays, Tuesdays, and November through March; admission charge. From Ries it's another 4 miles (6 km) on the left bank of the river to Cochem.

COCHEM This attractive medieval wine town with a year-round population of 6,000 has evolved into a bustling (but still appealingly small) tourist destination. Its distinguishing feature, a restored 950-year-old castle, complete with ramparts, towers, and turrets, dominates the town from its perch high on a steep, vineyard-covered hill. Most of the original 11th-century structure was destroyed in 1689 by French troops of King Louis XIV; in the 19th century it was rebuilt in the style of a 14th-century fortress. The *Burg* (fortress; phone: 2671-255) is a half-hour walk from the Marktplatz on Schloss Strasse. Guided tours of the fortress (in German only) are conducted daily from March 15 through October; admission charge. Below the serene fortress setting, Cochem resembles most major cities—with traffic backed up in both directions and parking virtually nonexistent (although there's free parking in a lot behind the railway station, a fair distance from the river). The city is particularly crowded on weekends and late August through mid-October, when the grapes are harvested and turned into wine. Unfortunately, crass commercialism has not passed Cochem by: Souvenir shops and ice-cream and sausage stands abound, but the fortress and the views of the surrounding countryside soften the sometimes tacky trade.

BEST EN ROUTE

Alte Thorschenke A 14th-century inn and wine restaurant located by the Mosel near the city gates, this property offers 34 well-appointed guestrooms. There is also a pretty garden area and parking. Open mid-March through mid-January. 3 Brückenstr., Cochem (phone: 2671-7059; fax: 2671-4202). Moderate.

Am Hafen A small, modern family-owned and -operated hotel located on the opposite (quieter) side of the Mosel. The 20 rooms are nicely furnished; those in front look out on the river, the bridge, the fortress, and the vineyards. The hotel restaurant, *Zur Hafenschenke,* serves home-cooked regional cooking and wines from the owner's vineyard. 4 Uferstr., Cochem (phone: 2671-8474; fax: 2671-8099). Inexpensive.

En Route from Cochem Leaving Cochem, the scenery becomes more dramatic—steep promontories punctuated by sharp curves in the road, slopes rising practically straight up from the river, vineyards clinging steadfastly to the rocky soil. Take Route 49 along the left bank of the river for 3 miles (5 km) to the bridge at Ernst; cross to the opposite side and proceed another 3 miles (5 km) to Beilstein, one of the Mosel's lesser-known attractions.

BEILSTEIN At the base of a mountain, this medieval market town, with its narrow cobblestone streets, ancient archways, and centuries-old gray stone houses, seems almost untouched by time (the only modern element is that the former stables at street level have been converted into residences). High above the town, the ruins of the 12th-century *Schloss Metternich* (Metternich Castle)—still within its original walls—stand silent vigil. Far more serene than neighboring Cochem, the town remains relatively unspoiled. Orchards line the riverside against a backdrop of vineyard-covered hills, pleasant cafés are set up in leafy courtyards, and cozy wine rooms afford a welcome respite from a day's touring. Beilstein also boasts a fine inn, *Haus Lipmann* (see *Best en Route*).

BEST EN ROUTE

Haus Lipmann Dating from 1795, this timbered inn with an adjoining vineyard has been in the same family for six generations. There are only five tastefully furnished rooms looking out on the Mosel. Restaurants include the antique-filled *Rittersaal,* a rustic tavern, and a grape-arbored terrace café that looks out on the river. All offer such local specialties as eel with dill sauce, trout, game in season, and homemade sausages, as well as breads and cakes baked on the premises and wines from the family vineyards. Open mid-March through mid-November. No credit cards accepted. 3 Marktpl., Beilstein (phone: 2673-1573). Inexpensive.

En Route from Beilstein Continue on Route 49 for 4 miles (7 km) to the bridge at Senheim; cross back to the left bank. Six miles (10 km) farther is the village of Alf, nestled in a woodsy setting at the base of *Schloss Marienburg* (Marienburg Palace; phone: 6542-2382); the castle, built in 1127, affords sweeping panoramas of the Mosel River and the valley, including several vineyards on the far side of the river. Tours (available in English) are given several times daily. There's also a good restaurant. The palace is closed mid-November through mid-March; admission charge. Take Route 53 for 5 miles (8 km) to Zell, crossing back to the right bank of the Mosel.

ZELL One of the prettiest—and least-crowded—wine towns in the area (and one of the most charming places on this route), Zell is distinguished by red-roofed houses and remnants of 15th-century fortifications lining the riverbank. Its vine-covered hills produce the grapes that are made into the renowned Schwarze Katze (Black Cat) wine. An annual wine festival is held here in mid-October. The town has several hotels that will put you up in style and comfort, and restaurants that serve fine food.

BEST EN ROUTE

Graacher Tor At this dining spot, you can get a variety of local specialties prepared with Spanish touches; especially good are the snails cooked in garlic oil and *Weincreme,* a custard flan. Closed Mondays. Reservations advised. Major credit cards accepted. 3 Graacherstr., Zell (phone: 6531-2204). Moderate.

Am Brunnen This small hotel in a townhouse on the bank of the Mosel has been in the same family for over a century. There are 19 attractively furnished rooms and a good restaurant offering nouvelle cuisine and Mosel wines at moderate prices. No credit cards accepted. 51 Balduinstr., Zell (phone: 6542-4060). Inexpensive.

Stadtschenke This small, no-frills family-run restaurant is the perfect place to stop for a quick lunch of home-cooked German fare, along with draft beer or Mosel wine by the glass. In summer, there's a popular salad bar. Closed Thursdays year-round and Fridays in winter. Reservations advised. No credit cards accepted. 78 Baldungstr., Zell (phone: 6542-4736). Inexpensive.

Zur Post A small, family-run place with 16 guestrooms, a terrace café overlooking the Mosel, and a rustically furnished restaurant. The hotel and restaurant are closed February; the restaurant is also closed Mondays. 25 Schlossstr., Zell (phone: 6542-4217). Inexpensive.

En Route from Zell Continue along Route 53 for another 11 miles (18 km) to Traben-Trarbach, passing through such colorful age-old market towns as Pünderich, Enrich, and Starkenburg.

TRABEN-TRARBACH Actually two towns situated on opposite sides of the river connected by a bridge, Traben-Trarbach is headquarters of the Mosel wine trade; there's a major wine festival held here each July. As befits a wine town, Traben-Trarbach is rich in taverns and wine rooms; as for its scenic appeal, its surrounding hills are studded with remains of fortified castles, the most important being the ruins of *Grevenburg,* high on a hill behind Trarbach with a view across the river to Traben.

BEST EN ROUTE

Rema-Hotel Bellevue Housed in the oldest Art Nouveau structure on this route (built in 1900), this elegant hotel on the Traben side of the river offers 50 attractive, well-appointed guestrooms; ask for one of the antique-filled rooms in the older section. Amenities include a restaurant and an indoor pool. Am Moselufer, Traben-Trarbach (phone: 6541-7030; fax: 6541-703400). Expensive.

Zur Goldenen Traube On the Trarbach side of the river, this hotel has 15 spartan rooms, along with a fine (moderately priced) restaurant featuring regional cooking—cream of sorrel soup, baked pike-perch with potatoes and sauerkraut—plus good local wines. Open daily. Reservations advised. Major credit cards accepted. 8 Am Markt, Traben-Trarbach (phone: 6541-6011; fax: 6541-6013). Inexpensive.

En Route from Traben-Trarbach Bernkastel-Kues, the next stop, is located 15 miles (24 km) south of Traben-Trarbach on Route 53. Villages worth a brief look in this area include Kröv (with exquisite 200- and 300-year-old homes) and Urzig (with more of the same).

BERNKASTEL-KUES Another combination of two wine villages on opposite sides of the Mosel connected by a bridge, Bernkastel-Kues is more popular than Traben-Trarbach; in fact, it is the most visited place along the river, a favorite weekend destination with a wide range of accommodations and fine restaurants. There's ample parking (for a fee) at riverside next to where the bridge crosses to Kues, and free parking along the opposite shore. The tourist office (5 Gestade; phone: 6531-4023; fax: 6531-7953) is closed Sundays.

A medieval town, Bernkastel survived the ages with most of its Old World charm intact, spared the ravages of the 17th- and 18th-century wars that decimated so many other places in the Mosel and Middle Rhine region. As a result, the town looks much as it did five centuries ago. Narrow streets no wider than alleyways are lined with late Gothic and early Renaissance houses, some with painted or carved façades, others half-timbered with sharp gabled roofs. Other houses frame cobblestone squares with fountains and statuary. Note the graceful *Michaelisbrunnen* (Michael's Fountain) in the main market square; the work was completed in 1608 by Hans Hoffmann, a renowned Trier sculptor. As part of the annual wine festival (the first week in September), the fountain spews a stream of wine instead of water.

A local wine that gained international fame is Bernkasteler Doktor, so named because it is said to have saved the life of an ailing church dignitary after all other medication had failed. Legend has it that after drinking a glass of wine from a neighboring vineyard the man got up from his deathbed, and went on to live to a ripe old age. The wine was also a favorite of England's King Edward VII, who served it at state functions. If you're interested in wines and wine tasting, Bernkastel-Kues has two must-see attractions. The *Mosel Wein-Museum* (2 Cusanusstr.; phone: 6531-4141) explores the history of wine from the 14th century to the present, with exhibits ranging from bottles and wine presses to displays on the art of wine making. There's also a bar for tasting. The museum is closed November through mid-April; admission charge. Also be sure to visit *Weingut Dr. Pauly-Bergweiler* (15 Gestade; phone: 6531-3002), a charming vintner that offers tours (available in English) of its wine cellar and samples of its wines. If notified in advance, the proprietors also will prepare food for visitors to enjoy with the wine. It is closed Sundays and late October through mid-May, except by appointment. (Also see *Visitable Vineyards* in DIVERSIONS.)

A worthwhile side trip is to the remains of *Burg Landshut* (Landshut Fortress). Perched on a promontory high above Bernkastel, it is one of the few local structures that did not escape the ravages of war; built in the 11th century for the bishops of Trier, it was partially destroyed in 1692. Sections of fortress walls are all that remain. The view of the Mosel from this vantage point is merely superb.

BEST EN ROUTE

Doctor Weinstuben On the Bernkastel side of the river, this historic house (dating from 1668) offers 18 guestrooms with most modern comforts (but no TV sets) and plenty of traditional European hospitality; there's also a restaurant. Open April through December. 5 Hebegasse, Bernkastel-Kues (phone: 6531-6081; fax: 6531-6296). Moderate.

Drei Könige On the Kues side of the river, right next to the bridge across the Mosel, it has 40 plushly furnished rooms with a choice of either river or vineyard views. Also on the premises is a wine bar and a subterranean dance hall. Open mid-March through mid-November. 1 Bahnhofstr., Bernkastel-Kues (phone: 6531-2035; fax: 6531-7815). Moderate.

Römischer Kaiser An old-fashioned resort hotel on the main street overlooking the river on the Bernkastel side, it has 35 comfortable rooms and the *Kaiser Keller* restaurant. There's also a bar with live music. Open March through December. 29 Markt, Bernkastel-Kues (phone: 6531-3038; fax: 6531-7672). Moderate.

Zur Post A former coaching inn (ca. 1827) on the Bernkastel side, this is one of the best places along the Mosel. Family owned and operated, it offers 42 nicely furnished rooms, comfortable public areas, the rustic *Poststube* bar and *Weinstube* restaurant, and friendly, efficient service. Restaurant specialties include local trout, eel from the Mosel, grilled steaks, rack of lamb with herbs, and fine wines. The hotel and restaurant are closed January. Reservations advised. Major credit cards accepted. 17 Gestade, Bernkastel-Kues (phone: 6531-2022; fax: 6531-2927). Moderate.

En Route from Bernkastel-Kues From here the winding river road threads through a countryside dense with vineyards for another 40 miles (64 km) to Trier, passing many towns that gained fame on the labels of some of the Mosel's finest wines.

Brauneberg, 6 miles (10 km) from Bernkastel, was once known as Dusemond, from the Latin *dulcis mons* (sweet mountain). It was already known during the Roman period for producing exceptionally rich wines, of which today's Brauneberger Juffer is a fine example. A little farther on is Piesport; another former Roman settlement, its Piesporter Goldtröpfchen is considered among the finest of Mosel wines. Back on the east bank, Neumagen-Dhron also dates from the Roman era and has been the site of a number of recent archaeological findings. The carved relief of a Roman wine ship discovered here several years ago is on display in Trier's *Rheinisches Landesmuseum* (Rhine Regional Museum; see below); a replica graces Neumagen's main square. Trittenheim, at the next sharp bend of the river, is the last major wine center along this route. After Schweich, Route 53 changes to Route 49 for the final 6 miles (10 km) into Trier.

TRIER In comparison with the bucolic Mosel Valley, with its beguiling vineyards and romantic villages, Trier looks like a major contemporary urban center—minus the bustle. But few cities boast such a long heritage: According to medieval chronicles, Trier dates to prehistoric times. Legend relates that more than 2,000 years before the birth of Christ, Trebeta, the son of the Assyrian queen Semiramis, explored the banks of the Mosel and established a settlement on this site, which became known as "Treveris" due to its association with him. If the story is true, Trier would be the oldest city in Europe. At any rate, an inscription facing Trier's Hauptmarkt (Market Square) reads, *Ante Romam Treveris stetit annis mille trecentis*—which translates as, "Before Rome, Trier stood for 1,300 years."

In 16 BC, during the reign of Emperor Augustus, Treveris was established as a Roman colony and renamed Colonia Augusta Treverorum (Augustus's Colony of Treveris). Largely destroyed in battle in the 3rd century, it was subsequently rebuilt and elevated to the capital of the Western Roman Empire. At the time, the city (now called Trier) was considered one of the greatest in the world, in the same league as Rome, Alexandria, and Byzantium. (For more information about Trier's Roman heritage, see *Memorable Monuments and Museums* in DIVERSIONS.)

Although many ruins from the Roman era remain in Trier, there are plenty of monuments to more recent history as well. The city boasts visible elements from medieval and Renaissance times, as well as works of art and architecture in Baroque, rococo, and French and German classical styles. Yet, in spite of all its historical treasures, Trier should not be considered a sterile museum relic lost in its past. The dominant impression it makes upon a visitor is of a lively and charming German city that has managed to escape the ravages of war. This is the way Germany used to look—at least in part—and still does, here along the Mosel.

Despite the scope of its history, Trier is a relatively small city (only 90,000 residents) that is easily explored on foot. Most of the main sights can be visited in a few hours; be sure to wear comfortable shoes.

Begin the walking tour at the 2nd-century *Porta Nigra* (Black Gate; Porta-Nigra-Pl.; phone: 651-978080; fax: 651-44759), the largest city gate the Romans ever built and one of Trier's (and Germany's) most striking Roman monuments. Still perfectly intact, the gate was not originally black; it was built of a light gray, locally quarried sandstone that took on a dark patina with time. The gate is closed weekends; admission charge. Beside the *Porta Nigra,* the *Städtisches Museum* (Municipal Museum; Porta-Nigra-Pl.; phone: 651-718-2449) is situated in the former *Simeonstift* (St. Simeon's Cloister), with Romanesque galleries surrounding an inner courtyard. Collections chronicle the history of Trier from the Middle Ages to modern times. The museum is closed Mondays; admission charge.

From the *Porta Nigra,* walk along the traffic-free Simeonstrasse toward the city's center. Along the way, note the 13th-century *Dreikönigenhaus* (House of the Three Kings), a fine example of a typical merchant's house in medieval times. It is still a private residence and cannot be visited. A short walk farther, and Simeonstrasse opens onto the Hauptmarkt, the heart of Trier. Dominating the square is the *Marktkreuz* (Market Cross), which was erected by Archbishop Heinrich I during the market's dedication in 958. A market is still held here daily.

Just a few steps off the Hauptmarkt is Trier's *Dom* (Cathedral; Sternstr.; phone: 651-75801), a towering, fortress-like structure of rough stone. Originally the site of a palace in the 4th century, the building has undergone several incarnations over the centuries; several churches occupied this spot before construction began on the present cathedral in 1034. Parts of previous buildings were incorporated into its design: Touches of Gothic and Baroque coexist comfortably, for the most part, with the classical architecture. Note the exquisite tympanum in the south aisle. The *Domschatzkammer* (Cathedral Treasury) contains a remarkable 10th-century golden altar, as well as other priceless relics. Not on view—except on rare occasions—is what is purported to be the Holy Robe worn by Christ at his trial before Pontius Pilate. (It is scheduled to be on view next year.) The *Domschatzkammer* is closed weekends; admission charge.

Directly next door, the *Liebfrauenkirche* (Church of Our Lady) is one of the oldest Gothic churches in Germany. Dating from the 13th century, it has an elegant interior with several noteworthy funerary monuments. Across the street, the *Bischöfliches Museum* (Episcopal Museum; 6-8 Windstr.; phone: 651-710-5255) houses some extraordinary 4th-century frescoes, including one presumed to represent Emperor Constantine's wife, Fausta, in the company of St. Helen. The museum also displays several examples of sacred art and statuary from the Middle Ages. It is open daily; admission charge.

From the *Liebfrauenkirche,* cross the plaza and continue via Mustorstrasse and Konstantinerstrasse to the *Basilika* (Konstantinerstr.; phone: 651-72428). It was originally part of the *Aula Palatina* (Palace Hall), which served as the Emperor Constantine's residence from 310 to 316. Most of the palace no longer stands; the huge basilica is the only surviving part. Its interior space is the second-largest of any existing ancient structure in the world (topped only by the Pantheon in Rome). Painstakingly restored, the *Basilica* now serves as a Protestant church.

Walk a short distance south through the *Palastgarten* (Palace Garden), a pleasant green space with pools and Baroque statuary, to the *Rheinisches Landesmuseum* (Rhine Regional Museum; 1 Weimarer Allee, phone: 651-42588). This museum houses an impressive collection of art and artifacts from the Rhine-Mosel region, including a carved Roman relief portraying a ship transporting wine on rough Mosel waters. The museum also boasts the world's largest collection of gold coins—numbering around 175,000 at last count. Exhibits range from prehistoric times through the Bronze and Iron Ages to the medieval period. The museum is open daily; no admission charge.

A short walk south along Weimarer Allee brings you to the ruins of the *Kaiserthermen* (Imperial Baths), one of the largest spa facilities in the entire Roman Empire. The baths are closed weekends; admission charge. Three other Roman relics are also in the vicinity. To the southeast are the remains of the *Amphitheater,* which once seated some 20,000 people. It is closed weekends; admission charge. To the west, near the banks of the Mosel, stand the ruins of the *Barbarathermen* (St. Barbara's Baths), which are closed Mondays and holidays; admission charge. Just beyond the *Barbarathermen,* the medieval Römerbrücke (Roman Bridge) spans the Mosel.

As you head back toward the city center, stop at *Karl-Marx-Haus* (10 Brückenstr.; phone: 651-43011). The author's birthplace is now a museum devoted to his life and work. On view here is a signed first edition of *Das Kapital,* as well as biographical documents, photographs, and memorabilia of the social economist who changed the course of modern history with his ideas. It is open daily; admission charge.

Just a 15-minute walk from town (beyond the *Porta Nigra*) are formal gardens adorned with Baroque statuary; continue to the river's edge to see two loading cranes, dating from the 15th and 18th centuries, which were used to lift wine barrels onto barges plying the river.

For a panoramic view of the town and its surroundings, walk across Kaiser-Wilhelm-Brücke (Kaiser Wilhelm Bridge) and climb the stairs of the *Mariensäule,* a column on a hill that affords broad views of the city and the river valley (open daily; no admission charge). For scenic hilltop views from the Trier side of the river, drive out from the city a short distance to the upper reaches of Petrisberg.

For information about Trier, contact the tourist information office, directly next to the entrance to the *Porta Nigra* (on Porta-Nigra-Pl.; phone: 651-978080; fax: 651-44759); it's open daily. Here you also can get excellent brochures, city and area maps, information on concerts, wine tastings, and wine seminars. The office also arranges for guided walking tours in English and sells tickets to the regular concerts given by Trier's excellent symphony orchestra performed in the *Stadttheater* (on Augustinerhof).

Don't be discouraged if time doesn't permit your "seeing" all of Trier. Roman monuments aside, the pleasure of strolling these ancient streets, stopping for refreshment at an open-air café, and crossing a nearly 2,000-year-old bridge to the other side of the river to take in the view is more food for the soul than most take in in a year, much less in a day. Enjoy a glass of Mosel wine and watch the rest of the world go by. Victor Hugo was enchanted by Trier. Goethe waxed philosophical about it. We think it's a fitting close to this route along one of Europe's loveliest river valleys.

BEST EN ROUTE

Dorint Ideally located across from the famed *Porta Nigra,* this undistinguished-looking box-like structure has 106 spacious rooms—some with romantic views of the *Porta Nigra*—bars, a coffee shop, several restaurants, and even a casino. 1 Porta-Nigra-Pl., Trier (phone: 651-27010; fax: 651-270-1170). Expensive.

Pfeffermühle Trier's culinary favorite, it features nouvelle cuisine such as filet of turbot from the Atlantic, monkfish in champagne sauce, and a seven-course "tasting" menu, plus the finest of Mosel wines. Closed Sunday lunch, Monday lunch, and three weeks in July. Reservations necessary. MasterCard and Visa accepted. 76 Zurlaubener Ufer, Trier (phone: 651-26133). Expensive.

Petrisberg High on a hill along the outskirts of the city, its 37 rooms and three apartments are housed in a cluster of villas in the midst of pine woods. An obvious labor of love of the Pantenburg family, each of its rooms has been individually decorated by a family member: Hand-crafted woodwork and original artworks are finishing touches. Though there is no restaurant, an elaborate buffet breakfast is served, and wine and snacks are offered in the afternoon. No credit cards accepted. 11 Sickingenstr., Trier (phone: 651-41181). Moderate.

Zum Domstein An extensive menu offering German cooking—wurst and sauerkraut and boiled beef with horseradish sauce—and excellent Mosel wines. Open daily. Reservations advised. MasterCard and Visa accepted. 5 Hauptmarkt, Trier (phone: 651-74490). Moderate.

Brunnenhof The setting is what matters here, in the *Simeonstift* next to the *Porta Nigra,* with courtyard dining (on traditional German fare) alongside the ancient stones of the massive Roman gate. Closed for three weeks in January and all of February. Reservations advised. Visa accepted. Simeonstift an der Porta Nigra, Trier (phone: 651-48584). Moderate to inexpensive.

En Route from Trier On the return trip to Koblenz you can take the same river roads, perhaps spending another night in Bernkastel-Kues or Zell. The express route to Koblenz, about 77 miles (124 km) north on the autobahn (E44), will get you there in little over an hour. Another alternative is to take a side trip southwest into the capital of Luxembourg (also called Luxembourg), which can be reached in a matter of minutes on another autobahn E44.

Glossary

Useful Words and Phrases

Germans don't really expect foreign visitors to speak or understand their fairly difficult language, although they certainly are pleased and appreciative if you try. While it's true that you could probably spend a week or more in Germany without ever having to resort to using the kind of basic words and phrases indicated below, to do so will surely give you pleasure on your stay and add an extra dimension to the foreign travel experience. Certainly just about everyone involved in the hospitality trade—in the hotels, restaurants, car rental agencies, tourist information offices, railway and bus depots listed in this guide–will deal with you in excellent English. Still, there's a thrill to pulling up at a gas station and jauntily commanding, "*Volltanken mit Super, bitte,*" or ordering a restaurant meal from soup to nuts in German.

Be advised that German tradition and protocol calls for greater politeness and formality than is customary in the US, both on a social and business basis, with frequent use of the terms *bitte* (please) and *danke* (thank you), and attention paid to titles. A word to the wise for the business traveler: For strangers to be on a first-name basis after short acquaintance is unheard of. In any transaction, you deal with *Herr, Frau,* or *Doktor* So-and-so. On a professional level, any woman who is an executive or is in charge of a department is invariably addressed as *Frau* (Mrs. or Ms.); *Fräulein* (Miss) is reserved for the very young, secretaries, and waitresses.

You also might consider taking a course in German before you go. Language courses are offered at some adult education and community colleges. *Berlitz,* among others, has a series of teach-yourself language courses on audiocassette tapes. They are available for $15.95 from Macmillan Publishing Co. (100 Front St., Riverside, NJ 08075; phone: 800-257-5755).

The list below of commonly used words and phrases can help get you started.

Greetings and Everyday Expressions

Good morning!	*Guten Morgen!*
Good day, good afternoon!	*Guten Tag!*
Good evening!	*Guten Abend!*
How are you?	*Wie geht es Ihnen?*
Very glad to meet you!	*Es freut mich sehr!*
Goodbye!	*Auf Wiedersehen!*
Yes!	*Ja!*
No!	*Nein!*
Please!	*Bitte!* or *Bitte sehr!*
Thank you!	*Danke!* or *Danke schön!*

Thank you very much!	*Vielen Dank!*
You're welcome!	*Gern geschehen!* or *Bitte sehr!*
Very nice!	*Sehr schön!*
Excuse me!	*Verzeihung!*
It doesn't matter.	*Es macht nichts.*
I don't speak German.	*Ich spreche kein Deutsch.*
Do you speak English?	*Sprechen Sie Englisch?*
How do you say . . . in German?	*Wie sagt man auf Deutsch . . . ?*
Please speak a little slower.	*Etwas langsamer, bitte.*
I don't understand.	*Ich verstehe nicht.*
Do you understand?	*Verstehen Sie?*
My name is . . .	*Ich heisse . . .* or *Mein Name ist . . .*
What is your name?	*Wie heissen Sie?* or *Was ist Ihr Name?*
Miss	*Fräulein*
Mrs.	*Frau*
Mister/sir	*Herr*
open	*offen*
closed	*geschlossen*
entrance	*Eingang*
exit	*Ausgang*
push	*drücken*
pull	*ziehen*
today	*heute*
tomorrow	*morgen*
yesterday	*gestern*
Help!	*Hilfe!*
ambulance	*Krankenwagen*
Get a doctor!	*Holen Sie einen Artz!*

Checking In

I have (have not) reserved a room here.	*Ich habe bei Ihnen ein (kein) Zimmer reserviert.*
I would like	*Ich möchte*
I would like to have	*Ich hätte gern*
a single room	*ein Einzelzimmer*
a double room	*ein Doppelzimmer*
a quiet room	*ein ruhiges Zimmer*
with bath	*mit Bad*
with shower	*mit Dusche*

with air conditioning	*mit Klimaanlage*
with balcony	*mit Balkon*
overnight only	*nur eine Nacht*
a few days	*ein paar Tage*
a week (at least)	*(mindestens) eine Woche*
with full board	*mit Vollpension*
with half board	*mit Halbpension*
Does the price include breakfast?	*Ist Frühstück in den Preis einbegriffen?*
Is everything (service, taxes) included?	*Ist alles (Bedienung, Steuern) einbegriffen?*
Can I pay with traveler's checks?	*Kann ich mit Reiseschecks zahlen?*
Can I pay with a credit card?	*Kann ich mit Kreditkarte zahlen?*

Eating Out

ashtray	*Aschenbecher*
bottle	*Flasche*
(extra) chair	*(noch ein) Stuhl*
cup	*Tasse*
fork	*Gabel*
spoon	*Löffel*
knife	*Messer*
plate	*Teller*
napkin	*Serviette*
table	*Tisch*
coffee	*Kaffee*
black coffee	*schwarzer Kaffee*
coffee with milk (cream)	*Kaffee mit Milch (Sahne)*
tea	*Tee*
juice	*Saft*
fruit juice	*Fruchtsaft*
orange juice	*Orangensaft*
tomato juice	*Tomatensaft*
orangeade	*Orangeade*
lemonade	*Zitronenlimonade*
water	*Wasser*
mineral water (carbonated or non-carbonated)	*Mineralwasser (mit or ohne Kohlensäure)*
beer	*Bier*
port	*Port*
sherry	*Sherry*
vermouth	*Wermut*

wine	*Wein*
red wine	*Rotwein*
white wine	*Weisswein*
dry wine	*trockener (or herber) Wein*
(very) dry	*(sehr) trocken*
bacon	*Speck*
ham	*Schinken*
bread	*Brot*
butter	*Butter*
jam	*Marmelade*
eggs	*Eier*
soft boiled	*weichgekocht*
hard boiled	*hartgekocht*
fried	*Spiegeleier*
scrambled	*Rühreier*
omelet	*Omelett*
honey	*Honig*
sugar	*Zucker*
salt	*Salz*
pepper	*Pfeffer*
cold	*kalt*
hot	*heiss*
sweet	*süss*
Waiter!	*Herr Ober!*
Waitress!	*Fräulein!*
I would like	*Ich möchte*
a glass	*ein Glas*
a bottle	*eine Flasche*
a half bottle	*eine halbe Flasche*
a liter	*ein Liter*
a quarter liter	*ein Viertelliter*
The check, please.	*Die Rechnung, bitte.*
I'd like to pay.	*Ich möchte zahlen.*
Is everything (service) included?	*Ist alles (Bedienung) einbegriffen?*
This doesn't seem to be correct.	*Das scheint nicht zu stimmen.*
Do you accept credit cards?	*Nehmen Sie Kreditkarten?*
Do you accept traveler's checks?	*Nehmen Sie Reiseschecks?*

Shopping

bakery	*Bäckerei*
butcher shop	*Fleischerei*
delicatessen	*Metzgerei*

grocery store	*Lebensmittelgeschäft*
pastry shop	*Konditorei*
supermarket	*Supermarkt*
bookshop	*Buchhandlung*
camera shop	*Fotogeschäft*
department store	*Kaufhaus*
drugstore (pharmacy)	*Apotheke*
drugstore (cosmetics)	*Drogerie*
jeweler	*Juwelier*
newstand	*Zeitungshändler*
shoe store	*Schuhgeschäft*
cheap	*billig*
expensive	*teuer*
large	*gross*
very large	*sehr gross*
too large	*zu gross*
small	*klein*
smaller	*kleiner*
too small	*zu klein*
long	*lang*
short	*kurz*
old	*alt*
new	*neu*
used	*gebraucht*
handmade	*Handarbeit*
Can you wash this in a machine?	*Ist das maschinenwaschbar?*
How much does this cost?	*Wieviel kostet das?*
What kind of material is this?	*Was für Stoff ist das?*
cotton	*Baumwolle*
corduroy	*Kord*
jersey	*Jersey*
leather	*Leder*
linen	*Leinen*
silk	*Seide*
synthetic fiber	*Kunststoff*
wool	*Wolle*
pure wool	*reine Wolle*
pure virgin wool	*reine Schurwolle*
gold (plated)	*Gold (vergoldet)*
silver (plated)	*Silber (versilbert)*
wood	*Holz*

Colors

black	*schwarz*
blue	*blau*
brown	*braun*
gray	*grau*
green	*grün*
orange	*orange*
pink	*rosarot*
purple	*lila*
red	*rot*
yellow	*gelb*
white	*weiss*

Getting Around

Where is . . . ?	*Wo ist . . . ?*
north	*Norden*
south	*Süden*
east	*Osten*
west	*Westen*
right	*rechts*
left	*links*
straight ahead	*geradeaus*
near	*nah*
far	*weit*
How far is it to . . . ?	*Wie weit ist es bis . . . ?*
map	*Landkarte or Karte*
city map	*Stadtplan*
airport	*Flughafen*
airport gate	*Flugsteig*
bus stop	*Bushaltestelle*
gas station	*Tankstelle*
train station	*Bahnhof*
main train station	*Hauptbahnhof*
train platform	*Bahnsteig*
track	*Gleis*
subway	*Untergrund-Bahn or U-Bahn*
Does this train (bus) go to . . . ?	*Fährt diese Bahn (dieser Bus) nach . . . ?*
What time does the train (bus) leave?	*Wann fährt die Bahn (der Bus)?*
ticket for streetcar or underground	*Fahrschein*
ticket for train, boat, plane	*(Fahr)karte*
one-way ticket	*Fahrschein/Karte einfach*
round-trip ticket	*Fahrschein/Karte hin und zurück*

in first class	*erster Klasse*
in second class	*zweiter Klasse*
gas	*Benzin*
regular (leaded)	*Normalbenzin*
high test (leaded)	*Super*
unleaded	*bleifrei*
diesel	*Diesel*
Fill it up, please.	*Volltanken, bitte.*
oil	*Ol*
tires	*Reifen*
Caution!	*Vorsicht!*
Danger!	*Gefahr!*
Detour	*Umleitung*
Dead End Street	*Sackgasse*
Do Not Enter	*Einfahrt Verboten*
No Parking	*Parkverbot*
No Passing	*Uberholverbot*
No Stopping	*Halteverbot*
One Way	*Einbahnstrasse*
Steep Incline	*Steigung*
Stalled Traffic	*Stau*
Stop	*Halt or Stop*
Yield	*Vorfahrt gewähren*
Intersection	*Kreuzung*

Personal Items and Services

absorbent cotton	*Watte*
aspirin	*Aspirin*
condoms	*Kondome*
diaper	*Windel*
razor (blade)	*Rasierapparat (Rasierklinge)*
sanitary napkin	*Damenbinde*
shampoo	*Shampoo*
shaving cream	*Rasiercreme*
shower	*Dusche*
tampons	*Tampons*
tissues	*Papierhandtücher*
toilet paper	*Toilettenpapier*
toothbrush	*Zahnbürste*
toothpaste	*Zahnpaste*
toilet	*Toilette*
Where is the toilet?	*Wo ist die Toilette/das WC?*

barber shop	*Friseursalon*
beauty shop	*Damenfriseur*
dentist	*Zahnarzt*
dry cleaner	*Reinigung*
laundromat	*Waschsalon*
post office	*Post* or *Postamt*
postage stamp (via airmail)	*Briefmarke (mit Luftpost)*

Days of the Week

Monday	*Montag*
Tuesday	*Dienstag*
Wednesday	*Mittwoch*
Thursday	*Donnerstag*
Friday	*Freitag*
Saturday	*Sonnabend* or *Samstag*
Sunday	*Sonntag*

Months

January	*Januar*
February	*Februar*
March	*März*
April	*April*
May	*Mai*
June	*Juni*
July	*Juli*
August	*August*
September	*September*
October	*Oktober*
November	*November*
December	*Dezember*

Seasons

Spring	*Frühling*
Summer	*Sommer*
Fall	*Herbst*
Winter	*Winter*

Numbers

zero	*null*
one	*eins*
two	*zwei*
three	*drei*
four	*vier*
five	*fünf*
six	*sechs*
seven	*sieben*

eight	*acht*
nine	*neun*
ten	*zehn*
eleven	*elf*
twelve	*zwölf*
thirteen	*dreizehn*
fourteen	*vierzehn*
fifteen	*fünfzehn*
sixteen	*sechzehn*
seventeen	*siebzehn*
eighteen	*achtzehn*
nineteen	*neunzehn*
twenty	*zwanzig*
twenty-one	*einundzwanzig*
thirty	*dreissig*
forty	*vierzig*
fifty	*fünfzig*
sixty	*sechzig*
seventy	*siebzig*
eighty	*achtzig*
ninety	*neunzig*
one hundred	*hundert*
1995	*Neunzehnhundertfünfundneunzig*

WRITING RESERVATIONS LETTERS

Restaurant/Hotel Name
Street Address
Postal Code, City
Germany

Dear Sir:

Please reserve a table for (number of) people on (day and month), 1995, at (hour) o'clock, for lunch/dinner.

or

Please reserve a room for (number of) days from (day and month), 1995 for (number of) people.

and

Please confirm my reservation as soon as possible. Thank you.

Very truly yours,

(Signature)

Sehr geehrter Herr:

Können sie bitte für mich einen Tisch für (number of) *Personen am* (day and month)*, 1995, um* (hour using the 24-hour clock) *Uhr für ein Mittagessen/Abendessen reservieren.*

or

Können sie bitte für mich ein Zimmer für (number of) *Tage von* (day and month)*, 1995, für* (number of) *Personen reservieren.*

and

Könnten sie bitte meine Anfrage so bald wie möglich bestätigen. Vielen Dank.

Ihr ergebener,

(Signature)

(Print or type your name and address below your signature.)

Climate Chart

Average Temperatures (in °F)

	January	*April*	*July*	*October*
Baden-Baden	29–38	43–61	59–77	45–58
Berlin	27–36	40–56	58–76	43–56
Cologne	31–40	41–58	58–76	45–58
Dresden	25–36	40–58	56–76	41–56
Düsseldorf	32–40	41–58	56–74	47–59
Frankfurt	29–38	43–61	59–77	45–58
Hamburg	29–36	38–56	56–72	43–56
Heidelberg	40–47	45–61	58–74	41–48
Leipzig	27–36	40–58	58–76	43–58
Munich	23–34	38–58	56–74	40–56
Nuremberg	25–36	38–56	56–74	41–56
Stuttgart	27–38	41–58	58–76	43–58

Weights and Measures

APPROXIMATE EQUIVALENTS

	Metric Unit	Abbreviation	US Equivalent
Length	1 millimeter	mm	.04 inch
	1 meter	m	39.37 inches
	1 kilometer	km	.62 mile
Capacity	1 liter	l	1.057 quarts
Weight	1 gram	g	.035 ounce
	1 kilogram	kg	2.2 pounds
	1 metric ton	MT	1.1 tons
Temperature	0° Celsius	C	32° Fahrenheit

CONVERSION TABLES

METRIC TO US MEASUREMENTS

	Multiply:	by:	to convert to:
Length	millimeters	.04	inches
	meters	3.3	feet
	meters	1.1	yards
	kilometers	.6	miles
Capacity (liquid)	liters	2.11	pints
	liters	1.06	quarts
	liters	.26	gallons
Weight	grams	.04	ounces
	kilograms	2.2	pounds

US TO METRIC MEASUREMENTS

	Multiply:	by:	to convert to:
Length	inches	25.0	millimeters
	feet	.3	meters
	yards	.9	meters
	miles	1.6	kilometers
Capacity	pints	.47	liters
	quarts	.95	liters
	gallons	3.8	liters
Weight	ounces	28.0	grams
	pounds	.45	kilograms

TEMPERATURE

Celsius to Fahrenheit	(°C x 9/5) + 32 = °F
Fahrenheit to Celsius	(°F - 32) x 5/9 = °C

Index